FIRE AND MOVEMENT

FIRE AND MOVEMENT

THE BRITISH EXPEDITIONARY FORCE
AND THE CAMPAIGN OF 1914

PETER HART

OXFORD
UNIVERSITY PRESS

OXFORD
UNIVERSITY PRESS

Oxford University Press is a department of the University of Oxford.
It furthers the University's objective of excellence in research, scholarship,
and education by publishing worldwide.

Oxford New York
Auckland Cape Town Dar es Salaam Hong Kong Karachi
Kuala Lumpur Madrid Melbourne Mexico City Nairobi
New Delhi Shanghai Taipei Toronto

With offices in
Argentina Austria Brazil Chile Czech Republic France Greece
Guatemala Hungary Italy Japan Poland Portugal Singapore
South Korea Switzerland Thailand Turkey Ukraine Vietnam

Published in the United States of America by
Oxford University Press
198 Madison Avenue, New York, NY 10016

Library of Congress Cataloging-in-Publication Data
Hart, Peter, 1955–
Fire and movement : the British Expeditionary Force and the campaign of 1914 /
Peter Hart.
pages cm
Includes bibliographical references and index.
ISBN 978–0–19–998927–0
1. Great Britain. Army—History—World War, 1914–1918. 2. Great Britain.
Army. British Expeditionary Force. 3. World War, 1914–1918—Campaigns—
Western Front. 4. World War, 1914–1918—Campaigns—France. 5. World War,
1914–1918—Personal narratives, British. 6. Germany. Heer—History—World War,
1914–1918. 7. France. Armee—History—World War, 1914–1918. I. Title.
D546.H44 2015
940.4'21—dc23
2014008945

1 3 5 7 9 8 6 4 2
Printed in the United States of America
on acid-free paper

CONTENTS

LIST OF MAPS

PREFACE

WHEN THE BRITISH went to war in August 1914, they didn't send an army but an expeditionary force, which was dwarfed by the massive armies lined up against each other in France. Little wonder that the British Expeditionary Force (BEF) would become the very stuff of legend – a British David sent against a German Goliath – and the early month of the war proved a self-contained military and human drama. The fighting in 1914 indeed had almost everything: high hopes and crushing disappointment; moments of sheer horror and nerve-shattering excitement; pathos and comic relief; occasional cowardice and an awful lot of selfless courage. For the men who fought in the campaign, whose centenary we now commemorate, it was a terrifying experience, one that tested them to their limits. It is a truly epic story.

Although part of a series of battles between the Allies and the Germans collectively known as the Battle of the Frontiers, the exploits of the BEF have an inherent exhilaration and raw emotion all of their own. In its way, theirs was a war within a war. The 'Old Contemptibles,' they proudly called themselves in proud rebuttal of the Kaiser's supposed dismissal of them as 'A Contemptible Little Army'.[1] Yet all too few of them were still fighting at the front when the year ended with the false dawn of the Christmas Truce.

Many of the senior commanders of the BEF believed to the end of their days that one more vigorous push by the Germans would have condemned the force to an ignominious defeat. There is no doubt that his experiences at Ypres in the autumn of 1914 lingered long in the mind of Field Marshal Sir Douglas Haig, and he certainly called upon those memories in penning his inspirational Order of the Day during the German offensive of April 1918.

Many amongst us now are tired. To those I would say that victory will belong to the side which holds out the longest. The French Army is moving rapidly and in great force to our support. There is no other course open to us but to fight it out. Every position must be held to the last man: there must be no retirement. With our backs to the wall and believing in the justice of our cause each one of us must fight on to the end. The safety of our homes and the freedom of mankind alike depend upon the conduct of each one of us at this critical moment.[2]

Haig had been only a corps commander back in 1914, but every word reflected the desperate situation he had faced as his exhausted men sought to cling on to the low ridges in front of Ypres.

The British part in the 1914 campaigns has long been veiled in layers of self-congratulatory myth, which have become accepted as the 'truth'. This version of events supposes an unprepared Britain, reliant on the peerless class of her regular soldiers to bolster the rabble of the unreliable French Army. At the Battle of Mons on 23 August, these 'old sweats' slaughtered the teeming hordes of Germany – firing at such a speed that the Germans imagined they were being fired on by massed machine guns. The BEF had been forced to retreat only by the 'collapse' of the French forces on their flank. Next, a further glorious stand at Le Cateau, which gave the hapless Germans such a bloody nose that they never again pursued the British so closely. Then the 'Great Retreat', before a stunning reversal in fortunes with the 'Miracle of the Marne' when – for apparently inexplicable reasons – a gap suddenly opened up between the onrushing German armies into which the British poured, forcing the Germans into a chaotic retreat. After a valiant pursuit by the British, the Germans turned and finally stood firm on the Aisne. Thwarted, both armies engaged in the tumultuous 'Race to the Sea' before the final drama on the battlefields of Ypres ending on 22 November. Here the BEF held back the tide and ensured that Germany could not win the war in 1914. As far as this fairy-tale version of 1914 is concerned, Britain's sacrifice and military prowess were second to none.

The aim of this book is to place the British role in 1914 into a proper historical context. Indeed as a narrative it has a far greater resonance when we are truthful about the manifest deficiencies of the small numbers of the BEF – just 120,000 when the fighting started – when caught up in a vast continental war where armies marched in their millions. The British regulars were skilful soldiers, courageous and adaptable in the near-impossible circumstances they found themselves. But they and their commanders lacked practice in many of the disciplines of modern warfare. We learn the truth about the German Army they faced, not the caricature of hordes of automatons, but the reality of a well-trained and superlatively equipped force that outfought the BEF in the early battles. We can also come to a full appreciation of the role of the French Army. Brave soldiers – if anything too brave – marching to their deaths in their teeming thousands in August 1914. But the French Army dug deep within itself. Led by the determined figure of General Joseph Joffre, the French would in the end outmanoeuvre the German armies at the Battle of the Marne. By this time, some of the harsh lessons of modern warfare had been grasped by the more adaptable British commanders, and from that time onwards the BEF demonstrated its value on plentiful occasions during that fraught autumn and desperate winter.

Overall, we can admire the achievements of the BEF in conjunction with those of their allies on the long, hard road that led to Ypres in November 1914. Here, fighting side by side with the French, the 'Old Contemptibles' engaged in a defensive clash that at times defied belief as the Germans pressed forward in huge numbers desperate to secure a decisive victory before the end of the year. Although the Battle of Ypres cannot really be seen as a victory, at least the Allies managed to avoid a defeat that would have been calamitous. The war would go on and the Germans *would* lose. The BEF played a full and splendid part in this epic tale: there is no need for vainglorious embellishment.

The most vibrant depiction of war incorporates the personal experience of the men who actually did the fighting, within a solid framework based on recent research. Every soldier has his own story, but I have chosen accounts that blend together to give a coherent idea of what was really happening in 1914, avoiding getting too bogged down in layers of detail that confuse far more than they can ever elucidate. In a war of such a size and intensity, it is impossible to cover every battle, every unit, every incident, but I have tried to give a representative picture without disrupting the narrative of this remarkable story.

1

SMALL BEGINNINGS

Therefore I say that it is a narrow policy to suppose that this country or that is to be marked out as the eternal ally or the perpetual enemy of England. We have no eternal allies, and we have no perpetual enemies. Our interests are eternal and perpetual, and those interests it is our duty to follow.[1]

Lord Palmerston, Secretary of State for Foreign Affairs

THE BRITISH EMPIRE WAS NOT founded on the strength of its armies. Britain's power as an island nation was maritime, with the domination of the world's sea lanes by the Royal Navy underpinning her mercantile endeavours and colonial acquisitions. Global preeminence had been achieved through a series of naval battles culminating in Trafalgar in 1805. As a whole the British had avoided – as far as possible – overt entanglement in the wars raging across Europe, normally getting involved only to ensure that no one country could attain domination. Traditionally, this had involved creating and financing coalitions against France or Spain, whilst contributing a small army which was often engaged only on the periphery of the conflict. Even at the much-vaunted dénouement of the Napoleonic Wars at the Battle of Waterloo in 1815, Wellington's army was a polyglot confection, far more reliant on support from Blucher's Prussian Army than he would subsequently care to admit. While France, Spain, Holland, Austria, Russia and Prussia fought it out toe-to-toe in Europe,

Britain used her naval power to harvest the colonies of her enemies all around the world. Behind the sturdy shield of the Royal Navy, troops could be deployed at key strategic locations, while in times of peace the intervention of a humble gunboat could stem a localised confrontation before it could get out of hand.

Over the years a series of underlying British foreign policy precepts had been hammered out, centred on the necessity of maintaining the essential status quo on mainland Europe by acting to contain the expansion of any wayward power that appeared to be threatening a domination. Outside of Europe, Britain continued to seek the expansion of the Empire, with particular regard to the perceived opportunities for growth in Africa, the Middle East and China, while simultaneously engaging in what was euphemistically termed the 'Great Game', seeking to maintain a healthy buffer zone protecting India, the so-called 'Jewel in the Crown', by thwarting Russian expansionary aims in Central Asia. There was supposed to be an underlying favouritism towards the liberal democracies, but when push came to shove this was not one of the primary planks of British foreign policy. As an economic power Britain favoured negotiation and peaceful persuasion, but all the while prepared for the possibility of war by an ongoing heavy investment in her navy. As a general rule-of-thumb it was considered necessary that the Royal Navy should be equal, or superior, to the combined fleets of the next two strongest naval powers. In marked contrast, the British Army remained a tiny force, more akin to a colonial police force than a continental army. This was not an accident: successive British governments were unwilling to bear the additional cost of a 'proper' army in addition to the huge outlay on the navy. Britain was not ill-equipped for war: she was well prepared for the traditional maritime role that has served her well over centuries. Regrettably, the exigencies of the Great War would demand a great deal more from the British, that or an acceptance of the utter overthrow of the status quo in Europe.

British policy may have been consistent for the best part of 200 years, but British fixations were almost an irrelevance to the deep wrangles that haunted mainland Europe in 1914. Ultimately it would be the rise of the German Empire that would prove the catalyst for war. Under the presiding hand of Chancellor Otto von Bismarck, Prussia had converted the loose confederation of German states into a serious force right at the heart of Europe. Following the Austro-Prussian War of 1866, the crushing defeat of France in the Franco-Prussian War of 1870–1871 indicated a new pecking order in Europe. Henceforth, the problems tormenting the Great Powers were easy enough to catalogue, but almost impossible to resolve. The new Imperial Germany became rudderless after Bismarck was jettisoned prematurely by Kaiser Wilhelm II in 1890. Failing to gain the friendship of Russia, Germany still faced the enmity of a France which burned for revenge and the reclamation of the provinces of Alsace-Lorraine lost in 1871. The French soon capitalised on German irresolution and in 1894 signed the Franco-Russian Dual Alliance. This left the German military facing the grim prospect of a war on two fronts: east and west. As a partial compensation, Germany had an alliance with Austro-Hungary signed back in 1879, but this once great power brought with it a terrible baggage through the seething cross-currents of the Balkans. Riddled internally with nationalistic unrest and divided constitutionally, the Austrio-Hungarian Empire proved a faithful friend, but a fast-declining power – that ultimately only added to the problems faced by Germany. A third country completed the Central Powers when Italy formed an unlikely defensive Triple Alliance with Germany and Austro-Hungary in 1882. Given the enduring tensions over border issues that remained between Austro-Hungary and Italy, this was a paper alliance which offered little to Germany in the event of a war.

In the meantime, Germany also managed to earn the distrust, edging into outright enmity, of the British Empire. Given the mores of the age it was not unreasonable for Germany, a late-comer to the imperial banqueting table, to seek to gain new colonies and economic spheres of influence to reflect her vastly increased status in the world. Like Britain, Germany was awake to the colonial possibilities in Africa, the Middle East and China, but it was a misfortune that the bombastic personality of Wilhelm II lent an overly aggressive feel to the manoeuvrings intended to satisfy these ambitions. Time and time again, as crisis followed crisis, the Kaiser engaged in needless sabre-rattling that exacerbated already tense situations. There was also a significant degree of economic competition between the two countries, as Britain's aging factories and infrastructure were first challenged and then overhauled by the 'new' powerhouse German economy.

Yet the most significant area of disagreement proved to be the German decision to construct a fleet that would directly challenge the Royal Navy. The Kaiser had long been an admirer of the teachings of the American naval historian Alfred Mahan, whose influential studies had pinpointed the crucial role of maritime power in creating and maintaining colonial empires. Wilhelm II already had tremendous military and economic strength at his fingertips, but he could not resist the temptation to add a naval string to his bow. The results were the Navy Acts of 1898 and 1900, which created a construction programme of some thirty-eight battleships – a fleet which had as its very purpose a threat to the naval hegemony exercised by the Royal Navy. The German intent became known as the 'Risk Theory'.

> To protect Germany's sea trade and colonies in the existing
> circumstances there is only one means – Germany must have a battle
> fleet so strong that even for the adversary with the greatest sea power a
> war against it would involve such dangers as to imperil his position in
> the world. For this purpose it is not necessary that the German battle
> fleet should be as strong as that of the greatest naval power, for a great
> naval power will not, as a rule, be in a position to concentrate all its
> striking forces against us. But even if it should succeed in meeting
> us with considerable superiority of strength, the defeat of a strong
> German fleet would so substantially weaken the enemy, that in spite of
> victory he might have obtained, his own position in the world would
> no longer be secured by an adequate fleet.[2]
>
> Memorandum, Naval Act, 1900

This changed the British perception of Germany from irritating rival to dangerous foe. Taken as a course of action it had a major flaw in that there was no allowance for the obvious British reaction, which was to seek a diplomatic solution by converting her former enemies into friends. Spurred by the explicit naval threat to her very being, Britain became receptive to diplomatic overtures from France. The colonial disputes and historical enmity that dogged relations between the two countries soon evaporated once they realised that they now had a common enemy in Germany. The Anglo-French Entente Cordiale signed in April 1904 would develop into a closer relationship, encompassing naval and military agreements which, while not binding, nonetheless would place a very significant moral obligation upon the British to side with France in the event of any war resulting from German aggression.

A very real tension still existed between Britain and her other historical 'enemy', Russia, over the latent Russian threat to India and long-standing attempts to secure Constantinople, thereby gaining unfettered access to the Mediterranean. But the idea of a Europe dominated by Germany and above all the threat of the new German fleet proved far more potent. The diplomats managed to overcome, or at least stifle, their long-standing differences, working to define borders and allot areas of influence in a manner that dampened down the old enmities, thus allowing the signing of the Anglo-Russian Convention in 1907. Now there were three: the Triple Entente between France, Russia and Britain was born.

Diplomatic manoeuvrings were not the only British response to the spectre of a growing German Navy. The Royal Navy was not a luxury to the British: it underpinned the whole edifice of the British Empire. As such there had to be a direct naval response to the challenge. The result was a significant step forward in battleship design as the First Sea Lord, Sir John Fisher, responded with a new breed of 'all big gun' battleships armed with ten 12" guns, powered by the very latest turbine engines to generate 21 knots, all attained without loss of armour or defensive capabilities. From the moment of her launch in 1906, the *Dreadnought* rendered all previous battleships obsolescent – indeed henceforth they would be known generically as pre-dreadnoughts. This was followed by the advent also under Fisher's hand of the battlecruiser *Invincible* in 1908, the first of a class of fast, powerful, heavily armed vessels capable of hunting down and destroying the slower armoured cruisers. The Germans could have accepted the rebuff, but they chose instead to see this great leap forward as a chance to bridge the gap between the fleets. The naval race became ever more intense, as both sides struggled to build the new dreadnoughts and battlecruisers that acted as an index of naval power. The delays caused as the Germans assessed the new designs and prepared their own versions, coupled with the grim determination of the British to maintain their naval supremacy, meant that the Royal Navy still retained a numerical lead in 1914. Here at least there was no stinting; what was required had been provided.

Thus, from a traditional British perspective, it cannot be said that the British Empire was unprepared for war in 1914: the massed squadrons of Grand Fleet dreadnoughts offered tangible evidence of a country that had done all in its power to counter the perceived German naval threat. Yet when the Great War broke out it would not be remembered for its gigantic naval battles. For the Germans had another naval theory, that of the 'Fleet in Being'. When it came to war, the Kaiser and his admirals valued the latent threat posed by his fleet far too much to offer it up as a hostage to fortune in battle. The High Seas Fleet therefore stayed in port. The Nelsonic response of a perpetual close blockade was rendered impossible by the advent of submarines, mines, the threat of destroyers and the constant requirement to refuel. Instead, the Royal Navy would exercise its grip by means of a distant blockade based on the vast anchorage of Scapa Flow in the Orkneys and the closure of the English Channel with minefields and light forces. This sealed off Germany from the oceans of the world and allowed the bounties of maritime supremacy to be harvested by the Allies throughout the Great War. But there was to be no 'Armageddon', no decisive naval clash at sea. Attention must therefore turn to the British *military* preparations for war. Huge sums had been spent on the Royal Navy, but were they willing to make the commensurate investment in the British Army? The answer was no.

THE LAND CAMPAIGNS OF 1914 WERE inevitably going to be dominated by the gigantic German, French and Russian continental armies. The German plans originated in the thinking of General Albert von Schlieffen, who had been appointed Chief of the General Staff in 1891. He was faced with the dread possibility of war on two fronts with the French and Russians, under circumstances where Germany would be badly outnumbered if the Russian Empire was given the time to mobilise its millions of men. A quick decision was therefore essential – but how to achieve it? Warned off by the lessons of history that indicated the near impossibility of swiftly defeating a Russia blessed with its vast hinterlands and inexhaustible manpower, Schlieffen resolved to leave only a holding force facing Russia to stall any invasion of East Prussia, while the bulk of the German Army would strike at France to secure a quick victory before turning on Russia. But here too he was faced by problems, for the French in the aftermath of their 1871 defeat had built a line of strong modern fortresses along their border with Germany. Thinking laterally, von Schlieffen decided to circumvent the problem by attacking through Holland, Belgium and Luxembourg, sweeping into northern France, seeking to envelop the French armies and thereby securing a crushing victory that would knock France out of the war at a stroke.

This 'plan' was not the detailed construct of popular imagination, but rather more a key plank in the whole planning process which was still being tweaked by von Schlieffen until he handed it over to his successor as Chief of the General Staff, General Helmuth von Moltke (the Younger) in 1906. Constant revision was necessary in an ever-changing world. The speed with which the Russian Army recovered after the chastening defeat of the Russo-Japanese War of 1904–1905 was one factor, while French investment designed to improve Russian rail communications to the German frontier further weighted the dice against Germany. The French Army was also indulging in a major expansion, as the new conscription measures of 1913 increased the length of time men served with the colours. In the absence of any alternative solution, Moltke stuck to the framework of the Schlieffen thinking, which was developed into full-blooded operational war plans. However, three major adjustments were made by Moltke in response to shifting circumstances: the threat of a French drive into Alsace-Lorraine made him strengthen German forces held on the Franco-German border, he decided not to add to his enemies by the invasion of Holland, and he scheduled an immediate attack to remove the problem posed by the Belgian forts at Liège some twenty miles from the frontier. The threat of a more-rapid Russian deployment also had the side effect of forcing Germany and Austro-Hungary closer together in an effort to secure the Eastern Front. Yet Moltke remained mordantly aware that the ongoing French and Russian army reforms would begin to maximise the opposing forces arraigned against him from around 1917. For Germany, hamstrung by the incompetence of her foreign policy and the intransigence of the French, time was running out. If there was to be war then it had to be soon.

French plans mutated as the strength of her armies, shattered in the Franco-Prussian War, was restored. At first they were defensive in tone while a new system of conscription was introduced, the process of modernising the army begun and a series of modern fortifications constructed at key points along the German border. Once the alliance with Russia had been secured, the French high command became far more ambitious, creating a series of plans devoted to a major cross-border offensive designed to reclaim the 'lost' Alsace-Lorraine provinces. The French general staff were aware of the threat of a German assault through Belgium and began to strengthen the forces held in the north of France, but preferred to believe that their own assault driving into Lorraine would be the decisive stroke. The increasing optimism of the French was enhanced by the development of a powerful cult of the offensive, which espoused the belief that a combination of powerful new weapons systems to break the will of defenders, coupled with the incomparable morale of the French troops, could attain victory against almost any odds.

The signing of the Anglo-French Entente was a step forward, but the French wanted far more: they sought to inveigle the British into committing an expeditionary force on the European continent early in the war. This was a major decision for the British as it would reflect a clear break with their traditional military and maritime policies in time of war. But in the event the decision was taken in secret, with very few people being consulted, and, indeed, without the knowledge of many of the government ministers and senior officers of the day.

The first steps occurred in 1906, after a signed letter of agreement between the British Foreign Secretary Sir Edward Grey and the French Ambassador Paul Cambon. This was actually a very guarded affair, which merely delineated the self-evident fact that both countries were free to decide whether or not to assist each other in the event of war. Yet the French regarded this as a signal that the British were likely to play their part should the Germans attack, and exploratory staff talks began to hammer out what might – or might not – be expected from the British Army in the event of war.

This dialogue had achieved little of any note, until a relatively junior British officer began to influence events. Brigadier General Sir Henry Wilson was born 5 May 1864 and educated at Marlborough. Having inexplicably failed to qualify for entrance to Sandhurst, he served in the militia to gain his commission in 1884. Service in India with the 1st Rifle Brigade followed but he was wounded with a slash above his eye in the 1887 campaign against the Dacoits in Burma. His injuries took time to heal and – rather cruelly – caused him to be dubbed 'the ugliest man in the British Army'. He attended Staff College from 1892 and moved on to a string of staff appointments, including service in the Boer War and then on to the War Office, where his growing reputation for intelligence was enhanced, although he was also acquiring a name as a 'political' officer, who was not always entirely 'straight' in his dealings. In 1907, he was promoted to acting Brigadier General in command of the Staff College. By this point, Wilson had been convinced that, in the event of a continental war with Germany, it was Britain's destiny to stand alongside the French. He devoted much time to tours of the Franco-Belgian/German borders, and in 1909 he paid a fateful visit to his opposite number General Ferdinand Foch at the École Supérieure de Guerre. In addition to professional discussions on their staff courses, they also talked at length on the threat posed by a German invasion via Belgium – and of the possible role of a British deployment on the French left flank to help counter such a move. The two men established a warm relationship and exchanged several meetings. It was at one of these that Foch defined the French attitude towards British involvement. Wilson asked him bluntly, 'What would you say was the smallest British military force that would be of any practical assistance to you in the event of a contest such as we have been considering?'[3] Foch's answer was all too revealing: 'One single private soldier and we should take good care that he was killed!'[4] Foch knew that once committed the British would inexorably be drawn further into the conflict.

When, in 1910, Wilson was promoted to be Director of Military Operations at the War Office, he was horrified at what he found. Discussions so far had been hypothetical in character, lacking in any real urgency, and no practical arrangements had been undertaken. To Wilson it was axiomatic that the early despatch of a BEF to assist France was not only the only logical course of action, but a simple matter of duty to Britain's main ally. He thus went to work and produced timetabled plans for the despatch of six infantry divisions and a cavalry division to France ready to be enacted in the event of war. He also began a further series of secret talks with his French opposite numbers. It was as well he had done this preparatory work, because in the summer of 1911, a crisis arose following the German despatch of the gunboat *Agadir* to Morocco to press overt colonial ambitions in the region. There was consternation at the heart of the British government. This was Wilson's chance.

> We had the emergency meeting of the Committee of Imperial Defence to consider the problem of what we should do in the event of a war

between France and Germany. Asquith (chair), Lloyd George, Haldane,
Chief of Imperial General Staff, self, Bethell, Sir A. Wilson, McKenna,
Winston Churchill, Sir Edward Grey, Sir John French. Asquith asked
me to explain my proposals. I had all my big maps on the wall and
I lectured for 1¾ hours. Everyone very nice.[5]

The Home Secretary, Winston Churchill, left his own description of this
important meeting.

Standing by his enormous map, specially transported for the purpose,
he unfolded, with what proved afterwards to be extreme accuracy,
the German plan for attacking France in the event of a war between
Germany and Austria on the one hand, and France and Russia on the
other hand. It was asserted that, if the six British divisions were sent
to take position on the extreme French left, immediately war was
declared, the chances of repulsing the Germans in the first shock of
battle were favourable. Every French soldier would fight with double
confidence if he knew he was not fighting alone. Upon the strength
of Russia, Wilson spoke with great foresight, and the account that he
gave of the slow mobilization of the Russian army swept away many
illusions.[6]

After a break it was the turn of the Admiralty to present their vision
for war. But the First Sea Lord Sir Arthur Wilson was ill-prepared. All he
could offer was a vague rehash of his predecessor Admiral Sir John Fisher's
unrealistic schemes for amphibious landings on the German Baltic coast.
This proved almost entirely unsatisfactory to the committee members
and Churchill was unimpressed.

Sir Arthur Wilson, with another map expounded his views of the
policy we should pursue in the event of our being involved in such a
war. He did not reveal the Admiralty war plans. These he kept locked
away in his own brain, but he indicated that they embodied the
principle of a close blockade of the enemy's ports. It was very soon
apparent that a profound difference existed between the War Office
and the Admiralty view. In the main, the Admiralty thought that
we should confine our effort to the sea; that if our small army were
sent to the Continent it would be swallowed up among the immense
hosts conflicting there, whereas, if kept in ships or ready to embark

for counter-strokes on the German coast, it would draw off more than its own weight of numbers from the German fighting line. This view, which was violently combated by the General, did not commend itself to the bulk of those present, and on many points of detail connected with the landings of these troops the military and naval authorities were found in complete discord. The serious disagreement between the military and naval staffs in such critical times on fundamental issues were the immediate cause of my going to the Admiralty. After the council had separated, Mr Haldane intimated to the Prime Minister that he would not continue responsible for the War Office unless a Board of Admiralty was called into being which would work in full harmony with the War Office plans, and would begin the organization of a proper naval war staff.[7]

In the event the *Agadir* crisis soon faded away following successful negotiations, which compensated Germany with other territories in Africa and allowed free rein to the French in Morocco, but the effects would linger. Churchill was duly installed as First Lord of the Admiralty, where he would form a close and enduring relationship with Henry Wilson.

Churchill was soon engaged in a conversation with the French naval authorities with the intention of establishing a framework for joint naval action in the event of a possible war with Germany. France was faced by a possible combination of both the Austrian and Italian fleets in the Mediterranean, while the Royal Navy needed to concentrate most of its strength facing the German High Seas Fleet across the North Sea. The answer was clear: the French would retain all their main fleet units at the naval base of Toulon, taking the bulk of the responsibility of defending British interest in the region, while the Royal Navy would protect the French maritime interests in the Atlantic and English Channel. This was difficult for traditionalists of both countries to stomach, but the agreement was a logical answer to their mutual problems. It was an agreement based on mutual convenience and, in theory at least, did not affect the political independence of either country.

The Royal Navy also had a great deal of preparatory work in order to ensure that the safe embarkation, transportation and disembarkation of a BEF across the Channel was actually feasible in the event of war. Although the Admiralty was naturally somewhat preoccupied with the dreadnought naval race with Germany, they still managed to have everything in readiness by 1914. Meanwhile, Henry Wilson too had been working hard to render the mobilisation process as smooth as possible, slotting into place the logistical framework for the rail transport and rapid embarkation of the BEF to France. A War Book was established and published every year from 1912, detailing the exact steps needed to secure the efficient mobilisation of every element of the army in time of war. Above all, Wilson ignored constitutional niceties, missing no opportunity to assure the French General Staff that the BEF would indeed be deployed alongside the French Army when it came to the crunch. Whether he had the right to make such assurances was a very different matter. His maverick approach was typified in a meeting with key members of the French General staff in 1911.

> They were most cordial and open. They showed me papers and maps, copies of which they are giving me, showing the concentration areas of their northern armies. Intensely interesting. Then they showed me papers and maps, copies of which they are giving me, showing in detail the area of concentration for all our Expeditionary Force. We had a long discussion. In fact, by 12.30 I was in possession of the whole of their plan of campaign for their northern armies, and also for ours. I never spent a more interesting morning.[8]

Thus it was that the French generals revealed their intention that the BEF would be concentrated around Maubeuge. Wilson's Francophile nature had prevented any serious British role in the consideration of where exactly they would be deployed. While this was an incredible scenario, an even stranger was to follow. As was his wont, Wilson then began a cycling tour of frontier areas where he made a visit to the patriotic French memorial erected on the 1870 battlefield of Mars-la-Tour. 'Paid my usual visit to the statue of "France" looking as beautiful as ever so I laid at her feet a small bit of map I have been carrying, showing the areas of concentration of the British forces on her territory.'[9] Few, if any, of the British high command who would have to lead the BEF were privy to this information so lightly cast to the winds. And in fact the final decision as to whether – or where – the deployment of the BEF would actually be made in the event of war was still not resolved; the British Cabinet still retained its absolute right to decide only at the moment of truth.

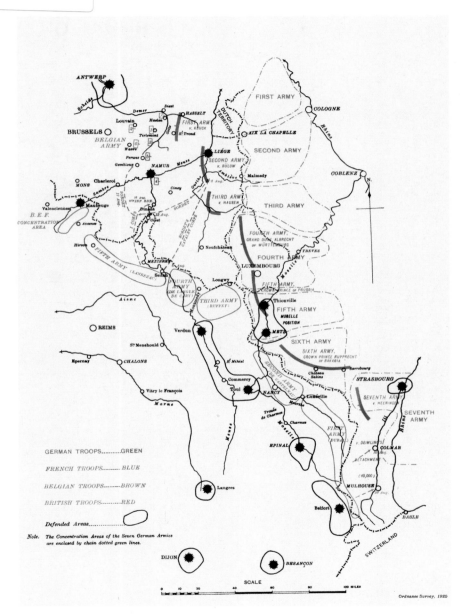

Map 1 The Concentration of the Armies, August 1914

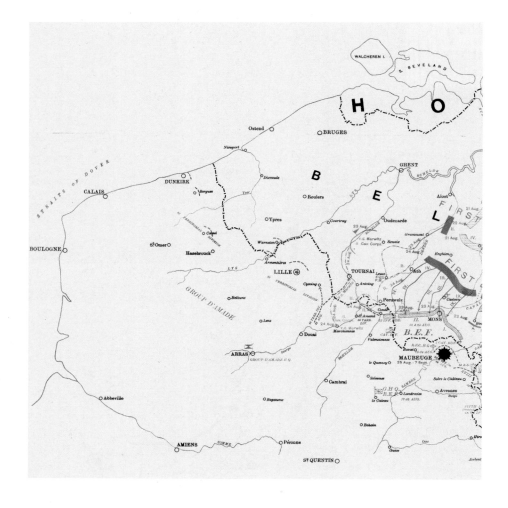

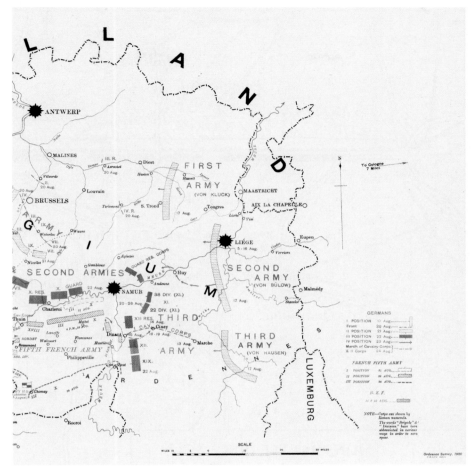

Map 2 Situation 17–24 August 1914

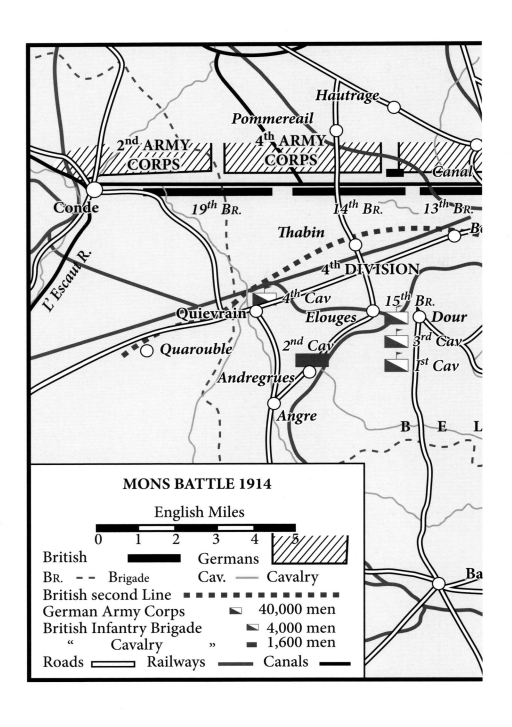

Hautrage

Pommereail

2nd ARMY CORPS

4th ARMY CORPS

Canal

Conde

19th BR.

14th BR.

13th BR.

L' Escaut R.

Thabin

B

4th DIVISION

Quievrain

4th Cav

15th BR.

Elouges

Dour

Quarouble

2nd Cav

3rd Cav

Andregrues

1st Cav

Angre

B   E   L

MONS BATTLE 1914

English Miles

0   1   2   3   4   5

British ▬▬▬   Germans

BR. - - Brigade   Cav. ▬▬ Cavalry

British second Line ■ ■ ■ ■ ■ ■ ■ ■

German Army Corps   ◣ 40,000 men

British Infantry Brigade   ◣ 4,000 men

"   Cavalry   "   ▬ 1,600 men

Roads ▭▭▭   Railways ▬▬   Canals ▬▬

Ba

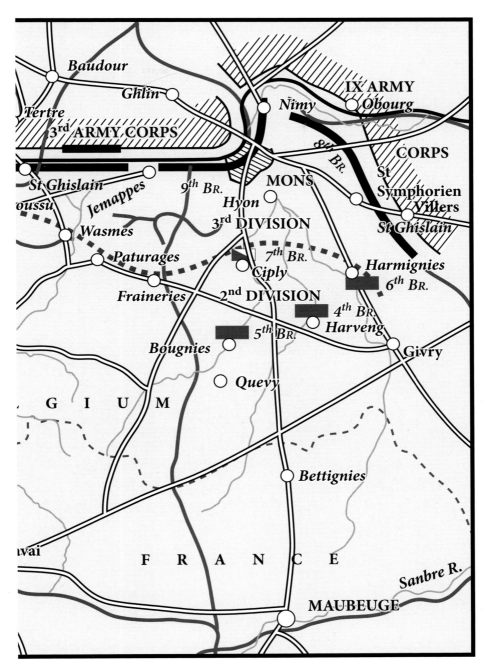

Map 3 Battle of Mons, 23 August 1914

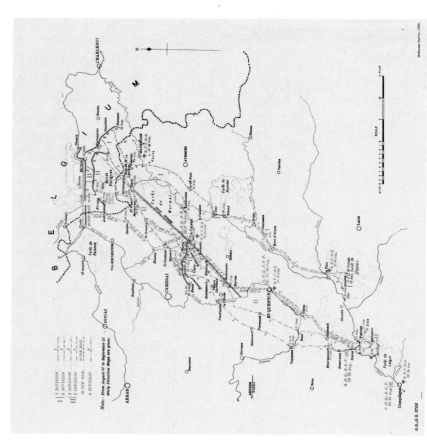

Map 4 Retreat from Mons

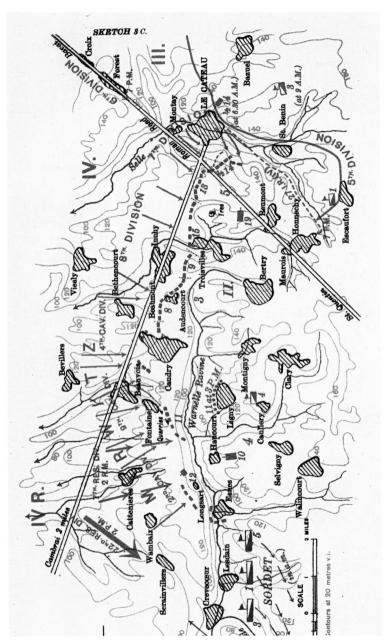

Map 5 Battle of Le Cateau, 26 August 1914

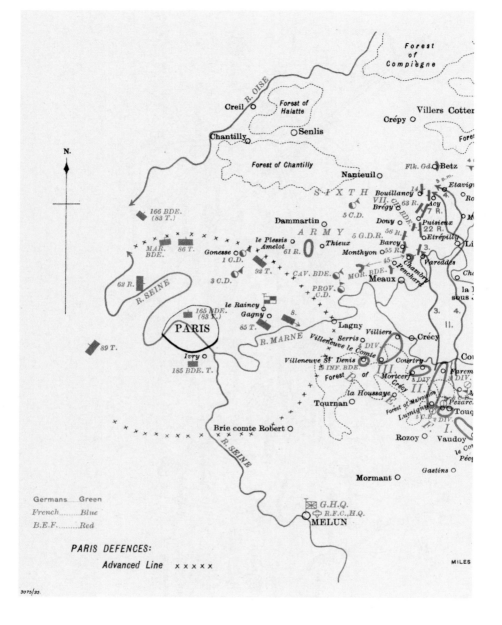

Forest
of
Compiègne

R. OISE

Creil ○

Forest of
Halatte

Villers Cotter

Crépy ○

Chantilly ○

Senlis ○

Forest

Forest of Chantilly

Flk. Gd ○ Betz

Nanteuil ○

5 p.m.

N.

S I X T H

Bouillancy ○ 14

Etavig

VII. ⚔ ○ 63 R.

Acy

Ro

Brégy ○

7 R.

166 BDE.
(83 T.)

Dammartin ○

A R M Y

Douy ○

BDE.

Puisieux

22 R.

M

5 C.D.

5 G.D.R.

56 R.

Etrépilly

Li

MAR.
BDE.

86 T.

le Plessis
Amelot

Thieux ○

Barcy

5 G.D.R.

45

Chambry

Cha

62 R.

Gonesse ○

1 O.D.

61 R.

Monthyon ○ 55 R.

Penchard

Varreddes

3.

R. SEINE

3 C.D.

92 T.

CAV. BDE.

MOR. BDE.

Meaux ○

la I
sous

89 T.

le Raincy

3 C.D.

PROV.
C.D.

3.   4.

165 BDE.
(83 T.)

Gagny

8.

Lagny ○

11.

PARIS

85 T.

R. MARNE

Villiers ○

Crécy ○

Serris ×

Ivry ○

Villeneuve le Comte

4 DIV.

Cou

185 BDE. T.

Villeneuve St. Denis

Couilry ○

III.

Farem

Forest   of

10 INF. BDE.

Crécy

3 DIV.

II.

Moricerf ○

la Houssaye ○

Pezarc

Tournan ○

Forest of Malvoisine

Luzignin

Toug

5 B.

3 DIV.

F. I.

Brie comte Robert ○

Rozoy ○

Vaudoy ○

R. SEINE

le Co
Péc

Gastins ○

Mormant ○

Germans ___ Green

French ___ Blue

B.E.F. ___ Red

⚑ G.H.Q.
✠ R.F.C.H.Q.

MELUN ○

PARIS DEFENCES:

Advanced Line   × × × × ×

MILES

3075/33.

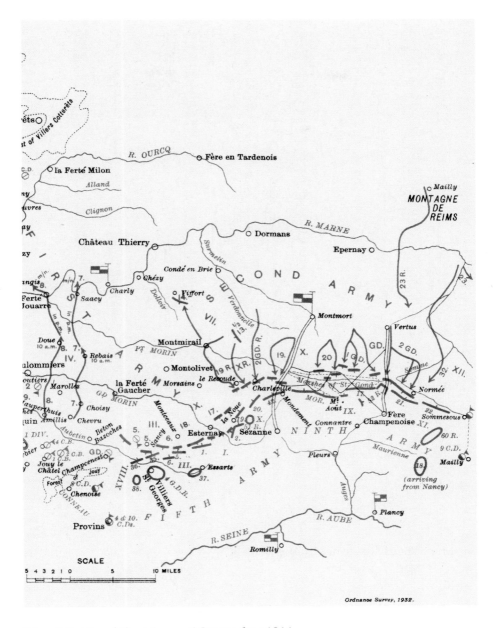

Map 6 Battle of the Marne, 6 September 1914

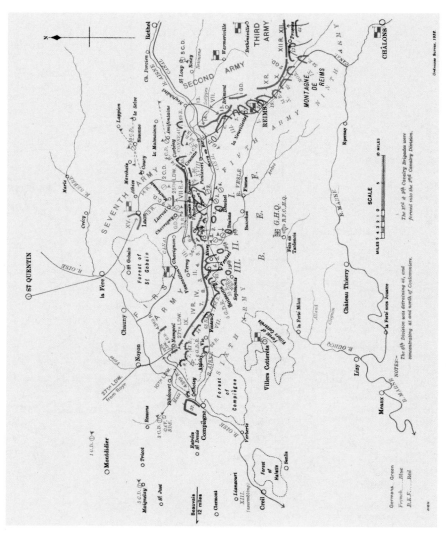

Map 7 Battle of Aisne, 13 August 1914

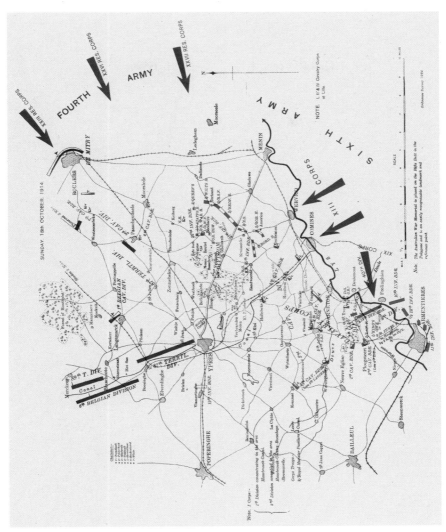

Map 8 First Battle of Ypres, 18 October 1914

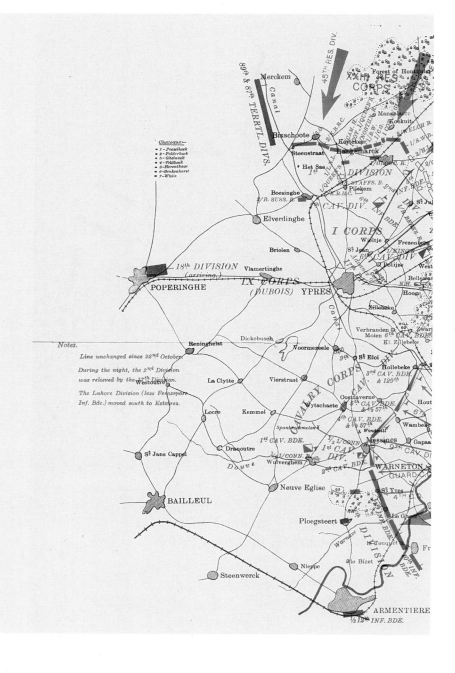

Chateaux—
1 — Poezelhoek
2 — Polderhoek
3 — Gheluvelt
4 — Veldhoek
5 — Herenthage
6 — Beukenhorst
7 — White

89th & 87th TERRIL. DIVS.

Merckem

Canal

45TH RES. DIV.

Forest of Houthulst

XXIIᴺᴰ RES. CORPS

Kortekeer

Mansshare

Koekuit

Bixschoote

Steenstraat

Langemarck

Het Sas

1st DIVISION

Boesinghe
2/R. SUSS. R.

Pilkem

CAV. DIV.

Elverdinghe

I CORPS

Wieltje

Frezenberg

Brielen

St Jean

6th CAV. DIV

18th DIVISION
(arriving.)

Vlamertinghe

POPERINGHE

IX CORPS
(DUBOIS)

YPRES

Hooge

Zillebeke

Verbranden
Molen

6th CAV. BDE.

Kl. Zillebeke

Notes.

Line unchanged since 22ⁿᵈ October

During the night, the 2ⁿᵈ Division
was relieved by the 17ᵗʰ Division.

The Lahore Division (less Ferozepore
Inf. Bde.) moved south to Estaires.

Reninghelst

Dickebusch

Voormezeele

9th

St Eloi

Hollebeke

3rd CAV. BDE.
& 129th

La Clytte

Westoutre

Vierstraat

Wytschaete

CAVALRY CORPS

Oosttaverne

6th CAV. BDE.

Locre

Kemmel

Spanbroekmolen

4th CAV. BDE.
& ½ 57th

Windmill

Messines

Hout

Wambele

9th CAV. DIV

St Jans Cappel

Dranoutre
½ 1/CONN. R.

1st CAV. BDE.

1st CAV.
DIV.

2nd CAV. BDE.

WARNETON

GUARD

Wulverghem

Douve

Neuve Eglise

St Yves

4th

BAILLEUL

Ploegsteert

Wormhe

le Touquet

Fr

DIVISION

INF. BDE.

la Ghee

Nieppe

le Bizet

Steenwerck

ARMENTIERE

½ 12th INF. BDE.

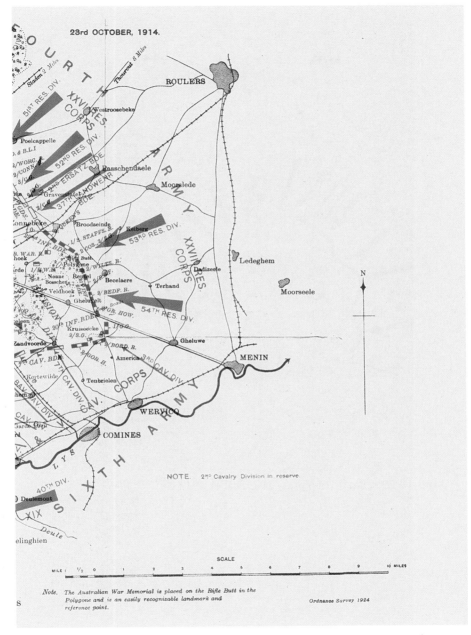

23rd OCTOBER, 1914.

ROULERS

Westroosebeke

Poelcappelle

Passchendaele

Moorslede

Gravenstafel

Broodseinde

Keiberg

Zonnebeke

Becelaere

Terhand

Ledeghem

Dadizeele

Moorseele

Polygone

Nonne Boschen

Reutel

Veldhoek

Gheluvelt

Kruiseecke

Zandvoorde

Gheluwe

MENIN

Kortewilde

Tenbrielen

America

WERVICQ

COMINES

N

NOTE. 2ND Cavalry Division in reserve.

Deulemont

elinghien

SCALE

MILE ½ 0 1 2 3 4 5 6 7 8 9 10 MILES

Note. The Australian War Memorial is placed on the Rifle Butt in the
Polygone and is an easily recognizable landmark and
reference point.

Ordnance Survey 1924

Map 9 First Battle of Ypres, 23 October 1914

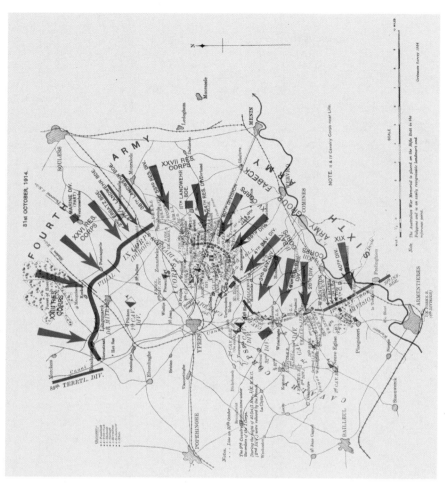

Map 10 First Battle of Ypres, 31 October 1914

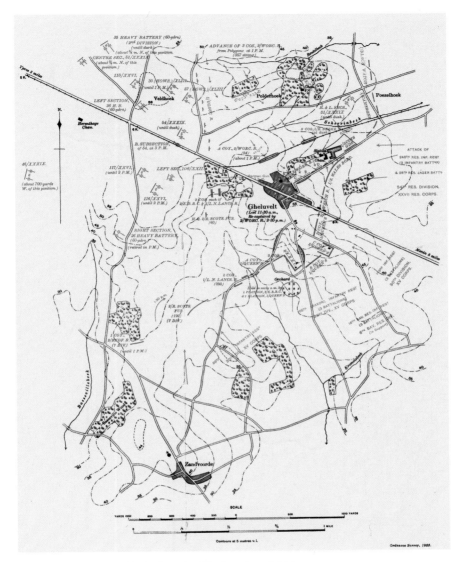

Map 11 Defence of Gheluvelt, 31 October 1914

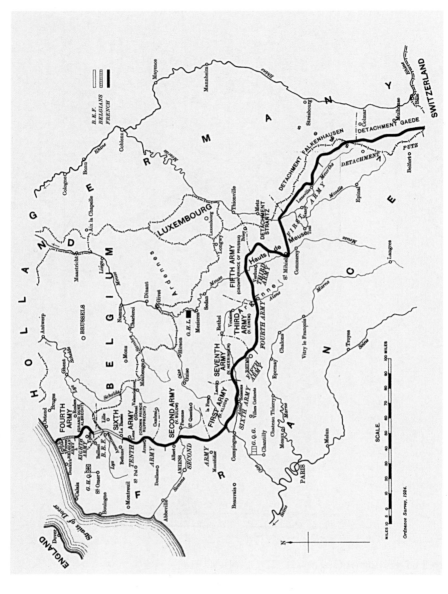

Map 12 Situation on the Western Front, December 1914

2

READY FOR WAR?

When it comes be assured it will come suddenly. We shall wake up one night, and find ourselves at war. Another thing is certain. This war will be no walk-over. In the military sphere it will be the hardest, fiercest, and bloodiest struggle we have ever had to face; let us fully make up our minds to that, and probably every one of us here to-night will take part in it. We need not be afraid of overdoing our preparations.[1]

Major Herbert Musgrave, Experimental Flight, Royal Flying Corps

THE IDEA OF THE BRITISH Expeditionary Force fighting in mainland Europe had thus been established in considerable secrecy between 1906 and 1914. One key question remained: how well prepared were the British Army and its commanders for the challenge of fighting in a continental campaign? Modern warfare was a complex business, made more confusing by the contradictory lessons that could be drawn from various conflicts over the last hundred years. Had modern weapons really rendered existing tactics redundant? Did the application of the power of concentrated quick-firing artillery, machine guns and magazine bolt-action rifles mean that defenders would be rendered helpless and vulnerable to their attackers once the firefight had been won? Or was an attack under fire across open ground no longer a feasible proposition? What was the role of artillery in battle? Were cavalry doomed as an anachronism, or did the necessity for speed under fire give them a new lease of life? Would the success of fast-moving cavalry columns point to a new type of mounted infantry? Did the new aeroplanes and airships have a role in warfare? Answers to these questions seem obvious in hindsight, but at the time no one knew what would happen. Some had a strong inkling and indeed were right; others were all too certain and were wrong. Most were half-right and half-wrong – it was indeed all terribly confusing.

The British Army had undergone a considerable learning experience during the Boer War of 1899–1902. The details of the traumas, tragedies and ultimate 'success' of the British in the Boer War are not really relevant here. But it was a vital part of the development of several officers who would go on to hold senior roles in 1914. Of these the most obvious is Sir John French. Born on 28 September 1852, he briefly enlisted to train as a midshipman in the Royal Navy in 1866. A combination of seasickness and vertigo rendered a life on the ocean wave a matter of great discomfort, so he left the navy and after serving in the militia was commissioned into the 8th King's Royal Hussars in 1874. Following successful periods of regimental service, he fought in the Sudan in 1884–1885 and was promoted to command the 19th Hussars in 1888. After service in India, where an adultery case against him might have derailed his career but for the support of senior officers, he achieved the command of a cavalry brigade at Aldershot in 1899. French would excel as a dashing cavalry leader throughout the Boer War, especially at the Battle of Elandslaagte on 21 October 1899. He rose to command the Cavalry Division and began to be seen as the 'coming man' in the army when a column under his energetic direction was successful in relieving the besieged town of Kimberley on 15 February 1900. Ultimately, he was promoted to lieutenant general and appointed to the Aldershot Command in 1902. His reputation was such that he was included on the Committee of Imperial Defence and thus played a part in helping shape the role of the army in the Great War. French became the Chief of the Imperial General Staff in 1912. Finally in 1913 he was made a full field marshal and designated as the commander of the BEF if the need should arise. Although undoubtedly a distinguished cavalry officer, few would have considered French as a military theoretician – indeed his own words mark him out as a more intuitive commander.

> A life-long experience of military study and thought had taught
> me that the principle of the tactical employment of troops must be

instinctive. I knew that in putting the science of war into practice, it was necessary that its main tenets should form, so to speak, part of one's flesh and blood. In war there is little to think and the right thing to do must come like a flash – it must present itself to the mind as perfectly obvious.[2]

In truth, French was not a serious student of war and merely rationalising his personal self-assurance that a 'happy instinct' would guide him in the absence of hard graft. This conviction was a significant hostage to fortune given the uncertainties and complexities of modern warfare.

In sharp contrast to French was Sir Douglas Haig, one of the most influential of the senior officers in 1914. Haig was born in Edinburgh on 19 June 1861 to a prosperous middle-class family involved in the whisky trade. He was thus by no means the upper-class scion of legend. Educated at Clifton College in Bristol, he attended Brasenose College at Oxford University, before becoming a cadet at the Royal Military College, Sandhurst from 1884–1885. He was commissioned into the 7th Hussars in 1885. After a successful regimental stint in India and various staff postings, he returned to attend the Staff College at Camberley in 1896. By this time he had begun to gain a reputation as a very capable officer, blessed with a capacity for hard work and a mind that could cut through irrelevancies to focus on what was important.

> If a scheme interested him he took tremendous pains with it; if he thought there was no profit in working it out, he sent in a perfunctory minimum. I remember a road reconnaissance sketch on which most of us lavished extreme care, marking all the letter-boxes, pumps, gateways into fields and such-like. Haig handed in a sheet with a single brown chalk-line down the centre, the cross roads shown and the endorsement, 'Twenty miles long, good surface, wide enough for two columns with orderlies both ways!'[3]
>
> Captain James Edmonds, Staff College, Camberley

In 1898, Haig was selected for duties in the Sudan, where he experienced active service for the first time, demonstrating a coolness under fire that would serve him well. Haig then served with distinction during the Boer War, both as staff officer under the command of Sir John French and whilst leading a cavalry column, before promotion to colonel and the prestigious command of the 17th Lancers in 1901. His abilities were evident and as a result he would be given several key staff appointments in the years that followed. First he became Inspector General of Cavalry, before promotion to Major General, acting in the capacity as Director of Military Training at the War Office from 1906–1907. This was followed by the role of Director of Staff Duties in 1907–1908. Next came the challenging appointment of Chief of the General Staff in India from 1909. Finally he was promoted to Lieutenant General and in 1912 given the Aldershot Command. This was a crucial appointment as he would henceforth be responsible for the preparation and training of the 1st and 2nd Divisions, which would form I Corps under his command in the event of war. Throughout his career, Haig had prepared diligently for war, studying military history and in particular German military doctrine. To that end he had attended their manoeuvres and could read German. He was also reasonably proficient in French – the language of his likely allies. Not for nothing would he be known as 'The Educated Soldier'.[4] Haig's importance does not just rest on his contributions during the war as commander of I Corps (1914), the First Army (1915) and ultimately the whole BEF (1915–1919), but also reflects his pre-war work in preparing the army for the campaigns that lay ahead. Just as a sympathetic understanding of Haig and his command role is the litmus test of competence for military historians of the Great War, so his pre-war career can be used as a prism to refract light on the development of the British Army in the years leading up to 1914.

When it came to military doctrine, Haig, like many others, had been greatly influenced by the teaching he had received at the Staff College during the formative years of his intellectual development as a soldier. Throughout his career Haig was not generally an original thinker per se but he proved receptive to the ideas of others, which, once tested and found sound, he would adopt and then develop, or modify, to meet his needs. Thus Haig became an adherent of the standard Staff College interpretation that any battle would go through distinct stages: initial manoeuvring to gain a tactically advantageous position, the first encounters, followed by a wearing out phase of indeterminate length before one side or the other starts to lose cohesion in the field, at which point the decisive stroke could be launched and followed by the exploitation of victory to the maximum effect. When working as Director of Staff Duties he would encapsulate this approach into the revision of Field Service Regulations

Part I and II, manuals issued in 1909 by the Army Council that sketched out general tactical principles to govern the conduct of the British Army in future conflicts. Haig was convinced that these basic premises were a sufficient espousal of all the doctrine required. This was in contrast to the more developed theoretical approach of both the German and French military schools of thought.

> While the German General Staff preaches the doctrine of envelopment, and the French General Staff advocates a large general reserve with a view to a concentrated blow at a decisive point of the enemy's battle order, the critics urge that the British General Staff hesitates to publish and to teach a clear line of action. The reasoning appears to be that unless some such definite doctrine is decided and inculcated in peace, action in war will be hesitating and mistakes will be made. The critics seem to lose sight of the real nature of war, and the varying conditions under which the British Army may have to take the field. It is neither necessary nor desirable that we should go further than what is so clearly laid down in our regulations. If we go further, we run the risk of tying ourselves to a doctrine that may not be always applicable, and gain nothing in return. An army trained to march long distances, to manoeuvre quickly, and to fight with the utmost determination, will be a suitable instrument in the hands of a competent commander whether the situation is to be solved by 'envelopment' or 'penetration'.[5]

In view of the way that warfare developed over the next ten years, it is worth noticing that the Field Service Regulations laid special emphasis on the necessity of all the component parts of the army acting together in concert on the battlefield.

> The fighting troops of the army are composed of cavalry, artillery, engineers, infantry, mounted infantry, and of cyclists. These arms are in certain proportions, which have been fixed as the result of experience. Each has its special characteristics and functions, and is dependent on the assistance of the others. *The full power of an army can be exerted only when all its parts act in close combination,* and this is not possible unless the members of each arm understand the characteristics of the other arms. Infantry depends on artillery to enable it to obtain superiority of fire and to close with the enemy. Without mounted troops the other arms are hampered by ignorance of the enemy's movements, cannot move in security, and are unable to reap effectually

the fruits of victory, while mounted troops are at a great disadvantage, unless accompanied by horse artillery, which assists them to combine shock action with fire. Artillery and engineers are only effective in conjunction with the other arms, and all their efforts must be directed towards assisting the latter to secure decisive success.[6]

General Staff, War Office, Field Service Regulations, Part I

Such a sensible ideal was a long way from fruition in 1914, five years after publication. The army was still in thrall to the cult of the regiment, which were the individual fiefdoms of the lieutenant colonel in command, and there was little consideration as to how they could liaise together to fight effectively as a brigade, never mind a division or corps. There was no real grasp of how to properly coordinate the operations of infantry, artillery and cavalry, a situation exacerbated by the lack of training areas of sufficient size to accommodate realistic large formation exercises.

The infantry division was the building block of both corps and army commands in the European armies. In the British Army a division was composed of three infantry brigades, (each of four battalions), three brigades of field artillery (each of three batteries), a howitzer brigade (three batteries) and a single heavy battery. Each division had its own integral divisional engineers, medical services and lines of communications troops. The cavalry division was made up of three cavalry brigades (each of three regiments and a battery of horse artillery). But the trained staff required to allow the constituent elements to function smoothly in accordance with the intent of the Field Service Regulations were sadly lacking. Staff work was widely perceived as a dull necessity, to be avoided if possible, and regimental duty was seen as the highlight of an officer's career – particularly in time of war.

In devising a modern tactical approach, one complication for the British Army was the considerable confusion caused by the Boer War in the proper analysis of field tactics. The highly mobile mounted Boer commandos were a far from typical opponent, but of course they still had to be effectively countered. Unfortunately, the successful response, involving the use of chains of blockhouses coupled with the operation of columns of cavalry, mounted infantry and horse artillery, had skewed tactical thinking towards the value of mobility in the field. But such tactical considerations were a short-term fix, irrelevant to the kind of fighting between continental armies that would be likely in a European conflagration. Indeed the 'lessons' of the Boer War were equally opaque to German and French military theorists.

For the British infantry, 'fire and movement' was still the characteristic mode of attack. An assault would be launched once 'fire superiority' had been achieved, the attack going in, if possible from the flanks, with continued heavy supporting fire directed at the enemy positions.

> The essence of infantry tactics consists in breaking down the enemy's resistance by the weight and direction of its fire, and then completing his overthrow by assault. Although the enemy may not await the assault, infantry must be constantly animated with the desire to close with him. Troops under cover, unless enfiladed, can seldom be forced to retire by fire alone, and a decision by fire, even if possible, takes long to obtain. To drive an enemy from the field, assault, or the immediate threat of it, is almost always necessary.[7]
>
> General Staff, War Office, Field Service Regulations, Part I

Many British officers had a respect for the firepower of modern weapons, having seen the effects inflicted by their own fire in various colonial encounters or the bitter fruit of attacks across open ground on Boer entrenchments. One answer to the problems of such an attack in the future was that they intended to 'win' the firefight that would precede any assault. To help them in that task the British infantry were equipped with an admirable weapon in the .303 Short Magazine Lee Enfield Mark III rifle introduced to the army in 1907. Its magazine could hold two clips of five rounds, with an efficient bolt action to load and extract rounds. It had a range that reached out to around 2,800 yards but the Field Service Regulations defined up to 600 yards as 'close' and 600–1,000 yards to be 'effective'. These ranges were far more relevant to the wide-open veldts of South Africa than the closed-in rural and industrial landscapes of Western Europe, where a clear shot of even 600 yards could be difficult to obtain. Cults of both marksmanship and rapid fire had developed with the men expending up to 250 rounds a year in refining their skills on the rifle ranges. They were taught to be capable of measured firing at targets at long range, snap-shooting at nearer moving targets and the famous 15–20 rounds in the 'mad minute' of rapid fire to provide a wall of fire to stem an enemy assault at close range. Such a rate could not be exercised for long as the rifles would soon overheat and run out of ammunition – the individual soldier only carried 120 rounds in his webbing pockets with an additional 100 rounds in cloth bandoliers.

The days of close-order attacks had been ended by the brutal realities of the Boer War. The Boers had dug systems of well-concealed trenches that had provided safe refuge from British infantry and artillery fire, thereby allowing them to conserve their manpower until the moment came to open fire and rebuff frontal attacks. In the aftermath of that war, infantry assault tactics were refined to try to solve the conundrum of getting men across open ground to defended positions. The solution adopted was to make the initial approaches in widely extended order, with the men up to ten yards apart, often employing a series of successive rushes at the double covered by heavy covering fire. This was the 'fire' that allowed the 'movement' by forcing an enemy to keep their heads down. The men advanced as individuals, making their way forward in accordance with their orders, but allowed to take cover if it became really necessary. Once close enough to the enemy positions they would establish a firing line and then they in turn would provide the covering fire as more troops were fed forwards, thus gradually building up their strength for the decisive firefight that if successful would precede a final assault.

Sadly, there was nowhere near this awareness from the British Army of the tactical requirements for a successful defensive action. The construction of realistic trenches was rarely at the heart of peacetime exercises for a variety of reasons that combined the lazy avoidance of hard physical graft, the lack of a suitable training environment and the overall concentration on the offensive at the expense of defence.

The abandonment of close formations, coupled with the difficult command and control environment expected on a modern battlefield, meant that it was a concomitant necessity to inculcate qualities of intelligence and resourcefulness amongst junior officers, NCOs and private soldiers. Men had to be able to think for themselves in the press of action, for although orders were still there to be obeyed, when they were deprived of orders for whatever reason there was no point in milling round like sheep. Individual soldiers had to step up to the mark and take control of the situation. Yet to do this they had to have practice: if they were to act as an elite force, there had to be a commensurate investment in education and training. The balance between maintaining firm discipline and encouraging initiative was difficult to achieve, especially given the widespread distrust in 'polite' society of the working classes, exemplified by a scepticism that they could ever exercise free will in a responsible fashion. This reluctance to hand over power, coupled with the usual budgetary restraints, impaired the tactical training of NCOs. Nonetheless, there was an improvement in the overall skill and initiative of the trained regular soldiers in the years leading up to the Great War.

The value of machine guns as a concentrated essence of infantry had long been appreciated within the British Army. Officers like Haig saw the value of such a deadly weapon, and before leaving for Egypt in 1898 he had visited the Royal Ordnance Factory to study the working mechanism of the Maxim. He would even employ them in battle to some considerable effect in repelling an attack by the Dervish infantry and cavalry on 5 April 1898. The usage of the machine gun was encapsulated into the Field Service Regulations.

> The machine gun possesses the power of delivering a volume of concentrated rifle fire which can be rapidly directed against any desired object. Rapid fire cannot be long sustained owing to the expenditure of ammunition involved, and it is therefore necessary that the movements and fire action of these weapons should be regulated so as to enable them to gain their effect by means of short bursts of rapid and accurate fire whenever a favourable opportunity arises. Surprise is an important factor in the employment of machine guns, which should be concealed, and whenever possible provided with cover from fire.[8]
>
> General Staff, War Office, Field Service Regulations, Part I

The battalion machine gun sections were armed with two belt-fed Maxim machine guns, which was equivalent to the provision in both the French and German armies. There had been calls for more machine guns, but these were resisted on the grounds of cost, as was the suggestion of their replacement with the much lighter Vickers machine gun. The recent re-equipment with a new rifle and artillery pieces had evidently plumbed the shallow pockets of the army budget. While the potential worth of machine guns had been accepted, the tactical employment of them as a weapon was still in its infancy. The importance of locating machine guns to take an attacking force from the flank was not always grasped, nor was the danger of putting such valuable weapons in the front line, where they could be soon located and targeted. It would take time to learn how best to employ this deadly weapon to best effect.

Overall, when it came to infantry tactics, there is no doubt that many of the senior officers of the British Army were at least partial adherents to the cult of the offensive battlefield tactics as espoused by many of the leading generals of the French Army, of which one of the most eloquent was Ferdinand Foch in his capacity as commandant at the École Supérieure de Guerre. It was believed that modern weapons would permit such a devastating concentration of firepower on defending troops that they would break under the strain and thus be rendered vulnerable to the assault by determined troops. The concept of the 'spirit of the offensive' and ability to overcome obstacles was explicitly referenced within the Field Service Regulations.

> Decisive success in battle can be grained only by a vigorous offensive. Every commander who offers battle, therefore, must be determined to assume the offensive sooner or later. If the situation be unfavourable for such a course, it is wiser, when possible, to manoeuvre for a more suitable opportunity; but when superiority in skill, morale or numbers has given a commander the initiative, he should turn it to account by forcing a battle before the enemy is ready. Superior numbers on the battlefield are an undoubted advantage, but skill, better organization, and training, and above all a firmer determination in all ranks to conquer at any cost, are the chief factors of success. Half-hearted measures never attain success in war, and lack of determination is the most fruitful source of defeat. A defensive attitude at the outset of a battle should not be assumed except when it is advisable to gain time or to utilize advantages of ground for some special reason, e.g., to compensate for inferiority of numbers.[9]
>
> General Staff, War Office, Field Service Regulations, Part I

While there is some truth in these precepts, they had not taken into account the devastating power of bolt-action rifles, machine guns and artillery fire deployed from covered positions by an equally well-trained and motivated force – for instance the German Army. Where there is no flank to turn or more 'suitable opportunity' then an attack over open ground would result in nothing but slaughter. The narrative of much of the fighting from 1914–1916 would see the British slowly come to terms with this new reality.

The tactical development of the Royal Artillery was complicated by the failure to grasp properly either the naked power of the guns or their potential multifarious roles in battle. During the Boer War, the fatal consequences of placing two batteries well within rifle range of the Boer lines had been exposed at the Battle of Colenso, when the gun detachments had soon been shot down and most of the guns lost. Yet some of the impact of this salutary lesson had faded and much more attention had been drawn to the value of light guns to accompany the mobile columns chasing after the Boer Commandos. These confusions were only made worse by the failure to digest the lessons emanating from the Russo-Japanese War of 1904–1905. One of the official British observers, Sir Ian Hamilton, brought back reports that could – or perhaps should – have prompted a change in attitude to the potential of the guns. At the Battle of Yalu, the Japanese had numerous guns and 4.7″ howitzers hidden in concealed positions with carefully thought-out arrangements for concentrating indirect fire.

> These observation stations were connected with the howitzer batteries by telephone, and both batteries and observation stations having duplicate maps of the enemy's position marked out in small squares, the observers on the southern heights were able, by merely telephoning down the number of a square, to switch the whole fire effect of the masked batteries on to any spot where they from their elevation could see a suitable mark present itself. Platforms were also erected in trees on the flanks of the batteries, from whence officers would be able to make local observations of the effect of their fire. All this was accomplished in one night, and, although the soil was light and easy to dig, yet, when I saw those deep trenches, the platforms, and the enormous baulks of timber I confess I was fairly surprised.[10]

The Japanese batteries proved capable of inflicting devastating counter-battery fire once they managed to locate the Russian opposing guns on the opposite bank of the river.

> No guns in the world could resist a couple of large pontoon boats full of men rowing quietly about on a broad river within very easy range of their muzzles. Therefore inevitably the Russians opened on

the boats, and instantly seventy-two guns and twenty howitzers were at them. The Russians never had a chance, but just for the first ten minutes the *rafale* of their quick-firing artillery enabled them to look dangerous to the anxious headquarters staff and infantry looking on at a distance. After that, not only the overwhelming superiority of the Japanese in batteries and in weight of metal, but also all their careful preparations told with crushing effect. The Japanese were invisible and comparatively invulnerable, the Russians were conspicuous and everywhere most vulnerable. In thirty minutes the Russian guns were silenced. At 11am they brought up a fresh battery on to the knoll east of Makau and opened fire, but these guns were also silenced in a couple of minutes by two or three batteries of Guards artillery, which had that morning advanced on to Kyurito island. Thus, in an easy triumph ended the anxiously anticipated artillery duel, probably the last of its sort that will ever take place.[11]

The trouble was that there were so many lessons tucked away in such incidents that it was difficult for Hamilton, or anyone else, to decide what was of enduring importance – and what was a fluke, created by particular circumstances unlikely to be repeated. Hamilton himself was more taken with the question of whether the weaker Russian gunners should have declined the artillery duel at the Yalu River and instead reserved their fire for the moment when the Japanese infantry attacked. The value of the Japanese concealed positions and indirect fire was referenced, but not emphasised, in his arguments.

In the aftermath of the Boer War, the Royal Artillery remained locked into a tactical perspective which looked to direct fire from the guns in close support of an infantry assault – or to repel an opposing enemy attack. Mobility was regarded as a prerequisite for the guns which otherwise would not be able to keep up with the envisaged fast-moving operations. Heavier guns would be slower, so there was a built-in bias towards light field guns with gun carriages that sacrificed extra range for mobility. As a result in 1904 the Royal Artillery settled on the 18-pounder (84mm) as their main field artillery piece. This was a quick-firing gun, a relatively new technology, where, upon firing, the gun barrel recoiled within a buffer case, slowed and then halted before being returned to the original firing position by recuperator springs. As the gun carriage remained static there was no need to relay the gun before each shot. This allowed a rate of fire of up to twenty rounds a minute. They fired a shrapnel shell that weighed just over 18 pounds and contained 374 spherical lead-alloy bullets. The shell was detonated by a time fuse, set by the good judgement of the gunner to explode in the air just in front of the target. This propelled forward the bullets much akin to a shotgun charge which would scatter the ground to deadly effect for any infantry caught in the open. There was no provision of high-explosive shells. The 18-pounder proved to be a fine field gun with a range of up to 6,500 yards, comparable to its equivalents, the French 75mm (which had a much faster rate of fire but fired a lighter shell) and the German 77mm. The British standard field howitzer was the excellent 4.5" howitzer (114mm) first brought into service in 1909. With a range of 7,300 yards, capable of firing up and over obstacles that would thwart the flat trajectory of a gun, it had a firing rate of four rounds per minute and fired a high-explosive (HE) shell weighing 35 pounds. Each division had three brigades of three six-gun batteries (a total of fifty-four 18-pounders), with one brigade of three batteries of 4.5" howitzers (a total of eighteen). In addition, there was one battery of four 60-pounder guns, the sole concession to any heavy artillery support. Weighing some 4½ tons, they were slow-moving beasts pulled by a large team of horses. Firing a 60-pound shell of HE or shrapnel, it had a range of 10,300 yards, but as a gun it had a flat trajectory which rendered it incapable of plunging fire. The cavalry divisions were equipped with 13-pounder guns, a slightly lighter version of the 18-pounder firing a shell just under 13 pounds to a maximum range of 5,900 yards.

As far as field artillery went, the divisional establishment of guns was adequate compared to French and German practice. The problem came with the lack of mobile heavy howitzers. The Germans in the pre-war years had a much greater interest in the capabilities of such weapons, seeing them as vital to breaking down permanent or temporary field works in order to restore mobility to the battlefield. Long-range howitzers also offered a superb counter-battery capacity to win any artillery duel preceding a battle. It would be fair to say that few appreciated the pressing need for heavy howitzers for prolonged periods of trench warfare.

It should nonetheless be recognised that much of the individual training of the gunners in the Royal Artillery was excellent. Gun drill may have been repetitive but it worked, allowing impressive rates of fire to be achieved. The gun detachments could drop swiftly into action and the officers had mastered the methodology of direct ranging, with a section of two guns firing using a 100-yard bracket system until the range of the target was established, at which point the whole of the battery would open up a rapid fire. Simple skill levels were good, even if there was no real understanding of the more arcane elements of gunnery that would be required in the battles to come. Of course, if artillery actions were to be fought at close range, then relatively simple adjustments of range and direction could be made from the gun position itself. There was the acknowledged possibility of communicating with observers in positions of vantage by telephone, but these forward observation officers were usually still located close to the gun line. However, there was a widespread ignorance of the diverse techniques required for *accurate* indirect fire, to be employed when a target was invisible from the guns. First, the maps and surveying techniques were far too inaccurate to allow for 'shooting off the map' by estimating exact locations, ranges and angles. Second, the science of individually calibrating guns to allow for different barrel characteristics and rates of wear was not generally understood. Third, the importance of making allowance for meteorology, and in particular changing barometric pressures, was not yet grasped. There was even a shortfall at the battery level of the required telephones and reels of telephone wire, which made communication with a forward observation post difficult except in ideal circumstances.

Summing up, as far as most Royal Field Artillery (RFA) and Royal Horse Artillery (RHA) officers were concerned, the concept of registering an invisible target from concealed gun positions lay in a glum future when mathematics and science had overwhelmed the gentlemanly pursuit of warfare. After all, in the envisaged fast-moving battle there simply wouldn't be the time for complicated indirect fire arrangements. Many were more interested in the French methodology of employing the 75mm guns to deliver a blizzard of shells in the general area of the target. Only the lesser-status officers of the Royal Garrison Artillery and Coastal Artillery seemed to take the science of gunnery seriously. Even the shells fired by the guns betrayed their purpose: shrapnel shells were deadly against infantry or gunners in the open, but of far more limited use against troops or guns under cover. The Royal Artillery lacked the HE shells necessary to destroy trenches, buildings and covered gun positions. Indeed the worst possible scenario for them would be to encounter an enemy equipped with long-range heavy howitzers engaging in indirect fire from gun pits behind a hill. In truth they had a limited supply of *any* shells as there was no concept of sustained fire either in a continuous engagement or to break down strong enemy defence works. Each 18-pounder gun had only 176 rounds held at the battery, part of a total of just 1,000 shells per gun in France, with a meagre 300 more back in Britain and theoretically another 500 due from the munitions factories within six months. During the later stages of the Great War, guns could easily have to fire 500 rounds in a single day – accurately in complex barrages – without the gun detachments ever seeing a German. All told the Royal Artillery had a lot to learn in 1914.

One bitterly contested area of 'doctrine' was over the role and nature of cavalry in war.[12] The dispute had a particular importance to officers like Haig and French, who were by their origins 'cavalry generals' whose rise at least in part reflected the long-standing social cachet and prestige of the cavalry regiments within the army. Cavalry had traditionally been charged with the role of reconnaissance, feeling their way forward, carefully probing to determine the movements and strength of the enemy. At the same time they were expected to establish a screen to deny the self-same intelligence to the opposing cavalry. Before the advent of aeroplanes there was really no other method of determining what was going on. There was also the concept of the bold cavalry raid, penetrating deep into enemy territory with a potentially devastating effect on lines of communications and rear-echelon formations. Finally, the cavalry were considered to be 'shock' troops, the *arme blanche* capable of charging enemy formations and shattering their cohesion. It was this last that triggered most controversy. It was apparent that the advent of modern weapons had thrown a considerable question over the feasibility of the classical knee-to-knee charge. It seemed evident that few charging troopers would survive given exposure to quick-firing artillery, machine guns and magazine rifles, especially if they were held up by barbed wire defences.

One recent development was an interest in the potential of mounted infantry or mounted rifles, capitalising on the perceived success of such hybrid cavalry in the Boer War. It was accepted that there was a continued necessity on the modern battlefield for effective reconnaissance and screening, but there was great scepticism in some quarters as to the need for dashing charges to achieve significant military results. At the centre of this campaign was Lord Roberts, the Commander-in-Chief of

the British Army from 1901–1904. This distinguished officer had come
to view cavalry officers as hidebound idiots, unable to grasp the new
realities of the battlefield. He launched a series of attacks or reforming
initiatives (depending on perspective) on the cavalry, demanding the
abandonment of the lance and the sword in favour of a concentration on
the rifle. He triggered a splenetic debate amongst the cavalry fraternity,
which then spilled out into the popular press. Roberts had the unfortunate knack of alienating not only the more reactionary officers opposed
to any change per se, but also the more progressive officers like Haig who
had already adopted a far more nuanced position looking to the future.

The tactical response of intelligent cavalrymen was to ensure that
any charge would be covered by intense fire in an attempt to prepare the
way for success. Indeed, following the failure of the Russian cavalry to
achieve much of note during the Russo-Japanese War of 1904–1905, some
speculated that in a full-scale battle cavalry might have to be kept back
until the decisive firefight had been already won by the combined action
of the infantry and artillery – only then would the cavalry be released to
fall on their broken enemies. There was also an increased awareness of
the necessity of seeking concealed or sheltered approach routes, coupled
with the evident desirability of taking artillery from the flank and the
importance of speed in execution across open ground.

Overall it was clear that the timing of a cavalry charge was crucial.
But at the crunch it was clear: the cavalry did not want to lose the option
of the charge – to lose the chance to break the morale of an enemy by
inflicting upon them the terrific kinetic impact of man and horse at full
pelt, with the additional atavistic fear of cold steel driving deep into their
vitals. There was no denying the importance attached within cavalry regiments to the sword and the lance for reasons of prestige and morale, as
summed up by French in 1904.

> It is difficult to define what one means by the 'cavalry spirit', but it is
> a power which is felt and realised by those who have served much in
> that arm. Its attributes are 'dash', 'élan', a fixed determination always to
> take the offensive and secure the initiative. Such a spirit can never be
> created in a body of troops whose first idea is to abandon their horses
> and lie down under cover in the face of a swiftly charging mass of
> horsemen.[13]

Many senior cavalry officers feared that if they surrendered the option of the charge then they would lose that offensive spirit, that instead of attacking their enemies on sight, they would dismount and commence a fire-fight, thereby losing any opportunity to attack before the enemy was entrenched.

Ultimately, once the saddle burr of Roberts' relentless negativity had been – at least partially – removed upon his retirement, the end result of all the sound and fury was a sensible compromise. The regular cavalry would be trained for all eventualities and thus capable of performing the full range of roles ascribed to it, while the yeomanry, colonial mounted rifles and any units generated in wartime were not supposed to be trained in 'shock tactics', although this restriction was often breached in practice. This meant that the training of a regular trooper remained a slow business, but the end result was surely worthwhile: a skilful horseman, with the practical knowledge to care for his animal in the field, trained to a proficient standard on his rifle – the same .303 Lee Enfield rifle carried by the infantry – and accomplished in all the 'bread and butter' cavalry duties of outposts, screening and reconnaissance patrols. The cavalry were able to deploy rapidly for dismounted action to act as infantry in any emergency, but equally equipped to launch a raid far behind enemy lines, and of course still capable of launching an 'old-fashioned' charge with sword or lance should the opportunity ever arise as a result of maintaining an offensive attitude. As such the cavalry would prove to be valuable troops who could turn their hands to almost anything.

In the event in 1914, a swollen cavalry division of five brigades would accompany the BEF, supported by two Maxim machine guns per regiment and four batteries of the light quick-firing 13-pounder guns of the RHA. It is undeniable that modern cavalrymen had grasped the innate power of modern weapons, but at the same time they were aware that all European armies were planning for a short, fast-moving war of manoeuvre, avoiding entrenchment wherever possible, and therefore promising plenty of opportunity for cavalry action. They knew it would be risky and appreciated that casualties might be high, but they still believed that the results of the cavalry charge could be worthwhile. The question was would the war be as they, and almost everyone else, imagined? Only time would tell. This was not a case of boneheaded cavalrymen opposing all reason, but rather more a desire to preserve all possible capabilities of cavalry as the only truly mobile force available on the contemporary battlefield.

Whilst the generals pondered on the future of cavalry, a certain degree of mental agility was required as they simultaneously struggled to appreciate the almost immediate impact that would be made by aeroplanes on the practice of warfare. The first aeroplane had only fluttered into the air in 1903 but already there was much interest in the military potential of both aeroplanes and airships. Although ideas of effective bombing and the use of machine guns to strafe troops from the skies were still in the future, the aerial reconnaissance possibilities were immediately obvious. Previously there had been experiments with tethered observation balloons, but airships and aircraft offered a far more free-ranging area of vision. In the 1910 divisional and army exercises, both a single aeroplane and the airship *Beta* had been deployed in an experimental fashion. Although there was an awareness that the technology was at an early stage and that aircraft were still unreliable in all but the mildest weather conditions, it was evident that the army was monitoring the advance of aviation. Flying trials were also held in India in 1911, which impressed Haig enough for him to recommend that officers be sent back to Britain to learn to fly. Very early on, experiments began to investigate the possibilities of aerial photography, the observation of artillery fire and the feasibility of ground-to-air and air-to-ground signalling. There was also interest in seeking the best way of disguising the presence of troops and temporary field fortification from the eyes in the sky.

In consequence there is no doubt that the aerial dimension of warfare was very much at the forefront of many military minds during the manoeuvres held September 1912. Although the exercises were severely restricted by a grievous lack of space, budgetary considerations and the restrictions imposed by the continuation of civilian life within much of the area, there was still something to be gained as senior officers and their staff could practice the multifarious disciplines required in controlling operations conducted by large numbers of troops. The scheme featured Haig in command of the Red Force, while his opponent in command of the Blue Force would be Lieutenant General Sir James Grierson. This distinguished officer was born in 1859 and had been commissioned into the Royal Artillery in 1877. He served with distinction in various staff capacities, including active service in both Egypt and Sudan. In 1896, he became the Military Attaché in Berlin, before service in the Boer War. In 1904, he was made Director of Military Operations, following which he commanded first the 1st Division at Aldershot from 1906 and then Eastern Command from 1912. Fluent in both German and French, he was tactically astute and a worthy opponent for Haig, who had only just taken over the Aldershot Command. At this stage of their careers, this was very much a battle between equals.

Historically there has been much exaggeration as to the results of these manoeuvres, often presented as a huge success against the odds for Grierson through his innovative use of aerial reconnaissance.[14] Haig's Red Force (1st and 2nd Divisions plus a cavalry division) was playing the part of an invader, landing in East Anglia and advancing on London, which the Blue Force (3rd and 4th Divisions plus two cavalry brigades) was defending with a concentration area to the south of Cambridge. These were the exceptionally large (by the standards of the British Army) peace-time manoeuvres and included aerial observation as supplied by aerial detachments from the newly formed Royal Flying Corps (RFC). Indeed, prior to the 'battle' both generals had emphasised the importance of using aircraft to supplement the more traditional cavalry reconnaissance. Once the manoeuvres began, Haig placed a great deal of reliance on his aerial scouts and – at first – all seemed well as their initial reports allowed him to locate the bulk of Grierson's force. Using this intelligence, Haig planned to pin these forces with the 1st Division, while his 2nd Division and the Cavalry Division launched a flanking attack.

However, it would prove critical that Haig's aircraft failed to detect the 4th Division (commanded by Major General Sir Thomas D'Oyly Snow), which had been ordered to stay concealed in daylight, even employing early camouflage and deception methods to blind or confuse the observers above them. Perhaps they had been inspired by Grierson's colourful advice that they should mimic as accurately as possible the appearance of toadstools! More prosaically, they were helped by the onset of mellow autumn mists which thwarted the airship and pair of aircraft sent by Haig to check that the key sector was clear of any significant Blue Forces. His cavalry patrols were equally unsuccessful. Haig himself also tried to use deception, openly advancing a cavalry brigade as a feint to be detected by the Blue aircraft, but the overall pattern of his manoeuvring was discerned by Grierson – after all, as the 'attacker', Haig had much further to march and as such his columns of troops were impossible to disguise, in contrast to the far more static defending units. As a result, on the last day, Grierson was able to launch a surprise counter-attack by the 4th Division, which threatened a serious defeat for the Red Force. In fact the exercise ended before the 'battle' was resolved, but it was generally considered that Grierson had 'won'. In analysing his success Grierson paid tribute to the role of aircraft.

> The impression left on my mind is that their use has revolutionised the art of war. So long as hostile aircraft are hovering over one's troops all movements are liable to be seen and reported, and therefore the first step in war will be to get rid of the hostile aircraft. He who does this first or who keeps the last aeroplane afloat will win, other things being approximately equal. The airship, as long as she remained afloat, was of more use to me for strategical reconnaissance than the aeroplanes, as, being fitted with wireless telegraphy, I received her messages in a continuous stream and immediately after the observations had been made. It is a pity that the airship cannot receive messages by wireless, but doubtless modern science will soon remedy this defect.[15]

Grierson's comments presage a new era of aerial combat with the development of dedicated fighter aircraft to bring down reconnaissance aircraft. But this still lay in the future. For the moment, as Haig had discovered to his cost, aerial reconnaissance was still a fairly haphazard affair: 'The information brought in was, as a rule, so reliable that there seems a danger in taking it for granted that if no enemy are seen by the observers none are there.' French, in his capacity as the overall exercise director, seemed to appreciate both the exciting possibilities and inherent limitations of aerial scouting, stating in his report both that 'Aerial reconnaissance had added so much to the difficulty of deceiving an enemy as to the nature of the force by which he is opposed' and also that 'Even in favourable conditions it is not safe to rely entirely upon air reconnaissance, and that in close country it is possible for large bodies of troops to escape observation for some time.'[16] Senior officers also had to bear in mind that the wastage rate endemic in regular flying operations would gradually erode their air detachments; at this early stage aircraft were not robust and the accumulated stresses of pilot error, poor weather conditions and rough landings all took their toll.

Meanwhile far more junior officers were busy exploring many other military possibilities of aviation, with an experimental branch of the RFC working flat out on possible usage of balloons, kites, wireless, aerial photography, bomb-dropping, night-flying and flirtations with the possibility of fitting machine guns to aircraft. This was the future writ small, but at least the work had begun. Often these matters were considered the province of the airship. Aeroplanes were still far too underpowered to carry much weight, seeming to preclude the carrying of wireless, machine guns, or a worthwhile payload of bombs. There were also experiments in cooperation with artillery. This would prove one of the most significant aerial contributions during the Great War. Captain Sefton Brancker, an artillery officer, flew as a volunteer on numerous trial flights to determine how best to communicate between an observer in the sky and the gunners on the ground.

> Experiments were carried out from Larkhill in observation of artillery fire, and I was nominated one of the observers. Our two great difficulties were first to persuade the artillery to treat us seriously, and secondly, to communicate with them. There was never any difficulty in actual observation in the ideal conditions which prevailed on Salisbury Plain. But our progress was slow, for on account of bad weather and shortage of machines we did not accomplish much flying. We started by trying to drop messages to the battery commander, but this method was far too clumsy and slow, except as a means of indicating where the target was. Smoke puffs, lamps and other forms of visual signalling were suggested and tried, I remember General Rawlinson being much impressed by our ability to locate targets, but this was about as far as we got, and I fear the results of these experiments only made the conservative gunners still more sceptical of the value of aviation to them. It was obvious then that the ideal method of communication between the air and the ground must be wireless, and at that early date Lefroy, James and Lewis of the RFC and the Sappers were already experimenting in this direction with the very cumbersome and unreliable wireless sets which then existed.[17]

These experiments presaged the rapid developments that would be made once the experience of war revealed the importance of indirect firing, thereby creating the motivation to release appropriate resources to overcome the complex cross-disciplinary problems that had plagued

them in peacetime conditions. This was another example of the cata-
lytic effect of war.

As to the progress amongst the generals, Grierson had done well in
the 1912 army manoeuvres, but Haig had learnt his lesson and took care to
utilise more aircraft in future to reduce the chances of such an 'ambush'.
In the smaller-scale exercises of 1913, designed to test the deployment
of an expeditionary force, it was Grierson that came unstuck. On this
occasion, French was in overall command (with Grierson acting as his
Chief of Staff) of the Brown Force composed of I Corps (Haig), II Corps
(General Sir Arthur Paget) and the Cavalry Division (Major General
Edmund Allenby). Facing them was the White Force, an amalgamation
of Territorial and Yeomanry units designed to provide only a skeleton
opposition, for the exercise was largely to test the readiness for action of
the various components of the command structure. Grierson and French
soon clashed when French ordered an impractical move directly across
the front of an opposing force in an attempt to turn the flank. Such a
manoeuvre would have been disastrous in the presence of a real enemy
and Grierson objected strenuously, forcing amendments to French's
plans. The result was that Grierson, despite his good reputation, was no
longer considered suitable as the Chief of Staff at General Headquarters
in 1914, but would instead be appointed to command II Corps in the BEF
in the event of war.

There were plenty of lessons to be learnt even at this late stage: Major
General Sir Thomas D'Oyly Snow (commanding 4th Division) noticed
one failing and took care to see that it was addressed. He had discerned
in previous years that there had been a distinct reluctance to practice the
methodology of a retreat in the annual manoeuvres and could not help
but notice that when unexpected circumstances compelled his division
to retreat it had been a chaotic affair. He was determined to redress this
failing in the staff rides carried out without troops in the spring of 1914.

> The mess we got into and the number of unexpected difficulties that
> presented themselves made me determined to practise that particular
> manoeuvre. I therefore made a scheme for this staff tour which brought
> about a hasty retirement for 2½ days after an unsuccessful action. We
> had out at this tour our complete war staff. We learned a great deal
> and found out what the difficulties were which we should encounter

in a retreat, how to overcome those difficulties, and the duties of every member of the staff in a retreat. I shall always be thankful we selected this particular exercise and what it must have saved us both in lives and work when we took part in the real thing it is impossible to say.[18]

It was planned that the main annual manoeuvres for 1914 would feature a retreat in the face of superior forces, but by then, it was too late; the war had already been underway for two months. The question was how many other failings had not been detected?

THE BOER WAR HAD ALSO DEMONSTRATED that there were huge systemic problems in rapidly assembling extra forces to quickly reinforce the Regular Army in any long-term war or where serious reverses were suffered. Recruiting was voluntary and men joined the infantry for a minimum of seven years with the colours and then five more as reservists liable to be called up in the event of war. It was these reservists that would complete the battalions to form any expeditionary force and provide reinforcement drafts to restock the existing overseas units. This had proved entirely inadequate to the escalating manpower demands of the Boer War. The ad hoc response of calling on various amorphous bodies of militia, yeomanry and volunteers was also clearly not enough when even the Boers had stretched Britain's military resources to the limit. It was evident that something had to be done to rapidly channel reinforcements and volunteers to the army in times of need. Two Royal Commissions had considered the options and made various suggestions, but little was done before the advent of the Liberal Government in 1906. The man henceforth responsible would be Sir Richard Haldane, the new Secretary of State for War. Aware of the contentious nature of some of the intended reforms, Haldane made a distinct attempt to get the senior army officers 'on side' right from the beginning. This is typified by his initial meetings with Haig, who was to be his Director of Military Training and as such would become his right-hand man. The two got on right from the start: 'Mr Haldane is a fat, big man, but with a kind, genial face. One seemed to like the man at once. . . . I had two walks with Mr Haldane, before and also after lunch. He seems a most clear headed and practical man, very ready to listen and weigh carefully all that is said to him.'[19]

The army had been divided up into county-based regiments, which generally maintained one battalion on overseas service in the Empire, mostly in India, while the second battalion served at home and funnelled through enough drafts to keep the overseas unit fully up to strength. The inevitable result was that the home battalions were well below the required numbers. The question was how to create an expeditionary force of six fully equipped and manned divisions without denuding the Empire, or abandoning home defence entirely. Most of all there was to be no increase in government spending, and indeed reductions in the overall budget were sought.

Haldane's answer lay in the rationalisation of the mishmash of voluntary formations – the Volunteers, Yeomanry and Militia – into a new Territorial Force, which would be responsible for the defence of Britain, but with the intention of providing an additional force which, when properly trained, could be deployed overseas in times of war (subject to the men volunteering for that service). It was Haig's role to pull together the details of the new system and to resolve any snags that arose. One story from this busy period concerns Haig attending a medium's spiritualist sessions at the behest of his – evidently – gullible sister Henrietta. The incredulous Haig asked the medium whether the spirits had any cogent advice as to whether the new Territorial Force should be organized on a company rather than battalion basis. The spirits seem to have plumped for the company option! But there was more to follow, as the medium was apparently guided by none less than Napoleon, who perhaps had too much time on his hands in afterlife.

> It was in my power to be helped by him for good affairs but I might repel him if his influence was for bad though he had become changed for better in the spirit world. I was destined to do much good and to benefit my country. Asked by me how to ensure the Territorial Army Scheme being a success, she said, 'Thought governed the world. Think out the scheme thoroughly, one's thoughts would then be put in so convincing a manner that the people would respond (without any compulsion) and the national army would be a reality!' She could not bring Napoleon to me, but I must think of him and try to get his aid as he was always near me.[20]

Sadly, not everything could be left to the spirit world, and Haig pressed on with the hard graft required to turn Haldane's concepts into reality. There were of course objections from entrenched bastions of privilege within the militia and volunteer forces. Then again, some supporters of conscription, such as Lord Roberts, poured scorn on the scheme, questioning the military worth of part-time soldiers. Yet there was no political will, inside or outside of Parliament, for conscription. Even more importantly there was an unwillingness to face the exorbitant expense of a huge conscripted army. Further concerns were also expressed as to whether the new territorials could be entrusted with an artillery role. Through it all Haig persevered, determined to press on, and the end result of his labours was the Territorial and Reserve Forces Act of 1907. This created a structure for fourteen regional-based infantry divisions and fourteen cavalry brigades, all with the associated artillery, medical and logistical units.

The Territorial Force finally came into being on the inauspicious date of 1 April 1908. The territorial units were to be locally raised and part-funded by County Associations, but in time of war would come into the ambit of the War Office. The act also established a Special Reserve. Under this, men could enlist as special reservists and after six months of basic full-time training, usually with the 3rd (Reserve) Battalion of the regular regiments, topped up thenceforth by annual training periods, they would be eligible for call up for a period of six years. An Officer Training Corps was created, operating in public schools and universities to provide a ready source of young officers for both the regular and territorial armies. The Territorial Force was not originally intended to serve overseas but in the event, after the majority of the men had volunteered, the best trained of the territorial battalions would make a very welcome appearance to help bolster the line on the Western Front in the winter of 1914.

The Boer War had made clear the importance of improving the education and training of all ranks within the army. This most emphatically included the high command and their senior staff officers, for it was apparent that they had much to learn. Yet the Treasury blanched at the cost of establishing a fully functioning permanent general staff. One early vocal supporter was the ubiquitous Henry Wilson, who put forward an excellent summation of their intended role.

> The objects to be kept in view in forming a General Staff: (a) To gather the ablest men in the army together, and by some system of advancement and promotion to make sure that the fortunes of the army are always in their hands; (b) By means of these men, to form a

school of military thought which shall be abreast, or ahead, of that of any other army. It is impossible to secure unity of policy and action without reasoned and well-ordered thought. At present every officer has his own opinion on every conceivable military subject, the net result being that there are as many opinions as there are officers. Hence the advice tendered to the Secretary of State by his responsible military adviser is the individual advice and opinion of the officer concerned, and is not the carefully balanced opinion, after mature thought and deliberation, of a collective body of experts. Thus, continuity of thought and of action are wholly impossible, and in their place we find disjointed and unconnected plans, still-born for the most part and leading nowhere except indeed to chaos.[21]

Eventually, the proposals were accepted, but delays multiplied and it was not until September 1906 that a General Staff was created, officers of which would man the 'G' Branch at the War Office in Whitehall, which encompassed the Directorate of Military Operations, covering broad strategic and operational planning and associated intelligence; the Directorate of Staff Duties, covering the definition of war establishments, staff training and training manuals; and the Directorate of Military Training, covering home defence and the training of troops.

It was during Haig's period of work under Haldane that he orchestrated a significant step in recognising the growing importance of the colonies in providing armed forces to assist, at least in part, in their own defence. Not only would the colonial units be raised on the standard British divisional model, they would also contribute officers to an Imperial General Staff. This whole process was intended to be undertaken without interfering with the autonomy of the self-governing dominions such as Canada, Australia and New Zealand.

Haig was at the heart of reforms introduced to facilitate the creation of an Indian Expeditionary Force during his tenure as Chief of Staff India stretching from 1909 to 1912. He had taken a stiff broom to the meandering bureaucracy that clogged the system and enjoyed quoting a fine example of civil service-style circumlocution: 'Continuity of policy is not sacrosanct against diversity of circumstance.'[22] Haig sought simpler procedures, encouraging direct lines of communication between officers, to lay out clear alternatives and to define a coherent policy. In considerable secrecy he had plans produced defining in every detail the despatch of an Indian Expeditionary Force to fight alongside the BEF in France. This culminated in 1911 with a staff exercise in which they ran through the whole process to check if the plans were feasible. Contingency plans were in addition prepared for expeditions to Mesopotamia and East Africa. When Lord Morley, the Secretary of State for India, discovered what was happening, he took fright at the very idea of Indian troops serving outside the borders of India and ordered the immediate destruction of the plans. However, it would appear that Haig was also not above a degree of dissembling, for the self-same plans duly reappeared – as if by magic – when war loomed. The result would be the timely despatch of the Indian Corps to the Western Front in the late autumn of 1914.

FOR ALL THE EFFORTS TO PREPARE for war, in March 1914 a fearsome crisis threatened to undermine the whole of the British Army. Reliant on Irish Nationalist Catholic MPs to maintain his government in power, the Liberal Prime Minister Sir Herbert Asquith had introduced a Home Rule Bill which would have granted an autonomous Catholic-dominated parliament based in Dublin, thereby exercising control over the Protestant 'majority' in the Ulster provinces in Northern Ireland. The bill passed through the House of Commons and although delayed by the House of Lords, it was due to be enacted in June 1914. The Protestants were aghast and accelerated their preparations for armed resistance through the medium of the Ulster Volunteer Forces, which had attained a strength of some 100,000 men by March 1914. Several senior British officers, such as French, Wilson and even Lord Roberts, were of Irish Protestant stock and were ambivalent at the spectre of armed revolt over the prospect of Home Rule for Ireland. This was an extremely sensitive state of affairs.

In mid-March, General Sir Arthur Paget, General Officer Commanding Ireland, was given Cabinet instructions to move troops into the northern provinces as a precautionary measure to defend government buildings and armouries. Although the exact blame for what follows is difficult to apportion, the situation was exacerbated greatly when Paget demanded that the officers under his command give a categorical statement as to whether they would – or would not – obey orders if ordered to take military action against the Ulster Volunteers. Only those who actually lived in Ulster would be allowed to 'disappear' – the rest must decide, one way or another. Not unnaturally, given the substantial Protestant, Conservative and Unionist element within the British Army officer corps, this caused an immediate furore. At the epicentre of it was Brigadier General Hubert Gough, commanding the 3rd Cavalry Brigade. An Ulsterman through and through, but not domiciled there, he was thereby forced to choose and resolved to resign his commission – as did no less than fifty-seven of the seventy officers in his brigade. Gough was a man not without humour – unconscious or otherwise – and he explained that they had not mutinied, 'The truth was that *we had obeyed orders*. We had been ordered to make a choice between two alternatives which were forced on us.'[23] This spread through other units in the Curragh. Second Lieutenant Rory Macleod was serving with a battery of field artillery when he was called to a meeting of officers where the government's ultimatum was placed before them.

> All officers of the brigade at Kildare were summoned to the Colonel's office at 7pm. He sat there looking very grave with a paper in his hand and said, 'Gentlemen, I've got a very serious communication to make – I'm not going to give my own opinion – after I've read it I will give you five minutes to make up your mind and then you must tell me what you intend to do!' He then read the paper. He first of all asked the senior officers what they would do. Most of them said they couldn't afford to be instantly dismissed because they'd lose their pensions and other privileges. When it came down to me I said I would be instantly dismissed, because I knew my father had signed the Ulster Covenant and would fight on the other side.[24]

The sinuous tendrils of this affair spread through the army and it was explained somewhat belatedly that the government had only intended to protect the armouries in Ulster from the very real possibility of raids by the Ulster Volunteers.

Further complex wrangling ensued as to whether a promise should be given that Gough's cavalry would not be employed to enforce Home Rule. When such a written guarantee was conceded, it was then the turn of Asquith to be incandescent and several of the senior figures responsible – including the Minister of War Sir John Seely and Sir John French – were forced to resign in the ensuring recriminations and backtracking that ensued. French was replaced as Chief of the Imperial General Staff by Sir Charles Douglas and appointed Inspector General of the Home

Forces, although he was still earmarked for service as commander in chief of the BEF in the event of war. The whole affair heightened tensions between nationalist and unionist factions across Ireland, with both sides continuing to raise paramilitary forces in the aftermath. Although the Home Rule Bill was approved in May 1914, progress then stalled while the Liberal Government considered some form of Irish partition. Eventually the whole issue was subsumed in the turmoil surrounding the start of the Great War in August. Yet the 'Curragh Mutiny' had generated much resentment and suspicion amongst the senior ranks of the army and undoubtedly had the potential to damage their relationship with the Liberal Government.

3

LIGHTS OUT, 4 AUGUST 1914

It appears to me that things have now come to such a pitch that we cannot now abstain from joining in the war and still hold up our heads in honour. In fact, if we stay out, whoever wins, we shall presumably take it in the neck soon. The war will be a terrible business though, won't it?[1]

Lieutenant Rowland Owen, 2nd Duke of Wellington's Regiment

THE ASSASSINATION OF THE ARCHDUKE Franz Ferdinand on 28 June 1914 would provoke the outbreak of the Great War. The nationalist tensions in the Balkans were already boiling up nicely when the Bosnian Serb, Gavrilo Princip, shot dead the archduke and his wife during a visit to Sarajevo. Once Princip and his co-conspirators were arrested, interrogations by the Austro-Hungarian authorities soon revealed that the Serbian state had been deeply implicated in the plot. To the Austrians, the Serbian state represented a focus of discontent and covert support for all the Slavs within the Austro-Hungarian Empire who sought unification or independence. The enraged Austrians consulted their German allies, who promised them backing and, thus bolstered, issued a harsh ultimatum to Serbia on 23 July. In turn, Serbia was preparing to cow-tow to the demands when, on 25 July, they received the startling news that Russia was prepared to support them and indeed had begun early preparations for mobilisation. This put renewed pressure on Germany – for if it came to war, German plans were reliant on the slowness of the Russian mobilisation to assist them in striking France a fatal blow first before turning east. Emboldened by Russian support, the Serbs had the temerity to reject various aspects of the Austrian ultimatum and a state of war appeared imminent. At this point the British tried to cool the rising temperature by proposing a Four Power Conference – Britain, France, Germany and Italy – to give everyone a chance to think and seek a compromise solution avoiding war. Sadly, the Austrians by this time had the bit between their teeth and declared war on Serbia on 28 July. Last minute negotiations between Germany and Russia were doomed to failure; the wheels of war had already begun to turn. On 31 July, the Germans began to mobilise and at the same time demanded both immediate complete Russian demobilisation and a declaration of neutrality from France. France naturally refused, unwilling to fracture her precious alliance with Russia, although at the same time anxious not to be seen to be actively seeking war. On 1 August the German Empire mobilised and declared war on Russia. Immediately, German troops began to cross the Luxembourg border in the preparatory stages of the great right hook that would punch through neutral Belgium. On the same day the French Army had no choice but to mobilise for a war that now seemed inevitable. On 2 August the Italians deserted the Triple Alliance and on 3 August the Germans completed the formalities by declaring war on France. The Great European War had begun. The only question that remained was what would the British do? They had formed a loose entente with both France and Russia, but this did not mean that they *had* to fight.

There were several issues for British politicians to consider in making their decision. First, there were obligations under the 1839 Treaty of London to guarantee the neutrality of Belgium from any aggressor – which Germany clearly was, her troops already streaming across the Belgian border. Even more serious was the threat the Germans were posing to the status quo in Europe. If they emerged victorious from a war with France and Russia, then they would secure the utter domination of mainland Europe for the conceivable future. They would gain unfettered access to the Channel ports, a particular *bête noire* for the British who feared for the future with a powerful German fleet poised to strike across the English Channel. The British Secretary of State for Foreign Affairs, Sir Edward Grey, summed up the dilemma: he did not want war, but how could he avoid it?

There is but one way in which the Government could make certain at the present moment of keeping outside this War, and that would be that it should immediately issue a proclamation of unconditional neutrality. We cannot do that. We have made the commitment to France that I have read to the House which prevents us from doing that. We have got the consideration of Belgium, which prevents us also from any unconditional neutrality, and, without those conditions absolutely satisfied and satisfactory, we are bound not to shrink from proceeding to the use of all the forces in our power. If we did take that line by saying, 'We will have nothing whatever to do with this matter' under no conditions – the Belgian treaty obligations, the possible position in the Mediterranean, with damage to British interests, and what may happen to France from our failure to support France – if we were to say that all those things mattered nothing, were as nothing, and to say we would stand aside, we should, I believe, sacrifice our respect and good name and reputation before the world and should not escape the most serious and grave economic consequences.[2]

Britain had indeed made promises to France. These were not perhaps legally binding, but the naval agreement had left France wide open to attack if Britain reneged on the understanding.

Ever since the Entente matured, the whole distribution of our fleets and the French fleets has been based on our mutual cooperation. We withdrew our fleet from the Mediterranean, and the French withdrew practically all their battleships from the Channel. If we were to declare our neutrality, the German fleet would be free to do what they like. We could never look a Frenchman in the face again, and we should be hated and mistrusted by the whole world.[3]

Captain Henry Jackson, Military Aeronautics Department, War Office

One first step had already been taken by Churchill and the Admiralty as early as 26 July, when it was decided not to disperse the fleet, which had been gathered together for a royal review. This was undoubtedly a sensible precaution. At least the fleet was in a state of near-readiness and the country was safe from an unlikely surprise invasion.

Taken all in all, there was a widespread feeling that the crisis had gone too far, that to back out at that point would expose Britain to ridicule and ultimately leave her without a friend in the world.

Overwhelming opinion amongst the 'man in the street' that we must help France. It is not a question of national honour any longer, but of national welfare and actual life in the future. If we climb down (which is thought almost impossible, as it is completely unthinkable) then we must be done. Canada might join USA, Australia set up on its own, anything, in short, might be the outcome of such a degrading performance. As far as the French authorities are concerned, they want our fleet, and would like a force also; they don't want numbers; ten boy Scouts and British flag is all that is wanted. The whole thing lies in the moral support and the fact of the British flag assisting on French soil. As a matter of fact, 120,000 or 160,000 troops from us at Maubeuge would mean a very real help to France, although people talk about our army as a drop in the ocean. At present, granted that Germany will violate the neutrality of Belgium, France must prolong and therefore weaken her lines to a certain extent. There are only two ways of a flanking movement for Germany: 1) By Sea; 2) By Belgium. The first we ought to be able to settle, the second we should be able to assist France very materially in preventing by the above mentioned force. For every man we send over there Germany must tell off so many more to face us.[4]

Lieutenant Sir Edward Hulse, 1st Scots Guards

The politicians could delay no longer – they had to make their minds up one way or the other. So it was that when Germany formally declared war on Belgium on 4 August, a British ultimatum was issued at 19.00 the same day demanding the immediate withdrawal of German forces from Belgium. Of course Germany could not conform and by the end of the day Britain was at war with Germany. The Great European War was now a World War – the Great War.

As the politicians expected, the brutal realities of the German invasion of Belgium cleared away many of the doubts that might have existed within the civilian population as to whether Britain should plunge into a continental war. The British obligations had been a partial consideration in the decision to go to war, but proved a gift for the politicians who could stir the emotions of the general public with emotive calls to defend Belgium. The speeches of the Chancellor of Exchequer, Lloyd George, caught brilliantly the mood of the country and were typical of the rabble-rousing tone employed in the months that followed the declaration of war.

Belgium has been treated brutally. How brutally we shall not yet
know. We already know too much. But what had she done? Had she
sent an ultimatum to Germany? Had she challenged Germany? Was
she preparing to make war on Germany? Had she inflicted any wrong
upon Germany which the Kaiser was bound to redress? She was one
of the most unoffending little countries in Europe. There she was –
peaceable, industrious, thrifty, hard-working, giving offence to no one.
And her cornfields have been trampled, her villages have been burnt,
her art treasures have been destroyed, her men have been slaughtered –
yea, and her women and children too. Hundreds and thousands of
her people, their neat, comfortable little homes burnt to the dust, are
wandering homeless in their own land. What was their crime? Their
crime was that they trusted to the word of a Prussian King.[5]

http://archive.org/stream/greatwarspeechde00lloyuoft/
greatwarspeechde00lloyuoft_djvu.txt

The impact of the speech on the audience are evident in a transcript littered with 'hisses', 'laughter' and 'cheering' as the audience responded
to Lloyd George's undoubted eloquence. There was dissent, and even
counter-demonstrations, but the anti-war movement was swamped by a
wave of popular enthusiasm for the great adventure.

The regular army units responded with a considerable degree of
enthusiasm to the news of war. Regimental Sergeant Major Arthur Denton
of the 2nd Seaforth Highlanders was relaxing at Shornecliffe Camp when
he got his first inkling of what was happening.

I was watching a cricket match. My Colonel was a good player, an old
Hampshire player – Sir Evelyn Bradford – and the garrison team in those
days could get a good team out. The Brigadier was there – Haldane[6] –
and Bradford came off the field, in flannels. Then the Brigade Major
came out, who happened to be an officer in my regiment. He said, 'You'd
better stay here, the Colonel might want you in a minute!' The Colonel
did come out. We went across to the barracks and he said, 'Sound the
mobilisation call!' Which was a regimental call – four 'G's. That was
the first we heard of the war – it was as casual as that. The men in the
barracks heard it and gave a yell – they knew what it was![7]

The government had already undertaken a series of precautionary measures to ensure that the army was ready for mobilisation.

Aldershot was shaken from its usual calm. Officers thronged the main streets buying in a hurry the things they needed, and the outfitters, outside whose shops there were regular queues, were very quickly sold out of everything useful. Officers dismantled their rooms and packed their effects, and the mess rooms rapidly assumed a most forlorn appearance, denuded of pictures and regimental property. Although the actual order for mobilisation had not been proclaimed, preliminary orders were sent round which enabled the work to be got well on the way. When the final order did come, everything went without a hitch.[8]

Lieutenant Joseph Dent, 2nd South Staffordshire Regiment

Key personnel had already been called up and protective guards had been placed on places of military value from 27 July. Two days later all the men home on leave were recalled and on 30 July, Field Marshal Sir John French was duly informed that he would indeed have the responsibility of commanding the BEF.

The proclamation authorising full mobilisation was signed at 11.00 on 4 August and the first mobilisation telegrams began to flood out from 16.40 that afternoon. Within just a couple of hours they would begin to be delivered to reservists all over the country. The essence of the mobilisation scheme was that the reservists would report in the first instance to their regimental depots. They already had in their possession orders telling them where to report and the appropriate travel warrant. One of the reservists called up was Private Edward Roe. An Irishman from Westmeath, he had served his time as a regular from 1905 to March 1914. Now, after a relatively short break at home, Roe was called back to resume his service with the 1st East Lancashire Regiment.

After breakfast I went around and shook hands with all the neighbours. One or two asked me, did I think I would be killed? The only answer I could give was that I did not know, quite a number will be killed for certain. I wended my way to the village smithy after duly fortifying myself with the necessary amount of *esprit-de-corps* in Mrs Early's pub *en route*. I found quite a considerable gathering there considering the early hour and the fine working day it was. No one was getting horses shod or farm implements repaired, but all were talking war. Fifteen pairs of critical eyes were directed on me simultaneously to see how I was 'taking it'. Would I break down and cry? Would I start blubbering because I was going out to be killed? Well I did not start crying, neither did I 'blubber'. I was quite cheerful.

I told them it would be over in six months and that I would consider myself lucky if I could get a shot at a Jerry before it was all over. Tom the blacksmith stated that it would not last three months. How could it last any longer with millions of Prussians on one side and the French, English and Belgians on the other side? We'd go through them like a 'dose of salts'! Well, let us hope so![9]

He eventually boarded the Dublin-bound train which he found to be crowded with large numbers of fellow reservists. At that time Ireland was a major recruiting ground for the British Army.

Every unit in the army is represented; the majority are uproariously drunk. I was struck by the various stages of prosperity displayed by the reservists. Some were well dressed and looked exceedingly smart, some just managed to maintain an appearance of respectability, whilst others had not a boot on their foot and just the semblance of a coat on their backs. The latter category were almost stupefied with liquor and gave me the impression by their general run down appearance that they could not stick a long march in full marching order. The occupants of every carriage were singing. The crowd of country people who were assembled on the platform were truly amazed, I overheard such observations as, 'They must all be mad; fancy men singing and they going off to be killed, for killed they will surely be as the English always put the Irish in front of the battle!'[10]

The reservists were taken in at their regimental depots, where they were to make up the war strength of the home service regular battalions that would constitute the BEF.

I arrived at my depot, and, after reporting myself at the guardroom, made my way toward the block of buildings which my unit occupied, these particular barracks being the depots of three units. I met on arrival several old faces, and, after renewing our acquaintances, I there and then fell in with a batch of men going up for medical inspection. We were then examined by two doctors very thoroughly.[11]

Private Frederick Bolwell, 1st Loyal North Lancashire Regiment

It was unfortunate, but probably inevitable, that many in sedentary occupations had allowed their physical condition to degenerate somewhat. For some this 'softening up' process – or their waistlines – had reached critical dimensions and such men were weeded out for immediate discharge, or a brisk period of remedial training to bring them back up to a military standard of fitness. The reservists were kitted out with a uniform, rifle and all the equipment they would need. At the same time the existing regulars had everything checked and anything missing, or worn, was replaced without the usual defrayments from their pay. Everything was chaotic but the arrangements just about worked.

> We have been issued with a little tin disc with our number, name and regiment on which we have to wear round our necks so they can tell who we are if we get killed. This is a place to be in, we have to fight like tigers to get our food here soon as ever it comes up about fifty make a grab at it – some get a lot and some don't get any! If we have money it is a hard job to spend it, if you go the coffee shop or canteen you have to wait about two hours before it is your turn to be served. If I get through this lot, no more for me.[12]
>
> Private Harry Lincoln, 1st Bedfordshire Regiment

Before they left, everyone was issued with their emergency rations consisting of a tin of bully beef (corned beef), dry biscuits, meat extract, tea and sugar.

One unpopular precaution was the vaccination programme. This triggered an amusing incident with the 1st Northamptonshires.

> The whole battalion paraded for inoculation against enteric. All company officers had been warned to parade their men in the morning, explain to them what inoculation was, and what for, that there was nothing to be afraid of, etc., and that, while it was not compulsory, it was expected that every man would be done for his own future good. The battalion duly paraded and formed up outside the camp hospital. Lloyd, the Adjutant, went in to be done first and to show a good example. I may say that his usual complexion was distinctly on the healthy side! When he came out, looking extremely green in the face, I was standing at the bottom of a few steps running up to the door of the hospital. I said, 'Are you all right, Lloyd? You look a bit dicky!' He replied, 'Yes, quite all right!' and fell down the steps in a faint! That did it! There was a mighty rushing sound and we saw numbers of men legging it back to barracks as hard as they could go. But they were taken to the slaughter again the next day! The

authorities, in the comic way authorities sometimes have, delayed this inoculation till three days before we were to sail, though they had had a complete week to do it in before. One usually has two goes of inoculation at about a week's interval, but we were all given a double dose, with the consequence that the next day half the battalion could not hold a rifle, or do anything. I know I had seldom felt so ill as I did; I spent most of the day in bed![13]

Lieutenant Evelyn Needham, 1st Northamptonshire Regiment

As to the overall state of morale, the men seem to have been in a slightly febrile state with an understandable tangle of conflicting emotions. Most were excited, but some were filled with a nagging awareness of their personal mortality.

It was curious to see the mental attitude of all ranks of the battalion to the coming adventure. I think the majority looked forward to it as a relief to the dull monotony of the peacetime life of a soldier, but there were those who seemed to lose all interest in life and appeared to have some foreboding of the awful times to come and obviously dreaded it.[14]

Lieutenant Kinglake Tower, 4th Royal Fusiliers

The idea that everyone thought the war would be 'all over by Christmas' is soon exposed as an exaggeration when looking at contemporary documents. Private Harry Lincoln of the 1st Bedfords had been given an inkling of what was to come when he wrote home to his wife Clara.

This war is going to be worse than I thought. Some seem to think it won't last a month and some say it will last three years. Our officers told us this morning it would be a hard and long war. If I never come home again, I leave the boy in your charge and I know you will do your best to him. I have got to make my will this afternoon, I shall make it out to you – everything of what I possess – so if I go under and you do not get anything you must apply for it. If I get killed in active service there will be a medal for me somewhere and I hope you will try and get it and keep it for the boy to wear when he grows up.[15]

Though some were well aware of the seriousness of the situation, many others were caught up in a fever of impatience, as if afraid that they might 'miss' Armageddon. Lieutenant Rowland Owen had done nine months training and attended summer camps since his commission into the Special Reserve of Officers in 1911. As such he was immediately mobilised with the 2nd Duke of Wellingtons, but was soon fuming at what seemed like endless delays in getting off to France.

> This existence is simply awful – I think I may fairly say that I have tasted of the horrors of war now. Just hanging round, getting things done, sometimes in a great hurry, and generally feeling very fed up and weak. We were to have departed tomorrow, and I had calculated that I could just last out that time, and now there is a rumour that we are not going till Thursday.[16]

The war would wait for them.

ONE DECISION THAT HAD TO BE made was whom to appoint as Secretary of State for War. The Prime Minister Herbert Asquith had been standing in, since the resignation of Sir John Seely over the Curragh Mutiny, but this was obviously impractical in a wartime situation. Many sensible military observers were keen that the Lord Chancellor Lord Haldane should resume his position as Secretary of State for War and were wary of the popular calls for the appointment of Field Marshal Lord Kitchener. Haldane, the urbane politician, definitely had the experience required for the post, as he could be considered the 'father of the BEF', given the impact of his eponymous reforms and the additional creation of the Territorial Force. He had a deep knowledge of the issues likely to be encountered in any rapid expansion of the army. In contrast, Kitchener was the gruff martial hero of the Empire. Born in 1850, he had commissioned into the Royal Engineers, before service in the Middle East and rising to command the Egyptian Army, which he led to triumph against the Mahdi of Sudan at the Battle of Omdurman in 1898. He had then served as first Chief of Staff and then Commander in Chief in South Africa during the Boer War from 1899–1902. Here his effective policies in response to the Boer guerrilla tactics had involved criss-crossing the country with chains of blockhouses, whilst utilising the mobility of mounted troops to harry the Boers and imprisoning the civilian population in concentration camps where poor hygiene led to an unacceptable number of deaths. Kitchener followed this with a period as a modernising Commander in Chief in India from 1902–1909. In a subsequent tour of the Far East he had acted as an advisor to both Australia and New Zealand in the formation of their armed forces, before returning to his first love as Consul General of Egypt from 1911–1914. By coincidence he was back in England on leave and thus close at hand. Kitchener had enormous prestige and possessed a formidable intellect, but also defects that perhaps rendered him unsuitable for a *civilian* role as Secretary of State: as a soldier he was autocratic by nature, not used to persuading rather than ordering and found delegation difficult. Furthermore he had little experience or knowledge of home service, the existing war plans, or the wider military situation in Europe.

Although Asquith seems to have leaned towards appointing Haldane, the barrage of frenzied newspaper editorials demanding Kitchener proved too much to withstand – sometimes politicians simply have to give the people what they want. Kitchener himself was not overly keen on the role, probably recognising the scale of the task, but acquiesced when Asquith presented it to him as his 'duty' to the country. He took office as Secretary of State for War on 5 August. Kitchener's well-documented dislike of politicians meant that he never grasped his own new 'civilian' status as a Secretary of State and he remained at heart a military man. He endorsed the necessity of standing beside the French in Europe; but did not believe that Britain was properly prepared for war. As he put it: 'I am put here to conduct a great war, and I have no army.'[17] He bluntly announced to the Cabinet that Britain must raise an army of over a million men and prepare for at least a three-year war, but the obvious solution – conscription – was not considered politically viable by Asquith. Kitchener's solution was typical of the man: he launched a massive recruiting campaign, but at the same time improvised a structure for the New Armies, thereby ignoring the existing Territorial Force organisation put in place by Haldane and Haig. Kitchener was prejudiced by his previous experience of such volunteer bodies and, having been out of the country, was unaware of the progress made by the territorials since 1908. He sought a fresh canvas to start all over again, raising fresh formations in tandem with the existing territorial structure. In fairness there was also the very real fear that the existing Territorial Force battalions would have been overwhelmed by the rush of recruits, but many considered Kitchener mistaken.

> I always thought it the greatest mistake to want Kitchener at the War Office. His place at this time is in Egypt, where there might be trouble

if the Turks go in with the Germans; he knows nothing of modern war; he knows nothing of our schemes. What they should have done was to put back Lord Haldane. The handling of the Expeditionary Force is now in the hands of the soldiers and the French – and it is the putting to the test of his pet scheme the Territorials. And it is surely no time for a new broom and a pig-headed one at that. Kitchener's first move is to raise another Regular Army of 100,000 recruits, with a sprinkling of ex-soldiers, officered by leavings of the Regular Army and the Territorials. This force will be *useless* for six months, and not as good as the Territorials will be by then.[18]

Captain Henry Jackson, Military Aeronautics Department, War Office

Brigadier General Sir Henry Wilson, the original architect of British plans, had been appointed onto the staff of the BEF and he was soon seething with rage at what he regarded as Kitchener's 'lunacy'. He believed that the French Army needed help as soon as possible and that all this planning for the future was a waste of time.

Kitchener's 'shadow armies' for shadow campaigns, at unknown and distant dates, prevent a lot of good officers, NCOs and men from coming out. It is a scandalous thing. Under no circumstances can these mobs now being raised, without officers and NCOs, without guns, rifles, or uniforms, without rifle ranges or training grounds, without supply or transport services, without moral or tradition, knowledge or experience, under no circumstances could these mobs take the field for two years. Then what is the use of them? What we want, and what we must have is for our little force out here to be kept to full strength with the very best of everything.[19]

Although Kitchener's methodology in raising and administering his New Armies has been questioned, there is no doubt that his view of the war proved far more perceptive – and realistic – than that held by Wilson. Kitchener was indeed a difficult man in various ways, but he had numerous qualities, and this was after all going to be a very *difficult* war. Perhaps he was indeed the man for the job.

There are those who try to belittle his work, but, 'Heavens!' where would we have been without him? So far as my experience goes, I would say unhesitatingly, '*Beaten*, sure!' I met most of the men who became great, were called great, or called themselves great during the war, and Lord Kitchener towers above them all in my memory. His prophetic insight: his quick understanding: his indomitable courage: his unity of purpose: his untiring energy: his subtle cunning: his vast sense of humour: all were magnificent in 1914. He had an almost impossible task – member of a Cabinet of twenty-three who made political speeches at him; head of a War Office which had been deprived of almost all its best brains – anyway, on the general staff side; chief of an organisation in which he had never served, and which he had never been allowed to approach before; confronted with an enemy who suffered from none of these disabilities, and had, to boot, the biggest and best equipped army in the world and a clearly thought out plan of campaign. He was much harassed by the endless quibblings and discussion of the Cabinet at this time, and I remember his bursting out to me one day that you never knew where you were with these damned politicians.[20]

Lieutenant Colonel Sefton Brancker, Military Aeronautics Department, War Office

One thing that was agreed is that Kitchener's Army would never be ready for deployment in 1914. It was an army for the future.

HAIG WAS NOT PARTY TO THE secret plans to deploy the BEF to France, but on 4 August he wrote a prescient letter to the Lord Chancellor Lord Haldane on what would turn out to be the last day of peace. From his detailed pre-war studies of the German Army, Haig was well aware of the threat it posed, the improbability that it could ever be swiftly defeated and the sheer mayhem that would be unleashed in the opening exchanges of the war. There was clearly a real risk that the tiny BEF could be swept away and destroyed in this battle between the 'big battalions' of France and Germany. Even the Belgian Army dwarfed the British contributions. Would it not be possible to 'keep their powder dry' and join the fight a little later when fully prepared?

> The war will last many months, possibly years, so I venture to hope that our only bolt (and that not a very big one) may not suddenly be shot on a project of which success seems to me quite doubtful – I mean the checking of the German advance into France. Would it not be better to begin at once to enlarge our Expeditionary Force by

amalgamating less regular forces with it? In three months' time we should have quite a considerable army, so that when we do take the field we can act decisively and dictate terms which will ensure a lasting peace.[21]

Like Kitchener, Haig believed that the imminent war would be a fraught affair and that neither side would give in without a long and grinding struggle. However, French, who was far more conversant with the existing plans, disagreed with Haig's assessment.

> Personally, I was opposed to these ideas, and most anxious to adhere to our original plans. Any alteration in carrying out our concentration, particularly if this meant delay, would have upset the French plan of campaign and created much distrust in the minds of our Allies. Delay or hanging back would not only have looked like hesitation, but might easily have entailed disastrous consequences by permanently separating our already inferior forces.[22]

In fact Haig would change his mind almost immediately, indeed just as soon as he had been made fully aware of the scope of the BEF deployment plans and the French reliance on that British contribution. The silken binds of alliance warfare, the necessity of contributing – and being seen to contribute – to the overall effort, were already evident. Sometimes the most logical path is not possible: Haig would find that the requirements of his Allies would radically curtail his own freedom of action when he became Commander in Chief later in the war.

On the afternoon of 5 August 1914, Asquith held a meeting at 10 Downing Street. Several of the Cabinet were there including the designated Secretary of State for War Lord Kitchener, and the three main BEF generals: French, Haig and Grierson. The debate at first centred on the composition of the BEF.

> It was generally felt that we were under some obligation to France to send as strong an army as we could, and there was an idea that one cavalry division and six divisions of all arms had been promised. As to the exact number, it did not appear that we were under any definite obligation, but it was unanimously agreed that we should do all we could. The question to be decided was how many troops it was necessary to keep in this country adequately to guard our shores

against attempted invasion and, if need be, to maintain internal order. So far as the Navy was concerned, he considered Home Defence reasonably secure; but this consideration did not suffice to absolve us from the necessity of keeping a certain number of troops at home. After this discussion it was decided that two divisions must for the moment remain behind, and that one cavalry division and four divisions of all arms should be sent out as speedily as possible. This meant a force of approximately 100,000 men.[23]

Field Marshal Sir John French, General Headquarters, BEF

This was an egregious decision: there was no real threat of invasion to the British homelands and it was thus a betrayal of the 'promises' made to the French. On the other hand there is no doubt that Kitchener was very worried by the nature of the plans being revealed to him for the first time. A second point of debate was as to where the BEF should be deployed. This was a moment of truth.

The British and French General Staffs had for some years been in close secret consultation with one another on this subject. The German menace necessitated some preliminary understanding in the event of a sudden attack. The area of concentration for the British Forces had been fixed on the left flank of the French, and the actual detraining stations of the various units were all laid down in terrain lying between Maubeuge and Le Cateau. The headquarters of the Army were fixed at the latter place. This understanding being purely provisional and conditional upon an unprovoked attack by Germany, the discussion then took the turn of overhauling and reviewing these decisions, and of making arrangements in view of the actual conditions under which war had broken out. Many and various opinions were expressed; but on this day no final decisions were arrived at. It was thought absolutely necessary to ask the French authorities to send over a superior officer who should be in full possession of the views and intentions of the French General Staff. It was agreed that no satisfactory decision could be arrived at until after full discussion with a duly accredited French officer.[24]

General Sir John French, General Headquarters, BEF

Kitchener expressed his concern that Maubeuge was too far forward should the Germans be intending to sweep through Belgium, and he very much preferred a concentration area further back around the Amiens rail-head. Haig too was worried and rather taken aback at some of the views expressed by French during the wide-ranging debate.

> He spoke about his hopes of now going to Antwerp and operating with the Belgian and possibly Dutch Armies. I trembled at the reckless way Sir John French spoke about 'the advantages' of the BEF operating from Antwerp against the powerful and still intact German Army! So, when it came to my turn to speak, I formulated a number of questions to bring out the risk we would run of 'defeat in detail' if we separated from the French at the outset of the campaign, 'Have we enough troops, with the Belgians, to carry on a campaign independently of the French, or do we run excessive risk, if we act separately, of defeat in detail?' and 'What does our General Staff know of the fighting value of the Belgian Army?'[25]

Although Haig now accepted that the BEF had to be deployed at once, he, like Kitchener, still had his eyes firmly fixed on a long war, requiring a British Army of up to a million in strength.

> We only had a small number of trained officers and NCOs. These must be economised. The need for efficient instructors would become at once apparent. I urged that a considerable proportion of officers and NCOs should be withdrawn from the Expeditionary Force. This latter suggestion met with much opposition from Sir John French, with the result that only three officers per battalion were retained in England from the battalions now ordered to France. Lastly, my advice was to send as strong an Expeditionary Force as possible and as soon as possible, to join the French forces and to arrange to increase that force as rapidly as possible.[26]

Haig's argument had already shifted: he now wanted to use a pool of well-trained regular officers and NCOs left behind out of battle as 'yeast' in the process of growing a vast new army that could hold the balance of power in the crucial later stages of the war. The bickering generals were at least relieved to receive an assurance from the First Lord of the Admiralty Winston Churchill that the Channel had been sealed to prevent any possible German raid on the BEF transports as they made their crossings. After a further War Council meeting with the French liaison officer, Colonel Victor Huguet, it was finally agreed to adhere to the original plan of a concentration at Maubeuge, and the date of embarkation for the BEF headquarters was fixed for 14 August.

French and Haig had worked closely together in South Africa, and both had fought hard to defend a valid role for the cavalry. Superficially they had much in common. But they had also grown apart as Haig gained in seniority and self-confidence. The pressure of war triggered a degree of antipathy that Haig did not always manage to keep secret, and indeed the cracks gaped open in front of the King during his inspection of Haig's Aldershot Command on 11 August.

> His Majesty joins me in an open car and we motor round the lines. The troops turn out and line the roads and give their Majesties a cheer as they pass along. Their Majesties, too, say goodbye to the senior officers as they pass along in front of their Headquarters. The King seemed delighted that Sir John French had been appointed to the Chief Command of the Expeditionary Force. He asked me my opinion. I told him at once, as I felt it my duty to do so, that from my experience with Sir John in the South African War, he was certain to do his utmost loyally to carry out any orders which the Government might give him. I had grave doubts, however, whether either his temper was sufficiently even, or his military knowledge sufficiently thorough to enable him to discharge properly the very difficult duties which will devolve upon him during the coming operations with Allies on the continent. In my own heart, I know that French is quite unfit for this great command at a time of crisis in our nation's history. But I thought it sufficient to tell the King that I had 'doubts' about the selection.[27]

This was hardly loyal of Haig, but in truth French had already given him numerous reasons over the last few years to have severe reservations as to his suitability for such a key role. Perhaps Haig himself realised he had gone too far in his criticism, as in his diary he resolves to try harder to make the relationship work.

> I have grave reason for being anxious about what happens to us in the great adventure upon which we are now to start this very night. However, I am determined to behave as I did in the South African War, namely, to be thoroughly loyal and do my duty as a subordinate should, trying all the time to see Sir John's good qualities and not his weak ones.[28]

All in all, it was not an auspicious start between two men required to work together in harmony at the highest levels of command in the BEF.

4

ROAD TO MONS

The first fight! How would it turn out? How would the men shape? Could the ammunition supply be depended upon? But above all, what would he be like? Would he feel afraid? If so, would he be able to hide it?[1]

Second Lieutenant Arnold Gyde, 2nd South Staffordshire Regiment, 6th Brigade, 2nd Division, I Corps

THE WAR HAD NOT WAITED for the BEF to arrive. The British mobilisation had begun a couple of days behind the French, and the Battle of the Frontiers had already started well before the BEF could arrive at the front. In a war between such colossal armies, the BEF of just four divisions was really neither here nor there, dwarfed by the seven German and five French armies, which averaged out at five corps apiece. Even the relatively small Belgian Army managed to deploy a total of six infantry and one cavalry divisions, which was the original promised size of the BEF. The French and German general staffs had toiled for years preparing the war plans that would now decide the fate of their respective countries. The German Army was swollen on mobilisation to a staggering 2,292,000, organised into seventy-nine divisions of which the vast majority – sixty-eight – would be facing the French and Belgian Armies on the Western Front. The French Army expanded on mobilisation to 2,944,000 in some seventy-five divisions. Yet this huge force contained serious weaknesses. In particular, a lack of effective field training of the French reserve forces meant that General Joseph Joffre did not intend to use them in the front line, in marked contrast to the front-line role of the far better trained German reserve formations. This left just forty-six active French front-line divisions to face the Germans when the storm broke.

The German strategy was still based on the Schlieffen Plan, as tweaked and developed by General Helmuth von Moltke the Younger. After stamping down the Liège fortresses, the First and Second Armies would hammer through Belgium before sweeping down into northern France. The Third Army would break through the Belgian Ardennes region, while the Fourth and Fifth Armies would push through Luxembourg and the French Ardennes. Five huge armies would be launched in a single wheeling manoeuvre seeking to overwhelm the French left flank, while along the Alsace-Lorraine frontier the German Sixth and Seventh Armies would simply stand fast to absorb the weight of the expected French offensive.

Plan XVII was the latest version of the French campaign plans as configured by General Joseph Joffre. Born in 1852, Joffre had early active service as an officer cadet fighting the Prussians during the siege of Paris in 1870–1871. After this chastening experience he served as an engineer officer in French Indo-China and North Africa. In 1904 he was appointed Director of Engineers, after which promotion was rapid. Politics of all kinds was rife in the French Army, but Joffre was not connected to any political or religious faction and seemed to slip through unscathed by the infighting. His promotion was not based on allegiances, but on his evident qualities: a phlegmatic attention to detail and a driven determination to succeed. In 1911, he became Chief of the General Staff, in which capacity he would be Commander in Chief in the event of war. Joffre was aware of the possibility of the Germans violating Belgian neutrality and had even explored the idea of moving into Belgium to counter the threat head-on. In this he was somewhat restricted, because the French government, understandably wary of international repercussions, had insisted that no French troops could enter Belgium before the Germans crossed the border. As a result Plan XVII concentrated four armies along the German, Luxembourg and Belgian borders with another army behind them held in reserve, with the intention of driving into Alsace-Lorraine, but with the option of deploying two armies to counter German forces attacking through Belgium and northern France. Facing almost the full strength of Imperial Germany, the French were dependent on an agreement that the Russians would launch an offensive into East Prussia with between 700,000 and 800,000 men some fifteen days after mobilisation had begun.

The Germans struck first with their attack on the Liège fortress, commencing on 5 August. The great reinforced concrete forts dated back to 1888–1892 and were built to resist shells of up to 210mm calibre. The German plans had been juggled specifically to allow the earliest possible attack on Liège; it was regarded as crucial to overwhelm them quickly and not allow delays to hold up the German juggernaut. The Belgian field army had been placed in defensive positions behind the Gette River, leaving the forts in the front line. As the German attacks began, the Belgian commander, Lieutenant General Gérard Leman, decided to move out the defending 3rd Belgian Division while he still could, so the battle resolved itself into German attempts to destroy the fortifications and their garrison. To do so they brought up gigantic 420mm mortars – double what the forts had been designed to withstand. Leman was trapped inside Fort Loncin as the shells crashed down on 15 August.

> They burst with a thunderous roar, raising clouds of missiles, stones, and dust. After some time passed amid these horrors, I wished to return to my observation tower; but I had hardly advanced a few feet into the gallery when a great blast passed by, and I was thrown violently to the ground. I managed to rise, and continued my way, only to be stopped by a choking cloud of poisonous gas. It was a mixture of the gas from an explosion and the smoke of a fire in the troop quarters. We were driven back, half-suffocated. Looking out of a peephole, I saw to my horror that the fort had fallen, slopes and counterslopes being a chaos of rubbish, while huge tongues of flame were shooting forth from the throat of the fortress.[2]

The last fort surrendered on 16 August. The Belgian garrison had fought bravely, but they had not managed to hold up the German advance to any great extent. Indeed, the First Army had already begun crossing the Meuse on 13 August after the fall of the forts that actually dominated the river.

Meanwhile the French offensives had commenced on 7 August with an exploratory incursion towards Mulhouse in southern Alsace by the

First Army. Just one corps was pushed forward and after a brief success they were rebuffed two days later by German counter-attacks, which forced them right back to the border. It was an inauspicious beginning, but this was only the aperitif. Joffre planned for his main offensive to take place in two distinct phases. First, he would launch the First Army through the Vosges Mountains heading towards Sarreburg and the Rhine while the Second Army would push towards Morhange. Second, when he had divined the line of the German assault into Belgium, he planned to attack with the Third, Fourth and Fifth Armies north of Metz-Thionville, intending to strike at what he believed would be the weakened 'hinge' of the German attack. No one was waiting for the BEF.

THERE WAS AN ENTHUSIASTIC RECEPTION FROM the assembled French civilians as the troopships carrying the first troops of the BEF began to pull into Le Havre on 13 August. Cheers emanated from bobbing fishing boats, while on disembarkation the marching columns were surrounded by crowds shouting variations on the general theme of 'Vive l'Angleterre'. Amongst them was Lieutenant Joseph Dent and the 2nd South Staffordshires aboard the *Irrawaddy*.

> We were awakened soon after dawn by the sound of unmistakably foreign cheers, *'Eep! Eep! Oorah!'* coming across the water, and, on hurriedly looking out of the port hole, discovered that we were slowly making our way into Le Havre, welcomed by enthusiastic coastguards, waving flags of the Allies, gesticulating and cheering. We landed, and, without waiting for our transport to disembark, we proceeded to march to the Rest Camp, which was situated about six miles away on the summit of a hill commanding the harbour. We had to march through the town most of the way, and our reception was truly terrific, beggaring description. The town was *en fête*, flags and banners welcoming *les braves Anglais* were displayed on all sides, and our march became a triumphal procession between cheering crowds. We had been to some pains in teaching the men the Marseillaise and there were a good many mouth organs amongst the company, so that, when we struck up, there was a tremendous burst of enthusiasm, and the crowds nearly went mad, flinging flowers down for us to walk over. The march did not, however, end very gloriously. The men had had

two bad nights and little food on the boats; the heat was absolutely
terrific, and the march between dense crowds through narrow streets
was almost suffocating. In addition, the weight of the equipment
carried was found very trying by the reservists, and it was a steady pull
up steep hills over cobble stones the whole way. The men soon became
exhausted, and it was impossible to prevent the well-meaning populace
from pouring wines and liqueurs down their throats whenever there
was a halt.[3]

The situation soon got out of control as many of the NCOs and officers
were themselves tired and uncertain as to what they should do.

Ladies pursued them with basins full of wine and what they were
pleased to call beer. Men were literally carried from the ranks, under
the eyes of their officers, and borne in triumph into houses and inns.
The men could scarcely be blamed for availing themselves of such
hospitality, though to drink intoxicants on the march is suicidal. Men
'fell out,' first by ones and twos, then by whole half-dozens and dozens.
The Colonel was aghast, and very furious – he couldn't understand it –
he was riding![4]

Second Lieutenant Arnold Gyde, 2nd South Staffordshire Regiment, 6th
Brigade, 2nd Division, I Corps

Over the next few days the BEF continued to disembark. The plans were
for I Corps (1st and 2nd Divisions) to concentrate around Wassigny, the
II Corps (3rd and 5th Divisions) at Nouvion and the Cavalry Division at
Maubeuge. The men were jam-packed into troop trains, which provided
little in the form of comfort, or speed, as they juddered along.

We paraded again that night at 11pm and marched down through
the town to Havre station. This was the battalion's first introduction
to French railway rolling-stock, and the covered vans for 'Hommes 40,
Chevaux 8' which were afterwards so intimately known to the British
Army. We duly entrained men and horses, amidst a lot of laughter
and backchat from the men at their novel travelling accommodation,
and steamed out at about 1 am. Young Gordon, Joe Farrar, Wauchope,
Jervois and myself had a first-class carriage to ourselves, and proceeded
to make ourselves fairly comfortable. The train crept slowly through
the night, as only a French train knows how, through Rouen, Arras,
Douai, etc. All along the line, and at every station we stopped at

were crowds of men, women and children all shouting and cheering, *'Vivent les braves Anglais!' 'Vive l'Angleterre!' 'A bas les Boches!'* The last accompanied by graphic gestures of cutting the throat! They thrust bread, cakes, fruit, chocolate, wine, flowers, etc., on all, officers and men alike. The journey seemed interminable, and we were all getting stiff and cold, and were dog-tired; and the wretched men in the cattle trucks, who had been singing ceaselessly the whole day, sitting each side of the trucks in the open doorways, with their feet hanging out, had relapsed into silence and, I expect, painful slumber![5]

Lieutenant Evelyn Needham, 1st Northamptonshire Regiment, 2nd Brigade, 1st Division, I Corps

Once they had reached the railheads, then they would march the rest of the way.

Sir John French had come ashore at Boulogne on 14 August and began a series of meetings with the French authorities. His two corps commanders, Haig and Grierson, disembarked the next day at Le Havre, then at 01.00 on 17 August boarded a train to experience the relative luxury of a first-class carriage for the journey to the Amiens area. Haig and his Chief of Staff, Brigadier General Sir John Gough, had an amusing escape from minor harm when the train lurched to a stop at around midnight. Haig's diary drily records that, 'Gough's portmanteau placed in overhead rack (contrary to my advice) came down with a bang, luckily on the floor of the carriage.'[6] But a few hours later something a good deal more serious had befallen the party. James Grierson, a stout, if not portly man by nature, had suffered a fatal heart attack at around breakfast time. This represented a blow to the BEF, disrupting the command arrangements at a crucial time. Yet speculation as to the possible impact of Grierson if he had survived on the history of the BEF at war are surely irrelevant: Grierson had fallen at the very first hurdle, well short of the intensive physical and mental tests to come.

The question of Grierson's replacement caused considerable friction. General Sir Ian Hamilton, who had just been appointed to command the Home Defence Central Force (chiefly the Territorial Force divisions), pressed his case, sending an immediate telegram as soon as he heard of Grierson's demise. Hamilton was difficult to ignore, being one of Britain's most highly regarded soldiers, but French clearly did not want the vastly experienced Hamilton at II Corps and fended him off by pointing out that the role was far too junior for a man of his rank. Instead, Sir John French requested the services of Lieutenant General Sir Horace Plumer, but Kitchener preferred – and indeed insisted upon – the appointment of General Sir Horace Smith-Dorrien.

Smith-Dorrien was another officer of huge experience: born to an army family in 1858, he was educated at Harrow before entering Sandhurst as a cadet in 1876. Commissioned into the infantry, he had the notable experience of being one of the very few to survive the disastrous Battle of Isandlwana on 22 January 1879. He then served in Egypt before attending Staff College in 1887. He returned to Egypt and participated in the Battle of Omdurman on 2 September 1898 before active service in the Boer War. He was promoted to major general and in several incidents demonstrated the independent streak of a man who would not necessarily blindly follow orders if there was a better alternative. Service in India followed, before he returned to take over the Aldershot command from French in 1907. Here Smith-Dorrien instituted several reforms to improve both military efficiency and the living conditions for the men, but in doing so aroused the enmity of his predecessor, who chose to see these changes as an implied criticism of his regime. In particular, Smith-Dorrien was determined to improve the prowess of cavalry rifle shooting, while he also had a keen interest in exploring the nature of infantry tactics in the face of increased firepower and trench systems. Alongside his trenchantly held opinions, Smith-Dorrien also gained a reputation for his choleric temper, which made him a testing colleague. In 1912, Smith-Dorrien took over Southern Command and was promoted to full general, following which on the outbreak of war he had been given command of the Home Defence Army, a subordinate under Hamilton's command. Given the poor relations between French and Smith-Dorrien, there has been some speculation as to the nature of Kitchener's motives in foisting him into the command of II Corps. In the absence of any real evidence, it seems likely that Kitchener wanted someone capable of making his own decisions and standing up to French should the need become apparent.

The senior commanders and staff of the BEF were now all in place. At the General Headquarters (GHQ) of the BEF, which was established in the French town of Le Cateau, Field Marshal Sir John French had Lieutenant General Sir Archibald Murray as his Chief of Staff, with an additional Sub-Chief in the form of Major General Sir Henry Wilson. The operations staff included Colonel Montague Harper as GS01 (Operations) and Colonel George Macdonogh as GS01 (Intelligence). The Adjutant General was Major General Sir Nevil Macready, while the Quartermaster General was the reassuring figure of Major General Sir William Robertson, a man who had risen from private to major general and would one day be a field marshal. Although it was once considered fashionable to decry staff officers, without them an army cannot move, feed itself, or indeed conduct any operations in accordance to a plan, as Robertson later explained.

> The staff of an army, according to the British system, is composed of three branches: the General Staff deals with training, operations, intelligence, and general military policy; the Adjutant General with recruiting, mobilisation, discipline, medical services, and the chaplains' department; the Quartermaster General with supplies and transport, and the issue of all military stores. Stated in a simpler form, the Adjutant General recruits the men with which to fight, tends to their spiritual needs, tries them by court-martial when accused of breaking the regulations, takes care of them when sick or wounded, and buries them when they die. The Quartermaster General clothes, arms, feeds, and houses them, and supplies them with all they need with which to fight, viz. horses, motors, lorries, bicycles, ammunition, guns, entrenching tools, barbed wire, bombs, and a thousand other things. He also moves them, according to the direction of the General Staff, by rail and sea. The staffs of the Adjutant General and Quartermaster General thus put and maintain the army in the field ready for use by the General Staff, who arrange, according to the instructions of the Commander in Chief, all matters connected with the actual fighting.[7]

All this was manifestly important, but the pre-war disputes between French and Grierson, followed by the chaos generated by the Curragh Mutiny, meant that the GHQ staff had to be hastily cobbled together on the outbreak of war, which was not conducive to efficiency under pressure. The late appointment of the stolid Murray as Chief of Staff, with the more mercurial Wilson acting in an ill-defined role as his Sub-Chief, was also unfortunate. Murray would soon be side-lined, acting as a workhorse, toiling away, while Wilson seemed to have far more influence over French when it came to making the big decisions – in effect the reverse of a more conventional situation.

The orders from the GHQ of the BEF were channelled to two corps headquarters, who sent orders to their divisions, who in turn passed them to the brigades. Then it was the turn of the brigade staff.

The usual proceedings on the ordinary line of march were that, on receiving 'Divisional Orders,' which arrived at any time in the afternoon, or often at night, we compiled 'Brigade Orders' on them. 'Divisional Orders' give one first of all any information about the enemy which it is advisable to impart, then the intention of the Divisional General – whether he means to fight on the morrow, or march, or stay where he is, &c, &c.; and if he means to march he gives the direction in which the Division is to proceed, the order of march, by brigades, artillery, divisional troops such as Royal Engineers, heavy batteries, divisional cavalry, &c, &c, and generally says where and how the transport is to march, whether with its own troops or some way behind, and if so, where; and gives directions as to the supplies, where the refilling-point, rendezvous for supply carts, and railhead are, and many other odds and ends, especially as to which brigade is to provide the advanced- or rear-guard, who is to command it, at what time the head of the column and the heads of all the formations are to pass a given point, and so on. On receiving these orders we have to make out and issue similarly composed 'Brigade Orders' in detail, giving the order of march of the battalions and brigade headquarters, how much rations are to be carried on the men and in the cook-wagons, what is to happen to the supply and baggage wagons, whether 'B' transport (vehicles not absolutely necessary in the fighting line) are to be with the 'A' transport in rear of their respective battalions, or to be bunched up by themselves behind the brigade, with similar detailed orders about the advanced-guard or rearguard, and the time to a minute as to when each detail is to pass a given point, the position of the Brigadier in the column, the point to which reports are to be sent, &c, &c. These orders might be written in anything from fifteen to fifty minutes according to the movement required, and then had to be quadruplicated and sent out to the battalions by their respective orderlies, or by wire. By the time the battalions had written out and transmitted their own orders to their companies it was sometimes very late indeed.[8]

Brigadier General Lord Edward Gleichen, Headquarters, 15th Brigade, 5th Division, II Corps

All in all, moving an army was an extremely complex skill that needed years of experience and practice. Even then, there was an enormous amount that could go wrong, particularly when operating in a foreign country where there could be stiff competition to use the required roads.

The men themselves knew nothing of such administrative challenges as they moved off from the rail heads. Driver Frederick Smith long treasured the welcome he received from the French people as they passed through various villages.

> We have not so far had to beware of German bullets, but our chief danger has been from French apples, which the people threw at us as we pass. We get all sorts of things, such as kisses, apples, pears, peaches, apricots, nuts, bottles of wine, chocolate, cigs. and cigars, tobacco, nuts, flowers, &c. We decorate our lorries with the flowers. The people all flock into the streets as we pass. The nearest approach to our reception is like what the King got when he came to Nottinghamshire. There are hundreds of chaps in England who would give twenty years of their lives to get such a reception as we get wherever we go. I should advise any chaps coming to France to bring a corkscrew with them, because they will get loads of wine given them by the French peasants – they can't do enough for us. And the girls! By Jove, there are some beauties![9]
>
> Driver Frederick Smith, 67th Company, Army Service Corps

But there was a cost, as the French were simply insatiable in their hunt for souvenirs with which to cherish the passing moment.

> After our first few minutes on French soil there were very few of us who could truthfully say he could show a complete kit. The main objective appeared to be our cap badges, failing this, the 'RFA' from our shoulder straps and as a last resort the blighters had our buttons. We did attempt to preserve some of our property and perhaps, dignity, for a while, but it was a pretty hopeless task and we eventually gave way against hopeless odds.[10]
>
> Signaller John Palmer, 118th Battery, 26th Brigade, RFA, 1st Division, I Corps

The billeting officers had their work cut out in allotting the accommodation each night, but there was a general air of good humour, even when there were minor 'misunderstandings' as amusingly recounted by Captain Charles Paterson of the 1st South Wales Borderers.

> Discovered a lady next door wild with excitement trying to explain something to one of the men. It appeared that she had not been detailed to take anyone in and wanted to do so, and was showing him various beds and things, and naturally this had led to misunderstandings. When I arrived they were both in fits of laughter, she jabbering French and he a mixture of English, Welsh and Urdu.[11]

But, as with almost any military operation, there was the occasional tragedy. Some men were under great personal strain, perhaps worried about their response to the fighting that lay ahead, or concerned as to the future of the family they had left behind. On the night of 17 August, Private Harry Rowthorn of the 1st Northamptonshire Regiment had been placed on precautionary piquet duty by Corporal Ward, taking post on a grass verge about a mile forward of the overnight billets. With him was a reservist, Private William Marney.

> Marney, stood about 6 foot 2" but he had a queer sort of look about him. Ward said, 'Don't go to sleep and don't make a noise, if you should be attacked fire two shots down towards us and we shall hear it!' So we laid there. I couldn't see him and he couldn't see me. Then it must have been about 2am. I kept almost dozing off – when suddenly a big bang rang out. I thought Marney must have seen something or thought he did. I laid and waited some time, then I thought perhaps his gun went off accidentally, so I whispered, 'Marney, Marney, are you alright?' But I got no answer. He may be badly wounded in which case I shall have to fire the two shots in order to get an ambulance or he may lay there and die. Then I should cop out for not doing so. I thought I'd better make sure before getting all the regiment out. So I quietly crawled across the road on to the grass and was running my hand over his body. He never made a sound, then I found out why, as I reached his face, my hand fell into a large hole in his head and my fingers fumbled into a thick sticky mess, which I knew to be his brains. I rubbed my hands on the grass, but that was too wet with blood. It was quite evident there was no need to send two shots up now, he had shot himself. I got down in the ditch but couldn't find any water to wash my hand in. I found a bar of chocolate in my haversack but couldn't

get the wrapper off with one hand and didn't fancy using the other till I had washed it. So I thought, 'Orders or not I must have a smoke!' Even that was a job with one hand, but I had got to do something to calm my nerves down.[12]

In such sad circumstances, Private William Marney[13] became one of the first to die during the British campaign; there would be many more.

Even as the British were arriving in France on 15 August, the First, Second and Alsace Armies drove forward into Lorraine as the first phase of Joffre's great offensive. They were faced by the German Sixth and Seventh Armies who gave way before them, a controlled retreat, not allowing the French to really get to grips, but taking every opportunity to inflict heavy casualties by utilising the power of the German guns. The French found their forces being spread out across a wide front and gaps began to appear between the army corps. This offered a hostage to fortune that Crown Prince Rupprecht, commanding the Sixth Army, was keen to take advantage of. The plan, as given to him by Moltke, was that he should fall back, sucking in French reserves, while the main German effort was devoted to their right hook through Belgium, which it was intended would eventually swing round behind the French armies. But Rupprecht begged to be allowed to counter-attack and Moltke gave way. On 20 August a blistering attack was launched on the French Second Army in the Morhange area. The Germans used their longer-range artillery to beat the French guns into submission and then turned their attentions to the French infantry. As the Second Army was forced into retreat it uncovered the flank of the neighbouring First Army; soon they too were in full retreat and by 22 August they were all back at their start lines. It was at this point that the Germans lost the plot. They had already departed from the original script, but now Moltke allowed his army commanders to launch a full-scale offensive between Toul and Épinel on 23 August – almost as if he was attempting a double envelopment of the French centre. Now they were attacking French troops in previously prepared defensive positions and as a result German casualties began to mount. For four days they continued battering at the French lines but achieved little, other than expending precious German reserves.

Meanwhile, far to the north, the German plans were coming to fruition as their right hook swept through Belgium. On the right flank was the First Army (General Alexander von Kluck), with alongside him the Second Army (General Karl von Bülow) and on the inside of the wheel the Third Army (General Max von Hausen). All that seemed to face them was the French Fifth Army (General Charles Lanrezac), who with a force of some fifteen divisions found himself facing the thirty-eight divisions of the German Second and Third Armies, while the First Army was sweeping round his left flank. Lanrezac was born in 1852 and had seen action as a young officer in the Franco-Prussian War, then gaining steady promotion through the ranks. After a stint as a lecturer at the École Supérieure de Guerre, he had been raised to corps command before promotion to command the Fifth Army in 1914. There is no doubt that from a very early stage Lanrezac was extremely nervous about the threat to his exposed left flank. He considered Plan XVII to be a dangerous gamble, even if the Germans were not attacking through Belgium, and his frustrations with Joffre at the French General Headquarters were evident.

> It was my absolute conviction that our opponents, violating
> shamelessly Belgian neutrality, would take the offensive to the north
> of Metz with the major part of their forces and would stay on the
> defensive along the entire Metz-Strasbourg front. Such was my way
> of looking at things in May 1914; my predictions were fully realised,
> but I acknowledged that it was not absurd to conceive of the Germans
> taking another course of action. Let us only note that, from the fourth
> day of the war, the ultimatum sent to Belgium demanding that they
> allow German columns free passage through their territory and the
> surprise attack on Liège which followed immediately after the Belgian
> refusal, left no doubt as to the intentions of our adversaries. There was
> only GHQ who were still scornful there. Let us record that their error
> was prolonged right up to 15 August![14]

Lanrezac was convinced that the Germans were about to overwhelm his Fifth Army. Yet Joffre only responded in part, ordering the Fifth Army to move towards the northwest and establish a line along the River Sambre, ready to attack any advancing German forces they encountered. By 20 August, Lanrezac had taken up positions with his I Corps acting as a right flank guard looking east across the Meuse while the X, III, and XVIII Corps were spread along the Sambre looking towards the northeast. There is little doubt that Joffre had not recognised the scale of the German forces marching, not just towards Lanrezac, but circling round his left flank. Lanrezac's fears were not assuaged by promises that the BEF would soon arrive to cover his endangered flank, for the Fifth Army was a vast force in comparison to the diminutive BEF.

Meanwhile, French visited Joffre's headquarters at Vitry-le François at noon on 16 August. In the minds of many British historians, this is treated as a summit of equals, but nothing could be further from the truth. This was a meeting between a man who commanded five huge armies and the equivalent of a senior corps commander. Yet Joffre could afford to be magnanimous: his only real concern at this stage was the date by which the BEF would be ready for action.

> He gave me at once the feeling that he was a loyal comrade-in-arms, firmly attached to his own ideas and, while bringing us his full support, anxious not to compromise his army in any way. He let me understand that the instructions of his Government were specific in requiring him to consider himself wholly independent, and that he could only offer us the collaboration of his Army. I perfectly well understood this point; it was entirely natural that England should not consent to subordinate her troops to any Allied commander. I never had any illusions on this subject, although I realized that the absence of a single authority to direct all the Allied forces composing our left would be a serious cause of weakness. The only thing to do was to take things as they were and try to get the best results out of collaboration and mutual confidence. Our conversation then bore upon the date on which the British Army would be ready to start operations. I had counted on the 21st of August, but Sir John informed me that on that date his army would be ready only to push forward small detachments for the protection of the de-training of the main body, which would not be ready to move before the 24th. I pointed out all the unfortunate results that this delay would cause, and he promised to reduce it as much as possible.[15]

Next day, French visited Lanrezac's headquarters, whom Joffre had assured him would provide him with every cooperation. This could not have been further from the truth. For the over-stressed Lanrezac, his visitor seemed to bring nothing but more problems.

> I receive at Rethel a visit from Field Marshal French, who lets me know that he cannot get his army on the move before August 24th,

'And even then', he added, 'I would need a another week to train my infantry reservists!' It seems dangerous to me that our allies move so late and I ask the Field Marshal if he would not see fit to join his cavalry to Sordet's Cavalry Corps to cover our left flank? 'No!' he answers, 'I was to have had three army corps; by having only two, I shall keep my cavalry to use as a reserve!' I judge that it is useless to insist. I request the permission to make use of a few localities within the vast deployment area of the British Army, near railway stations allocated for the disembarkation of the XVIII Corps to avoid their units having to have their billets too far from their detraining point. I believe that the Field Marshal is willing and give orders accordingly; yet then, at around four or five o'clock, I was informed by General Mas Latrie, commanding the XVIII Corps, that his troops were face to face with the British soldiers in the billet they were allotted. Then one of my officers had to report to the English headquarters to bring an end to the dispute. The incident was nothing in itself, but it made plain that the military relations between the English and us would be difficult in spite of an undeniable mutual willingness: we did not speak the same language, and, furthermore, we had different ideas on war.[16]

The language difficulties between Lanrezac and French were real enough, and there is a famous account of this meeting that indicates that Lanrezac had very little patience for the stumbling French of the British commander.

There was a big map and the news had just come in that the German armies were making for a place on the Meuse called Huy – very difficult word to pronounce in English! French started off gallantly in French, turning to Lanrezac and said, 'Qu'est que vous croixaic que l'Allemand vont faire ä. . .' then he stuck, he just couldn't pronounce 'Huy' so after a moment's hesitation he said triumphantly, 'Hoy! What are the Germans going to do at Huy?' The Frenchman said, 'What's he say? What's he say?' Then very rudely, Lanrezac turned to somebody and said, 'Tell the Field Marshal, the Germans have come to the Meuse to fish!' This was very rude and as a matter of fact it was a most unfortunate incident because it was resented and remembered. It was the beginning of an extremely bad relationship between the two men![17]

Lieutenant Edward Spears, Headquarters, French Fifth Army

Spears cannot be considered an entirely reliable witness – indeed he often seemed to be remarkably well informed as to events where he was not himself present – but there does indeed seem to have been considerable antagonism between the two men. Lanrezac may well have given vent to his frustrations, for there is no doubt Sir John French took umbrage, as his subsequent description of the French general makes clear.

> His personality did not convey to me the idea of a great leader. He was a big man with a loud voice, and his manner did not strike me as being very courteous. When he was discussing the situation, his attitude might have made a casual observer credit him with practical powers of command and determination of character; but, for my own part, I seemed to detect, from the first time my eyes fell upon him, a certain over-confidence which appeared to ignore the necessity for any consideration of alternatives. Although we arrived at a mutual understanding which included no idea or thought of 'retreat', I left General Lanrezac's headquarters believing that the Commander-in-Chief had over-rated his ability; and I was therefore not surprised when he afterwards turned out to be the most complete example, amongst the many this war has afforded, of the Staff College 'pedant' whose 'superior education' had given him little idea of how to conduct war.[18]

It may be perhaps observed that French was never comfortable with 'educated soldiers' – whether French or British.

The next phase was intended by Joffre to be decisive: the great offensive on 21 August to be launched by the Third, Fourth and Fifth French Armies, designed to punch through the Ardennes area, driving in at the imagined hinge of the German manoeuvres. Joffre at this stage had not worked out the sheer monumental scale of the mailed fist that was swinging round his left flank. Joffre was far more focussed on his own plans for the Third and Fourth Armies to smash through the 'weak' German centre, thereby threatening the left flank of any German forces wheeling through Belgium. The problem was that he had totally underestimated the scale of the German forces in the Ardennes as well – the German Fourth and Fifth Armies were advancing through the Ardennes as part of the same gigantic manoeuvre. In part this was a technical misunderstanding as to the German method of using their reserves, allowing them to field a much larger number of army corps than the French were expecting.

In the great battles that followed, the French Fourth Army began to advance on Neufchâteau in the central Ardennes, while the Third Army pushed forward towards Virton and Metz. The two French armies ran straight into the German Fourth Army (Duke Albrecht von Württemberg) and the Fifth Army (Crown Prince Friedrich Wilhelm), which were cautiously advancing. The resulting encounter battles on 22 August were intensely sanguinary affairs that are collectively known as the Battle of the Ardennes. The Germans were in no hurry and had prepared defensive works at each stage of their advance through the wooded and hilly terrain of the region. In misty conditions, reconnaissance was difficult and the French found themselves tactically outwitted at every turn. The German troops were usually dug in along the front edges of the woodlands, condemning the hapless *poilus* to an advance across open ground. In their bright red and blue uniforms, their officers standing erect and proud, they were shot down in droves. The worst massacre – on a day of utter carnage – was in the attack by the 3rd Colonial Division on Rossignol, to the south of Neufchâteau. That single division lost some 4,083 men killed and a further 6,000 wounded or taken prisoner. And this is just one of many French divisions that were devastated on 22 August. Time after time the French launched fruitless attacks, failing to concentrate their forces, with little or no coordination between the infantry and artillery. In contrast, the Germans stayed under cover where possible, while their 77mm field guns would deluge the French infantry in shellfire. Where possible, concentrated machine gun fire would add to the deadly mix. Troops caught in the open had no chance.

> My company was sustaining heavy losses. Evidently its action was hampering the enemy who concentrated the combined fire of his infantry, artillery and machine guns on us. We were surrounded by a heavy cloud which at times completely veiled the battlefield from our eyes. Little Bergeyre sprang up, shouted, 'Vive la France!' at the top of his voice and fell dead. Among the men lying on the ground one could no longer distinguish the living from the dead. The first were entirely absolved by their grim duty, the others lay motionless. The wounded offered a truly impressive sight. Sometimes they would stand up bloody and horrible looking, amidst burst of gunfire. They ran aimlessly around arms stretched out before them, eyes staring at the ground, turning round and round until, hit by fresh bullets, they would stop and fall heavily. Heart-rending cries, agonising appeals and horrible groans were intermingled with the sinister howling of projectiles.

Furious contortions told of strong and youthful bodies refusing to give up life. One man was trying to replace his bloody dangling hand to his shattered wrist. Another ran from the line holding the bowels falling out of his belly and through his tattered clothes. Before long a bullet struck him down. We had no support from our artillery! And yet there were guns in our division and in the army corps, besides those destroyed on the road. Where were they? Why didn't they arrive? We were alone![19]

Major Alphonse Grasset, 103rd Regiment d'Infanterie, 7th Division, IV Corps, Third Army

The numbers of French casualties were simply terrifying. This was a tragedy of epic proportions for the French nation.

I was hit by a bullet in the left side, I felt a terrible pain as if I'd broken a bone. The bullet passed through the whole of my body, through the pelvis and lodged above the knee. Immediately I was suffering greatly with a burning fever. The bullets continue to rain down all around me, I may be hit again, so I do my best to drag myself into a hole, I find it hard to gain any comfort. The fight is over: all my comrades have retreated, and we wounded, are left without care, dying of thirst. What an awful night! Nothing but more shooting, every sound made by the wounded, triggered a resumption of fire. Machine gun swept the ground, bullets flying over my head, but they can no longer touch me in my hole. Thirst tortures me more. As I suffer, I think about my parents, especially my mother, remembering when I was sick and very young. It wasn't only me thinking of their mothers, for I could hear the wounded and dying calling out for their 'Maman'.[20]

Private Désireé Renault, 77th Régiment d'Infanterie, 18th Division, 1X Corps, Fourth Army

Soon the French were retreating, pursued by the Germans.

The planned attack by Lanrezac's Fifth Army had been overtaken by events as the German Second and Third Armies crashed into his positions along the Sambre and Meuse, in what would be the Battle of Charleroi. Here too the fighting had a stark brutality that mocked pre-war conceptions of the spirit of the offensive. There was nothing flesh and blood could do against concentrated rifle fire, machine guns and shrapnel shells.

Suddenly the enemy's fire became precise and concentrated. Second by second the hail of bullets and the thunder of the shells grew stronger. Those who survived lay flat on the ground, amid the screaming wounded and the humble corpses. With affected calm, the officers let themselves be killed standing upright, some obstinate platoons stuck their bayonets in their rifles, bugles sounded the charge, isolated heroes made fantastic leaps, but all to no purpose. In an instant it had become clear that not all the courage in the world could withstand this fire.[21]

Lieutenant Charles De Gaulle, 33rd Régiment d'Infanterie, 1st Division, I Corps, Fifth Army,

Vastly outnumbered, Lanrezac was in a desperate position with no chance of help from his neighbours in the Fourth Army, which was suffering its own disasters at the hands of the Germans in the Ardennes. In all, the French casualties in the Battles of the Frontiers would total some 200,000 men, of which more than 75,000 were dead. It is estimated that up to 27,000 died on the 22 August alone. As the French advance stalled and fell into reverse, the BEF was advancing towards potential disaster.

On 21 August, the Cavalry Division commanded by Major General Edmund Allenby began to cross the Belgian frontier with the intention of screening the advance of the BEF north of the Sambre. The division had been thrown together on the outbreak of the war and resembled rather more a collection of independent cavalry brigades than one formation. To add further confusion, the staff officers had little experience in their professional function, resulting in orders that were often vague in the extreme. Brigadier General Hubert Gough, commanding the 3rd Cavalry Brigade, was soon infuriated by the lack of clear direction or briefing received from headquarters.

Responsible commanders should have been informed in the clearest manner of the general plan of campaign and of the positions of all forces operating near us. Yet too often we only received such general orders as, 'March on X!' ' "Assemble at Y!" the object of the movement being withheld. A blindfolded man cannot move intelligently. Of the two dangers – the risk of one's own orders falling into the hands of the enemy, or the lack of intelligent and coherent initiative in commanders due to the absence of information – the latter is far the more serious. This complete secrecy about the general situation, the position of forces in our neighbourhood, and the plans of our commanders, was, I think, carried to excess, and it was contrary to all our staff training previous to the war. It undoubtedly prevented units from exercising their full powers on many occasions during those first critical days. We often groped about in the fog of war, not doing all we might have done – or sometimes doing too much![22]

One problem breathing down their collective necks was that the British cavalry were badly outnumbered by the German cavalry, who – in the first instance – would be their opponents as they sought to screen the advance of the BEF and determine the location of the German forces in front of them. On the German right wing there were both I Cavalry Corps (two cavalry divisions) and II Cavalry Corps (three cavalry divisions) facing the five brigades of Allenby's Cavalry Division. The Germans had adopted a different tactical approach from the British, attaching a battalion of *jäger* (light infantry) to each cavalry division to augment their fire power. Yet the British were not only armed with a proper .303 Lee Enfield rifle, but had also been exhaustively trained in both marksmanship and infantry tactics, even learning to dig in where necessary. They were also better horsemen and as such kept their horses in much healthier condition, often marching alongside them to conserve the finite energy of their steeds. The French cavalry were not so well-blessed, reliant as they were on a poor quality carbine with minimal stopping power, whilst collectively still imbued with a disdain for any form of dismounted action.

Given the emphasis on cavalry reconnaissance, it is amusing to relate that the most accurate information on the approach of the German First Army was amassed by the simple initiative of a somewhat unconventional intelligence officer, Lieutenant Colonel George Barrow, who made a series of telephone calls from Mons railway station on the morning of 22 August.

> I went into Mons in order to execute a novel plan I had conceived
> for ascertaining the positions the Germans had reached and of
> maintaining touch with his subsequent progress and the extent of the
> great left wheel he was evidently about to make. With the consent of
> the French authorities, I took possession of the railway telephone office.
> Here, assisted by Bertrand Stewart, I sat all day and far into the night
> ringing up all possible and impossible places in Belgium not known
> yet to be in German hands: Soignies, Braine-le-Comte, Hal, Tubize,
> Lens, Ath, Ghislenghien, Lessines, and many others. Replies took the

following forms: 'No signs of enemy here, but rumours they are in A'. 'Germans are five miles distant on road to B!' 'Have just received message from C that enemy close to town. Germans are on outskirts of town; we are closing down!' A German voice or failure to get contact told that the enemy had already arrived. It was easy from these replies to get a fairly accurate picture of the German line of advance. Allenby sent this information on to GHQ. It showed that the German right extended much further west than had been suspected. But GHQ preferred to rely on its own agents and more orthodox intelligence methods. It replied, 'The information which you have acquired and conveyed to the Commander-in-Chief appears to be somewhat exaggerated.'[23]

In fact, this exercise gave a good impressionistic picture of the real threat lurking behind the German cavalry screen. It was another sign that modern technology was creating new methods of gaining information and that the day of the cavalry might be all but done. There were a series of small cavalry skirmishes, which loom large in some British histories, but which were trivial in the extreme compared to the mayhem encompassing the French Army the same day. The first British shot was fired, the first casualty suffered in action, but Barrow had gained far more potentially useful intelligence at the Mons station telephone, only to have his initiative ignored by GHQ.

Meanwhile, behind the British cavalry screen, long columns of sweating infantry began to push forward into Belgium on 22 August.

It was a very hot day and the march proved particularly trying to the reservists – about 50% of the strength. As soon as the frontier had been crossed, and the column had entered Belgium, the general aspect of the countryside underwent a great change. This district, the southwestern outskirts of the Mons-Charleroi mining area, was industrial, and its villages were more densely populated than those on the French side of the frontier. For the first time roads paved with cobbled stones, very uneven and trying to the feet, were met with. The inhabitants from outward appearances gave the impression of being less friendly than the French peasants. They watched the passage of troops through their midst with marked indifference. Men of military age were numerous in the villages, lounging at the street corners as the troops passed. The distance marched was fifteen miles.[24]

Captain Algernon Ransome, 1st Dorsetshire Regiment, 15th Brigade, 5th Division, II Corps

Up above them all were the aircraft of the RFC. Frail in appearance, they had the power to influence the course of events, by what they could discern of the German plans. Given good visibility, little was hidden from them as they flew searching out the German columns.

> I started out that morning from Maubeuge and we were told to go to a given area – east – and we were told we should see advancing German troops. We were very, very excited as we looked for them. You were very limited in your facilities, you had a map strapped on one knee and a pad with a pencil on the other and it was rather wobbling about. As soon as we got over our area instead of seeing a few odd German troops I saw the whole area covered with hoards of field grey uniforms – advancing infantry, cavalry, transport and guns. In fact it looked as though the place was alive with the Germans. My pilot and I were completely astounded because it was not a little more than we'd been looking for – it was infinitely more. The main roads of Belgium were pavé in the centre, with two areas of a yard or two of dry earth, which in the winter were chewed all up, but which in the summer you could use. The Germans had their guns and heavy transport on the pavé to give them foundation, infantry walking along on this soft earth and on the field on either side in many cases there were cavalry. We very busily covered the area, made marks on the map, made notes as much as we could. After a little while we went away. I was completely horrified! We came roaring back and we landed whereupon I was put into a motor car by my squadron commander and taken off to general headquarters.[25]

Lieutenant Cuthbert Rabagliati, 5 Squadron, RFC

Like Barrow, Rabagliati would discover that intelligence is of little value of it is not appreciated or understood by those in command of events.

> As we arrived we were ushered in and we went into a room with a lot of elderly gentlemen covered in gold lace and all the rest of it. All these senior generals, it was Sir John French's own personal conference that was going on. Somebody announced us and he said, 'Well here's a boy from the Flying Corps, come here and sit down!' I was put to sit next to him rather terrified! I showed him a map all marked out. He said, 'Have you been over that area?' and I said, 'Yes, Sir'! I explained what I had

seen and they were enormously interested. Then they began reading the figures that I had estimated, whereupon I feel that their interest faded – they seemed to look at each other and shrug their shoulders. Then French turned round to me and said, 'Now, yes my boy, this is terribly interesting, but tell me all about an aeroplane, what can you do when you're in these machines? Aren't they very dangerous, are they very cold, can you see anything? What do you do if your engine stops?' I couldn't bring him back to earth because obviously he wasn't interested. I again tried and he looked at me and said, 'Yes, this is very interesting, what you've got but our information – which of course is correct – proves that I don't think you could have seen as much as you think! Well of course I quite understand that you may imagine that you have, but it's not the case!'[26]

It was evident at the conference held on the afternoon of 22 August that intelligence which disagreed with the perceptions of GHQ was treated with considerable scepticism.

Little attention seemed to be paid to the reports which have been coming in for several days that the enemy is moving in large masses on Tournai. The Commander-in-Chief had apparently not discussed the situation with his intelligence officer (Macdonogh) because the latter, who was not in the conference room, told me after the conference that aeroplanes reported all the roads running west from Brussels to Ath and Tournai were thickly covered with masses of German troops of all arms marching very rapidly westwards. This was indeed an alarming situation. Yet our C-in-C ordered my Corps to press on. Wilson had news that the French would re-establish the situation by a breakthrough in the Ardennes or in Alsace! De Castelnau was about to deliver an enormous attack which must succeed![27]

Lieutenant General Sir Douglas Haig, Headquarters, I Corps, BEF

However, Wilson's optimism would prove ill-founded. The Battle of the Frontiers had been a disaster, for the French and the Fifth Army had been treated very harshly in the Battle of Charleroi between 21 and 22 August, as was evident to the British liaison officer Lieutenant Edward Spears.

I had ascertained that General Lanrezac had no intention whatsoever of advancing, because of the orders he had given and I had been to see myself what the state of his army was: most of his troops were running away. Now it is quite obvious that an army that is running away isn't in a very good position to advance. I knew that the British Army was absolutely relying on this advance to complete its own movement. I was liaison officer and, on my own responsibility. I had come to tell Sir John French that he couldn't rely on the French advance and indeed that if he continued to advance as he planned to do it was the destruction of the whole of the British Army – we were walking straight into the mouth of an enormous trap. I walked into the house with Colonel Macdonogh who was the head of our intelligence, and Sir John French and his Chief of Staff, General Murray had come out of the dining room to listen to my news. I told Sir John French what I had seen. As I was speaking I was seized inwardly with an awful sense of panic! There was I – I had no instructions for anybody, I'd not been told anything directly by General Lanrezac – all this was based on my personal observations. I had no sort of backing, no sort of support and here was I telling the Commander in Chief of the BEF that he had to retire! It was a perfectly horrible feeling. But still I could only do what I thought it was right to do. Colonel Macdonogh and I left the study where Sir John French and Murray were looking at the map and walked straight into the dining room which they had left to meet us and hear my news. Macdonogh and I sat in a low couch, nobody paying any attention to us. The people round the table were the chiefs of staff from different corps who had come to get their final orders from the Commander in Chief to coordinate their plans, for the attack by the BEF next morning – they were just finishing their dinner. Coffee cups had been pushed back, notebooks were out and everybody was busy talking to their neighbour, settling the details. It was really a frightful sensation: Macdonogh and I knew that the planned offensive couldn't possibly take place because of the news I'd brought that the French were retiring in some disorder. But nevertheless, sitting on that couch, I had awful visions of Captain Nolan, who gave the wrong instructions to Lord Cardigan the Commander of the Light Brigade at Balaclava which led to appalling disaster! It really was awful. I was overwhelmed with the sense of responsibility – that I a subaltern – was the bearer of such overwhelming responsibility. We sat there for quite a long time, then suddenly General Murray appeared framed in the doorway and called to all these high ranking officers round the table, 'Look here, come in and see the Commander in Chief now! But remember, there must be no questions, the decision has been taken, there's going to be no advance tomorrow!'[28]

Despite the reports from cavalry and aircraft reconnaissance, despite the explicit warnings from Spears and the warnings from his own Intelligence Officer Colonel George Macdonogh, it is strange to relate that on the morning of 23 August French was still clinging to the hope that an advance might still be possible.

> About 6am the Chief appeared at my headquarters, and, addressing his corps and cavalry division commanders assembled there, told us that little more than one, or at most two, enemy corps, with perhaps a cavalry division, were facing the BEF. So it was evident that he too was in blissful ignorance of the real situation. Sir John was in excellent form, and told us to be prepared to move forward, or to fight where we were, but to get ready for the latter by strengthening our outposts and preparing the bridges over the canal for demolition.[29]
>
> Lieutenant General Sir Horace Smith-Dorrien, Headquarters, II Corps

A sense of reality would only dawn on French much later. It would be for others to extricate the BEF from its dangerous position.

5

BATTLE OF MONS

So did I first hear the song of the bullet and the howl of shrapnel.
I can't quite describe my feelings through this show, but
I somehow don't believe it dispelled the odd idea that we were
on some big sort of manoeuvres, which had idiotically been with
me since we started from the Curragh. The burst and hum of the
shrapnel surprised me, and the bullets made me duck my head!
It interested me, I think, when a bullet flicked the ground just
in front as I was riding along a road to get more ammunition.
I won't say I was not frightened, I'm sure I was, but I don't think
I knew it.[1]

Lieutenant Arthur Ackland, 1st Duke of Cornwall's Light Infantry, 14th
Brigade, 5th Division, II Corps

MONS WAS A SLIGHTLY STRANGE location for the first British battle of
the war. It was a coal-mining region with the associated slag heaps dotted around the small pit villages and towns. The II Corps would defend
a line along fifteen miles of the Condé Canal between Mons and Condé,
with the canal looping round Mons itself to create a difficult salient. The
canal itself was a significant obstacle, being about twenty yards across
and six feet deep, although there were a large number of bridges potentially available to the Germans. On the BEF left would be the French
84th Territorial Division, while Haig's I Corps was on the right, bending
back towards the already retreating French Fifth Army. It was a cluttered

countryside, a closed-in industrial landscape, largely built up and dominated by slagheaps west of the canal, but bespattered with patches of
woodland along the eastern side. There was no beauty here: this was a
landscape created by man.

Smith-Dorrien deployed the 3rd Division on the right covering the
Mons salient from Bois le Haut to Mariette, with the 5th Division holding
positions all along the canal to Condé. It is noticeable that Smith-Dorrien
therefore spread most of his available troops out thinly, failing to hold a
significant reserve at either divisional or corps level. This left them unable
either to stem an incipient German breakthrough or to counter-attack to
seize any fleeting opportunities to disrupt German attacks. This was not
in accordance with British doctrine as expressed in *Field Regulation Part 1*,
which was very firm on the importance of maintaining an aggressive
outlook.

The built-up terrain and pit heaps posed a particular problem for
the Royal Artillery. The batteries found it very difficult to find suitable
gun positions possessed of a reasonable arc of fire. Even moving the guns
about proved difficult, as there was a myriad of streams and drainage
channels. Observation was also severely restricted by the landscape. The
result was that very few guns were able to play any meaningful part in the
battle to come, especially on the 5th Division front stretched out along
the canal. As such, the defensive line chosen was unfit for purpose.

A further weakness in the British defensive plans was the indecision
over the demolition of the bridges. French may still have had dreams of
resuming the BEF advance, but bridges are a two-way street. Their continued existence offered a tempting focus for German attacks; if they could
capture a significant number of the bridges, then the British line would be
irretrievably broken. Although orders to *prepare* the bridges for demolition
were issued belatedly by Smith-Dorrien at 02.30 on Saturday 23 August,
that still left a great deal to be desired. The Royal Engineers representative
on his staff was just a single sapper colonel, with a lieutenant colonel, an
adjutant and clerk at each of his divisions. The orders had to percolate
right thought the staff to reach the Royal Engineers on the ground, where
there was a complement of two field companies for each of the 3rd and
5th Divisions. As the senior officers were urgently reconnoitring a second, more defensible, position further back from the canal, this meant
that the preparation of the demolition charges was left to subalterns. The

end result was that there was little time to prepare properly sited charges. Worst of all, the decision-making process as to when the bridges should actually be blown up was non-existent, with authority supposedly lying with divisional headquarters, but devolving in practice to the judgement of junior officers on the spot. This was a recipe for prevarication and disaster.

Yet General Alexander von Kluck, commanding the German First Army, was also approaching the battle from a position of disadvantage through his ignorance of the location of the BEF, which he imagined was gathering in the Lille area. Still smarting at having been placed under the overall command of General Karl von Bülow of the Second Army, there was an air of considerable tension between the two German commanders. Although aware of the skirmishes with British cavalry and the presence of British aircraft originating from Maubeuge, von Kluck appears to have had no real idea of what lay ahead of him in his approach to the Condé Canal, as expressed in his orders issued on the evening of 22 August.

1. A squadron of British cavalry was encountered today at Casteau, northeast of Mons, and a British aeroplane coming from Maubeuge was shot down near Enghien. In front of the Second Army there appear today to be only three cavalry divisions and a weak force of infantry.

2. The Second Army has advanced today to the line Binche-Mettet, northwest of Dinant, and tomorrow it is to press forward east of Maubeuge, its right wing, the VII Corps, moving from Binche through Solre.

3. The First Army will continue its advance tomorrow to the area northwest of Maubeuge, masking that fortress.

4. The II Corps will reach La Hamaide, marching from Ninove through Grammorit; the IV Corps will march to Basecles and Stambruges by Ath and Chievres; the III Corps will reach St. Ghislain and Jemappes by Lens and Jurbise. The rising ground on the southern side of the canal is to be occupied. The IX Corps will cover the movement of the Army towards Maubeuge, and for this purpose will advance across the line Mons-Thieu towards the north and northwestern front of Maubeuge, keeping its main force on its right flank. The line Ath-Roeulx will be crossed by the leading troops of the IV, III, and IX Corps by 8.30 am.[2]

The German First Army was still engaged in a gigantic wheeling manoeuvre, with IX Corps on the left flank, then III Corps, IV Corps and finally

II Corps on the right. This was a proper army, totalling an intimidating 142 battalions of infantry, 32 cavalry squadrons and 110 batteries of artillery. It was also ready for war, with highly motivated troops, well-trained before the war in full-scale exercises on the extensive training grounds in Germany. Such exercises featured an 'enemy' force and live-firing elements to create a sense of realism. The infantry were armed with the 8mm Gewehr '98, magazine bolt-action rifle, which, although not on a par with the .303 Lee Enfield used by the British, was still capable of a good rate of fire. The Germans practiced firing collectively onto targets to win the firefight that under German doctrine would precede most infantry attacks. To maximise the possible concentration of fire, they had collected the two Maxim machine guns allowed per battalion into machine gun companies, which were held back and only deployed when necessary to provide a decisive impact. The support from their artillery was even better, allowing heavy concentrations of fire from their 77mm field guns and 105mm howitzers. Once the firefight had been won, the German infantry would attack in open order, advancing in short bounds, before the final assault.

As von Kluck still had little, or no, awareness of where the BEF was located, the battle took the shape for him of an old-fashioned advance to contact. As the German corps wheeled round on their designated lines of march, so, one by one, they bumped into the thin British line. The first exchanges were between the troops of IX Corps (17th and 18th Divisions) and the British 3rd Division defending that Mons salient. What happened is indeed the stuff of legend, but there are two versions of this enthralling tale.

The British troops had prepared defensive positions, but for the most part had only time to dig shallow scrapes, take up positions in the scattered miners' cottages, or man improvised barricades thrown up to block the narrow streets. One of the most vulnerable locations was at the apex of the salient held by the 8th and 9th Brigades, where the canal bent round the town of Mons. Lieutenant Kinglake Tower describes the defences near the village of Nimy.

> We were ordered to take up an outpost position guarding the main road from Namur into Mons and the railway line about Nimy bridge. We started to put up what defences we could and it was a funny

sensation to do it in reality when one had been accustomed at manoeuvres in England to pretend to do it! I well remember smashing loopholes in the walls of a house with a crowbar and great fun it was! However, when we had been at work for about two hours, we were told to withdraw about 100 yards further back behind the Mons-Condé Canal, which ran along our front. That evening we commenced to dig up some protection on the canal bank with our entrenching tools which we carried. Very difficult little tools to use effectively, but sometimes invaluable when the big tools are not available. The battalion detachment of two machine guns was sent to us and took up a position on the bridge under the command of Lieutenant Dease. A detachment of sappers arrived and started to put up barbed wire entanglements along the railway line and sandbag protection for the machine guns. We worked away till about 9pm, but were told that we should be advancing again in the morning, so that we need not do too much. We lay down in our positions and talked, having put out three groups of sentries in advance of the canal.[3]

Lieutenant Kinglake Tower, 4th Royal Fusiliers, 9th Brigade, 3rd Division, II Corps

The idea of placing the precious machine guns actually on the bridge, was interesting. Although they could generate bursts of intense fire, the machine gun was best deployed in positions where it could take an advancing force from a flank. Placed on the bridge they were both easy to locate for German observers and vulnerable to capture if the Germans could gain fire superiority long enough to rush the bridge.

The battle had a low-key opening for Lieutenant Kinglake Tower, who seems to have encountered a German advanced cavalry patrol as he walked around the battalion outposts situated north of the canal.

I was out visiting my sentries in the woods about a 1,000 yards in advance of our position about 7am and was talking to an old reservist when we suddenly saw a horseman ride through the wood. He dismounted and tied his horse to a tree and advanced about 300 yards from us to the edge of the wood and stood looking at our position on the canal bank. My old reservist said to me, 'Is that a German, Sir?' I said, 'Yes, I expect it is!' Thereupon he said, 'Shall I shoot him, Sir?' And I said, 'Yes, have a try!' He picked up his rifle, took careful aim and fired. The man fell and we walked over to look at him. It was a trooper of the famous regiment of the Death's Head Hussars, the first German I had seen. We searched him and found only his pipe, so I took his horse and rode it back to our lines and made my reports.[4]

Subsequently, there were scattered outbreaks of firing as the advance guard of IX Corps encountered the forward detachments of the British line around the Mons salient. To Lieutenant Tower it all seemed faintly surreal.

> By this time the sun was getting quite hot. A gorgeous morning – the church bells were ringing for service and the Belgian peasants could be seen walking quietly to church. What a contrast and it seemed hardly believable that we were at war – and that men had just been killed only a few yards away.[5]

When the Germans reached the edge of the woods facing the canal they could take stock of the situation.

> The British had an excellent position, which nature might have designed for defence. Separated from us by the canal, they had barricaded the only two ways of crossing the canal – a railway bridge and a foot bridge – with strong barbed wire obstacles. They had also placed two machine guns on the bridge abutments. The machine gun on the railway bridge was at more or less at the same height as the flat top of the rise on which our skirmishing line was located and so was able to bring down fire on the entire hilltop. On the lower lying ground between the bridges the British had built sandbagged positions, whilst others took cover behind sheaves of oats, which were dotted close to one another in the fields and offered excellent cover from view. Of course we were dealing with troops with colonial experience who were therefore dangerous opponents.[6]
>
> Theodor Schröder, 84th Regiment, 35th Brigade, 18th Division, IX Corps

The first major German attacks at Nimy began at 09.30 as the 84th Regiment made a lunge for the canal.

> Some of the enemy appeared out of the woods. I gave the order to fire at the range of 800 yards and several were seen to fall, whereupon I ordered 1,000 yards and fire into the woods hoping to catch some more. The enemy was seen to retire at the double and bugle calls were

heard all through the woods. Shortly after this the enemy started to advance in mass down the railway cutting about 800 yards off and Maurice Dease fired his two machine guns into them and absolutely mowed them down. I should judge without exaggeration that he killed at least 500 in those two minutes. The whole cutting was full of bodies and cheered us all up. Soon however the enemy started debouching from the woods in all directions and we lay down and fired as hard and as fast as possible. Our shooting was very accurate and we did a lot of damage. The Germans still continued to advance: the more we shot the more appeared.[7]

Lieutenant Kinglake Tower, 4th Royal Fusiliers, 9th Brigade, 3rd Division, II Corps

The British, doubtless caught up in the excitement and confusion of the moment, tended to exaggerate the effect of their fire. The myth of Mons is encapsulated in the popular account written by Lance Corporal Alfred Vivian of the neighbouring 4th Middlesex Regiment at Obourg.

'Rapid fire!' That solid-looking field-grey wall was blasted away by the hail that leapt at them through the hedge, as powerful rifles, manipulated by men who, in pre-war days, depended on their skill at this exercise for their pay, pumped steel-jacketed leaden death into them, with never a miss, at the rate of at least fifteen rounds a minute per man. No troops on earth could have faced that murderous blast and existed, and within less than a minute of the order to fire, the only signs left of this futile attack, and of the terrible lesson the enemy had been taught, were the numerous, grey-clad figures that littered the ground between our hedge and the wood from which the enemy had launched his attack. Another calm period ensued, broken only by the pitiful cries of the wounded foe who had been left lying abandoned out upon the blood-soaked field.[8]

The idea that the Germans attacked in mass formation, after the fashion of the Napoleonic Wars, is one that it is difficult to shift. Research in the surviving German archives has revealed no sign of such suicidal behaviour at this stage of the war and it bears no resemblance to well-established German infantry tactics. To believe such stories is to believe that the Germans abandoned everything they had practiced pre-war. Yet, at the same time, there is no doubt that as the Germans attacked they did soon become very aware of the potency of the British rifles and machine guns.

> At that instant a skirmishing line leapt up and dashed forward led by my company commander, Hauptmann Stubenrauch, with his sword drawn. No sooner had Leutnant Matzen noticed this than he ordered us to rush forward and join the company skirmishing line. Setting us a good example, he took the lead, but within a few dashes the daring officer fell dead, hit by two bullets. Because we were under machine gun fire, we threw ourselves down and crawled forward the few paces which separated us from the skirmishing line. Here we made the bitter discovery that enemy fire had torn great holes in the ranks. I had just shouted the news of the death of Leutnant Matzen, when word was passed through the ranks that Hauptmann Stubenrauch was also seriously wounded.[9]
>
> Theodor Schröder, 84th Regiment, 35th Brigade, 18th Division, IX Corps

The Germans advanced in short bounds: rising in skirmish lines, running forwards under covering fire and then dropping back down to earth again. They were not advancing in a solid phalanx, although successive lines advancing may have conveyed such an illusion from the perspective of troops lying at ground level. When they dropped, they were taking cover, not all dead and dying as the British optimistically assumed. Nor did the Germans believe that they were facing excessively large numbers of machine guns, as is often boasted. The Germans knew full well that each BEF battalion only had two machine guns and had for the most part accurately located them.

In accordance with German standard doctrine, their forward skirmishing line was gradually edged forward and strengthened, before the serious business commenced.

> A lively firefight between us and the enemy now began. Because we were silhouetted against the horizon to the enemy troops in their lower lying positions, our casualties here were also significant. Death tore great gaps in our ranks, but help was on the way. In the heat of the battle, we had not noticed our comrades from the 5th and 8th Companies filling in the gaps in the firing line. Gradually we began to win fire superiority. Feldwebel Ehlers, took over command of the

company and the enemy riflemen and machine guns were brought systematically under fire.[10]

Oberleutnant Liebe, 84th Regiment, 35th Brigade, 18th Division, IX Corps

The marksmanship of the British regulars took its toll, but their defences were flimsy and not proof against serious shellfire once the German artillery intervened.

Guns had now been brought up and the deafening crashes of the shrapnel shells bursting on top of us was added to the continuous roar of rifle fire. Heavy shells were falling in the town of Mons about a mile behind us and I remember seeing a church tower collapse and fall into the street. The enemy was getting closer and closer to us and had begun to bring massed machine gun fire to bear on our slender parapets on the canal bank. The dead and dying were lying all over the place.[11]

Lieutenant Kinglake Tower, 4th Royal Fusiliers, 9th Brigade, 3rd Division, II Corps

To the right of the Fusiliers, the 4th Middlesex were also in desperate straits. The folly of relying on ad hoc demolition arrangements to destroy the bridges was soon abundantly clear as the canal line began to collapse around them.

Our next message was from the brigade as follows, 'You will decide when bridges and boats within your zones should be destroyed: acknowledge!' I acknowledged in the ordinary way. It was too late. The enemy were across or crossing. It was now about 1 o'clock and we saw a platoon of 'A' Company retiring under a sergeant. I think they must have seen Major Abell and Captain Knowles hit, and got jumpy. The former was seriously wounded and it was thought killed and the latter was killed. The C.O. said he would enquire into the facts afterwards and if the Sergeant had not had any order to retire, he would have him shot. We then went over to the track just west of the houses and east of the quarry (which we made our new headquarters) and caught all these fellows just getting on to the main road, and got them back to the line by the track in front of us. They did not seem to mind coming back in the least.[12]

Lieutenant Thomas Wollocombe, 4th Middlesex Regiment, 8th Brigade, 3rd Division, II Corps

Their opponents' tactics were proceeding smoothly. The German Army had invested a great deal of time and money in annual manoeuvres and exercises in readiness for just such tricky situations. As a result, they had the answer to the conundrum before them and, more to the point, the concentrated firepower to achieve it. They were not reliant on rapid accurate rifle fire alone, but deployed far more deadly weapons in the form of concentrated machine guns and, above all, artillery fire. Young Private William Holbrook of the 4th Royal Fusiliers found himself in a very tight spot close by the Nimy bridges.

> They had the worst part on the bridge, quite a number got killed and wounded. Lieutenant Dease in charge of the machine gun party, he wasn't with them at first, but when things got very close he was wounded about three times, but he still went to the gun. Godley was firing in. Dease died there, leaving Godley in charge of the gun. There were some village kids up there, quite near the canal bank and I remember Godley shouting at them, 'Get out of the way! Get away!' These kids were within about fifty yards – during the attack![13]

Perhaps because of his youth, Holbrook was picked to act as a runner.

> I was in Major Bowden Smith's company and I had the job of orderly. I only fired a bit because I was behind the company with the officers. I had to run back to take any message. It wasn't a very pleasant job. The first one I took, I don't know what it contained but I had to take this message from Nimy down near to Mons. I didn't know my way really. I came back and I'd been gone about half an hour I suppose, they were still firing there, we weren't firing much. I took up position there and shortly afterwards, about three in the afternoon, I had to take another message down. By then I'd got the impression there was something happening. I started going back and met some troops coming down. A fellow said, 'Where are you going!' They weren't my battalion. He said, 'You'll have a job – they're retiring from the village!' I suppose that was the message I took back – I don't know![14]

Back at the canal, the situation had indeed become desperate shortly after Holbrook's departure. Bullets and shrapnel balls lashed across the shallow trenches. It took real luck to survive.

> I had a shot which took off my hat, another through my sleeve, and two bits of shrapnel in my puttees – but unwounded. Captain Bowden

Smith[15] was hit with shrapnel in the stomach and lay at my feet in fearful agony. One could do nothing for the wounded and the enemy had now got right round on our right flank, driving in the Middlesex Regiment who retired without letting us know. We were now being shot at from all sides and the position was hopeless. I picked up a rifle and shot six of the enemy about twenty yards across the canal. Dease, all his machine gun crew and both guns had been knocked out. I went along under cover and saw his body.[16] He had been hit about a dozen times. I remember lying there wondering what it would be like to have a bayonet stuck into me and I admit that I have never felt so frightened in my life.[17]

Lieutenant Kinglake Tower, 4th Royal Fusiliers, 9th Brigade, 3rd Division, II Corps

From across the canal, Oberleutnant Liebe watched the exchange of fire with considerable satisfaction and was impressed greatly by an act of individual courage and sacrifice in the common cause.

After a lengthy firefight we gained the upper hand. A 2nd Battalion patrol under Sergeant Röver pushed forward to the bridge site and Musketier Niemeyer of 8th Company swam over, despite being under heavy fire, and succeeded in swinging the bridge, which the enemy had earlier swung back, across the canal once more, thus making it possible to get across. Unfortunately this brave man died a hero's death in the process.[18]

Oberleutnant Liebe, 84th Regiment, 35th Brigade, 18th Division, IX Corps

Once the first Germans managed to get across the canal, the resistance of the Royal Fusiliers soon crumbled. The German officers seized the chance to use their superior numbers in a direct assault.

Once a few German uniforms were spotted on the far bank there was no holding back. Feldwebel Ehlers ordered, 'On your feet! Double march!' We dashed down the bank to the canal and while some comrades kept the enemy under fire, the others climbed onto the bridges and forced their way through the barbed wire entanglements. This swift assault caught the British on the hop. They jumped up waving white cloths and surrendered. We took about sixty prisoners. Having reached the far bank we could see how well the company had operated. About three quarters of the British who had opposed our sector were lying dead or wounded. The sandbagged position was completely shot to pieces. Our victory was dearly bought.[19]

Theodor Schröder, 84th Regiment, 35th Brigade, 18th Division, IX Corps

The Germans reported the capture of up to ninety Fusiliers, as well as both of the exposed machine guns. This despite the fact that Private Sidney Godley[20] has been credited in British accounts with throwing his machine gun into the canal before his position was over-run. In the final moments, Lieutenant Tower realised that it was hopeless and that he had little option but to retreat. It was evident that there was no chance of getting any of the seriously wounded away.

> Collecting all I could of the company, which was only about six men under the bridge I told them we had got to run for it! I first went and saw Bowden Smith who was very slowly dying[21] and did what I could to make him comfortable. We dashed off under a hail of fire and I don't know how on earth we ever got away – only one man of my six being hit.[22]

The battle then slipped into street fighting in Nimy itself. Here there was still determined British resistance, but when it came to the crunch the German gunners had the whip hand.

> Towards 4.00 pm the battalions forced their way over the canal and occupied the houses. Held up by enemy fire, the leading companies on the far bank were all jammed together. It was only thanks to the determined intervention of Oberst von Amelunxen and Hauptmann Hofmeister that we drove on ruthlessly into the village of Nimy. Shots came from every building and numerous brave Mansteiners fell victim to this fire. In the face of tough defence, every house had to be stormed one after the other. Because the attack was supported by the artillery, the whole village caught fire. We deployed our attached engineers and the street fighting continued accompanied by the sounds of doors being blown in, firing and the cries of the wounded. By 5.00 pm the village, now a huge sea of flames, was in our hands.[23]

Oberleutnant Liebe, 84th Regiment, 35th Brigade, 18th Division, IX Corps

While the German 18th Division attacked the Mons salient, the 17th Division had pushed forward, crossing the undefended canal to the right of the 4th Middlesex Regiment. As they swung round towards Mons, they were able to threaten the exposed right flank of the 3rd Division, which was protected only by the 1st Gordon Highlanders and 2nd Royal Scots who were stretched very thinly over nearly four miles, angled back towards I Corps and facing the villages of St Symphorien and Villers St Ghislain.

> From the farthest point of the wood, at a range of 1,200 yards, a large body of troops marched out into the open in column, moving across our front to our left flank, evidently for the purpose of reinforcing the attack on 'C' Company. At 1,200 yards rifle fire, even at such a target, is practically useless. It was impossible to resist the temptation to open fire with the hope of breaking up the column formation and thus delaying the reinforcement operations. 'No. 1 Section, at 1,200 yards, three rounds rapid!' I bent over the parapet, glasses fixed on the column. They were not quite clear of the wood and marching along as if on parade. At the first volley the column halted, some of the men skipped into the wood, and most of them turned and faced in our direction. With the second and third volleys coming in rapid succession they rushed in a body for cover. All our shots seemed to have gone too high and none found a billet, but the enemy made no further attempt to leave the wood in close formation, but presently advanced along the edge of the wood in single file, marching in the same direction as before, and affording no target at such a distance.[24]

> Captain Malcolm Hay, 1st Gordon Highlanders, 8th Brigade, 3rd Division, II Corps,

Close behind the Gordon Highlanders, the 6th Battery, RFA was in forward positions on the eastern shoulder of the hill of Bois la Haut. They opened fire on the approaching German infantry at a range of 3,200 yards.

> Firing the first round at the enemy was an impressive moment. We had all fired hundreds of rounds at dummies at practice camps and thought nothing of it, but sending off a round knowing that it might possibly kill somebody – and that you hoped that it would – gave one for a moment a curious feeling. An even more curious feeling was to come shortly afterwards. Evidently we were getting on to something worthwhile as for some time we had been firing rounds of gunfire at infantry targets, the range to which was continually decreasing. While we were firing merrily away, I suddenly saw a burst of white smoke fairly close in front of the guns. I thought at first it was a 'premature',

but shortly a shell whizzed over us and burst on percussion a few yards behind. Evidently a German battery had got a bracket on us, which in two rounds was pretty good shooting. Realisation that someone was really out to kill one was a solemn thought. In coming into action, I had in order to clear the crest of this very steep hill, to put the guns rather nearer the crest than one normally should and our flashes must have been visible to the enemy for he proceeded to put a good deal of very accurate shrapnel into us.[25]

Lieutenant Sidney Archibald, 6th Battery, 40th Brigade, RFA, 3rd Division

In poor positions and harassed by German counter-battery fire, few of the 3rd Division guns were able to come into action to any real effect.

At around 14.00, the Gordons were reinforced by the 2nd Royal Irish Rifles, further extending the line to the south. The 8th Brigade managed to beat off the initial tentative German attacks even as the pressure began to grow after 16.00. In this achievement they were greatly assisted by the failure of the German artillery in this sector to find suitable observation posts and battery positions to allow them to first pinpoint and then destroy the shallow British trenches. In the absence of effective artillery support the Germans had no crushing advantage in the fire-fight and their attack stalled till nightfall. This was important as it prevented a further threatening incursion into the right flank of II Corps.

Nevertheless, it was evident that the Germans had entirely broken the right flank of the British positions and in consequence the whole canal line was no longer tenable. To the west of the Mons salient, the canal line was being held by the rest of 9th Brigade from Nimy to Jemappes. The German attack progressively moved westwards as the First Army wheeled round like a closing door hinged on Mons itself. After IX Corps initial attacks, first III Corps and then finally elements of IV Corps came into line and began to launch their attacks. One-by-one the British battalions faced the purgatory of German shellfire followed by the challenge of a German assault. The story was in many places the same: the Germans over-ran outposts on the north bank, took up positions firing from close range across the canal, brought up artillery where necessary and ultimately breached the canal line.

On the left of the 9th Brigade, was the 1st Northumberland Fusiliers who were occupying positions covering the Mariette bridge. They had detachments on the north side of the canal, but the defences relied on a solid barricade across the main road that crossed the canal and loop-holed cottages. As the Germans closed up there was a vigorous exchange of fire.

> My barrier across the road was getting rather crowded with the incoming detachments, who all seemed to desire to be near an officer and disliked the idea of going into any more houses. However, I got some of them away into the prepared houses in rear of the barricade. On the other hand one or two of the men on the barrier ware convinced that it was nicer to be in a house with all these nasty shells flying about in the open, and the house on the right of the barrier was getting quite full when a high-explosive crumped right into it doing a lot of damage. The nervous ones came tumbling out of it again. Under cover of this artillery fire the Germans had occupied the houses at the end of the main road, and when it stopped for a bit they sniped at us out of the windows making the barricade rather unpleasant, though most of their shots were going high. We were doing some damage too and any German who showed himself got a very warm reception.[26]

> Captain Beauchamp Tudor St John, 1st Northumberland Fusiliers, 9th Brigade, 3rd Division

Street fighting was always a brutal business: right up close and personal, often at point-blank range. Second Lieutenant Eric Dorman-Smith was in command of the barricade directly facing the bridge.

> I saw – directly in front of me – a German soldier sitting astride a low 3-foot wall at the bottom of the gardens of the houses directly across on the north side of the canal – about 200 yards away – rather less! He sat there looking, quite motionless, resting almost on the garden wall – he'd probably had a lot of marching. I said to the Fusilier next to me, 'Private, shoot that man!' Then the voices from either side of me said, 'Oh no, the officer must have first shot!' Someone said, Take my rifle, 'Sir, it's a good one!' I realised it was up to me. So I shot him! He fell down on our side of the wall and lay quite still. Almost at once another German got up onto the wall, sat on the wall, looking down at my victim! The voices said, 'Go on Sir! Have another shot!' I fired again and shot him! A third man did the same and I shot him! After that I handed back the rifle, saying, 'Really it's somebody else's turn for this war now!' Then quite a number of Germans came over the

wall in a rush and ran forward into the long grass and rough ground just between the garden walls and the canal. There of course they stopped – there was nowhere else to go. We could see them all in this grass and we shot them one by one, one or two rifles at a time – I think we probably killed the lot. Meanwhile the fighting was going on round the bridge. After a short pause they began shelling from German field guns, they were falling back round by the station in Mariette which was about 300 yards back behind me. The next thing I knew was there was the most appalling bang on my left, down by my barricade. They'd manhandled a field gun to within 200 yards of the canal and were fighting at us direct over open sights. We couldn't see the gun, it was shooting at an angle from behind the cover of some sheds. That altered the situation quite a lot![27]

The orders to retire issued by 9th Brigade headquarters at 14.30 had still not got through due to a broken telephone line, which left the 1st Northumberlands grievously exposed. By around 16.00, Captain Beauchamp Tudor St John realised the situation was clearly untenable.

One of their bullets hit my sword and tore away the scabbard thereof, so that I had to discard the weapon to my great relief. We had orders to retire as soon as there was any indication of the enemy getting round our flanks, but it was impossible to say how things were going on either flank. Toppin and I held a council of war together and as the flank bridges were very silent the people in front of us were more and more active, we decided to try and get some definite information. But at the same time the Germans opened fire on us at point-blank range with a field gun they brought down to within 400 yards of us. Fortunately they had a very bad field of fire but it was very unpleasant as they were firing shrapnel burst at the muzzle. We also got a report from Boyd who was with a detachment on our left, that the Germans were massing men and some artillery in and near the coal sheds. We decided, therefore, to commence a retirement and I began to send men back in small driblets down a side street. When most of the men had gone – in fact, only the quartermaster sergeant and myself were left – the Royal Engineer officer[28] and a staff sergeant arrived to blow up our bridge. He reported to me that the Germans were over the bridges on both our flanks so that things did not look too rosy, however he got to work on his job, but found that the man who had laid the charge had only provided leads for the main canal and had not taken the second waterway into consideration. Nothing daunted he went out in front of the barrier and got under the bridge of the near canal, dragged himself through the water to the centre towpath and wriggled about that trying to find the leads which connected the charge. Unfortunately he could not find them and so he returned. It was a plucky action particularly as he was wounded at the time. I reported this instance and was glad to see that the officer got the VC for it, although, poor chap, he was afterwards killed.[29] Meantime the Quartermaster Sergeant and I had been doing what was possible in the way of covering fire and our barrier was getting most unhealthy, so as soon as he got back we cut and ran for it and luck being with us we got away without being hit.[30]

The efforts of Captain Theodore Wright, the adjutant of the 3rd Division Royal Engineers, to blow up the Mariette bridge were valiant indeed, but it was the culture of neglect of the whole issue of demolition by high command and the engineers which had rendered his desperate efforts necessary in the first place.

All along the canal line held by 3rd Division the sappers were in desperate straits as they attempted to carry out last-minute demolitions, hampered by the total lack of instantaneous fuses and criminally short of exploders, electric firing apparatus, safety fuse and explosives. As there were far more bridges to destroy than officers available, it forced a reliance on junior NCOs, who had even less idea of what was happening. Orders were left too late or not received at all. The result was that by the time the sections got to the bridges they were often already under heavy fire from the Germans and attempts to fix the charges under close-range fire were often near-suicidal. Some demolition parties were rushed by the Germans even as they struggled to set the charges. On the front of 57th Field Company, just one of the eight bridges was actually blown up. Only on the 5th Division front, where they had more time to prepare, were the sappers more successful. This is an indictment of British military competence, for the minimum requirement when defending a canal or river line against vastly superior forces is to destroy all (or at the very least most) of the bridges. And in truth the British had had the time, but had failed to provide the necessary resources, to make the essential preparations or take the decisions when required. However, it should be noted that even where the sappers had succeeded, the German war machine was prepared for such eventualities, and their sappers had soon thrown temporary pontoons across the canal before nightfall on 23 August.

To the left of the 9th Brigade was the 5th Division, defending from St Ghislain to Condé. Along this front the German 12th (Brandenburg) Grenadier Regiment suffered a severe bloody nose in its attacks against the 13th Brigade just over a mile west of St Ghislain. Key to this success was a machine gun post established in the sandbagged window on the top floor of a white house.

> We could see the Germans debouching in extended order across a road 900 yards straight to our front. I did not open fire as the target did not seem to warrant the exposure of my positions. Unfortunately a large number of them were able to approach into a wood behind the houses in front of me, without coming under fire. 'A' and 'C' Companies took these on. Sergeant Gilmartin pointed out to me two groups of two Germans, each lying in the open. We thought they might be machine gunners and decided to fire on them. I took the range accurately and we laid out all four in the first traverse. This was our first experience of killing people: it was rather horrible, but satisfactory.[31]
>
> Lieutenant James Pennyman, 2nd King's Own Scottish Borderers, 13th Brigade, 5th Division, II Corps

It was by no means so satisfactory for the Brandenburg Grenadiers, who had failed to coordinate their attacks with sufficiently close artillery support and thereby paid a terrible penalty.

> We had no sooner left the edge of the wood than a volley of bullets whistled past our noses and cracked into the trees behind. Five or six cries near me, five or six of my grey lads collapsed on the grass. Damn it! This was serious. The firing seemed at long range and half-left. 'Forward!' I shouted, taking my place with three of my 'staff' ten paces in front of the section leader, Holder-Egger, and the section in well-extended formation ten paces behind him again. Here we were, advancing as if on a parade ground. 'Huitt, huitt, srr, srr, srr!' about our ears, away in front a sharp, rapid hammering sound, then a pause, then more rapid hammering – machine guns. Over to our left the rifle and machine gun fire was even more intense, the roar of guns and bursting shells increasing. A real battle this time![32]
>
> Captain Walter Bloem, 12th Grenadier Regiment, 5th Division, III Corps, First Army

Quotes, from Bloem, a German novelist, have been at the centre of British attempts to portray the Battle of Mons as a rampant massacre of naive German troops. Yet even in this text, held in almost sacred regard, there is plentiful evidence as to the real nature of German tactics, with explicit mention of advancing in a 'well-extended' formation. The Brandenburgers suffered serious casualties because they failed to follow many of their own precepts and also faced close-range fire from two Royal Artillery guns which had been dragged forward right to the very canal towpath. The three battalions of the 12th Grenadier Regiment did indeed suffer severe casualties, totalling over 600 men, but this was only 20% of their total strength and nowhere near the fantasy figures such as 3,000 which are often quoted.[33] Bloem and his comrades failed to get across the canal and eventually dug in some 200 yards away, where they would remain until the general advance.

The 120th Battery, RFA had provided vital support for the infantry in the St Ghislain sector from the two forward guns, but also from guns perched high on a nearby slagheap, that had used accurate counter-battery fire to seriously disrupt the deployment of the German artillery. Yet this was the exception that proved the rule, as it was the only 5th Division battery seriously involved in the fighting. The rest were thwarted by a combination of poor fields of fire and a lack of observation.

Next in line, along the canal to the left, was the 14th Brigade. Lieutenant George Roupell of the 1st East Surrey was refreshingly honest as to the initial quality of his men's musketry as the Germans approached his men lining the canal bank.

> Soon after we had got into position the enemy started to come through the wood about 200 yards in front. They presented a magnificent target and we opened rapid fire. The men were very excited as this was their first 'shot in anger'. Our men had a good firing position and a clear target at short range but in spite of this a number of them were firing high. I could only tell this from seeing the branches fall from the trees above the Germans' heads, but I found it hard to control the fire as there was so much noise. Eventually, I drew my sword and walked along the line beating the men on the backside and, as I got their attention, telling them to fire low. So much for all our beautiful fire orders taught in peacetime![34]

To their credit, the East Surreys held their positions for several hours, repelling various attacks. However, communication problems meant that half of their 'C' Company stationed in an outpost on the north side of the canal found themselves fatally marooned later on that afternoon.

> About 5pm the order to retire was eventually given. It never reached us and we were left all alone. The Germans got right up to the canal on our right, hidden by the railway embankment and crossed the railway. Our people had blown up the bridge before their departure. We found ourselves alone and I realised we had about 2,000 Germans and a canal between myself and friends. We decided to sell our lives dearly. I ordered my men to fix bayonets and charge, which the gallant fellows did splendidly, but we got shot down like ninepins. As I loaded my revolver I was hit in the right wrist. I dropped my revolver; my hand was too weak to draw my sword, this afterwards saved my life! I had not gone far when I got a bullet through the calf of my right knee, which brought me down. Those who could walk the Germans took away as prisoners. As regards myself, when I lay upon the ground, I found my coat sleeve full of blood, so I knew an artery of some sort had been cut. The Germans had a shot at me when I was on the ground to finish me off; that shot hit my sword, which I wore on my side, and broke it in half, just below the hilt. This turned the bullet off and saved my life. We lay out there a night, for 24 hours. I had fainted from loss of blood and when I lost my senses I thought I should never see anything again.[35]
>
> Captain William Morritt, 1st East Surrey Regiment, 14th Brigade, 5th Division, II Corps

Captain Morritt was indeed severely wounded. Although he was briefly found and sheltered by local Belgians, he was soon uncovered and taken into captivity by the Germans.

At the end of the long British line were the 19th Brigade, an extra reserve brigade attached to II Corps, which had been brought up mid-afternoon to extend the line along to Condé as a replacement for the 5th Cavalry Brigade. Their lines came under fire as the Germans approached about two hours later, but the Germans made no serious attempt to force the passage of the canal. By then the battle had already been decided further to the east.

The initial orders to retire may have been given but they were enacted at various times, depending on a combination of the prevailing circumstances and the state of communications up and down the line. Some units were extremely hard pressed as the Germans probed forward against their rearguards.

This retirement was one of the most exhausting things I remember. We had no time to waste and my job was to post covering parties. We had to defend every street corner until the column had turned the succeeding corner and the result was that by the time I had placed one post I had to run on and catch the column up and tell off and place the next. I would have given my kingdom for a horse and no mistake.[36]

Captain Beauchamp Tudor St John, 1st Northumberland Fusiliers, 9th Brigade, 3rd Division, II Corps

In some cases, there was little chance of escape for such small detachments. Captain Eben Hamilton was kept extremely busy in his capacity as a medical officer, but he had time to notice the courage of the men chosen to stay behind.

From 3 to 5.30pm we were retiring – or rather we were dressing the wounds of retiring men up and down the road. I remember standing on the road and looking along to see if any more of our men were coming and could see none. There were a few men, possibly six, stationed at various points under what cover they could find along the road. These were really being sacrificed, but every man went to his post without a murmur as soon as he was told. To all appearances they might have been merely chosen to get a message to the next village – they just went and lay down behind a stone, or in a ditch, or something and kept a look out for the first of the Germans, determined to get as many as possible before they were 'got' themselves.[37]

Captain Eben Hamilton, 7th Field Ambulance, 3rd Division, II Corps

As Hamilton and his men fell back, there was a significant development that tested his own personal commitment, as he was required to put himself in grievous danger to bring succour to the wounded.

Then a mounted bugler of the Gordons galloped up from the direction of the road we had left knocking sparks from the cobbled pavement as his horse dashed along. He pulled up with a final slide as he saw me and said that a Major of the Gordons was lying along the road with his leg smashed up. I asked for two stretcher bearers and a stretcher and sent the rest in charge of the sergeant straight back to camp. I and these two followed the bugler who got rid of his horse somehow. It was awfully hot and as we were expecting rifle bullets all the time we took what cover we could – rested a few seconds – and then ran on as fast as the load of stuff we carried would allow us. We pressed on expecting to find the Major on the side of the road somewhere. Someone told us he had been taken into the chateau – it had a large Red Cross flying in front. The three of us went in. A scene of disorder met me in the hall and was visible in the room opposite: men, some bleeding from visible wounds, some collapsed and apparently dead were lying about on the floor, or on beds and chairs, and a crowd of women mostly in white overalls were excitedly doing their best to fix them up – but in an obviously amateurish way. I saw there was a lot of work for me, but, I realised that it probably meant being taken prisoner.[38]

His personal duty was clear and after sending his two stretcher bearers off to relative safety, he got down to treating his new patients.

I went first to see the fellow I had come after. He turned out to be Major Simpson[39] of the Gordon Highlanders. His right leg was smashed and he had small shrapnel wounds – only skin deep on the backs and sides of his thighs. He was glad to see me and asked at once if I had a cigarette. I gave him one and fixed up his leg and got him into bed. I then fixed up the others as fast as possible and tried to get out. I walked round the corner of the chateau towards the steps down to the road at and as I got half way across a sudden whizz of bullets past my ear and into the bushes and against the wall made me stop. I turned round with the idea of showing my left arm with the brassard on to the people firing and walked back to the chateau. As I did so I could see Germans down by the gate. I went upstairs to the top room and from there (all the shutters were shut) looking through the crack I could see columns of Germans advancing along all the roads and across the fields in the valley between the hill where we were and the hill on which Mons is built.[40]

Over the next few days, Hamilton would provide medical treatment to British and German wounded alike as they were brought to him at the St Symphorien chateau. He was hence mortified when on 5 September he was taken off to Germany as a prisoner of war, considering that he should have been released. His spirited protests eventually resulted in his repatriation via the Netherlands in January 1915.

As II Corps fell back there was incredible confusion and it was very difficult for the constituent units to find out exactly what they were meant to be doing, or indeed where they were supposed to be going.

> About eight o'clock we were joined by a battery of the brigade, who, like ourselves, were without orders and without any knowledge of what was happening. After a hurried consultation between the two captains – the Major of the battery had been killed – it was decided to send out search parties to locate brigade headquarters, and in consequence I found myself stumbling and groping through the obscurity of an exceedingly dark night. For an hour or more I wandered fruitlessly about the strange country. Once I ran into an unknown battery, where an electric torch was flashed suddenly in my face, and a voice demanded harshly who I was. Once I was stopped at the point of a bayonet by a picket on a road. Occasionally I met straying groups of men who had lost themselves in the retirement, and were now trying to rejoin their units. I returned, unsuccessful in my mission, and as we were without orders and within a few hundred yards of the infantry outposts, it was decided to move back a mile or so and bivouac where we could. In the darkness, stabbed by flashes of light from an electric torch, and amid the imprecations of exasperated men, the horses and vehicles filed out of the meadow down a lane and on to the pavé highroad up which we had marched so confidently the day before.[41]
>
> Captain Cecil Brownlow, 40th Brigade, RFA, 3rd Division, II Corps

The Germans had followed up until night fell, when, perhaps wisely, they refrained from pursuit until they could see what they were doing. Although there was some confusion, von Kluck was now far better aware of the location of the BEF and resolved to push round its left flank on the morrow. The Battle of Mons, such as it was, was over.

THE TOTAL BRITISH CASUALTIES AT THE Battle of Mons were estimated to be 1,638. By later standards of fighting in the Great War, this much vaunted 'battle' is little more than a skirmish. As to the German casualties, the general approach adopted by British historians has been to take any high random number and simply double it. Aware of the total of British casualties and taking as gospel the tales of devastating rifle fire ripping apart massed German ranks, they have simply extrapolated from the fact that the German casualties must be higher – a lot higher – even reaching as high in some guesstimates as 10,000. Bald conjecture replaced any kind of research and over the years unreferenced assertions came to be regarded as facts. Only recently has the truth emerged from the work of historians burrowing into the German archives. The results are chastening: the true total of German casualties seems to have been between 1,900 and 2,000 on 23 August.[42] This is more than the British lost, but then again, the Germans were advancing to contact in an assault across open ground against defended positions. Such a casualty exchange reveals the accounts of mass slayings by the trusty Lee Enfields to be nothing more than a fantasy. Most of the British riflemen could indeed fire the much-vaunted fifteen aimed rounds a minute, offering the prospect of a hail of well-directed bullets onto a target, but they could not keep this up for long. Physical considerations, such as tired hands and red-hot rifles, were augmented by the simple fact that they would very soon run out of ammunition, as each soldier only carried 220 rounds. The Germans suffered, sometimes badly, but the performance of the British was, in the final analysis, merely dogged, with the evident musketry skills failing to counterbalance other military failings. Most of all, the narrative of the battle emphasises that the British fought as a disparate collection of battalions, not even as brigades, but as isolated units, reacting to the situation as it developed rather than cooperating together in concert to secure and retain control of the battlefield situation. The Royal Artillery was hampered by the exceptionally difficult and cluttered ground configuration, which prevented them from taking up good gun positions. This unavoidable problem was then exacerbated by their own lack of training in the vital battlefield skills of target acquisition, indirect fire and liaison with the infantry. These handicaps for infantry and artillery alike originated in the lack of opportunity for large-scale exercises back in Britain. Yet we must not forget that the British were outnumbered, though not by twelve to one as some would have it by adding together every German unit anywhere near the battlefield, whether or not they took part. But where it counted at the pinch-points like Nimy, the BEF were facing odds of three or four to one. They were also well aware that the German battalions attacking them had plenty of reserves within easy reach. As individuals, the British regulars fought bravely and skilfully, but as trained bodies of soldiers harnessed to a single cause, they collectively lacked too many of the basic disciplines.

One characteristic of the battle is its confused nature. No one seemed to have much executive control of what was going on. From the very start von Kluck had no idea where the BEF was located, failed throughout to understand their dispositions and was unable to seize any kind of command initiative. He was also thwarted in efforts to uncover the left flank of the BEF by the endemic fatigue amongst the units of his right wing, who had much further to march as they wheeled round in their approach to the battlefield. His subordinate commanders seem to have succeeded in deploying their troops in accordance with peacetime drills and manoeuvres, but an encounter battle like Mons gives few opportunities to shine, other than by uncovering and enveloping the opponent's flank. If anything, Sir John French was even more at sea. Dangerously delusional the previous day and in the early morning, he then, in effect, absented himself from the position of responsibility in this, the very first battle of the BEF. He failed to exert any form of command and control over I and II Corps, leaving the decision making and responsibility to Smith-Dorrien and Haig. As Haig was preoccupied in maintaining the link with the French, Smith-Dorrien took the whole weight of the battle on his shoulders. Yet, even here, he was neutered by his failure to keep back any effective reserve: the passive nature of II Corps plans and dispositions meant that his main role lay in deciding when to withdraw. Even then he was left helpless by the vagaries of an inexperienced staff and severe communications problems.

THE FIRST STEP OF THE GREAT retreat was but a short one. The BEF gradually pulled back from the canal on the afternoon of 23 August, falling back about two or three miles to a new defence line that had already been sketched out as a possibility by Smith-Dorrien, running through the villages of Nouvelles, Frameries, Wasmes, Élouges to Audregnies. However, the ground was already moving beneath Smith-Dorrien's feet. Late on 23 August, French made an important decision having 'discovered' that there were four (not two) German corps facing the BEF and that Lanrezac's Fifth Army was already retiring. French's own intelligence and liaison officers, his RFC observers and even – belatedly – the French High Command had all confirmed in explicit terms the dire situation that faced the BEF. It was apparent that French was out of his depth. He could get little coherent advice from either his ineffectual Chief of Staff, Major General Sir Archibald Murray, or the overly optimistic Sir Henry Wilson. Now at last realisation had dawned, and it was decided that they must withdraw still further from the Nouvelles to Audregnies positions, initiating the first steps of what might be a lengthy retreat. Even when the decision had been taken, the staff arrangements for disseminating the orders to corps commanders were shambolic, as was bitterly recalled by an aggrieved Smith-Dorrien. He had good reason to be irate.

> At about 11pm a message from GHQ summoned my chief staff officer to army headquarters at Le Cateau, about thirty miles away, and it was past 3am on the 24th when Forestier-Walker returned to my headquarters to say that the commander in chief had, in view of fresh information, decided that instead of standing to fight, the whole BEF was to retire. I naturally asked him for the plan of retirement, and was told that GHQ were issuing none, though he had gathered that the idea was for the I Corps to cover the retirement of the II, but that I was to see Haig and arrange a plan with him. There must have been some very good reason why four or five hours of valuable time had been lost by sending for staff officers instead of sending the order and plan for retirement directly the chief had decided on it. It must be remembered that we had prepared for continuing the fight and our fighting impedimenta, such as ammunition columns, were close behind the troops and blocking the roads, and before a retirement could commence, these would have to be cleared away; also that it would take a long time to get the change of orders to the troops, and lastly that I had to find out what Haig was going to do. All this could have been done and the retirement actually begun before dawn had we known in time. As it was, daylight was already breaking when the order reached me and some hours must elapse before the retirement could commence, by which time we should be in deadly grips with the enemy and would have to carry out one of the most difficult operations in war, namely, breaking off a fight and retiring with the enemy close on the top of us. Such were the thoughts which flashed through my mind.[43]

Haig's chief of staff, Brigadier General Johnnie Gough, had attended the conference, but as his headquarters had managed to establish

communications with GHQ, Gough was able to wire direct from Le
Cateau, allowing Haig to issue orders for the retreat at 02.00. Even so
there were often considerable delays before the orders actually reached
the troops on the ground.

> At about 6am we suddenly got the order to retire, which I thought a
> most pernicious order. We had to abandon about eighty rounds per
> gun, and the horses were up before we could strap on all our digging
> tools. All the mess stuff had to be left behind, and both the officers'
> and battery dixies. We drove out of action under a heavy fire, one
> shell bursting just above 'C' Sub-Section gun team, but the bullets
> all carried over. One horse only was hit by a shrapnel bullet in its
> quarters. There were a lot of spare gunners who had been brought up
> for digging and replenishing ammunition, etc., and in the hurried
> departure the coats and blankets had not been very well tied on, so
> we lost a good number. The thing that really mattered was leaving the
> ammunition, about three hundred and fifty rounds or £700 worth.
> It was the fault of the staff making us believe we were going to be in
> action all day.[44]
>
> Lieutenant Francis Le Breton, 50th Battery, 34th Brigade, RFA, 2nd
> Division, I Corps

For all that, most of the 1st and 2nd Divisions were able to move off in
relatively good order. This did not improve their mood: as far as they
were concerned they were not defeated, they had not even been in serious action at Mons. They had also to endure the muted reproach of the
Belgian civilians they were abandoning to the tender mercies of the
advancing Germans.

> Our retirement, without firing a shot, was bad for morale, and the
> heat was overpowering. It was very difficult to keep the men together
> and maintain march discipline; every man who fell out was bound
> to become a prisoner. We marched back for about ten miles pursued
> by shrapnel fire the whole way, finally evading pursuit and obtaining
> a short halt for water and rest. The men were parched with thirst.
> We were only allowed twenty minutes, after which we fell in and
> proceeded in the direction of Bavai, I shall never forget the march, the
> terrible heat, the feeling of disaster which one scarcely dared admit,
> even to oneself, the struggle to maintain march discipline and keep

the men going at all, and the terrible sight of the villagers crying and rushing to pack their belongings, realising what our retirement meant. My spirits reached the lowest ebb when I heard some villagers who had shouted, '*À Berlin!*' to us the day before, murmur, '*À Londres!*' when we passed.[45]

Lieutenant Joseph Dent, 2nd South Staffordshire Regiment, 6th Brigade, 2nd Division, I Corps

There was nothing quite so hurtful as the truth.

The men of II Corps faced a much more problematic situation. By the time Brigadier General George Forestier-Walker had driven all the way back to Smith-Dorrien's headquarters from Le Cateau, it was already after 05.00. The German guns were already opening up with a dawn chorus and it was evident that a rearguard action would be required to allow the retreat of II Corps. Thus it was that the 5th Division was ordered by Smith-Dorrien to take action to cover the retirement of the hard-pressed 3rd Division. Once the 3rd Division had disengaged, then the 5th Division would begin to pull out, covered in turn by the 15th Brigade, which, having been in reserve on 23 August, was now given the onerous task of acting as a flank guard against the malevolent intent of the German IV Corps, which was trying to uncover the exposed left flank of II Corps.

At first all went well given the difficulty of the operations attempted. There were brisk rearguard actions as the 3rd and 5th Divisions began to fall back from Ciply, Frameries, Paturages and Wasmes. Both sides suffered losses: some German units were caught crossing open ground, the German artillery took its toll and at other times elements of British battalions mistimed their exit and found themselves cut off. Across the board though this can be seen as a successful operation, as the hard-punching rearguards allowed an orderly retirement.

Meanwhile von Kluck's orders indicate he was set on pushing hard at the exposed left flank of the BEF, intent on cutting it off from a retreat to the west and thereby shepherding French back towards the false security of the Maubeuge fortress.

Exploitation of to-day's successes by continuing to exert a uniformly strong pressure with the IV, III and IX Corps. Main objective of the operations to force the enemy into Maubeuge, each corps having a sharply defined zone of manoeuvre. Avoidance of any bunching of troops west of Maubeuge. Cutting and otherwise obstructing the communications.[46]

The left of II Corps lay in the direct line of advance of the German IV Corps. When the threat became apparent the commander of 5th Division despatched two battalions from 15th Brigade (the 1st Norfolks and 1st Cheshires) accompanied by the 119th Battery, RFA to take up positions around the village of Élouges. In addition, the 2nd Cavalry Brigade were sent up as additional support to the village of Audregnies, with the 3rd Cavalry Brigade tucked in not far behind them. Sadly there was considerable confusion from the outset between the two infantry colonels, who had very different impressions of their task. Thus Lieutenant Colonel Colin Ballard commanding the Norfolks was aware that they were merely a flank guard, but Lieutenant Colonel Dudley Boger of the Cheshires was under the misapprehension that they were to hold the position at all costs. The Norfolks and Cheshires took up positions between Élouges and Audregnies facing almost due west in the direction of IV Corps advancing from Quiévrain and the neighbouring Baiseux. As the German attacks began to develop from Quiévrain at 12.45, Brigadier General Beauvoir de Lisle commanding the 2nd Cavalry Brigade decided to commit the 9th Lancers and two troops of the 2nd Dragoon Guards to an attack which was intended to strike deep into the German flank as they advanced. His orders belonged to another age of warfare, one where cavalry were not threatened by modern weapons.

> I saw a strong enemy force advancing southeast from Quiévrain, and heavy infantry fire opened at 800 yards. I rode back to the village, met Colonel Campbell, commanding 9th Lancers, and ordered him at all costs to check the hostile advance, adding, 'It may be necessary for you to charge!' I ordered Colonel Mullens, 4th Dragoon Guards, to support 9th Lancers.[47]

The charge came under heavy fire and it swiftly degenerated into a somewhat embarrassing affair. Afterwards, de Lisle later tried to evade any personal responsibility for his role in despatching his squadrons across 1,200 yards of open ground against a much stronger German force. Those men who took part were generally left bemused.

Then we came under a terrific infantry fire – Micheleau – French interpreter fairly grovels. Suddenly one squadron (we are in squadron column) moving out a gallop – have a good start of me – what the hell are they doing? On we go thro' a hail of bullets and shrapnel – must be charging – find my sword and draw it – cannot see any Germans.[48]

Second Lieutenant Basil Marden, 9th Lancers, 2nd Cavalry Brigade, Cavalry Division

Captain Francis Grenfell summed up the futility of it all. 'We simply galloped about like rabbits in front of a line of guns. Men and horses falling in all directions. Most of one's time was spent in dodging the horses.'[49] They were stopped in their tracks by a combination of barbed wire and a railway embankment. Nothing whatsoever was achieved and German accounts do not even recognise that they were being 'charged', with some gunners reporting cavalry movements 'apparently at random.'[50]

The Norfolks on the right nearer Élouges were barely aware of this excitement, for they had had little time to dig in before the German shells started to splatter around them.

There was such a pandemonium that one could only know in the firing line what was going on just around one. We lay there in the potato crop like partridges. I think we were all too petrified to move. We lay under that shell fire for three hours and I think that none of us will ever forget the feeling of thinking that the next moment we might be dead – perhaps blown to atoms. I kept wondering what it was going to feel like to be dead and all sorts of little things that I had done and places I had been to years ago and had quite forgotten kept passing through my mind. I have often heard this happening to a drowning man but have never experienced it before and don't want to again! I think you get so strung up that your nerves get into an abnormal condition. My brain seemed extraordinarily cool and collected which I was proud of, but I looked at my hands and saw them moving and twisting in an extraordinary way, as if they didn't belong to me, and when I tried to use my field glasses to spy at the Germans, it was as much as I could do with the greatest effort to get them up to my eyes and then I could scarcely see.[51]

Lieutenant Evelyn Broadwood, 1st Norfolk Regiment, 15th Brigade, 5th Division, II Corps

Throughout the bombardment, Broadwood claims never to have seen a German. He and his men lacked any opportunity to open fire on their tormentors to relieve the building tension. The engagement was being decided by the concentrated fire of the German artillery. At first, the 119th Battery, RFA performed sterling service in supplying artillery support, but as the Germans brought up more batteries, they found themselves being overwhelmed. At around 16.00 they were forced to pull back, but the loss of many of their horses meant they had great difficulty in getting away. Lacking sufficient manpower, Major Ernest Alexander called upon the nearby remnants of the 9th Lancers to assist in manhandling the guns to safety. Captain Francis Grenfell had already been wounded, but he leapt to the task.

> I ordered the regiment to dismount in front of their horses, and then called for volunteers. I reminded them that the 9th Lancers had gained the eternal friendship of the gunners by always standing by the guns in South Africa. Every single man and officer declared they were ready to go to what looked like certain destruction. We ran forward and started pushing the guns out. Providence intervened, for although this was carried out under a very heavy fire and the guns had to be slowly turned round before we could guide them, we accomplished our task. We pushed out one over dead gunners and I do not think we lost more than three or four men, though it required more than one journey to get everything out.[52]

Grenfell and Alexander were both awarded the VC for their inspirational example to the men under their command. Grenfell retained a sense of proportion commenting, 'I never felt such a fool in my life! After all, I only did what every other man and officer did who was with me.'[53]

Meanwhile, Colonel Ballard of the 1st Norfolks had realised that if they waited any longer then the Germans would cut off their retreat. Even so it was a close-run thing as his men dodged back through the refuse stacks and railway lines of the colliery behind them. Lieutenant Evelyn Broadwood had a narrow escape.

> I stopped behind to collect stragglers and to carry in a couple of wounded into the house where the doctor was seeing to them and I believe that I was the last to leave. By this time the bullets had

begun to sing around us and the German infantry were getting close, so it was high time to clear out. But the shelling was ceasing lest they should hit their own men. I could not get some of the men along. They were too dead beat, as it was a broiling day and all the time the sun had been beating on us, but I and a last party of five climbed up a pear tree and over a garden wall, and so creeping along with bullets now flying all around we got over another wall and so up a path exposed for a short way. We ran along this and I remember – as an instance of the stupid things one does in moments of excitement – my little hair brush jumped out suddenly from my haversack and I ran back five or six yards to pick it up, and risked a life for a hair brush! I found subsequently two holes in my haversack where a bullet had passed through just grazing my clothes, and it may have been then that it went through. We ran into a cutting where there was a railway line for shunting coal and ran along this, I went over an embankment to my right front and dropping down the sheltered side I turned round to fire at the enemy to cover the rest if I could. The rest of our small party went along the cutting under the bridge. I never saw any of them again, and none have been seen since, so I almost wish they had waited for me. I fired twenty rounds and dropped two Germans. Then I turned – sharp left and ran along below the embankment to put them off the scent. I think my running has scarcely ever come in more useful than that day. After a bit of dodging about I got to the village where I caught up with some of the fragments of the regiment.[54]

Broadwood believed that the Norfolks had lost some 400 men killed, wounded and missing – it was later assessed as 250. In the mad confusion, despite Colonel Ballard's best efforts, the 1st Cheshires had failed to get the orders to retire. This was particularly serious as their commander, Colonel Dudley Boger, was still under the mistaken impression that this was a fight to the finish. For him, retreat was not an honourable option.

I found on our right the Norfolks had retired or been scuppered and the Germans enfiladed us from the railway and had got almost to our rear. Very decent order was maintained by Sergeants Meachin, Rothwell and Dowling but all three were wounded and nearly all the men. I was very lucky to be hit three times and none serious. Hand by shrapnel and thro' foot and flesh of thigh by bullets. We had no chance, no information and no instructions, except to guard the road.[55]

Boger himself was captured along with most of his men. Only around 200 of the Cheshires escaped this debacle to rejoin the main body of the BEF.

The II Corps had managed to disengage successfully, although at some significant cost. Too many battalions had been fatally ensnared in fights to the finish. As a result, the British casualties actually exceeded those suffered at Mons the previous day.

AFTER CONSIDERABLE VACILLATION FRENCH DECIDED THAT not only was von Kluck threatening the BEF left flank, but he was also deliberately shepherding them back towards Maubeuge. This was a superficially attractive option for the BEF, as it was a fortress town that might offer a safe harbour. Yet taking refuge there would also lead to isolation from the French Fifth Army. French was not blind to the lessons of the past as to the fate of besieged armies, and he had the recent reduction of the Liège fortresses to remind him that the German super-heavy artillery had the power to make the walls come tumbling down. Instead, therefore, he would march the BEF back to Le Cateau, with a view to taking up new defensive positions there. The decision was made, but there were still serious practical difficulties to overcome. Between the BEF and Le Cateau lay the significant obstacle posed by the Forest of Mormal. Unsure of the state of minor roads passing through the woods, French decided to split his force and determined that I Corps would move east of the woods, while II Corps took the roads down the western side to reunite only when they got to Le Cateau. Yet even these orders could not be given without yet another example of the lack of urgency demonstrated by GHQ.

At 6 pm, hearing the chief had come up from Le Cateau to his advanced head-quarters at Bavai, I sought him out and found him in the Mairie, and, describing the action of the II Corps and its positions, asked for instructions as to our further retirement. The Chief replied that I could do as I liked, but that Haig intended to start at 5am. I remonstrated, saying that unless we moved early we should have a repetition of that day (the 24th) when orders had been issued too

late to avoid the enemy coming to close grips. He asked me what
I proposed. I replied that I wished to start off my impedimenta, which
had already been in bivouac several hours, soon after midnight,
followed by the troops at such times as would ensure my rear-guards
being south of the Valenciennes-Jenlain-Bavai road by 5am. Sir John
concurred, remarking that Haig could still do as he intended. I then
crossed the room to the table where Sir Archibald Murray, the Chief
of the Staff, was working, and asked him to induce the Chief to issue
an order for the whole force to move early and simultaneously. Murray
said he would see what he could do later on, and he was evidently
successful.[56]

General Sir Horace Smith-Dorrien, Headquarters, II Corps

Eventually, at 20.25, the orders for a much earlier move on 25 August
were issued by French's headquarters. This lack of grip by GHQ was rife.
Time and time again throughout the retreat it would appear that the
tail was wagging the dog, with Smith-Dorrien or Haig taking the initiative. This lackadaisical approach by GHQ was evident in the treatment
of Major General Sir Thomas D'Oyly Snow. Snow was commanding the
newly arrived 4th Division, which had belatedly been despatched to
France on 23 August, moving up next day by train to Le Cateau. From
here Snow was ordered forward to the town of Solesmes towards the left
flank of II Corps.

It was very lucky it arrived when it did and it was pure luck. No
pressure was brought to bear from GHQ, France, on the War Office
to hurry up the division, neither, when the division embarked, was
there any reason to believe that its presence was so urgently required.
Had we arrived 24-hours later we certainly could have taken no part
in covering the retirement of the 3rd and 5th Divisions on to the Le
Cateau position.[57]

This would be a recurrent theme in his memoirs written after the event.
Snow was operating in the dark, ignorant of even the most basic intelligence as to the overall situation.

The difficulty was to find out what was going on. We got no news from
GHQ or from any other troops we were trying to get touch with. GHQ
must have been getting information, but certainly they sent none on to

us. We had no way of getting information ourselves, except by sending out staff officers in motor cars.[58]

Snow was not alone in his perplexity. No one seemed to know what was going on and many normal staff functions broke down completely.

> Started the day badly as I got no orders from the Brigade Major or information as to the movement of the different units and it is obviously impossible to keep communication if one does not know the position of the troops. However went direct to the place which I knew the main body must pass which proved right. Again I could do little as the General would never stay in his place for more than a minute.[59]
>
> Lieutenant Alexander Johnston, Headquarters, 7th Brigade, 3rd Division, II Corps

The correct location of commanding officers of units was a moot point; if they continually moved about in an effort to determine what was going on for themselves, then of course they could not be contacted when required by their own subordinates, who were equally desperate for orders and information.

As Smith-Dorrien intended, II Corps had managed to make a very early start on 25 August, although there were some delays caused by the passage of General André Sordet's French Cavalry Corps moving across the line of march to take up a flanking position to the west. The II Corps marched down two main roads towards Le Cateau: one passing along the Roman road just west of the Forest of Mormal and the other via Solesmes. They were naturally disappointed to be retreating and well aware that the Germans were not that far away. The question was just how far?

> We continued our retirement which went on without incident for some time. The heat was awful and the march seemed endless. A certain number of men began to tail off and straggled in an appalling manner. A retirement certainly seems to have a most demoralizing effect, discipline seems to relax, little attempt seems to be made to keep to the ranks and men fall out to get drinks or food or to lie down. We had not been worried in the rear at all, and it was obvious now that the danger was to our left flank. We therefore stopped taking up a series of positions, closed up the column and pushed on as fast possible, leaving the 2nd Royal Irish Rifles as rearguard. Just after passing Romeries, the brigade got checked on the high ground above Solesmes which is in a

deep hollow with steep and narrow streets resulting in the transport etc getting blocked. Every minute's delay was making things more serious, our cavalry could be seen in action on our left. Yet there we waited right out in the open along a road which could be seen for miles, the artillery and infantry in column of route affording an excellent target to the enemy's artillery should they spot us; this they eventually did and promptly sent over some shrapnel which luckily did no harm.[60]

Lieutenant Alexander Johnston, Headquarters, 7th Brigade, 3rd Division, II Corps

Throughout the retreat, Allenby's Cavalry Division was performing a role that often goes unappreciated. Fending off the attentions of superior numbers of German cavalry they dropped into defensive positions to cover the retirement of the infantry, forcing the Germans to deploy and bring up their guns, before, once again resuming the retreat.

A rear guard carries out its mission best by compelling the enemy's troops to halt and deploy for attack as frequently, and at as great a distance, as possible. It can usually effect this by taking up a succession of defensive positions which the enemy must attack or turn. When the enemy's dispositions are nearly complete, the rear guard moves off by successive retirements, each party as it falls back covering the retirement of the next by its fire. This action is repeated on the next favourable ground. All this consumes time, and time is what is most needed by a retreating force.[61]

General Staff, War Office, Field Service Regulations, Part I

It did not have the glamour of 'last-ditch stands' but it was far more effective in slowing down the German advance. The cavalry were worked hard, acting as flank guards, scouting and patrolling to determine the location of the Germans, then dropping into action to allow the infantry rearguards to make their escape. The British cavalry prided itself on horsemanship in the wider sense of looking after the horses to avoid riding them into the ground, by dismounting to walk whenever feasible to allow the horses some chance to rest. Yet even so both men and horses were becoming exhausted. Worse still the cavalry brigades and squadrons were getting isolated, thoroughly mixed up and out of touch with Allenby at divisional headquarters.

The town of Solesmes marked the point where several of the main roads converged and the town soon resembled a teeming ant heap. The cavalry were also struggling as gaps appeared in the rearguard and battalions of the 7th Brigade, and some field artillery batteries were swiftly deployed to check the German advance.

> The confusion in the town was appalling, the place being packed not only with our fellows but with civilians and the remnants of the French territorial regiment, and the traffic was continually being blocked, if the Germans had driven in our rearguard and got onto the hill above the town sooner, they would have had us at their mercy.[62]
>
> Lieutenant Alexander Johnston, Headquarters, 7th Brigade, 3rd Division, II Corps

The screen held until nightfall, when the town was once again clear of troops, and a potential disaster had been averted. Yet, there was little doubt that the Germans were getting closer.

The retreat of Haig's I Corps, east of the Forest of Mormal, was bedevilled by the necessity of sharing roads with the French. This was a major problem because it triggered seemingly endless delays, which enhanced the understandable tension amongst men expecting to be attacked at any moment by the Germans. This led to a series of near-comic interludes amid various false alarms.

> Just as we were emerging from Noyelles and were passing through a cutting, rifle fire sprang up just ahead of us. We were halted, and then the order, 'Reverse, gallop!' came down. I was rear-section. I started reversing. Then seeing some signs of a panic, gave, 'As you were!' This was greeted with howls of, 'Go on! Gallop!' from the front. I looked ahead over the battery, and right at the head of the battery saw someone giving the signal reverse, so. I let them reverse. The baggage waggon, water cart, and the rear waggon of my section, under Corporal Randal, all being behind, went off at full gallop before I could stop them, and I'm afraid caused rather a panic amongst the infantry transport in Noyelles. 'D' gun was now leading, and we cantered down the road, met some infantry doubling up, so we pulled up to let them pass. A large force of German cavalry was reported to be in front of us, and there was a lot of firing going on. The 22nd Battery had dropped some guns in action at Noyelles itself, but these could be of no use as they would only have killed our own troops if they had been fired. It would have been better to get them out of the way to make room, for

the infantry. Some of the transport people panicked, and in one case I saw an infantryman slip off his pack and run, and in another case a rifle was lying in the road. Our G. S. waggon also panicked rather, and dropped a case of maps off it. This got smashed up, and the maps scattered by the following transport. Dropped a gun into action at the first side-road we came to, but it was rather far back. The French were behind just where we were. Bugle calls came down for more men at the double for the front. David Sherlock tried to persuade the French to go on; but first they lost their Colonel, and then they lost his horse, and they all lost their heads, and they talked and chattered, and it was about ten minutes before anyone made a move. I believe there were not nearly as many German cavalry about as was thought at first, and the whole thing was rather disgraceful, and shows the moral effect of a retirement.[63]

Lieutenant Francis Henry Le Breton, 50th Battery, 34th Brigade, RFA, 2nd Division, I Corps

As night fell so the potential for tragic misunderstandings and panic increased dramatically.

Two shots rang out at the top of the street, and then hell was let loose! There was a terrific uproar of galloping horses on the paved roadway, crashing of vehicles, shouting and swearing, and a fusillade of rifle firing! Our men came through the archway with a rush and I found myself lying full length in a water-trough in the yard with about six men on top of me! After a while the noise quietened down and Tony Parker and I went out into the street to see what had happened, giving orders that nobody was to leave the yard until we returned. What had happened was that two inoffensive French troopers had ridden into the top end of the village. Some Army Service Corps privates and others on one of the wagons saw them and promptly took them for Germans – everybody's nerves were somewhat on edge, it was very dark and no one knew where we were, where the enemy were, or what was happening – and fired two rounds, killing one trooper and wounding the other. Probably in the ordinary way they could not have hit a haystack, however hard they had tried! The transport and Royal Engineer horses promptly bolted in every direction, wagons were crashed and men rushed out of the houses and started shooting indiscriminately. The result was that several horses were badly injured and had to be shot, several of the men also were badly injured, and at least three were killed! I shall never forget that scene or that indescribable uproar![64]

Lieutenant Evelyn Needham, 1st Northamptonshire Regiment, 2nd Brigade, 1st Division, I Corps

Despite all the alarums, I Corps was largely undisturbed during its retreat on 25 August. But the rate of progress had been dreadfully slow, dropping below two miles per hour, and they were well short of Le Cateau when they went into billets.

Haig set up his headquarters at Landrecies just south of the Forest of Mormal at 14.00 on 25 August. He himself was somewhat under the weather, having contracted a stomach bug which was having a pernicious effect on the previous day. Haig's diary makes reference to a two-hour bout of sickness and diarrhoea, as does his Intelligence Officer Colonel John Charteris, a man never afraid to gild the lily when putting forward a story.

I was awakened by Secrett[65] to say that D.H. was very ill; had shut himself up in his room, and given orders that he would see nobody. I got hold of Micky Ryan[66] and went in to D.H. and insisted that he must see Ryan. D.H. was at his worst, very rude but eventually did see Ryan, who dosed him with what must have been something designed for elephants, for the result was immediate and volcanic! But it was effective, for D.H. ultimately got some sleep, and in the morning was better but very chewed up, and ghastly to look at. He wanted to ride as usual, but Ryan insisted on his going in a car that day.[67]

This affliction may have had an impact on Haig in his subsequent conduct the night of 25/26 August. Haig himself is silent on the matter in his diary.

Unknowingly, Haig had placed his headquarters very close to the front line, for although Landrecies was occupied by the 4th Guards Brigade, the German 27th Infantry Regiment was fast approaching with the intent of securing the bridge over the Sambre and billeting for the night in the village. The German advance guard blundered straight into the barricades defended by the Guards and was met with a blast of fire. As they brought up more troops and the exchanges of fire continued, the situation became excessively confusing. No one knew what was happening, which promoted a considerable degree of alarm on all sides, especially as there were reports of a similar skirmish from the 6th Brigade billeted at Maroilles. Amongst those often accused of panicking was Haig, who, unaware of the strength of the attacking force, telephoned Sir John French at 01.35 on the morning of 26 August to suggest that not only was I Corps under a serious attack, but subsequently at 03.50 requested urgent assistance from II Corps. This was clearly an overreaction in the sense that Landrecies was a mere skirmish with both sides losing under two hundred casualties apiece. The incident was trivial but has attained a degree of notoriety, mainly due to pleasure taken by Haig's detractors in an incident where he did not seem to perform with his normal high standards of imperturbability. In the event though, Haig's appeal came to nothing; by this time Smith-Dorrien had rather more important things on his mind.

6

BATTLE OF LE CATEAU

About quarter past six the Germans made a great rush under cover of their guns; it was at this moment when a shell struck within five yards of us, covered us with dirt, but never exploded. Half past six they made another attack with their machine guns, and at this moment they swept the whole lot of us out, the butt of my rifle was split to pieces and I was wounded in both legs, twice in the left arm, and clean through the mouth which left me helpless on the ground with the loss of blood and unable to move. Just getting dark and the Germans came through us and handled us very rough.[1]

Private Charles Fussell, 1st Somerset Light Infantry, 11th Brigade, 4th Division

HINDSIGHT IS A WONDERFUL THING. It is the habit of crusty academics and popular authors alike to write as if they had the intelligence and decisiveness of a latter-day Napoleon with the ability to penetrate the multiple confusions of the battlefield to produce a perfect tactical solution to any calamitous state of affairs. The reality of war is often one of complete chaos. Indeed, the smokescreen is often near impenetrable, with little enough known of the location and condition of one's own units, never mind the blank ignorance of what your opponent is really up to. Before the Battle of Le Cateau, General Sir Hubert Smith-Dorrien commanding II Corps found himself in a terrible dilemma facing a situation so complex that ex post facto arguments are rendered superfluous. All we can do is look at the rationale for his actions and examine what actually happened in order to assess whether the decision was reasonable given what he knew at the time. GHQ had originally envisaged making a stand when I and II Corps met up at Le Cateau but, in view of the continued retreat of the French on the right flank and the demonstrable threat emanating from the German forces massed on the BEF front, French had ordered the retreat to be continued right back to St Quentin and Noyon. Smith-Dorrien had received his orders from French to continue the retreat at 21.00, and soon afterwards the appropriate orders had duly been issued by II Corps headquarters. It was only after this that Smith-Dorrien began to seriously reconsider his course of action as he began to receive a series of disturbing reports that made him realise the critical nature of the situation. His first concern was the whereabouts of I Corps, which had clearly been delayed in its progress towards the rendezvous.

> I counted on the I Corps coming into line with us on the Le Cateau
> position in accordance with GHQ operation order, and that I sent
> back weary troops to the east side of the town of Le Cateau to look
> out for them and to guard the flank until they appeared. Whatever
> the cause, the delay was of very serious moment to the II Corps, and
> indeed to the whole BEF. Had it not occurred the actions at Landrecies
> and Maroilles would not have taken place, and, instead of being out
> of touch with each other for the next six days, the two Corps would
> have had a united front on the night of 25th August under the hand of
> the Commander in Chief and the decision to fight at Le Cateau would
> not have rested with me. As things were, however, as will be seen later,
> the news that the I Corps was heavily engaged and the fear that their
> safety might be endangered unless the II Corps made a stand, though
> not the deciding factor, carried weight with me in coming to the
> decision I took in the small hours of the morning of the 26th.[2]

This was one anxiety for Smith-Dorrien, but the real trigger for his decision to turn and fight in defiance of the orders from French seems to have been a meeting held with Major General Edmund Allenby at 02.00 on 26 August. The Cavalry Division was meant to be covering the retreat but it was at the end of its tether.

> General Allenby told me his division had had an exhausting time, that 2½ brigades were about Catillon and 1½ brigades about Caudry and Ligny, and that he could get no orders from general headquarters, whereupon I asked him if he would act under my orders if I decided to fight and he agreed. As a matter of fact it was General Allenby's report of the scattered and tired state of the Cavalry Division which was the deciding factor as to whether I should attempt to go on with the retreat or not. My impression is that General Allenby was relieved by my decision – and certainly did not argue that I should go on retiring.[3]

There was no time for a detailed staff analysis and discussions, no time to scour round and locate missing units, no time for proper reconnaissance of a strong defensive position: a decision had to be made then and there. Just one man, Smith-Dorrien, bore the responsibility.

> The following arguments passed through my mind: (a) It must be a long time after daylight before the whole force covered by rear-guards can get on the move. (b) The enemy are in force close to our billets (for such Allenby had impressed on me). (c) To turn our backs on them in broad daylight with worn-out men suffering from sore feet will leave us a prey to hostile cavalry supported by infantry in motors. (d) The roads are encumbered with military transport and civilian fugitives and carts, some still on the enemy side of our position, and time to allow them to clear off is essential. (e) The I Corps is reported to be engaged some miles northeast of us and to retire would expose their flank to the full brunt of von Kluck's troops. (f) The Cavalry Division can be of little help in covering our retreat, for this Allenby had told me. (g) Our infantry have proved their staunchness and astounding accuracy with the rifle, our gunners are a marvel, and if Allenby and Snow will act under me, and Sordet will guard my west flank, we should be successful in giving the enemy a stopping blow, under cover of which we could retire. Well do I remember the dead silence in the little room at Bertry when I was rapidly considering these points and the sigh of relief when, on my asking Allenby if he would accept orders from me, and he replied in the affirmative, I remarked: 'Very well, gentlemen, we will fight, and I will ask General Snow to act under me as well.' The die was cast.[4]

Smith-Dorrien deserves considerable credit for his courage in taking such a momentous decision. In disobeying GHQ orders he was accepting personal responsibility for whatever might occur. The intention was to deliver a blow that would stop the Germans in their tracks and allow II Corps to

resume the retreat under reduced pressure. News of the decision to fight
was despatched by car to the GHQ at St Quentin where it was received
with some considerable consternation and only grudging acceptance.

About 6.45am, a cyclist brought me a message from Bertry station,
distant about half a mile, saying Sir John French wished to speak to
me on the railway telephone. I motored there immediately and heard
the voice of sub-chief of the general staff Sir Henry Wilson, who had a
message to give me from the chief to the effect that I should break off
the action as soon as possible. I replied that I would endeavour to do
so, but that it would be difficult, and that I hoped to be able to hold on
until evening and slip away in the dark. Henry Wilson then asked me
what I thought of our chances, and when I replied that I was feeling
confident and hopeful of giving the enemy a smashing blow and
slipping away before he could recover, he replied, 'Good luck to you;
yours is the first cheerful voice I have heard for three days!'[5]

Lieutenant General Sir Horace Smith-Dorrien, Headquarters, II Corps

Smith-Dorrien was after all the man on the spot; in accordance with
accepted practice he had the final say.

Yet coming to the conclusion to stand and fight was just part of the
difficulty: the next predicament, given the urgent nature of the new
orders, was the necessity to secure their rapid transmission to the headquarters of his 3rd and 5th Divisions, Snow's 4th Division and Allenby's
Cavalry Division.

The order to stand and fight drawn up by Forestier-Walker was clear
and to the point, but the difficulty was to get it to the troops in time.
It was fairly easy for corps headquarters, as they had simply to send
copies of the order to the four divisional headquarters and the 19th
Brigade, but the difficulties increased in mathematical progression
when it came to informing the smaller units, many of whose positions
were only very roughly known.[6]

Lieutenant General Sir Horace Smith-Dorrien, Headquarters, II Corps

This then was the crux of the matter. The choice had perforce to be
taken very late, but then the intent was undermined by the inability
to disseminate it to the toiling columns of men. Even divisional commanders were often in the dark. For many of the officers lower down
the chain of command, the night's work can be neatly summed up as

order, counter-order and disorder – a cliché perhaps, but one that fits the situation perfectly. It was not just a matter of telling the fighting units, as the modern army needed its support services if it was not to struggle.

> A mile or so further on, drawn up in a field by a cross-roads, we met the Divisional Ammunition Column, and as we required ammunition we took the opportunity to replenish our wagons. While the long line of vehicles were halted along the road, and while the gunners, sweltering in the heat, stowed away round after round of shrapnel, a motorcar swung round a bend of the road and drew up with a shriek of brakes. A staff officer of the division got out, and, approaching the Captain, said, 'You must return at once and at top speed. We are not retiring today according to the original orders. It has been decided to stand and fight!' Nosebags were whipped off the horses' heads, limber lids were shut with a clang, amid curses and imprecations the wagons were reversed on the road, and, with every vehicle bumping and rattling, we trotted as fast as we could towards the sound of the guns, which every moment grew louder and louder. Owing to the distance we had to go and to the exhaustion of the horses, it was necessary to march by alternate periods of trotting and walking, but even so the horses were soon black with sweat and flecked with foam.[7]

> Captain Cecil Brownlow, 40th Brigade, RFA, 3rd Division, II Corps

Their haste was understandable: the battle would have been short and swift indeed if the guns had run out of ammunition.

The II Corps took up hastily selected positions on a ten-mile front stretching due west from the town of Le Cateau, along the Caudry Ridge to Esmes, from whence the line was prolonged by the French 1st Cavalry Corps commanded by General André Sordet. The 4th Division were on the left, the 3rd Division in the centre, the 5th Division on the right flank with behind it the reserve force of the 19th Brigade held at Reumont. The infantry battalions had often only got their orders to 'stand and fight' at the very last minute; as such they were totally unprepared. Prior to this their main preoccupation had been to facilitate an easy exit covered by small rearguard parties on the morning of 26 August. In some cases the exhausted troops had failed to take even the most basic military precautions – as Snow found when he paid a visit to his 12th Brigade around Esmes on his left flank.

I was much horrified when I went to visit them to find that they had piled arms in an open space on a slope facing the direction of the enemy and had taken off their accoutrements and hung them up on the piles of rifles. Had artillery fire been opened there would have been a disaster. I was very angry and such a thing never happened again: but I quote it to uphold the statement I made earlier, namely that an Englishman has very little imagination. I rode round the troops who were supposed to be entrenched. In spite of what troops had learned in the Boer War, in spite of what they had been taught, all they had done was to make a few scratchings of the nature of a shelter pit, of no use whatever against any sort of fire. I came to the conclusion then, and never altered it during the war, that unless driven to it by his officers, the British soldier would sooner die than dig, but whether the reason for this was stupidity, lack of imagination or laziness I don't know, but probably it was a little of all three.[8]

Worse still, having arrived in pouring rain in the pitch dark, many of the units had taken up positions on the forward, rather than reverse, slopes of the Caudry Ridge line.

There was, however, little time for preparation. My division was again on the flank, and our line had to be extended to some five miles. The previous plans for the distribution of the artillery had to be discarded and all that could be done was to allot brigades to the different sections as we rode rapidly along the front – and they had little time to select positions and get the guns unto action and some hasty cover thrown up before the Germans opened.[9]

Brigadier General John Headlam, Headquarters, RFA, 5th Division

Here, come the dawn, they would be in full view of the German artillery. There was no time to reorganise the positions to secure the best possible fields of fire and minimal time left to dig in. This was a direct consequence of the absence of any coherent planning ahead of the battle. There was also the pernicious effect of the desire to provide close physical support to the infantry. It had not yet been recognised that it was the shells that were the weapon of the artillery, not the guns.

On the left, Snow was haunted by his almost complete ignorance of the 'bigger picture'. He was operating almost completely in the dark.

I had not been told anything about overwhelming forces being in the neighbourhood, or that there was any chance of an encircling movement from the north-west, all of which was known at GHQ and probably at Headquarters, II Corps. Why this information was not passed down I do not know, but I presume it was bad staff work, everyone being strange to the job. I was certainly very nervous of my left flank, not because I was led to expect a turning movement but because my flank was in the air, and I imagined it much more in the air than it really was. I had no divisional cavalry or cyclists with which I could guard my flank, and our eyes from where we stood were our only means of piercing the fog of war.[10]

It would not be long before the Germans announced their presence in no uncertain fashion.

At 7.45am three shells burst over us, in quick succession, and hit three men and alarmed the rest horribly. We all got our heads down behind our head cover, scraped up with our entrenching tools, just enough to stop a bullet, if you throw the earth well out to the front. I had just borrowed a tool from a man, and scraped up a bit before the firing began. This cover is no good against shrapnel, which bursts overhead. Luckily after those three shells, the Germans fired on the supports; otherwise we should have been wiped out in a quarter of an hour. The Germans had the range plumb. Then the Rifle Brigade retired across our front and got fired at by some of us, not knowing who they were. Then there was a lull. At about 8.45am a skirmishing line came across the road, in front of the German guns, and I gave my first fire order about five minutes later, 'Enemy advancing 1,500 – distribute fire!' I don't think we hit anyone as the range was very long and I couldn't see the bullets strike anywhere to correct the range. I shouted back to the machine gun, who had a rangefinder to give the ranges, but I couldn't make them hear. Two German guns then walked quietly along the distant road and came into action with the others behind them. I tried to fire on them, but it was 1,800 or 2,000 yards, and again I could make no one hear behind me. I saw the guns come into action and the observer in his sort of scaffold arrangement. I could see him through my field-glasses turn and shout when a shell pitched short. A few more men were hit by shrapnel and the nerve of the others shaken badly – which is what shrapnel is for. Then a machine gun started on our right and hit a few more, and I looked at my watch wondering how long we could stay there. So far very few infantry came at us, mostly going to the left of us where the rifle and machine gun fire was very heavy.[11]

Lieutenant George Parr, 1st Somerset Light Infantry, 11th Brigade, 4th Division

In the early stages this was mainly an artillery battle, as the Germans sought to establish a supremacy in the firefight, before launching any infantry attacks. Along the centre of the ridge was the 3rd Division, occupying shallow trenches from Caudry through Audencourt to Troisville. Here, too, there is evidence of some degree of panic as the men came under heavy shellfire.

The German was obviously acting up to his principles in his textbooks in which he always advocated having lots of guns near the head of his columns. There were a lot of men making their way back in a disgraceful manner even NCOs. I managed however to stop them quite easily and to get them back into the firing line without trouble. It makes one sad and anxious for the future to see Englishmen behave like this, and the fire was not really heavy, nor the losses great. Of course these were only the bad men or men whose officers had been hit and were therefore out of control, and one always found plenty of splendid fellows holding on gamely even if their officers had gone. Eventually it got so bad in the centre, that I collected some men of about five different regiments and ran forward to get them into the fields in front of the buildings where we would not be easily seen and where we would avoid the German fire which was mostly directed on the buildings. The position otherwise was not a very good one and there was not a good field of fire, But I thought from the point of view of 'morale' alone that it would be a good thing to get some of the men pushed forward. We lay out here in the turnips about a couple of hours and had a very hot time of it.[12]

Lieutenant Alexander Johnston, Headquarters, 7th Brigade, 3rd Division, II Corps

This reaction to artillery fire in poorly constructed, badly sited or non-existent trenches is hardly unnatural, but is often brushed under the carpet in British accounts of the Le Cateau fighting. The Germans were engaging in their classic tactic of developing the firefight, attempting to beat down the resistance from the British defenders before considering an attack.

On II Corps right flank, close to Le Cateau, was the 5th Division, which was in a dangerous state of flux as many units had only received their orders to stand at 06.00 – about the same time as the first shells began to fall amidst them. Some units never received formal orders at all. With no time to select proper defensive positions, they would have to fight where they found themselves. There was a further serious complication for the 5th Division in that they were still expecting to have support from I Corps on their right flank. Yet Haig had already confirmed that II Corps would fight alone: there seemed little point in putting the whole of the BEF at risk. The right flank would now – nominally – be protected by the Cavalry Division.

It was also on the 5th Division front that the artillery in forward positions found themselves excruciatingly vulnerable, not only to counter-battery fire, but also the machine gun and rifle fire of German infantry. The three batteries of the 15th Brigade RFA were stationed just southwest of Le Cateau and firing in a northeasterly direction. They had no time to prepare any kind of proper gun pits and in many cases had to make do with corn sheaves to partially conceal their guns.

We were told that the I Corps was going to be on the right of us on the high ground beyond the River Selle. It was a very misty morning, you couldn't see much. In front of our battery we had a nice little ridge, but the difficulty was there that we couldn't clear the crest at under 1,500 yards and the infantry were along the top of it. We were a 100 yards behind them, in fact all the batteries were almost in the infantry front line. When the mist cleared we could see this high ground beyond the River Selle on the right and nobody on it as far as we could see. About 06.00 in the morning we opened fire, our Major observing from the trench in front, on Germans massing north of Le Cateau, we fired at a range of about 4,000 yards. Very soon the Germans started answering back and salvoes of shells fell all round the place; especially in the 11th Battery on our right. Then the mists cleared further and we could see a place called Rambourlieux Farm on our left flank, completely looking down our line of guns![13]

Second Lieutenant Rory MacLeod, 80th Battery 15th Brigade, RFA, 5th Division, II Corps

The Rambourlieux Farm position lay on the Viesly spur running north-west from Le Cateau. Such errors in deployment might have been avoided in good visibility. Now there was little that MacLeod or his gunners could do as they came under heavy enfilading fire.

> More and more German batteries came into position and more and more shellfire came on us – very heavily indeed. Then some German aeroplanes came over and dropped what looked like long streamers of silver paper and very soon after an intense fire was opened all along the line of guns. Evidently this aeroplane was giving the range to the German gunners. Gun after gun went out of action – the 11th Battery suffered terribly heavily.[14]

At the Battle of Le Cateau the German artillery proved themselves a fearsome opponent. The Germans had far more long-range howitzers that could fire effectively from concealed positions tucked away from harm in deep folds in the ground.

> The thing that struck me most was the rapidity with which the German artillery got on to their target. It appeared to me as if they always got the bracket in two rounds and then the next round was plumb on the target. At one time I and a good many of my staff were dismounted in the open and our horses were being led about nearby. We were spotted and had fire opened on us very quickly. No damage resulted though the shells were all around us. We galloped away as quick as possible and were followed by shrapnel till we took refuge in a fold of the ground. Even then the hollow we had disappeared into was searched up and down. The way the Germans picked up targets seemed to me at the time almost uncanny, but it really was because they made use of aeroplanes.[15]
>
> Major General Sir Thomas D'Oyly Snow, Headquarters, 4th Division

Lieutenant William Read of the 3 Squadron, RFC had an unusual perspective to these artillery exchanges. He had been sent up on an early morning reconnaissance flight over Le Cateau. However, the RFC, unlike the Germans, had not yet developed the capability to provide any artillery observation from their aircraft, and Read was a passive witness.

> The whole sight was wonderful. It consisted of a fierce artillery engagement for the most part, but we were getting the worst of it. We

had all the German army corps against our little force. The French seem to be doing nothing to help us. We could see nothing of them. The German artillery fire was deadly accurate. I watched one battery of ours put out of action. It had only just opened fire when it became the target of the enemy's artillery. Shell after shell burst over it and in between the guns, and then there was silence except from one gun. Then another bunch of shells burst over this gun also, and then everything became quiet until more men, probably, were sent up and the battery opened fire again. One could see red patches on the ground round the guns showing what an awful hell this battery had gone through.[16]

The RFC learned quickly: within a month they too had developed the capability to correct the fall of shot of the Royal Artillery.

At about 10.00, the first German infantry attack on the right flank came, pressing up onto and around the Montay Spur, which was initially defended by the 2nd Suffolks and the 2nd King's Own Yorkshire Light Infantry. At the same time, German batteries began to appear on the hills east of Le Cateau on the far side of the River Selle – exactly where the men of 5th Division had fondly hoped they would see the arrival of I Corps. Soon the 15th Brigade, RFA were in desperate straits, yet still MacLeod's gunners stuck to their task.

The Germans started working round our right flank and right rear and enfilading us from behind. The 11th Battery had to turn a section right completely round to engage them. My battery also tried to engage the Germans on the right – my section I had to run up by hand, turning almost at right angles to the right to shoot at the Germans beyond the River Selle. Meanwhile more and more German batteries were appearing at Rambourlieux Farm, enfilading our position from the left. My battery were getting more and more casualties and we could see the German infantry advancing. The telephone line went and nearly all our signallers became casualties trying to signal by flag – well that went! Finally, the Major came down from the observation post and ordered gun control – one officer to each gun. We only had four guns left in action because of casualties. I had No. 4. We started engaging these Germans over open sights, swung the guns right round to the left, so that one gun was firing almost over the top of the other and the Germans went to ground behind a road embankment and some corn stooks – they were very poor cover for them! We started firing at them at a range of 2,400 and gradually reduced to 1,600 – we were firing so fast that we were running out of ammunition. So the Captain sent for one ammunition waggon for each section. Well the ammunition wagons for the two right-hand sections came up and got away all right. The ammunition waggon for my section came up – unfortunately the horses got entangled with the telephone wire running through the standing corn behind and started plunging and kicking. I shouted to my men, 'Go and unhook the horses!' Well they were plunging so heavily that they couldn't do very much, so I went myself and started pulling ammunition out of the waggon body.[17]

All the over-exposed 5th Division batteries were receiving a terrible pounding.

It was now getting terrible. Shells came all ways in sixes and tens at the time. They were bursting all over the place – on the tops of our guns, and over our wagon lines, with plenty of spare rifle bullets flying about. Men and horses were getting wounded and killed. We received the order to get mounted. It was terrible. Shells were still bursting over the top of us. Other batteries were getting smashed to pieces. Lumps of shells and bullets were flying down in between us. We could not get anywhere for shelter, so we had to sit on our horses with our heads bent down between the animals. Most of our drivers got wounded and we had given up all hope of escape, and only waited for our turn at any moment to come. The shells burst like rain. Our Major, who was at the observing station, sent down the order that the 37th Battery would never retire. Our Captain then took control of the battery. We stayed in action until we had lost nearly half our men, which was about sixty or seventy, killed or wounded. The cries of the wounded and the shouting of the men was something terrible. I do not think there was a man on the field that day who did not say his prayers.[18]

Driver Job Drain, 37th Battery, 8th Howitzer Brigade, RFA, 5th Division, II Crops

However brave they were, their initial dispositions had been faulty. Headlam had made a fatal mistake in allowing his guns to be deployed so close to the front line – and hence the Germans. An intelligent, indeed cerebral officer, he had lacked the time for proper consideration. Perhaps over-tired as well, he had simply made a blunder. He would learn from the bitter experience.

On the left of the British line, the 4th Division was also threatened by German outflanking movements from the 2nd and 9th Cavalry
Divisions. Apart from an initial disaster when the 1st King's Own Royal
Lancasters were caught in the open before they had chance to adopt
defensive positions, the dismounted cavalry were held back with little
difficulty. However, Snow was still almost entirely baffled as to the
overall plan.

> I was heavily handicapped by the absence of my signal company, as
> I was unable to get messages to the brigadiers, except by sending off
> my staff to carry such messages. The brigadiers were even worse off
> than I was, as, having a smaller staff, it was as much as they could
> do to get their orders to the troops without worrying about sending
> back information, the consequence being that I was very much in
> the dark as to what was going on in the front line. I had never been
> told that the enemy were in overwhelming numbers, and I was never
> made to understand that, whatever the result of the battle, retreat was
> inevitable. This omission might have had a serious effect as at about
> 1pm I was convinced that I was fighting a winning action and indeed
> my left was advancing. Had I not stopped this advance, and I did so
> because I heard that the whole front was to retire, my left would have
> been advancing at the very moment the enemy were in position to
> turn it and I should have been making his task easier.[19]

In the circumstances, Snow was fortunate in the resistance on his left
flank in the Cambrai sector of three French divisions under the command
of General Albert d'Amade. These troops successfully engaged elements
of the German II Corps which must otherwise have enveloped the British
left flank to disastrous effect.

In the centre the 3rd Division watched the approach of the German
infantry edging forwards towards them. Captain Malcolm Hay of the 1st
Gordon Highlanders was just to the west of the village of Audencourt.

> The German infantry first came into view crossing the beetroot fields
> on top of the hill on our right front, where the telegraph poles acted
> as the 1,200 yard mark. Through these fields they advanced in close
> formation until disturbed by the attentions of a machine-gun either
> of ours or of the Royal Scots (who were holding the other side of
> the village of Audencourt). It was not long before we had a chance
> of getting rid of some ammunition. German troops, debouching

from the little wood where the cows had taken refuge earlier in the day, now advanced across the stubble field on top of the hill, moving to their left flank across our front. My glasses showed they were extended to not more than two paces, keeping a very bad line, evidently very weary and marching in the hot sun with manifest disgust. The command, 'Five rounds rapid at the stubble field 900 yards!' produced a cinematographic picture in my field-glasses. The Germans hopped into cover like rabbits. Some threw themselves flat behind the corn stooks, and when the firing ceased got up and bolted back to the wood. Two or three who had also appeared to fling themselves down, remained motionless. The enemy, having discovered that we could be dangerous even at 900 yards, then successfully crossed the stubble field in two short rushes without losing a man, and reinforced their men who were advancing through the beetroot fields on our right.[20]

By and large Germans did not press home their attacks in the centre, cautiously respectful of the skill of the British riflemen. The first real assaults were only launched on Caudry and Audencourt in the early afternoon. Hay watched them come.

Great numbers of troops now began to appear on the ridge between Bethancourt and the little wood. They advanced in three or four lines of sections of ten to fifteen men extended to two paces. Their line of advance was direct on the village of Audencourt and on the low plateau on our right, so that we were able to pour upon them an enfilade fire. They were advancing in short rushes across pasture-land which provided no cover whatever, and they offered a clearly visible target even when lying down. Although our men were nearly all first-class shots, they did not often hit the target. This was owing to the unpleasant fact that the German gunners kept up a steady stream of shrapnel, which burst just in front of our trenches and broke over the top like a wave. Shooting at the advancing enemy had to be timed by the bursting shell. We adopted the plan of firing two rounds and then ducking down at intervals, which were determined as far as could be arranged for by the arrival of the shell. But the shooting of the battalion was good enough to delay the enemy's advance.[21]

As the German infantry drew closer, so Hay noticed the intensity of the small arms and machine gun fire began to increase.

The bullets began to spray too close to my left ear, and laying my glasses on the parapet I was about to sit down for a few minutes' rest, and indeed had got halfway to the sitting position, when the machine gun found its target. Recollections of what passed through my mind at that moment is very clear. I knew instantly what had happened. The blow might have come from a sledge-hammer, except that it seemed to carry with it an impression of speed. I saw for one instant in my mind's eye the battlefield at which I had been gazing through my glasses the whole day. Then the vision was hidden by a scarlet circle, and a voice said, 'Mr H. has got it!' Through the red mist of the scarlet circle I looked at my watch (the movement to do so had begun in my mind before I was hit); it was spattered with blood; the hands showed five minutes to four. The voice which had spoken before said, 'Mr H. is killed!' Before losing consciousness, and almost at the same time as the bullet struck, the questioning thought was present in my mind as vividly as if spoken, 'Is this the end?' and present also was the answer, 'Not yet!'[22]

Malcolm Hay was right for he did come round. He had been severely wounded and was being tended in the front line by Private Robert Sinclair.

My first consciousness was of intolerable cramp in the legs. When Sinclair saw that I was breathing, he laid me down on the straw at the bottom of the trench and tried to give me a drink out of my water-bottle. I was unable to move any part of my body except the left hand, with which I patted the right-hand pocket of my coat, where I had carried, since leaving Plymouth, a flask of old brandy. Red Cross books say that brandy is the worst thing to give for head wounds; but Sinclair poured the whole contents down my throat, and I believe the stimulant saved my life.[23]

While Hay received treatment, the German attacks faltered away, for the most part beaten back, although they did manage to penetrate into Caudry.

On the right flank of II Corps, the situation was growing even more desperate. Not only was the 5th Division artillery being pounded by the German guns, but it soon became apparent that they were also well within the range of machine guns, which were banded together to deploy concentrated firepower to maximum effect.

We could see no trace of any trenches. The British had a brilliant understanding of the art of digging in. The eerie emptiness of the battlefield, was very evident here. All we could make out, because of the muzzle flashes, were the enemy artillery positions. To our half-right we could see a battery which, according to our doctrine, was located far too far forward, in amongst the line of infantrymen, to which we had already approached very closely. To our front, by the village, we could see several batteries preparing to move off. Right! Sights at 1,400 metres! Rapid fire. Slightly short. Higher! Soon we could observe the effect of the fire. There could not be greater activity around an upturned ant heap. Everywhere men and horses were milling around, falling down and, in amongst all this brouhaha, was a constant 'Tack! Tack! Tack!' Soon many had disappeared.[24]

Lieutenant Schacht, 26th Infantry Regiment, 7th Division, IV Corps

The Germans were feeling round the exposed right flank of II Corps where elements of 2nd Argyll and Sutherland Highlanders and 2nd Manchester Regiment had been deployed forwards to help support the position of the Suffolks.

Then the party started! And I mean the party started! The Hun came along, in his hordes. I was with my platoon officer, a gentleman by the name of Campbell, and a young Sergeant called Johnny Fair[25], who got killed. We were just lined up in a cornfield. I shall never see a picture like this in my life again – these Germans literally came in their hordes and were just shot down. But they still kept coming. There were sufficient of them to shove us out of the field eventually. Then, the realisation of what war meant: when you see my Company Sergeant Major Sim, wounded in the mouth, going back dripping blood. There were various people getting killed and wounded – quite a sizeable amount. What I shall never understand is what I was supposed to do with a bugle in the front line, except to blow if my platoon officer told me to blow. But what would you be asked to blow? I mean I couldn't blow cease fire because it didn't mean a thing.[26]

Private Charles Ditcham, 2nd Argyll and Sutherland Highlanders, 19th Brigade, II Corps

As his right flank began to crumble away, it was apparent to Smith-Dorrien that he had achieved all that he could hope for. To stay any longer was to risk being encircled and overwhelmed.

The strain was beginning to tell on our exposed east flank, and at 1.40pm, Colonel Gathorne Hardy, of my staff, who was watching events for me at 5th Divisional Headquarters at Reumont, brought me a message from Sir Charles Fergusson, saying his troops were beginning to dribble away under their severe punishment, and he feared he would be unable to hold on until dark. The Germans had already penetrated between his 13th and 14th Brigades, had practically wiped out the Suffolks, had brought up guns to short ranges, and were shelling heavily his own headquarters at Reumont. The division had stood to the limit of human endurance, and I recognised that the moment had arrived when our retirement should commence, and, requesting Gathorne Hardy to hurry back to Fergusson and tell him to order an organised retirement at once as the best means of saving a disastrous rush to the rear, I put in motion the plans already in possession of divisional commanders. These were to the effect that, when they got the order, they were to commence retiring by divisions along the roads allotted to them. My chief staff officer thereupon sent out the necessary instructions, saying the retirement would commence from the right.[27]

Smith-Dorrien's orders reached the beleaguered 5th Division at about 14.00 and then there were the inevitable further delays of up to an hour in passing them on to brigade headquarters, which themselves were under heavy fire. The guns were removed from their forward positions first, but it was already far too late. The effect of German machine gun fire hosing across the exposed batteries was devastating. Lieutenant Lionel Lutyens was with the 122nd Battery, 28th Brigade, RFA supporting the infantry of the 13th Brigade.

I heard the ' Pop- Pop- Pop- Pop!' of a machine gun and a perfect hail of bullets started coming over. The Germans had pushed a machine gun, or a couple, on to the knoll, 500 or 600 yards to our right front and had turned straight on to the battery. This machine gun fire had been incessant for five or ten minutes, when I heard a shout of, 'Limber up, we're going to retire!'[28]

Thus Lieutenant Schacht bore witness to a dramatic spectacle as the desperate British gunners tried to prevent their guns falling into German hands.

Among the flashes appeared a dark mass. It was the teams approaching at a mad gallop. We could not help but think, 'Are they mad?' No, with extraordinary bravery they were attempting to pull out their batteries at the last minute; to save what was left to save. 'Half-right! 1.000 metres! Double-tap! Rapid fire!' and in a hectic rhythm, twelve machine guns poured bullets at the sacrificial victims. What a dreadful tangle there was up there. One vehicle was ready and drove off, with three horses in front and one man on and managed to get away. A second dashed up; six riderless horses, tripping and stumbling, emerged over the hill. A third could not get away. Men lashed out at the poor creatures, but soon could do no more as they were hit and fell. One remained standing in amongst this wild hail of fire from batteries and machine guns, started to graze, whinnied for water and shook its head tiredly. What a cruel ironic fate. The other three guns and teams were one dark, confused mass.[29]

Lieutenant Schacht, 26th Infantry Regiment, 7th Division, IV Corps

Lieutenant Lionel Lutyens had dreadful trouble as his gun teams came up to the gun positions just in front of the sunken road. As they breasted the ridge they came under heavy fire. One team managed to get a gun away without trouble, but the next was well and truly caught.

They got as far as the sunken road and then the leaders jibbed. The driver flogged them into the road and then one leader fell. A Sergeant of mine and myself had just pulled him out of the way when the other leader fell, and then the driver. We were busy at the second horse when down came the near centre, and down came the off centre and the driver. The horses fell so quietly it was hard to realise they were shot. We couldn't save the guns now.[30]

Lieutenant Henry O'Kelly of the 2nd Duke of Wellington's Regiment was looking from a very different perspective, as he watched the gun detachments struggling to get their precious guns away. For the Royal Artillery, the guns were considered as their regimental colours and to lose them was an absolute disgrace.

I saw that day the gunners doing the most extraordinary feats of bravery. I saw one officer with his arm blown off still riding his horse giving instructions. Of course, he soon fainted from loss of blood, but just imagine doing your duty with your arm blown off in most awful agony, knowing that you had only a few minutes more to live. I also saw batteries blown to pieces, one gun being left intact in one battery;

immediately a team of gunners galloped out with their horses and hooked in and galloped back with their gun safe. I saw an artillery major blown high in the air and falling down in pieces.[31]

The 37th Howitzer Battery was one of the last to leave. This would trigger yet another heroic episode in which Driver Job Drain took a significant role.

> The 18-pounder battery on the right of us went up to get their guns, but most of them were blown to pieces. Two teams only escaped, and they came down to our battery, and our Captain claimed them to take two of our guns away. There were now four guns left in action and the question was what was to be done. The Captain sent down for wagon teams and gun limbers, and we made a dash for it. Only two teams reached the guns; they were 'F' and 'B' Sub-Sections. We managed to get two more guns away safely and took them to the nearest village. Then our Captain said, 'We must have more guns', so 'F' and 'B' turned round and went back at a mad gallop. This time the German infantry were only 100 yards off our guns. Driver Luke and myself went back at a mad pace, but Driver Cobey, my centre driver, was shot from his horse. There were then only left myself and Driver Luke, Captain Reynolds and two or three others. It was the worst time of my life. Shells and bullets were flying like rain from the clouds.[32]

Against all the odds they managed to rescue two howitzers. Captain Douglas Reynolds, Driver Fred Luke and Driver Job Drain all lived to be awarded the VC. Poor Driver Benjamin Cobey[33] was forgotten and has no known grave – the fortunes of war.

The troops left battling it out on the isolated Montay Spur just above Le Cateau on the far right flank were in desperate straits. Although some of the Suffolks and Argylls managed to escape, the bulk of the 2nd King's Own Yorkshire Light Infantry never got the orders to retire and considered it their collective duty to fight on.

> About 2.30 the situation was as bad as it could be. The ridge on our right, which was held by 14th Brigade, was shelled to pieces, and we were getting it from the Maxims half-right at about 900 yards, as well as volumes of shell: HE and shrapnel. Half the men were hit and the ammunition was running out. I signalled myself to 'B' Company – though I though it must be certain death – that the enemy were about

150 yards from our front trench and asked them to assist. They then poured in a very hot fire on the ridge on the right about 800 yards from us. One battalion had held up its hands and I remember watching the German Guards coming up and taking them prisoners. Then I put down my glasses, tore up every piece of paper I had, and made up my mind that the end must come any minute. I saw that in a few minutes the remainder of us in the second line would be prisoners, or dead, as we were hopelessly enfiladed from the ridge on our right. To get up and try to retire seemed the only chance – and yet the ground was a perfect hail of bullets and it seemed 1000 to 1 that anyone could get out alive. The regiment on our right had retired, or were prisoners. The West Kent Regiment half a mile to our rear was retiring – so I started with my little band to try it on. Two men on each side of me were instantly killed. However we retired at a walk in true Aldershot fashion and three times we turned and tried to answer the fire. Then it became a case of each man running and so on and so on under a murderous fire: a few of us escaped. I can hardly tell you how much the loss of my four officers and most of my best NCOs upset me. I felt that I too ought to have been killed.[34]

Major Bertie Trevor, 2nd King's Own Yorkshire Light Infantry, 13th Brigade, 5th Division, II Corps

The remnants were finally overrun and most of the battalion had been captured by 16.30. Their stand had acted as a thorn in the side of the Germans, thereby allowing the rest of the 5th Division to make a relatively untroubled escape.

The 3rd Division was nowhere near so hard-pressed and its retreat progressed smoothly from right to left with the covering force being provided by the 8th Brigade at Audencourt. But here too there was a breakdown in communications and the 1st Gordon Highlanders failed to get the orders to retire even after the bulk of the division had safely departed. They fought on for hours before finally starting to pull out at around midnight. The severely wounded Captain Malcolm Hay by this time knew little or nothing of what was happening and his story is related by Private Robert Sinclair.

We held the trenches till about 12pm, when we got the order to retire. When the officer heard that we were to retire he seemed very much cut up about it, as it meant that he would be left behind to be taken prisoner. We did not care to leave him, so four of us put him on a coat and carried him about ¼ mile to where the regiment was to meet; when we got there we found there were no stretchers to put him on, so another officer gave us an order to leave him, and then decided to leave two men with him. Well, as we were left to do our best for him, by this time the battalion had passed, and not a stretcher was to be found. Hearing another regiment passing, I sent the other man to try and get a stretcher or a horse; but when he asked for a stretcher, the officer of the other regiment asked what it was for, then told him he was to go back at once and leave a water bottle and take any message, and that both of us were to fall in rear of his battalion at once. When our officer heard of this he told us to obey orders, so what could we do? We made him as comfortable as possible, then went to rejoin the battalion, but found that we had missed the road they had taken.[35]

Left alone, the helpless Hay was swiftly captured by the Germans. Most of the rest of the Gordons were ambushed a couple of miles further back at Bertry and very few escaped capture.

On the left flank the 4th Division were hampered in their retreat by the determined attacks on Ligny by IV Reserve Corps, which had been moved up to replace the rather lacklustre German cavalry. As the 4th Division withdrew, it was evident that many units had lost their cohesion.

There is no doubt that there was considerable confusion amongst the retreating II Corps in the aftermath of the Battle of Le Cateau. Many battalions had lost touch with their brigades and few officers has any clear idea as to what they were meant to be doing.

This retirement was made along the main road southeast for about a mile and a half. Major Finch and I were very busy collecting men all the way after we had gathered together those we could find at the first halting place. There were bullets and shells flying about all over the place, but no one seemed to get hit after we had got clear of the village. We could not make head or tail out of this situation, as men were being collected by other regiments in a similar way and the officers were shouting orders all at the same time and odd collections of men were gathered together in little bunches and led off to various positions hastily selected and facing in all directions. It was hard to tell what to do.[36]

Lieutenant Thomas Wollocombe, 4th Middlesex Regiment, 8th Brigade, 3rd Division, II Corps

Only a few of the 2nd King's Own Yorkshire Light Infantry had got away, and their medical officer recorded the mayhem as they joined thousands of men trying to escape down the same narrow roads.

> The road was now in a most indescribable state of confusion: infantry, cavalry, guns, limbers, waggons, ambulances, staff cars and every other conceivable form of vehicle, all going as hard as they could and all mixed up together. Things were not improved by the fact that the Germans were starting to shell the village and the word came along that the General had said that there was no time to be lost and every man was to shift for himself. I looked into the church which had been used as a dressing station and found it packed with wounded, who together with three Royal Army Medical Corps officers, eventually fell into the hands of the Germans. All cases that could stagger along were taken on limbers, etc. all the ambulances having been sent back full of wounded some time before. It was impossible to find my battalion as there was none as such, only a few groups of men scattered about the endless retreating column. I suppose the average pace was about 1½ miles per hour. As luck would have it, I managed to find my horse; that was the most extraordinary piece of luck, as many officers and men were left behind on the road absolutely worn out through want of rest and food.[37]
>
> Lieutenant Cyril Helm, 2nd King's Own Yorkshire Light Infantry, 13th Brigade, 5th Division, II Corps

Hanging over them all was the uncertainty as to the whereabouts of the Germans. It was almost impossible to gauge how close a pursuit was being made. As such, Second Lieutenant Henry O'Kelly of the 2nd Duke of Wellingtons was given a dangerous task when ordered to take part in an improvised rearguard.

> We had gone about three miles we were stopped by a General, who asked for the senior officer. The General told him he wanted an officer to stay behind on the crest of the hill with some men to protect the column which he feared would be followed up by cavalry. The Captain was ill, so of course there was nothing but for me to say I would do it. The General stopped about 130 men of all regiments, and pushed them into a field. I found that we had a machine gun with us and another very young officer. I don't know what regiments were with us. I was too beat to notice particulars, only I saw about seven men of our own

regiment, whom I called together and asked to show a bold front and give a good example. I also told them that they would probably be motored back. Well, it was getting on towards twilight, with no sign of the enemy in sight. The infantry and cavalry had mostly, except stragglers, passed on, when I saw Germans bringing a big gun down a laneway with twelve horses attached. I got the machine gun on them and shot most of the horses. They brought up another lot and tried to harness them; of these we also shot some and were beginning to enjoy it when a shell burst amongst us. This came from a gun they had brought from the other side of the road. This shell blew up the machine gun and killed seven or eight men, including the little officer. Immediately three other shells burst in our midst, doing frightful havoc, and everyone ran for cover, myself included. When we collected together I halted them about thirty yards back in a cave and found only eleven men and myself; we sat there until it was dark, and then I crept back and found a good many were only wounded but found none who could walk. We then started to try and rejoin our units and I decided to do so across country. The first village we came to was deserted, and as I had neither map nor compass I had not the slightest idea where we went.[38]

After many adventures, threading their way through the German Army, O'Kelly's group of stragglers managed to rejoin the retreating columns some four days later.

SOME MYTHS OF THE BATTLE OF Le Cateau have endured right to the present day. Foolish analogies with the Battle of Crécy based on a mere coincidence of date have no credibility and add nothing to our understanding of what happened. The traditional British boast is that the mighty German hordes were given a collective bloody nose, slaughtered in their droves and henceforth so chastened that they never again dared pursue the BEF with real vigour, allowing the retreat to continue relatively unmolested. The reality is far more that, in accordance with their doctrine, the Germans only pressed home their attacks on the flanks and that they actually suffered far fewer casualties than II Corps. The British were officially estimated to have some 7,812[39] casualties in addition to the thirty-eight guns which had been left on the field of battle. Of these some

2,500 had been taken prisoner. The Germans had a total of around 2,000 casualties. By any standards the Germans had won the day: they had by far the best of the fighting, but at the same time II Corps had managed to make its escape. This was because von Kluck had a mistaken appreciation of the BEF movements thinking the II Corps would be retreating towards what he fondly imagined to be their base at Calais and thus 'pursued' them to the south-west in the general direction of Péronne, when in fact they were falling back to the south towards St Quentin.

For the British, it is fair to comment that the tactics employed by Smith-Dorrien did not really conform to the tenets of the Field Service Regulations. Le Cateau was a full-scale battle rather than a series of token deployments by mobile forces designed to force a time-consuming deployment of the pursuing German forces. Yet the whole point of the decision to disobey the orders to continue the retreat was that there was simply no room or time for such tactics to be successfully employed. Surely the real question was whether Smith-Dorrien's decision was justified. Did it save II Corps? The only possible answer is that they did escape – if only more by luck than judgement. There is little value in 'guessing' what might have occurred if Smith-Dorrien had not stood and fought. The situation was too complex, with far too many random cross-cut factors tangled up, to allow anyone to accurately divine the incidental effects of alternative scenarios. One thing is sure: it is difficult not to admire the courage demonstrated by Smith-Dorrien in making his bold decision. Smith-Dorrien was lucky for sure: he had survived the Zulu assegais at Isandlwana in 1879 and now his II Corps had escaped the German grip at Le Cateau.

7

GREAT RETREAT

As we march through the villages the inhabitants are the picture
of despair. What a contrast: thirteen days previously we were
hailed as the deliverers of France, 'Long live England! *Vive
la Angleterre!*' Instead of delivering France, we are retiring by
forced marches in the direction of Paris. There is no enthusiasm
now, no '*Vive la Angleterre!*' no 'Tipperary!' No – nothing but
black despair. The Prussian jackboot, Prussian soldiers and
the Prussian cannon are going, so it seems, to repeat the
performance of 1870. The oldest inhabitants of the villages, who
remember that black page in France's history, ask us as we march
through, 'Are the Prussians going to take Paris?'[1]

Private Edward Roe, 1st East Lancashire Regiment, 11th Brigade, 4th
Division

THE BRITISH AFFECT TO TAKE pride in their calamitous retreats: they
admire Moore's desperate trek back to Corunna during the Peninsula
Campaign in 1809, romanticise the doomed retreat from Kabul in the
First Afghan War, 1841, and in more modern times indulge in vainglorious bluster over what can equally well be portrayed as the shameful
abandonment of their French allies at Dunkirk in 1940. The story of the
'Great Retreat from Mons' has become a cherished part of this celebration
of failure, claiming the endurance of unique trials, while all oblivious to
the fact that the French of the Fifth Army falling back alongside them

were undergoing equal tribulations. In the aftermath of the Battle of Le Cateau, the Germans were all but convinced that the British had been soundly defeated and were finished as a serious military force. However, von Kluck was again misled as to the direction of the British retreat. He was convinced that they had fallen back to the south-west as opposed to the southerly line of march adopted by II Corps. His cavalry and airmen seemed incapable of providing the intelligence needed, and the misconception encapsulated within his orders for the pursuit on 27 August towards Péronne meant a gap opened up between the pursuing Germans and the II Corps, who were actually retiring on St Quentin. As a result, with the exception of occasional skirmishes, the bulk of the BEF retreat was carried out unmolested.

The British High Command was equally confused by the situation. French believed that the II Corps had been soundly thrashed and was incapable of battle.

> More or less detailed reports had arrived, which showed the shattered condition of the troops that had fought at Le Cateau. All idea of making any prolonged stand on the Somme south of St Quentin, which had during the day seriously entered my mind as a possibility, was definitely abandoned. The first necessity was to rally and collect the troops which had become mixed up and scattered.[2]

Yet there was no stream of orders emanating from GHQ to resolve the situation, no guidance or leadership at all. The lacunae made the situation of subordinate commanders very stressful, as exemplified by the predicament of Brigadier General Hubert Gough commanding the 3rd Cavalry Brigade. Desperate to discover what was going on, he managed to place a telephone call through to GHQ, who at that stage were still at Le Quentin. After a long wait the urbane and charming voice of Sir Henry Wilson came on the line. After sketching out the situation for the 3rd Cavalry Brigade, which was at that stage situated in the gap between I and II Corps, Gough asked for orders. The conversation as related by Gough was symptomatic of the complete loss of control by French and the senior staff officers at GHQ.

> I knew nothing of the situation of our own troops except what I had seen with my own eyes: nor had I any information as to the direction

of the retirement, or of the intentions and plans of our commanders. 'Could he enlighten me so as to enable me to play my part as effectively as possible?' But I could get no information or orders from him. GHQ did not know – or at least Wilson could not tell me – what roads the II Corps was using, or by what stages the retirement would be conducted. He could not tell me what line to occupy as a rearguard, and had no information whatever as to the positions and intentions of the I Corps. The lack of this knowledge caused me great uneasiness and anxiety for my right flank and rear – though these were actually perfectly secure, owing to the presence of the I Corps. I did get some instructions from him at last – though hardly of the kind I had anticipated or needed. For Wilson's final words were, 'As you are on the spot, do what you like, old boy!'[3]

This may have conformed to some idea of leaving things to 'the man on the spot' on the grounds that he knows best, yet Gough had made it clear that he had no idea what was happening – and no information on which to make a rational decision. It should be noted that, since the fallout from the Curragh incident a few months before, Gough could not be considered a sympathetic witness towards French. Yet this was not an isolated voice railing against the GHQ, for, as we have seen, Major General Sir Thomas D'Oyly Snow often expressed similar complaints. Gough's response showed that he was more than capable of a little disingenuity, for he soon managed to make contact with Haig's staff, placing himself within the orbit of I Corps command. Gough found this far more congenial as his brother, Brigadier General John Gough, was Haig's Chief of Staff and there may – or may not – have been a touch of nepotism, which caused him to contrast the situation he found in I Corps with the shambles at GHQ or indeed the scattered Cavalry Division.

We remained under the orders of the I Corps for several days and during all that time I was clearly informed of the position of the I Corps and the intentions of its commander, receiving precise orders as to my role. It was a great relief and gave me a feeling of confidence to find myself under the orders of a commander like Haig, who understood the handling of troops, knew what he wanted them to do, and clearly directed them to do it. The voluntary placing of my brigade under Haig's command was sound and justified, but it had not been directly sanctioned by GHQ – although my sole instructions from Henry Wilson, 'Do what you like, old boy!' could be claimed as covering the move.[4]

The headquarters staff of I Corps had been in place pre-war, with both 1st and 2nd Divisions under Haig's Aldershot Command. This was in contrast to the situation at both II Corps and GHQ, where the staff had been thrown together ad hoc on the outbreak of war. As such, the staff work within I Corps triggered far less resentment amongst the constituent units.

> Haig keeps his head better than any other and remains unusually cool in his judgement. He stops to talk to me occasionally on the line of march and I must say he is the only superior officer who appears to me to grip hold of the essential points. Sir John French has not been seen by anyone in this Army Corps since we started! He lives in a headquarter camp containing 300 people and goodness only knows what they are all doing![5]
>
> Brigadier General Ivor Maxse, 1st Guards Brigade, 1st Division, I Corps

Early on in the march, elements of II Corps passed through St Quentin on 27 August. The town was the scene of considerable reorganisation as staff officers attempted to sort out the badly dispersed units.

> As we approached the town the entrance had got rather blocked with troops. This was rather a good thing, as it enabled the stragglers behind to close up and find other portions of their own regiments; and, extraordinary as it seemed, whole companies had now got together and in some cases had even coagulated into battalions. I found most of the Norfolks collected together in a field by the side of the road, and a stray Bedford company or two looking quite fresh and happy. At last in the middle of the town, I managed to collect some instructions, and was told that the 5th Division was to form up in a field near the railway station the other side of the town. There were also staff officers at different points, calling out '5th Division this way, 3rd that', and so on; and as the men, now more or less in columns of fours, passed them, they perked up and swung along quite happily. We were now outside the region of our maps, so I asked my way to a stationer's, which luckily happened to be open, though it was barely 7.30 a.m., and bought all

the local maps I could get hold of: they were only paper, not linen, but they proved extremely useful.[6]

Brigadier General Lord Edward Gleichen, Headquarters, 15th Brigade, 5th Division, II Corps

Many of the junior British officers did indeed not have the appropriate French maps – after all they had only needed maps of Belgium under the original plans!

Later in the day, things began to deteriorate as the streets of St Quentin Grand Place gradually filled up with stragglers who seemed to have given up all hope and were listlessly waiting to be captured by the Germans. Worse than this, Lieutenant Colonel John Elkington of the 1st Royal Warwicks and Lieutenant Colonel Arthur Mainwaring commanding the 2nd Royal Dublin Fusiliers (both of 10th Brigade, 4th Division) were guilty of a terrible error of judgement. Totally exhausted themselves, they could see no solution to their problems. With their men seemingly unable to march any further, they had tried and failed to secure transport by train. Unable to summon the motivational willpower to get their men going, they were also being besieged by local French politicians desperate to avoid a bloody destructive battle on their doorsteps. In the end, Elkington and Mainwaring reluctantly came to a written agreement with the French mayor to surrender their battalions to the Germans in order to avoid the spectre of the shelling of St Quentin. Their intentions were good, but this was an unfortunate dereliction of duty.

I felt if I argued as to conditions, it might leave an opening for the Germans to shell the town and kill the civilian population and I then felt my duty was to make no attempt at terms. Prostrated with mental and physical exhaustion, I wrote those words convinced I was doing my duty and a noble act.[7]

Lieutenant Colonel Arthur Mainwaring, 2nd Royal Dublin Fusiliers, 10th Brigade, 4th Division

There was a great deal of subsequent controversy and a painful court-martial, but it is clear that the actions of men in such an abject state are not easy to reconcile after the fact. Neither wanted to accept the responsibility, but there is little doubt that, however understandable the circumstances, the actions of the two colonels went well beyond what was acceptable.

Colonel Mainwaring proceeded to the mayor with an interpreter and signed a paper to the mayor. This paper I never saw till the trial and did not know till then how it was worded. I am sure when [he] signed it he did so under great mental and physical strain and did not realise the consequences. I thought at the time the mayor was exaggerating the situation.[8]

Lieutenant Colonel John Elkington, 1st Royal Warwickshire Regiment, 10th Brigade, 4th Division

While the station area was full of disarmed Warwicks and Dublin Fusiliers waiting like sheep for the Germans to arrive, the Grand Place was also beginning to fill up with rootless stragglers who had lost their battalions and had nowhere to go. They had lost the will to struggle on and they no longer cared what happened to them. All they craved was an end to the torments of physical exhaustion and mental uncertainty that plagued them.

The whole square was thronged with British infantrymen standing in groups or wandering about in an aimless fashion, most of them without either packs or rifles. Scores had gone to sleep sitting on the pavement, their backs against the fronts of the shops. Many exhausted, lay at full length on the pavement. Some few, obviously intoxicated, wandered about firing in the air at real or imaginary German aeroplanes. The great majority were not only without their arms, but had apparently either lost, or thrown away, their belts, water bottles and other equipment.[9]

Captain Arthur Osburn, 4th Dragoon Guards, 2nd Cavalry Brigade, Cavalry Division

It was at this point that Captain Thomas Bridges also of the 4th Dragoon Guards arrived. Appalled by the news of the imminent surrender, he wrested control from the two broken colonels and retrieved the incriminating surrender document from the French mayor. He then used a mixture of cajoling and threats to finally get the Warwicks and Dublin Fusiliers back on their feet and once more stumbling on their way out of St Quentin.

I sent an ultimatum giving them half an hour's grace, during which time some carts would be provided for those who really could not walk, but letting them know that I would leave no British soldier alive in St Quentin. Upon this they emerged from the station and gave no more trouble.[10]

The resourceful and dynamic Bridges then turned his attention to the dispirited rabble in the Grand Place.

> The men in the square were so jaded it was pathetic to see them. If only one had a band, I thought! There was a toy shop handy which provided my trumpeter and myself with a tin whistle and a drum and we marched round and round the fountain where the men were lying like the dead, playing *The British Grenadiers* and *Tipperary* and beating the drum like mad. They sat up and began to laugh and even to cheer. I stopped playing and made them a short exhortation and told them I was going to take them back to their regiments.[11]

It was an incredible scene, soon woven into the narrative of the 'Great Retreat' as Bridge's crazy impromptu gesture – against all the odds – struck just the right chord and got most of the shattered men back on their feet.

> They were in a bad way some of them were sitting at the side of the road crying. There was a toy shop and Bridges went in the shop and got this drum out of the shop window – whether he paid for it or not I don't know! He came out, 'Come on, we're all right now!' He got this drum going, got them together and they marched behind the drum! One helped another; the more fit stragglers helped the elderly one. Some were left behind – you couldn't get them all back.[12]
>
> Private William Holbrook, 4th Royal Fusiliers, 9th Brigade, 3rd Division, II Corps

Yet for all Bridge's success on this occasion, it was evident that morale was going to be a key factor: a retreat is one of the most difficult military manoeuvres simply because it erodes the self-belief of the men and can dissolve units before the eyes of the officers. To make it more difficult, the senior officers could not provide any real guidance as to when the ordeal might end. Attempts to give them hope could often prove counterproductive.

> The rumour, started at GHQ, got about that we were to halt behind the River Oise to rest and refit. Why the Oise was supposed to afford us protection I don't know, and as it turned out we hardly halted there at all, but similar rumours kept on being circulated, and the Aisne, and

afterwards the Marne, and later the Seine, were all held out as havens of rest which we were marching for. It was not good for the troops. The mention of rest and refitting began to be a subject for joke and the men were quite certain that it was intended to retire to Marseilles with every river between held up as haven of refuge, a refuge which they knew would never materialise. At first I was taken in myself and did forced marches to reach these havens, but when I found that these havens of rest disappeared when one reached them I soon attached no importance to rivers.[13]

Major General Sir Thomas D'Oyly Snow, Headquarters, 4th Division

Perhaps one reason for the lack of 'grip' exerted by GHQ was the inability of Sir John French to grasp his real function as Commander in Chief. A brilliant cavalry commander during the Boer War, he still inhabited a world where generals could inspire their troops man-to-man by moving amongst them on the battlefield and somehow 'sensing' what was going on.

I spent several hours of the 28th in going the round of the troops, as it was possible to intercept various columns on the march or at their temporary halts. I was able to get the men together on the roadside, to thank them for the splendid work they had done, to tell them of the gratitude of the French Commander-in-Chief, and the immense value of the service they had rendered to the Allied cause. I charged them to repeat all this to their comrades, and to spread it throughout the units to which they belonged. There was neither time nor opportunity for any formal inspection or set parade. The enemy was on our heels, and there was little time to spare, but it touched me to the quick to realise how, in the face of all the terrible demand made upon their courage, strength and endurance, these glorious British soldiers listened to the few words I was able to say to them with the spirit of heroes and the confidence of children.[14]

It is apparent that he was indeed capable of evoking a considerable response from the men, who generally were pleased to see him.

We halted in an orchard outside La Fere for two hours at about 12 noon, and had dinner. General French came round and personally addressed each unit. He told us he had never been prouder of being a British soldier, and that the Army had saved the French from annihilation, after having undergone the most terrible test an Army could experience. We cheered him heartily on his departure, and everyone felt much better; after all we had done something, and everything pointed to a turn in the tide.[15]

Lieutenant Joseph Dent, 2nd South Staffordshire Regiment, 6th Brigade, 2nd Division, I Corps

Yet, in truth, French's words were nothing more, nor less, than meaningless platitudes designed to bolster the confidence of his men – or his 'children'. Whatever the temporary restorative effect his visits to the retreating battalions may have had, they were not an effective use of his time. In this new form of warfare the 'Chief' must not stray too far from the network of phones and staff officers that allow him to control the whole of his force. He must be located at a spot where he can be reached easily when an urgent decision was required to facilitate the complex functions of command in the twentieth century. Indeed, even as he reassured his men, French himself was becoming increasingly aware of the desperate state of affairs.

It was during Friday the 28th that I fully realised the heavy losses we had incurred. Since Sunday the 23rd this had reached, in officers and men, the total of upwards of 15,000. The deficiency in armament and equipment were equally serious. Roughly, some eighty guns and a large proportion of our machine guns, besides innumerable articles of necessary equipment and a large quantity of transport, had fallen into the enemy's hands. It became quite clear to me that no effective stand could be made until we were able to improve our condition.[16]

THE FRENCH HIGH COMMAND WERE ALREADY very sceptical as to the British capacity to recover from the blow dealt them by the Germans at Le Cateau. To Lanrezac it merely confirmed his belief that Joffre and GHQ had got everything wrong from the start of the campaign. He was a man mired in a degree of depression mixed with a desire to point out that he had forewarned it all.

Attacked from the front and outflanked on its left, they could disengage only with great difficulty after suffering cruel losses; the opportune arrival of Sordet's Cavalry Corps to their left helped ease their retreat. The British Army fell back to the south, with its left flank on St. Quentin, the right passing through the Oise valley, thereby clinging to the left of the Fifth Army. This was inevitable from the moment it had become impossible to amass on the left of our allies a force capable of containing the movement of an overwhelming opponent.[17]

Joffre was well aware that the onus of defeating the German Army must of necessity fall upon the French Army; the BEF was just a useful adjunct, an investment for the future, perhaps, should the war not be over in 1914. Plan XVII was abandoned, never much more than a concentration plan, to be followed by crushing offensives, and it was clear that the bones crushed had been French. First, Joffre cleared the decks by engaging in a thorough clear out of officers not considered up to standard. At the same time he tried to address some of the underlying tactical failures that had condemned the French to such unbearable casualties in the Battle of the Frontiers.

It was apparent that the principles of the offensive which we had tried to inculcate in the army before the war had often been poorly understood and badly applied. From all points of the front came reports of mistakes made in handling troops, mistakes which had brought about heavy losses and sometimes reduced to nought the offensive and defensive qualities of the men. I was told that advanced guards, through a false comprehension of the offensive spirit, were nearly always sent into action without artillery support and occasionally got caught in close formation under the enemy's artillery fire. Sometimes it would be one of the larger units which, moving forward with its flanks unguarded, would suddenly become exposed to unexpected and costly fire. The infantry was almost always launched to the assault when at too great a distance from its objective. Conquered ground was never organized before starting off to the attack of a new position; in this way, if the latter failed, the troops were driven back without even reaping the fruits of their first effort. Far and beyond all, the cooperation of the infantry and the artillery was constantly neglected.[18]

Joffre had very little time left to respond to the threat of the looming German right hook swinging round through Belgium and northern France. To his eternal credit he stayed calm, where a lesser man would surely have panicked. His response was one steeped in the classical tactics of a war of movement; as a plan it was simple, but it had great virtue in that it charted a possible course out of the dreadful imbroglio that had engulfed the French Army.

> My own preference consisted in creating on the outer wing of the enemy a mass capable, in its turn, of enveloping his marching flank. If we were to have time to assemble in the region of Amiens a force large enough to produce a decisive effect against the marching flank of the enemy, it was necessary to accept a further retreat of our armies on the left. But we had reason to hope that by making good use of every obstacle by which the enemy's advance might be retarded, and by delivering frequent counter-attacks, these armies need not fall back further than the general line of the Aisne, prolonged by the bluffs running from Craonne to Laon and La Fere. The Third Army would rest on the fortifications of Verdun, which would thus serve as a pivot for the general movement in retreat. The French Fourth and Fifth Armies, the British Army and the Amiens group, constituted with forces taken from our right wing, would furnish a mass capable of resuming the offensive at the moment the enemy, debouching from the wooded regions of the Ardennes, would have to fight with this difficult ground lying behind him. My conception was a battle stretching from Amiens to Rheims with the new army placed on the extreme left of our line, outside of the British and in a position to outflank the German right.[19]

Having taken the decision, Joffre had to be equally decisive in creating a new army. The French armies in the Ardennes and Lorraine would have to take up a defensive posture to allow divisions, or even whole corps, to be stripped out and despatched north, where, as part of the new Sixth Army, they would lurk on the right flank of the onrushing German First Army. Joffre originally hoped this could be done from a concentration area in the Amiens area, but as the Germans pressed deeper and deeper into France, they would eventually be gathered near Paris ready for what would become known as the Battle of the Marne. While Joffre grappled with these gargantuan problems, he was not helped by the parochial attitudes displayed by French, as evinced in their meeting held previously on 26 August.

> French came in, accompanied by General Murray, his Chief of Staff. I expected to find the same calm officer whose acquaintance I had made a few days before; but, to my great surprise, the British Commander-in-Chief started out immediately in a rather excited tone

to explain that his army had been violently attacked, and that, the evening before, General Haig's corps had been obliged to fall back on Guise and the Cavalry Corps on Bohain (that is to say, into the zone assigned to the French Fifth Army); that his II Corps and General Snow's 4th Division were being pressed by the enemy in the direction of Le Catelet. He explained to me that since hostilities had begun his troops had been submitted to such hardships that he could not for the moment contemplate resuming the offensive. He considered the situation as being very delicate. More than once he made complaints concerning the manner in which the Fifth Army, his neighbour, had acted. He accused this army of having broken off the fight and left him completely isolated. In reply, I said to the Field Marshal that all the Allied troops without exception had been pushed hard by the enemy and that he must not suppose that the British Army was the only one which had suffered from the severe conditions of the campaign.[20]

General Joseph Joffre, General Headquarters, French Army

This somewhat chastening rebuttal seems to have gone right over the head of French, which was perhaps just as well given his somewhat volatile temperament. The report Joffre received on 27 August from Colonel Huguet, his liaison officer, at the GHQ was deeply disturbing.

I have the honour to confirm my telegram of last evening, August 26th, informing you of the defeat inflicted yesterday upon the British Army. Later information which has just reached me indicates that the situation is extremely critical. For the moment, the British Army is beaten and is incapable of any serious effort. The right column – 1st and 2nd Divisions – now retreating on Origny-Saint-Benoit, still presents some aspects of cohesion; the same may be said of the 4th; but the 3rd and 5th Divisions, most severely tried, having lost a great many men, a large part of their artillery and transport and having been subjected to a most violent artillery fire during nearly thirty-six hours, are now nothing more than disorganized bands, incapable of offerings the smallest resistance and not in a condition to take their place again on the field of battle until they have been rested and completely refitted. Fortunately the pursuit has not been vigorous. Conditions are such that for the moment the British Army no longer exists.[21]

Huguet may have been eaggerating, but there is little doubt that, from the French perspective, the BEF was not contributing a great deal to the joint effort; indeed by the final days of August, it was actually retreating faster than Lanrezac's much-maligned Fifth Army. The pressure on the British was such that on 28 August, in an effort to regain some of the initiative and to assist his stumbling allies, Joffre felt obliged to order Lanrezac to launch a counterattack by the Fifth Army against the German Second Army. This triggered a huge row between an increasingly resentful Joffre and his by now openly disdainful subordinate. Lanrezac was furious when a staff officer arrived from Joffre to explain exactly what was required.

> Colonel Alexander, who was speaking to my Chief of Staff, General Hély d'Oissel a few paces from me, exclaimed at one point, 'You have not understood General Joffre's instructions! You must not simply retreat, but must fight back and contain the enemy with strong counter-attacks supported by strong artillery!'. . . I wanted to use this plan only in exceptional circumstances, judging it dangerous given the state of my troops, and thinking that it could be achieved as well and with less risk through the successive defensive actions by our rearguard. The time to take the counter-offensive should, in my opinion, be delayed until we reached Laon. There, the ground seemed favourable, and above all I hoped we could have time to rally the English and to reinforce Maunoury's [Sixth] Army, so that I did not expose my left flank to the prospect of a sudden and overwhelming attack.[22]

Despite his misgivings, which encompassed requests for direct written orders and a fraught meeting with Joffre on 28 August, Lanrezac was bluntly told, 'Make a substantial offensive as soon as possible on St Quentin, without concerning himself about the English!'[23] The still-reluctant Lanrezac eventually launched the Battle of Guise on 29 August. Yet this counter-stroke, designed to save the BEF, also provoked a considerable row within the British camp. Lanrezac had asked Haig to provide assistance from I Corps. Haig could see considerable tactical opportunities as the German Second Army, in concentrating on the French Fifth Army, was inadvertently presenting a left flank to Haig's forces. He thus decided to offer support conditional on the approval of French, and duly contacted GHQ for confirmation.

> Reference by General Lanrezac for support of our First Corps on left of attack which begins at 5.30 a.m. tomorrow, I replied that infantry must

have day's rest, but that support by the whole artillery and machine guns of the corps with suitable infantry escort could be given provided Field Marshal approves. Infantry would be ready to support tomorrow evening and in any case could join in pursuit. Please telephone Sir John French's instructions. I consider infantry will be able to go forward after 24-hours rest.[24]

The reply from French's headquarters was brusque and clearly reflected not only his visceral dislike for Lanrezac, but also a complete lack of tactical awareness.

Commander-in-Chief does not approve of any active operations on the part of our I Corps tomorrow and has already ordered a halt for one day's rest. . . . The Commander-in-Chief repeats the order that no active operations of any arms except of a defensive nature will be undertaken tomorrow.[25]

French's 'vision' encompassed nothing more than a continued withdrawal with the Utopian ideal of securing a safe locality where the BEF might secure up to ten days for rest and recuperation, whilst refitting and reorganising before rejoining the fray. To add insult to injury, French followed this up with a querulous note effectively accusing Haig of acting above his station.

Please be good enough to inform C-in-C how it was that any confidential promise of support by I Corps was made to General Lanrezac or why any official exchange of ideas was initiated without authority from headquarters.[26]

Unsurprisingly, Haig was livid and his own reply was a stinging riposte in a distinctly insubordinate tone.

I do not understand what you mean. I have, 'initiated no official exchange of ideas.' GHQ not having secured from the French roads for the retirement of my Corps, I had for my own safety to enter into relations with the nearest French force on my right. As far as it was possible I have maintained touch with the left of these French troops – and due to the presence of this Corps their left has been protected ever since we left Maubeuge. My Corps in its present position still protects their left, and if the enemy advances from St Quentin southwards, I shall have for my own safety to deploy guns, etc., without asking for the authority of GHQ to do so. The extrication of this Corps from the false position in which it was placed still demands the greatest exertion from us all, and my sole objective is to secure its retreat with honour to our arms. I therefore beg you will not give credit to such allegations as the one under reference without first ascertaining whether it is true or not.[27]

The waspish exchange shows that Haig's working relationship between Sir John French was fraying away under the extreme tensions of the campaign. Haig had expressed his doubts on his superior's capabilities at the outbreak of war and he was clearly finding his self-imposed oath of loyalty somewhat frustrating

When the Fifth Army unleashed its offensive by XVIII Corps against St Quentin on 29 August, little was achieved, but on the right the X and III Corps had a significant success in forcing the German Second Army to withdraw some three miles towards Guise. Next day the Fifth Army resumed the retreat, but it had showed spirit in administering a sharp reverse to the Germans. In some ways this can be considered a demonstration of everything that the Battle of Le Cateau was not: a vigorous counter-attack, exploiting an identified weakness, handing out a severe thrashing to elements of von Bülow Second Army, followed by a smooth disengagement to continue the retreat. Yet, despite this encouraging performance, the rift between Joffre and his recalcitrant subordinate was by this time unbridgeable and, on 3 September, Lanrezac was replaced with the more overtly aggressive General Franchet D'Esperey, who had distinguished himself as the commander of I Corps during the Battle of Guise.

AS THE WEARY COLUMNS TRUDGED BACK along the dusty roads, the men could not but be aware of the sad plight of the French and Belgian refugees who had not chosen to await the arrival of the German forces. Many were haunted by the harsh treatment meted out to civilians by the Germans during the Franco-Prussian War, when the German fear of *franc-tireurs* led to some unpleasant reprisals, including the shooting of considerable numbers of hostages. Sometimes the roads were almost choked with refugees and stern measures had to be taken to secure the passage of the British troops.

One of the saddest sights of that day, was the huge columns of refugees on the main road to Guise. Carts heaped with household treasures led by crying women and frightened children. These carts were ruthlessly swept off the road to make a passage for the troops. This was absolutely necessary, of course, in spite of its cruelty. None of these poor people could have crossed the river at Guise, as we had to blow up the bridge after crossing – and held back the fugitives to do it.[28]

Captain Herbert Rees, 2nd Welsh Regiment, 3rd Brigade, 1st Division, I Corps

The refugees were faced with a terrible quandary: whether to leave their homes and most of their possessions or to stay and risk harsh treatment. Lieutenant Duncan Laurie had been much impressed by the hospitality of a pretty wife of a French farmer serving with the French Army. On an impulse he decided he had to try and help.

Wood and I were having dinner and as we had heard such dreadful stories of what the Germans were doing to the women we decided we would try and go back and get the women from the farm at Ham. After great difficulty we persuaded Smith to let us have a car. Which he said he would do when the staff had gone to bed. By 11pm we started back along the road to Ham. We got through to the farm house at Ham and banged on the door of the farm. Presently a lady put her head out of the window and we asked her to come down to the door. Lots of English soldiers were lying down on the pavements of the street sleeping as they were dead-beat. We told the lady the Germans were about three miles outside the village and would be in at dawn and that if she liked to leave within half an hour we would take her to Noyon. She went up to consult with some relation and came down to say that if we would take her and two other ladies, they would be ready to start in twenty minutes. The three of them came down with what they could carry in their hands and left a most beautiful farm and everything in it. They were very plucky. We squashed them down in the back of the car and got them through to Noyon. There would have been a fearful row if we had been found out. One old lady in the next house to the farm begged us to take her also, but it was quite impossible, and as she was old and plain we did not think it mattered so much leaving her.[29]

Lieutenant Duncan MacPherson Laurie, General Headquarters, BEF

The closing remark is more than a little unfortunate!

Meanwhile, the tightly packed columns marched on and on: collective bodies, but within which every individual was fighting a personal battle to counter the overwhelming fatigue that seemed likely to drag them down. Every so often a battery of guns, a troop of cavalrymen, or a batch of rattling general service wagons, would force them to stand aside to let them pass. Occasionally they would stop and begin to dig in – back-breaking work that was of course essential in case the Germans caught up, but all that hard graft was rendered frustratingly redundant the moment the orders passed down the line and the long march began again. Above them the August sun blazed down, while their own marching boots raised clouds of choking dust. Their packs pressing down on weary backs, they endured as best they could the ever-growing pain from their feet. Many of the reservists reported severe problems with their boots.

> We were all walking like drunken men. I said to 'Timber' Woods, 'Are your feet hurting?' He said, 'Yes, the nails are playing me hell!' I said, 'So are mine!' Then the bloke in front of me fell smack on his face. I went to step over him, but went sprawling on the grass, owing to his pack being too high to get my leg over. Up came Captain Cartwright shouting, 'I'll shoot the next man who falls out!' I was pretending to try to bring the man round, but really it was just an excuse to have a little rest. Cartwright said, 'And what are you supposed to be doing?' I said, 'Trying to bring him round, Sir, but he's unconscious, Sir!' 'Roll him out of the way, let the Germans look after him, we can't have the whole company stopped for one man!' And he rode off to the front again. I thought that sounds a bit callous, but when I come to think of it, it wouldn't be right to risk the lives of two to three men for the sake of one, so he must be right – I didn't like leaving him but I had to. The others were about half a mile in front of me and I couldn't catch up with them and the nails were sticking into my feet. Every mile or two I came across others that had dropped out, then I simply had to do something with my feet. I sat down and took my boots off and the one putty. My socks were all holes where the nails had torn them and my feet were bleeding so I bound the putties round them and threw the boots over the hedge, and when I started walking again it seemed lovely the only thing now was they would keep slipping off the toes, time after time I would keep pulling them up again but within a few yards they

would be off again so in the end I left them off it wasn't very nice but better than nails.[30]

Private Harry Rowthorn, 1st Northamptonshire Regiment, 2nd Brigade, 1st Division, I Corps

Such makeshift palliative measures could only ever be a temporary respite and at the next halt Rowthorn sought out the battalion medical officer.

He looked down at my feet and said, 'What happened to you then?' After I explained, he got half a bucket of water out of the river and put about half a teaspoon of Condes fluid in it and said, 'Put your feet in that while I go and see if I can get you some shoes!' He came back about quarter of an hour later with a pair of brown canvas gym slippers – size about '10'! He said that was the best he could do, I thanked him, but said, 'Sir, they are much too big!' He said, 'No they won't be, I've got them too big on purpose as you will have to have some bandages round them!' Then the doctor came back with a large roll of bandage and a half-inch layer of cotton wool, which he put under my toes which had been exposed and then brought this layer up the front of the toes and over the top as far as the ankle and told me to hold it in place while he bound it round the toes and up the ankle then slipped the foot inside the canvas slipper in which he had cut four small holes two in each side thus lacing it up like a shoe lace, and tied it as a lace. He wanted to know how it felt. I said very comfortable thank you. He said, 'There is just one thing, you must never take your slippers off, because if you do you will never get them on again because all the packing will fall off and I want you to give those toes a chance to heal up. Even if you get another pair of boots, carry them about with you, but don't put them on for at least a fortnight!'[31]

Private Harry Rowthorn, 1st Northamptonshire Regiment, 2nd Brigade, 1st Division, I Corps

Some men could not cope. Younger or older, or just constitutionally less strong, their comrades would try to help, but they eventually came to the end of their physical and mental reserves.

It was about here that Worthington fell out. He was a little fat Dublin fellow, stiff on the march and easily distressed with the heat. As his platoon sergeant I regarded him as a minor nuisance; a young soldier not yet broken in to the march. I remembered him staggering along.

Sometimes one of the lads took his rifle and the little fellow took hold of a comrade's shoulder, sometimes one on each side. As we passed through villages, the women raised their hands in pity at the sight of him, *'Ah! Le pauvre garcon! Le petite garcon!'* Two good women gave him a jug of beer while we jeered at him being petted and passed on. He must have been picked up by an ambulance.[32]

Sergeant John McIlwain, 2nd Connaught Rangers, 5th Brigade, 2nd Division, I Corps

In 1914, Private James Worthington was just a boy at fourteen years old and a mere 5 feet 4 inches tall. By the time McIlwain next saw him in Dover in 1918, Worthington had transmogrified into a great hulking full-grown man of some 6 feet 2 inches.

Feeding an army of tens of thousands is complicated, but feeding an army in the midst of such a chaotic retreat posed a serious challenge. Fortunately, in Quartermaster General Major General Sir William Robertson, the BEF had a truly competent staff officer, a man who had had a lifetime to thoroughly master his trade, and he was possessed of the capacity for lateral thinking to provide solutions to the most intractable of problems.

The distribution of supplies after they reached railheads was another difficulty, as the ever-changing situation and frequent interruption of communication made it impossible to know where particular units might be at any given time. I could only guess as to the place where they might be, send their food to it, and a further supply to other probable places, in the hope that if the first consignment did not reach them the second would. The expedient was also adopted of dumping supplies – flitches of bacon, sides of beef, cheese, boxes of biscuits – alongside the roads so that the troops might help themselves as they passed. Much of the food thus deposited had to be left where it was put, either because it was not found in the darkness, or from want of time to use it or of means to carry it away, but on the whole the object of ensuring that plenty of food should be obtainable when and where wanted was fairly well achieved. Compliance with routine regulations, and the extra expense incurred by issuing double or treble the normal allowance of rations, were not considerations to be taken into account.[33]

The rationale was that it was better to waste some supplies than for units to further degenerate through not getting their rations and adding hunger to exhaustion. It certainly came as a welcome surprise for the men of 6th Battery, RFA.

> A message was passed down verbally with orders to pass it on, 'Spies on the road ahead!' While wondering why, if that were so the people in front hadn't done something about it, everyone assumed an attitude of extreme alertness and perhaps I surreptitiously grasped my revolver. Shortly afterwards a blessed sight appeared. Lying by the side of the road and obviously left there for us by the Army Service Corps were cases of bully beef and biscuits. For 'Spies' read 'Supplies' and there you have it![34]
>
> Lieutenant Sidney Archibald, 6th Battery, 40th Brigade, RFA, 3rd Division

It may not have been the most tempting of foods, but for hungry men it was good enough.

> You got bully beef in seven-pound tins – we used to open our tins and get on with it. We ate on the march. You had to cut it open, dish it out as fair as you could, you couldn't expect a man to carry a seven-pound tin, particularly hot weather – it was jolly hard work. Well, that was the ration: bully beef, biscuits and water, no time for anything else![35]
>
> Sergeant Thomas Painting, 1st King's Royal Rifle Corps, 6th Brigade, 2nd Division, I Corps

As ever, some men attempted to take advantage of the situation. Captain Hubert Rees watched as one Welsh soldier greedily took on a load that his enfeebled body could not long endure.

> Our rations were dumped for us along the road and every man took anything that struck his fancy. It was rather amusing to see what the men selected. One man near me had seven tins of bully beef and not a single biscuit. He threw one tin away per mile on the average as he grew tired![36]
>
> Captain Herbert Rees, 2nd Welsh Regiment, 3rd Brigade, 1st Division, I Corps

There was also chance for that rare beast, the unprincipled quartermaster, to take advantage of the situation as Lieutenant Harry Yates of the 2nd Royal Welsh Fusiliers gleefully recorded. This gruff old regular had been a long-standing regimental quartermaster-sergeant and knew exactly how to gain best advantage.

We received orders to go to different dumps to get rations. I never took any notice of the orders, but as soon as I had delivered one lot to the battalion I filled up from the first dump I came to. The officer would say, 'Are you such-and-such a division?' Answer was always, 'Yes!' And away I went loaded![37]

Robertson's experiment was a success but there were still occasions when battalions went hungry. Inevitably, in such circumstances, the men would indulge in a little foraging, at times upsetting the local French population, who considered it rather more in the nature of looting and pillaging.

Regret to state that I came off very much second best in a thrilling encounter today. Acting on instructions, I popped over a garden wall where I had spotted a number of tame rabbits in a hutch. I was closely followed by my chum who was going to explain the method of killing them. After taking his advice I was in the act of proudly surveying my handiwork when suddenly the explosion occurred. The cottage door flew open and a regular torrent of abuse issued from the lips of a buxom French damsel. Luckily I could not understand French but she also conveyed her feelings by her frantic gesticulations. How were we to know the cottage was occupied? I only have a very dim recollection of the latter part of the interview, suffice to say we beat a hasty retreat leaving, as they say 'several dead on the field'. My chum appeared highly amused when I told him I thought the lady was annoyed.[38]

Signaller John Palmer, 118th Battery, 26th Brigade, RFA, 1st Division, I Corps

Less controversial was a degree of harmless scrumping from the bountiful fruit harvest in the orchards and gardens on every side as they marched through the French countryside.

The 1914 fruit season was a record one, and we had had, and we continued to have, many occasions to congratulate ourselves on the fact during the retreat. Our diet of bully and biscuits could almost always be varied by pears and apples, and the abundance of fruit helped to mitigate the terrible difficulties of maintaining the water supply. We were, however, careful to prevent any wholesale looting of orchards, and confined our attentions to the windfalls. Those inhabitants who had not fled were only too ready to offer us all they possessed, but it was bad enough for them to have to bear a German occupation, without our adding to their difficulties by taking away one of their few means of subsistence.[39]

Lieutenant Joseph Dent, 2nd South Staffordshire Regiment, 6th Brigade, 2nd Division, I Corps

Thirst was a particular problem as the arrangements for the normal water carts often fell through. The dust got everywhere, sticking to their parched and cracked lips. Sometimes the only drink available was beer, not something which troubled most of the men, but a problem for a tee-totaller such as Private Arthur Cook.

On our midday halts food was ready for us including barrels of French beer. Nothing was arranged for teetotallers like myself to drink. I stuck it out for several days in spite of the size of my thirst. I sat and watched the boys as they filled up their mess tins with beer and came back to drink it, all frothy, in front of me, pulling my leg. Today it was especially hot and my resistance weakened. When the order came to fall in with mess tins, I was in the queue like a shot and came back with my tin full and running over. I thought to myself, 'If I get intoxicated the boys will help me along!' Down it went, all honey-sweet and I smacked my lips. To my astonishment I felt no ill effects and could walk in a straight line. I shall be in the beer queue every day in future.[40]

Private Arthur Cook, 1st Somerset Light Infantry, 11th Brigade, 4th Division

The combination of lack of sleep, exhaustion from the endless marching, the burning heat of the sun, occasional hunger and frequent thirst, was enough to bring strong men to their knees. Soon it was not just the old, the young, the weak, or the badly led that were faltering: almost everyone was reduced to a shell of their former selves.

Men were observed staggering about on the roads – falling out apparently as they wished and rejoining – often with units not their own. Men threw away equipment and clothing. Men lost their caps and girls' sunhats became quite a fashionable article of wear. These were looted from houses and shops. Special instructions were afterwards issued condemning this eccentricity of the British soldier.[41]

Sergeant John McIlwain, 2nd Connaught Rangers, 5th Brigade, 2nd Division, I Corps

At times the officers had to rely on intimidation and threats to get the men moving again.

> When the whistle blew for, 'Fall in!' many of the men lay where they were, not in any mutinous spirit but just because they were physically incapable of getting up. My platoon was the rear platoon of the company, which was the rear company of the battalion. Parker and I went round actually kicking the men till they got up and threatening, with our revolvers drawn, to shoot any man who did not fall in at once. We were reeling about like drunken men ourselves, past hoping for any rest, but knowing we had to go on.[42]

Lieutenant Evelyn Needham, 1st Northamptonshire Regiment, 2nd Brigade, 1st Division, I Corps

Although exhausted himself, Brigadier Aylmer Hunter-Weston tried his best to inspire his tired men, keep up their morale and most of all keep them moving along at the best pace possible. In some cases his well-meaning efforts fell on stony ground.

> The Brigadier is a pest. For the past two days he has been riding up and down on the flanks of the Battalion shouting, 'Cover off, by the left, hold your heads up, swing your arms! Left, Right, Left, Right!' Everyone is grumbling and remarking, 'It's all right for you Hunter, you're on horseback, your feet are not sore, you have not averaged thirty-five miles per day for the last nine days in full pack and almost nothing to eat, if we had, we had no time to cook or eat it. If you cannot give us encouragement for Christ's sake don't bully us!'[43]

Private Edward Roe, 1st East Lancashire Regiment, 11th Brigade, 4th Division

The officers themselves were by no means immune from the deadening fatigue that sucked all the life from their limbs. This was the kind of tiredness that few – if any – would ever experience in their civilian lives.

> The average man is, I am sure, quite ignorant of the effect which extreme exhaustion has on the brain. As the weary hours drag by, it seems as if a deadness, a sort of paralysis, creeps up the limbs, upwards towards the head. The bones of the feet ache with a very positive pain.

It needs a concentration of mind that a stupefied brain can ill afford to give to force the knees to keep from doubling under the weight of the body. The hands feel as if they were swelling until the boiling blood would ooze from the finger-tips. The lungs seem too exhausted to expand; the neck too weary to support the heavy head. The shoulders ache under the galling weight of sword and haversack, and every inch of clammy skin on the body seems ten times as sensitive as it normally is. The nerves in the face and hands feel like swelled veins that itch so that they long to be torn by the nails. The tongue and eyes seem to expand to twice their usual size. Sound itself loses its sharp conciseness, and reaches the brain only as a blurred and indistinct impression.[44]

Second Lieutenant Arnold Gyde, 2nd South Staffordshire Regiment, 6th Brigade, 2nd Division, I Corps

The August sun was beating down, giving them little respite, as they plodded along. Even officers lucky enough to be mounted found they were utterly done.

At about 9am it began to get frightfully hot, the hottest day I have ever known. The heat was too dreadful for words. The C.O. came back and rode with us for a while. He looked at me and said, 'You haven't been getting enough sleep, my boy!' I said I wasn't feeling very grand and told him I had a little rheumatism. The heat was suffocating and at every halt I sort of rolled off my saddle and sat in the hedge or ditch feeling half-dead. It was about all I could do to climb up into the saddle again. How the men stuck it I don't know, but they were coming along quite well. I was continually sleeping in the saddle and expected to fall off sooner or later – but I couldn't get off and walk. The C.O. came along again now and asked me if I was better. I said I should be all right with a little rest. He said, 'You must not do anything when we get in, I'll get you a bed and get a Medical Officer to give you a sleeping draught!' I said I thought I could sleep all right if I was given the chance![45]

Lieutenant Thomas Wollocombe, 4th Middlesex Regiment, 8th Brigade, 3rd Division, II Corps

The colonels and senior majors were older men and sometimes, despite their very best efforts, they could stand no more. Lieutenant William Synge of the 1st King's Liverpool Regiment watched the sad physical disintegration of his proud company commander, reduced to pale insubstantial shadow of his former self.

> I eventually found him walking up and down, his hands in his greatcoat pockets. His eyes were half-open and he was keeping up a continuous muttering to himself. And yet he was asleep. He took no notice of me, even when I pinched and kicked him, and eventually I took him by the arm and led him before the Colonel. I stood him up in front of him and saluted, whereupon he collapsed on the ground and snored at the Colonel's feet. We put him on the mess cart where he lay like a log until the evening, when, at about 6pm, he woke up as fit as anything.[46]

One man who was lasting the course was Smith-Dorrien. Although he was fifty-six years old, he was surprisingly resilient under circumstances of great personal stress.

> Six days fighting and marching without a moment's rest. I don't suppose I have managed two hours sleep a day, but I am gloriously fit and well – and in splendid spirits.[47]

Young and old, back, back they went, across the Somme, the Aisne and towards the Marne.

On 30 August, as the British fell back across the Aisne, Lieutenant Roger Rolleston West of the Intelligence Corps discovered to his considerable alarm that the bridge over the Oise at Pontoise was still intact, leaving the way open for the fast-approaching German cavalry.

> It was a suspension bridge and the charge intended to cut the strap had failed, while a fire lit in the roadway to burn it down had gone out without damage. It seemed a pity to leave this bridge intact when all others were down.[48]
> Lieutenant Roger Rolleston West, Intelligence Corps

West dashed off to make a report and to try to secure help to get the bridge blown up. About eight miles further back he reported the situation to Major Walker of 59th Field Company, Royal Engineers.

> I thought it might just be possible for me to get there before the Germans did. But I would need a supply of gun cotton, primers, fuses

and detonators. He gave immediate orders for this. Then I told him that with my rusty knowledge of demolitions I would much like to have an expert engineer along with me if he could spare one. He hesitated evidently thinking that this would probably be suicide, so did not give an order, but called for a volunteer, from among the group of officers, Lieutenant J. A. C. Pennycuick stepped forward, and said he would go with me on the carrier of my motorcycle. So we heaved my baggage hurriedly onto a waggon and strapped on a 14-pound tin of gun cotton, fuses and primers to the back. Pennycuick put the detonators carefully in his breast pocket, lest they go off with the jolting. We were riding I thought straight into the German army, and the hints of our impending suicide did not add to my peace of mind. Afterwards I think far the most dangerous part of the trip was the ride, as we were in a hurry, and the roads were full of troops, guns limbers and horses. I could fully sympathise with Pennycuick as I know of nothing more terrifying than sitting on the back of a motorcycle, behind an unknown rider at desperate speed through traffic. I felt his hands grip on my shoulders in anguish at some of the narrower escapes, but with a pocketful of temperamental detonators he could only sit still and take it![49]

After a journey of some eight miles, at last West and Pennycuick got to Pontoise.

Some of the inhabitants were now up and about, as it was, I suppose, 6.30 or 7am. 'Est-ce-qu'il-y-a-des Allemands dans la ville!' We asked, 'Non, pas encore, mon Capitaine!' We unpacked the gun cotton and primers and pointed the machine for 'home' before walking out to the bridge. It was all quite still, and there may not have been any Germans for miles, but it would not do to waste time. After examination we decided to blow up one of the suspension pillars, as we had not enough gun cotton to smash both, and a second attempt to break the strap might meet with no more success than the first. I swarmed up to the top of the pillar and Pennycuick threw up the gun cotton slabs. By the merest luck the slab fitted tightly without tamping between the steel blocks, over which the straps passed. When they had been fixed Pennycuick scrambled up with the detonators and fuse and cast an experienced eye over my efforts. Having fixed the fuse and detonator he climbed down again. Lighting it up I slid down after him and we ran for a neighbouring house where we waited for it to go off. After a bit there was a feeble bang. The primer must have been wet or something.[50]

Cursing vigorously, the two officers ran back to the bridge and fixed another detonator and fuse. West realised they were running out of time.

> There was a sudden burst of rifle fire somewhere behind the river, where some stragglers or ours had probably butted into an advancing German patrol, but it may have been a long way away on such a still morning. However there was not much time to waste, and anyway the fuse was now fizzling again at the top of the pillar and Pennycuick was sliding down to get away. At this moment an aged paralytic old dame arrived at the head of the bridge. She had heard the 'Pop!' and thought it was all over, so had come out to see what the bridge looked like broken. Her fastest sprint would I daresay, only have reached two miles an hour, so there was nothing for it but to push her into the toll house beside the bridge and run. With unerring instinct we were lucky enough to enter an estaminet and got a couple of ciders. We were just drinking to the success of the demolition, when a tremendous crash announced that this time it had gone off. We ran out and found the straps had thrown clear of the pillar, and the whole roadway slid sideways into the river, forty feet below. One of the steel straps had whipped back in breaking and gone straight through the roof of the toll house. I do not know what happened to the old dame.[51]

Well pleased with their morning's work they dashed back to their motor-cycle and sped into the distance. When later they reported their success to their general, he laughed and said, 'Now that's a funny thing, that was the very bridge we wanted to use for our advance!'[52] Truly, the task of bridge demolition was fraught with hazard. But their work was appreciated, for both officers were subsequently awarded the DSO, a rare thing for men of such junior rank. Sadly, as at Mons, many of the other bridges over the Oise were not destroyed.

There was generally very little to celebrate, but on 1st September, two small skirmishes gave some heart to the retreating British. At Villers-Cotteret a vigorous – and competent – rearguard action by the 1st Guards Brigade successfully covered the withdrawal of the 2nd Division. This was encouraging enough, but the sheer drama of the action at Néry on that morning seemed to raise spirits all round. The 1st Cavalry Brigade (the 2nd Dragoon Guards, the 5th Dragoon Guards, the 11th Hussars and the associated 'L' Battery, RHA) had been billeted overnight in the valley in which nestled the small village of Néry, when they had, metaphorically at least, a rude awakening on the arrival of the German 4th Cavalry Division, which had decided to push on through the night to Néry, even in darkness and the prevailing foggy conditions. Having made a silent covert approach, the Germans deployed three batteries of guns on the hills east and southeast of Néry.

> We had earlier on orders to saddle-up but because of the mist we couldn't move, so we were dismissed had breakfast and watered the horses. Suddenly we heard the sound of an explosion and then a barrage of shells. I am sure it was about five o'clock in the morning. We rushed to see what was happening and found that shells had burst amongst our horses. They belonged to 'C' Squadron. A lot of them were terribly injured and killed and many of them had stampeded off with fright. There were men hanging on to them but they couldn't stop the horses bolting. We had no idea what was really happening, just that we had been shelled.[53]
>
> Trooper William Clarke, 2nd Dragoon Guards, 1st Cavalry Brigade, 1st Cavalry Division

As Clarke and his fellows attempted to control their horses, it was apparent that they had been totally surprised. The German cavalry were treated to scenes of total chaos.

> Suddenly, our artillery and machine guns began to pour fire at very close range at two British bivouacs, which they destroyed. It was as though we had poked a stick in a hornets' nest. There we were, right in the middle of the enemy army which was carrying out its morning toilet.[54]
>
> Leutnant von Zitzewitz, 2nd Kürassier Regiment, 3rd Cavalry Brigade, 4th Cavalry Division

The men of 'L' Battery were equally shocked by the burst of German fire lashing all around them.

> Got up at 4am with orders to be ready by 5am to move at a quarter hour's notice, we had the teams all hooked to their carriages, poles down and everyone dismounted on our bivouac. I was trotting a

horse down the road for lameness and was examining his hind fetlock, when suddenly a terrific burst of shrapnel and rifle and machine gun fire was opened onto us at a range of 600 to 800 yards. No one had the slightest idea of there being any Germans in the vicinity, and I am not sure if it was the fault of our own cavalry or the French outposts. The horse was killed at the first burst and I and Sergeant Weedon dropped onto the road and crawled along to one side of the camp and got up close to it under cover of some stacks. We found Bradbury, John Campbell and Mundy and about a dozen men there or so, we rushed out and got two guns into action, myself on one with half-a-dozen men and Brad[bury], John, Mundy, the Sergeant Major and Sergeant Nelson on the other.[55]

Lieutenant Jack Giffard, 'L' Battery, 7th Brigade, RHA, 1st Cavalry Brigade, 1st Cavalry Division

With three of the 13-pounder guns manhandled into action, 'L' Battery began to return fire as best they could. The gun under the command of Lieutenant Campbell was knocked out almost immediately by a direct hit. Then it was Jack Giffard's turn.

I had only fired a few rounds when the whole of my crew were wiped out, so I went on till I'd finished the ammunition and then got hit through the left leg above the knee by a splinter and peppered on the right arm and back and grazed along the hip bone by a whole shell or a very large fragment. Then a shell pitched on the gun wheel and smashed it, something getting me on the top of my head, as I could do no good there, I crawled back to stack where some of our wounded were sheltering, they were terribly knocked about most of them. A few minutes later a shrapnel swept along our side of the stack, a fragment going clean through my right leg, missing the main artery by an eighth of an inch and I think missing the bone. Two or three more pieces pierced the leg as well, several fellows were killed by it and horribly wounded.[56]

For a while the third gun, commanded by Lieutenant Edward Bradbury, continued the unequal battle with the three German batteries. Bradbury lost a leg as shells dropped all around, but continued directing his gun detachment until he died.[57] Battery Sergeant Major George Dorrell then took over command as he and Sergeant David Nelson, although both wounded, continued to serve the gun until they ran out of ammunition. The cavalry themselves had not been inactive.

> Then troopers improvised a firing line. Lieutenant Lamb, the machine gun officer got some of his men together and got a couple of guns going along the sunken road, helping the other gunners with their guns. I think another enemy battery started firing on the village then and the 5th Dragoons engaged them. I was one of a small party of about fifteen men who were ordered forward to try to stop a German advance towards the sugar factory. The Germans had occupied some buildings alongside it. Lieutenants de Crespigny and Misa, and a Sergeant Major led the attack. We managed to stem the Germans advancing for a time, but due to casualties we had to withdraw.[58]
>
> Trooper William Clarke, 2nd Dragoon Guards, 1st Cavalry Brigade, Cavalry Division

Meanwhile reinforcements began to arrive, in the form of the 4th Cavalry Brigade, the 'I' Battey, RHA and the 1st Middlesex Regiment. Gradually the situation began to turn against the Germans, who found themselves remote from any support.

> The Germans were machine gunning us from the sugar factory and I remember that the Germans were finally shelled out of the factory and outbuildings by 'I' Battery of the Royal Horse Artillery. Our casualties were heavy, Lieutenant de Crespigny[59] was killed, and so were two or three other men and the rest were wounded. Lieutenant Misa, myself and one other man were the only ones to come back unwounded. I was incredibly lucky. Everything seemed to happen so quickly, events were out of our control. I know that I felt frightened and excited at the same time. We were a very highly-trained and efficient Regiment and we did as we were trained to do, responding quickly to a situation without question. And if you wanted to live you had to kill in order to do so.[60]
>
> Trooper William Clarke, 2nd Dragoon Guards 1st Cavalry Brigade, Cavalry Division

Surprised or not, the British had fought back hard, and eventually the Germans were forced to withdraw.

The battle flared up, quickly increasing to extreme intensity. 4th Squadron provided our artillery with protection and took up positions just behind our batteries. Now the enemy artillery opened fire; the exploding shells showering us with sand, earth and stones. There was activity behind every hedge and corn stack. It was a favourite trick of our opponents to lurk in cover and open fire from the rear. The artillery lost many horses and seven guns. We dismounted and fought on foot, deploying in a skirmish line against enemy infantry. Masses of shells and small arms fire whistled past. Suddenly shells landed amongst our lead horses. The horses reared up and the few handlers were powerless to stop them. Then a strong patrol raced by, spreading alarm and total confusion amongst the horses. They bolted, throwing their riders, and set off at a mad gallop. After some time the division disengaged from the enemy and pulled back.[61]

Kürassier Soltzien, 2nd Kürassier Regiment, 3 Cavalry Brigade, 4th Cavalry Division

The heroism of the men of 'L' Battery struck a chord and Battery Sergeant Major George Dorrell and Sergeant David Nelson were both subsequently awarded the VC, which Lieutenant Edward Bradbury was also granted posthumously. In all, the battery suffered fifty-five casualties.

Over the next five days the BEF continued to retreat, falling back well beyond the Marne. Covered now to some extent by the French on either flank, they were little troubled by the Germans. But exhaustion was ever present. By the time the retreat came to an end on 5 September they had marched up to 200 miles in distance on the ground, or 136 miles as a crow flies. Against the odds they had survived, but were they still a coherent fighting force? Even amidst the chaos of the retreat, there were inklings of the answer. For the process of forming a III Corps had begun with the arrival of the designated commander Major General William Pulteney on 31 August. Born in 1861, Pulteney was an officer in the Scots Guards and had active service experience in both Egypt and South Africa before promotion took him to the command of the 6th Division in 1910. Pulteney was a contemporary of Haig, Grierson and Smith-Dorrien, but he lacked their cerebral qualities, apparently uninterested in military theory and missing their high-level experience as staff officers. The theoretical establishment of his III Corps included the 4th Division, which had already been much involved in the fighting, and the imminently expected 6th Division. However the exigencies of service meant that for a while III Corps would act as little more than a pool of reserves for I and II Corps. The BEF was starting to show a capacity for growth. The more pressing question was: could it start to fight as more than a sum of its parts?

8

BATTLE OF THE MARNE

He begged Sir John to cooperate with all his might. He said, 'The lives of all French people, the soil of France and the future of Europe depended on the coming battle.'[1]

Brigadier General Sir Henry Wilson, General Headquarters, BEF

THE EPIC TALE OF THE Battle of the Marne is one best recounted in French. It was General Joseph Joffre who settled on the plan for the battle, French generals who led the way and French troops who did most of the fighting. For admirers of the BEF, there are many embarrassments to be overcome before they can relish its relatively minor role in one of the great battles of the twentieth century, one that truly changed the fate of the world. It is difficult not to find the surname of the British Commander in Chief, Sir John French, somewhat ironic, for before the battle began he had never been more British, never more limited, in the scope of his mental horizons. Out of his depth, he sought only a shelter from the storm that raged around the BEF. Twisting and turning, he tried to evade any commitment to serious fighting in a manner that brought to mind the old slurs of 'Perfidious Albion'. Mercurial as ever, French was assailed by deep pessimism, and on 31 August he made his doubts clear to Lord Kitchener back in London.

> General Joffre appeared to me to be anxious that I should keep the position which I am now occupying north of the line Compiegne – Soissons. I have let him know plainly that in the present condition of

my troops I shall be absolutely unable to remain in the front line, as he has now begun his retirement. I have decided to begin my retirement tomorrow in the morning behind the Seine, in a south-westerly direction west of Paris. This means marching for some eight days without fatiguing the troops at a considerable distance from the enemy. It will be possible for us to commence our reorganization on the road. My base is now in the neighbourhood of La Rochelle, and I am now forming an advanced base at Le Mans. All that we need to refit and to make good our deficiencies can be sent; from this latter place up to meet us at points behind the Seine which I select, and which will be quite safe under the outlying forts of Paris.[2]

Kitchener was appalled: he could clearly see 'the bigger picture' and his telegram in reply was fairly unambiguous.

I am surprised at your decision to retire behind the Seine. Please let me know if you can all your reasons for this move. What will be the effect of this course upon your relations with the French Army and on the general military situation. Will your retirement leave a gap in the French line or cause them discouragement, of which the Germans might take advantage to carry out their first programme of first crushing the French and then being free to attack Russia?[3]

The reply by Sir John French was petulant, more redolent perhaps of the playground than the battlefield.

If the French go on with their present tactics, which are practically to fall back right and left of me, usually without notice, and to abandon all idea of offensive operations, of course, then, the gap in the French line will remain and the consequences must be borne by them. I can only state that it would be difficult for the force under my command to withstand successfully in its present condition a strong attack from even one German army corps, and in the event of a pause in my retirement I must expect two army corps at least if not three.[4]

To this he added in a further telegram in which he dismissed Joffre's plans for an offensive in scathing terms: 'I have no definite idea of General Joffre's general plan; its general result is the advance of the Germans and the retreat of the Allies.'[5] The impact of such messages was predictable. Kitchener hastened over for a face-to-face meeting with French at the

British Embassy in Paris. The meeting must have been a tempestuous affair. Kitchener arrived in uniform, adopting rather more the manner of a commander in chief than the demeanour of a civilian politician. Although Kitchener was within his rights as a field marshal to do so, the uniform raised French's hackles and a vigorous discussion followed.

> Lord Kitchener appeared to take grave exception to certain views which I expressed as to the expediency of leaving the direction of the operations in the field in the hands of the military chiefs in command in the field. He abruptly closed the discussion and requested me to accompany him for a private interview in another room.[6]

What followed would be characterised in modern military parlance as 'an interview without coffee'. French left a blustering account in his memoirs claiming to have reached an 'amicable understanding'[7] implying Kitchener had accepted his reasoning. This is clearly nonsense – the evidence shows that it was French that had buckled under, as demonstrated in Kitchener's curt telegram back to the government that very evening.

> French's troops are now engaged in the fighting line, where he will remain conforming to the movements of the French army, though at the same time acting with caution to avoid being in any way unsupported on his flanks.[8]

This was followed up by French's meek acquiescence on 3 September: 'I fully understand your instructions. I am in full accord with Joffre and the French.'[9]

The problems facing General Alexander von Kluck were of a different nature. He was approaching the denouement of the campaign, but he had concerns as to whether they were asking too much of the men.

> The requirements of the strategic situation made it impossible to give any rest days in the true sense of the word. Marches and fights, battles and marches, followed one another without interval.[10]

There was also an awareness that Moltke had already removed two corps from the strength of the wheeling right wing formed of the German First, Second and Third Armies in their advance. In his memoirs, von Kluck claimed to recognise that, instead of weakening the right wing,

Moltke should have been strengthening it, by bringing in troops from the Alsace-Lorraine front.

> The necessary force should have been taken away from the opposite flank of the armies, which was wheeling up against the line of fortresses in Lorraine, a movement which might well have been discontinued. For the situation in the West was only just reaching its full development, and in order to be prepared for it the transference of several divisions, with, if possible, heavy batteries, from the left wing of the German Armies would have been welcomed, in order to form an echelon behind the right wing.[11]

Against this background his mood was still generally optimistic. Although the German Supreme Command had originally intended the right wing to swing round Paris, they had approved the move south by the Second Army in pursuit of the French Fifth Army and the move southeast in front of Paris by the First Army. In essence there were simply too few German troops to allow them to sweep round Paris without leaving enormous gaps between the armies.

> It was therefore decided to move the two corps on the left wing, the III and IX, in the general direction of Chateau Thierry against the flank of the French retreating from Braisne-Fismes on Chateau Thierry-Dormans in front of the Second Army. In co-operation with the Second Army it might be possible to damage the French western flank very considerably. The First Army by its deep formation was in a position both to cover the flank and rear of such an attack and also to hold in check the garrison of Paris and the British.[12]
>
> General Alexander von Kluck, Headquarters, First Army

Then, on the night of 2 September, the German Supreme Headquarters issued wireless orders that formally changed the direction of the wheeling armies: 'The French will be forced away from Paris in a southeasterly direction. The First Army will follow in echelon behind the Second Army, and will be responsible henceforward for the flank protection of the force.'[13] However, the Supreme Command order left von Kluck in a real quandary: his First Army was actually already a day's march ahead of von Bülow's Second Army, which had been held back by the earlier clash with the French Fifth Army at the Battle of Guise. Thus the First Army was in by far the best position to push the Fifth Army to the southeastwards, and von Kluck could hardly stand still for two days without losing the initiative. But at the same time the orders left him responsible for guarding the right flank as they swept past Paris.

> It fell to the First Army to apply the principal pressure in forcing back the enemy, as it was the only force that was immediately on his heels and that could exert the necessary compulsion on his line of retreat. On the other hand, if it halted for two days so as to get in echelon behind the Second Army, the enemy's Higher Command would regain the complete freedom of action of which it had been deprived. Should the First Army hold back, the great success for which the Supreme Command was confidently striving by 'forcing the enemy in a south-easterly direction' could no longer be hoped for. It was therefore fully in keeping with the spirit of the often-mentioned wireless order for the First Army to continue the pursuit as before across the Marne. The protection of the flank of the armies on the Paris side appeared to be provided for if the IV Reserve Corps with a cavalry division and the brigade expected from Brussels, together with the II Corps, halted echeloned towards the fortress capital, and if a thorough cavalry and air reconnaissance was insisted on.[14]

In other words, von Kluck's response was to try to square the circle. The end result was that only IV Reserve Corps stood to guard their exposed right flank, with the possible assistance of II Corps, as the main force of IX, III and IV Corps were all committed to thrusting ever further to the southeast in an attempt to finish off the Fifth Army.

THE SCENE WAS SET FOR JOFFRE to spring his trap on the Marne, and the Germans seemed to be walking straight into it. By now the hastily assembled Sixth Army was in place, lurking and ready to strike at the right flank of von Kluck's First Army as it wheeled round to pass to the east of Paris. Meanwhile the BEF continued to retreat faster than the French Fifth or Sixth Armies on either flanks and were under little threat. Joffre now diverted much energy to ensure the participation of the BEF in the imminent offensive, and in the end decided to make a personal visit to French at the Vaux le Pénil Chateau at Melun. Sir John French left a short description of the meeting.

Later in the day Joffre came to Melun, and I had a long conference with him. We again went over all plans, and it was definitely arranged that the attack was to commence all along the line next day, the 6th. Joffre was full of enthusiasm, and very hopeful of success if we all fulfilled our respective *roles* and attacked *au fond*. Thus ended the Great Retreat.[15]

This seems straightforward enough, reflecting a meeting between two near equals, both committed to putting their shoulder to the wheel. But there are other accounts of that meeting that prove omission can be a useful art in memoir writing.

Without any preamble at all General Joffre unfolded this plan for the Battle of the Marne. It was extraordinarily impressive, very clear – he outlined the movement of the troops, the army corps that had come from Alsace-Lorraine in the east, grouping in Paris for the thrust into the German flank. The certainty that the Germans have changed their line of advance, making the mistake which enabled Joffre to plan his thrust. It was a very strange thing to see a single man exercising his will on a mass of about a million men with the fate of his country in the balance; having to face a catastrophic situation and never, never getting rattled. There was this man, with his muted voice, talking very slowly, never raising his voice once. As we listened, we saw the manoeuvre unfolding, saw into the future, saw what was going to happen next day. Then Joffre turned to the fact of the essential role the British Army must play in this offensive: without them the manoeuvre was impossible! They faced the gap in the German line which if it wasn't filled by us would mean that the whole manoeuvre would simply fail altogether.[16]

Lieutenant Edward Spears, Headquarters, Fifth Army

But Joffre's own account is the most remarkable. This phlegmatic man had to conjure up raw emotion and all his powers of persuasion to persuade his recalcitrant allies.

I put my whole soul into the effort to convince the Field Marshal. I told him that the decisive moment had arrived and that we must not let it escape – we must go to battle with every man both of us had and free from all reservations. 'So far as regards the French Army,' I continued, 'my orders are given, and, whatever may happen, I intend to throw my last company into the balance to win a victory and save France. It is in her name that I come to you to ask for British assistance, and I urge it with all the power I have in me. I cannot believe that the British Army will refuse to do its share in this supreme crisis – history would severely judge your absence.' Then, as I finished, carried away by my convictions and the gravity of the moment, I remember bringing down my fist on a table which stood at my elbow, and crying, 'Monsieur le Marshal, the honour of England is at stake!' Up to this point French had listened imperturbably to the officer who was translating what I said, but now his face suddenly reddened. There ensued a short impressive silence; then, with visible emotion he murmured, 'I will do all I possibly can!' Not understanding English, I asked Wilson what Sir John had said. He merely replied, 'The Field Marshal says, 'Yes!'' I had distinctly felt the emotion which seemed to grip the British Commander in Chief; above all, I had remarked the tone of his voice, and I felt, as did all the witnesses to the scene, that these, simple words were equivalent to an agreement signed and sworn to. Tea, which was already prepared, was then served.[17]

The reference to the serving of tea surely convinces that the truth lies in the Joffre version of events. Whatever the truth of the matter, there is no doubt that the protagonists were finally agreed and the Battle of the Marne would indeed begin on 6 September 1914. Joffre summed up the importance of the battle in an inspirational, but chilling order of the day.

We are about to engage in a battle on which the fate of our country depends and it is important to remind all ranks that the moment has passed for looking to the rear; all our efforts must be directed to attacking and driving back the enemy. Troops that can advance no further must, at any price, hold on to the ground they have conquered and die on the spot rather than give way. Under the circumstances which face us, no act of weakness can be tolerated.[18]

Joffre had triumphed and the BEF would join the French armies in the great offensive.

So it was that French issued his orders that marked the end of the Great Retreat at 17.15 on 5 September.

The enemy has apparently abandoned the idea of advancing on Paris and is contracting his front and moving south-eastward. The Army will advance eastward with a view to attacking. Its left will be covered by the Sixth French Army also marching east, and its right will be linked to the Fifth French Army marching north.[19]

Haig was eating his breakfast in an orchard at the village of Maries when a staff officer, Major Dawnay, arrived with orders to advance on 6 September. He was delighted.

> No words could have been more welcome to the troops. For thirteen days, broken only by a short rest at St Gobain, the I Corps had retreated without a check and had fought a continuous series of rearguard actions, some of them serious. The total distance covered was not less than 160 miles, and there was not a man in the force who had not covered considerably more than this distance. The total losses in action throughout this period were 81 officers and 2,180 non-commissioned officers and men. These figures, however, give no idea of the demands which were made upon the force under my command. The actual fighting was the least of our difficulties.[20]

Brigadier General Hubert Gough was less impressed, even though his command had been expanded by the addition of the 5th Cavalry Brigade to his 3rd Cavalry Brigade. Gough was assigned a covering role during the advance and furthermore required to maintain contact with the French Sixth Army as it hammered into von Kluck's exposed flank. Gough pointed to a continued lack of urgency, clarity, or detail in the orders received from GHQ.

> Why were we not warned? Joffre's instructions for the counter-offensive were issued to his Army Commanders at 10pm on 4th September: this attack was to take place on the 6th and Sir John French had agreed to conform. Yet no attempt was made by GHQ to explain to the corps and divisional commanders the extraordinary opportunity now available for a decisive blow at the enemy. The GHQ operation order issued on the evening of 5th September merely stated in a matter-of-fact way that the enemy was, 'Contracting his front and moving south-eastward. The Army will advance eastward with a view to attacking.' These words failed to convey an adequate view of the position, and gave no inkling of the fact that the situation had changed from an apparently hopeless retreat to a vigorous offensive, offering every opportunity of turning it into a great victory. We, the advanced troops, were left in complete ignorance of these very important decisions, and had

to gather them as best we could from the information of our patrols and the observations of our own eyes. Valuable time was necessarily lost while we were ascertaining the situation. With how much more decision, rapidity and advantage could we have acted had we been kept informed of the change in plans.[21]

But the real importance lay not in the BEF staff work, but in the orders issued by Joffre and the French headquarters. What really mattered was the BEF participation as a small cog in the 'wheel' of the stupendous co-ordinated advance of the French Sixth, Fifth, Ninth and Fourth Armies, all pivoting round the hinge of the Third Army around the Verdun fortress, while the Second and First Armies continued to hold fast in the south.

On 4 September, the Germans had become belatedly aware of the looming threat from the French Sixth Army lurking around Paris, and orders were issued to try to get the First and Second Armies to turn and face Paris. This was almost impossible to achieve, and von Kluck still considered that he would be best served pushing the French Fifth Army back behind the Seine, before turning to face Paris. A bitingly sarcastic message sent by von Kluck to the German Supreme Headquarters demonstrated his continuing frustration at the lack of briefings as to the real progress made in the fighting elsewhere along the front.

> The First Army requests to be informed of the situation of the other armies, whose reports of decisive victories have so far been frequently followed by appeals for support. The First Army, which has been fighting and marching incessantly, has reached the limits of its endurance. It is through its efforts alone that the crossings of the Marne have been opened for the other armies, and that the enemy has been compelled to continue his retreat.[22]

By the time the message from Supreme Command was received at First Army Headquarters on the morning of 5 September it was already too late. The German II, IX, III and IV Corps were all well south of the Marne, approaching the Grand Morin River. That evening a staff officer despatched from Supreme Command, Lieutenant Colonel Richard Hentsch, arrived to brief von Kluck.

> To the amazement of First Army Headquarters, who believed all the Armies to be advancing victoriously, it appeared that the left wing of

the German Armies namely, the Fifth, Sixth, and Seventh Armies was held up in front of the French eastern fortresses, so much so that it could scarcely pin the enemy in front of it to his ground. There was consequently a possibility that the enemy would move troops by rail from his eastern wing towards Paris.[23]

New orders to fall back to meet the threat could not be disseminated until 6 September. The stage was set for one of the most significant battles of the twentieth century.

General Michel-Joseph Maunoury and his Sixth Army had actually begun the first steps of the offensive on 5 September, driving into the inadequately guarded German right flank on the line of the Ourcq River between Senlis and Reims. Soon they were threatening to overwhelm the IV Reserve Corps and then began gradually sucking in the other corps of von Kluck's First Army. Even as von Kluck's units performed a backwards wheel to turn back to the north to face the threat of the Sixth Army, so the gap between the German First and Second Armies lay wide open behind them. It was into this inviting opening that the BEF and the Fifth Army poured.

The British advance was covered by Allenby's Cavalry Division and Gough's two cavalry brigades. Sure enough they found that the German First Army was already dropping back, intent on facing Maunoury's thrust. Joffre had set the scene for the 'Miracle of the Marne', not by divine intervention but by keeping his calm, adopting a feasible plan and managing to exert a firm 'grip' on his field commanders – even Sir John French. In the end the battle would see something like forty-nine Allied divisions and eight cavalry divisions take the field against forty-six German divisions and seven cavalry divisions. This was a huge battle – yet tactics is not just about bludgeoning exchanges; sometimes there is room for finesse. There will always be many who claim credit for any success, and few authors of failure, but there is no doubt that in defeat Joffre would have been pilloried.

One thing evident to Haig was the critical importance of the speed of the BEF advance, and he too was soon chafing at the unnecessary delays in issuing orders from GHQ, as demonstrated again on 7 September.

At 6.45am (no orders having been received from GHQ) I ordered divisions to advance to the line Maupertuis-Dagny, with advanced

guards beyond. Operation orders were not actually issued from GHQ till 8am on the 7th and reached me at 9am. I thought our movements very slow today, in view of the fact that the enemy was on the run.
I motored and saw both Lomax and Monro and impressed on them the necessity for quick and immediate action.[24]

Haig was right to be pushing his troops forward, but the continuing dissatisfaction with the performance of French and GHQ was self-evident. Delays multiplied as they passed down the command chain and the result was that most of the morning was wasted. Inefficiency of staff functions aside, Haig has himself been blamed for adopting a cautious approach at some phases of the advance over the next week. But it should be remembered that this was not the pell-mell pursuit of a beaten enemy. The Germans were still under discipline, still fighting rearguard actions and far too dangerous to treat lightly. A degree of caution by both Haig and Smith-Dorrien was not unnatural, especially after their tortuous experiences over the last month. It was the unnecessary extra delays that chafed.

On 8 September, the BEF faced the obstacle of two tributaries of the Marne flowing across their path. The Grand Morin was crossed without trouble, but there were some stiff skirmishes with the German rearguard forces along the Petit Morin. Then it was on to the Marne itself.

The Germans had fled, leaving the bridge at Charly for some unknown reason intact. It was evidently the original intention of the enemy to dispute the crossing, for the houses wore loop-holed, and there were barricades in the street. German writing was chalked on the houses where the enemy had billeted, and we saw many evidences of the hurried nature of their retirement. The doors of houses were open, and inside was chaos: chairs overturned, tables crowded with empty bottles and unfinished food, and mattresses and straw dragged out on to the ground floors to provide sleeping accommodation. Charly and the villages on the road presented a pitiable sight: houses were burnt, and looted, and their contents scattered everywhere.[25]

Lieutenant Joseph Dent, 2nd South Staffordshire Regiment, 6th Brigade, 2nd Division, I Corps

The tide seemed to have turned. But were the Germans beaten or was this a temporary reverse?

Within a couple of days it seemed evident to many of the German commanders that the situation was still spiralling out of control. On the night of 8 September, von Bülow was clearly depressed by reports from his air observers that reported columns of marching men pressing into the void between the First and Second Armies.

> In these circumstances the probability of a break-through of strong enemy forces between the First and Second Armies had to be reckoned with, unless the First Army decided to retire in an easterly direction and regain touch with the Second Army.[26]

As von Kluck was actually still engaged in turning to the west to face Maunoury's Sixth Army, the situation simply got worse, and to the exhausted von Bülow it seemed that nothing less than a full-scale retreat could rescue the situation.

> When early on the 9th September numerous enemy columns crossed the Marne between La Ferte sous Jouarre and Chateau Thierry, there remained no doubt that the retreat of the First Army was, for both tactical and strategical reasons, unavoidable, and that the Second Army must also go back, in order not to have its right flank completely enveloped.[27]

Around midday on 9 September, Lieutenant Colonel Richard Hentsch once again arrived at First Army headquarters, seemingly having been verbally instructed by von Moltke to try to coordinate the retreat of the First and Second Armies if either should be forced to fall back. Be that as it may, Hentsch's words were carefully recorded for posterity by the First Army headquarters staff.

> The situation is not favourable. The Fifth Army is held up in front of Verdun and the Sixth and Seventh in front of Nancy-Epinal. The retreat of the Second Army behind the Marne is unalterable: its right wing, the VII Corps, is being forced back and not voluntarily retiring. In consequence of these facts, all the Armies are to be moved back: the Third Army to north-east of Chalons, and the Fourth and Fifth Army,

in conjunction, through the neighbourhood of Clermont-en-Argonne towards Verdun. The First Army must therefore also retire.[28]

So the die was cast: within a few hours von Kluck had issued the orders for the retreat to the Aisne River. The memoirs of the time reveal the tensions between all the German commanders: proud of the achievements of their men, unwilling to accept responsibility for failure, and desirous of blaming someone else. All of this was entirely natural. In the final analysis they had been collectively out-manoeuvred by Joffre. In trying to counter the attack from Maunoury's Sixth Army, they had merely exposed themselves to great danger from the BEF and the Fifth Army. In the end there was no option; they had to retreat.

Once the retreat proper began, the Germans employed a light cavalry screen to try to hold up the BEF, performing the same function that the British cavalry had during their own retreat over the previous month. Amongst the German cavalry was Rittmeister von der Horst of the 15th (Hanover) Hussar Regiment.

> When we heard that the British had crossed the Marne, we had to pull back in order to avoid being cut off. This was a real shame, because I had just decided to feed and water the horses and to have some rations cooked. Everyone was extremely hungry and completely done up. During the afternoon we were in action together with the jägers, but we broke it off towards dusk when we heard that more British had got across. Later it emerged that Second Army had withdrawn in the face of superior enemy forces, so First Army had to do the same so as to conform. There followed a truly awful night march: tired out, nothing to eat, the roads jam packed with troops. It was sad to see how tired and worn out the men were. Finally we could get no further, so we lay down in the road for about two hours. About 4.00 am we arrived in St Gengoulph, fifteen kilometres northwest of Chateau Thierry, where we bivouacked. The troopers just threw themselves down on the ground; there was absolutely nothing there.[29]

It is often forgotten that the Germans had marched further and fought just as hard as the BEF in the previous weeks. They had marched all the way across Belgium before they even reached Mons.

As the British troops moved forwards they looked on aghast at the destruction left in the wake of the retreating Germans.

Away again as late as 12 noon. A real hot day and a most trying march, seeming interminable. Today showed us the real horrors of war, a none too pleasing picture to be presented with as a birthday gift! All sorts and conditions of abandoned things: wagons, guns, horses, lives (if one may put it in that way); wreckage of every description – human and material – strewn on all sides. The most maddening wreckage was that of the farms and animals. Houses wantonly broken up, each room a mass of debris, heads and the useless parts of the limbs of cattle, pigs and sheep, filing indiscriminately about around the buildings; furniture taken out of the cottages, (some of it old and perhaps priceless), broken and thrown aside, and, most blatant of all, – and possibly the cause of it all – piles of wine bottles, outside and inside every house! Every little cottage seems to own lots of *Vin Rouge* and *Vin Blanc* and I think the Germans like it very much. By the number of empty bottles about I feel certain of it. Another and most objectionable feature of a pursuit of the German Army is the most unpleasant smell which greets one at every one of their halting places – and we seemed to be passing their bivouacs perpetually. Anyhow, the stench which was eternally in our nostrils was disgusting beyond words.[30]

Lieutenant Arthur Ackland, 1st Duke of Cornwall's Light Infantry, 14th Brigade, 5th Division, II Corps

These references to a distinctive German 'smell' could perhaps be countered by reference to the existence of a uniquely British 'odour', but they are frequent in accounts of the time.

We came to the first German bivouac; it was a choice sight. The remains of cattle, geese, chickens, etc. which they had stolen and killed were lying all over the place, intermingled with old paper and every kind of rubbish. Amongst other things there was a dead horse, the smell of which, together with the stink peculiar to any place the Germans had been in, nearly made us sick, hardened as I was to most things by that time. They seemed to make a point of leaving a dead horse or two whenever they could; some of them could be smelt nearly a mile away. I do not know what the smell is which one connects with the Huns; it was very definite and everybody who was on the Retreat will tell you the same. I used to make a point of leaving the column and riding through these bivouacs, partly out of curiosity and partly to study their field sanitation which appeared to be non-existent, as I never saw a trace of any. That evening we passed through

Coulommiers and halted for the night just the other side. The town was a pitiable sight and some of the worst orgies the brutes ever had had taken place there. I believe they had committed some of the most appalling atrocities. The Germans had only been there one night but they had made the most of it, having broken into every shop in the place, got blind drunk and afterwards proceeded to amuse themselves in the ways which have now become so notorious.[31]

Lieutenant Cyril Helm, 2nd King's Own Yorkshire Light Infantry, 13th Brigade, 5th Division, II Corps

A slightly more restrained view of the German conduct was taken by Lieutenant James Pennyman of the 2nd King's Own Scottish Borderers.

Since coming home I have heard nothing but 'atrocities', but I never saw signs of any. The Germans always took all edible matter and searched the houses for socks, etc. I did hear of their taking the peasant's jewellery, and they made an awful mess of houses by putting straw down to sleep on, but the natives never complained of cruelty. What surprised me was rather how little harm they had done. The side of the road the whole way was littered with bottles, but they could not have got drunk, or we should have caught them. This seems to point to organized distribution of liquor rather than indiscriminate looting. The peasants were always so very glad to see us, and when they saw the prisoners, they laughed at them. This shows here that at any rate there had been no misbehaviour amongst the German troops, or the women would have been making frenzied signs of hatred.[32]

As they advanced many of the troops came into contact with the French cavalry, whose gilded cuirassiers still dressed much as their predecessors had at Waterloo. Their presence brought a different age of warfare to the battlefield.

Our advance guard consisted of French cavalry. It reminded us of the civil war, we seemed to have gone back to the days of King Charles. Imagine them scouring the country infested with the enemy, dressed as though they were proceeding to a fancy dress ball. Burnished helmets and breastplates and red trousers – what a target! The rejection from the sun was enough to blind us.[33]

Signaller John Palmer, 118th Battery, 26th Brigade, RFA, 1st Division, I Corps

The Germans had not seriously contested the Marne crossing, but were now falling back in a controlled manner towards the Aisne River, leaving behind rearguards to delay the BEF pursuit. For the men involved in these skirmishes, these were life or death affairs, and sometimes the fighting could be vicious. One such action occurred on 10 September near the village of Hautevesnes. For Sergeant Thomas Painting of the 1st King's Royal Rifle Corps it was one of those rare days when everything seems to go just as it was practised in peacetime training.

> We halted at Hautevesnes and the Colonel come along to see me and said, 'Who's in charge here?' I said 'I am, Sir'. He said 'Right, down the road a little way, turn left-handed, join up with 'C' Company in the next attack, range 1,500 yards!' Well, we formed up on the right of 'C' Company and made the attack on the Germans, a German Jäger Battalion, a rifle battalion same as we were. They were in a sunken road which was good cover. We'd got to go 1,500 yards over a cornfield which had been cut and cleared. It was just stubble, no cover at all! We had two machine guns in the battalion but our machine gun Sergeant was killed, so one of our machine guns was out of action. We advanced by covering fire. One section would advance under the covering fire of another section, leapfrogging each other as the others were firing to keep Jerry's heads down. When we got to within 200 yards of them my company was going in with the bayonet, on the flank of them. Jerry put white flags up, surrendered. After we roped them up and disarmed them we said 'Well, why did you surrender?' Their casualties were about a 180 – and we took 450 prisoners. We said 'Well, why did you pack up when you've got so much ammunition?' They said 'Well, your fire was so accurate we couldn't put our heads up to shoot at you!' It was absolutely a field day: fire and movement, fire and movement; one section firing while the other moved – inter-communication with each other – extended order – leapfrogging. That was why our casualties weren't so great, you see, because they were pinned down. That was the basic training. We were all trained to fire fifteen rounds a minute rapid – all aimed shots. We only had twelve killed and sixty wounded.[34]

Coming up in support of the 1st King's Royal Rifle Corps were the 1st King's Liverpool Regiment, also of the 6th Brigade. Lieutenant William Synge was also aware of the comparison that could be made with the halcyon days on the Wiltshire training grounds.

We saw a crowd of some two or three hundred Germans standing in the open in front of the cutting with their hands above their heads. Some of them had even got their shirts off, which they were waving as white flags. When I arrived about 150 yards from them I was rather at a loss as to what to do next. On field days at Aldershot we had never reached the stage of capturing prisoners wholesale. I remember turning round to my platoon sergeant and asking him what was the procedure for taking prisoners. He suggested that it might be as well if I drew my revolver. As I was entirely unarmed I thought this was good advice, but on doing so, the Germans nearest to me set up a wail and so I put it away again. I then advanced a little way and beckoned to them to come over to me. Finally one very dirty little man came timidly forward, and when about a yard away, made a dart forward and began shaking me warmly by the hand. This was embarrassing, but I do not quite know what made me give him a biscuit, which was my next action. This was too much for him altogether, and I believe he would have embraced me if I had not handed him over to two men to be searched. After this they came in quietly enough and were searched. As the officer next me had more prisoners than I had I handed over my lot to him together with my platoon to guard them. I then went up to have a look at the cutting. There is no object in describing it, but its appearance fully explained the absolutely dazed look on most of the prisoners' faces.[35]

When they moved forward, another King's Liverpool officer, Captain Thomas Sheppard, was appalled at the shattering effects of modern weaponry on the human body.

The road was a horrible, terrible sight, my first real dose of horror, and I remember poor Kyrke-Smith advising me not to go over the bank at a certain place because just over it was a man with his head blown off. As it was I had to see enough to sicken me – the whole road literally a shambles, bodies and blood everywhere, and some appalling scenes of dying men.[36]

The German retreat continued, but they were approaching the intended stopping point to take up positions on the ridges behind the Aisne. The question was would they be able to hold back the French and British Armies?

On 11 September, there was a controversial intervention in the British line of march, when Joffre requested that the BEF wheel in northeasterly direction to make room for the advance on their left flank of the French Sixth Army. French issued the necessary orders, but Haig considered that this surrendered the initiative and allowed the Germans to gain a day's march on the BEF – a day the German troops would put to good use digging themselves in over the next couple of days.

> I think it is a mistake to have changed direction now, because the enemy on our front was close to us last night and was much exhausted. Had we advanced today on Soissons, with cavalry on both flanks, large captures seemed likely.[37]

But for all the inevitable recriminations – and few if any military operations are perfect in both conception and execution – there was no doubt that the advance from the Marne had been a tremendous victory. General Ferdinand Foch, the newly promoted commander of Ninth Army, knew exactly who was responsible for that victory.

> It was the work of the man who, as early as August 24th, had begun to plan it and who had carried it through to the end, the Commander-in-Chief, General Joffre. Immediately after our repulses on the frontier, he had clearly perceived wherein the game had been poorly played. He therefore broke off the action, with the idea of resuming it energetically as soon as he had repaired the weaknesses discovered. Clear as to the enemy's intentions, fully unveiled as they now were by his powerful manoeuvre across Belgium, he did not hesitate to undertake a new distribution of his forces, as well as a reassignment of General Officers, made necessary by several proofs of incapacity. He created an army of manoeuvre on the west and then continued his retreat until a favourable moment for halting his forces should present itself. When this moment arrived, he judiciously combined the offensive with the defensive, after executing an energetic 'about turn'. By a magnificently planned stroke he dealt the invasion a mortal blow.[38]

As the British advanced formations approached the Aisne it soon became apparent that the Germans had decided that far and no further. The Allies were confident of victory, optimistic that the worst was over. How wrong they were.

9

BATTLE OF THE AISNE

Everywhere the same hard, grim, pitiless signs of battle and war. I have had a belly full of it. Those who were in South Africa say that that was a picnic to this and the strain is terrific. No wonder if after a hundred shells have burst over us some of the men want to get back into the woods for rest. Ghastly, absolutely ghastly, and whoever was in the wrong in the matter which brought this war to be, is deserving of more than he can ever get in this world.[1]

Captain Charles Paterson, 1st South Wales Borderers, 3rd Brigade, 1st Division, I Corps

THE BATTLE OF THE MARNE had been fought and won. But the might of the Imperial German Army was such that no mere reverse, no matter how serious, was sufficient to secure outright victory. This was not a game. The Germans simply knuckled down to repairing the situation. This was going to be no ordinary war; this was after all the 'Great War'. As von Kluck put it when he reached the Aisne, 'There was no sign of uneasiness or anxiety, and everywhere the same keen, enterprising spirit in spite of the need for a rest.'[2] This was not even the end of the beginning. But one thing had been finished by the Battle of the Marne: the career of General Helmuth von Moltke the Younger as Chief of the Imperial German General Staff. The retreat marked the overthrow of the Schlieffen Plan as developed by von Moltke. The failure was absolute. Germany was not defeated, but von

Moltke had been reduced by a combination of stress and poor health to the point of collapse. At times he was said to be teetering on the point of tears – not the ideal state for a German warlord at a crucial phase of a campaign. This could not be allowed to continue and on 14 September,[3] General Erich von Falkenhayn was appointed to replace von Moltke as Chief of the General Staff.

Falkenhayn was born in 1861 and had a sound career behind him as a staff officer as well as active service with the German expeditionary force fighting alongside the British during the Boxer Rebellion in China in 1900. He had been promoted to lieutenant general before being made the Prussian Minister of War in 1913. Falkenhayn was an intelligent, independent-minded and energetic leader with the innate strength of character to grow into the taxing role of Chief of the General Staff. Over the next two years he would prove a formidable opponent to the Allies.

The inability of the Allies to maintain close contact with the main body of the retreating German First and Second Armies meant that the German forces had time to prepare defensive positions along the Chemin des Dames escarpment rising up from the north bank of the Aisne River. The Aisne was a serious obstacle in its own right: an unfordable water-course about 170 feet across and up to 15 feet deep, it meandered slowly through a wide, flat-bottomed valley, with wooded hills rising up to 400 feet on either side. To make matters worse there was also a canal to cross in most sections of the valley. In the segment approached by the BEF there were some twelve bridges, which the Germans had demolished with a fair degree of efficiency in contrast to the efforts of the BEF at Mons. Nonetheless, it is extremely difficult to destroy bridges in their entirety when acting in haste. Charges fail to detonate, some parts of the structure remain standing, the rubble forms 'islands' in the stream – thus there was often enough left of the bridges to give the British sappers a good start at rebuilding.

The weather had changed and was dismal, unseasonably cold and dank, with torrents of rain pouring down, as on 12 September the BEF approached the Aisne, with I Corps on the right, II Corps slightly further back in the middle, and III Corps on the left. Acting in accordance with Joffre's 'suggestions', French issued his orders at 19.45 that evening for an advance commencing at 07.00 next day, with the intention of reaching the line of the road running along the heights of the Chemin des Dames. In essence, this envisaged breaking the German defence lines at a bound.

Although these plans, with hindsight, were optimistic in the extreme, the operations got off to an outstanding start, when elements of the 4th Division, III Corps, on the left of the BEF, took a bold action acting under the initiative of the ebullient figure of Brigadier General Aylmer Hunter-Weston, who was commanding the 11th Brigade. Captain Francis Westland of the 9th Field Company had been despatched ahead to investigate the condition of the designated bridges at Venizel. Arriving at about 20.00 on 12 September, Westland quickly found that the Germans appeared to have had some difficulties in carrying out an effective bridge demolition, as only two of their charges had gone off. Although some of the girders had been severed, the reinforced concrete of the actual road-way had partially survived and was still strong for men passing over in single file. Hunter-Weston, as a sapper officer, had no hesitation in ordering his men forward. This was not a popular decision with everyone in his long-suffering brigade: Second Lieutenant Tennyson had conceived a marked dislike of Hunter-Weston and was markedly unenthusiastic as he and the 1st Rifle Brigade had already endured a testing a march of some twenty-seven miles in the pouring rain and had been exhausted when they filed into their billets in a mustard mill. Tennyson was a man possessed of an august name as the grandson of the poet Lord Alfred Tennyson, but he also had the considerable personal distinction at twenty-four years old of having already played test matches for England on the winter tour of South Africa in the winter of 1913–1914. Indeed he had been selected as one of the five Wisden 'cricketers of the year' for 1914.

> We were about to settle down for the night having taken off some of our wet clothes, when the order came we were to be prepared to move off at once. Tired as we could be – and a mournful sight to look at – being still very wet. We paraded at 10pm and had about another eight-mile march in the pouring rain until we reached the River Aisne at a place called Venizel. Here we found that the bridge over the river had been blown up, but the Germans had done it so badly that they left one girder which was still holding the left side of the bridge partially together. We never know till this day if our General had reconnoitred this bridge and the country the other side of it – or not! It seemed to us all an absolute risky slapdash proceeding. However, about

1am, the whole of 11th Brigade went over the bridge one by one in the middle of this pitch-black night, in the pouring rain. The bridge, which was some sixty feet above the river, quivered and shook as every man went over, but luckily it bore us and eventually the whole brigade got across – though it was a pretty dangerous proceeding. The men were so tired they fell asleep as they stood or marched, and one felt oneself walking along and reeling like a drunken man.[4]

They were advancing into the dark, but by 03.00 on 13 September they were all safely across and pushed on up the steep side of the escarpment. The orders given to the 11th Brigade by Hunter-Weston were reported as a masterpiece of succinctness – commencing with the memorable: 'You see that there are three 'bumps' in front of you?'[5] He then sent forward one battalion up each of the spurs leading to the crest, retaining the fourth in reserve. To Tennyson's relief, there was no sign of opposition from the Germans.

As soon as the whole brigade were across the river we advanced across the open ploughed and stubble country, through the village of Bucy-le-Long with bayonets fixed, to the top of the ridge of hills overlooking the Aisne. As it turned out, if we had not crossed tonight over the river, and this flat open country, we must have lost hundreds of men doing it, as the Germans had a wonderful position, and never till this day shall I know why they had no outposts out tonight, except they thought they had blown up the bridge.[6]

This represented a superlative start, but the main German trench lines remained inviolate in front of them. Furthermore, Tennyson, who as we have seen was never an admirer of Hunter-Weston, blamed his brigadier for fatal confusion when the Royal Artillery gunners awoke to find a tempting target in their sights, across the Aisne valley and up on the ridge.

Everything went more or less calmly till 9.30am when our own guns spotted us in our waterproof sheets, as it was still raining, from the opposite side of the river, and thinking we were Germans started shelling us with lyddite. Of course our General – I imagine – had never let these gunners know that we had crossed the river. These shells were particularly well aimed, and though we tried to signal to them who we were, the shells came thicker and thicker until my captain, Jimmy Brownlow, signalled to me to retire to where he was. Across this open field we went, doubling as fast as we could, and the shells falling all amongst us. We lost a very good corporal – acting Corporal Gregory[7] – a signaller, who had his head blown off right close to me, and three more men severely wounded as well as one or two others killed, and several more wounded. My servant Welch, who was close to Gregory when he was killed, had all his hair stained absolutely yellow by the lyddite, which was still that colour for weeks afterwards, and he couldn't get it off. I had great luck just before we managed to get under cover as I was hit in the back on the burberry by a bit of a shell, which burst between a rifleman called Hall and myself, but never hurt either of us.[8]

Elsewhere the crossing of the Aisne did not commence until the morning of 13 September.

On the right flank of the BEF, I Corps followed up behind the Cavalry Division, which, despite a certain amount of confusion, had managed to force a passage using the canal aqueduct where it crossed the river at Bourg. Brigadier General Beauvoir de Lisle then led them up onto the ridge and deployed with I Battery, RHA.

Reveille 3am – saddle up – counter-order arrives – saddle down – ordered to move at 6.45 – at 6.25 new orders to move at once – off in confusion at 6.35 – good work by regimental staff! We then attack Bourg and the crossings of the Aisne and parallel canal – the further bridge of the two having been blown up. We go to the right and cross by sixes in a ferry under an irritating sniper's fire from a church tower – gave the ferry boy a franc for courage. De Lisle orders the 4th Dragoon Guards to gallop the bridge – they gallop into a barricade and come under a hot fire – Fitzgerald and three men killed. We come into action from the right and the 4th Dragoon Guards cross directly. We then climb up a hill and form up in mass behind a battery in action – our usual unusual procedure! Naturally we receive several hostile over-shoots aimed at the battery. We hastily pack up our lunch and, having mounted, retire in open order at a walk for 300 yards. Six horses in my troop wounded, Lucas killed,[9] two men wounded. The General thinks it a brave thing to do: to sit down behind a battery in action in close formation. Anyhow he has thrown away his best squadron leader – feel very depressed as I was very fond of Lucas.[10]

Second Lieutenant Basil Marden, 9th Lancers, 2nd Cavalry Brigade, Cavalry Division

Another officer reacted badly to what was clearly intended to be an 'inspirational' oration from de Lisle.

> He wound up with, 'You must stay here at all costs! Everything
> may depend on you! Don't give an inch of ground. You may have
> to sustain seventy or eighty per cent of casualties! Remain and die
> like gentlemen!' We looked at one another, 'Like gentlemen!' How
> else do people usually die? If, during one of our rapid retreats in
> August, we had all been shot in the back, would that death have been
> gentlemanly? And why so much talk about dying? Death was the end
> for us all, in any case – even civilians. It is living – especially in war –
> that is so difficult, so tiresome and tedious. Dying is absurdly easy.
> Anyway, I hated this kind of speech; I thought it melodramatic, like a
> penny novelette.[11]
>
> Captain Arthur Osburn, 4th Dragoon Guards, 2nd Cavalry Brigade, Cavalry
> Division

If anything, Osburn was made rather more nervous than reassured by de Lisle's speech.

The 1st Division were following up, assisted by their sappers, who conjured up a variety of methods of crossing the river. Gaps were bridged, while rafts and boats plied their way backwards and forward carrying the men to the north bank. Further to the left the 2nd Division managed to make a crossing using the remnants of the Pont d'Arcy bridge,

> Some of the girders of the broken bridge were showing above water.
> The crossing was at once taken in hand, and, as best they could, the
> men crawled across by the broken girders. The first man over was
> Private Hayes. On the whole company crossing, they deployed and dug
> in. There they held on all day.[12]
>
> Captain Charles O'Sullivan, 2nd Connaught Ranger, 5th Brigade, 2nd
> Division, I Corps

The Connaught Rangers then dug in along the bank of a canal running parallel to the river in order to allow them to cover the crossing of the rest of their brigade. Then they advanced across the flat valley bottom before ascending the steep sides of the ridge and up onto the plateau, where they reached the deserted village of Soupir at around 21.00.

A similar situation faced the men of II Corps in the centre as they crossed the remnants of the bridge at Vailly. The soldiers needed a steady head for heights as they teetered above the 'abyss' and Private William Holbrook paints a vivid picture of the challenge faced by the 4th Royal Fusiliers.

> The Germans had left the canal bridge intact, but had blown up the bridge over the river. It was very, very high. What the engineers had to do was throw a bridge from one side to the other – a distance of ten to fifteen feet. We had to cross these planks next afternoon – it was half dark when I got across. No railing, just bare planks. They kept moving as you walked: no supports, no rope to hold on by. As you put one foot down, the weight of your body, as you lifted your foot, the plank sprang up and met your other foot before you could get it down. It was a hell of a job. One or two shells coming over! You could hear the roaring water of the river rushing by twenty or thirty feet below. We lost a few men drowned, fell over from the plank. Colonel McMahon went across first and stood the other side, calling out the names and helping. Sergeant Jarvis in front of me was very, very timid. As he went he halted and stopped, I heard the Colonel say, 'And what's your name?' 'Sergeant Jarvis, Sir?' 'Are you all right?' 'Yes, Sir!'" Eight or nine hundred men across a plank, marvellous it was really![13]

The II Corps was also plagued by harassing fire from German heavy guns. When the Royal Artillery batteries deployed and tried to respond they found themselves totally outranged – it would be another sign of what was to come. Nevertheless, the BEF had done well in securing a crossing that might well have been far more problematic. The question now was whether they could get a grip on the crest of the Chemin des Dames ridge.

AT THIS STAGE NEITHER JOFFRE NOR Sir John French had realised that the Germans had stopped retreating and were intent on making a determined stand behind the Aisne. Allied orders for 14 September were thus marked by a jovial optimism with a move forward to a line reaching from Laon through Suzy to Fresne. This envisioned an advance of up to twelve miles, an ambition that bore no relation to the real situation on the ground. Matters were not helped by the continuing grim state of the weather, which prevented aerial reconnaissance to see what was going on ahead of the cavalry. Indeed high winds, lashing rain, mingled with copious early morning fog and a generally gloomy outlook, combined to restrict even localised visibility on the ground. On receipt of their orders from GHQ, Haig, Smith-Dorrien and Pulteney decided to take things in stages and made it their first objective to complete the crossing of the Aisne and capture the Chemin des Dames ridge. But what lay ahead of them was a nightmare.

The main problem faced by the German High Command had been how to close the gap between their First and Second Armies in the Aisne area, but they were fortunate that the VII Reserve Corps, commanded by General Johann von Zwehl, had been released by the fall of the Maubeuge fortress on 8 September. Rapidly redeployed, they managed to arrive just in time to take up their place in the line on the heights of Chemin des Dames by the early afternoon of 13 September.

> The hurricane force winds continued to blow. It was as though we were on the steppes of Russia, rather than 'Sunny France'. We were falling asleep on our feet and were fearful that we would collapse. Voices came from the rear, 'Slow down! We have lost contact!' At every such halt men fell to the ground in a deep sleep. The column stumbled on. Some were overcome by exhaustion and lay collapsed on the ground, but the majority stuck it out. The first glimmer of dawn announced the arrival of morning. The cloudburst eased a little, then reduced to a drizzle. There was a wood to our front which, as we passed through it, provided some protection from the icy wind. As it became light the road dropped down and we passed the first houses of Festieux. The place was dead; the road wound downwards. To the front on a hill were our commanders. All the officers remounted, the column braced up and everyone put their last reserves of strength into it as we reached the hill. Marching to attention, 159th Infantry Regiment gave an 'eyes left' to General von Zwehl, who was casting an anxious eye over the column. His personality filled each man with renewed courage, but who knew what he was feeling inside, or how the burden of responsibility was weighing him down? Would the troops be able to go into battle after such a strenuous, forced march like this?[14]
>
> Major Maywald, 2nd Battalion, 159th Infantry Regiment, 28th Brigade, 14th Reserve Division, VII Reserve Corps

The two divisions of the VII Corps represented a severe obstacle to further British and French progress once ensconced up on the ridges towering above the Aisne. In some ways the Battle of the Aisne was decided before it began. Indeed the German High Command were already turning their minds to the possibility of resuming the offensive.

If the British generals were left groping in the dark as to what lay ahead of them, then their subordinate commanders had no idea of what was happening. Thus it was not surprising that Lieutenant William Synge gained little or nothing from the briefing given by the Colonel of the 1st King's Liverpool Regiment.

> I lay stress on the fact that all these arrangements were made on the map, as the subsequent events of the day show how different everything becomes when you get on to the ground, and how difficult it is to keep to the 'picture' arranged on the map beforehand, once you get spread out amongst woods, and under fire. Owing to the situation it was not possible to examine the ground except from the map, and I assume the factor of time prevented a systematic reconnaissance of the position. At all events with these few words of guidance, we set forth, with very little idea of the nature of the ground which we were going to cover, and no idea as to how many of the enemy were in front of us, or where they were.[15]

This state of ignorance was typical for most officers involved in I Corps attacks on the Chemin des Dames made that day. In the prevailing circumstances there was very little that could be done to alleviate the confusion.

As I Corps moved forward, the 1st Division were attacking on the right. They sent the 2nd Brigade forward while it was still dark at 03.00 acting as a covering force to rush the sugar factory that lay close to the village of Cerny. The 1st Northamptonshires made their approach climbing up the spur above Moulins. At first, in the dark, shrouded by mist and rain, the leading battalions made solid progress as they advanced from Vendresse via Troyon and up onto the high ground.

> The ground here was dead ground from the enemy, and we could not be seen by them. We halted on the road for a minute and straightened up our line with the Queen's; then on we went. About 150 yards beyond the road the gradient began to flatten out, and it was soon pretty evident that we had now been seen! Everything seemed to open on us at once – rifles, machine guns, artillery, etc. The noise was deafening, the rifle and machine-gun bullets made a noise like a stockwhip being cracked in one's ear as they passed. The shrapnel seemed

worse – it never seemed to stop. Nothing seemed to stop. Men were falling now right and left. We were advancing in two lines, and my platoon was in the second line. On we went – it seemed like miles that we advanced, whereas it was only about 300 yards. Men continued to fall, the noise continued deafening, but we could see no shells from our guns bursting over the enemy, and we were cursing them accordingly. On we went until we got to the skyline, to find the Germans entrenched almost at our feet! Then what had gone before in the way of fire and noise was as nothing: there was just one continuous roar of firing, and we flung ourselves to the ground. The German machine gun fire was terrific and incessant. It would have been utter madness to try to advance any further, as even to raise one's head brought a storm of bullets immediately. We lay where we were for about twenty minutes, being utterly unable to find out what was happening elsewhere, or what we were to do – advance, retire, or stay where we were. Then the rain stopped and the mist began to clear, and presently to our joy shrapnel started to burst about twenty to thirty yards in front of us, right over the German trenches. Our guns were in action at last, and making the most wonderful practice.[16]

Lieutenant Evelyn Needham, 1st Northamptonshire Regiment, 2nd Brigade, 1st Division, I Corps

As the covering force of the 2nd Brigade fought to hold the ring, the 1st Guards Brigade was moving forward in turn with the intention of prolonging the line held by the 2nd Brigade to the west along the Chemin des Dames Road, with the 3rd Brigade still waiting near Moulins. The fighting was such that the 2nd Brigade had to call forward the 1st Loyal North Lancashires from their place held back in brigade reserve at Vendresse. As the Loyals emerged onto the plateau, they too came under a vicious fire as they prepared to make the next bound from the transient security of a road bank.

A terrific fire of all kinds sweeps over our heads, and we know that we shall be exposed to it in a very few minutes. The signal to advance is given and Loomes is the first to take his platoon over the bank and into the inferno. For a minute or two I have a clear picture of him with his sword drawn, leading his men forward and waving them on with words of encouragement, to which they respond without the slightest hesitation. This is the last glimpse I have of him.[17] My turn comes next, and I draw my sword and call on my men to follow me. We leap on the bank and begin to rush forward, and are immediately exposed to a devastating fire. Many men fall, but we go on, nevertheless, by rushes of from 60 to 80 yards. We have only gone a few paces when two shells pitch into the left half of my platoon, and seven or eight men disappear entirely. We continue to double forward, although as yet I can see nothing of the enemy. We pass scores of our dead and wounded, and many of the latter are calling out for water, but it is impossible for us to help them and we have to go on. Suffering severe losses, we at last reach the firing line. Here the casualties are appalling, and our men are literally lying on the ground in heaps. We lie down in the open, as there is not a vestige of cover of any kind. I order the men to use their hand shovels to dig themselves into the ground. The noise of the battle is, however, so great that only the men nearest to me can hear me, and I therefore have to crawl round to give them my instructions. By this time the rain has ceased altogether, and visibility is distinctly good. I look round and try to grasp the situation.[18]

Lieutenant James Hyndson, 1st Loyal North Lancashire Regiment, 2nd Brigade, 1st Division, I Corps

Despite taking heavy casualties, the 1st Loyals, the 2nd King's Royal Rifle Corps and the 2nd Royal Sussex managed to capture the sugar factory buildings and began to dig shallow trenches in the fields beyond at around 09.00. The question was whether they could stay there? When the BEF had held the line at Mons and Le Cateau, theirs had been a static defence lacking uncommitted reserves. The Germans had a different and far more effective tactical approach. Wherever possible, they took care to maintain an adequate tactical reserve at all levels, enabling swiftly organised counter-attacks to be generated before the British could consolidate their gains. It was not long before they attacked the Loyals in great force.

They come on bravely, surging forward in mass formation, scores of them being shot down. They manage to get to within 200 yards of our firing line, but the reception they get is too hot, and the survivors fall back rapidly to their original starting-point. Once more the Germans pour a terrific fire of all arms into us. Our numbers diminish but we hang on grimly, digging ourselves further and further into the ground, until the whole of our bodies are under cover of mother earth. By this time I have only about twenty men left unwounded, and ammunition is running short. In anticipation of being attacked again, I order the men to get all the ammunition they can from the dead and wounded, as there is no other method of getting a fresh supply. At the same time, I myself acquire a rifle in exchange for my sword, which I discard in order to camouflage myself as much as possible. We are now too far forward, and Allason orders me to withdraw and go back to a new alignment, to conform with the troops on our right. Gathering my command together, I double back under a perfect tornado of shell and bullets. By a miracle I am not hit, but all my men except ten are shot down. With the survivors, I seek shelter in a nullah,[19] which we fortunately happen to stumble on, and I decide to remain there, as it is impossible to move either backwards or forwards under the hail of shot and shell.[20]

Lieutenant James Hyndson, 1st Loyal North Lancashire Regiment, 2nd Brigade, 1st Division

Even a desperate state of affairs failed to suppress the natural wry humour of the men.

At one time we were in a swede field, and a large shell burst in front of us, covering us with dirt. A chum of mine, being hit very forcibly with a flying swede, up he jumped, shouting, 'I'm hit! I'm hit!' but came to the conclusion that he wasn't as bad as he had thought![21]

Private Frederick Bolwell, 1st Loyal North Lancashire Regiment, 2nd Brigade, 1st Division, I Corps

By this time the Northamptonshires had also been forced back to the road. Here they dug in as best they could.

A lot of shrapnel was bursting over our heads all the time we were digging, which was far from pleasant. Young Gordon would insist on walking up and down his platoon while they were digging and exhorting them to further efforts. Finally, Parker and I damned his eyes and told him too, 'Get down and dig himself, instead of turning himself into a walking target for the Huns!' He was a plucky young devil and did not care a tinker's curse for shell fire or anything, but appeared to be thoroughly enjoying himself all the time, laughing and joking with the men.[22]

Lieutenant Evelyn Needham, 1st Northamptonshire Regiment, 2nd Brigade, 1st Division, I Corps

What followed in the fields around the sugar factory was a real old-fashioned 'soldier's battle' in the thick fog which caused a great deal of confusion to both sides. As the 1st Guards Brigade arrived, they prolonged the 2nd Brigade line to the left stretching out along the slightly sunken Chemin des Dames road.

> We had a ding-dong battle under heavy German artillery fire to which our gunners could not then reply. The result was that we lost about 33% of my brigade in killed, wounded and missing in about a couple of hours or so. With the remainder we stuck to the ground we had gained, aided by two battalions of the 2nd Brigade who also suffered as heavily as we did. It was absolutely essential to the whole Allied Army that we should not give way one inch of ground because we thus held an indispensable bridgehead over the River Aisne. If we had been driven off this bridgehead, the Allied line was cut in two and each wing would be dealt with separately, but probably with success. This I knew but most of the brigade did not at the time. Since the 14th we have continued to hold onto the same ground and the bridgehead over the Aisne is now secured, I think.[23]

> Brigadier General Ivor Maxse, 1st Guards Brigade, 1st Division, I Corps

At this point the bulk of the 3rd Brigade was moved forward to take up a defensive position to the left of Maxse's brigade from about 10.30. Amongst them were the 2nd Welsh on the Beaulne Spur.

> We were holding a steep bank on the near crest of the ridge, with the Germans among some corn stooks, only about 150 yards away. Eventually we rushed the Huns and the remnants of them fled. The ground was littered with their dead. We continued to advance with most of 'C' Company and about half some other company, across the top of the ridge, until we passed a line of apple trees on the further side. As soon as we passed the apple trees, a perfect storm of shells struck round us. Luckily few, if any, burst. I fancy we must have nearly surprised a field gun battery, who fired at us with badly timed shrapnel. Anyhow two shells struck the ground on either side of me and I threw myself flat in the long grass for the storm to pass. When things had quieted down, I crawled over to talk to Moore and we agreed that our

present position was hopeless. We therefore decided to retire the 250 yards across the ridge, to the bank we started from. We started back in small groups from the right. Unfortunately the German gunners saw the movement and opened fire with every form of projectile. It seemed to me that every yard of that plateau top was blowing up. I hurled myself down the bank head-first, closely followed by a Lance Corporal who had his arm practically blown off. The Huns deluged the bank with shells. I saw Moore and ran over to him. We both threw ourselves flat as we heard the scream of a shell, and it burst a few yards below us, killing Fitzgerald and four or five men. Moore's first comment was: 'Well, I thought they would hit *you* anyhow!' was hardly satisfactory.[24]

Captain Herbert Rees, 2nd Welsh Regiment, 3rd Brigade, 1st Division, I Corps

That same day Rees saw an excellent demonstration of infantry working well with their support weapons. To his right were the battalion machine guns under the command of Lieutenant George Melville who deployed his two machine guns to deliver a devastating fire from the flank on a German trench.

Suddenly, to my intense excitement, observed the German trenches on my right filled with troops prepared to repulse the attack of the South Wales Borderers. Ranging very carefully with my Barr and Stroud, I started vertical searching from both my guns. As the range was only about 700 to 800 yards, the execution was terrible. Eventually the Germans could stand it no longer, and breaking from their trenches ran back over the crest of the hill like a football mob, both my guns pumping into them, as hard as they could fire. I then saw a most beautiful exhibition of shooting by the 113th Field Battery, which was supporting us in the valley below. As soon as the enemy broke from their trenches, the guns opened on them with shrapnel. The slaughter was terrific.[25]

Lieutenant George Melville, 2nd Welsh Regiment, 3rd Brigade, 1st Division, I Corps

Throughout, the British gunners tried their best to support the infantry, but they found themselves operating at a severe disadvantage. Often they were forced to pass through terrible bouts of shellfire even before they could drop their guns into action. The shattering crash of the shells right in amidst men and horses was terrifying in its abruptness.

> That day the battery first came under fire, its baptism being a salvo of four 8-inch toys slap in the middle as we were just wheeling to come into action. One officer was sick on the spot! Jones' horse was killed under him, mine was blown – or shied – aside and I fell off! In the ensuing mêlée both my guns got turned over coming down a steep bank. I saw one, but didn't know about the other, as I was leading the battery at the time and when I finally got them into the next position I found my section was gone. Before we fired a round in the new position, the infantry came back through us and we loaded up with Fuse '0' expecting the [Germans] to be following. However as they didn't roll up, the Major thought we'd better get back to the crest behind and went on to find a spot telling Jones or me to bring on the battery. The teams came up and we got them away somehow. I gave Jones my horse and I waited with a couple of gunners to get away on the last wagon. However the team had been killed earlier and they didn't roll up, so we left the damn thing there and did a two-mile run back with bullets thick all over the country. I've never heard anything to approach the rifle and machine gun fire on that day. We got to our new position and we subalterns went out in turn to the forward crest to try and find out something or observe something. Forward observing wasn't the clear cut game and I'm afraid I was so scared and absolutely ignorant of where our 'feet' were or where the Bosches were that I didn't do as much good as I might have.[26]
>
> Lieutenant Ralph Blewitt, 54th Battery, 39th Brigade, RFA, 1st Division, I Corps

Perhaps Blewitt had more excuse than he might have imagined. It was difficult to secure a decent observation post up on the ridge: no one knew where the British front line was, never mind the German positions, there was a shortage of telephone wire to run back to the battery and above all the visibility was often terrible. The German guns were in well-concealed positions on the back slopes of the ridge and their heavier guns easily outranged the British field artillery.

The 2nd Division were advancing to the left of the 1st Division, pushing through the village of Soupir, up onto the Soupir spur, but there was a complication in that two brigades had not yet crossed the Aisne to join the 5th Brigade covering their crossing from positions between Moussy and Verneuil at the bottom of the spurs reaching down from the main ridge. Unsurprisingly there were delays in crossing the bridges under considerable harassing fire from the German gunners. In the interval the 2nd Connaught Rangers were despatched up to try and secure the Soupir spur. They took up positions on either side of the La Cour de Soupir Farm but soon were exposed to determined German counter-attacks.

> By 9 o'clock we were in the midst of the hottest fight so far witnessed in the battalion. We had no cover of any description and the ground was perfectly flat for 800 or 900 yards in front of us and for 500 or 600 yards behind us, until one reached the steep ground leading down to the river valley. The German fire was not very accurate, but, even so, we suffered fairly severely. They attempted to advance by short rushes of small parties at a time, but did not succeed in getting on very far. It was the first time that most of us had been under a really heavy infantry fire. There was one constant crackle of the firing, and the hiss of the bullets was like the hiss of steam escaping! At about 10 o'clock the company on our right, which had lost its commander and most of its officers, was forced back to a wood, so that both my flanks were exposed. Shortly after this we found that we were being fired at from the direction of our left flank, so we had to retire to a position further back. I ordered the left half-company to retire, and as soon as they got up the German fire became simply appalling. The right half-company, with which I myself was, kept up as rapid a fire as we could until the other half had got back about a 100 yards. Then they got down and opened fire whilst we retired. In this way we got back about 300 yards to where there was some cover of sorts, and there we started improving the cover with our entrenching tools. It is surprising that we did not lose more men whilst falling back, but the enemy's fire, although very heavy, was very inaccurate. I suppose they got excited and fired wildly; however, whatever the cause, we had very few men hit. At about 11 o'clock the Guards began to arrive.[27]
>
> Captain Ernest Hamilton, 2nd Connaught Ranger, 5th Brigade, 2nd Division, I Corps

At last the 4th Guards Brigade arrived and took up positions on either side of the farm. The murderous to and fro of attack and counter-attack began anew, concentrated particularly around the farm itself. The Guards lunged forward supported by elements of the Connaught Rangers and finally managed to retake the farm. By this time it was a scene of slaughter.

> I and two or three other officers went back to the farm. There were some 150 wounded men of my own regiment there and about 250 of the Guards Brigade, besides 200 Germans. In a house belonging to the farm were some twenty wounded officers and six wounded German officers. Dead men were lying about in the yard, and just outside the gate of the courtyard there was a whole pile of dead. When it got dusk I went out to where my company had been to see if there were many of them there. I found about eighteen of them, all dead and all in a straight line – the line we had occupied early in the morning. About 300 yards in front of them were piles and piles of German dead. In one spot, about the size of a small room, there were at least twenty.[28]
>
> Captain Ernest Hamilton, 2nd Connaught Ranger, 5th Brigade, 2nd Division, I Corps

The 6th Brigade and part of the 5th Brigade moved up onto the ridge and managed to secure positions on the Beaulne spur on the right, but that was the limit of their achievements in the face of severe shelling and relentless German counter-attacks.

It is chastening to consider that in making what limited progress they did, I Corps had suffered some 3,500 casualties on 14 September, more than twice the numbers suffered by II Corps at the far better known Battle of Mons just three weeks earlier. The war was expanding in scale and deadly scope for the BEF as it began to experience serious contact with the German Army. This was an attack, not a retreat. They could not minimise casualties by stealing away: they had to stand toe-to-toe with their opponents. It was a truly painful business.

Elsewhere along the line, the attacks of II Corps achieved nothing of any importance, although again the cost was high. The 3rd and 5th Divisions had only established small unconnected bridgeheads across the Aisne. Further west III Corps had already got the 4th Division up onto the edge of the ridge but failed to make any further progress. The French also had a mixed day, with their Sixth Army next to III Corps unable to discover an open flank to the German First Army and failing in its efforts against strong German positions. The French Fifth Army, to the right of I Corps, had more success attacking towards Craonne at the end of the

Chemin des Dames and securing the capture of Berry au Bac and the city of Rheims.

Whatever the Allied High Command had expected on 14 September, this was not a case of mere 'light resistance' from the Germans; they were clearly present in strength and by no means passive. Indeed the counter-attacks launched on the British line had been of an extremely threatening nature. French assessed the situation and at 23.00 issued verbal orders to his three corps commanders that they were to entrench where they stood. This decision was entirely endorsed in orders received from Joffre a couple of hours later.

> It seems as if the enemy is once more going to accept battle, in prepared positions north of the Aisne. In consequence, it is no longer a question of pursuit, but of a methodical attack, using every means at our disposal and consolidating each position in turn as it is gained.[29]

This marked the end of open warfare on the Aisne front. All along the BEF front lines the men were digging trenches; in doing so they accepted tacitly that the time spent in improving their defences would without doubt be matched in a similar manner by the Germans. This had happened already along much of the battle-line between the French and German armies all the way from Alsace to the Aisne. There had been plenty of trenches in the history of warfare. They had been an integral part of siege warfare from medieval times. The use of trenches during the American Civil War had encompassed prolonged periods with the Confederate and Union armies staring across at each other's inviolable fortifications. Trenches had also been widespread at various times in the Boer War and during the Russo-Japanese War. Only the Anglocentric believe that trench warfare started on the Aisne – but it did indeed start in earnest for the men of the BEF on that miserable night of 14 September in the aftermath of a truly dreadful day.

While the soldiers tried their best to scratch out trenches with their entrenching tools, one man under severe pressure was Captain Robert Dolbey, the medical officer of the 2nd King's Own Scottish Borderers. The battalion was trapped in a wooded area just the other side of the Aisne to the right of the Missy bridge. As Dolbey moved amongst the wounded, he frequently encountered the broken bodies of men that he had known in happier times.

There were wounded men everywhere and one didn't know where to begin. Then a Corporal spoke to me and I turned aside to a little hollow; and there lay young Amos, one of our junior subalterns. Only the day before I had spoken to him as we lay lazily listening to the overhead shelling in the woods behind La Sermoise. He had behaved most gallantly at Mons, bringing in a wounded man of his platoon under a very heavy fire at a range of less than 50 yards. I remember I told him that he must have had a very watchful 'Guardian Angel'. Now again had his 'Guardian Angel' come to him; but with a wreath. He must have died very swiftly, for the aorta had been severed.[30] He was the most promising of our junior subalterns, just from Sandhurst; yet he had become, already, a capable officer.[31]

His first priority was to find somewhere that could be pressed into service as a regimental aid post, where the stretcher bearers could bring the wounded for assessment and emergency treatment.

At the edge of the wood, in a line with the shallow shelter trenches that our men had thrown up, was an old stone barn; clearly the one place in all that wood for my dressing station. Established there, the wounded were brought to me, dressed, and such crude surgery as was possible attempted. We had only the small surgical haversack, but it did good work that day. All day long the firing was incessant; and our two companies, spread out along the fringe of the wood, were badly enfiladed. Steadily the stream of wounded poured in until, in the shelter of that wall, there were soon over 150 wounded and dying. But our morphia never gave out, and my orderly was a very great help. All the time the rifle bullets cracked like whips above us. Then an enfilading machine gun worked steadily round our right flank, and the wounded, behind the wall, were in danger. Out we went and fetched them into the narrowing angle of shelter that was left; still the angle of safety narrowed, until I thought we should never keep our wounded whole.[32]

In front of them the men of the 2nd King's Own Scottish Borderers were engaged in a terrible battle. Pinned down by heavy fire, Lieutenant James Pennyman was using the massed firepower of his two machine guns to try to force the Germans to keep their heads down.

Every now and then, when the fire against us increased, I swept the whole ground in front of us with machine-gun fire, and this each time lessened the volume of their fire. One of the guns jammed (the first time this had happened since we started) but I believe they soon put it right. There was such a noise going on that verbal communication was almost impossible. A bullet went into the ground very close to me as I was working the other gun. I thought it might be a sniper who had seen us, so we moved three or four yards to our right. The next thing I remember was a sensation like a blow with a cricket ball in the chest. It knocked me clean down, and I remember shouting as I fell and bleeding profusely at the mouth. I felt quite certain that I was a 'goner', but managed to get up and give some directions to the gunner, then I flopped down again. Four men picked me up and carried me to a place about twenty yards back where the fire was not quite so severe. The next thing I remember was being handled by the doctor in twilight.[33]

Pennyman was carried into his aid post, where he was immediately recognised by Captain Dolbey.

Then Pennyman was brought in, all limp and grey and cold; there was blood on his shirt in front, and my orderly, seeing the position of the wound, said, too loudly, that he was gone. This roused him, and I knew that the age of miracles was not past and that the bullet had just missed the big vessels at the base of the heart.[34]

As Pennyman struggled to his senses he discovered that although he was still in great danger, he was at least in good hands.

I was surprised to find myself alive, and more so when the doctor began to treat my hand, as doctors don't bind corpse's thumbs. I began to have a feeling of terrific cramp all over my chest, and a difficulty in breathing. I was told that my only chance was to lie absolutely still and flat, and a healthy dose of morphia helped me to do this, I was put on a stretcher and carried into a building of some sort, where I lay that night and all the next day.[35]

Dolbey and his assistants worked deep into the night, surrounded by broken dreams and shattered bodies. Darkness brought no relief; that came from the doctor's opiates that could equally soothe the pain or the passage from earth depending on the severity of the wounds. To Dolbey the plight of the crippled wounded, lost and alone in the tangled under-growth of the woods, did not bear thinking about.

> The wood was full of groans; of cries of men who thought they had been forgotten; of stertorous snores of unconscious brain cases. Never could one forget such a night as this: pitiless rain; no lights we dared to show for fear of bringing upon us the machine guns that were so near; no stretchers. Hastily improvising from waterproof sheets and blankets, stretched on saplings, we gradually got the wounded to our hospital. There tea was ready and grateful warmth and more morphia and soft straw. The stretcher bearers now across the river, worked like the good fellows they were and toiled up the slippery clay banks with their painful freight all through the night. But it was hard to find the wounded in the dark and some were very still; and those that lay far out in the wood kept silent, when help was so close, for fear we were an enemy patrol that had come searching through the wood. Wounded men, like wounded birds, creep into ditches and bushes to hide. Wounded men in a wood at night. The recollection yields nothing in horror to Dante's *Inferno* itself.[36]

The British far too often drift into the unwarranted assumption that it was the BEF, and the BEF alone, that was fighting on the Aisne front in September 1914. It is a useful corrective to examine a poignant German account of the bitter fighting with the French to the right of I Corps.

> The platoons were deployed in steps, one behind the other, but each platoon was on higher ground, so all had clear fields of fire when the enemy attacked. Soon we observed individual enemy columns appear in the low ground and begin to dig in. We opened fire immediately. From my position I could see the enemy assaulting our first battalion. I watched how their regiments deployed and how their artillery galloped up, went into action and began to fire. In short, the place was teeming with 'Red Trousers'. One battery after another drove up. We poured fire at them and soon my company was out of ammunition. "Volunteers to collect ammunition, step forward!' Schwender and I volunteered, but the ammunition wagons were nowhere to be seen. After a lengthy search we came to the aid post and took all the ammunition off the wounded. We took this back to the company, distributed it and set off once more. On our third journey the ammunition wagons were there, thank goodness. We took as

much as we could carry and brought it to the company. By now it was beginning to get dark. The intensity of firing reduced, but did not stop completely. Advanced sentry posts were manned and the company set about improving its positions.[37]

Musketier Kubina, 3rd Battalion, 159th Regiment, 28 Brigade, 14th Reserve Division, VII Reserve Corps

Next morning they found the French had managed to improve vastly their tactical position and now it was the turn of Musketier Kubina and the rest of 159th Regiment to find themselves being overlooked.

The following morning the situation had changed. The enemy had entered the village and established themselves in our rear. It was not long before the French began firing at us from the church tower and the roofs. We had dug in a little during the night, but it did not help, because we were being fired at from above. All that the company could do was to lie there calmly and await nightfall when we should be able to escape. Casualties mounted. About midday I was hit in the left upper arm by a ricochet then, a few minutes later, in the left thigh. I lay at the fork in the road under machine gun fire. The remainder raced back further into the sunken road, but could not even consider getting me out of the danger area, because the machine gun never stopped firing. About 5.00 pm the remainder of the company got away, leaving we wounded behind. I had been lying there under machine gun fire for nine hours, awaiting the bullet that would kill me. When it finally went dark the fire stopped. I attempted to get up so that I could rejoin the company, but it was hopeless; I could not move. To my front was a pile of dead and another wounded man. I shouted to him, asking him if he could stand. He had been creased in the back by a bullet and had been shot through the calf. He got to his feet, came over to me and hauled me upright. We wanted to get away, because the French could appear at any moment. I could not take single step. There was nothing for it but to lie down again and wait for whatever might transpire.[38]

Kubina would lie there untended for three days, for the most part ignored by the French soldiers, who were otherwise engaged in fighting his comrades. Fed just a few scraps of bread by a kindly Frenchman he somehow survived, still unable to move, just lying there until rescued by a German counter-attack.

It was evident on 15 September that both sides were all but played out. Everywhere men were digging; they would be digging one way or another for four years. The first trenches were little more than ditches.

> The trench would be about four feet deep, that's all, with sandbags on the front. In between us and the German trenches there were some potatoes growing. One chap said, 'I'm going to have some of those potatoes if they blow my blinking head off!' He got out of the trench, he got the potatoes but a shell took his head clean off his shoulders. That happened, it sounds a bit fantastic but it's true![39]
>
> Lance Corporal Joe Armstrong, 1st Loyal North Lancashire Regiment, 2nd Brigade, 1st Division, I Corps

That night in the orders issued at 20.30 French upgraded his instructions: 'The Commander in Chief wishes the line held by the Army to be strongly entrenched.'[40] It was of course his intention to resume the offensive at the first opportunity, but there was no doubt that for the moment his priority was defence. The chances of a successful British attack were clearly remote. Next day French visited his allies to see how they were progressing.

> On the 16th I went to see General Maunoury at his Headquarters. I found him watching an attack of the 61st and 62nd Divisions on the village of Nouvron and the plateau above it. The General and his Staff were standing on a kind of grassy tableland on the edge of a wood. I remember that a French staff officer who was there spoke English fluently. I threw myself down on my face on the grass and watched the battle taking place on the other side of the river. I spent an hour or two with the General at this spot and discussed the situation with him. From all I could see the French appeared to be getting on very well. On my way back I visited the corps commanders again, and they all expressed the utmost confidence in their ability to hold their positions.[41]

However, the passive approach adopted by the BEF, while on either flank the French continued to attack, caused some consternation amongst his subordinates. One bright staff officer, Lieutenant Colonel Stanley Maude at III Corps headquarters, reviewed the situation.

> French are taking the offensive all along the line today but we can only hang on by our eyelids to the edge of the plateau we are holding. Our

position is tactically a bad one but we must do the best we can as it would expose the French position if we were to retire now. Enemy less active in front of us today though they shelled us pretty continuously.[42]

So the British engaged in a root and branch process of extending and deepening their trench system. Where possible some barbed wire was put out in between the British and German lines in No Man's Land.

My Section Sergeant, coming to me just after dark, said, 'Do you know anything about barbed wire? Well, out in front about forty yards you will find a lot of stakes and two reels of barbed wire. Now you go out and I'll send another fellow to knock in the stakes while you can twist the wire round them and make some entanglements!' I can't say I liked the job, because I didn't! The enemy lay only a few hundred yards away, and I had to go out there attracting attention by knocking in stakes and twisting barbed wire around them, a thing the enemy would be sure to try their best to prevent. But it had to be done, so off we started, creeping over the top. We were looking for nearly an hour for this wire and, after twice nearly walking into the enemy's lines, we at length found it, and managed, after several volleys from the enemy, to accomplish our task, and rig up some sort of defence. Every night after that, whenever we occupied the front line, I was one of the men erecting the barbed wire entanglements, and many were the narrow squeaks I had at the hands of the Germans.[43]

Private Frederick Bolwell, 1st Loyal North Lancashire Regiment, 2nd Brigade, 1st Division, I Corps

This process of improving the trenches went on throughout the British stay on the Aisne. They took great pride in their work, and Second Lieutenant Lionel Tennyson even presciently speculated as to the future as an attraction to sightseers.

At dawn we move back to our forward trenches by a wonderful communication trench about 300 yards long, which we had dug. If the farmer is not a fool he will keep these trenches after the war – and would make a fortune by tourists coming to see them. Even our General, who is not given to praise anyone much, said they were very fine trenches and the best he had ever seen![44]

Second Lieutenant Lionel Tennyson, 1st Rifle Brigade, 11th Brigade, 4th Division, III Corps

Even today, a century since, people still make pilgrimages to view the outlines of the trenches and the graves of the men that defended them.

WHILE THE BRITISH DUG deeper and deeper, the Germans were intent in deploying their artillery to blast them off the top of the ridge. In this they had a potent new weapon in the form of the heavy 8" artillery pieces brought up to the Aisne front after the fall of the Maubeuge fortress to rain their enormously destructive shells down on the British trenches.

> The first surprise came when the 'Jack Johnsons' began to fall. This was a nickname given by the men, 'Black Marias' was another, to a high-explosive shell fired from 8" howitzers, which had been brought down from the fortress of Maubeuge to support the German defensive position on the Aisne. They were our first experience of an artillery much heavier than our own. Although these guns caused considerable damage and many bad casualties, they never had any very demoralising effect upon the troops.[45]
>
> General Sir John French, General Headquarters, BEF

French was being fondly optimistic, for although many of the men had coped quite well under shell fire from the German field artillery, the concentrated fire of the heavier 150mm (5.9") gun/howitzer and 210mm (8") heavy howitzers was a shattering experience.

> The whole place seamed alive with bursting shrapnel and high-explosive shell. One burst a few feet over the crest line, hitting gun, horses and my own poor horse. I had just time to call to the gunner drivers that it was no use running about, when another 5.9" H.E. shell came just right for us! It struck a little tree about twelve foot up its trunk and exploded. I felt something hit me on the left breast and on right instep, no pain and did not think I was wounded. I looked up and heard Corporal Jack saying his leg was broken, and the lad lying next to me looked pitifully round and I saw he was practically disembowelled by the base of the shell. Then I opened my shirt, found a fair hole about four inches above the left nipple and a lot of blood flowing, foot only bruised, but very painful and end of left spur shot away. The bullet, or shell fragment, had gone through my medal-ribbons. Did not feel sick and was not spitting blood, so concluded it

was not serious, but as well to clear out; picked up my kit, got out the field dressing and stepped off down the road.[46]

Lieutenant Colonel Sir Cecil Lowther, 1st Scots Guards, 1st Guards Brigade, 1st Division. I Corps

Attempts to invoke religion, the fates, humour, lucky charms or logic to evade the 'Black Marias' were ineffectual. Men lived or died according to no discernible pattern.

Our machine gun officer – Mr Cecil – a very brave man who told his men not to 'bob' as shells and bullets would not hit them unless their name and address was on them, but five minutes after he was hit by a shell himself and killed instantly.[47] We had just heard the news when a shrapnel burst just over us and knocked out forty-three men, many of whom were my personal chums. It completely disembowelled an ammunition mule, and although I was right under it and men killed all around me, yet I was unscratched. It was a fearful sight: groans, screams, legs, arms, heads cut off, blood and gore all around.[48]

Private Frederick Firks, 2nd Grenadier Guards, 4th Guards Brigade, 2nd Division, I Corps

The sheer concussive power of an exploding shell generated shock waves passing through the air to kill a victim without leaving a trace of a wound. Proximity to such a blast could also scatter the senses, triggering an episode of what would be known as 'shell shock'. Private Samuel Knight was lucky in that he was only dazed for a while after one such close escape.

Artillery duel subsides somewhat. I am told off to fetch water from the village. We make out way down the hill. We pass two comrades in a sitting posture. One has a cigarette between his fingers. I see no trace of blood. But their souls have fled. I wonder as to the cause of their death. I am soon to find out myself. I have filled my bottles at the well. It is in a farmyard. I see nothing but graves, with their simple crosses bearing the names in indelible pencil. I fill my pockets with apples, which I pluck from the trees. I raise the water-bottles. There's a terrific crash! Then whizz! Something strikes a comrade's hand very near my face. A spurt of blood is followed by a groan. Something seems to clutch at my throat. I fall to the ground. I have a vague recollection of falling into line with my comrades and of marching back to the trenches. I am brought to myself by a touch on the shoulder and a question, 'What's the matter, old boy?' They tell me I've been babbling to myself. Such is the effect of concussion brought about by a bursting shell. It was a narrow shave.[49]

Private Samuel Knight, 2nd Welsh Regiment, 3rd Brigade, 1st Division, I Corps

One possible source of relative safety from the constant shelling was a line of caves in the rocky outcrop just below the crest of the ridge. Sergeant John McIlwain and his men took shelter in one such cavern near Verneuil.

The caves – which the German gunners have the range of to a foot – though formed of powerful stone, are precarious enough. In the largest a company of 200 men can shelter, cook and sleep. The roof, in places is twenty feet high. During the five days we were in and out of this cave, the shelter became less secure. On our last day the continual bombardment had so loosened the rock, that when a particularly good hit by a German gunner broke off a huge boulder, the sudden darkening of the light within indicated to us the unpleasant possibility of being buried alive.[50]

Sergeant John McIlwain, 2nd Connaught Rangers, 5th Brigade, 2nd Division, I Corps

It was sobering thought for McIlwain when he subsequently heard a rumour that a few days later a group of Cameronian Highlanders were trapped in that same cave when the roof collapsed on them.

Even further behind the line, on 29 September Medical Officer Captain Arthur Osburn witnessed an appalling incident at Longueval sur Aisne which presaged an awful future. The 9th Lancers were in billets, seemingly safe some two miles south of the Aisne River when a giant shell sought them out.

Down the wind from the side of the village which looked towards the heights on the further side of the Aisne came a low moaning sound, ominous to anyone familiar with the sound of long-distance artillery fire. The moan narrowed to a whining scream. There was a flash, a terrific metallic detonation, the walls of the building shook, and the air was full of dust. Fragments of stone, manure, pieces of clothing and hair came falling all about me as I ran through an archway into the yard and beheld one of the most heartrending sights I have ever seen, even in war. The detachment of the 9th Lancers had almost completely disappeared. In the centre of the yard there was now a mound four or five feet high of dead men and horses, all too obviously dead, yet still they were moving, men and horses twitching and sliding over one another with slow writhing movements, the men's faces purple, crimson or ash-grey. For a moment, rooted to the ground, I stared at this heap – a moving mound of death. Then, from all sides of the yard, a chorus of screams, shouts and groans. Around this central heap of dead men the wounded lay on all sides. Some had been blown to the other end of the yard, their backs broken. One sat up dazed and whimpering, his back against a wall, holding part of his intestine in his hand. Those nearest to the heap, with terrible stomach wounds, or with legs and arms torn away, were only moaning and writhing; it was those further off, comparatively speaking the least damaged yet terribly injured, who shouted and screamed in agony.[51]

The horrors faced by Osburn that day in dealing with individual cases are beyond comment. Men lived on for the cruellest time despite the wounds that surely doomed them to death.

One, terribly wounded, lay with both legs partly torn away at the knee, one arm broken and other wounds; he was still conscious. 'Oh! My God! Shoot me! Shoot me!' he moaned. 'Quick!' I injected some morphia into his breast. It had no effect. Someone who had rushed into the yard was standing, breathless, horror-stricken, beside me. The tortured man recognized him – his brother! 'Shoot me, Tom! Oh! Shoot me! For the love of God! Shoot me, will you! WILL YOU!' he began to scream piteously. Irresolutely, the man appealed to, fumbled with his revolver and looked at me rather wildly. He was trembling, and his face was very white. Then, suddenly dropping his revolver, he covered his face with his hands and staggered away. I hastily soaked with chloroform a piece of clothing that had been literally blown from one of the other wounded, and doubling it, I laid it over the mouth of the agonized man beside whom I was kneeling.[52]

That one shell killed Second Lieutenant George Taylor-Whitehead[53] and seventeen more men. A second a few minutes later doubled the casualties. This was a war that pitched high-explosive heavy-calibre shells against frail bodies.

The possession of such heavy artillery gave the Germans an enormous advantage in the fighting on the Aisne. Any attempts to retaliate by the

Royal Artillery were hampered by the lack of heavy guns or howitzers. All they had were a smattering of 60-pounders with the later addition of a few obsolescent 1896 6" howitzers. Then there was the problem of trying to get what guns they had into reasonable firing positions. The 18-pounders had a flat trajectory and found themselves either too often exposed to the full view of the Germans, or relatively hidden, but unable to clear the crest of the ridge. For the most part they would be firing 'blind' from the gun positions and forced to use the indirect fire techniques decried before the war. As such, it was necessary to establish forward observation posts.

> Two men were wanted to go forward to where the infantry had dug their trenches. It was necessary to have someone to observe as the German trenches were but a little way in front and the artillery had to be on the alert for an attack. Arrived at a rick near our trenches just before dawn. Dug some cover to protect us from shell and rifle fire.[54]
>
> Signaller John Palmer, 118th Battery, 26th Brigade, RFA, 1st Division, I Corps

These observation posts were linked to the battery by long telephone lines that had to be rolled out and maintained by signallers like Palmer. Amongst the batteries moved up as soon as possible were the 4.5" howitzers of the 31st Howitzer Battery. Their natural high trajectory made them invaluable.

> On the 15th September the brigade, being howitzers, had taken up a position at Bucy le Long, under cover of a spur of the high ground occupied by the enemy, and by careful forward observation had very successfully engaged the enemy's guns. In order to locate our howitzers an aeroplane was sent out to 'spot' our positions. I was sitting with the Battery Commander in our observation post in the rear of the battery, and I very clearly saw the plane drop a signal when over the battery. This was soon followed by a salvo from the heavy guns. We certainly never expected the enemy to use the heavy siege artillery prepared for use against Paris, in the field and the Major and I were astonished actually to see the projectiles coming over us. The range was plus and these first few salvoes fell on the wood in which the wagon line had been placed. The casualties at the gun position were very slight but unfortunately seventy or eighty horses were killed or injured. The Major's plucky, little trumpeter was killed – he held on to three

of the horses – mine, his own, and the Major's. I had the sad job of accompanying our Captain, who passed through the wood shooting all the very badly injured horses. It was our first bad day, and the battery was badly shaken at the loss of so many old friends.[55]

Sergeant Frank Pusey, 31st Howitzer Battery, 37th Brigade RFA, 4th Division, III Corps

The gunners of both sides fought intense private duels in their attempts to gain a superiority of fire. It was by no means unusual when Lieutenant Francis Le Breton of the 50th Battery came under heavy fire from the dreaded 'Black Marias'.

They started firing large-size explosive shells at us. They burst with a terrific crash amid volumes of dense black smoke, and throw up quantities of mud, which rain down on one for about half a minute after the shell has exploded. After one or two of these, the Major told us to take cover under the big bank on the right of the battery. And it was lucky he did, as just afterwards one fell right under 'E' Sub-section limber, picked it up and hurled it fifteen feet, leaving it lying on its back riddled with holes. It also made several holes in the spring case of the gun. Sat under the bank for some time, and had our lunch there. During the afternoon they fired some more heavy shell at us, but as we were firing ourselves we did not mind so much. One fell about ten yards in front of 'C' gun, behind which I was kneeling; it covered us all with mud. These big shells are worst when one is doing nothing, as one hears them coming nearer and nearer through the air, and one never quite knows, if they will pitch on you or not.[56]

It was apparent that counter-battery fire – the deliberate-aimed destruction of an opposing battery – was going to be a very important part of the fighting in trench warfare. One response was to take extreme care in preparing gun pits protected from the front. Camouflage was employed to conceal the guns from sight, using bushes, foliage and straw. The gun detachments were provided with sheltered positions, either simple dugouts or use of the existing caves on the reverse slope.

It was during the Battle of the Aisne that the RFC first began to carve out a vital role within the all-arms battle. Up until then it had been a useful adjunct to the cavalry, bringing in long-range reports that indicated where large formations of the Germans were to be located, in what direction they were heading and much other valuable intelligence. As we have seen, it was not always believed by French and Wilson. But now the devastation raining down on the British positions at the Aisne demanded the inclusion of aviation in a coordinated response.

> They have 8-inch guns which fire an enormous shell, 2 foot 11 inch long. Yesterday they knocked out one of our howitzer batteries in about three minutes, German aeroplanes signalling to direct the fire of the batteries. Some better cooperation between our flying men and the batteries is necessary and we are trying to work this up.[57]
>
> Lieutenant Colonel Stanley Maude, Headquarters, III Corps

Three were several important technical problems that had to be overcome before the aircraft could achieve its potential worth in both aerial observation and artillery ranging. But war is a powerful catalyst for change, and already the first steps had been taken that would make the RFC indispensable to the Royal Artillery for the rest of the war. The problem was simple: the Germans were up on the heights looking down on them and even had an observation post in the seemingly invulnerable tall chimney of the sugar factory above Troyon. They also had the use of observers in the baskets hoisted aloft by kite balloons (*drachen*), which facility the British still lacked at this stage of the war. Thus the Germans could see their targets, often in plain view, while the British could only see the crest of the ridge and nothing beyond it. The location of the German gun batteries tucked behind the ridge was a mystery – and would remain so without the use of aircraft that could soar above it all.

It was soon the acknowledged role of the RFC to fly over the German lines to detect and record the exact position of any located German batteries on a map. This would then be handed to the Royal Artillery. Knowing their own position on the map, the gunner officers could work out the angle and range to the target. Although the maps were not accurate enough to allow for real precision shooting, the gunners could at least try to get their shells in the general area of the German batteries. Lieutenant William Read of 3 Squadron was up on such a mission, flying in a Henri Farman biplane with his observer. As they flew over the German lines they soon became aware of the increasing accuracy of the German anti-aircraft batteries.

At 2pm we got orders to do a reconnaissance between Soissons and Vailly, north of the River Aisne. When we were 4,000 feet over Vailly the Germans opened fire on us with anti-aircraft guns and they made surprisingly good shooting for the first few shots. The first shell was the nearest, it burst about twenty feet below us and I felt the machine shake and the left wing was boosted a little. I made rapidly for a thick white cloud on my right and as soon as I came out of it they were at us again, but the shots were wide. They fired at us again over Aizy. We got back to our landing ground at 4.15pm with our report.[58]

On 20 September Read was up again with his observer. This time he employed a simple system of firing Very lights to indicate necessary corrections to the aim of the gunners.

The sky cleared and we went off to try and locate a battery of artillery which has been causing our troops a good deal of annoyance. We discovered the battery just as their anti-aircraft guns opened fire on us. Their shells burst all round us but we did not offer them a very good target as we were well above the clouds, and only showed ourselves occasionally. We gave in our report to a Major belonging to one of the 60-pounder battery and soon after we went up again to observe the fire and get them onto the battery which we had spotted. We soon got them onto it by the aid of Very lights and our shells must have caused them a good deal of annoyance.[59]

A few days later Read had another success.

We located exactly the positions of two batteries. On our information the 60 pounders were told to shell these batteries and we went up again to direct their fire and get them on with Very light signals. Just as we were going over the guns and all ready to observe the engine started missing badly, also Walker found that his Very pistol had jammed. So down we came again to put things right. We then went up to try again with much better success. We got our battery onto them and our shells were just right, and I think we must have paid them back for the bad time they have been giving our troops in Missy. All the while we were circling about and observing, the enemy plastered us with their anti-aircraft guns until the air all round was thick with shell bursts, I kept turning, diving and climbing so as to offer as difficult a target as possible but we lost height a good deal, and when we were at 3,500 feet they managed to burst a shell near enough to put a piece of it through our propeller. So, having got our battery the range we decided to get away and land.[60]

Having been released from his staff duties at Whitehall, Captain Henry Jackson was also flying on these early artillery observation missions with 3rd Squadron, RFC. He soon found that his chronically underpowered aircraft struggled to gain much altitude and in consequence Jackson often came under Germans small-arms fire as they flew over the heights of the Chemin des Dames ridge.

> A bullet from a rifle went through the back of my seat, through my leather flying coat, but was turned off by a steel rib in my Sam Bowne belt – and I was none the worse except a bruised back. There are generally shots through our wings, but they do no harm. There are four pilots with whom I fly – all youngsters – but with good heads on their shoulders and unsurpassed in the air. I have not had an encounter with a German airman yet – of course one always has to be on the lookout for them – but I think they are a bit afraid of us and don't worry us at all.[61]

Towards the end of September the German anti-aircraft guns had become far more threatening. The young RFC pilots bestowed the guns with a suitably ironic name : 'Archibald' or 'Archie', derived from a wonderful monologue performed by the musical hall artiste George Robey concerning a nagging wife.

> Archibald, certainly not!
> Get back to work at once, sir, like a shot.
> When single you could waste time spooning
> But lose work now for honeymooning!
> Archibald, certainly not![62]

The first pilot reputed to have used the term was the eighteen-year-old Lieutenant Amyas Borton, serving with 5 Squadron, RFC, who was renowned for shouting out, 'Archibald, certainly not!' when a shell burst near his aircraft. Perhaps such an innocuous nickname was meant to diminish the growing effect that the bursting shells all around their flimsy aircraft was having on the personal morale of pilots – including Lieutenant William Read.

The Germans are getting awfully energetic with their anti-aircraft guns. Their zeal is worthy of much praise and it is not for want of trying that they have been unsuccessful in bringing any of us down with shell fire so far. They will get somebody soon with 'Archibald' as their shooting is improving every day. We ought to have some anti-aircraft guns also. All we have is a miserable pom-pom which is no use for putting the fear of God into one, in the way that 'Archibald' does. 'Archibald' can reach you at 10,000 feet, and belches forth dirty yellow and black smoke and chain shot – and the noise of the shell bursting is almost enough to make one stall the machine with fright. The pom-pom shell on the other hand only bursts on percussion and its maximum height of smoke trail is only 4,500 feet.[63]

Even as the artillery observation work using simple Very light signals continued, the next advance was already underway with experiments to get a wireless transmitter up into the skies. This would allow Morse code signal corrections sent back directly to the British batteries. The first wireless artillery observation flight took place on 18 September by Lieutenants Donald Lewis and Lieutenant Baron James of 4 Squadron, RFC. This was not a sophisticated matter, as can be seen by the record of their wireless messages on their mission on 24 September.

4.2pm.	very little short. Fire. Fire.
4.4pm	Fire again. Fire again.
4.12pm	A little short; line O.K.
4.15pm	Short. Over, over and a little left.
4.20pm	You were just between two batteries. Search 200 yards each side of your last shot. Range O.K.
4.22pm	You have them.
4.26pm	Hit. Hit. Hit.
4.3 pm	About 50 yards short and to the right.
4.37pm	Your last shot in the middle of three batteries in action; search all round within 300 yards of your last shot and you have them.
4.42pm	I am coming home now.[64]

This was a great step forward once a method of accurately describing where the shells had landed in relation to the target could be devised.[65]

The value of aerial artillery observers able to guide shells right on top of the target was appreciated by the more intelligent artillery officers.

> Without air reconnaissance no accurate artillery work at long ranges is possible. We have now had some excellent results with an air observer (James, Royal Engineers) who controls his machine, observes fire and signals results by wireless alone. The other day James put heavy battery on to target in three rounds. An exceptional man is evidently needed for this. I reported effect of wireless work to Sir Douglas Haig and has ordered us to apply for more equipment.[66]
>
> Major John Mowbray, Headquarters, Royal Artillery, 2nd Division, I Corps

There were still teething problems to overcome, but the process had begun; soon the exceptional was mere routine as more and more pilots and observers mastered the skills of artillery observation.

Fertile minds also leapt on the idea of taking up cameras to accurately record what the pilots themselves could see. The first experimental photographic reconnaissance was undertaken on 15 September by Lieutenant George Pretyman and Sergeant Frederick Laws of 3 Squadron, RFC. The results were fairly blurred, but this too was the start of something significant. The first step was crucial, as once the idea had taken hold, it was merely a matter of resolving the practical details of sourcing the right kind of camera/lens and a functional method of fitting the camera to the aircraft. Then there had to be photographic laboratory facilities to develop the photos and arrangement made to ensure the rapid dissemination of photographic prints to the relevant army headquarters. Within a few months the RFC would have pin-sharp glass-plate photos that went a long way to lifting the curtain as to what the Germans were doing – and where. It was soon found that photographs taken from directly above and at a consistent height could be patched together in a fantastically detailed mosaic-map of the whole front line area. A new art – or science – of photographic interpretation would soon evolve to tease out the location of German headquarters, machine gun posts, dugouts and – most important of all – gun batteries.

The end result of a month of experimentation, reorganisation and sheer hard work was a quantifiable improvement in the performance of the Royal Artillery. Together with the RFC they were charting away through this new form of warfare – one in which the guns and their 'hand maidens' in the RFC would become the dominant destructive weapons system of the Great War. But there was still a long way to go. One essential was to develop the ability to concentrate the fire of divisional artillery onto an identified corps target worthy of a sustained heavy barrage. This was the future, but shortages of telephone wire hampered experiments launched as early as 16 September by Haig and the I Corps Commander Royal Artillery, Brigadier General Henry Horne. There were so many difficulties to be overcome. Practical minds were identifying the needs, the problems and the solutions. But it would all take time and resources.

Of course both sides were engaged in overcoming the same problems. The British could not but be aware that their opponents were already adept in artillery observation. German aircraft were frequently sighted over the British lines, unveiling the few secrets not already visible to the observers up on the ridge and hanging from the *drachen*. The Germans used a system of light signals to correct the range, or angle, of fire for their gunners.

> Next morning a German aeroplane, when immediately above our trench, let something fall which we took to be a bomb as it appeared to be dropping right on top of us it fell about half way and burst giving out a shower of silvery lights, this we afterwards found out was a signal to the German gunners as to the effect of their firing and accuracy of their aim. The shelling then became more accurate and the shells seemed to lift you up and drop you down again so terrific was the concussion.[67]
>
> Lance Corporal Edward Luther, 3rd Rifle Brigade, 17th Brigade, 6th Division, III Corps

Not unnaturally, the infantry and artillery looked at the RFC to counter the depredations of their opposite numbers. There had already been some clashes in the air between British and German aircraft, but from this time these would increase exponentially. The problem was that the aircraft were not powerful enough to take up even a light machine gun, but rifles, shotguns and revolvers were difficult to use in the air, especially in a single-seater.

> About 4pm a German aeroplane flew over the battery and dropped balls of light. We fired at it with our rifles, but it took no notice. As

a result, a few minutes later, the German heavy howitzers opened fire on us, just after we had taken post on the guns to fire at some target or other. One gets quite used to being covered with earth from explosions of shells close by, but the awful sound of these heavy shells coming straight at one, is the most terrifying noise imaginable. All our guns have holes through their shields and spring cases, and every wheel has one or more spokes shot away. This aeroplane then came back over us, and a British biplane came up from the other side of the Aisne, and the two aeroplanes had a duel. We could hear the shots fired. After a little manoeuvring the British machine suddenly tilted up sideways and started falling: it recovered partly, however, and flew back in a rather slanting attitude whence it came. Heard later that Mapplebeck[68] was the pilot of this machine, which was only a single-seater, and that he had some bombs but no rifles, so he could not expect to do much against the two-seater Albatros, whose observer had a repeater rifle. Mapplebeck was hit in the thigh; but managed to land the machine all right.[69]

Lieutenant Francis Le Breton, 50th Battery, 34th Brigade, RFA, 2nd Division, I Corps

One other aviation development was an increasing interest and experimentation in dropping bombs on the German trenches. Although a simple concept, the actual practicalities of designing a fool-proof bomb release mechanism were considerable as Lieutenant Cuthbert Rabagliati of 5 Squadron, RFC discovered to his disquiet.

When we were operating from the Aisne in September we were served out with various kinds of bombs which we used to carry in our machines and drop on likely targets whenever we found any. I and my co-pilot were using a French shrapnel bomb, it was a contraption about four inches wide and about eight or ten inches long. We used to dump it over the side hoping that you wouldn't hit one of your own wires or your wheels as it went. I thought we could improve on that and I made in the squadron workshops a metal tube which I put through the floor of my seat right down and fastened it on to the central skid of my Avro machine. We could drop bombs right through it without entangling ourselves with anything. On that day I dropped two, and all went well. I dropped the third – but it wasn't apparently the same size as the others and to my horror it stuck in the tube. Not only did it stick in the tube but it stuck with the detonator of the bomb lower than the level of my wheels – which was a bit exciting. We tried everything we could think of and I couldn't get it out. I even tried to climb out over the side but I couldn't. I passed a note back to my pilot telling him what had happened and I watched him read it and I watched his face – it was a sight! We flew round for a long time. Then we came back to the squadron, came very low and I wrote a message. I put it in a message bag and dropped it down in front of the hangers telling them what had happened and saying that when we landed to keep well away, because obviously the whole thing was going to blow up. Then we landed right away at the far end of the aerodrome – as far away as we could possibly get – we were for it but we didn't want to blow up the whole squadron as well! I suppose my pilot was a bit scared and he landed much faster than usual. We skimmed along at practically ground level and the edge of the aerodrome was covered in uncut corn so that it was quite high. The stalks of corn wrapped themselves round the detonator of the bomb and had wrenched it right out of the bomb so that when we finally landed we had no detonator and it did nothing. You can imagine the feeling of touching the ground, drawing your feet and knees up – knowing perfectly well that that was the end – and suddenly there was a bounce, then another bounce, then you began running along – your reaction! All I know is I leapt out of the machine when it was still running and I gather my pilot did too, because when it finally came to a stop there we were lying with complete silence. I got up to try and go to it, whereupon my pilot called out, 'For God's sake stay still, you've done enough damage for one day!'[70]

Aviation was making great leaps forward across the skies above them, but somehow the British were often strangely unwilling to believe that it was not German 'eyes in the sky', but rather some hapless French peasant acting as a devilish spy with some weird, wonderful and – let it be said – totally unpractical method of communicating with his German masters.

We are much bothered by spy scares. The Germans seem to have an uncanny knowledge of what goes on this side of the river, and it certainly must be largely due to spies, and not only to aeroplanes. In Chassemy village, it was noticed that one man had horses and cattle left him. This looking suspicious, he was arrested and searched. On him they found a large sum of money – much larger than he could have come by honestly; they then searched his house and found in the cellar a German working a telephone, the line of which went over the river. Both were given short shrift. Altogether in the last ten days we have caught and shot sixty spies, most of them bribed peasants. They are usually handed over to the French authorities for justice, which is less merciful than ours, as a matter of fact. It is extraordinary that Frenchmen, who one would think had a good reason to loathe Germany, should help them – yet many do.[71]

Lieutenant William Congreve, Headquarters, 3rd Division, II Corps

This was the equivalent of the modern urban legend, something people seem to want to believe is true no matter how unlikely. This would be nothing but amusing were the suspects not usually reported to have been shot out of hand.

THROUGHOUT SEPTEMBER THE GERMAN ATTACKS CONTINUED. Although they were still intent in throwing the BEF back across the Aisne in disarray, the Germans were also beginning to work towards a new plan of campaign, so that they were increasingly intent on pinning as many French and British forces on the Aisne as possible, whilst they amassed strength preparation for a lunge northwards and then westwards around the relatively unguarded Allied left flank. As a result the fighting remained intense. There were long slow bombardments rising to shattering climaxes, the gradual sapping forward of the German trenches, and sudden desperate attacks across the narrow No Man's Land. One allegation made frequently by the British throughout the Aisne fighting was that of treachery or immoral conduct by Germans pretending to surrender and then opening a deadly fire at their all-unsuspecting captors. One of the best documented incidents occurred on 17 September when the Germans made an attack on the extreme right of the British line where it joined with the trenches held by the French troops. In conditions of dire visibility the Germans managed to occupy a trench that enfiladed the British line. The 1st Northamptonshires were ordered to retake the trench.

Then Parker gave the order to fix bayonets and a few minutes later to charge. Over the low bank we went, Parker shouting, 'Come on, the Cobblers!' and the men cheering like hell. I ran as hard as and as best I could over the roots with my drawn sword in one hand and my revolver in the other, stumbling over and cursing the roots and expecting every moment to be tripped up by my sword scabbard! We charged through heavy rifle and machine-gun fire and men were dropping off in every direction. We got to about 30 yards from the trench which we had passed over on the Monday and which was now strongly held. By now everyone was pretty well blown, and I was thankful when I saw the whole line to my right throwing themselves down flat. I shouted out, 'Down!' to my men, and suited the action to the word; in any case, nobody could have heard me over the appalling din of firing. After what seemed hours, I saw young Gordon crawling along towards me from the right flank of the company on his tummy; he eventually reached me and told me that poor dear old Parker[72] had been killed leading the charge and that I was in command of the company and also of the company of the 60th Rifles on our right, all of whose officers had been either killed or wounded![73]

Lieutenant Evelyn Needham, 1st Northamptonshire Regiment, 2nd Brigade, 1st Division, I Corps

They lay there for about an hour. A further attempt to advance aroused such a storm of fire that the attack broke down before it started. Then Needham had a welcome surprise.

Suddenly I heard the men shouting, 'They're surrendering!' and, looking up, I saw a line of white flags, or rather white handkerchiefs or something of the kind tied to the muzzles of rifles, held up all along the German trench from in front of us right away to the left. I shouted out to the men to cease fire and stop where they were. After a few minutes I saw a large number of Germans, two or three hundred at least, moving forward from their trench towards 'A' Company on the road, some with their rifles, but many with white flags tied to them, and many with their hands up. They got down to 'A' Company's trench and stood there for some time, apparently conversing. All this time the white flags in front of us continued up and many Germans were standing with their hands up. All of a sudden a burst of heavy firing broke out down by 'A' Company and we saw the Germans and our men engaged in a hand-to-hand fight. Still the white flags in front of us remained up![74]

Second-Lieutenant Lancelot Burlton was amongst the Northamptons surprised by the 'change of heart' amongst the Germans.

We saw the enemy in front of us making signs of surrender by putting their hands up. Their fire stopped and I ordered my men to do likewise. I stood up on the parapet and called for an officer to meet me. An individual, I think a private, who spoke English, responded to the call, and I went out some forty yards ahead of my trench to make the necessary arrangements. On finding out that he was not an officer, I ordered him to return and tell his officer to replace him. A sergeant or under-officer next turned up, but was also returned as 'not wanted,' after which an officer did materialize. He appeared to find great difficulty in understanding me. I agreed to accept surrender, but, as a preliminary thereto, naturally ordered him to make his men lay down their arms. Our conversation took place half-way between the opposing trenches and, to my annoyance, I saw a large number of the enemy detach from their trenches before my arrangements were completed. Most of them had their rifles, but many had not and many had their hands up. I tried to make the Bosche officer understand that I would order my men to fire if his men continued to advance with their arms. All this time, the enemy continued to advance and the officer appeared quite willing to surrender, but unable to grasp my idea of his men putting their rifles down as a preliminary. I found myself being surrounded by the advancing Germans, and, as there was no officer in our trench, I could not afford to remain out in No Man's Land, which was rapidly being overwhelmed by the advancing Huns. I was, at the time, quite sure of their *bona fides* as to surrender, and did not want to open fire for two reasons. Firstly, many of the enemy came without arms and with their hands up; and, to make the illusion complete, some of them who were armed handed their rifles over to some of our Tommies who had come out to meet them on their own. It would have been a dirty business to have opened fire on men who were advancing with their arms because they did not understand English.[75]

Then the situation spiralled out of control and a bloody hand-to-hand battle began in the middle of No Man's Land, even more vicious than usual, fuelled as it was by intense feelings of betrayal and a visceral desire for vengeance which resonate through Burlton's account.

A German quite close to me shot one of my men dead, and the officer, on my saying that if he did not order an immediate cessation of his fire, I would order mine to open, informed me I was his prisoner! We then all got to in earnest, so to speak, and at point-blank range, of course: no accuracy of shooting was necessary – the men used their butts and bayonets lustily. We were, however, far outnumbered, being but some seventy-odd against, I believe, four hundred. Then the most wonderful thing happened. The Queen's on our right, seeing we were in trouble, and seeing that the Bosches were, for the most part, standing on our parapet and firing down on us in the road, turned on their machine gun and the spectacle was one never to be forgotten. They fairly enfiladed the Huns on our parapet, and the execution can only be compared to that of a harvesting machine as it mows down wheat. A regular lane was cut – those Bosches on their side of the lane (perhaps some hundred strong) made their best pace back to their trenches; those on our side of the lane threw down arms and surrendered; but we declined their offer, and, in fact, I think only kept one prisoner – a souvenir no doubt![76]

The end result was a reprehensible slaughter, but the feelings of those involved ran high beyond liberal reasoning. One of the Northamptons who received appalling wounds in the bitter fighting was Sergeant John Stennett.

I received fourteen wounds, commencing at the spine, shattering my right shoulder. The sensation was a shell had burst very close and I thought a piece of brick had hit me in the back of the neck. Of course I was knocked down. The fire was too heavy for me to try and get to the dressing station. I laid still for about twenty minutes then thought I would try and get back. I just managed to get up, but was promptly sent down again with another in my back. This put me down for the count.[77]

Another victim of the incident was Second Lieutenant Cosmo Gordon, the young officer who just four days before had refused to take cover while trying to inspire his men at the height of the fighting. Now he was sorely hit during the sudden burst of firing from the Germans. It was a sad and terrible end as witnessed by Lieutenant Evelyn Needham.

Gordon and I had been kneeling up trying to make out what was going on, and were still doing so when the Huns opened fire. Gordon, who was not a foot away from me, suddenly pitched forward on his face and yelled out, 'Oh, my God, I'm hit!' He writhed about on the ground in agony and I tried to keep him quiet. He assured me again and again that he was shot through the stomach and that he was going to die. Poor devil, it was hell being able to do nothing for him and to see and hear him in such agony. I could only try to reassure him. We got poor Gordon[78] on to the stretcher. He made me promise to see that his sword was sent back to his family and his batman took it. They carried him off and I never saw him again. Poor boy, he died at the casualty clearing station, as he said he was going to, having suffered terribly, and was buried there. A typical, cheery, plucky boy, straight from Sandhurst, gazetted only that January, to whom everybody had taken a great fancy, and whom I had particularly liked.[79]

The grieving Needham never really understood what had happened.

To this day it is a mystery to me. Did the Germans really mean to surrender, but on getting down to 'A' Company to do so and finding so few men there, change their minds and try to reverse proceedings and take them prisoner, or was the whole thing a put-up job? We shall never know.[80]

Many histories are dogmatic in assigning blame, but the tangled nature of the situation on top of the Chemin des Dames ridge made such fatal mis-understandings nigh on inevitable. Other German units with no inten-tion of surrendering could easily have been involved with no intention of 'treachery'. Indeed German accounts make remarkably similar accusa-tions of British troops failing to respect a white flag.

The troops in the trenches were still enduring an unprecedented amount of shell fire from the German artillery, though burrowing deep into the ground had at least given then a reasonable amount of protection.

I wonder how many thousands of shrapnel bullets must have been fired at us during the last 24-hours. It is a wearing trying job and gets on one's nerves fearfully. How long can it go on, I wonder, and how long can one's nerves stand it. Of course, one is safe enough as far as things go in trenches with cover, etc., but it is the noise and shock that tires one. A whistle and a bang, and a noise that sounds like a shower of hail as the shrapnel comes through the branches of the trees, and then all is over for a minute and then at it again.[81]

Captain Charles Paterson, 1st South Wales Borderers, 3rd Brigade, 1st Division, I Corps

Many were beginning to show classic signs of mental strain, with almost uncontrollable reactions to sudden, or loud, noises. They certainly had good reason.

> When I get home, I hope you will not take it amiss if I dive down under the sofa when the servants slam the attic door, or fall down flat in New Street when I hear an errand boy whistling; as these things are rather apt to get on one's nerves.[82]
>
> Lieutenant Rowland Owen, 2nd Duke of Wellington's Regiment, 13th Brigade, 5th Division, II Corps

Signaller John Palmer had no chance to react when a shell descended close to him as he carried out a small gesture of comradeship that could easily have lost him his life.

> Decided to go up to the observation post with some provisions for the lads. Put a tin of jam in each pocket, some bully, and carried an armful of bread. Add to this a dixie of hot tea and you might imagine I was fully loaded. Got to within 100 yards of the position when it happened. Only heard a sudden roar and crash then darkness descended. When I awoke I found I was on the edge of a glorious shell-hole, several horses dead, a despatch rider and his motor cycle in a horrible mess and my bread well in the mud. The dixie was or course overturned and all that seemed to remain was the jam in my pockets. I certainly felt groggy on my feet and I suddenly became aware of that wet sticky feeling on my face and neck which denotes blood. Where my wound was I did not know, I had pain all over and was not sorry when I staggered into headquarters again. I was greeted with 'Hello Jack, what the hell have you been up to?' I told him as best I could and said I thought I must have lost a lot of blood as it was all over my tunic and neck. To my utter astonishment he burst out laughing and asked me when I was going to learn the difference between jam and blood? It was quite correct. As the shell exploded a fragment had burst open one of the tins in my pocket. The jam had been forced but all over my tunic and in my dazed condition I had mistaken it for blood! Then an order to present myself in front of the Colonel – all he wanted was to appreciate my jam episode to the full! I suppose it will be months before I hear the last of this![83]
>
> Signaller John Palmer, 118th Battery, 26th Brigade, RFA, 1st Division, I Corps

Trapped in the line for days on end, with only infrequent reliefs, whole units began to betray clear signals that their morale was fading. When units broke there were always excuses to be made and brickbats to be thrown, but the men needed a chance to rest away from the constant fear of sudden death or terrible maiming injuries.

> A very lively fusillade started in front of the Liverpools on our right. It became so violent, and so many spent bullets came whistling past us, that the Major ordered all the rifles off the guns and we lined the edge of the bank. A good many Liverpools came running back along the top of the hill, and some through the battery. We argued with those that came through us, and some went back again, but others insisted that they had been ordered to retire – liars! After about half-an-hour the din subsided, and finally ceased. I'm afraid the nerves of the Liverpools are rather the worse for wear. I wish they would relieve them, as it would not need much force to get through them in their present state, and then we should be captured, as I don't think we are more than 400 yards from their trenches.[84]
>
> Lieutenant Francis Le Breton, 50th Battery, 34th Brigade, RFA, 2nd Division, I Corps

But it was not just the relentless shelling or the sudden German attacks that made life almost unbearable. Lieutenant William Synge, of the self-same 1st King's Liverpools, reflected on the multitude of miseries that they had to endure in their open trenches.

> The whole time that we were here it rained incessantly; the nights were very cold, and for reasons of safety we were unable to light a fire at which to dry our clothes. We had no chance of a hot meal or drink, and lived on biscuits and jam for the most part. We had bully beef too, but as far as I was concerned, I found that my tongue got so sore from eating it continually in an uncooked state, that I gave it up altogether. Rum was our one expedient, and, much as I detest it, I must say that it has a most soothing and warming effect on a cold night. For the first three or four days I had not got my mackintosh or my great coat, and I used to wring the water out of my breeches in the morning. When I got up, in order to stand to arms an hour before dawn, my legs used to be quite numb, and it was sometimes a quarter-of-an-hour before I could stand up without falling down again. The extraordinary thing was that none of us, not even the older men, got colds or rheumatism.

A doctor said the reason was that we and our clothes were so dirty and full of grease that we were waterproof![85]

But even as they enjoyed the occasional periods without shell fire, they were by no means out of danger. Trench warfare brought with it the concept of the sniper, the concealed rifleman picking off the unwary soldier.

When one does at long last come under a bit of rifle fire, in one's delight one treats it as child's play. Some of the enemy are only about 60 yards away from our position, and the rest only about 300 yards. There are snipers all over the place, in the woods and up trees; and they carry on a hearty old shoot all day. The first man that had a shot at me I had such a contempt for, that I absentmindedly turned round and cocked snooks at him, to the huge delight of my platoon – and then it suddenly struck me that he was probably going to try another and I ducked into a doorway.[86]

Lieutenant Rowland Owen, 2nd Duke of Wellington's Regiment, 13th Brigade, 5th Division, II Corps

Second Lieutenant Arnold Gyde of the 2nd South Staffordshire Regiment was not so lucky, getting shot by a German sniper early in the morning of 22 September. He recorded his tangled impressions in the third person, strange for such a deeply individual experience, but his words even so have a jarring immediacy and ability to conjure up the terrible shock as the bullet struck home.

He almost reached the end of his trenches. There was a crisp crash, a blinding light flew up like a circular sunset around him, a dreadful twinge, as of hair and skin and skull being jerked from his head with the strength of a giant! For the millionth part of a second he was at a loss to understand what had happened. Then, with sickening horror, he realised that he had been shot in the head. It is impossible to convey with what speed impressions rushed through his mind. The flaring horizon tilted suddenly from horizontal nearly to perpendicular. His head rushed through half a world of black, fury-space. His toes and finger-tips were infinite miles behind. A sound of rushing waters filled his ears, like deathly waterfalls stamping the life from his bursting head. Black blurred figures, nebulous and meaningless, loomed up before his face. 'Hit in the head – you're done for.' The inadequate thought chased through his brain, 'What a pity, what a shame; you might have been so happy, later on! What a pity, what a shame; you might have been so happy later on!' He was conscious that it was a foolishly futile thought at a supreme moment. His life seemed pouring out of his head, his vitality was running down as a motor engine, suddenly cut off. He felt death descending upon him with appalling swiftness. Where would the world go to? And what next? He was afraid.[87]

Gyde fell unconscious and when – somewhat to his surprise – he awoke, he found that his right side was paralysed. Then he thought he saw something moving towards him. After a long wait he was evacuated, then operated upon and would eventually begin a long recuperation back in England.

THE GERMAN ATTACKS ON THE AISNE petered out on 28 September. Throughout, the British had devoted themselves to improving their defences rather than engaging in their own offensive operations or in combining with the French. This uncooperative approach was noticed by the somewhat despairing Brigadier General Stanley Maude, who references several of the problems that had dogged the BEF right from the start.

> Went with Du Cane to GHQ to get instructions as regards possible advance tomorrow. GHQ have too little grip on the army, which is not commanded as a whole but separately as three distinct Corps. Also there seems to be scarcely enough determination to support the French when they decide to attack. We always seem to be waiting till they have done something.[88]

Another example of the continued British failure to support the French was noticed by Maude a couple of days later.

> We are not very good allies in that sort of way as we only co-operate when it suits us. It must be rather disheartening to the French and the reason for acting so seems difficult to follow. Surely when one makes war, one should be more resolute and put every effort forward to beat the enemy as quickly as possible.[89]

It is evident that the British approach embarrassed Maude. However, it should be noted that one hampering factor in any kind of offensive capability by the BEF was the serious lack of shells. The Royal Artillery had not planned for either sustained fire or a long war. Here they had both to contend with. The gunners were soon lacking in every kind of shell and without an armaments industry geared up to meet their needs, they were condemned to an informal system of rationing, only permitting firing at tempting targets or in circumstances of real need. It was a problem that would dog them throughout for the remainder of 1914.

Overall, this was a new kind of warfare for the BEF. In taking on the Germans, they were fighting an opponent of equal or greater military aptitude, an army counted in millions, with individuals equally convinced of their superior morale. The failed assault of 14 September had persuaded French and many others in the BEF command structure that they could not break through the German line on the Aisne: it was simply impossible. But one last hope remained: if they could not go through the German trenches, perhaps they could go round them. Perhaps there was one last hope to be home for Christmas.

10

RACE TO THE SEA

It was his right wing that we attempted to outflank and envelop.
When he outstripped us, it was his effort to outflank us that
we warded off. For he was trying by increased speed to envelop
us in a manoeuvre similar to our own. This produced on each
side a race towards the northern wing of the opposing army.
At the same time, we had to check the enemy's advance and
immobilize him on the remainder of the front; and this front
was getting longer and longer. As a result of this symmetrical
manoeuvre, the northern wing moved at an ever-increasing
speed through the Ile de France, Picardy, Artois and Flanders,
up to the North Sea. In this way, the sea marked the end of the
manoeuvre, though it had never been its aim.[1]

General Ferdinand Foch, Headquarters Northern Group of Armies

DEADLOCK ON THE AISNE WAS not the end of open warfare. The
German plans encompassed strong attacks by their Second, Seventh and
First Armies in an effort to pin the French armies in place, while they
gathered ready for a lunge around the northern flank of the French. There
is no doubt that both sides had become keenly aware of the open flanks
to the north. It was obvious that if they could not push forward to overwhelm by brute force, then they would have to go round. It is therefore
unsurprising to discover that Joffre was planning the mirror image of the
German plans.

> I had the distinct impression that the Germans were going to accept a new battle on the line where they now stood. To my mind there could be no question of our beginning a general action, for it would cost us heavy losses and use up most of our ammunition. My intention was, while maintaining an aggressive attitude which would keep the enemy constantly under the threat of a general attack and prevent him from sending forces to strengthen his right wing, to undertake a powerful action with my left against the German right, by means of units which I would withdraw from my centre and right.[2]

Joffre decided to create a new Second Army under General Édouard de Castelnau to operate to the north of the Sixth Army in the Picardy area from 20 September. The Second Army ceased to exist on the Lorraine front where it was in the line facing Metz, with the remaining units being assigned to the neighbouring First Army. Meanwhile the headquarters and the XX Corps were moved north, to join the XIV, IV Corps and XIII Corps, where they were to carry out an enveloping attack against the German right wing, manoeuvring north to ensure that they still outflanked any additional forces the Germans might add to their right wing. While the fighting continued on the Aisne the Second Army sent its corps, one by one, to the north and northeast. Yet at every turn they found themselves blocked by the equal and opposite manoeuvre by their German counterparts. They leapfrogged north reaching the Somme, then Arras, then Lens and even the Lille area. At times the situation appeared desperate, but Joffre drove his commanders on by a mixture of encouragement, cajolement and naked threats – and by this time his subordinates were well aware that dismissal was no idle threat. To keep everyone up to the mark, on 4 October, General Ferdinand Foch was appointed as Assistant to the Commander in Chief, with the responsibility for coordinating the operations of the Northern Group of Allied Armies in what would be erroneously forever known as the 'Race to the Sea'. Although just weeks before, Foch had served as a corps commander under de Castelnau, this was nevertheless an excellent appointment, due to his relentless forceful attitude, unwillingness to accept defeat and, above all, a demonstrable ability to inspire subordinates to feats they would otherwise never have considered possible.

Meanwhile, Sir John French was attempting to secure the immediate move of the BEF to the left of the French armies, up into the northern coastal areas, where they could protect British interests and have the (unmentioned) option of an easy escape should the situation deteriorate again.

> So long as the Germans were being driven back, whether by frontal
> or flank attack, the Channel ports might be considered comparatively
> safe. I had arrived at the conclusion that a frontal attack was hopeless;
> whilst it began to appear that any threat against the German flank
> would be effectually countered if not turned against ourselves.
> This, then, was my great fear. What was there to prevent the enemy
> launching a powerful movement for the purpose of securing the
> Channel Ports, whilst the main forces were engaged in practically
> neutralising one another? From this time I sent constant and urgent
> warnings to London by wire and by letter to look out for the safety of
> these same ports. It was just about now that I began to conceive the
> idea of disengaging from the Aisne and moving to a position in the
> north, for the main purpose of defending the Channel ports and, as a
> secondary reason, to be in a better position to concert combined action
> and cooperation with the Navy.[3]

However, the diary entries of Henry Wilson for 24 and 25 September give an idea not only of the degree of vacillation that plagued the decision-making process of GHQ, but also the influence exerted by Wilson, who claims that it was he who had first implanted the idea in his superior's mind.

> Told Sir John. . . said it was his idea (!) and let the proposal mature.
> All day passed and Sir John came to no decision. Before dinner he
> told me that he had given up all idea of going on the left because
> the Indian divisions could not be here until the middle of October.
> There was nothing new in this, but the silly man[4] had at last realised
> that he had not got those divisions in the field. He said he would not
> go on the left with three corps and two cavalry divisions because he
> would be afraid after his Mons and Le Cateau experience. I pointed
> out that the German corps of today were very different indeed to the
> corps of a month ago and that they were no longer an avalanche. After
> considerable argument I nearly got him round to my way of thinking.[5]

Four days later, it was indeed all change as French put forward the latest version of his views to Joffre in a memo, pointing to the imminent arrival on the Western Front of the 7th and 8th Divisions, the 3rd Cavalry Division, the Indian Corps (two divisions) and one Indian cavalry division. This would raise the BEF strength from six divisions and two cavalry divisions, to ten divisions and four cavalry divisions. Joffre conceded the logic of the case, but disputed French's bold statement that 'There remains the question of *when* this move should take place. I submit that *now* is the time.'[6] Amidst all the enormous problems of funnelling a substantial portion of the French army north, while at the same time countering the simultaneous German offensives, here was Sir John French agitating to be moved *at once* next to the sea. Furthermore, Joffre had not forgotten – or more to the point forgiven – the BEF for its lacklustre performance during the Great Retreat, nor the special pleading required to 'stiffen' them enough to secure their participation in the Battle of the Marne. Joffre preferred to see the BEF, as an unreliable ally, sandwiched between the French Fifth and Sixth Armies, where it could be closely monitored for backsliding during the critical phase of operations. Nevertheless he reluctantly agreed - with strings attached.

> The manoeuvre now being executed, I wrote him, requires the constant reinforcement of our left wing by withdrawals from various parts of the front; as the transport of the British Army has prevented, during nearly ten days, all transfers of French units, it is of capital importance for the outcome of our operations that all the movements of troops effected towards the north be made to collaborate without exception and immediately in the same task, viz., the arrest and outflanking of the German right wing. I, therefore, asked the Field Marshal not to wait until all of his forces were reunited before employing the units which had already moved.[7]

As Joffre icily remarked, 'Thus a fresh problem was added to all the others.'[8] His solution was a compromise: in effect to transport the BEF north in stages. The Cavalry Division could move north to act as a liaison between the Belgian Army and the French Second Army, then the newly arriving 7th and 8th Divisions could be deployed in the Dunkirk area prior to moving in the direction of Lille, the Indian Corps would link up with them, before the divisions of II, III and finally I Corps would be despatched to join them, as and when it was possible to transport them from the Aisne.

Despite this compromise offer, French and his staff remained unrelenting in their campaign to accelerate the move north of the forces left on the Aisne. Joffre was furious at this British intransigence and although he did to some extent give way, he would later blame the resulting delays in French troop movements for the loss to the Germans of the valuable manufacturing and industrial heartlands of the Lille area. The replacement of the BEF by relatively weak French forces also led to the subsequent loss of valuable tactical positions on the Aisne, ground that would turn into one of the bloodiest battlegrounds in the whole war. The BEF had done well on the Aisne, but once again were blotting their collective copybook.

ONE LAST GREAT PROBLEM DARKENED JOFFRE'S stormy horizon. Having occupied Brussels, the German III Reserve Corps (commanded by General Hans Hartwig von Beseler) was turning its attention to besieging the Belgian port of Antwerp from 30 September. The Belgians appealed for assistance to both their French and British allies. Joffre announced that he would send what troops he could, mainly light and territorial forces, but he had no army to spare, due to the tremendous pressure imposed by the 'Race to the Sea'. The Belgians were told brusquely that they must evacuate Antwerp and concentrate what remained of the Belgian Army on the north flank of the allied line. Joffre was adamant that the real battle was taking place elsewhere in northern France and that Antwerp was a lost cause, as it was apparent that reinforcements could not be organised and deployed in time to save the port. The Belgians were appalled at the thought of abandoning Antwerp, as indeed were the British, partly because of their fixation with preventing hostile powers gaining control of major Channel ports. This was of particular concern to the mercurial Winston Churchill, the First Lord of the Admiralty, who had long been concerned by the apparent vulnerability of the Belgian port. Churchill despatched several machine guns, 4.7" naval guns and some anti-aircraft guns to Antwerp and was keen to despatch more reinforcements. Kitchener and the British Cabinet baulked at the idea of sending the regular troops of the 7th Division to bolster the defence, reasoning that this would court disaster if they became trapped – as seemed very likely. It was, however, agreed that the 7th Division and 3rd Cavalry Division (banded together to form a makeshift IV Corps) could operate in Belgium to threaten the besieging German forces, yet it was clear that they could not be deployed for several days and time was in short supply for the Belgian defenders of Antwerp. It was at this point that Churchill became more intimately involved, in that he had his own military force available to deploy.

The Royal Naval Division (RND) was a curious creation initiated by Churchill at the outbreak of war. On reviewing the naval mobilisation plans, he had become aware that there would be over 20,000 reservists for which there would be no ships immediately available, and he decided to form them into a division for emergency deployment ashore as a potential augmentation to the six divisions of the Regular Army. In consequence, once the Royal Navy began mobilising, a large body of reservists was soon established in camps near Deal. The officers and NCOs originated from the Navy, although stiffened by the addition of a judicious sprinkling of officers detached from the Guards. The training had proceeded in a thoroughly disorganised manner and, other than some basic foot drill, little progress had been made in the first two months of the war. Two naval brigades had been formed from the new volunteers and reservists, but to give the RND more backbone, a Marine Brigade was attached to complete the division, although only around half the complement were serving regular personnel. Overall this remained a ramshackle formation possessed of minimal military value. Yet, in the mind of Churchill, the RND was a valid resource that could be utilised in emergency.

An eclectic force was gathered together and despatched on 21 September to Dunkirk, consisting of the regular Marine Brigade from the RND, the Oxfordshire Hussars and a number of Royal Naval Air Service armoured cars manned by marines. The *Boy's Own* antics of the armoured cars have been much celebrated, but the Marine Brigade achieved little, hampered by a nervous awareness of the high number of new recruits lurking within the ranks. On 27 September, they moved forward to an advanced base at Cassel, where they remained as the Antwerp crisis took shape. To Churchill, the question was reduced to the danger of the Allied line being outflanked, which directly threatened the safety of the Channel ports. In his mind, Antwerp remained the key to the strategic situation; wiser heads such as Joffre saw other options to resolve the situation. As a result, Churchill despatched the Marine Brigade by train to Antwerp, where it arrived early on the morning of 4 October, moving into trenches on the west bank of the Petite Nethe to take its place in the line alongside the already fatigued Belgian infantry.

So far so good, but at this point, Churchill resolved to deploy the two remaining brigades of the nascent RND to prevent the Germans from capturing Antwerp and help create a tenable line running across via Ghent to Lille. Thus it was that on Sunday morning, 5 October, the untrained recruits of the 1st and 2nd Royal Naval Brigades were rudely awoken from their slumbers.

> I woke up about 5.30 am and thought with joy of the extra hour in bed. But it wasn't to be. At 5.45 a stentorious voice shouted at the outside of our tent, 'Get up – show-a-leg!' and, what is more, continued to shout. We answered back in none too polite language, telling the unknown visitor to take his unwelcome presence elsewhere. He then began to undo the tent ropes; we resisted, till, recognizing the voice as that of some superior, we let him in. It was no less a person than Commander Fargus himself. He ordered us to get up without delay, and proceed at once to the parade ground. Everyone was fairly buzzing with excitement, and we dressed in record time, doubling up to the parade ground, finishing our hurried toilet as we ran. In about five minutes the whole battalion was on parade, and Commander Fargus told us that in a very few hours we were to embark for France. He couldn't tell us where we were going to, or what we were going for. We were to be ready to fall in at 11am. This was a regular bomb-shell to us. Mad with excitement, we rushed back to our tents and packed our gear.[9]
>
> Able Seaman Edward Lockwood, Benbow Battalion, 1st Naval Brigade, RND

They had no idea what they would be facing, but were armed with an enormous self-confidence, born of the inner certainty that, trained or not, the British soldier was the equal of any number of Germans. Many were caught up in the romance of war, encouraged on by the warm approbation of the crowds.

> The neighbouring battalions were also lined up. And a really fine show they were. All the blue uniforms – the smart upstanding of the men (for we had learnt to drill in our short training, and drill well, too) – the various bands playing. A sharp order of command, and the head of the column swung out towards the Dover road, everyone in the crowd cheering and waving handkerchiefs. Old women weeping – the

yearning sad look of the wives – and we marched at attention through them. I have never felt such a thrill before – to be actually one of these men – to be actually going to France; it made one thank Heaven to be alive at that moment.[10]

Able Seaman Edward Lockwood, Benbow Battalion, 1st Royal Naval Brigade, RND

Amongst them, serving with the Anson Battalion, was the distinguished poet Rupert Brooke, who could not help but think of the trials that awaited them.

I felt very elderly and sombre and full of thoughts of how life was like a flash between darknesses, and that 'X' per cent of those who cheered would be blown into another world within a few months; and they all seemed to me so innocent and patriotic and noble, and my eyes grew round and tear-stained.[11]

Soulful thoughts may have been in the air, but the journey that followed was more prosaic.

We reached Antwerp at 5am after a night of extreme discomfort, packed like sardines in a wretched Belgian train. Our kit was dumped at the station; we had, incidentally, taken everything we had with us. The people received us with ecstasy, and we marched about 5-miles through cheering crowds, being looked on as saviours of the town. Cigars and wine were lavished on us. On arriving somewhere at the outskirts we were sent into billets, and had just comfortably settled ourselves when the order came that we were immediately to parade in the market square. There we were told by Commodore Henderson that we were to go into the line at once, and 300 rounds of ammunition were served out to each man. We were also told that the Germans in front of us were of very inferior quality, and that the appearance of the well-trained Naval Brigades would be quite sufficient to induce them to retire! These remarks of the Commodore were received with cheers, and off we went in high fettle. Unfortunately we lost our way, and after wandering through the outskirts of Antwerp (where, incidentally, we saw Winston Churchill in a car looking very worried) we were halted on a country road, and told to 'pipe down' for the night. This I, for one, did in a ditch, which, luckily, was fairly dry. At 3am whispered orders were passed down the line that we were to 'march away' immediately.

Apparently we had wandered near the German lines! After marching away most of the night, we eventually reached our position, Forts 3 and 4, about 8am.[12]

Leading Seaman Robert Shelton, Hawke Battalion, 1st Naval Brigade, RND

Churchill was present in person as he had abandoned his responsibilities as First Lord to take up an ill-defined role coordinating the defence of Antwerp, even postulating vainly that he should be appointed as the field commander. This was met with considerable amusement by the Prime Minister Herbert Asquith and other ministers.

I regret to say that it was received with a Homeric laugh. Winston is an ex-Lieutenant of Hussars, and would if his proposal had been accepted, have been in command of two distinguished major generals, not to mention brigadiers, colonels &c: while the Navy were only contributing its little brigades.[13]

By the time the 1st and 2nd Naval Brigades arrived at Antwerp, the Germans had already forced the Belgians and the Marine Brigade back from the Petite Nethe river line. Thus the callow new arrivals soon found themselves occupying a system of shallow-dug trenches in the Vieux Dieu sector amidst the inner ring of Belgian forts.

Our marine Sergeant went round instructing the men how to fill their magazines with clip ammunition, as some of us had never seen this modern device before! The only redeeming feature was provided by some remarkably fine wire entanglements in front of us to a depth of 50 yards; these made us feel very safe. Nothing happened during the day, but at 12 o'clock, midnight, the Germans fired the first 11" shell into Antwerp, about 4 miles away. This was repeated through the night at 2-minute intervals. The following morning heavy shelling stopped, but we were visited with a few shells of smaller variety, which did little or no damage – to the Hawke, at any rate. During the preceding night there was a heavy fusillade from one of the battalions on our left. Report has it that they saw movement behind the wire.[14]

Leading Seaman Robert Shelton, Hawke Battalion, 1st Naval Brigade, RND

The men were close to panic, seeing imaginary Uhlans everywhere and ready to open fire at the slightest pretext.

It was the first time most of us had ever fired a rifle but we got some practice that night, I can assure you. The marksmanship was not brilliant! About the middle of the night someone noticed a white thing moving about halfway between us and the wood and the order was given for the Collingwoods to fire at it. We did so; there were about 1,000 of us and we fired about 200 shots apiece. Towards dawn the firing gradually died away and we saw our object, an old white cow, still calmly grazing away![15]

Ordinary Seaman H. Mellanby, Collingwood Battalion, 1st Naval Brigade, RND

Whether imaginary Uhlans or cows, the targets were relatively immune to harm from such raw soldiers. The palpable inaccuracy of such panicked rifle fire was not surprising, as shooting high was an endemic problem for all untrained troops. And there is no doubt that many of the troops were nervous.

There's the excitement in the trenches we weren't attacked seriously in our part – with people losing their heads and fussing and snapping. It's queer to see the people who do break under the strain of danger and responsibility. It's always the rotten ones. Highly sensitive people don't, queerly enough. 'Nuts' do. I was relieved to find I was incredibly brave! I don't know how I should behave if shrapnel was bursting on me and knocking the men round me to pieces. But for risks and nerves and fatigue I was all right. That's cheering.[16]

Sub Lieutenant Rupert Brooke, Anson Battalion, 2nd Royal Naval Brigade, RND

From the Belgian perspective, the situation had not been much improved by the arrival of this enthusiastic, but woefully inexperienced, body of troops. It was clear that neither the 7th Division nor French reinforcements was going to arrive in time to save Antwerp from the Germans. The Belgians thus soon reverted to their original plan of abandoning Antwerp and withdrawing their surviving field army units behind the River Scheldt towards Ostend. The emphasis then turned to the necessity of evacuating the RND from what was an impossible situation, and an ignominious retreat began on the evening of 8 October. The Marine Brigade and 2nd Naval Brigade managed to reach the pontoon bridge across the Scheldt at Burght, but then found themselves condemned to a long march in roads almost choked with Belgian civilian refugees from Antwerp. Sub Lieutenant Rupert Brooke left a picturesque account.

> The march through those deserted suburbs, mile on mile, with never a living being, except one rather ferocious looking sailor, stealing sulkily along. The sky lit by burning villages and houses; and after a bit we got to the land by the river, where the Belgians had let all the petrol out of the tanks and fired it. Rivers and seas of flame leaping up hundreds of feet, crowned by black smoke that covered the entire heavens. It lit up horses wrecked by shells, dead horses, demolished railway stations, engines that had been taken up with their lines and signals, and all twisted round and pulled out, as a bad child spoils a toy. And there we joined the refugees, with all their goods on barrows and carts, in a double line, moving forwards about a hundred yards an hour, white and drawn and beyond emotion. The glare was like hell. We passed on, out of that, across a pontoon bridge, built on boats. Two German spies tried to blow it up while we were on it. They were caught and shot. We went on through the dark. The refugees and motor-buses and transport and Belgian troops grew thicker. After about a thousand years it was dawn.[17]

To Brooke, it seemed as if the whole civilian population of Antwerp was fleeing, unwilling to take their chances with the Germans. Brooke was a jovial correspondent but his letter could not hide his distress at what he saw.

> That was like Hell, a Dantesque Hell, terrible. But there – and later – I saw what was a truer Hell. Hundreds of thousands of refugees, their goods on barrows and hand-carts and perambulators and wagons, moving with infinite slowness out into the night, two unending lines of them, the old men mostly weeping, the women with hard white drawn faces, the children playing or crying or sleeping. That's what Belgium is now: the country where three civilians have been killed to every one soldier.[18]

The roads were packed and chaotic and disorder spread through the ranks to such an extent that the marching columns were in disarray by the time they reached St Gillaes-Waes. Here the bulk of them were entrained and whisked to safety by 09.00 on 9 October.

Far worse befell the 1st Naval Brigade, which had a much delayed start, due to poor staff work in passing on the requisite orders. By the time the rear columns reached the Burght bridge it had been destroyed and they were forced to cross by boat. Then they too belatedly commenced the wearisome march to St Gillaes-Waes.

> As map-reading was not a strong point, we successfully lost our way. At one period we marched at least six kilometres along a straight, dusty road, only to have to turn back. During the afternoon a report was received from the scouts in front that a party of mounted Uhlans were barring our way. The whole battalion promptly lined a turnip field two deep, and started to blaze away, the rear ranks firing in very unpleasant proximity to the front ranks' heads. Commander Beadle dashed out in front (how he escaped being shot, the Lord only knows!) and shouted orders to stop fire. It was then discovered that we were firing at some Belgian cavalry, who had returned our fire hotly. No damage was done to either side.[19]
>
> Leading Seaman Robert Shelton, Hawke Battalion, 1st Naval Brigade, RND

The military competence of both sides in this fire fight may be impugned by the lack of casualties. All cohesion was lost in the rampant confusion, units straggled their way, vital hours slipped away. Many isolated elements would later fall prisoner to the advancing Germans. When they arrived at St Gillaes-Waes they found that the Germans had cut the train line and, with his units widely dissipated, Commander Wilfred Henderson, commanding the 1st Naval Brigade, was left in a dreadful position.

> The road to Holland was still open – the question was, should it be surrender to the Dutch or attempt to cut through the German line, and then came the question – what were the chances of success if we attempted to cut through? Was it possible, with about 1,000 men, to cut through the German Line? The Germans we had against us were regular troops of all arms, flushed with victory, organised to the last button, and with the advantage of being already in position waiting for us. Presumably they would be entrenched, and as we could hear guns in action to the westward of us, it was certain that they possessed artillery with which to receive us. The war had by that time been long enough in progress to exclude any doubt as to their being well supplied with machine guns, and we were already well acquainted with

the German tactics of carrying out all movements behind swarms of screening cavalry. What had we to oppose to such troops? Of these 1,000, perhaps 50% might have been relied upon to deliver fairly effective rifle-fire – the remainder simply didn't know their rifles or how to use them, and would have been a danger to those who did. When the men left the trenches at Antwerp they were not only hungry, but thirsty, and since then they marched about 30 miles. By the time the column got to St Gilles-Waes, it was more like a mob on the verge of panic than like troops – the poor fellows were demoralised by utter fatigue. The few officers we had were as exhausted as the men and they hardly knew their men – and the men hardly knew them. But apart from exhaustion, demoralisation, lack of training, lack of officers, faulty and deficient equipment, no water bottles, no entrenching tools, our food and ammunition had been taken away to Ostend that morning. Under the conditions I have described, to have attempted to go forward, with troops in the last stages of exhaustion and whose morale I simply could not trust, without artillery support, with the certainty of having to fight a determined action against fresh regular troops, deliberately entrenched, was in my judgement senseless and a useless sacrifice of the lives for whom I was responsible. There was therefore nothing to gain by heroics – the inevitable result would have been sheer slaughter purposeless sacrifice, and for those who survived the hostilities the brutalities and miseries of German prison camps. Had we even had the faintest hope of relief, we might perhaps have improvised some sort of laager and held out as long as possible, but we knew by that time that every minute was taking British troops further away from rather than nearer to us – they had left for Ostend. So I had to bow to the inevitable, and took the remains of my brigade into Holland.[20]

The men were for the most part baffled by what was going on. The majority were too exhausted to do anything but acquiesce, but a few brave spirits were determined to try and escape the trap they had fallen into.

Lieutenant West came up to me, and said that he would not go across, further suggesting we should get as many men as possible to stay on the Belgian side. About forty men decided to stay with us. During the night there was a lot of firing at the back of the village; one by one the men went across, and when dawn broke there were three of us left: West, Petty Officer Stewart, and myself. We were too tired and too cold to sleep. Poor West was practically delirious throughout the night, but still undaunted.[21]

Leading Seaman Robert Shelton, Hawke Battalion, 1st Naval Brigade, RND

After many adventures the three escaped on a boat disguised as gas-fitters, dressed in workmen's clothes and carrying a cosmetic length of lead piping. All the rest of the Hawke Battalion were interned in Holland for the duration of the war, alongside the Benbow and Collingwood Battalions. Of the 1st Naval Brigade, only the Drake Battalion escaped relatively unscathed.

The RND had contributed little or nothing to the defence of Antwerp; indeed, their participation had been an utter disaster. The troops were raw and untrained, but they had a potential military value that had been cast away on a whim. The Marine Brigade were trained men, but as to the deployment of the two naval brigades, Asquith neatly summed up as a, 'Wicked folly', further commenting: 'It was like sending sheep to the shambles.'[22] Churchill would later seek to analyse military operations on the Western Front using a fanciful 'blood test' based on the casualties suffered. It is ironic that such a scrutiny of his Antwerp adventure does not bear up too well: the RND lost some 2,613 men, of which only 138 were wounded – the rest were killed (57), interned (1,479), or became POWs (936)[23] – and hence some 2,472 were out of action for the duration of the war. This was far more than had been lost in the Battle of Mons – and all for nothing. As an operation of war it was conceived and driven by Churchill's restless spirit, cursed by his sense of inner certainty that sadly bore little resemblance to the situation on the ground. The remnants of the 'division' were finally evacuated from Ostend back to Britain on 10 October, on which same date Antwerp fell to the Germans. This would not be the last time that Churchill's overweening confidence in his own strategic insight led to severe casualties – the raw tragedy of Gallipoli still lay ahead for the men of the RND.

IN THE REAL WORLD THE FRENETIC leapfrogging of the 'Race to the Sea' in an effort to turn the opponent's flank was still proceeding apace. As each French or German corps was brought north, they were countered by their opposite numbers. From mid-September, severe fighting had raged across the Somme region. It was soon apparent that the operations of the French Second Army had been countered and Joffre was forced to create a new Tenth Army (under the command of General Louis Maud'huy) to move into the line still further north, beyond the city of Arras. Yet when Maud'huy attempted an offensive from 1 October, he was thwarted by the arrival of three more German corps; indeed, the Tenth Army was hard pressed to hold the ground it held. Yet beyond, still further to the north, was the spectre of no less than three German Cavalry Corps sweeping round the open flank. It was this desperate state of affairs that, quite naturally, distracted Joffre from the doomed attempts to save Antwerp. The German cavalry in turn were baulked by the arrival of the French XXI Corps as they arrived in the Béthune area on 7 October; next day the Germans XIV Corps arrived – and so it went on.

It was at this point that the BEF became actively involved as II Corps was quietly removed from the line on the Aisne by 2 October and, after a day's rest, it was entrained for Abbeville. They then began to march on Béthune to add a little more muscle to the French left flank. Behind them III Corps would begin to move north to the Hazebrouck railhead on 6 October, while I Corps remained *in situ* for another week. The II Corps, covered by Allenby's newly formed Cavalry Corps (1st and 2nd Cavalry Divisions), began to arrive in the Béthune area from 11 October, thereby prolonging the Allied line north. All too aware of the difficulty in breaking through German trenches and barbed wire, Foch sought to catch the German units while they were still manoeuvring and before they had time to entrench. After a conference with Foch (appointed as commander of the Northern Group of Armies on 11 October), French ordered Smith-Dorrien to advance eastwards on 12 October feeling for the German northern flank. The result was the Battle of La Bassée fought in the flat ground stretching between Béthune and the low Aubers Ridge some ten miles to the east. At first II Corps advanced, pivoting on the village of Givenchy and pushing towards Aubers. Private Dominik Richert of the German 112th Infantry Regiment remembered an early encounter with the BEF at Richebourg village.

> Suddenly the English artillery started to shell us heavily. Large numbers of artillery and shrapnel shells exploded, scattering death and destruction. Soon lines of English infantry appeared and

approached us by leaps and bounds. We fired heavily at them, but as they outnumbered us we withdrew. Quite a lot of us fell before we could reach the houses. We withdrew at the double through a drainage ditch which had been planted with willow stumps, while the English shrapnel shells continued to burst overhead. A number of us fell before they were able to reach the houses. A shrapnel shell cut off the upper part of a rotting willow stump above my head. As a result of the explosion and the shock, I fell flat into the dirty ditch, but then I got up again immediately to get out of the dangerous line of fire. Now the English took over the village, but they did not try to chase us any further. We dug ourselves in and spent several days facing the enemy. We had to be very careful, because the 'Tommies' – as we called the English – were good shots. As soon as one of us showed himself he would lose something.[24]

Private Dominik Richert, 1/112th Infantry Regiment, 58th Brigade, 29th Division, XIV Corps

As II Corps advanced there were many small actions, now forgotten. On 17 October the 1st Northumberland Fusiliers were advancing towards Aubers Ridge. Captain Beauchamp Tudor St John was detached to take up flanking positions on the high ground to the north of Aubers close by the village of Fromelles.

We were at the foot of a ridge which was I suppose about 50 feet in height and to the north of Aubers in between that town and the village of Fromelles. I got the half a company I was with together and put them under cover and was going on to the top of the ridge where the leading platoon had already arrived, when I was unexpectedly fired on from the direction of Fromelles. As I had been told the French had cleared this village and that there was no one in it excepting perhaps a few wounded Germans I did not think much of this fire to begin with. However it became more intense and as it became very persistent I decided to swing round the rear half-company and advance towards Fromelles with the idea of finding out what the bother was about. As we advanced the fire became heavier and more accurate but I could not see anything to fire at in return. When we were within about 500 yards of the outskirts of the village I halted and we made ourselves snug while I sent back a signal for supports. We had had eight or nine casualties and I could not yet see a sign of the Germans. The field we were in being ploughed land it was easy to entrench ourselves sufficiently against rifle fire and so far we had not encountered any shellfire. I waited here for an hour or two for the supports I had asked for but none came and eventually I got a message to say I was to stay where I was and the French were going to clear the village. If you can imagine the village to be in the middle of a square of which my Company formed one side and the French advance an adjacent side you will see that I was in a position to see a very pretty fight and I settled down to enjoy myself. In the middle of the village was a church with a spire and on this the French artillery began to range. Two or three rounds wore enough to burst shrapnel quite close to the spire and then the real business began. The French infantry were about 800 yards away from the village and between them and the village the 75's placed first one and then a succession of curtains of shrapnel fire which steadily advanced right through the village and which spread right across it. Germans came tumbling out of trenches in front of us and running back at least some ran back, others remained where they fell. We then grumped rifle fire into them too and they got a very hot time of it. I believe there were about 3,000 of them in the village and they lost nearly 1,000 in killed and wounded before the French had finished with them. When the fire from the 75's had ceased the French infantry advanced and some came over to where I was and 1 thought were going to 'coupe ma gorge' but I was able to reassure them that we were English before any accident of that sort occurred.[25]

As his regimental history wryly retorts, 'Captain St John's early grounding in French irregular verbs once again proved equal to the occasion!'[26]

As the Germans moved up their reserves to counter II Corps, the fighting took on an increasingly bitter flavour. The medical officers were amongst the first to realise that the scale of casualties was rising.

I took over the cottage which the medical officer of the battalion we were relieving had used as a regimental aid post. It was by no means an ideal spot and he told me it was in full view of the Germans and only about 300 yards away. Among other delights he left me fifty severely wounded cases which had not been collected by the field ambulance the night before. They completely filled the place and were a serious handicap for me when my men began to come in later on in the day. We spent several hours getting things into ship-shape condition and luckily nothing much happened but in the afternoon things were very different and rather unpleasant. Men started to crowd in and I was working hard right up until the middle of the night. Shells were falling all round us but that day none actually hit the house. The ambulances luckily came up well and by daybreak I had got rid of all the wounded. Next day, 18th October, the scrapping started off very early and we were pounded away at all day. Casualties poured in and I was soon working all out with coat off and sleeves rolled up. About four o'clock in the afternoon I was sitting down just inside the door when there was an awful crash and I thought the whole place was coming down. Looking out at the back door I saw the cause of it. A small high-explosive shell had burst on the ground about two feet away from the back wall. This worried me a good deal as the place was full of wounded with no protection for them. I knew what the Germans were trying for. There was a battery of field guns about 200 yards behind us placed in between some stacks. Shells were coming over pretty rapidly and as I returned to the front door I saw a direct hit on one of the guns. A few minutes afterwards I thought our end had come! A shell went slap through one of the rooms full of wounded without bursting. It was a narrow escape as two great holes were torn in the walls and nothing could have saved us if it had exploded. Two officers who were leaning outside with their backs against the wall were both killed. I am glad to say nothing more touched us. The joyful news that we were to be relieved that night came round soon after this. It was none too soon either as we had had two hundred casualties in the two days.[27]

Lieutenant Cyril Helm, 2nd King's Own Yorkshire Light Infantry, 13th Brigade, 5th Division, II Corps

Immediately to the north, III Corps had moved up from Hazebrouck to the Armentières area in order to prolong the allied line northwards. On the afternoon of 18 October, Sir John French went into Armentières hoping to get a good view of the local area from the high buildings. The town was under shellfire with large shells crashing down amidst the helpless civilian population.

The day being Sunday, everyone was wearing his best clothes. The scenes in the streets were extraordinary. Some of the men seemed to have gone mad with either rage or fear. Women rushed to and fro, screaming, with babies in their arms. Close to the look-out post where I was standing, a priest in his altar vestments dashed out of a church with the sacred vessels in his arms, and tore in panic down the street in front of me, followed by large numbers of his flock. A great deal of damage was done to the town, and there were many casualties amongst the civilians.[28]

All along the line the BEF was facing increasing growing pressure from German attacks, which seemed ever more insistent. And of course soon the heavy artillery was spewing shells out with a stomach-churning abandon. By this time, Helm had moved his aid post to a farm cellar at Richebourg L 'Avenue.

> The Germans started to register on our trenches with eight- and twelve-inch guns. All round us they fell, behind, in front and on both sides. Three fell in the little garden at the back, the ground round was dotted with shell craters. Many fell in our front line trenches, causing awful casualties. Men were buried alive whilst others were just dug out in time and were brought to, unable to stand with their backs half broken. My cellar was soon packed but I could not put up with any wounded upstairs as any minute I expected the place to be blown up. In the 'apology' for a cellar, our chances seemed to be extremely poor but it was the best that could be done. All day this went on and we listened for the shriek of the shells which came over in salvoes about every three minutes. There is nothing that I know of more trying to the nerves than to sit listening to the shells and wondering how long there is before one comes and finds your hiding place. The wounded were praying to be taken out as they knew they were really no safer here than in the trenches. When I was hard at work dressing, the shelling did not affect me but when I sat down and listened, trying to be cheerful for the sake of the men, my feelings were indescribable. We all counted the minutes until sunset as then we knew the shelling would slacken. At last when the sun went down and there was peace the sigh of thankfulness that went up from everybody was worth hearing.[29]

Even up aloft in the clouds in his Henri Farman aircraft, Lieutenant William Read could find no respite from the shelling, as he found that the once-derided German 'Archie' was beginning to tell on his nerves.

> It took me forty minutes to climb to 4,000 feet on my brute of a Henri. They are rotten machines. My opinion of Henri goes down daily. It *won't* climb on some days, and it isn't good enough going over 'Archie' at 4,000 feet. I wonder how long my nerves will stand this almost daily

bombardment by 'Archie'? I notice several people's nerves are not as strong as they used to be and I am sure 'Archie' is responsible for a good deal, I would not mind quite go much if I were in a machine that was fast and that would climb a little more willingly. Today we both had a good dressing down by 'Archibald' and some of the shells burst much too near and I could hear the pieces of shell whistling past – and they have to burst very close for one to be able to hear the shrieking of loose bits of shell above the noise of one's engine. Well, well, I suppose the end will be pretty sharp and quick if one of 'Archie's' physic-balls catches one. I think I would rather 'Archie' caught me than crumple up [the] Henri [Farman], because one would have too long to think when falling from 4,000 feet![30]

On 22 October, Private Dominik Richert recalled the bitter fighting as the German 29th Division launched an attack on the village of Violaines defended by the 1st Cheshires.

In a field they got us to form up in lines abreast while it was still dark. Then we advanced. As the dawn approached, we started to see houses and fruit trees. It was the village of Violaines. We attached our bayonets to our rifles and headed towards the village at the double. Instead of keeping silent, our young soldiers shouted 'Hurrah!' as they had been trained to do. As a result of their shouts, the English troops in the village were alerted. Soon single shots fired towards us, one minute later shots crackled out of all the windows and doors and from behind hedges and walls. One of the first bullets hit the man next to me in the stomach. He plunged to the ground uttering a terrifying scream. August Zanger turned to me and called: 'Have they hit you?' Just at that moment, three bullets ripped through his pack and his canteen, without injuring him. The man next to him was shot in the shoulder and fell to the ground. We ran behind a thorn bush as quickly as possible. We all hid behind the hedge, so the English soldiers concentrated their fire on it. Soon several comrades lay motionless. Together with further lines of advancing troops we charged through the hedge and stormed through the gardens towards the houses, in the course of which more of our people were hit.[31]

Captain Robert Dolbey, the medical officer of the 2nd King's Own Scottish Borderers, watched the development of this German attack on the neighbouring Cheshires with considerable concern.

They poured out of the ends of the trenches, spread out into most perfect open order and advanced at the double; nor was any officer visible. Some ran and dropped, so that I thought the whole line had been wiped out by our fire, but these men were foxing; and those who fell face downward soon got up to run forward again. Not so with the killed or wounded, they lay on their sides or, spinning round in the air, they fell supported by their packs, in a half reclining position. They were sitting with their backs to our trenches, their heads dropped forward, and they looked as if they were asleep. We saw that that was the sleep that knows no waking; for they stayed like this, quite still, all the afternoon. Taking the cover of every natural object, they got behind trees or wagons or mounds of earth; so they advanced up to within 100 yards of our position, and our field of fire not being good, there they found shelter.[32]

As the Germans edged closer, Dolbey realized that the Cheshires were unlikely to be able to withstand the next full-fledged assault. The scene being played out before his eyes was typical of the situation all along the line as II Corps was – understandably – fading fast after more than two months of incessant fighting.

The Cheshires were very weak – none of us had supports – and if the line gave on our right, our flank would be turned. I was not without grave misgivings, so intense was the machine gun fire and so unusual these strange explosions on our own front and over all the way to Violaines. The stretcher bearers were so exhausted that we should have to keep for the night any wounded that might come in. In their dug-out behind the hospital they lay down to sleep. All was quiet, save for the restless groaning of the wounded just brought in, but I was uneasy and could not sleep. The sense of impending disaster oppressed me, and though we were accustomed to sleep through anything in perfect security behind our infantry, there was an ominous sound in the rising machine-gun fire. More of the big booming; the big shells were falling near the hospital now.[33]

Then his worst fears were justified, as he saw the Germans overrun the remnants of the Cheshires.

A German cheer, and something moving on our right against the red glare that was Violaines on fire. There was no mistaking the spiked helmets. If I did not run for it I should be cut off from the hospital. It was 2am, and the enemy were through and behind and around the hospital. I barred and bolted the door and turned to wake Thompson. Our only chance in the world was to get out by the back, but the wounded were awake and frightened, and our job was to stay with them. A glance through the back windows showed us the yard full of Germans firing through the windows, charging round the house. Then I realised in a flash that we had no Red Cross flag; nothing to show that we were a hospital. But still they hesitated; they feared an ambuscade. They came close to the windows that were on both sides of the main room where our wounded lay, and fired point blank inside. Then they burst in; still quite dark. How could they know we were a hospital? One could not have blamed them if they had bayoneted us. Again they feared an ambush and would only come to the top of the cellar steps, firing at us through the barrels. This, I thought, is the finish! But contenting themselves with placing a guard on the top of the cellar steps and over the cellar window that opened to the grass outside, they left us. Then came the dawn and they saw the bloodstained dressings, the medical equipment, the surgical panniers. It was clearly only a hospital.[34]

Once Richert and the 112th Regiment had taken Violaines they were ordered to press home a follow-up attack on a trench lying some 300 yards in front of them.

We were met by a fearful barrage of machine-gun and infantry fire. Despite heavy losses we stormed the trench. Some of the English soldiers surrendered, while many of them fled, but were almost all gunned down due to the lack of cover on the flat ground. In order to escape the artillery fire, Zanger and I took a wounded soldier back to the village and carried him to the doctors. Then we hid in the cellar of a house which had been stocked with food by its inhabitants. The village was continuously under English artillery fire. Our house suffered several hits, and on one occasion bricks fell down the steps to the cellar. On the evening of the third day we heard footsteps crashing down the stairs. It was a Lieutenant, the adjutant of the regiment, 'You damned cowards, get a move on out of here!' he yelled at us.[35]

While they had been malingering, the rest of his regiment had managed to advance a couple of more fields towards the village of Rue D'Ouvert.

Back in the fold despite their misdemeanours, Richert and Zanger once again found themselves attacking the British trenches.

> We were to advance across the field in groups of eight to some willow trees and dig ourselves in. We did not know where the English troops were. The first group jumped. Soon we heard shots. We saw straight away that three men fell. The others ran behind a heap of wheat sheaves standing in the field. Now the second group, to which Zanger and I had been allocated, had to jump. I can't describe to anyone what my feelings were as I forced myself to do so. But the terrible force of circumstances prevailed. There was no argument. Just a quick prayer and off we went. We had barely become visible, when it felt like we were surrounded by a swarm of buzzing bees. The man ahead of me stumbled, threw his arms in the air, and fell on his back. Another man fell on his face. Then I noticed that no one from the first group apart from NCO Luneg was still alive. We threw ourselves to the ground and pressed our faces into the soft ground of the field. All the English soldiers in the trench now concentrated their fire on us. The bullets hit the ground all around us, showering us with earth. Now an English machine gun started up too. The bullets flying over us were less than a hands-breadth above us, and one after the other, people were being killed. I too felt that my final hour had come, thought of my loved ones at home and prayed. Zanger, who was lying near me, said 'We can't go on lying here'. He raised himself slightly and noticed a farm track with ditches on either side about fifty metres ahead of us. In one leap we jumped up and rushed towards the safety of the ditch. Although the English troops directed a rattling fast fire at us, we miraculously arrived unharmed. NCO Kretzer, the leader of our group arrived right after us. As the trench at this position was very shallow, we crept on our stomachs towards some foxholes which had been abandoned by the English soldiers. While we were creeping forward, NCO Kretzer was hit in the back, he said 'Please greet. . .' to me, and was dead.[36]

They dug themselves in as best they could, but they were still not safe, for the British seemed intent on justifying their reputation as excellent shots.

> As dawn approached I looked carefully over towards the English and saw their trench about 150 metres ahead of us. When the English soldiers spotted our mounds of earth they fired like mad at them for a while. They eased off and I saw that one of the young soldiers who,

with two others, had occupied the hole next to ours was cautiously looking towards the English lines. I quickly called to him to take cover, which he did. But his curiosity was too great. After a while he wanted to look across again. Almost as soon as his head was visible, he fell down dead, shot through the forehead. His two comrades wanted to put his corpse into the field behind them as there was not enough room in their foxhole. One of them got up too high and was shot in the back. He fell down dead in the hole and the corpse tumbled down on top of him. Now there were two corpses and one living person in the foxhole.[37]

Richert found himself lying out in a field and in the circumstances he was distinctly rash in his choice of amusement as the hours drifted by.

I fitted my bayonet to my rifle, pierced a mangelwurzel, and pulled it into the hole. Then I stuck the bayonet into the mangelwurzel from below, put my helmet on top and raised the contraption up above the cover of the trench. The English soldiers thought it was a head and shot at it wildly. Very soon, both the mangelwurzel and the helmet were full of holes like a sieve.[38]

The British may have been fighting hard and with considerable skill, but the sheer weight of German numbers was pressing them back.

The Germans were pushing hard against II Corps – and III Corps, too, further to the north. Both corps found themselves enfolded into the fighting as part of the line rather than acting as a viable force able to threaten the German flank. Smith-Dorrien and Pulteney could try to stand, to hold fast against the vigorous German counter-attacks, but any idea of outflanking or overwhelming the German right wing was impossible. It took everything they had just to hold their ground. The last remaining chance of outflanking the Germans seemed to lie with I Corps, who had finally left the Aisne in mid-October. They were on the road to Ypres.

BATTLE OF YPRES: CONTACT

Grasping the firing handles and pressing my thumbs on the trigger lever, I fired without taking aim, into the grey mass in front of us. Steam was now coming from the escape plug near the muzzle, as the water in the barrel casing began to reach boiling point. Belt after belt of cartridges went through her, till I began to think our ammunition supply must be getting low. Still those grey-clad figures came on. Hundreds of them, dead and wounded, lay out in No Man's Land. Whereas before the attack I had been shivering, I was now wet with perspiration.[1]

Private William Quinton, 2nd Bedfordshire Regiment, 21st Brigade, 7th Division

ONE MIGHT HAVE THOUGHT FROM a casual study of Great War battles on the Western Front that Ypres was some fabled city, fought over by armies desperate to secure access to untold wealth or a commanding tactical position. Nothing could be further from the truth. Ypres was just an ordinary town, lying in the centre of the fertile western Flanders plain. Although it was true that Flanders was the 'cockpit of Europe', fought over in countless campaigns over the past thousand years, the strategic importance of Ypres for the Allies lay in what possession of the town denied to the Germans rather than to any positive benefit to themselves. Ypres lay squarely across the German route to the Channel ports: Dunkirk was thirty miles away and Calais just twenty miles beyond that. The low ridges, dotted with woodlands, that rose up to the east of Ypres represented one of the last feasible lines of defence. The British also saw the town, not as an end in itself, but as a stepping stone to more strategically important locations pushing eastwards, such as the rail centre at Roulers or the ports of Ostend and Zeebrugge. For both sides Ypres was on the road to somewhere.

The early operations in the Ypres area saw the first involvement of the 7th Division. This had been created in September 1914, under the command of Major General Thompson Capper, and, unlike the earlier divisions which had a large component of reservists, it was largely composed of regular battalions that had returned from imperial service in the colonies. It was despatched to France, crossing with the 3rd Cavalry Division, collectively under the command of Lieutenant General Sir Henry Rawlinson, landing on the Zeebrugge harbour mole on 7 October, before moving inland for Bruges. It was originally intended that they should be an independent command, receiving orders directly from Kitchener at the War Office, and charged with assisting the Belgian Army in the doomed defence of Antwerp, but, by the time they arrived, the situation had already degenerated beyond rescue. The two divisions were then formed into a makeshift IV Corps and placed under the overall command of Sir John French as part of the BEF on 9 October. With Antwerp beyond saving, Rawlinson advanced to Bruges and Ghent in an effort to cover the withdrawal of the Belgian Army.

> This march was one of the most extraordinary experiences I have ever had. The wretched Belgians, who for weeks had expected to be overrun by the Germans and treated in the usual Teuton manner, went absolutely mad at seeing the British troops. Passing through Blankenberg, we were fairly mobbed, and it was with the greatest difficulty that we forced our horses through the crowd, who pressed cigars, apples, and Belgian flags on us in thousands. This continued all the way, and by the time we had passed through the streets of Bruges we looked more like a bank holiday crowd than soldiers. Every gun and waggon was decorated with large Belgian flags; most of the men had given away their badges and numerals, and all were wearing flowers and ribbons of the Belgian colours. I shall never forget seeing Colonel Fasson riding at the head of his brigade, clutching an enormous apple in one hand, whilst the Belgian girls were stuffing cigars into his pockets.[2]
>
> Major Ralph Hamilton, Headquarters, 22nd Brigade, RFA, 7th Division, IV Corps

Sadly for the welcoming Belgian civilians, the British would soon abandon them once more.

The Germans were moving cautiously towards IV Corps. Once the Belgians had managed to retire towards the Yser River, then Rawlinson started to pull back through Ghent, via Roulers, towards Ypres. The Northumberland Hussars, a yeomanry territorial unit, had been attached to 7th Division and Trooper Henry Mattison left his wide-eyed impressions of the retreat.

> Orders were received to mount and keep silent, not a light was to
> be struck and talking was to be avoided. The infantry filed past us,
> battalion after battalion with bayonets fixed, and rifles slung, ready
> for immediate use. I shall never forget the impression the Gordon
> Highlanders made on my imagination. They walked so stealthily
> and quietly that to me they appeared more like phantoms filing
> silently past in the darkness, almost indiscernible except for the
> gleam of their bayonets. Batteries of artillery rumbled past, the gun
> carriages and wagons had their wheels muffled, and when the last
> of them had passed we moved off rearguard. The streets were, so far
> as I could see, entirely deserted of civilians, but at many a window
> I could discern the corner of a blind uplifted and white anxious
> faces peered out at us in bewilderment and wonder at our departure.
> I must confess we felt ourselves hypocrites at the thought that we
> were turning our backs on these hospitable people and leaving
> them to the mercy of the invader. Mile after mile we marched in the
> darkness, dismounting frequently to ease our horses. Foot-slogging
> is distasteful to infantrymen, but to a cavalryman it is something
> worse, especially when we had to march in the darkness and lead our
> nervous horses along uncertain ground.[3]

The first elements of IV Corps reached Ypres during the early afternoon of 14 October. The town had been occupied by German cavalry on 7 October and evidently some still lingered in the locality.

> The battalion marched with the brigade up the Menin Road and
> after a time I received orders to proceed to Kruisstraat and billet the
> battalion there. This village was about half a mile from the Ypres
> railway station on the road to Dickebusch. On arrival there I rode
> through the village in order to get an idea of the size of it and the type
> of houses it contained. I then came back to the Ypres side of the village

and commenced to mark up the houses for the battalion. Suddenly, a small boy appeared out of a by-road, shouting, 'Uhlan! Uhlan!' I had my regimental quartermaster sergeant with me, and Sergeant Bell was actually at the door of the house. I seized Sergeant Bell's rifle and some ammunition off him and dashed off to the corner of the road. There about twenty yards away were two Uhlans. My quartermaster sergeant and I dropped on our knees and blazed off. The Uhlans who, in my opinion, should have charged us, turned round, crashed into each other, and dashed away, but not before we had got them both in the back. A naval party, who had an aeroplane on the Dickebusch Road, was in Ypres when we started firing, and thought their aeroplane was in trouble, so dashed out in a light lorry. I told them what had happened and asked them to get down the Dickebusch Road as fast as they could and try and capture those two Uhlans. Off they went as fast as possible and returned about ten minutes later with the two. One was an officer who was very badly wounded and died shortly after in Ypres, the second was a non-commissioned officer who was also seriously wounded in the back.[4]

Major Edward Pickard, 2nd Green Howards, 21st Brigade, 7th Division, IV Corps

Despite success in such trivial skirmishes, IV Corps was in a somewhat exposed position, as III Corps had not yet come up on their right to the south and there was also a gap of indeterminate width to the north between them and the Belgian forces – the situation was thus by no means stable. And the Germans were once again on the move.

General Erich von Falkenhayn, the new German Chief of General Staff had created a 'new' Fourth Army under the command of Duke Albrecht of Württemberg, including the experienced III Reserve Corps, fresh from its capture of Antwerp, aided and abetted by the XXII, XXIII, XXVI and XXVII Reserve Corps. Their orders were crystal clear: 'The Fourth Army is to advance, without regard for casualties, with its right wing resting on the coast, first on the fortresses of Dunkirk and Calais, then to swing south at St Omer.'[5] The III Reserve Corps would strike to the north at the French and Belgian units, while the newer reserve corps would launch themselves at the British in Flanders. The strategic intention may have been clear enough, but the force generation to carry out this vision was poor in the extreme. The German Army was already extended almost to the limit and these new reserve corps formations levered into Fourth Army were manned for the most part by recruits and conscripts only called up since the start of the war. Like the British, the Germans suffered from a shortage of competent NCO instructors and they had had no chance to inculcate anything more than the very basics of soldiering into such raw recruits. They could march and carry out basic foot drills, and their fitness was improving, but they had minimal weapons skills and no training in field tactics. There was also a distinct shortage of basic equipment such as field kitchens. These reserve units were not ready for action, but there was no one else. Needs must when the devil drives, and Falkenhayn decided it was worth the risk for a last chance of a significant strategic victory on the Western Front in 1914.

Meanwhile, French was ignorant of the German plans, but, in the absence of any evidence to the contrary, was 'decidedly optimistic as to the possibility of carrying out a strong offensive eastwards.'[6] However, he was also becoming increasingly aware of the underlying weakness to the Allied position in Flanders.

> I was far from satisfied with the situation in the north. Although no
> reports had reached us of any great concentration of the enemy there,
> I had much reason to fear that troops were being moved east across
> Belgium to reinforce him. The French troops on the Yser were not
> numerous, and they included many Territorials, whilst the Belgians
> were completely tired out. On the right of the Belgians, as far as
> Menin, there were only the 3rd Cavalry and 7th Infantry Divisions,
> both of which stood in need of rest and refit. Ours was a tremendously
> long line to guard with so few troops available. If the enemy broke
> through the left flank all the British would be turned, the Belgians
> and the French troops with them would be cut off and the sea-coast
> towns would be gone. When I looked further south, the prospect was
> no better. The enemy was daily and almost hourly getting stronger
> in front of our line, which was held by the cavalry and by the II and
> III Corps. The endurance of these troops had been heavily taxed, and
> I had practically no reserves. Moreover, they were extended on a front
> much too wide for their numbers, especially north of the Lys.[7]

Although still concerned by the situation from La Bassée stretching north towards Ypres, Sir John French was determined to try to clear the ground as far as Bruges before significant German reinforcements could arrive. Thus a general attack was ordered for 16 October, when he required Rawlinson to advance IV Corps in an easterly direction towards the town of Menin. Rawlinson was notably unenthusiastic about the prospect, being rather more aware of the immediacy of a looming – if undefined – German threat. Nevertheless, by the morning of 17 October, the 7th Division had moved forward over the ridges east of Ypres, with the 3rd Cavalry Division edging alongside it towards Poelcappelle on their left flank.

> As dawn began to break, we found ourselves close to Zonnebeke and news was passed down the column that the village had been occupied without opposition. The artillery halted at the level-crossing south of the village, whilst the infantry proceeded to take up a position on a line from Zonnebeke station in the direction of southeast. We billeted in Zonnebeke that night. The town was full of its inhabitants; shops were open and life going on in a normal manner. Little did the townspeople imagine that 24-hours later they would be flying for their lives, with shells bursting all round them.[8]
>
> Major Ralph Hamilton, Headquarters, 22nd Brigade, RFA, 7th Division, IV Corps

It would prove fortunate that as a precaution Major General Thompson Capper ordered his men to dig in all along the ridge running from Zonnebeke, through Gheluvelt, to Zandvoorde. Behind them, the first elements of Haig's I Corps were entraining en route for Flanders, but it would take some time to actually deploy them in the field. On 18 October, the 7th Division again began to slowly push onwards, pivoting on Zandvoorde, to take up the required southeasterly axis of advance. However, in the early afternoon, reports began to come in that the Germans were present in considerable strength towards Morslade and north of Menin, so the attack was postponed.

The 18 October would prove to be the day when the German counter-stroke began to take shape. The most obvious initial manifestation was the attack by III Reserve Corps (on the right flank of the German Fourth Army), which advanced on the Belgian line along the Ypres Canal and Yser River from Boesinghe, just north of Ypres, to the sea at Nieuport. This whole area was flat and in many places below sea level at high tide. Indeed at Nieuport there were a complex series of locks and sluices designed to drain water away at low tide and keep back the sea waters when the tide rose. The first German attacks crunched into the Belgian line between Dixmude and the sea. The Germans were determined, but the Belgians were fighting to keep control of the very last segments of their homeland and were resolute in their resistance. As the Germans tried to press forward, their troops nearest the sea were harassed by enthusiastic shore bombardments from a mixed Royal Naval flotilla under the command of Rear Admiral Horace Hood.

It is apparent – in retrospect – that, once the fighting in Flanders had begun, both sides had similar plans to break through their opponent's line and then wheel round to roll them up by thrusting down from the north. Foch planned for the Belgian Army to hold the line of the Yser while the BEF and the French pushed eastwards towards a line stretching between Lille and Courtrai. Sir Henry Wilson was still very much in thrall to Foch and lost no opportunity in pressing forward his viewpoint on to the malleable mind of Sir John French. It was apparent that Wilson had not lost an iota of his insouciant optimism in the face of depressing intelligence reports. As a result the GHQ orders issued to Rawlinson for 19 October were similar in tone and intent to the orders given the previous day. As far as French and Wilson were concerned nothing much had changed.

The situation on the ground was very different. As Rawlinson began his attack a string of disconcerting reports began to come in from the 3rd Cavalry Division of strong German columns advancing from the general direction of Roulers. On the left of the 22nd Brigade was the Northumberland Hussars, who came into contact with a German cyclist battalion at the village of Ledgehem. Trooper Henry Mattison left his impressions.

> Under heavy fire we galloped pell-mell into the village, dismounted and took up a defensive line on the outskirts. Alnwick Troop was lining the ditch, running along the side of the road and from it we had a clear line of fire on the Germans who had ensconced themselves, and both sides kept up a steady fire. Some of our troop climbed into a windmill nearby and blazed away with better advantage. A white-haired old man suddenly dashed out from the buildings occupied by the Germans and in spite of the firing he reached us in safety. He was too excited and

nervous to be able to speak for a long while, but eventually he told us of the long grey columns of German infantry which were marching towards the place.[9]

From his position in the village, Mattison watched the 22nd Brigade coming under heavy artillery and infantry fire. The German attack was abandoned at 13.05, but Capper ordered the 7th Division to fall back, swinging round to face to the east. As the 3rd Cavalry Division also began to retire in the face of sustained German pressure, Capper withdrew still further, eventually taking up a line based on the trenches his men had dug two days before from Zonnebeke to Zandvoorde. As the Germans followed them, Major Ralph Hamilton watched his field artillery going into action – at first to little effect.

> Standing in the trench, with nothing but my eyes showing, I watched the enemy's infantry trickling over the skyline. They came into view at 3,400 yards, but as they were in very open order and came on in short rushes, they did not present much of a target for artillery; and, owing to the farms, woods, and hedges, we could only see them here and there as they crossed open patches. This ridge they were crossing was under fire of our guns, and whenever we saw enough of them bunched together, we let off a few rounds at them.[10]

Then Hamilton noticed a considerable gathering of German troops taking shelter behind a clump of bushes. As they were not visible to the designated observation officer, Hamilton took personal control of the guns.

> One of the ambitions of my life was realised in that I ranged a battery of guns in action. Measuring off the angle between the place at which we were then firing, and the place where I had seen the Germans bunching, with the graticules of my glasses, I gave the necessary switch of some five degrees, and ordered a round of battery fire. The ground sloped away from left to right. The range on the left was about right, but the right section were short. This was owing to the angle-of-sight being different for the two flanks of the battery. However, as I did not wish to upset the battery angle-of-sight, I increased the range in the right section by fifty yards, and then ordered a round of gun-fire. This was completely successful, two shells bursting in the clump of bushes in which I had seen the Germans collecting. I think that some twenty

or thirty of them must have been in these bushes, and when the shells
burst I saw only two or three run out. One ran away altogether; the
other two, after staggering a few yards, collapsed. The remainder,
I think, must have been knocked out at once.[11]

The intended attack on Menin had been a total failure, but French still
envisioned a successful advance could be made next day, as he laboured
under the misapprehension that the German strength only amounted
to a single corps on the whole front from Menin to Ostend. He therefore decided to push I Corps into the line north of Ypres, moving them
up between the 3rd Cavalry Division and the French cavalry on the left
flank, with Haig being given orders to advance on Bruges.

The nature of the fighting that ensued was very different from
French's fanciful projections. On 20 October full-scale German assaults
had begun to develop all along the line: the attacks on II Corps in the La
Bassée area, as already recounted, but there were also heavy attacks on
III Corps between Armentières and Ploegsteert Wood, the Cavalry Corps
located in front of the Messines Ridge, IV Corps and 3rd Cavalry Division
covering Ypres, and the French cavalry north of Ypres. As the German
artillery moved up in force, so the power of the guns began to dominate
the battlefield. Major Ralph Hamilton watched aghast at the gradual veritable demolition of the buildings of Zonnebeke.

About midday, the enemy began to bombard the town itself for some
hours, but only with shrapnel. This did not do very much damage,
but was very alarming, as the bullets from the shrapnel and the
pieces of the shells flew about the streets like hail. They were firing in
bursts – that is to say, six shells arriving at a time. The air was thick
with the flying lead, fragments of steel, slates from the roofs, glass and
bricks. The noise was appalling: one could hardly hear oneself speak.
One really wondered how anything could live in such an inferno,
the more so as the main street of Zonnebeke was a prolongation of
the German line of fire, and rifle bullets were continuously whining
down the street. About 3 o'clock in the afternoon the 'Black Marias'
started. Zonnebeke has a church standing in a small place, with a very
high steeple, and evidently the German gunners, knowing that our
headquarters were in the centre of the town, were using the church
steeple as a target. This bombardment in the streets of a town by
high-explosive shells was, I think, the most alarming part of the whole

experience. Everything in the town shook when one of these shells burst. The whole ground appeared to tremble as in an earthquake, even when the explosion was 100 yards away.[12]

On 20 October, IV Corps could do nothing more than hold the line round Ypres, while I Corps started to move forward ready for their 'offensive'. On their left flank the situation was fast deteriorating as the French cavalry were forced back from the Houthulst Forest and the village of Passchendaele on the summit of the ridge was lost. In consequence, the 3rd Cavalry Division was forced to pull back to take up a line bending back from Zonnebeke through St Julien to Langemarck. Only the emergency despatch forward of the 2nd and 3rd Coldstream Guards helped stabilise the position, as the 2nd Division of I Corps moved into positions behind them.

Despite it all, French still planned for I Corps and 3rd Cavalry Division to advance on 21 October, while the rest of the British line held firm in the face of attacks of varying strength. As I Corps moved forward on the left flank around Ypres, it soon became manifest that Haig, like Rawlinson before him, placed little credence in the easy assurances from French that they were only facing one German corps. All the same, having been given his orders, Haig had little option but to issue orders for the advance of both 1st and 2nd Divisions to Passchendaele and beyond. The 2nd Division was on the right and advanced as far as Zonnebeke before increasing German fire brought it to a standstill on a line from just northwest of Zonnebeke across to the Poelcappelle–St Julian road. To their left, the 1st Division pushed forward to Langemarck and then launched an attack on the strong German forces occupying Poelcappelle village. Captain Hubert Rees of the 2nd Welsh soon found that the situation appeared a lot worse than some of his divisional staff appreciated.

I was ordered to move with my company through the village and support the attacks of the South Wales Borderers who were said to be doing splendidly. Ferrar was convinced that we should capture a hostile battery, which was shelling the village, and urged me to hurry up. I met Colonel Morland on the road, when I got on to it, and he gave me what information we had, which he admitted was very limited and urged me to proceed with due caution. We shook out into artillery formation and managed to dodge the enemy's shells in the village. The road out to Poelcapelle on the east ran across very open ground and I halted, when I saw it, to explore. I was promptly urged by some staff officer to go straight up it 'in fours', as the SWB's were in a bad way 500 yards up the road. I refused to move without putting out an advance guard and started off half a dozen scouts up the road. They had not got ten yards away from the cover of the last house before a machine gun opened on them at close range and they threw themselves flat. I yelled directions to them, until they got back under cover, and then turned to express my views to the staff officer, but he had disappeared.[13]

While he sought out the staff officer, his men addressed the advancing Germans with murderous intent.

They are 400 yards in front of us. They appear to be in confusion. We bang away like mad. It is fascinating. I concentrate my fire on a space between a farm house and a hay rick. They are seeking shelter. I am 'potting' them one by one into this space. Bullets fall amongst us. Some of my comrades are wounded. I am unhurt.[14]

Private Samuel Knight, 2nd Welsh Regiment, 3rd Brigade, 1st Division, I Corps

The German attacks proliferated in number with new threats appearing all around the 1st Division. Yet the Germans were also suffering terrible casualties as their inexperienced troops walked forward to the slaughter. Vizfeldwebel Frischauf of the 236th Reserve Infantry Regiment was leading his men towards the Hannebeek stream. At first all went well as they moved unseen through a village landscape of gardens and hedges. Then they came out into clear view of the British.

Then, when we crossed the crest and tried to jump down into the streambed, we were spotted by the enemy. Salvo after salvo was fired at us and shells almost parted our hair. As though blown apart, we lay there widely scattered. All around there was moaning and groaning; a shell had landed in amongst us as we leapt and now the men became panicky. 'Back!' came a shout, 'Back, behind the hedge!' I could not halt the withdrawal. The overpressure of the exploding shell had hurled me into the stream bed. One of my arms and a leg were stuck in the mud and I had to be pulled out by two of my men. Wounded as I was, I could not move myself. A shell splinter which had hit my stomach had paralysed my right leg. Some of my men carried me back into cover and bandaged me up then I was carried through heavy shell fire through Poelcappelle on a stretcher. I saw no more of my platoon. I was delivered, semi-conscious, to the regimental aid post.[15]

Such incidents were repeated all along the line. This was the kind of slaughter that British propagandists had boasted had happened at Mons back in August; now it had become a reality as hordes of barely trained German troops stumbled forwards across open fields straight into the sights of well-concealed British troops.

We had imagined that our baptism of fire would be somewhat different. There can be nothing more depressing that the very public failure of an attack launched as though on exercise against an invisible enemy. Unthinking, section after section ran into the well-directed fire of experienced troops. Every effort had been put into our training, but it was completely inadequate preparation for such a serious assault on battle-hardened, long-service colonial soldiers. We had just reached a meadow on a hillside, which was surrounded by trees and hedges, when the first British caps came into view. Forgotten for a moment was that little we had learned about modern battle drills, cover and exploitation of ground. In two ranks and, in some places three, keeling or standing, we poured down fire with an abandon which can only be understood by the excitement of the first great moment of this day of assaults. After hours of demoralising hopelessness, here was a task which was visible and achievable. After two rounds fired standing unsupported, as if on the range, the inevitable happened. Just as I was taking the first pressure on the trigger, I was hit in the left buttock and I immediately felt the effects of the last strenuous days of marching – days for which we had not in the slightest been prepared – and the loss of blood from the wound weakened me far more than should have been the case. Everywhere there was confusion. Men were flooding back from the front.[16]

Private Willi Kahl, 236th Reserve Infantry Régiment, 51st Reserve Division, XXVI Reserve Corps

It was a total disaster for the inexperienced German formations, and in the face of such a massacre some German units began to break, running back in disorder.

To the north of 1st Division, the pressure of the relentless German attacks emanating from the green fastness of the Houthulst Forest was such that the French cavalry were forced back towards Bixschoote. This withdrawal uncovered the whole left flank of the 1st Division and Haig had no choice but to suspend any remaining thoughts of an attack; indeed, it was soon obvious that the bulk of the 1st Division would be needed to cover his flank. Amongst the reserves sent forward to restore the line was Lieutenant Evelyn Needham and the 1st Northamptonshires.

> The Germans had attacked the 1st Brigade, who were holding the line in front of the road running between Langemarck and Steenstraat, and the line to their left, which was held by dismounted French Cavalry. These latter, having no entrenching tools of any description, had been unable to 'dig themselves in' and were soon driven out of their line. The Huns had occupied this and had enfiladed the left of the 1st Brigade line, held by the Cameron Highlanders, who in their turn were driven out of their trenches. 'C' Company was to lead the way, and I was told, not at all to my satisfaction, that I was to go ahead with the 'point' of the advance guard, taking every possible precaution, as nobody knew just where the line was, just where the Camerons were, or where the enemy were. It was now pitch dark, in fact one of the darkest nights I have ever known in my life. It was impossible to see more than a yard in front. I think that for the next half-hour or so I was more thoroughly frightened than at any other time during the war. Moving up a lane in the inky darkness, not knowing where one was going to, but only that somewhere ahead were the enemy, waiting for us. We moved along the ditches on each side of the road, so as not to give away our advance by the sound of our feet tramping along the hard surface of the lane![17]

Eventually they got through and located the Camerons, reinforcing their line and digging in. But it was not long before Needham's luck ran out.

> We could see large bodies of Germans collecting in the wood on the ridge opposite, and 'Jumbo' Bentley and I knelt up in our ditch so as to be able to see better what they were up to, and both scanned the wood closely through our field-glasses. Suddenly I felt a terrific blow on my right arm, just as if somebody had hit me on the funny bone as hard as he could with a sledgehammer. It spun me round like a top and I collapsed in the bottom of the trench. The man next to me rolled me over and said, 'You ain't 'alf bloody well got 'it in the 'and, Sir!' and on

looking down I saw that my right hand was a mass of blood. My arm still felt numb from the blow, and I could hardly realize that it was my hand that was hit, as it did not hurt at all. However, this man cut my field dressing out of my tunic, and after dousing my hand with iodine, which did hurt, he bound it up very well; he then made a sling out of my woolen scarf which I was wearing, insisted on giving me one of his own cigarettes and lighting it for me, and told me not to worry, I was, 'For 'Blighty' all right with that packet!' This sounded too good to be true, and I felt distinctly better. He also said, and I then realized it for the first time, that I had been very lucky not to be killed, as I had my field glasses up to my eyes and the bullet which had hit my right hand would have got me in the head if it had been one inch further to the left! He told me my right collar badge was badly dented and the bullet must have hit this after hitting my hand.[18]

By the afternoon Haig's main preoccupation was to hold the ground they already held: this phase of the fighting would become known as the Battle of Langemarck.

The 22 October brought further evidence that, while French might continue to underestimate the strength of the forces the Germans had amassed against the BEF, on the ground the situation was increasingly obvious. Indeed, it was not long before heavy German shells began crashing down on British positions at Langemarck.

> I was standing at the door when I heard a coal-box (the first of the day) coming towards us. He pitched in a house about twenty yards up the street and simply blew the whole house away. Tables, chest-of-drawers, etc., etc., came hurtling through the air. Every window in the place was broken, then they began in earnest. Coal-boxes (big and small), shrapnel (percussion and time fuse) all came shrieking through the air and crashing round us. The Welsh headquarters ran like hares.[19]
>
> Captain Charles Paterson, 1st South Wales Borderers, 3rd Brigade, 1st Division, I Corps

Captain Rees of the 2nd Welsh witnessed the discomfiture of Lieutenant Colonel Charles Morland by a spray of German shells that seemed to follow him wherever he went as he moved around Langemarck.

> I saw a field gun shell strike the spire of the church just below the cross and send the cross some twenty yards into the air. The church

shortly afterwards caught fire, and went up in a sheet of flames. A little time afterwards, Colonel Morland and battalion headquarters came to my headquarters. He had had two houses blown down over his head in succession in the village and as he remarked, 'It was safer in the front line!'[20]

The heavy German barrage continued all day. Major Frederick Packe found himself in a very exposed salient around the very end of the village.

The position of my company was at the apex and they went to attack first on one flank and then on the other, – and sometimes all round – so it happened that at times there was less than a quarter of the whole circle from which bullets and shells were *not* coming at us. The effect of lying out in the trenches under the fire of these 'crumps' is awfully trying to the nerves as one is absolutely helpless against them. They also turned their attention to the town which they simply and literally destroyed – each house in turn appeared to get a shell in it and when it did that house ceased to exist. The fine old church was set fire to by a shell and we saw it blazing behind us – may England never see the horrors we see in this country! I am glad to say my nerves are very good – this is nothing to do with pluck or anything of that sort, but simply being the lucky possessor of a somewhat phlegmatic temperament.[21]

Packe may have maintained his nerve under pressure, but he had only just joined the 2nd Welsh and he was still 'fresh'. Methodical devastation by shellfire was a new concept to most of the BEF; this was not how they had envisioned the use of artillery, and many were shocked at what they witnessed.

We sat and saw the total destruction of the village. The Germans went for the church spire until the whole church was in flames and falling to pieces, and then they turned their attention to the rest of the town and simply blew it to pieces. I went in the evening to see it. Practically every house ruined and all round the church on fire. A wonderfully awful sight in the night with the church one glowing mass and showers of sparks coining up as some house fell in somewhere in the town. There was absolutely no reason for the continual bombardment. Of course, if we use buildings we can't expect them to keep their shells off them; but this was such wanton destruction. They went at the church and continued at it long after the spire, which of course might have had one of our artillery or observation officers in it, was blown away. Up till a very late hour they went at it, and now the nice little place is simply one ruin.[22]

Captain Charles Paterson, 1st South Wales Borderers, 3rd Brigade, 1st Division, I Corps

The fighting was desperate: a mixture of shells crashing down upon the British trenches, followed by sudden German attacks. Many of these were primitive affairs, with little element of sophistication or military skill. Indeed, Captain Hubert Rees was somewhat shaken by the carnage inflicted by his men during the suicidal mass attacks launched on his positions.

At the corner of my hedge, we had a machine gun. Colonel Morland and I stood by this gun for about an hour. We actually saw the Germans form up for attack and opened fire on their first line at 1,250 yards. From that time onwards, we had every form of target from a company in mass, who tried to put a large haystack between us and them, but who formed on the wrong side of it, to a battalion in fours near the edge of the Houthulst Forest. Sergeant Longden, who was firing the gun, told me that evening that he reckoned he'd killed a thousand Germans – I put it at four or five hundred casualties. The enemy, who had not properly located us before the action began, started shelling, and one shell practically burst on this machine gun, killing or wounding the whole crew, except Longden and one other man. By this time, the attack had obviously been disposed of and with practically no loss to us. I never saw the Germans make a worse attack or suffer heavier losses.[23]

For the supporting artillery gunners, it was a grievously confusing situation as the lines see-sawed backwards and forwards in circumstances of near-total confusion. In the midst of this pandemonium, Signaller John Palmer and his companions almost made a fatal mistake.

Laid out wires from the telephone cart under shell and rifle fire. We had been given instructions by the Colonel and went off at a rare pace, we had just emerged from the cover of a small wood when Fritz let it rip. Our off horse dropped and we had to get the harness off in full view of the Germans. My chum and I expressed a hope that if this was under cover – as stated by the Colonel – then thank goodness it was not in the open! We were just giving instructions to the driver to get the cart back to headquarters when we were accosted by an infantry officer who inquired as to 'What the bloody hell we thought we were doing there?' We told him that we had had a bit of bad luck in losing a horse, but were going to lay the last ¾ mile of wire by hand. He was wonderfully sarcastic, pointing out that the position we expected to reach had passed into the enemy's hands about an hour before we arrived![24]

Signaller John Palmer, 118th Battery, 26th Brigade, RFA, 1st Division, I Corps

Palmer's mood was by no means improved when he realised they would then have to go back and recover some two miles of telephone wire – a vital resource that was still in very short supply at that stage of the war.

By 22 October, the position had further deteriorated for the Allies: the BEF was faltering under the pressure and further to the north the Belgians were struggling to keep the Germans east of the Yser. Thus it was that the arrival at Ypres of the French IX Corps (17th and 18th Divisions, plus the 6th and 7th Cavalry Divisions, under the overall command of General Pierre Dubois) was probably crucial to the course of events. It mirrored the arrival of the first elements of the Indian Corps on the same day to rescue the II Corps further south and the deployment of the French 42nd Division to bolster the Belgians in the Nieuport area. Without the arrival of these French reserves the fight would have been all but over – whatever the British or Belgian heroics that might ensue. In a battle between armies of millions size does matter.

Yet Foch's instructions to IX Corps betray his continuing failure to grasp the true seriousness of the Allied position, as he attempted to grasp the initiative by ordering a renewed offensive for 23 October towards Roulers. This was to be carried out by the newly arrived French 17th Division pushing out through the centre of I Corps. Foch also requested a supportive attack by the entire BEF all along the line. As the British were only informed of this prospective attack at 02.00 on 23 October, it was by then administratively impossible for the staff to issue the required orders and make the necessary preparations. In the end the French 17th Division only advanced as far as a line between Zonnebeke and St Julien. It was decided to abandon any pretence of an attack and instead they relieved the 2nd Division from their front-line positions. The 2nd Division, together with the French 18th Division, 6th Cavalry Division and 7th Cavalry Division, were then gathered to form a useful tactical reserve held further back towards Ypres.

During this dramatic phase of the fighting, the British had nothing more than improvised trenches, about three feet deep at most, usually lacking in any proper barbed wire protection in front of them. The 'line' was often riddled with gaps that could stretch for hundreds of yards and which were only covered by either the artillery or small arms fire. Captain Harry Dillon was in such a position on the 2nd Division front on the evening of 23 October.

> The night came on rather misty and dark, and I thought several times of asking for reinforcements, but I collected a lot of rifles off the dead, loaded them and put them along the parapet instead. All of a sudden about a dozen shells came down – and almost simultaneously two machine guns and a tremendous rifle fire opened on us. It was a most unholy din. The shells ripped open the parapet, and trees came crashing down. However, I was well under ground, and did not care much, but presently the guns stopped, and I knew then that we were in for it. I had to look over the top for about ten minutes, however, under their infernal Maxims, before I saw what I was looking for. It came with a suddenness that was the most startling thing I have ever known. The firing stopped, and I had been straining my eyes so that for a moment I could not believe them, but, fortunately, I did not hesitate long.[25]
>
> Captain Harry Dillon, 2nd Oxford and Bucks Light Infantry, 5th Brigade, 2nd Division, I Corps

Dillon only had a blurred impression of what was coming towards him: perhaps that was just as well.

> A great grey mass of humanity was charging, running for all God would let them, straight on to us not fifty yards off. Everybody's nerves were pretty well on edge as I had warned them what to expect, and as I fired my rifle the rest all went off almost simultaneously. One saw the great mass of Germans quiver. In reality some fell, some fell over them, and others came on. I have never shot so much in such a short time, could not have been more than a few seconds and they were down. Suddenly one man – I expect an officer – jumped up and

came on. I fired and missed, seized the next rifle and dropped him a few yards off. Then the whole lot came on again and it was the most critical moment of my life. Twenty yards more and they would have been over us in thousands, but our fire must have been fearful, and at the very last moment they did the most foolish thing they possibly could have done. Some of the leading people turned to the left for some reason, and they all followed like a great flock of sheep. We did not lose much time, I can give you my oath. My right hand is one huge bruise from banging the bolt up and down. I don't think one could have missed at the distance and just for one short minute or two we poured the ammunition into them in boxfuls. My rifles were red hot at the finish. The firing died down and out of the darkness a great moan came. People with their arms and legs off trying to crawl away; others who could not move gasping out their last moments with the cold night wind biting into their broken bodies and the lurid red glare of a farm house showing up clumps of grey devils killed by the men on my left further down. A weird awful scene; some of them would raise themselves on one arm or crawl a little distance, silhouetted as black as ink against the red glow of the fire.[26]

Some of the Germans had got within twenty-five yards of Dillon's line. It had been a close-run thing and, after they had been relieved by the French later that night, the French reported that some 740 German corpses littered the ground in front of the trenches held by the Oxfordshires. Not too far from Dillon was Sergeant John McIlwain of the 2nd Connaught Rangers, who gives a fine impression of the feelings of men under heavy shellfire in shallow trenches that were totally unfit to provide any real cover.

The shelling is more deadly than ever. We have nothing else to do but chew biscuits and bully, work with the spade when we can to improve cover and wait for death – or soldiering on. Many trenches are blown in. Sergeant Banks and six men are killed together – the old story told to relatives could truthfully be said of him – 'he never felt it' – his head was neatly taken off at one slice! Crouched and pondering the best position, I watch for hours, for the shell that is coming to me. Closer each one came after the other, by inches getting nearer. I decide that with the same elevation the next one will do it. Then by some means that dogmatists might explain the German gunner alters slightly his elevation, the dead ground in front or rear is raked – and I am saved again.[27]

As they sat in their shallow, muddy trenches, men could not help but ponder on the grim situation they found themselves in. Dillon's emotional response was not unusual.

> It all fills me with a great rage. I know I have got to stop my bullet some time and it is merely a question of where it hits one, whether it is dead or wounded. I don't care one farthing as far as I am concerned, but the whole thing is an outrage on civilisation. The whole of this beautiful country is devastated – broken houses, broken bodies, blood, filth and ruin everywhere. Can any unending hellfire for the Kaiser, his son and the party who caused this war repair the broken bodies and worse broken hearts which are being made – being made this very minute – within a few hundred yards of where I am sitting?[28]

Dillon was beginning to realise the sheer scale of the gigantic undertaking that was the Great War. This would be no short-term conflict, easily resolved by a couple of 'decisive battles'. This was 'Armageddon' writ large and it looked like few of them would survive it.

> Dead Germans wherever one goes. I suppose 5,000,000 men take a lot of killing, but we ought to have accounted for a good few by now. I suppose this is one big battle that has been going on for about six days. It is certainly bloody enough for anything. I am now second in command of the regiment, so if the Colonel gets hit I take command – rather too much responsibility for my liking; still, it might be a chance of doing something.[29]

The only consolation for many of the British troops was the evident youthfulness and inexperience of the majority of the German troops they encountered.

> All the prisoners we have taken have been either old men or boys of fifteen up to twenty. They can't have a man left in Germany now, I should think. And to think that we haven't started with all our hundreds of thousands which are in the making. They are beaten I am sure; they must be beaten, and I have no doubt that they will be beaten properly.[30]

Captain Charles Paterson, 1st South Wales Borderers, 3rd Brigade, 1st Division, I Corps

The determination was admirable; but the human cost would be frightful. A week later Paterson himself was dead.[31]

THE 24 OCTOBER SAW THE FRENCH take up the baton and attempt to attack. Prodded on by Foch, the commander of the French Eighth Army, General Victor d'Urbal, in turn issued his orders to General Dubois of IX Corps. These orders proved fanciful given the extreme situation at Ypres.

> As we stand now the tiniest rupture of equilibrium at any point may incline the balance definitely in our favour. The enemy troops which you have on your front and on your left appear to belong for the most part to newly-raised corps without great value. Take advantage of this to press your offensive on Roulers with the greatest vigour, without troubling whether this carries you faster than the rest of the Allied line or not. Secure your flanks by flank guards on both sides and push on, whatever your neighbours right and left may do, without troubling about them except to ascertain what they are about. Try to make a gap. Attack tomorrow, as soon as it is possible.[32]

This was bold; the German troops were largely inexperienced, but it was still far too confident. Indeed, d'Urbal also planned for French troops to relieve the 1st Division from their positions around Langemarck to allow them to join the 2nd Division in reserve. It was then planned to deploy the whole of I Corps in the proposed attack eastwards. Sadly for the French, when it came to the crunch they were unable to make any serious progress, merely edging forward a few hundred yards and managing to recapture the smoking ruins of Zonnebeke. Further round the salient, the 7th Division was once again involved in fierce fighting with elements of the German XXVII Reserve Corps. They first lost and then recaptured Polygon Wood, although only with the help of the 5th and 6th Brigades of 2nd Division, which had to be deployed forward from Haig's precious reserves.

There was, however, beginning to be a discernible pattern to the vicious battles that raged on the low ridges east of Ypres. The Germans were seeking to bludgeon their way through the thin defence lines by means of mass assaults using tens of thousands of half-trained troops.

> Owing to these repeated attacks by overwhelming odds our infantry were somewhat disorganised and units were intermixed. There was, as yet, no sign of any relief and our infantry were fighting a desperate battle against these columns of grey which rolled up time after time, like crowds from a football match. Dead and wounded strewed across the ground round the woods where most of the fighting took place and the pitiful, and at times, horrifying, sights we came across I shall not attempt to describe. Some of the infantrymen I saw appeared to have lost their reason owing to the immense strain of continuous fighting day and night. The act of pouring lead continually into visible masses of men is in itself repulsive even to a fighting man and no wonder many of the men of the 7th Division who managed to come through the fight lost their reason – I saw some of them and they certainly aroused one's sympathy.[33]
>
> Trooper Henry Mattison, Northumberland Hussars, 7th Division, IV Corps

By now it was clear that although the inexperienced German troops could take an objective – often at a terrible cost – they lacked the essential military skills required to organise the captured position for effective defence. Trenches had to be 'turned round' to face the British, proper interconnected fields of fire defined, machine guns sited to best effect with opportunities for enfilade fire, reserves distributed, links with the artillery established and communications checked. Many of the new artillery units were not sufficiently skilful to be able to swiftly change targets, or indeed to respond as appropriate to a changing situation. The Germans were also tiring as the relentless battle ground them down; they too were suffering horrendous losses.

Yet the Royal Artillery was also facing severe problems. The heavier German long-range howitzers were establishing a clear dominance over the whole battlefield, capable of projecting shells all the way back into the city of Ypres itself.

> Saw the result of his latest shell – 'Black Jacks' they call them. I only hope Jack's name is not written on them! The sight of the shell holes certainly does make one feel a bit funny under the waistcoat. One hole in the road and that road is out of action for traffic! One

disadvantage of the heavy type of shell is that they can be heard long before they arrive. We get many a creepy feeling down our spine as we hear the shell roaring towards us. In some cases it bursts several hundred yards away but we still get the creepy feeling. The only advantage is that one can get down flat and in that way take advantage of all the cover possible. You never get killed by the shell you can hear. They tell us that but that idea may go bust at any moment and I should not like to rely on it! The streets of Ypres are now littered with smashed wagons, dead men and horses and it is distinctly unhealthy to loiter there.[34]

Signaller John Palmer, 118th Battery, 26th Brigade, RFA, 1st Division, I Corps

But there was another, increasingly desperate problem for the Royal Artillery as they attempted to counter the German guns. The pre-war presumptions of the role of artillery on the battlefield, the likelihood of short engagements and the length of the war were all exposed as erroneous and the consequences were unavoidable.

Certain shortages in 18-pounder and 4.5" lyddite ammunition; our arrangements do not contemplate battles lasting a month! Most inconvenient at this time![35]

Major John Mowbray, Headquarters, Royal Artillery, 2nd Division, I Corps

This was symptomatic of a much wider problem for the whole BEF. French sent desperate telegrams back to Kitchener claiming that there were only 150 rounds per gun that had not been issued from the ammunition parks on the Western Front, while the number reaching the front from Britain only amounted to a paltry seven rounds per gun per day. All that could be advised in return was the practice of economy; it may be considered a truism that the Battle of Ypres was not the ideal place to try to conserve shells. Of course they were not the only army caught in this trap: the French and Germans were also running short of shells. No one had expected either a long war or this intensity of fighting.

Yet the British and French High Commands remained in good spirits. They had managed to hold the German attacks and had now amassed a considerable tactical reserve, which they felt meant they were poised to wrest the initiative from the Germans. On 25 October, D'Urbal intended to resume IX Corps attack up onto the Passchendaele Ridge and advance towards Roulers. If they were successful then first I Corps and then the whole British line would follow up, domino style, with each corps awaiting the success of their neighbours before launching their own attacks. However, the French progress proved dreadfully slow, and the 2nd Division on their right flank only began to attack in tandem from about 15.00, and by then nothing could be achieved. Further south, on the 7th Division front, it was the Germans who attacked, pressing hard all around the exposed salient around the village of Kruiseecke thrusting out about two miles southeast of Gheluvelt, the village which dominated the main road leading from Menin to Ypres.

Despite all the disappointments of the day, optimism was still unduly prevalent within the Allied High Command. Little notice was paid to air reconnaissance reports indicating that columns of fresh troops were on their way to reinforce the faltering German Fourth Army. Indeed, the orders issued for 26 October bore a remarkable similarity to those of the day before. The French IX Corps was again to have the major role, this time in advancing on both Poelcappelle and Passchendaele, while the British would fall in from the left as they moved forward together. Hampered by effective German resistance from well-organised defences in the Poelcappelle sector, the French failed to make any appreciable progress. The 2nd Division tried to press on, but had achieved no success, when Haig received a worrying message.

A report from IV Corps reaches me that the 7th Division which is holding line from crossroads southeast of Gheluvelt to Zandvoorde is giving way. I send staff officer to find out whether they are being attacked by infantry or whether they are merely leaving their trenches on account of shell fire. He reports several battalions in great disorder passing back through our 1st Brigade. By 4 pm the bulk of the 7th Division had retired from the salient about Kruiseecke, most units in disorder. One brigade came back to the vicinity of Hooge Chateau where I had my 'reporting centre'. I rode out about 3pm to see what was going on, and was astounded at the terror stricken men coming back. Still there were some units in the division which stuck to their trenches. I arranged for the necessary number of   units from the 1st Division to support the latter, and hold a line from Poezelhoek to the left of the Cavalry Corps near Zandvoorde. It was sad to see fine troops like the 7th Division reduced to inefficiency through ignorance of their leaders in having placed them in trenches on the forward slopes where enemy could see and so effectively shell them.[36]

There is no doubt that the German artillery superiority was beginning to have a corrosive effect on morale in the 7th Division. As Haig suggests, this came to a head on 26 October. Battered, bruised and exhausted by a week of constant fighting, they began to give way under the never-ending torrent of heavy shells crashing down on their all-too-inadequate trenches. Their trenches had been dug in haste and without much consideration early in the fighting. Many were placed on the forward slopes of the ridges: this gave them good fields of fire, but on the other hand they were a 'sitting' target for the German artillery, who could carefully range their shells right onto – and into – the trenches. Looking back to the half-digested lessons of the Russo-Japanese War, Capper believed that covered trenches were more effective, but given the preponderance of German high-explosives shells they proved a veritable deathtrap. By this time almost half their officers and a third of the men of the 7th Division were casualties.

Haig sent forward several units from the 1st Division, who managed to stem the German tide and establish a line just in front of Gheluvelt, accepting the loss of the salient stretching forward to Kruiseecke. However, the situation was hardly secure, and already air reconnaissance reports were suggesting the approach of considerable German reinforcements. The remnants of the 7th Division were thus moved sideways to hold the line to the south of the Menin Road, while the 1st Division was moved into the line on their left flank.

For a moment in time, the situation froze. The further French attacks made on 27 and 28 October were unable to make any progress and the British line in consequence also remained static. French visited Haig at I Corps headquarters in Hooge Chateau and transferred the 7th Division to his command, as the 3rd Cavalry Division had already been attached to Allenby's Cavalry Corps. Rawlinson meanwhile returned to Britain to supervise the formation and training of the 8th Division, which would ultimately, alongside the 7th Division, constitute a 'new' IV Corps. The situation may have quietened down but there were still reports coming in of German transport and troop movements towards Ypres. Both sides seemed to be waiting for the next stage to commence. As he waited back in reserve, Captain Harry Dillon recorded his private thoughts, which reflected the duality of mankind at war: cloying sentimentality mingled with a murderous hatred.

> I heard a poor kitten mewling in a cottage and went to its rescue, I found the poor little beast starving – also lots of rabbits, pigs and goats all of which I let out. I took the poor kitten to some friendly gunners who gave her of the best that they had. The whole ground round the place was covered with dead etc, etc but I don't know why – perhaps because one has got so used to this sight – one did not feel it. It does seem hard though that these poor animals should suffer because men are such foul creatures. I do hope however that before the inevitable bullet or shell comes my way I shall get my bayonet into a German.[37]

12

BATTLE OF YPRES: BEDLAM

His plan aimed at breaking through the Allied front at Ypres, the gateway to French Flanders and the starting point of many roads that lead from this region to the Channel ports. The clash of the two forces resulted in a shock of supreme violence and brutality as well as of amazing duration. The enemy was playing his last card and attempting his last manoeuvre on the western theatre of operations.[1]

General Ferdinand Foch, Headquarters, Northern Group of Armies

THE GERMANS HAD NOT GIVEN UP. This Flanders offensive was the culminating effort of the whole German campaign on the Western Front: the last chance for real success. They would throw every last resource into this desperate bid for victory. So they brought up yet more troops to smash down the British and French defences and to secure the gateway to the Channel ports. At the close of the assaults on 24 October, Duke Albrecht of Württemberg realised that his Fourth Army was not going to get through the British and French lines as things stood. Although his forces on the Ypres front (XXIII, XXVI and XXVII Reserve Corps) still attacked vigorously in an effort to gain key tactical locations, at the same time they began to consolidate and strengthen their positions, intent on holding what they had already gained pending the organisation of a new assault force. Exactly the same fate had befallen the Sixth Army

(Crown Prince Rupprecht) in their efforts to break through the British II and III Corps to the south. Falkenhayn's reaction was to introduce a new Army Group in between the Fourth and Sixth Armies with the intention of finally breaking through between Ypres and Zandvoorde He took units from all along the German line to create the eponymous Army Group Fabeck (II Corps, XV Corps, I Cavalry Corps and the 26th Division) under the command of General Max von Fabeck. While this force was being amassed ready for a coordinated attack with the Fourth and Sixth Armies on 30 October, the Fourth Army was to launch a covering attack on Gheluvelt on 29 October.

As ever, French seemed oblivious to any threat and, despite intelligence warnings that a German attack was looming, his mind was still dominated by plans for a renewed offensive. Haig had no choice but to order the necessary reconnaissance, and indeed dutifully issued orders for an attack, but his attention was rather more firmly focussed on defence. The British trenches were still not in good shape, many had originally been support or communications trenches, and there were still problems with having to occupy exposed trenches lying on forward slopes. Haig was still deeply concerned at this and had despatched his senior Royal Engineer officer to examine the potential for improvement. The real answer was to dig a better-sited line further back, but it was unlikely that the Germans would be accommodating enough to give them the necessary time.

When it came at 05.30 on 29 October, the German attack was squarely aimed at the junction of the 1st and 7th Divisions at the Gheluvelt crossroads, a mile east along the Menin Road from the village itself. The fighting was murderous: the temptation is to see it solely from a British perspective, but as the men in *feldgrau* attacked, they too were losing men in droves.

Suddenly someone shouted, 'Left, British dug in on top of the hill!' and the order came, 'Up! Double march! Down!' 'Sights at 400 metres! Aim carefully!' Using the first available cover, at first we all fired too short. We were right in their line of fire; were literally swamped by it. My friend Schram was the first to fall; shot straight through the centre of his head. He threw me an unforgettable glance as though he was trying to give me a message of farewell! A moment later came the order, 'Up!

Double march!' As I rushed forward I felt a violent blow to the stomach. Realising what had happened, I crawled as best I could in my weakened condition to a nearby ditch along the road towards Wervik. It was a miracle that I reached it still in one piece. I lay with my face down in the ditch whilst bullets whistled in all direction over me. Shells crashed down so close that I was sprayed with earth. Eventually, darkness fell and the shelling and machine gun fire died away.[2]

Lance Corporal Ludwig Klein, 16th Bavarian Reserve Regiment, 6th Bavarian Reserve Division, XIV Reserve Corps

Some 349 soldiers of the three battalions of Klein's regiment were killed on 29 October. Overall the German casualties were dreadful, but at the same time the pressure of the mass attacks was unceasing and it was a relatively thin British line. Much of the impact fell on the men of the 1st Guards Brigade.

At dawn the enemy came over, *en masse*, but were repulsed with heavy losses. Seven times they came with only a short interval, but every time they were beaten back. It was impossible to miss a target, they came in such dense mass. Then disaster came to us – news arrived they had broken through on our right. Finally, they completely encircled us, and about 11am we were forced to throw down our arms. Captain C. E. de la Pasture,[3] our own company commander, fell wounded, and died with the words, 'Tell my wife I died fighting!' He was a born gentleman and an excellent officer.[4]

Corporal Charles Green, 1st Scots Guards, 1st Guards Brigade, 1st Division, I Corps

By this time the front line trenches were veritable charnel houses as the piles of bodies mounted up – each of them a former comrade, now nothing but a corpse and a lifeless husk. The wounded could not be got away and had to just lie there and hope for salvation.

We had a large number of dead and wounded actually down in the trench with us. One Lieutenant Macdonald[5] was lying in the corner of my trench mortally wounded. I was standing in the blood that was running out of him, but could not stop to render first aid because of the scarcity of riflemen to repel the constant attack. My rifle barrel and breech used to swell and contract with the constant use, and often one could not work the bolt, it being stuck, we put the one so affected down and picked up a dead colleague's. Stringer, a man I had grown to love dearly, was killed about 1.30pm. He was shot through the left wrist and clean through the heart, in the final German breakthrough. He died in my arms with the loveliest smile on his face that I have ever seen.[6] Roff was shot in the throat but it was not much more than a flesh wound, although an artery was cut, for I hastily dressed it with my emergency dressing and the bleeding stopped. We took a quick glance along the trenches and, as we could not see a single man on his feet, we decided to retire to a farm building thirty yards to our rear, where we ought to find some cover. We dashed into the farmyard – to our surprise we saw that it was swarming with German infantry who ordered us to give up our arms at once. So we did. We were taken across the farmyard to be interviewed by a German officer who spoke a little English. He said, 'You are now prisoners of war. You will have to conform to our orders until the end of the war!'[7]

Private Joseph Garvey, 1st Scots Guards, 1st Brigade, 1st Division, I Corps

The prisoners received a rough treatment, although in fairness it could not be denied that the German troops had suffered much at their hands. Human nature can be unforgiving in such circumstances.

They bought us to our knees and we should have been dead men if a German officer had not intervened. They took away everything: money, smokes, pipes etc. But my luck was in. The Hun who searched me was a decent fellow – one in a million. He told me to put everything back in my pockets, which I gladly did. All of us, however, were ordered to discard our greatcoats. We felt the loss too, the weather was cold. The fellows who suffered most were those on whom German money etc. were found. We now commenced to march back to the enemy's headquarters. They forced us to march hands above heads the whole way. We stopped at a farm, and left our wounded, also all small books, photographs. On restarting, some of our escort were so kind enough as to give our fellows their packs to carry. Fighting had evidently been going on all around. We passed many wounded who made motions they would dearly like to cut our throats.[8]

Corporal Charles Green, 1st Scots Guards, 1st Guards Brigade, 1st Division, I Corps

Immediately south of the Menin road were the 7th Division who also came under heavy attack. Amidst the worst of the fighting was the 2nd

Gordon Highlanders. Sergeant James Bell had been ordered forward with the battalion reserves and on reaching the forward-most trench found the dead lying three deep. His account conjures up the desperation of counter-attacks arranged on the spur of the moment and carried out without much thought of the odds of success.

> After taking bearings, I told the men to keep under cover and detailed one man, 'Ginger' Bain, as look out. After what seemed ages 'Ginger' excitedly asked, 'How strong is the German Army?' I replied, 'Seven million!' 'Well,' said Ginger, 'Here is the whole bloody lot of them making for us!' We were driven from the trench, and those of us who were unscathed joined Lieutenant Brooke, who had come up with cooks, transport men, and men who had been wounded but could still use a rifle. Lieutenant Brooke was (outwardly) quite unperturbed, walking about the firing line issuing orders as if on the barrack square. I had served under him for nine years, and seeing him such a target for the enemy riflemen, I asked him to lie down as I felt if he was hit his loss at that particular time would be disastrous. He told me we must retake the trench I had been driven from, and to pick twenty men to do so. All the men were alike to me – men I had known for years – so I told ten men on my right and ten on my left to get ready to rush the trench. We succeeded in this. No artist or poet can depict a trench after fighting in its stark hellishness. If we could not be driven out of the trench, it seemed certain that we would be blown out of it. Shells kept landing near enough in front of or behind the trench to shake us almost out of it. Many got killed by rifle fire, 'Ginger' Bain[9] being the first, then 'Big' Bruce[10] whom I boxed in a competition before going to France. I passed a message to Lieutenant Brooke,[11] informing him our numbers were so reduced that if attacked we could not hold the trench, and received back word that he had just been killed.[12]

Shortly afterwards Sergeant James Bell himself was badly hit.

> I slipped over the rear of the trench, to cut across and meet the lads as they emerged from the communication trench, but had only gone about 6 yards when I received what in the regiment was called the 'dull thud'. I thought I had been violently knocked on the head, but, feeling I was not running properly, I looked down and discovered that my right foot was missing. Somehow, I stood watching men running

along the communication trench. My power of speech had left me, so I could speak to none of them; then I swooned into the trench. No one had seen me being wounded, but one of the men, 'Pipe' Adams, on missing me, returned to look for me. On seeing me lying quite helpless, he prepared to lift and carry me out of the trench. I told him I was too heavy, that it was too dangerous, and that in time our regiment would retake all the ground lost, when I would be safe. I then put a field dressing and a shirt from my pack over my stump and lay down to wait further developments. In this trench there would be about sixty badly wounded British soldiers, mostly Gordons, of all ranks. I noticed a watch quite close to me; on looking at it I found the time was 9am. I must have dropped into a kind of stupor, and I woke suddenly with the noise of great shouting. I thought it was our fellows returned to their old position, imagined I heard voices I knew, also that of my company officer, Captain Burnett, shouting, 'Where are you, Sergeant Bell?' I tried to rise, failed, but kept shouting, 'Here I am, in this trench, Sir!' Judge my surprise when two German infantrymen jumped into the trench. One of them got quite excited, raised his rifle, levelled at and within a yard of me, but the other knocked his mate's rifle up and asked me when and where I was wounded.[13]

Bell was a prisoner of war, but the Germans could not get the wounded away amidst the frenetic fighting so Bell and the other badly wounded Gordons had to lie abandoned and unattended in that trench for the rest of the day and all night.

There were periods of heavy gun fire, periods of silence, periods when all the wounded – those still alive – were shouting for stretcher bearers, praying for death, moaning noisily and quietly with pain. Strange the thoughts that pass through one under such circumstances. I thought of a great-grandfather of mine who fought in the Peninsular War, and was badly wounded at the Battle of Waterloo. Then I would think of a picture I once saw of a trench during the Balkan War. I had considered the picture was overdrawn, and now I knew that it was not horrible enough for the real thing. The Germans had taken a lot of ground, were busily consolidating their new position, and all morning (the 30th) groups of them and individuals kept looking into the trench. Two German officers slowly and quietly walked along the trench, and when they saw me still alive they appeared greatly surprised. Each of them spoke to me in English, enquiring how long I had been lying there. They informed me that there were fifty-seven of my comrades dead in the trench, and that I was one of three still alive. One of them promised to send someone to pick me up, but I had doubts about him doing so. However, about an hour later, four German private soldiers arrived, bringing a waterproof sheet to carry me off. One of the Germans could speak English, and in his deep-spoken voice said, 'Ah! Scotlander, you lucky man. Get out of this damned war. It last long time. What we fight for? Ah! German Army and English Navy, both damned nuisance!' They carried me with great care to a barn about half a mile away that was being used as a dressing station.[14]

Meanwhile the situation at Gheluvelt had for a while looked grim, but at about 14.00 a counter-attack was launched by the 3rd Brigade.

On reaching the further end of the village we met the German infantry advancing in rather a dense line. On the appearance of our men the enemy hesitated, some stopped and opened fire, and some continued advancing slowly. We had great difficulty in getting into any position where we could use our rifles, as anyone showing himself clear of the houses and enclosures received a hail of bullets. The men behaved splendidly, Sergeant Peoples particularly distinguishing himself, and we managed to establish a thin line, whence we were able to stop the enemy. In getting through the village we had to keep clear of the main road which was swept by fire, platoons and sections keeping together in spite of other troops straggling back in a disorganised condition. We now found ourselves in a nasty salient. We got in touch with 'C' Company on our right, which appeared to be holding their own, but on the left we could only hear rifle fire, but not see what was happening. It was here that Melville under heavy fire established two machine guns on a mound from which position he was able to enfilade the Germans advancing north of the village, and did such execution that the enemy fell back, taking with them those in front of the village.[15]

Captain Christopher Berkeley, 2nd Welsh Regiment, 3rd Brigade, 1st Division, I Corps

Berkeley himself was hit in the neck during the attack, but stuck to the task until the scant reserves arrived and the village of Gheluvelt was once more secure. In the circumstances, there is no doubt that Lieutenant George Melville had done exceptionally well to position his machine guns where they could take the Germans from the flank. Fired at a frontal attack they were a deadly enough weapon, but machine guns only came into their own when they could rake the whole line of advance from the flank – then they were lethal. Gradually the BEF was learning hard practical lessons through combat experience.

The German attacks had widened from the epicentre at Gheluvelt, but in general the line had held. After the dust died down, the British had lost their trenches in the vicinity of the Gheluvelt crossroads, being forced back towards the village itself. That night, the tired troops were heavily engaged in digging – as best they could – a new line of trenches ready for whatever the Germans had in store for them. The French attacks further to the north could make no progress against the well dug-in German troops supported by copious heavy artillery. The parameters of what was – and was not – possible were being defined for both sides.

The ground was moving beneath the feet of the British and French commanders. The misty and cloudy weather conditions hampered their aerial reconnaissances, while the Germans had learnt the wisdom of concealing their major troop movements, moving mainly by night and resting up in concealed positions in woodlands or villages. But the five new divisions of the Army Group Fabeck were gathering and beginning to take over the line from the exhausted divisions that had by this time given their all. The German artillery began to bombard the 2nd Division front early on 30 October.

Jerry hit my platoon four times in one morning with heavy shells. The first one hit the trench, blew it in. Well, we dug them out and built up the trench. One of my lads he was lying back there, I couldn't see a wound on him, but he couldn't move. I think the explosion had blown him against the wall of the trench and had dislocated his spine because he had no feeling downwards. Anyway, we couldn't do anything for him – we left him lying there. The last shell found me 'at home'! It blew the platoon's ammunition sky high, smashed my rifle in front of me, buried me in the trench – and didn't hurt me! They came and dug me out. What grieved me was my rations had gone! A bit of reserve, you see, that you kept in the side there. I was a bit shook up. I went along to company headquarters. The officer in charge was a Second Lieutenant Slater.[16] He'd just had his commission on the 1st October and we had been pals – sergeants together. He was wounded in the head. I sat down there with him in this company headquarters. He said, 'You been having a rough time along there, Tom?' He gave me a drink of cherry brandy and a bully mutton sandwich. It was nectar![17]

Sergeant Thomas Painting, 1st King's Royal Rifle Corps, 6th Brigade, 2nd Division, I Corps

Despite the bombardment, when the German assaults finally came on the 2nd Division and the neighbouring French IX Corps, they were generally unsuccessful.

The main German effort on 30 October would be directed at the 7th Division and the 3rd Cavalry Division, which were stretched thinly between Gheluvelt and Zandvoorde. Here Fabeck had moved up his 260 heavy artillery pieces and used them to unleash a devastating bombardment from 06.45 with huge shells crashing down on the British trenches, particularly on the Life Guards of the 7th Cavalry Brigade on the Zandvoorde Ridge. When the Germans attacked in great force at 08.00, the dazed cavalrymen simply could not hold and were forced back behind the village of Zandvoorde and right off the crest of the ridge. Desperate measures were made to send up reserves to try to carve out a defensible new front line. Meanwhile, further to the south the 3rd Cavalry Brigade of the 2nd Cavalry Division was also forced back from Hollebeke. Gradually they fell back to a line along the Messines Ridge just in front of the village of Wytschaete. Here they stood, sensing a slight reluctance from the Germans to push on their attack. But the line was far too thin and the last of the Cavalry Corps and I Corps reserves were being sucked into the battle. Despite the desperation of the situation, there was still the occasional outbreak of modest levity.

An officer of the Household Cavalry Composite Regiment, whom I happened to know, turned up and actually made me laugh. He told me his regiment was in the front line, which he did not consider was at all a nice or proper place for anybody, least, of all the 'Tins.' He said their swords were an awful nuisance, because when they moved they made such a noise, tripped them up when they tried to run and caught in everything in the trenches – and were too big to be useful even in opening bully beef tins! He also said that if we wanted any more men in the front line we had better go across and see if the Germans would lend us some as they seemed to have so many, whereas he did not think there were any on our side between us and Calais! Somehow he introduced a breath of Piccadilly into the air.[18]

Lieutenant Cuthbert Baines, 2nd Oxford and Bucks Light Infantry, 5th Brigade, 2nd Division, I Corps

The British cavalry were proving themselves crucial to the defence of Ypres. Although a brigade was less in strength than two ordinary infantry battalions, their inherent mobility meant that they could be deployed *where* they were needed *when* they were needed. This gave them a far greater value than might otherwise have been imagined. Once in position, the infantry skills inculcated into the cavalry would finally justify all that expensive training.

Haig was keenly aware of the importance of keeping reserves to hand in order to counter any German breakthrough. But, even with the best intentions, the situation was spiralling rapidly out of control. He had already been forced to send almost every spare battalion to strengthen the line between Gheluvelt and the Messines Ridge. Thus it was that twice during the course of that longest day Haig was forced to turn 'cap in hand' to his French allies – who proved to be well up to the challenge. First, they dispatched a cavalry brigade forward to fill a gap, then Dubois sent several battalions of his IX Corps across to cover the Zillebeke village just in front of Zandvoorde Ridge. As it happened the Germans made no more serious efforts to break through but it was a superb example of willing cooperation between allies.

Another example of self-sacrifice in the common Allied cause was evident on the Belgian front, which stretched along the Yser from Nieuport on the coast to Dixmude. The Belgians had earlier requested assistance from the Royal Navy, who initially sent a mixed squadron of monitors, light cruisers, destroyers and sloops, under the command of Rear Admiral Sir Horace Hood, to provide shore bombardments to try to impede the progress of the German advance. This had been done to some considerable effect, helping in the defence of Nieuport. As the battle reached a crescendo the pre-dreadnought *Venerable* was sent out to join them.

We steamed to a suitable position off Nieuport and when we had finished breakfast we opened fire with common shell from the after turret. The Germans were entrenched along the Yser and they must have had a very nasty time of it. Later on they closed up the port 6" guns crews and the fore turrets crew and started bombarding in earnest. We had hardly been at anchor an hour when our destroyers sighted a submarine about 1,000 yards away from our ship and they opened fire on it. We immediately weighed anchor and without waiting steamed away from the spot. After the submarine scare we no longer tried to anchor while bombarding, but steamed to a suitable spot, fired about twenty rounds and then steamed away again. All the time we were steaming we steered a zigzag course in order to make it harder for the submarine to torpedo us. Firing was carried on during the greater part of the afternoon.[19]

Midshipman Percy Baldwin, HMS *Venerable*

The Royal Navy had become morbidly afraid of German submarines after the loss of over 1,400 lives when the armoured cruisers *Hogue*, *Aboukir* and *Cressy* were sunk whilst patrolling in the North Sea by the U-9 on 22 September.

Despite the coastal bombardment the German pressure was beginning to tell and the Belgians made a courageous decision which demonstrated their unwavering commitment. Even as they were forced back to positions along the raised embankment of the Nieuport-Dixmude railway line, so the plans were laid to inundate all the low-lying country in front of them, despite the inevitable devastation that the rising flood waters would cause. First the culverts passing through the embankment were systematically blocked. Then as the waters began to rise, the Belgians took the ultimate step and at flood tide on 27 October they opened the coastal sluices at Nieuport. It would take just two days to completely flood the area. The question was could the Belgians hold out long enough? Once again the *Venerable* and the monitors were vital in supplying a supporting bombardment to harass and disrupt the last German attempts to advance before the water got too deep.

We opened fire at 7.30 and this morning we got a reply to our fire, a battery of about four or six howitzers opening fire on us and several shots fell very close to us, only missing us by about twenty yards. Two French destroyers joined us in the early morning and helped in the bombardment. We tried to locate the position of the German battery and for this reason we bombarded part of Westende village, and it is believed that we did destroy the battery at the same time.[20]

Midshipman Percy Baldwin, HMS *Venerable*

After more submarine alarms, the crew of the *Venerable* had a shock as they encountered another of the perils of operations in shallow coastal waters.

> As we were circling we were startled by a sudden jolt and discovered that we had run aground in the bows, the engines were reversed, but the ship was immoveable. Everybody was sent aft, but this failed to bring her off. Both cutters were lowered, one taking soundings and the other took a 6½" towing pendant to the *Brilliant,* by means of a 6" hemp with which to haul the wire across. With the aid of the *Brilliant* we left the mud banks.[21]
>
> Midshipman Percy Baldwin, HMS *Venerable*

The efforts of Admiral Hood and above all the self-sacrifice of the Belgians ultimately paid results as the seawater swirled in, forcing the Germans to withdraw right back from the bank of the Yser River. The left of the Allied line had been firmly anchored. The only way through was at Ypres.

THE GERMAN THREAT HAD NOT ABATED. They were merely girding their loins ready for an even more powerful twin thrust on 31 October to grab the tactically significant village of Gheluvelt controlling the road route into Ypres and to seize the 'heights' of the Messines Ridge overlooking Ypres from the southeast. The attack on Gheluvelt attracts the eye, a story of outstanding courage and endurance by the men of both sides. The village was defended by the men of the 2nd and 3rd Brigades of the 1st Division. They found themselves at the very eye of the storm. The first attacks began with the first glimmerings of dawn at around 06.00 and were initially repulsed, but this was a mere aperitif. Lieutenant Thomas Marshall was located with a detached company some 400 yards in front of the village, just to the north of the raised causeway of the Menin Road. The outlook from his perspective was by no means promising.

> About 7.30am the German artillery started to bracket on my trench. About 7.45am they got their range, and proceeded to blow the trench

to pieces. Luckily, two things saved the company from complete annihilation for the time being. The Germans were so methodical and so accurate that the men in the traverses were able to bolt to the one which had just been shelled, and then back again and so on. Secondly, there were so few men, and so long a trench to dig that the traverses were really untouched ground with narrow connecting paths dug round them, so that the trench itself was very well adapted against shell fire. About 9am the bombardment lifted on to the top of the hill and the village, and German infantry were seen moving into the eastern edge of the wood on our left. Half-an-hour afterwards fire began to come from the direction of the wood on our left flank. We then found that the company which had dug in opposite to us was a machine gun company with shields in front of their guns, and their fire was so accurate and heavy that we soon lost a lot of men, and found it impossible to fire over the parapet. We also found that there were only a dozen rifles that would fire, the remainder being either completely clogged up with clay or damaged by shell fire. About 10am the Germans again bombarded the trench for a quarter-of-an-hour, and then lifted to the village again.[22]

Captain Thomas Marshall, 2nd Welsh Regiment, 3rd Brigade, 1st Division, I Corps

Marshall and the remnants of his men were overrun and taken prisoner. Behind him, Captain Hubert Rees was in command of the reserves, such as they were, in a sunken stretch of the Menin Road just in front of Gheluvelt. He was soon the recipient of panicked – and at least partially inaccurate – reports of what had happened to the advance company.

The trenches, the sunk lane and the village were deluged with shells of all calibres. It was impossible – to move in the sunk lane and many men were hit. A few slightly wounded men from 'B' Company came in to say Lieutenant Marshall had been killed and that practically the whole company had been destroyed. The sunk lane itself was indefensible so Colonel Morland decided to move back to the front edge of the village and hold that with what men he could collect.[23]

In conditions of utter chaos, the positions held by Rees proved near useless and soon the only priority was to rescue as many men from the debacle as possible while they pulled out of Gheluvelt, which fell to the Germans at around 11.30.

In no time flat our lines rushed it, tumbling forward one after the other. Everyone charged forward against Gheluvelt. For a moment there was a pause in the enemy fire, rather as if they were taking a deep breath, then down it came again, with renewed strength, like a violent storm. It was clear that the enemy could tell what was at stake! Suddenly the leading troops wavered then fell back into the hurricane of fire which was being directed at them. It was a truly critical moment. The trumpeters from the left to the right flank blew the call for the charge and, their blood up, everyone responded. Emerging from behind hedges and out of cover, the assault was carried forward: line after line pressed on, closing gaps – Bavarians, Saxons and Württembergers. A thousand shouts of 'Hurrah!' echoed over the battlefield in one great cry of victory, which could be heard above the rattle of machine guns and the thunder of the guns. Rolling forward violently in waves like giant breakers crashing ashore the storm formations forced their way into the village. Gheluvelt was ours! After a short period of fighting from house to house, the enemy pulled back, abandoning their positions.[24]

Captain Rubenbauer, 16th Bavarian Reserve Regiment, 6th Bavarian Reserve Division, XIV Corps

No one knew what was happening, but the reality was that the pathway to Ypres lay gaping wide open for the Germans. Many of the men of the 1st Division were at the end of their tether – the very few that had actually survived the maelstrom. Exhausted, filthy dirty, and unshaven, dressed in ragged uniforms, their senses scrambled by the shell explosions, the aggravated traumatic shock of a week of near-continuous battle meant that it was amazing they had anything left to give. Rees himself was all but finished.

Several of my dozen men had been slightly wounded by shrapnel, so, without seeing anyone at all, I went through the northern outskirts of Gheluvelt and finally arrived at the battery position of the 54th Battery RFA, commanded by Major Peel, to whom I reported that I did not think that there were more than a 100 men of the Welsh Regiment left. He obviously disbelieved me, and I fancy seriously thought of putting me under arrest for spreading alarmist report. I confess to being very badly shaken, the stock of my rifle had been shot through in two places and the strap of my water bottle cut. He directed me to stand by as escort, to the guns, and one of the officers brought me some food. I remained with the guns for some time, collecting stragglers until I had about forty or sixty men.[25]

Rees was definitely shaken by his experiences. Lieutenant Ralph Blewitt of the 54th Battery was shocked at his appearance.

> The first group of men properly under control came back and I saw it was Rees in the Welsh Regiment. He had, I suppose, about fifteen or twenty men with him. The Major asked me who he was and whether I knew him and whether he was the sort of man who would come back. As he had got a DSO only a few days before I was able to convince the Major that he was one of the best and that there was no question of his coming back unnecessarily. Rees then came over to the battery, I have rarely seen a man in a more pitiable state, he was muddy and unshaven of course, but barely able to talk for sheer weariness, his equipment had for the most part been shot off him and he was absolutely stunned and almost speechless. By good luck we happened to have some hot tea going in the battery at the moment and a cup and a slice of bread and jam and a cigarette worked wonders. After profuse thanks for the first meal he had had that day, on the Major's suggestion, he took his command forward to a half-dug trench which was on the crest about 200 yards in front of the battery and manned it much to the satisfaction of the battery.[26]

Blewitt himself was called into action to assist the infantry and he did not hesitate.

> An infantry officer came up and said that there were snipers in a house well out this side of Gheluvelt on the main road, and would we do something about it. After we had put about half-a-dozen rounds of P.S. and two H.E. into it the nuisance abated. I remember the fact that it was two H.E. as at that time we only had sixteen rounds per battery. Three rounds per subsection, they were experimental and had only to be shot off under the most careful circumstances, with a long report on its effect etc., and we hadn't shot any yet. We were highly elated at the effect on the house which gave forth clouds of brick dust. And the infantry officer was full of thanks and praise.[27]

Shortly afterwards the Germans occupied a former British barricade across the Menin Road close to Gheluvelt. Blewitt was worried that they might bring up a machine gun, which would make things very difficult and resolved to take action himself.

'B' Sub-Section teams were got up and moved, off along the track to the main road. The teams were away very quickly, though barring a few odd rifle shots we were not being shot at and there were no casualties. Everything was exactly according to practice camp tradition – the 'Long Bracket' obtained the first two shots, and the first of the 'short bracket' hitting the bottom of the barricade. There were one or two shells bursting amongst the trees round about, but nothing really close, but on putting up my glasses to observe the next round I saw a flash over the barricade and realised at once that it was a gun – at the moment I had the impression that it must be a howitzer – even before the crash which followed a few seconds later. It was close enough to obscure with the smoke the gun and even the fuse setter who was alongside me, however as is so often the case it was all noise and smoke and no damage was done. No time was to be lost and we shot down the road about fourteen rounds in all I should think, after which, in the absence of any hostile shells arriving to prove the contrary I thought one might stop for a moment to see the result as at the moment all was smoke. When it cleared there was the joyful sight of the barricade with a very hearty hole in it, through which one could see a gun down on one wheel and no signs of life at all.[28]

It had been a risky venture, but it had worked.

Just south of the Menin Road were the 1st Queen's Royal West Surrey Regiment under the command of Major Charles Watson, who found themselves badly isolated, as the British line had been shattered on both their flanks. German battalions seemed to mushroom around them, many supposed to have been singing as they charged, all-enthused by the presence of Kaiser Wilhelm himself at the headquarters of Sixth Army.

Our ammunition in 'B' Company was running short and Wood sent back two orderlies, each of whom we saw shot before they had run 20 yards. Regimental Sergeant-Major Elliott eventually came up with some, and stopped for two minutes for a breather. He then started back for battalion headquarters, zig-zagging as he ran, and we saw him pitch on the road after going a few yards, and I was certain he was killed as he lay quite still without a move. Fortunately the Germans thought the same, and to our relief he suddenly got up and ran on under cover without another shot being fired; he had been hit in the arm when he fell, but was otherwise all right. It was just about this time that battalion headquarters was set on fire by incendiary shells. Things now began to look pretty hopeless, as we were being plastered with machine gun and rifle fire from the two flanks and front without being able to retaliate on any visible target. Wood ordered me to take what was left of the platoon at the roadside and report to Watson what was happening. It was not a cheery prospect having to double along the road for about 50 yards under heavy fire all the way. Three men were all I could muster from the platoon, and we all started together, but when I reached the farm I found the only survivor of the three who had started with me, together with Drummer Williams, who was able to tell me where Watson was, and I reported the situation to him. We collected eleven men of 'A' Company and lined a hedgerow about 150 yards behind the battalion headquarters farm. Here Watson received a report from our left that the Welsh had been forced back and that 'D' Company was being enfiladed from the north. Immediately following this message we saw the enemy coming over the hill in rear of 'D' Company, having apparently come right round their flank. The Germans were already entering Gheluvelt from the north, so our small party fell back to the western side of the village and held a line of hedge immediately south of the Menin Road. Watson went back to report the situation to brigade headquarters while I took charge of a motley throng of various regiments, with only Sergeant Butler and thirteen men of The Queen's amongst them.[29]

Lieutenant John Boyd, 1st Queens Royal West Surrey Regiment, 3rd Brigade, 1st Division, I Corps

Just behind Gheluvelt were two companies of the 2nd King's Royal Rifle Corps and two more from the 1st Loyal North Lancashire Regiment. Here the stress and confusion led to a sharp exchange of views between the two colonels.

We saw the Germans coming – and they did come in their thousands. We kept them off for an hour or two when the C.O. of the King's Royal Rifles consulted us, or rather our C.O., about retiring. I remember the two officers having a heated argument over it, as they stood by a farmhouse immediately in rear of the line. I do not however, know what their argument was, but heard afterwards that the King's Royal Rifles had got short of ammunition. The words I did hear from our

C.O. were, 'It's the General's orders that we hold the position at all costs, and this I'll do if I lose the whole regiment!'[30]

Private Frederick Bolwell, 1st Loyal North Lancashire Regiment, 2nd Brigade, 1st Division

The regiments of the British Army have a long history of blaming their neighbouring units for disaster and this would prove no exception. Still, Bolwell and the Loyals fought on.

We continued to fire until the Germans were on our trenches and coming through the line the King's Royal Rifles had vacated on our left. Just in front of the King's Royal Rifles' trenches was a huge German officer waving with one hand to the retiring Rifles to surrender and with the other waving his troops on. It did not seem of much good for us few men to attempt to fight that dense mass of Germans, but we did – and out of the thousand, or thereabouts, that we lined up with a couple of nights before very few got away.[31]

Somewhere close to Bolwell was Lance Corporal Joe Armstrong, who took a realistic attitude to the situation he found himself in. Once he realised it was hopeless, and there was no real purpose to fighting on, then he was willing to surrender. The question was would the Germans, incensed at their losses, accept the surrender.

We heard such a hullabaloo on our left! They'd broken through, swept right through, captured our artillery, captured the headquarters and they just swept us all in! The officer in charge, when he saw them coming across this way, he tried to do a bunk that way, but he only ran into them – he scuttled back as quick as he could! What could you do! There was no point at all – resistance would have been suicide. I was in a trench with the others. Same as the others I scrambled out – I nearly got blinking bayoneted for having my rifle in my hand until I threw it down – you don't get any instructions as regards what to do in the event of being captured you know! They marched us a bit further along, put us in fives. I had a pipe in my mouth and when the officer came to me, I was flank man, he saw this pipe, grabbed hold of it and tried to tug it out. I thought, 'Good crikey, this is my pipe!' And I stuck to it! A Corporal Taylor behind me shouted, 'Let go of that bloody pipe, you fool!' It's a good job I did because almost at the split second I let it go, his revolver was round my temples. It must have been a near thing![32]

Private Bolwell was luckier in that he saw the brief glimmering of an opportunity to try to escape capture. As is so often the case with personal reminiscence, there is a surrealistic tinge to his memories of that life-or-death gamble.

> I had a run for my life that day. A chum of mine who was with us had a cock-fowl in his valise that morning from the farm; he had wrung its neck but he had not quite succeeded in killing him; and, as we ran, this bird began to crow. As for myself, I had no equipment; I had run having left it in the bottom of the trench. It is quite funny as I come to think of it now the old cock crowing as we ran; but it was really terrible at the time. We were absolutely overwhelmed.[33]

Somewhere in the front line that day was a young RFA signaller engaged in running forward the telephone line from the gun battery to the forward observation officer.

> They launched a huge attack while we were up the trenches and as usual, we were armed with nothing more deadly than a telephone and a small roll of spare wire, when we first spotted the grey waves sweeping towards us. We were well out in the open and our nearest cover was the infantry trench which we made safely in very quick time. Once there we were soon busy with a rifle each (there were soon plenty spare) and firing like madmen. There was no need to aim as we could not possibly miss, it was only a question of reloading quickly enough. The terrific rifle fire did not have the desired effect as the Germans still came on, nearer and nearer, just a slight slowing up as they stepped over the bodies of their own dead and wounded. It seemed that nothing short of a miracle could possibly save us. It was a ghastly and sickening sight to see this slaughter, but it was their lives or ours.[34]
>
> Signaller John Palmer, 118th Battery, 26th Brigade RFA, 1st Division, I Corps

As the pressure began to tell, Palmer was well aware that the infantry were desperate for artillery support.

Suddenly an infantry sergeant grabbed me shouting, 'For God's sake get your wire working, we have lost touch with the artillery!' Our effort to mend the wire under almost impossible conditions was the means of saving our lives as we had only reached a spot about 300 yards from the trenches when we saw the enemy absolutely sweeping over our trenches in waves. They did not stop at the trenches either, and we guessed that our period of life or freedom was just about up. Hastily dropping our phones in the half-way trench and kicking some dirt over them, we ran hell for leather to where we knew our reserve trenches to be. How we escaped bullets from friend and enemy I do not know.[35]

Despite it all and after several very close shaves, Palmer and his fellow signaller made it back to their battery positions, where he found some of the dishevelled and traumatised survivors of the Queen's Royal West Surrey Regiment.

If we thought we were going to have a rest we certainly made a mistake. The batteries were short-handed having lost so many men and were madly firing over open sights at a range of 500 yards, what a target. A target one might dream of but never see. The range kept dropping as the enemy got nearer and nearer. Eventually the shells appeared to burst as they left the muzzle of the guns: 'Fuse 0'. This was never used at target practice. Our only difficulty lay in the fact that we could not get the ammunition (from the wagons about 100 yards away) up quickly enough to feed the guns. Many of the Queen's Regiment lay in the shallow trenches around our guns but nothing on earth would make them help us. Some of them did eventually after one had been shot by one of our officers. Poor devils, they were just about all in. They had been in action for days and could just stand no more. I do not think they cared if they lived or died, we had seen what they went through up the trenches. It was just hell and impossible for any human being to stand for long. The open ground in front of us presented a shambles. As fast as we mowed them down so others came on. The heaps of dead and wounded seemed to increase every minute. They must be very brave unless they are being forced on by the weight of numbers in the rear.[36]

When they had fired their last shell the horses and limbers were ordered forward as the battery attempted to make its escape. They had left it very late indeed.

I wish I could describe in detail the limbering up of those guns. Only two guns were got away after all. Men and horses were dropping like flies all the time and it was a miracle that the two were got away. I remember jumping on the back of one of the horses and clinging on like grim death as we went down the main road at a mad gallop. We only went a short distance at that pace though as the road soon presented a scene of panic. It appeared that the whole of the British were retreating in disorder and all madly trying to get away from that inferno of shot and shell. It was evident that unless someone took a hand at organizing the retirement, none of us would get far. Riderless horses, wounded men looking a horrible sight, overturned guns and wagons, all tended to make us realise that we were being licked. It was not a nice feeling either. Nobody seemed to know where we were going or what we were doing. Get away from that hell was the first thought of us all. However we discovered that we do not retreat quite so easily, and on moving a short way down the road we found a group of officers who were busy sorting out the remnants. They also informed us that the enemy's advance had been stemmed as reinforcements had arrived in the nick of time. On every side men can be seen feverishly digging trenches. Found our headquarters staff, they seemed very surprised to see us again. They said they thought we had gone for good. They failed to recognise us until we spoke to them as we were covered in blood, mud and oil.[37]

Everywhere behind the 1st Division lines there were signs of panic. It was plain that unless the situation could be stabilised then the whole of the British line would be broken. Given the scale of the forces against them it would be difficult, if not impossible to re-establish a defensible line without time, something they did not seem to have. The last resort was to order a counter-attack from the last reserves of the 2nd Division held in the Polygon Wood area just to the north of Gheluvelt. The intention was to pile-drive down into the German right flank as they advanced from Gheluvelt. It was a forlorn hope.

As the battle boiled up to one of many climaxes, Lieutenant General Samuel Lomax (commanding 1st Division), General Charles Monro (2nd Division) and key members of their staff were ensconced in the Hooge Chateau, intent on monitoring the situation and coordinating the planned 2nd Division counter-attack, when at 13.15 a shell burst in amongst them. Several staff were killed and Lomax was mortally wounded.[38] Munro was badly shaken up by the blast but able to continue in command. This unfortunate incident would cause considerable extra disruption during the tense hours that lay ahead.

The situation of senior officers and their staff was already desperate, given the conditions that prevailed in October 1914. Telephone communications were fragile and almost non-existent forward of brigade headquarters. Few had grasped the vulnerability of telephone wires to shell fire and the everyday snagging accidents that were inevitable on a crowded battlefield. The further back the generals were stationed, the more confusing the event became, but if they moved forward they too would disappear into the fog of battle. It was a difficult balancing act.

Haig had his I Corps headquarters at the White Chateau, close to what would become known as 'Hellfire Corner'. As the verbal reports began to trickle in he could sense that the situation was desperate. French was also well aware that something untoward was afoot as he drove through Ypres on his way forward to visit Haig's headquarters.

There were manifest signs of unusual excitement, and some shells were already falling in the place. It is wonderful with what rapidity the contagion of panic spreads through a civilian population. I saw loaded vehicles leaving the town, and people were gathered in groups about the streets chattering like monkeys or rushing hither and thither with frightened faces. On reaching the eastern exit of the town, on my way to Hooge, I was stopped by a guard specially posted by I Corps headquarters, with orders to prevent anyone leaving the city. Satisfying them as to my identity, I proceeded on my way. I had not gone more than a mile when the traffic on the road began to assume a most anxious and threatening appearance. It looked as if the whole of the I Corps was about to fall back in confusion on Ypres. Heavy howitzers were moving west at a trot – always a most significant feature of a retreat – and ammunition and other wagons blocked the road almost as far as the eye could see. In the midst of the press of traffic, and along both sides of the road, crowds of wounded came limping along as fast as they could go, all heading for Ypres. Shells were screaming overhead and bursting with reverberating explosions in the adjacent fields. This spectacle filled me with misgiving and alarm. It was impossible for my motor-car to proceed at any pace, so we alighted and covered the rest of the way to Haig's headquarters on foot, nor did I receive any encouragement on the way to hope for better things. Shells were falling about the place, and the chateau was already beginning to show the effects of artillery fire. I found Haig and John Gough, his Chief of Staff, in one of the rooms on the ground floor, poring over maps and evidently much disconcerted. But, though much perturbed in mind and very tired in body and brain, Haig was cool and alert as ever.[39]

Haig had ordered that the line be held from Hollebeke through Klein Zillebeke and Westhoek to Frezenberg. But he and his staff were also examining the feasibility of establishing yet another 'last line of defence', just over a mile in front of Ypres itself and stretching from Verbrandenmolen via Zillebeke through 'Hellfire Corner' to Potijze. In the brief exchanges that followed, French was unable to proffer any reinforcements, so he immediately set off to see a man who could: General Ferdinand Foch, commander of the Northern Group of Armies. Of course, Foch was much further back, and, although in overall command of the whole area, he was almost blind to the situation as it developed during the two days of frenetic German attacks.

> Generally speaking, during a modern battle where nothing is clearly seen, especially in an enclosed country, the results obtained are learned only through reports which show what localities are held by the troops at the end of the day. But when the line has been pierced, or even merely thrown back, these reports come in slowly and are not clear and definite, since the touch between units in the field has been weakened. In fact, it is precisely when the situation is gravest that a commander gets the least information from the front and runs the greatest risk of having no time in which to make dispositions to repair the harm.[40]

What news Foch received made him deeply anxious. There were also disquieting rumours that the British were thinking of withdrawal to Boulogne. Despite the Entente Cordiale, the French always had a lingering suspicion that the British might abandon them. But Foch was utterly determined that there could be no retreat from Ypres, the last feasible line of defence. Any significant step backwards would lead only to catastrophe; as such Foch promised Sir John French his unstinting support in the climactic battle that engulfed them both.

In face of the tremendous assault which all were sustaining, any
voluntary withdrawal at any point would bring in its wake a great
converging flood of attacks which we would be utterly unable to stem.
In rear of our front line nature offered no obstacle. For want of time we
had not been able to organize a position to which we might withdraw.
Under these conditions, a retreat carried out in full daylight by our
comparatively weak effectives over open stretches of ground, wide
indeed but cut up by battle, would be rapidly converted into a rout.
Crippled and disorganized, we would be thrown back on the Flemish
plain and rapidly swept to the coast. Moreover, it was only the British
I Corps that was in retreat; our other troops were standing firm. The
French IX Corps could furnish some help with its reserves, and more
French reinforcements were due to arrive the following day. I therefore
asked that for the moment the British I Corps be ordered to hold on
at all costs, and I undertook to mount an attack as quickly as possible
with the purpose of extricating it from the enemy's embrace. While
I was formulating these ideas in my mind, I wrote out on a piece of
paper the general principles they involved. I did this as much to aid
in fixing my own ideas as to furnish them in definite and precise
form to my interlocutor. I there and then handed this informal scrawl
to Sir John French. It read as follows: 'It is absolutely essential not to
retreat; therefore the men must dig in wherever they find themselves
and hold on to the ground they now occupy. This does not preclude
organizing a position further in rear which could join up at Zonnebeke
with our IX Corps. But any movement to the rear carried out by any
considerable body of troops would lead to an assault on the part of the
enemy and bring certain confusion among the troops. Such an idea
must be utterly rejected. It seems particularly necessary that the 2nd
British Division maintain itself in the vicinity of Zonnebeke, keeping
in touch with the French IX Corps. The lateness of the day makes this
organization feasible. It is useless to fall back, dangerous to do so in of
broad daylight'.[41]

Surviving tense moments like this would help turn the Entente Cordiale
into a real alliance of flesh and blood, one based on trust and partnership
of soldiers under pressure, not the mealy-mouthed words and sub-clauses
of a diplomatic treaty.

Haig too was determined to draw a line in the sand; this far and
no further was the essence of the orders given at the height of the crisis

when Gheluvelt fell and the Germans seemed to have burst through the thin khaki line of the 1st Division. Colonel John Charteris, ever the dramatic witness, left a typically overwrought account of Haig's phlegmatic reaction.

> Haig moved the cavalry brigade, his last reserves, to the support of 1st Division. He traced across his map a line a little more than a mile from the walls of Ypres, to which the Corps should retire if it were driven back, 'And there,' he said, 'it must fight till the end!' Then, with his personal staff and escort, he rode slowly up the Menin Road, through the stragglers, back into the shelled area, his face immobile and inscrutable – saying no word, yet by his presence and his calm restoring hope to the disheartened and strength to his exhausted troops.[42]

The morale effect of Haig's presence is exaggerated, as few of his men would have had the chance to see him, but Haig was an experienced field commander intent on determining for himself as best he could what was really happening. It is foolish to suggest that he was removing himself from any real control of the situation; indeed, this reveals a misunderstanding of the situation. This was not grandstanding or panic: Haig was trying to keep a lid on a situation that was almost boiling over, bedevilled by fragile communications and with disaster having already befallen the headquarters of his 1st Division. This was not a normal circumstance, it did not call for a normal response. As he rode forward, he called in on the headquarters of his subordinate divisional and brigade commanders, thereby establishing exactly what was going on, while at the same time seeking to send forward any remaining scraps of troops hoping to attack the Germans before they could consolidate their position. Haig was aware that one more successful German attack would doom them all; this was not histrionics or panic but a measured assessment. If anything Haig was guilty of understatement in his diary that day.

> Troops very exhausted and two Brigadiers assure me that if the enemy makes a push at any point, they doubt our men being able to hold on. Fighting by day and digging to strengthen their trenches by night has thoroughly tired them out.[43]

Meanwhile, back at the front, the last-gasp counter-attack had been organised, throwing forward the 2nd Worcesters, the last available reserves of the 2nd Division, who charged forward from Polygon Wood towards Gheluvelt Chateau and then into the village itself. What happened must have seemed miraculous to those watching the charge. Just over 350 men of the Worcesters made the initial attack; Lance Corporal William Finch was one that lived to tell the tale.

> When the charge went, the bugle went, we had to go for them, that's all. You know an excited a crowd would be at a football match when they score a goal, tremendous uproar, that's just how the charge started. Shouting of course, make as much noise as you can. During the charge I couldn't tell you what ever happened. We all go into the Germans, charge into Germans – they were very close. I had control of myself all of the way, I knew what I was doing; like if you go mad at anything. But what happened I could never say.[44]

The charge should not have succeeded but it appears that the German 16th Reserve Regiment was caught unprepared and for once a suicidal charge brought success and not just pointless deaths. The Worcesters pushed on past the chateau and took up positions in the sunken road leading through to the village itself. But Lance Corporal Finch was soon in dreadful trouble; any triumphal feelings he may have had were soon cut short in a most brutal fashion.

> Jerry opened fire straight across the Menin Road at me, which was the other side of the hedge, with a machine gun. And that's when I got hit in the leg. As I dropped down, I called out for help. I had to lay on me back. As I got up, Jerry hit me in the back, and the metal ration tin saved me from having my backbone broken. Anyway, I was calling out for help and a fellow gets over to me, laying there by myself, gets me kit off, cuts me trousers off and tied just above me knee, then a second tie in the thick of my thigh. I saw the blood come down his shoulder, he'd been hit and I said to him, 'For God's sake, leave me! I shall be all right!' But he finished the tying of the second tie on the thigh. He said, 'Well Corporal Finch, I shall get you back again!' He went away with that.[45]

While Finch suffered, the Worcesters and the remnants of other battalions in the sector had secured the position. The crisis was over for the moment. On the battlefield the wounded did their best to endure the freezing cold and took what minimal shelter they could. Many were haunted by the fear that if they slept they might never wake up.

It was night time. I was still calling for help and another fellow came to me rescue, He got me on German oil sheet that was right by the side of me and dragged me across the other side of the Menin Road. Then as he walked away he said, 'I'll get the ambulance!' I never heard no more about the ambulance till next morning. With the rain I got this German oil sheet and kept myself covered. All of sudden in the daylight of the morning, this sheet was thrown off me and it was German officer stood by me with his revolver at my head. I shouted, 'Have mercy on me!' He searched me and I said, 'Well, I can't do you any harm now!' As he was going through he pulled out my wallet, two kiddies pictures. I was asking him for a drink of water and he wouldn't. Then he threatened me again as he walked away. I'd got to lie down. As I went back on me back, I happened to recognise as I lay, my memory came back to me of this ditch – in the direction I had come from in the charge. It was only a few yards, but it seemed a hell of a way to drag myself, but anyway with the aid of me gun under bad leg, my hands and elbows, I pulled myself into this ditch – where I lay for three and a half days without being found. The rain, I'd got a handkerchief in my pocket, and I put it into the sheet above me, into the puddle of water and kept squeezing it into me mouth and spitting it out. I'm still laying in the ditch with the water going under me. I was still watching the Germans running about attacking, I couldn't see who they were attacking but they were making moves and shooting. I daren't turn to me left, to look to me left to see what it was. As I lay there for the third day, I said, 'I hope, please God, I'll be found today!' Which I was – the German oil sheet was flung open and there was two bayonets towards my head. I shouted quick to the fellows with the bayonets, 'Have mercy, I'm English!' They said, 'What brings you here! What regiment are you?' I told them, 'The Worcesters!' They were two Coldstream Guardsmen. They went away and brought back a stretcher, put me onto it and carried me into their lines.[46]

Finch was clearly a man with an ability to endure trials that would have doomed most men. He and the rest of the Worcesters had helped stem the German tide and to some extent re-established the 1st Division line. Yet the Germans had taken Gheluvelt village; another milepost on the road to Ypres had been lost.

The 31 October was filled with desperate last-ditch battles all along the line stretching from Gheluvelt right to the end of the Messines Ridge. There is no room to describe these frantic engagements – suffice to sketch out the course of events and to allow the imagination to fill in the fraught nature of this fighting, which was not a whit different from the better publicised fighting at Gheluvelt. Just to the south, the ground up to the Comines Canal was held by elements of I Corps, several French units and what little remained of the 7th Division. The fighting took place on the three wooded spurs stretching down from the lost vantage point of Zandvoorde Ridge, now in the hands of the Germans. An attack had been ordered by Haig to retake both Hollebeke and Zandvoorde, but this was soon abandoned in the face of a long drawn-out German bombardment which began at 08.00. When the German attack commenced at 12.25 the British front line soon began to fray and fall apart under the pressure, but the support line took a severe toll on the onrushing Germans. Just as, further north, small bodies of reserves arrived 'just in time' to prevent disaster, so this seemingly desperate situation was stabilised by the success of small-scale counter-attacks which almost defied rational explanation.

> Things looked real nasty as the Germans by this time were pouring through the gap and filling the wood we were in. In the circumstances I thought to do something unexpected might upset their applecart – so fixed bayonets and went straight in. We soon came across them and had the finest fight that ever was fought. I make no pretence at liking the ordinary battle – and anybody who says they do is a liar – but this was quite different. We first came on some fifty of the grey swine, went straight in and annihilated then. Very quickly into the next lot and in a few minutes we were shooting, bayoneting and annihilating everything that we came across. To cut a long story short, we drove the whole crowd back and by 2am were back in our trenches again. Five holes in my coat as a souvenir.[47]
>
> Captain Harry Dillon, 2nd Oxford and Bucks Light Infantry, 5th Brigade, 2nd Division, I Corps

The murderous fighting went on, but when darkness fell much of the ground lost earlier in the day had been recovered. It was a truly remarkable effort. During the night, the Germans came on again and began to make some progress, spilling through the gaps in the line.

Further south again, the 4th Division and the Cavalry Corps (1st and 2nd Cavalry Divisions) were responsible for the defence of the line running through the villages of Messines and Wytschaete and stretching across to the Comines Canal. The first German waves attacked at around 04.30, swarming time and time again with grim intent towards the two villages. During the lulls, the shallow and disjointed British trenches were lambasted by heavy shells crashing down all around them. Gradually the British were forced back, house by house. Ad hoc reserves were deployed, including the Oxfordshire Yeomanry, who found themselves attached to Brigadier General Beauvoir de Lisle's 1st Cavalry Division. It was not long before they were unceremoniously thrust forward.

> Then de Lisle appeared and told us to advance up the hill and occupy a line of trenches on the right of Messines. This was disagreeable as projectiles of every variety were exploding with a disquieting regularity all over the ground of our advance, also had to leave our coats and tools. Off we went over some very holding plough, three squadrons in succession of rushes in extended lines, the regularity of which was soon disturbed by the wire. Never move without nippers on the Sam Browne belt! Luckily we had no one hit – I can't think why – which put some heart into the men. On arriving at the indicated position we found only trenches for one squadron, the other two lay about in the open scratching themselves in with bayonets. We had four or five men wounded, and lay there, getting occasional blows off at Germans at about 800 yards, under a really very heavy fire, only luckily all the shrapnel burst just behind us, and the 'Black Marias', just in front, so though horribly frightened, we weren't hurt. There we stopped – very hungry – till 11pm. We couldn't move, about to get food as they had two Maxims nosing on our line of retirement pretty continuously till dark. When relieved we were given one hour's rest by squadrons and then put on a barricade in Messines with the 4th Dragoon Guards and the 18th Hussars. This was frightening. All the houses were burning, the Germans were only about 500 yards away, and had a gun with which they kept blowing shrapnel at the barricade, but it was a stout obstacle! They kept popping away at our squadrons on the left of the barricade with rifles, and coming very close under the smoke, so we

began to wonder how to fix the bloody bayonets with which we had been issued two days previously.[48]

Captain Val Fleming, 1st Oxfordshire Yeomanry, 2nd Cavalry Brigade, 1st Cavalry Division

Fresh reserves were sought from here, there and everywhere, to plug the line. Several battalions had been sent across from II Corps to join the fray, while the newly arrived territorials of the 14th (London Scottish) London Regiment were thrust into the fray on the left near Wytschaete. They had been back at St Omer, when the orders came to move forward, moving up by bus the previous day into Ypres. Now they were going into action for the first time – the first time indeed for any battalion of the Territorial Force. It would be a rude awakening to the realities of war as they suffered terrible casualties that day. Further north, the 2nd Cavalry Division was bolstered by the arrival of a French brigade despatched from the 32nd Division. When the struggle died down the British and French line had been dented and although Wytschaete had been retained after a frenzied see-saw struggle, the bulk of the Messines Ridge had fallen to the German night mass attacks launched early on 1 November. The Oxfordshire Yeomanry had been briefly withdrawn from the fray, but within a couple of hours were ordered back in.

De Lisle appeared, told us that the line had been broken and that we must counter attack! This bloody prospect almost made us sick, however still with empty bellies we began plodding up the usual wire enclosed ploughed fields on the left of Messines, being pooped at by very high and wild rifle fire, till we found the troops on our left halted and those on our right coming back out of Messines, and the whole line fell back about a mile, under very heavy rifle and maxim fire. Poor Brian Molloy was killed and two or three more men wounded. The rest of that day we spent two squadrons in the advance line, one in the support trenches. We were extraordinarily lucky, the regiment on our left had one squadron practically wiped out, and the 9th Lancers on our right had a bad doing, and they kept missing us by really not more than four or five yards. We had several men buried and trenches blown in, but none hit! It was a very trying day for the men, they were damned hungry, cold, and kept seeing wounded men come hopping back, bleeding and howling, and swearing the German had broken through – which they very nearly did! In the evening our squadron crawled up and took over the trench of the 4th Dragoon Guards squadron which had been so knocked about. The Germans were only about 200 yards away and kept sniping as we went into the trench which was as you may imagine in a pretty bloody condition! Full of corpses etc. The men have realised the fact that it's safer to sit in a trench than to get out of it and run away, and really thanks to our extraordinary luck they keep very cheerful, but we have not yet had to stand a determined bayonet attack – nor to deliver one! So we must not be too sure either of them or ourselves.[49]

Captain Val Fleming, 1st Oxfordshire Yeomanry, 2nd Cavalry Brigade, 1st Cavalry Division

As the British began to run out of men, there was the chance of the Germans making a genuine breakthrough, but at the same time it was evident that this excruciating level of German casualties could not be endured for much longer. The constant mass assaults on British trenches coupled with the frequent exposure to the guns of the Royal Artillery were eroding the strength of the attacking formations. The question was who could endure the longest, whose morale would hold, whose leaders would fold under the relentless pressure. It would be a close-run thing.

Next day, the Secretary of State for War, Lord Kitchener, came out to check what was happening and had a meeting at Dunkirk with the French President Raymond Poincaré, Joffre and Foch. Kitchener was blunt in expressing his fears.

I am afraid that the British Army, which is still far too small, might give way under a heavy assault. We rely on you to reinforce us.[50]

Foch for one does not seem to have been overly impressed at the British attitude as expressed by Kitchener.

Kitchener was very anxious. He accosted me with the words, 'Well, so we are beaten!' I answered that we were not, and that I greatly hoped we would not be. I then related in detail the events of the last three days, which had brought such heavy losses to the Allied Armies. In finishing I asked him to send us reinforcements as soon as possible. On that first day of November, 1914, when each day seemed as long as a month, Lord Kitchener replied as follows, 'On July 1st, 1915, you will have one million trained English soldiers in France. Before that date you will get none, or practically none!' 'We do not ask so many, but we would like to have them sooner – indeed at once!' We all cried as if in pre-concerted union. 'Before that date, do not count on anything!' was all he vouchsafed in reply. There was nothing, then, for us to do but to look forward to getting along through many a trying day as best we could without any further help.[51]

It was inevitable that, given the forbidding situation at Ypres, the French would be tempted into an element of short-termism in seeking reinforcements from the British. And who could blame them, as it was evident that from this point the main burden of defending Ypres would fall on French shoulders.

In the event, 1 November marked a slight reduction in the overall tension of the situation. The French 32nd Division came into the line to help relieve the British cavalry, thereby stiffening and strengthening the line, but French attempts to take the offensive in response to orders from Foch were not successful in the face of continued German pressure. The German guns still raged, the attacks still went in, but little was achieved as the ferocity of German efforts began slowly to abate, and more and more French divisions reached the front to take up the brunt of defending Ypres.

At this point in the war, the problems of fighting on both the Western and Eastern Fronts were beginning to impinge severely on the German High Command. They could not deploy troops as they would wish on the Western Front without paying the penalty of weakening the Eastern Front – and vice versa. By November, the Russian Army was beginning to mobilise its full strength – soldiers counted in millions – and although it had suffered grievous defeats at the Battles of Tannenberg and the Masurian Lakes, it was slowly beginning to pull its weight. The September battles raging in Galicia had not gone well for the Austro-Hungarian Army, and the Germans had been drawn into serious fighting raging in Poland. Reinforcements were required here too: war on two fronts was a German nightmare made flesh.

But the thunder of the British guns was also faltering; the ammunition worries of October had turned into a full-scale crisis as the supplies of ammunition began to run down to the bare bones. A third of all Haig's field batteries had to be withdrawn from the line of fire to allow the consolidation of the meagre stocks that remained. Even then, the remaining field guns only had an extremely limited number of rounds, which restricted their ability to fire except in emergencies. The threadbare remnant of the 7th Division was withdrawn from the line and elements of the much-battered II Corps were moved up to take their place. All along the line the British battalions had been reduced to mere shadows of their former selves, and some were lacking any officers at all; indeed, at this stage the 1st Division numbered just 2,844 men, or one-seventh of the supposed establishment for a division. Even as battalions struggled to rebuild from the meagre new drafts from back home, or the returning recovered wounded, they were still liable to be recalled into action at a moment's notice, as happened to Captain Hubert Rees and the 2nd Welsh.

> I found a draft of Lieutenant Cornelius and 50 men waiting for me and by calling up all spare transport men and the collecting of a few stragglers, the battalion reached a total of 148 men and four officers. It was quite obvious that the battle was not quieting down at all and about 3pm, I received orders, to counter attack to retake the trenches we had just vacated, as the Berkshires had been driven out of them. We advanced under a good deal of shrapnel fire. Hewitt was hit on the leg, Corder retired with a ball through the forearm, and I got badly lamed by a bit on the foot. When we arrived at the edge of the wood, on the west side of Tower Hamlets Ridge, I was told that General Fitz Clarence had ordered the troops there to charge and retake the lost trenches. Before we had much grip of the situation, we found ourselves charging into the darkness, led by General Fitz Clarence – it was then quite dark – with the Gloucesters on our right. We promptly came under a storm of rifle and machine gun bullets and I found myself in a depression in the ground, lying extremely flat. The men whirled away back rather faster than they had come. When the air was not quite so full of lead, I had a look round and found one of my quartermaster sergeants, lying next to me. We agreed that we might as well return and crawled back. When we got back to the rifle pits along the edge of the wood, there was hopeless confusion. I met General Fitz Clarence and told him that each pit now contained representatives from six different regiments, with some Frenchmen thrown in. He remarked that I had better start in to put it right. We got straightened out somehow.[52]

In some hard-pressed units, the pressure became too much and there were instances of men abandoning their positions under shellfire, having been tested beyond their endurance. From the perspective of the men 'at the sharp end' there was little if any sign of a relaxation in German pressure. The state of morale for the most part was acceptable. It could hardly be expected to be much better in the prevailing circumstances: these men were not fools.

So the German attacks continued, with the occasional threatened breakthrough, followed, as day follows night, by French and British counter-attacks to restore the situation. The Germans nibbled at the Allied line but were unable to achieve anything of importance. The French were holding far more of the ring around Ypres and began to launch several quite major attacks along the line in order to test the strength of the German resolve. Yet, for all the sound and fury, over the next few days the front stayed relatively static. The German troops were flagging in their efforts and, although the British may have been too exhausted to sense the change in the air, the French realised that the worst was over. Joffre issued orders to Foch to consolidate the ground they had and to reconstitute the reserves ready for battles to come. In the fashion of the time there were soon a slew of messages despatched to pay tribute to the efforts of the units at the front. The reaction of Captain Hubert Rees was delightfully cynical when such missives reached the 2nd Welsh on 5 November.

> We had had numerous congratulatory telegrams from every
> commander in the field who had anything to do with us and their
> receipt always presaged some more diabolical battle than the last.
> I went down to see Grant who had returned to his job as brigade major
> and remarked that when we had a message from the King, it would
> be time to dig a very large hole in the ground and wait there until the
> storm had subsided. He said 'You had better start now. Here it is!'[53]

Rees was right. The Germans had not shot their bolt. Not quite.

FALKENHAYN STILL HAD NOT GIVEN UP. The Allies were praying that it was all over, willing it to be so: but the actions of the German Army rarely conformed to the wishes of its enemies. Falkenhayn and his staff went through the detail of his deployments on the Western Front, seeking to identify those units that could be spared for just one more attempt at

Ypres. Units from the Fourth and Sixth Armies were shuffled across, while the elite 4th Division was brought up into the line. Most significant of all was the deployment of the newly created Prussian Guards Division. This truly was the very last throw of the dice in 1914. As the Germans moved up, a series of holding attacks continued seeking to pin down and exhaust British and French troops prior to a final push on 11 November. The Allies had become aware of the new German concentration in Flanders, but had not been able to determine the strength of the forces opposing them. The German bombardment commenced in driving heavy rain at 06.30 and redoubled its efforts, rising to a crescendo with a veritable hailstorm of shells exploding around the Allied trenches at the moment of the attack at 09.00. For all that, the onslaught proved a damp squib among much of the intended nine-mile front. The Germans had also been fighting hard for weeks and they too were exhausted, unable to press home attacks with sufficient vigour to seriously threaten a breakthrough. The exception proved to be either side of the Menin Road, where the 4th and Guard Divisions were attacking.

They drove us back about 100 yards towards the Menin Road. It was Prussian Guard attack, big bloody fellows, thousands of them! You couldn't see them in the half dark, not only that they were among trees and bushes, no clear field of fire at all. You couldn't see them until they were quite near you, you heard the noise. You were more or less firing, not knowing what you were firing at. Down on the Menin Road the French had put to hold the road North African Zouave troops. Of course they were hopeless – as soon as they got heavy shelling they cleared off! So the Germans came down that road and encircled us. There was nobody to stop them. We had to hold that part of the road and our own positions as well! They drove us out of our trenches, killed Colonel McMahon.[54] I was about 20 to 30 yards along the line. A fellow named Corporal Chaney said, 'The Colonel's been killed!' 'Been killed! No! Just along here?' He said, 'Yes!' God, it frightened the life out of me! I looked upon him more as a father more than anything else! Chaney gave me his pocket book and revolver, so I knew he was dead. I didn't know what to do with myself for days, neither did the men that was left. When he got killed it was as if somebody had obliterated the whole battalion, they thought so much of him. No other officer made them feel like that! We got driven back, you see how far they got, right down to our dressing station and killed our Doctor–Major Macgregor–killed him looking after the wounded. We fell back. When the morning came we had no officers left and 34 men out of 900.[55]

Private William Holbrook, 4th Royal Fusiliers, 9th Brigade, 3rd Division, II Corps

Desperate measures would be required to stem the flow. One of the units sent forward were the 2nd Connaught Rangers.

Suddenly someone came running in to say that the Germans had broken through. The battalion was moved forward to meet the Germans, whom we could see advancing between the two woods. The Highland Light Infantry on our left, also in reserve, opened fire on the enemy, and so did we. It may have been for that reason that the attack edged off and went through the Nonne Bosschen Wood. Some of the Rangers, and some of the 5th Company Royal Engineers, moved further forward towards the Nonne Bosschen Wood and continued to fire into the enemy's flank. Eventually we saw the enemy emerge from the wood and make for Westhoek, about 1,100 yards behind the wood. Had they got there they would have been right through the British position in that sector. It was then that we had one of the few strokes of luck during the early stages of the war. The ground sloped downwards for about 500 yards from the wood and then gently upwards towards the village. Fortunately there was a whole brigade of Field Artillery (18-pounders) and a group (one brigade) of French 75mm guns just north of the village. All these guns could and did fire over open sights at the Prussian Guards, who continued to advance in more or less close formation. Some thirty guns firing at point-blank range as fast as they could was a very inspiring sight for us. The enemy suffered very heavy casualties and eventually withdrew back to the Nonne Bosschen Wood.[56]

Captain Ernest Hamilton, 2nd Connaught Ranger, 5th Brigade, 2nd Division, I Corps

Sergeant John McIlwain recalled the desperation of the fight as the Prussian Guards advanced on the Connaughts.

Great bursts of fire and screams of delight brought us to the firestep – to a sight every infantry soldier dreams about. The Germans were lumbering over towards us just 50 yards away, in any order, bunching together. We poured rapid fire into them. Nine out of every ten were hit. The dead piled up in heaps. In the heat and noise of the conflict, and while my rifle was roasting hot, I became aware of Mick Keating roaring in my ear, 'For the love of Jesus, Sergeant, give me your rifle for my own is blocked entirely!' He had been firing like hell, killing Germans for England. 'God blast and damn you!' He yelled at the rifle, battering the breech with his bare hand as if it was something alive! I took the rifle off him and gave him my own. I found his was choked with dirt and wasted precious minutes clearing it.[57]

At the height of the battle a counter-attack was ordered on the Nonne Bosschen Wood by what little remained of the 2nd Oxfordshire and Buckinghamshire Regiment.

I sent 'A' and 'B' Companies to clear the Nonne Bosschen, advancing from north-west to south-east. This they did most successfully, driving the Germans before them, and killing and capturing a good many. 'C' and 'D' Companies followed in support. When 'A' and 'B' came out on the south-eastern edge of the wood they were joined by the Northamptonshire on the right, and by some Connaught Rangers and sappers on the left. Led by Dillon, they charged the Germans out of the trenches, some of the enemy turning and running when the attack was 30 or 40 yards off, and others surrendering. Most of those who ran were shot. The men with whom we had this fight were the Potsdam Guards. They were very fine, big men, but by the time we came across them they did not seem to have very much fight in them, as they had been under our artillery fire for some time, and this, no doubt, had shaken them considerably.[58]

Lieutenant Colonel Henry Davies, 2nd Oxford and Bucks Light Infantry, 5th Brigade, 2nd Division, I Corps

Despite living on borrowed time, young Harry Dillon survived to tell the tale.

Fierce fighting this. They are at their last gasp and we go for each other all out as hard as God will let us. We had a furious attack on the Potsdam Guards – the best infantry Germany can produce. All the sapper officers killed and half our men and only Pepys and myself were left at the finish, out of the officers. Not one man of the Germans got back and so prisoners – mostly wounded – were all that lived. We have been taken out of the battle. I am awfully cut up about poor Pepys[59] who was killed, getting back into the trench which he and I shared.

He was the only other officer in my company and now I have to sit frozen to death all day alone. It does seem bad luck after going through so much to be killed on the verge of being safe for a fortnight. I have never been so upset about anything.[60]

The situation was at least partially restored and the British line, battered and torn though it was, still stood firm. Back at I Corps Headquarters, Haig was extremely concerned, as he felt that his men had nothing left to give and that one more severe German attack would break through. He was told that he must cling on and that the French and II Corps would soon relieve them. So the orders to stand fast were passed on through the chain of command, triggering some more mordant humour from Captain Hubert Rees of the 2nd Welsh.

The Germans made a bombing attack on our pits at our junction with the London Scottish. I got together thirty eight men, mostly orderlies and senior NCOs, and started off. I posted my two machine guns to check any advance beyond the wood, there being no reserves of any sort left then we got to the trenches, we found Private John had collected a mixed force and reoccupied them. I did some adjusting, then went back and wrote a letter to Lord Cavan describing the situation. Lord Cavan's reply to my letter made me laugh for the first time for several days. It ran, if I recollect aright, 'Dear Rees, Thanks so much for your encouraging note. Should the line be broken on your right or left, I am sure I can trust you to hold on. I hope I have a cavalry regiment arriving shortly.' Aldworth was now clamouring for assistance, having used up his support platoon. I had nothing whatever to send him, so taking my cue from Lord Cavan's letter, I sent him a similar one and hoped for the best![61]

In the event the storm had passed. Yet there were plenty of aftershocks, the German guns still blazed out, attacks went in to 'straighten the line', or seize some desirable tactical positions, but these attacks were mainly made on the French positions, who after all by this time held most of the salient that bulged out around Ypres. Commencing on 15 November, the relief of I Corps began as the whole of the BEF was moved away from Ypres, down to hold the sector between La Bassée and Kemmel. Finally there came the news that the British and French High Commands had been praying for: the German divisions were entraining for the Eastern Front.

There they would be a problem for the Russians, but at least the Western Front was finally secure from Switzerland to the North Sea. The battle for Ypres was over.

In many ways Foch had been the key player in the Allied defence of eastern Flanders in 1914. As Commander of the Northern Group of Armies he had a huge responsibility as the Germans made their last great efforts, straining every sinew to break through the thin line. Foch may have been under pressure, but he was able to appreciate the even greater pressures resting on the shoulders of Joffre.

> While he never failed to recognize the importance of the operations in Flanders, he was not able to give us all the forces we wanted. His armies were greatly fatigued by two months of heavy fighting, and they lacked ammunition. Moreover, he was forced to provide for the security of a front which was as yet only poorly organized, and whose length had rapidly increased, until now it reached from the Vosges to the Lys, a distance of 375 miles. On such a line, where both sides were everywhere in close contact, a surprise was possible practically anywhere. This fact explains the more or less piecemeal arrival of our reinforcements for the battle of Ypres; it also explains why the troops which had started the battle had to be kept in action for so long a time. The reason was simple – there were no others to take their place![62]

Foch had done well, but Haig had also excelled. Calm under intense strain, he had fought a brilliant tactical defensive battle, always mindful of the absolute necessity of amassing and controlling the deployment of local reserves to allow counter-attacks when things went wrong. His battalions were the size of a company, brigades had been reduced to the numbers of a pre-war battalion, divisions slashed down to little more than a brigade strength in manpower. But still Haig remained, outwardly at least, calm.

> I can see Sir Douglas Haig now as he appeared when he sent for me on such critical days as October 31st and November 1st, to see if any increase or readjustment of our artillery fire could be made to meet changing and mostly unfavourable situations. He stood leaning over his map, the only noticeable sign of unusual anxiety being a constant pulling of his moustache. At these times it was his custom to ride

quietly down the Menin Road, stopping now and again to speak to an officer or a man, or visiting a hard-pressed commander with a word of commendation and encouragement. His presence and demeanour on such occasions were a wonderful inspiration to each and all.[63]

Brigadier General Henry Horne, Headquarters, I Corps

Such remarks are often seen as mere flannel, parroting the stereotypes of leadership as flattery, but such views of Haig's performance were widely held by the men under his command in 1914.

After getting no rest the previous night we were all somewhat tired and not in the best spirits: the prospects of what was ahead of them did not appear very cheerful! In fact, to put it bluntly, we were all somewhat anxious. When we were well within the area of shell fire the Corps Commander Sir Douglas Haig – with one staff officer and one orderly carrying his corps commander flag – overtook us. He rode quietly on ahead of us as though nothing unusual was happening. I remember noticing how immaculately he was turned out and how cool and unconcerned he looked. I don't know whether his action was designed in order to create an effect, but it certainly had the effect of bucking us all up and steadying our nerves.[64]

Captain Ernest Hamilton, 2nd Connaught Ranger, 5th Brigade, 2nd Division, I Corps

Haig had also showed a considerable adeptness in controlling his subordinates, allowing them the freedom where necessary to make their own decisions within outlines that had been cogently defined by his Chief of Staff Brigadier General John Gough, who also excelled. Many of the most important decisions had to be taken locally, with no time, or method, of consulting higher authorities. In particular, his brigadiers had 'grown into' their role, providing real leadership for their battalions, now fighting as a brigade, not single entities.

Foch and Haig had performed one of the most difficult of wartime tasks in maintaining an effective and cooperative liaison with their allies on the field of battle under stressful situations. Throughout they had recognised that it was not just their men that were in distress, there was an equivalence of suffering and the problems had to be tackled together with a substantial degree of good will and mutual trust. Thus it was as a relatively unified force that the British, the French and the Belgians had achieved a stalemate in Flanders, which at the height of the crisis had seemed an improbable outcome. But by mid-November, the deed was done, as Foch swiftly recognised.

> I consider the German offensive as *definitely blocked in the West*. With troops of inferior quality, the Germans cannot resume the attempt on Ypres with the violence they displayed on November 1st. If they begin again, they will fail. They are necessarily condemned to the defensive on the Western Front. They can no longer manoeuvre except on the Eastern Front; and even there, can they?[65]

13

LIFE IN THE TRENCHES

Suddenly there was a sharp cry to the right, the sound of a fall and of men's voices. I turned a traverse and found a man lying dead in the narrow trench. He had been sniped, and the bullet, entering the forehead, had blown the back of his head clean off. I looked at the smashed and splintered skull, at the mess of brains and blood, and I said to myself, 'The glory of war.'[1]

Captain Cecil Brownlow, 40th Brigade, RFA, 3rd Division, II Corps

GIVEN THE PRESS OF EVENTS, British trenches had little chance to develop much in the way of sophistication since they were first established in mid-September on the heights above the Aisne. Although there were many variations depending on the terrain, tactical considerations and the state of the ground, the basic pattern was for a single narrow fire trench with a parapet in front. The trench was not straight but had a crenellated pattern with short traverses to prevent the Germans shooting directly along the front line should they attain an enfilade position. The sides were normally not revetted, except by brushwood where it was deemed absolutely necessary to prevent them from collapsing. The bottom of the trench was usually a slimy morass of mud and water in the absence of proper drainage or duckboards. Sandbags were in short supply and the parapets of soft earth, swiftly thrown up in front of the trench, were often pierced to deadly effect by German bullets. In front was a smidgeon of barbed wire, often anything but continuous, and rarely more than a few strands in total.

As the situation began to quieten down, the men began to work on improving their trench environment for both comfort and safety. The amount of physical labour this entailed was simply staggering.

> They were seldom more than four feet deep, so that it was necessary to walk about with head and shoulders bent. They were nothing but man-made ditches, and we had no materials for revetting the constantly slipping muddy walls. We started to improve our surroundings by breaking up ration boxes in order to make seats at the back of the trenches. A hole about two feet broad and eighteen inches deep was hacked out with an entrenching tool, and the end of a ration box completed the seat. Unfortunately, there was not sufficient wood, available to bank in the ever-slipping, slimy sides and back. In fact, often the seats had to be taken to light fires. However, experience soon taught us that it was safer to be near the front of the trench rather than the back, as all shrapnel and pieces of shell had a certain amount of momentum and therefore it was safer to be on the 'coming' side. Consequently, little alcoves called 'funk holes' became fashionable, those being small recesses where one could huddle during a bombardment. As it became more apparent that this life was likely to continue on into the winter mouths, doors and planks were taken from the neighbouring farms and cottages. Day after day we sat huddled up on our improvised seats, wishing that something, even an advance, would take place. Shelling soon taught us to dig still deeper, and make firing steps. We also introduced frequent traverses, so that shells bursting actually in the trench were able to do little damage.[2]
>
> Private Douglas Kingsley 1st Honourable Artillery Company, 8th Brigade, 3rd Division, II Corps

Behind the front line firing trench, there would sometimes be a parallel communications trench used to move men laterally up and down the line. Such dugouts as there were at the front consisted of little more than scooped-out cubby holes tucked under the parapet with the roof – such as it was – propped up with wood secured from a variety of sources – approved or not! Normally, there would be one or two more communication trenches reaching back towards the rear areas and the battalion headquarters. Otherwise the only route forward lay across wide-open ground.

That first journey up into the trenches of the front line could be a tense affair for any young soldier. Private Harold Stainton certainly found the whole experience very testing when moving up with the 1/10th King's Liverpool Regiment.

We were to take up a position right under the noses of the enemy in the neighbourhood of Wytschaete Wood so great caution and silence had been enjoined upon us. The night was uncannily still except for the rattle of musketry and the curiously plaintive whisper and whistle of bullets flitting past our heads. The gentle rise of the ground made it difficult to maintain one's balance on the slippery going and at one moment as I fell, I inadvertently drove the projecting part of my long-barrelled Lee Enfield rifle well into the mud, effectively corking the muzzle. As luck would have it, one of my 'dog biscuits' broke loose from its moorings in the mess tin and, at every jolt of the body, gave an alarmingly loud rattle like the tap-tap of a side drum. One felt that every German in Flanders could hear, and for a few minutes I must have suffered an unpopularity among my pals sufficient to wither me. Being in single file the man immediately in front of me tried to ram the butt of the rifle into my stomach by way of protest, but as a halt was impossible I had to continue still rattling! Presently the section halted and I collided in the darkness with my friend in front. Putting his mouth to my ear he whispered, 'We are here!' That was, perhaps, unduly obvious, but, as I correctly gathered that he meant the front line trenches I peered into the darkness and groped about in vain. Then a bullet cracked unpleasantly near me and I dropped quickly to the ground to find, more by touch than by sight that there was no trench except slits in the earth on our left and right, full of water and ice![3]

Private Harold Stainton, 1/10th King's Liverpool Regiment, 9th Brigade, 3rd Division, II Corps

Stainton was frankly appalled at the primitive conditions he found in the 'trench' that they were supposed to occupy. He had found very little in civilian life to compare with this kind of purgatory.

This, an ex-enemy trench, was merely a widened ditch between two fields. The old parapet, now the parados, was reasonably high. The

reverse side, now our parapet, was low and ineffective; out of it grew
a hedge of sorts offering no fire cover but some measure of protection
against surprise tactics. Apart from its garrison, the ditch contained
about eighteen inches of water and slime, numerous corpses, and the
most appalling stench. Dugouts lined the higher side intermittently
but, as those had been filled with the corpses of bayoneted Germans,
they were uninhabitable. By keeping one foot on a dead German and
lying diagonally along the clayey bank I was able to keep my body
out of the water and, at the same time, keep my head out of sight of
the enemy, who occupied a trench at the edge of the wood fifteen
or twenty yards away. Near me, half afloat in the water, was a dead
Tommy minus one leg. Beside him a dead Bosche, badly swollen by the
gases of decomposition and with parchment-like face, was threatening
to burst at any moment. I was convinced that only the buttons of his
mud-soaked tunic held him together.[4]

In these circumstances, the freezing cold may have been an advantage as
it reduced, at least in part, the stench emanating from decaying corpses,
food refuse, human excrement and the dead animals rotting in the fields
around them. As the rain poured down, there was no spare manpower
available to achieve any kind of proper drainage.

The first week's rain turned our trenches into canals. Bale out all
day and all night was the order. We are provided with scoops. They
are large ladles and are fitted onto a wooden handle about six feet in
length. Holes are dug at irregular intervals in the trench. The water
drains into those. You set to work with your scoop and empty the
water over the parapet. It percolates through the earth in time and
finds its way back into the holes in the trench floor; those holes are
called sump holes. The object of a six-foot handle is to enable you to
throw the water over the parapet without running the risk of getting
shot through the hand or arm. I have seen men deliberately hold their
hands over the trench parapet, when baling out, with the object of
getting wounded. Of course their heads were kept well down. Quite
a number get wounded in this manner. Our dugouts have caved in.
You lie down in the water for a couple of hours at night. You must fold
yourself up as neatly as possible; if you stretch your legs out they get
trodden upon by all who pass up and down the trench. Drip, drip, drip
on your ground sheet, that damned rain, will it ever cease? Every ten
minutes you have to scratch various parts of your body with dirty clay

stained hands. The infernal lice are marching all over your body by platoons. I felt an infinitive longing to be out of it, out of this useless slaughter, misery and tragedy. I feel that way that I would sign peace on almost any terms.[5]

Private Edward Roe, 1st East Lancashire Regiment, 11th Brigade, 4th Division, III Corps

When Lord Edward Gleichen and his 15th Brigade took over the line in front of Dranoutre on 29 November, he was confounded by the very ubiquity of the mud and water that surrounded him and his men. Conditions seemed to have taken on an almost biblical tinge.

Oh that mud! We have heard lots about Flanders mud, but the reality transcends imagination, especially in winter. Greasy, slippery, holding clay, over your toes in most places and over your ankles in all the rest – where it is not over your knees – it is the most horrible 'going' I know anywhere. Whether you are moving across plough or grass fields, or along lanes, you are perpetually skating about and slipping up on the firmer bits and held fast by the ankles in the softer ones. There is no stone in the district, nothing but rich loamy clay, alias mud. However much you dig, you never come across stone, nothing but sticky mud which clings to your shovel and refuses to be parted from it – mud that has to be scraped off at almost every stroke, mud that absorbs water like a sponge yet refuses to give it up again. Every little puddle and rut, every hoof-depression full of rain, remains like that for weeks; even when the weather is fine the water does not seem to evaporate, but remains on the surface. And when it rains, as it did all that winter (except when it snowed), the state of the trenches is indescribable. Some were, frankly, so full of water that they had to be abandoned, and a breastwork erected behind. But a breastwork is slow work, especially if you are less than 100 yards from the enemy. For weeks, indeed, the garrison of one particular trench had to lie out on the mud, or on what waterproofs they could get, behind a shelter two to three feet high – always growing a little, yet never to be made to a real six feet height for reason of conspicuousness and consequent clusters of 'Black Marias'.[6]

This was bad enough, but then the temperature began to drop below freezing. It was to be a truly awful winter. The cold penetrated their bones, reducing their awareness to little more than an agonised appreciation of the biting discomfort endured by their own bodies; there seemed to be no hope of remission. No chance in the trenches of a brisk walk or vigorous exercises to warm the blood. Here there was nothing but standing about in freezing water, black and dank. And then there was the snow.

> It has been snowing hard, after two nights' sharp frost, and it is lying about two inches deep, except in the foot of the trenches, where by the continual passage of men up and down, it has become a freezing cold slush of mud, and chills one's boots right through. We have not changed our boots or socks even, and far and away the worst part is the cold in one's feet at night, which makes sleep impossible for more than half an hour or so at a time.[7]
>
> Lieutenant Sir Edward Hulse, 2nd Scots Guards, 20th Brigade, 7th Division, IV Corps

In such conditions the nights seemed endless; dawn always seemed an eternity away. It was no real surprise when the men began to fall prey to an excruciating new ailment that afflicted their sodden feet.

> The bottom of the trenches became deep in icy mud. In this they stood, up to their knees, day and night, for we could not spare a man from the trenches, and soon we began to experience what we call now 'frostbitten feet'. No one quite knows what it is but I think myself it comes from the continual pressure of the mud and the lack of ventilation to the feet. Anyhow, it is a dreadful thing and the men suffered agonies from it. The only way we could combat the cold was to keep every man working with the shovel all night. The poor souls were deadly tired and worn but even that is better than to sit at the bottom of a muddy trench frozen to the marrow until there is no possibility of sleep or rest.[8]
>
> Lieutenant Arthur Ackland, 1st Duke of Cornwall's Light Infantry, 14th Brigade, 5th Division, II Corps

The severity of the frostbite, or less serious 'trench foot', ranged from a mere tenderness to the touch to a deadness with a loss of all feeling. The feet could become red and swollen with blisters and at worst the toes would turn black or the whole foot become gangrenous. Such severe cases could cripple a man for life. Prevention meant, first of all, avoiding immersion in cold water for long periods, but as this was not possible, then the feet needed to be well-rubbed dry and cleaned before dry socks were put on. In most cases this was equally unlikely in the conditions prevalent in the front line. Makeshift measures had to be taken.

> Am trying to make the bottom of the trenches better for the men, so as to arrest frost bite of which we have had several cases. Have therefore sent Dorsets to cut brushwood to line the bottom of the trenches and on this we can put planks and straw if necessary.[9]
>
> Brigadier General Stanley Maude, Headquarters, 14th Brigade, 5th Division, II Corps

The real answer to trench foot would prove to be the combination of a proper drainage system, the use of raised duckboards at the bottom of the trenches and the liberal – and regular – application of whale oil to the feet. But in the winter of 1914 it remained a terrible curse. Hundreds of men were evacuated to military hospitals.

> The first cases of frostbite arrive this afternoon. Poor men they said the water in the trenches was almost to their knees and then the frost came with disastrous results to the feet. The feet are dreadfully swollen and painful. They are in some cases too painful to be washed so after being soaked for about an hour in a warm Condy's fluid bath they are dried and painted gently with Iodine and methylated spirit and then wrapped up in plenty of cotton wool.[10]
>
> Sister Martha Aitken, British Military Hospital, Wimereux

The efforts of the 'good people' back home to send extra clothing to keep the troops warm were understandable and commendable but at times provoked considerable amusement amongst the men.

> One morning about this time the Quartermaster Sergeant, returning from the Army Service Corps dump with the daily issue of rations and forage, produced from a wagon two bulky packages which aroused our curiosity. The parcels, on being opened, were found to contain a quantity of underclothing which had been knitted and sewn by a Dorcas Society of an English village. The garments came at a most opportune moment, for the official supply was short and the winter was setting in. Many of them were of extraordinary shapes and sizes. Attached to many articles were little cards bearing messages of goodwill. One, from a maiden lady, said: 'I am a little doubtful as to the size of a man's sock, but I hope these will be large enough and will

keep you warm!' These happened to be so large that they were used as
sleeping helmets, and warmed not only our heads but also our hearts.
Another, written in a large and laborious hand, ran: 'Dear Mister Soljer,
I nitted this mitten myself, your affecshunate Betty!'[11]

Captain Cecil Brownlow, 40th Brigade, RFA, 3rd Division, II Corps

When at the front, the men had nowhere to go, nothing to do, other than
follow the relentless rhythms of trench life. Despair was a common emotion given the utter bleakness of a world full of mud, freezing water, biting
winds, and the all-too-real threat of cold steel from some German inter-
lopers if they failed to maintain a vigilant watch across No Man's Land.
Many a sentry must have pondered the feasibility of operating his rifle
bolt with hands reduced to helpless numbness. But still, for the most part,
the men stuck it out. Many went sick; of course they did. But the majority
endured. The only possible respite was when brief periods of drier ground
conditions allowed the construction of crude dugouts hollowed out into
the side wall of the trenches. These could make all the difference.

We are keeping pretty warm in our dug-outs, and are gradually getting
a bit of straw into them, where it keeps dry and is warm to lie on. We
get a certain amount of charcoal served out, but not much, and with
old mess tins, with holes punched in all over them, get the charcoal
going, spread two or three oil-sheets over the trench, and with three
or four men sitting round, they can get quite a degree of warmth out
of it. I believe blankets are coming up, but we must get them into the
trenches dry, or they will be no good at all.[12]

Lieutenant Sir Edward Hulse, 2nd Scots Guards, 20th Brigade, 7th Division,
IV Corps

When they had time Hulse arranged for more substantial dugouts to act as
battalion company headquarters and to accommodate the officers.

I found the accommodation in the trenches very bad and anything
but rain-proof. Having no time to dig myself, I got two defaulters on
to a new Ritz-Carlton, and the servants on to a kitchen and bug-hutch
for themselves, the whole connected by a neat little trench, and after
two days' hard work the new company headquarters were completed;
and having a little more time to myself, Swinton and I did the skilled
labour, namely fitting up the inside and roofing – the latter we did
quite extraordinarily well, and in the most scientific manner. It is quite

rain-proof and proof from shrapnel, and luxurious beyond words. Little recesses, cut in the walls, hold a young library, food, plum puddings, and all the more valuable comestibles and drinks, which we do not trust in the servants' cook-house dugout. The inside, well lined with straw, is warm and well lit by a small oil lamp, supplemented by candles, for which we have cut little recesses. In short, the interior looks exactly like a shrine in a crypt![13]

Perhaps not the London Ritz or Carlton but better than nothing.

In the conditions prevalent in the trenches it was a considerable physical challenge just to move around, and the ration parties suffered greatly in their wearisome task of carrying the food to the men in the front line. The vigilance of the Germans made movement nearly impossible by day, but by night they would be lucky to have even a glimmer of moonlight to guide their path across an incomprehensible landscape.

It is an agony of endurance trying to get rations up to the firing line. The nights are dark and wet; the turnip field is pitted with shell craters, which are full of water. The dykes on each side of the road to headquarters are full of water. The regimental transport dumps the rations on the road opposite headquarters in an indiscriminate pile, and get out of it as quick as they can. There is something dreadful about the sound of a Maxim. We shun the ground they cover as if it were plague infested, but on ration fatigue we cannot. As an alternative to the bullet swept road we can go through the wood, but we would never get through the wood and carry a box of biscuits or bully. The mud is knee-deep and the shell craters almost adjoin one another they are that numerous, so it must be the road then. The party gets loaded up and struggle towards the firing line. Will he open up with his machine guns before we get there? Or will we be lucky enough to get back to the trenches without coming under machine gun fire. Those are our thoughts as we struggle along with our loads. 'Ping! Ping! Ping! Swish!' Down go the boxes, sand bags and rolls of cheese. We dive into the dykes on either side of the road. We are up to our necks in water, but we're alive. He fires down the road, traverses left and right then stops. 'Come on lads let us get a move on before he starts again!'[14]

Private Edward Roe, 1st East Lancashire Regiment, 11th Brigade, 4th Division, III Corps

This task was no one-off ordeal – it had to be carried out each and every night. Come what may, the men had to be fed.

The daily routine in the trenches was unrelenting. Perhaps for the officers it was a little easier, but they still had the responsibility of ensuring that everything was in order and that everyone was performing their duties as expected.

Failing any night alarms the day began at 4.0am. At this hour the cookers used to come up to a point about a quarter of a mile behind the trench. Orderlies went down to this place and brought back hot tea with rum in it as well as the day's rations. At five o'clock we stood to arms during the hour before daylight, the theory being that the enemy creep up by night and attack as soon as it gets light. This standing to arms was very cold work. After this I very often used to dose until seven or eight o'clock when we officers had breakfast consisting of bacon or sausages, bread and jam and cocoa. After breakfast I usually walked along the trench to see if anything was going on; then I used to sit in my dugout and read, if I had anything to read, write letters, censor the men's letters, every two or three days (a laborious occupation). Or sleep a bit. About twelve or one we had lunch consisting of potted jam, or sardines or tongue and bread and jam. After this I went and had a look round again and then tried to while away the afternoon as I had tried to while away the morning. At dusk I used to go along trenches again and about six or seven we had dinner. At this meal Corporal Earl, our mess corporal, generally managed to bring up a hot dinner. He usually produced soup; then a stew, or perhaps chicken, if he had managed to strangle; once he rose to fresh beef, and once to pork. How we blessed the inventor of tinned foods. After a bit of talk after dinner, if the enemy was giving no trouble, I used to go to sleep with my accoutrements on, except my rucksack, making myself as warm and comfortable as circumstances permitted. When I awoke in the course of the night I used to go round the trenches to see that the sentries were alert and went out to one or more posts.[15]

Second Lieutenant Robert Synge, 3rd Coldstream Guards, 4th Guards Brigade, 2nd Division, I Corps

Of course not everything was always in good order. Many of the men were exhausted beyond measure, while the freezing cold could reduce even normally vigilant NCOs to a near lifeless torpor.

The other night, after two hours' sleep, I woke up and thought I had better go down the trenches to see that everything was all right. Of course I found one whole platoon in the most hectic state ever seen. Not a sentry on the alert, the NCO on duty sitting down instead of patrolling his lines, and a hundred other things. Any enterprising twenty or thirty Huns could have simply walked right in; unless one is at it day and night, nothing is done. There are individuals, scouts, etc., volunteers and picked men, who are priceless, and worth a whole platoon in themselves, but, by Jove, one has to work at the rest. The unfortunate part was having every single one of our serving NCOs knocked out when the battalion took the knock originally. As half of them don't seem to understand English, or any other language for that matter, I have kept myself busy in spare moments writing 'standing orders' for the trenches. They were circulated to all NCOs in the trenches, and I got much better results, and could drop on a fellow more heavily if they were not complied with. I have broken three this morning, and replaced them with three jolly good men from the ranks.[16]

Lieutenant Sir Edward Hulse, 2nd Scots Guards, 20th Brigade, 7th Division, IV Corps

In most battalions, the average period of sentry duty lasted for two hours, with one man per section on watch during daylight and one man in three throughout the night. This allowed men to get four hours sleep out of six – always assuming that there were no threatening German incursions.

In the first gleam of half-light before dawn when the trees of the Petit Sois were emerging from silhouette into things with shape and form, I was peeping over my sights through the base of the hedge when a large form silently rose and obscured my sight of the trees. It could only have been an enemy, and instinctively I took a quick rough bead on the massive target and squeezed the trigger. Whatever it was sank to the ground and out of my vision. Now I was tense with suppressed excitement, I felt sure that I had disposed of a murderous sniper and in a bated whisper told my neighbour so – but where was the evidence? I had to wait impatiently for dawn to break before finding it – the grey uniformed body of a big and bulky German lying silent and still three or four yards away.[17]

Private Harold Stainton, 1/10th King's Liverpool Regiment, 9th Brigade, 3rd Division, II Corps

There were also sudden panics for the sentries, when the night seemed to breed shadowy figures, creeping forward with malevolent intent. Sometimes, almost nothing at all could trigger an outbreak of firing that would spread up and down the line.

> A curious thing, this 'wind up'. We never know when it would come on. It is caused entirely by nerves. Perhaps an inquisitive Bosche, somewhere a mile or two on the left, had thought he saw someone approaching his barbed wire; a few shots are exchanged – a shout or two, followed by more shots – panic – more shots – panic spreading – then suddenly the whole line of trenches on a front of a couple of miles succumbs to that well-known malady, 'wind up'. The firing becomes faster and faster; then suddenly swells into a roar. Everyone stands to the parapet and away on the left a tornado of crackling sound can be heard, getting louder and louder. In a few seconds it has swept on down the line, and now a deafening rattle of rifle-fire is going on immediately in front. Bullets are flicking the tops of the sandbags on the parapet in hundreds, whilst white streaks are shooting up with a swish into the sky and burst into bright radiating blobs of light – the star shell at its best. Presently there comes a deep 'Boom!' from somewhere in the distance behind, and a large shell sails over our heads and explodes somewhere amongst the Bosches; another and another, and then all becomes quiet again. The rifle fire diminishes and soon ceases. Total result of one of these firework displays: several thousand rounds of ammunition squibbed off, hundreds of star shells wasted, and no casualties. It put the 'wind up' me at first, but I soon got to know these affairs, and learnt to take them calmly.[18]
>
> Second Lieutenant Bruce Bairnsfather, 1st Royal Warwickshire Regiment, 10th Brigade, 4th Division, III Corps

Being on sentry duty at night was nerve-wracking enough, but it was even worse to be assigned to a stint in the listening posts at the end of short saps protruding out from the front line. Here they were isolated from their comrades.

> A post of this sort consists of a shallow trench running out at right angles to the line, ending in a shallow hole about fifteen yards towards the enemy trenches. Sometimes this extended outside our barbed wire, and was occupied by two men, whose duty it was to give timely

warning of enemy approach during the hours of darkness. They were
prepared to open fire and sacrifice themselves if necessary. Lance
Corporal Merry and Private Keane, two pals, were occupying the post
one night, and when it came time to change them, usually two hour
spells, it was my duty to creep out and warn them to return, one at a
time, and see their reliefs properly posted. Upon reaching these men
I was surprised to get no reply from them, so reached out and tugged
a foot, but neither whispered an acknowledgment or stirred, and
I found out they were both dead. When they were recovered to the
trench immediately, it was found that a sniper's bullet had passed clean
through both their heads. Believe me it was decidedly unpleasant for
the relief men who had to take their places.[19]

Sergeant Frederick Brown, 2nd Monmouthshire Regiment, 12th Brigade,
4th Division

The four hours 'off' sentry duty was by no means what it seemed. Often
far more dangerous or physically exhausting tasks were assigned to the
men as they 'rested'.

In true army fashion, it was more than likely that a Sergeant would call
for volunteers, usually done by his saying, 'I want six volunteers – you
and you and you!' Possibly to take out barbed wire entanglements,
repair some part of the trench which had caved in under shellfire, or
take part in a burial party. In fact, so numerous were the daily toils
necessary for the maintaining of human life under such conditions
that it would be almost impossible to enumerate them.[20]

Private Douglas Kingsley, 1st Honourable Artillery Company, 8th Brigade,
3rd Division, II Corps

When the men were back in the support trenches they were even more
hard-pressed. The trench systems demanded incalculable amounts of
labour to maintain.

When in supports we have not half an hour to ourselves. If we are
not digging communication trenches or reserve trenches to get filled
with water as fast as we dig them, we are in Plugstreet Wood, cutting
down saplings to make what are called corduroys. They are something
similar to a ladder, if you nail the rungs as close together as possible.
They are made in sections and are laid on top of the sea of mud to
form pathways. There are miles and miles of those corduroy roads

laid in Plugstreet Wood. If there are no corduroys to be made, we are stretching fathoms and fathoms of barbed wire around trestles. These have to be carried up to the firing line at night and placed a certain distance in front of our first line trench.[21]

Private Edward Roe, 1st East Lancashire Regiment, 11th Brigade, 4th Division, III Corps

At night, patrols and raiding parties would occasionally be sent out to gain some information as to the identity and activities of the Germans occupying the trenches across no man's land.

We often went out patrolling and I usually took the same men with me, always volunteers at this time, and Corporal Parkes always came. We climbed out of our trenches, got through the wire and across the stream, and then started to crawl. As a rule we moved up one of the hedges to avoid being seen in the open field when a Very light went up. We could not do this every night as the enemy might have been waiting for in the hedge, so we varied this with a crawl across the open field. It was quite exciting work, every noise, even if it was made by one of our own men made us halt and we used to lie flat for ages.[22]

Lieutenant George Roupell, 1st East Surrey Regiment, 14th Brigade, 5th Division, II Corps

Their objective was to get a prisoner. Roupell managed to circle round behind an advanced German post and then crept back.

I had given orders that no-one was to fire or throw a grenade until I fired my revolver, then they were all to shoot. We crawled closer and closer and at last I saw the figure of a man standing up in the post. He was evidently facing his front and consequently had his back to us. On we went, a yard or two more, all flat on the ground, and I with my revolver cocked and pointing at the dark figure whose head and shoulders I could see. One in the patrol made a slight noise at once the German sentry challenged; it struck me that he wasn't quite sure whether he had seen or heard anything or not, so I waited to see if he challenged again. He did challenge again and one or two more heads appeared. My reply to his challenge was to fire my revolver into them – then things happened quickly. All my men let off something, either a rifle or a hand grenade. In the middle of the excitement I thought my revolver had jammed, but on examining it later I found I had let off six rounds – they had gone so quickly that I thought that I had only let off two or three rounds.

I had an impression of five or six figures appearing in the post, and of two of them escaping down the communication trench. It was a very dark night, we had got to within five yards of the wire running round their post, so it is more than likely that we accounted for the remainder. Suddenly I felt a sharp pain in my right forearm and it gave me such a shock that from a prone position I somehow leapt up in the air and landed on top of Abercrombie! This startled him almost more than the enemy's fire, and as the main German trench was now fully alive to the fact that something was happening to their post, and was opening fire all the way along, we beat a hasty retreat.[23]

In the end they had been thwarted in their attempt to take prisoners by the barbed wire which had been erected around the German post.

Prisoners were crucial, for through them the British intelligence officers could track the movements of the German units in and out of the line, then they could determine if reinforcements were pouring in, and hence if a serious attack was looming. One of those involved in this process was Captain James Marshall-Cornwall, an intelligence officer at 3rd Division.

I had to go round the trenches and find out from the battalion commanders whether they could capture any prisoners (which was a rare thing in those days) and if so interrogate them. We did have a few Alsatian deserters who came over of their own accord and then we had a great field day getting first-hand information, but of course it was at their own level and they couldn't tell us much about the intentions of the higher command. Trench warfare really became fixed and I felt that apart from the odd deserter coming over I must do something about getting in touch with the enemy officers. I found there was a cottage in our front line which had not yet been destroyed and which I could get into during the hours of darkness and there, with a powerful telescope, I could survey a sector of the German trenches and even read the numbers on the soldiers' shoulder straps telling me which regiment they belonged to. However that was only on a very limited sector. I also used to crawl out between the lines of barbed wire, armed with a revolver and a wire cutter and find stray Germans lying dead from which I took their shoulder straps and any papers on them.[24]

If new German regiments were identified, then this intelligence could save lives and prevent a catastrophe by allowing proper preparations to be made to repel an imminent attack.

In many places the front line had not yet been properly established and thus the chance of being surprised was still high. In mid-November, Second Lieutenant Basil Marden of the 9th Lancers was occupying trenches in the stables of the Chateau of Mme Mahieu near Zonnebeke, the chateau itself having already been destroyed by a *Minenwerfer* shell.

> On entering stables thro' shell hole we fall over what we imagine to be sacks of potatoes – they are corpses really – 120 dead Germans and over a week old. They provide some good souvenirs! My dispositions: one troop on the right, entrenched; half a troop in room; half troop in trench on left. In the trench on the right the Royal Engineers hurled out coils of loose barbed wire and we had an abattis made of trees – cut down where they stood. From the trench the R.E.s were digging out to cover the front wall of the stables. Two or three were hit. The enemy became very active with hand grenades – one nearly gets me and badly wounds two men whom I had placed in the top front room. I fire eight pistol shots rapid at the sight of a match – no corpses there next day – though match goes out! When these grenades get bad, I send for another troop and keep them in room with fixed bayonets for two hours sitting on dead Huns. When dawn arrives I post snipers at each hole and we bag ten to fifteen Germans – I personally get three – my first separate and sure bag of the war! Alan comes and in spite of my telling him that the front windows was dangerous, we go and peep thro' an iron loophole we had hoisted there. Then we both got wounded in the head by one bullet – I think it must be explosive to get through the wall – or else reversed. 'Lord, I'm hit!' 'So am I!' And off we crawl downstairs on hands and knees, pouring with blood. I feel very dizzy and cannot do much good.[25]

The somewhat chastened Marden made his way back and was soon evacuated by ambulance to Poperinghe.

The trenches were shallow, there were gaps in the parapet and moving about often necessitated desperate dashes across open ground. In such circumstances, German snipers were a deadly threat.

> Snipers are the great trouble. One gets bullets coming in from all sides. They apparently climb trees or live in the cellars of destroyed houses, and simply pop away all through the night, having first laid the rifle by day. In the German trenches also it seems as though they have tripods or fixed rests for their rifles, and have them sighted all

the time on a loophole or a tee just at the back of our trench, or any conspicuous mark along our front. One gets bullet after bullet coming through the same loophole during the night, and always hitting the same spot in the rear. Their trenches are only about 130 yards away and so far only one attempt has been made to attack us; and I am pleased to say that my platoon sergeant spotted them starting climbing over, and get 'em hell. They didn't try any more just there. Sorry to say we have lost two officers killed and one wounded so far. Snipers in each case did the business. During the day the enemy tries hard to be funny, and, if our fellows let fly at a loophole near to where earth is being thrown over, they signal with a spade that the shot was a miss. Our chaps have taken to answering them in the same way. In one place in my bit of front as fast as the men build up a loophole the Germans knock it down, and there is apparently great rivalry as to who will eventually win. So far no men have been hit just at that spot, but many have had very narrow escapes. Personally, I find the show anything but a picnic.[26]

Second Lieutenant William Smalley, 1st Sherwood Foresters, 24th Brigade, 8th Division

On 9 December, the very day after this letter home was published in the *Nottingham Daily Express*, William Smalley[27] was shot and killed by a sniper whilst crossing an exposed part of the line. In these circumstances of constant danger, it seems strange to record a risky amusement that was frequently practised.

It is peculiar how under strain and stress a sharpening of humour and wit seems to run through most Englishmen. A constant source of amusement was the placing of an old hat on a stick walking with it along it along the trench, or bobbing it up and down, to tempt a Hun to take odd pots at it, knowing perfectly well that one was quite safe. This was sometimes done purposely so that somebody a few hundred yards further up would be able to spot an enemy sniper being tempted to expose his position by firing at the moving target.[28]

Private Douglas Kingsley, 1st Honourable Artillery Company, 8th Brigade, 3rd Division, II Corps

When it came to snipers, some men took risks that were near suicidal; many of them paid the price.

The morning was extremely cold, and word had passed down the trench that an issue of rum was going to be served out. About 6.30, Trooper Boyce, an extremely good and reliable youth who had been in my 'C' Squadron at Windsor, came along with two jars of rum, carrying one in his hand, and one on his shoulder. As he passed us I took the jar from his hand, to serve it out to my machine gun detachments and others who were posted near me. Boyce was a very light-hearted individual, with a supreme contempt for the Germans. A few yards outside our section was the partial ruin of an estaminet, of which some of the walls remained, which were enough to support the timbers of the roof, with a few tiles still on it. In these rafters there lurked a sniper, who could get a short view of a break in the trenches parapet, so that anyone passing could be seen for about five seconds while he passed the four-foot opening. This sniper had been annoying us since daybreak by firing at anyone who showed over the trench, or in the parapet gap. He was given the name of 'Dick Deadeye' by us in the trench. He fired with deadly accuracy from a top window whenever he got a chance. We warned Boyce of this man, when he went on to the other end of the trench with the rum jar on his shoulder, to bob down higher up the trench as it was very exposed. He however didn't think it worthwhile to do so, and he hadn't passed us twenty seconds when we heard a 'phut' followed by a thud, and a white face looked round the corner of our dugout, and said 'They've got him, Boyce is hit!' We crawled up to him. He was making terrible noises, but we found that nothing could be done. He had been shot clean through the chest, and he died in about five minutes. The rum jar however was rescued and passed on. Boyce's[29] body lay where he fell all day until nightfall, when it was pulled out and buried.[30]

Captain Sir Morgan Crofton, 2nd Life Guards, 7th Cavalry Brigade, 3rd Cavalry Division, Cavalry Corps

Of course, the British responded in kind but sniping was a dangerous and cold-blooded business. A considerable patience and cold-blooded ability as a marksman was essential.

One morning Lieutenant Paton, platoon officer, sent for me. A German sniper was reported shooting from a small square window in a barn some 300 yards away. He could be seen easily through the officer's field glasses, but indistinctly with the naked eye. I took a careful sight

on the bottom centre of the window, fired, and Lieut. Paton watching
through his glasses, exclaimed, 'Good shot, Sergeant!' He saw him
threw up his arms and fall backwards. I was not yet hard-baked enough
to remain unmoved by this incident.[31]

Sergeant Frederick Brown, 2nd Monmouthshire Regiment, 12th Brigade,
4th Division

Many men could not overcome their scruples and forbore to take
opportunistic shots at an identifiable individual as opposed to the
anonymous surge of a German mass attack. Somehow it seemed far
too personal.

When going round the trenches, I asked a man whether he had had
any shots at the Germans. He responded that there was an elderly
gentleman with a bald head and a long beard who often showed
himself over the parapet. 'Well, why didn't you shoot him?' 'Shoot
him?' said the man; 'Why, Lor' bless you, Sir, 'e's never done me
no 'arm!' A case of 'live and let live,' which is certainly not to be
encouraged. But cold-blooded murder is never popular with our men.[32]

Brigadier General Lord Edward Gleichen, Headquarters, 15th Brigade, 5th
Division, II Corps

Even at the front, amidst the cold miseries of Ploegsteert Wood, Second
Lieutenant Lionel Tennyson of the 1st Rifle Brigade remained as ever the
consummate sportsman, to the unfeigned joy of his troops.

Just at dusk, a cock and hen pheasant came and sat up in a tree about
100 yards from our trenches to our rear. I borrowed a rifle and shot the
hen straight through the neck and it fell dead – then I had a shot at
the cock and he fell, but we never got him as he was a runner. It was a
wonderful fluke, as it was nearly dark, but the men were delighted as
they were betting against my hitting it![33]

It would have been foolish to bet against Tennyson's phenomenal
hand-eye coordination.

One risk was obvious to everyone at the front from the moment they
first approached the lines to the moment they took their leave. At any
moment German shells could crash down upon them, randomly killing
and maiming the wary and unwary alike.

Their shells were bursting now on the near edge of my trenches, then ten to fifteen yards to my immediate front, and at each tearing scream we all crouched close to the inner wall of the trench. Nearer, nearer, we heard the shell; after a time it was possible to tell whether it was coming to right or left of your position, but equally possible to say with certainty, 'There's one for us!' And the few seconds terrible wait! Would it burst in front or behind, or would it be the one. Somehow curiosity to see what happened, prevented one being afraid, and anyhow it was no use feeling afraid; we had to stick there. For the whole of that hour the din was awful, awe inspiring. The whole of creation was trembling, as does the whole interior of a church when certain low notes on the organ are sounded, and at the end we all got up, stretched ourselves, and shook the mud and filth off our caps, for the heavy shells were bursting so close to us, that columns of liquid filth mixed with stones and bricks were shot 200 feet in the air, to fall back on to our devoted heads.[34]

Major Gerald Burgoyne, 2nd Royal Irish Rifles, 7th Brigade, 3rd Division, II Corps

When they were relieved next day, even such a 'cool' customer as Burgoyne was in a real state: 'As I got out of the trench I could have stuck my fingers into my ears and screamed like a girl. Those bombardments had fairly strung my nerves real tight.'[35] No skill, no caution, no 'second sense' could do much to keep a soldier safe. A trifling adjustment to the dials of a German gunner a couple of miles away, or the wobble of a shell in flight, would make all the difference between life and death. There was nothing anyone – no matter how gilded a youth – could do about it. Thus it was that Lionel Tennyson nearly did not survive his twenty-fifth birthday.

About 7pm I was standing on a road showing my platoon sergeant where to dig a communication trench between the two trenches – and he being very dense could not understand where to start it! I therefore got down into the trench to show him. I had not been down there ten seconds before six shells burst in quick succession in exactly the place where I had been standing on the road and must have killed me had I still been there.[36]

Sheer chance had saved him. Even well behind the lines, the long-range German artillery could still cause havoc as the heavy shells rained down.

We settled down to sleep, some in the cellar and some, including me, in a ground floor room. Just as one was dropping off to sleep a shell would come extra near: the house opposite was hit, then a house about three doors off had its inside knocked out, then one dropped on to the top of our garden wall. Then a flax factory near caught on fire, and finally just when we were all about asleep a shell came shrieking over nearer than ever. I could feel the wind of it through the open window. It crashed through the glass conservatory, hit a wall about five yards off our window and exploded. All I could see was a cloud of dust and smoke and then came the smell of the brute through the window We sat up at that one and laughed a kind of laugh and settled down to sleep again. We slept intermittently being roused when the whole house shook as some neighbour's house got hit. About 6am it ceased and I believe about four or five hundred shells had come over. These shells have an extraordinary fascination and interest: I am not terrified exactly, one just listens and when one comes near one wraps one's coat and blankets round one and waits like a dog. The various escapes there have been are simply marvellous. I don't know which is the worst – high-explosive shells, shrapnel, or rifle bullets. The thing that upsets me most of all is the plight of the civilians and hearing the kiddies crying with fear. It is a strange and awful state of things.[37]

Captain Frederick Chandler, 19th Field Ambulance, 6th Division, III Corps

The Germans also had very effective trench mortars that lofted their high-explosive shells high into the air, plunging down right into the British trenches.

Needless to say, the enemy minenwerfer were really efficient. They threw a bomb which looked like an electric torch as it turned over and over in the air and burst with a tremendous bang. Captain Herd,[38] who had lately joined us, was killed by one of them. Our attempt at a trench mortar consisted of putting a charge of gunpowder at the bottom of an 18-pounder brass cartridge case and firing out a tin of guncotton with a time fuse in it. It was a matter of speculation whether it would burst before it started or how far it might go![39]

Captain Herbert Rees, 2nd Welsh Regiment, 3rd Brigade, 1st Division, I Corps

The British possessed no comparable weapons. They were not prepared for this kind of war and were forced to rely on makeshift measures which varied from the most simple of solutions to Heath Robinson contraptions of mind-boggling complexity.

> I inspected some trench mortars, which we are making in our Engineer workshops. They are made of steel piping, which we obtain in the district, about two feet long, with a movable support near the muzzle to alter the elevation. A kind of spade is fixed to the base to prevent the gun from sinking in to the ground. They fire a bomb of 2-pound weight. This can be thrown up to 300 yards by means of gunpowder charges. Each division has already made four of these guns and about 100 rounds of ammunition. I offered my trench guns, and four are to be sent to the II Corps and four to the III Corps. Neither Corps had apparently started to make any. They seemed to me rather slovenly in their methods of carrying on war.[40]
>
> Lieutenant General Sir Douglas Haig, Headquarters, I Corps, BEF

Yet such improvised weapons had no chance of being properly tested and could prove lethal to their own side. This applied most of all to the early British hand grenades, which combined an inherent unpredictability with the propensity of untrained men to make silly mistakes.

> The Germans have been using large numbers of hand-grenades and trench mortars with disastrous results to our men. So we too have to practise these weapons in order to be able to hold our own. Perhaps they will improve someday, but the type of bomb now produced for our edification is made from an ordinary 'plum and apple jam' tin with an attached fuse which has to be lit by a match before throwing. This is obviously unsatisfactory in wet or windy weather, when it is difficult to get the match to light, but it is the only sort available at present, and the troops have to be taught to use it. Strange to relate, they have had no bombing instruction during their peace training, and no one, except a few engineers, knows anything whatever about the bomb and its habits. Sometimes these are harmless enough. One of the first produced was put by some irresponsible idiot on the heating stove in the officers' mess, and then forgotten. It was not spotted for some time, not, indeed, until it was nearly red hot, and the individual in question was ordered to remove it and drop it in a bucket of water. During this process, most of us made ourselves extremely scarce, feeling profoundly grateful that it had not exploded in the mess.[41]
>
> Lieutenant James Hyndson, 1st Loyal North Lancashire Regiment, 2nd Brigade, 1st Division, I Corps

The British were not ready for trench warfare. They lacked much of the necessary equipment: not just mortars and hand grenades, but even the bare essentials like waders and ordinary digging tools. It would take months to put things right.

THE ROYAL ARTILLERY WAS ALSO STRUGGLING to come to terms with a war that had almost nothing in common with the precepts laid down in accordance with pre-war training and theory. In particular, the reliance on guns firing with direct lines of sight, able to observe and range onto targets, was clearly impossible in conditions of trench warfare. Indirect firing was soon the 'norm' and a whole new method of working had to be devised.

> The artillery had observation posts up near the front line manned by an officer and usually two signallers, in communication with the guns by telephone, which meant a line had to be maintained between guns and OPs. Signallers were responsible for maintaining lines of communication, which were often cut by shellfire. Infantry usually occupied front line trenches for a given period, sometimes for a few days, according to conditions, then so many days in support trenches, situated just to the rear. These troops were periodically relieved at regular intervals and to rest billets in the rear to recuperate. The artillery stayed put in their positions until the whole division was relieved, unless they were strafed so much that their position became untenable. Each battery covered a certain sector of the front, supporting the infantry in that sector. All were constantly on the alert and all means of communication was tested at regular short intervals. If the infantry were suddenly attacked, they alerted the artillery by firing SOS rockets into the air and the guns immediately gave support by firing on fixed and previously determined targets, some would shell No Man's Land, others strategic points to harass the enemy movements. Cross roads and trench junctions were vital targets, the Germans usually kept up a steady bombardment on roads approaching the line during darkness when supplies of all kinds had to be brought up from the rear.[42]
>
> Signaller Percy Whitehouse, 8th (Howitzer) Brigade, RFA, 5th Division, II Corps

At some stages in the fighting the location of the front line was not always certain, and on one occasion Whitehouse was sent forward with an observation post party to pinpoint where exactly the British forward positions were located. This proved a terrifying business.

> An officer, corporal and two signallers made up the party and we worked our way forward, using any cover we could. We entered a house that had been shelled but still had part of its roof and our officer intended to climb up and try to make some observations from a height. Enemy shells began to burst around and things became so uncomfortable we were driven to find cover and discovered a cellar which we were glad to occupy. The shelling got worse the house was hit and rubble and brickwork was heard tumbling about above us and the entrance to the cellar was blocked. We were unhurt but frightened of being trapped. The officer had a torch and we looked for a way of escape and were busy tearing away at bricks and rubble when we heard shouting above and the noise of running. It was evident that an attack had been made once again on this very bit of front. We kept quiet and listened for some time, and then we heard footsteps above and voices and to our surprise and disgust, foreign voices which our officer said was German, so, there we were as good as captured. It was decided we would lie low and endeavour to crawl out when darkness came and try to reach our own lines. It would have been a very risky thing to try but we couldn't bear the thought of capture. We did not get the chance. There was some more shelling and small arms fire, more shouting and running, then activity subsided and things grew quieter. We realised that a counter-attack had been made and that it was likely our infantry had re-taken what they had temporarily lost. With some difficulty and much quiet cursing we succeeded in making an exit from our hiding place, but we were wary of emerging until we knew who we would be likely to meet. Eventually some of our own troops came near and we recognised their speech and we quietly called to them. It was some time before we could convince them of our true identity and we were under strict escort until our officer had proved our real identity.[43]

The new reliance on telephone lines, to connect the batteries with both each other and the front line observation posts, made the life of the signaller linesman responsible for laying and repairing the lines a real trial.

> Soaked to the skin again. Laid wires to all three batteries by hand. Mud too deep to allow use of telephone cart. Shall have to change our names to Samson. It certainly needs a man of muscle to get this wire

out these days. This time we had to carry a spare mile with us. To do this and lay out wire at the same time through mud nearly up to our knees was indeed a task one did not enjoy. We accomplished it however by leaving the spare mile in one position, walking on a few hundred yards laying out wire, then returning for the spare drum. This was repeated all through the chapter the only variety being the few shells sent over. Happily they did no damage and for once they allowed us to continue on our way without incident. We were certainly assisted by the mud as the majority of the shells went far into the ground before exploding. Now and then one would hit something hard and cause a devil of a roar and we would get showers of bricks, but normally it was showers of mud. We spent a lovely night trying to have a doze between us and also take turns with the phones.[44]

Signaller John Palmer, 118th Battery, 26th Brigade, RFA, 1st Division, I Corps

The wires were constantly being cut by waggon wheels or German shells. Then the signallers would have to go out from their dugout, feel along the telephone wire to locate the break and then painstakingly repair it. This was not only difficult and tiring, but very dangerous as Palmer was often working in open ground.

We were about to cross the Menin Road. The blighters commenced sending shells in twos and we had a very warm time. Several times we were forced to drop flat in the mud to avoid splinters. Once we were within a few yards of an old disused trench when we heard the warning note of a heavy one approaching. Shouting, 'Come on Jack!' my chum disappeared into the trench. I 'came on' and landed in it almost as soon as he did. I afterwards wished I had been miles away from the blooming trench. It was very deceptive. This we found to our cost when we landed nearly waist deep in water. I will not repeat the subsequent conversation. Eventually we simmered down and seeing the funny side, if there was one, both broke into a roar of laughter.[45]

If it snowed then their job just got worse and worse.

We had a nice downfall of snow and the wire was covered. This entailed following the wire by trailing it through our hands, not a very nice procedure as we soon lost the feel of our fingers. It was actually broken where it crossed the main road and Fritz was sending shrapnel right down that road at about two each minute. We both climbed a tree, one each side of the road, both of us admitted afterwards that we were really windy. It is certainly a very uncomfortable feeling being perched up a tree with shrapnel bursting around! However we managed to accomplish our task in safety and it was music to me to hear both ends in conversation when I tapped in.[46]

Palmer would find himself still carrying out the same nerve-wracking work in the Ypres salient three years later. These painful routines would become the rationale behind his very existence.

The artillery were also struggling to adapt to the corrections from the aircraft of the RFC, although in bad weather there was small chance of the flimsy biplanes being able to take off, or they were foiled by poor visibility. There was another terrible risk for the low-flying aircraft as Palmer witnessed.

A plane with the union jack and the red, white and blue circles painted underneath, was working in conjunction with one of our heavy batteries, sometimes dropping a red light, sometimes a white. The plane was flying very low, in fact only just clearing the tree tops of a wood where some thousands of our infantry were sheltering in reserve. The constant circling and the dropping of the lights must have aroused suspicion in the minds of the lads in the wood. It should be borne in mind that they had never seen a plane working in conjunction with artillery. Anyhow, the first we heard was the sudden crackle of rifle fire which was soon to increase in volume to a terrific rattle as the remainder of the infantry opened up. A staff officer ran towards them, vainly imploring them to cease firing as it was a friendly plane. I doubt if any heard – if they did they took no notice. Suddenly the firing ceased and a great cheer went up as it was seen that flames had burst out of the plane. Poor misguided fellows, they were quite convinced that they had fetched down enemy pilots who were using one of our planes. One man jumped out but was killed as he hit the ground, the other perished in the flames. Two fine men lost through a tragic blunder.[47]

As a result of such incidents the RFC introduced new red, white and blue 'target' roundels, which were easier to recognise.

THERE WAS A STEADY TRICKLE OF casualties in the trenches even when the line was 'quiet', but during an attack by either side, it was swollen into a veritable torrent. One serious wounded case was that of Captain Beauchamp Tudor St John of the 1st Northumberland Fusiliers, who had seemed to bear a charmed life since his first scrap at Mons right through to the moment he was hit in the arm and neck neat Wytschaete on 1 November. The first problem for any seriously wounded man was how to get medical treatment before it was too late.

> One moment I thought I was gone and the next as it seemed to me
> I felt as if I was away up in the high Alps somewhere breathing breath
> after breath of invigorating air. This must have been caused by the
> cessation of the bleeding which enabled me to breathe not only
> through the nose and mouth but also through both the wounds in my
> neck. It was very cold and the ground was wet and I remember having
> fits of shivering either from cold or funk or both. I could not see what
> was going on in the way of fighting but once they searched the field
> I was in with shrapnel. I watched two salvoes burst in front of me and
> then thought I would surely get my quietus but the third effort went
> over me and all was well once again. I could not use my right arm at
> all but I could wave my legs about in the air and also could manipulate
> my walking stick with my left hand. When I had been there an hour
> or two I saw some gunners at the edge of the wood. I waved both stick
> and legs at them and they stopped and conferred about me but would
> not risk coming into the open to see what I wanted. My heart sank as
> I watched them go away. Help eventually reached me through one of
> my own Sergeants who came along. He gave me water and then went
> off for stretcher bearers who arrived with a doctor about half an hour
> later. My but I was glad to see them! I lay there for I suppose about five
> hours. They cut off all my equipment and got me on to the stretcher
> and carried me to the dressing station which was about two miles away
> so far as I could judge. From the lurid language of the stretcher bearers
> it might well have been ten miles and I might have been a ton of coals
> they were carrying.[48]

The advanced dressing posts were usually located in some convenient buildings as close as was possible to the front line. Thus Captain Arthur Martin-Leake VC was located with the 5th Field Ambulance in what remained of the White Chateau at Zonnebeke.

> At present I am living in quite a good house with every comfort and
> plenty of coal in the cellar. The only disadvantage is that it has been

smashed up a good deal by shells, and we have to be content without any glass in the windows. We have shelter-pits to go to in the daytime when they begin to shell. The nights are always quiet and, when the wounded have been sent off, we have great peace and comfort. We had roast pig for dinner today. The beast was reported officially to have died from shell wounds!! It is extraordinary how often edible creatures meet this end.[49]

When Sergeant John McIlwain of the 2nd Connaught Rangers was lightly wounded in the upper left arm, he made his own way as one of the walking wounded back some 500 yards to Martin-Leake's post.

> I trudged through mud on the way back to the White Chateau at Zonnebeke, which looms wanly in the mist. We parade in a corridor for the medical officer in charge – who is Captain Martin-Leake VC. He jokes with us and raises a laugh at the expense of a poor little stout soldier who got a bullet through both cheeks of his bottom – a painful wound, 'My word, but they caught you bending!'[50]

McIlwain and the other wounded men were placed in the stable to the rear of the chateau.

> We are alert at dawn and those able to sit up talking. There are over thirty in the stable, many on stretchers, some dying with bad abdominal wounds, or heavy loss of blood. There is some shelling near but we never dream of danger. It was therefore a tremendous shock when a high-explosive shell came through the gable with a deafening concussion. I get a mass of debris, broken brick and dust full in the body, which knocks me out temporarily. I act automatically, escape from the building and wake to consciousness while running – regardless of direction – in the open, gasping for breath. A private of the Royal Army Medical Corps, himself wounded, asks me where I am going. 'Are you a Sergeant? If so look after your men! Captain Leake wants you all to get down into these trenches'. In a bad temper on finding I am still alive and capable of breathing, I bluster at the implied reproof from a private soldier. We wrangle foolishly! However, I take command of the situation as well as I can, though badly shaken, so bad I cannot overcome my instinctive fear of entering the shelter trenches in the hospital grounds. Shells are pouring into the chateau. Though I pass the order for the men to enter the trenches, I do not feel able to go myself. Since that day I know I suffer from claustrophobia.

Captain Leake comes amongst us directing the operation of removing the badly wounded. His orderly, with whom I had had words, rather conspicuously assists. Captain Leake did wonders whilst his hospital was burning and being heavily shelled.[51]

As a result of his gallantry at Zonnebeke Chateau over this period Martin Leake would be awarded the bar to his VC. The chateau had become a legitimate target for the German gunners as several French artillery batteries had moved into the area.

Every wounded man had his own story, their lives all had an intrinsic value, but many needed urgent attention and not all would get it. The doctors had to be impartial, assessing the chances of recovery, performing a simple triage on the serious cases in order to determine how to use their talents and time to best effect.

One felt that one was very glad to be so close up and to be so helpful, and yet one felt so strangely helpless. There was so much to be done, and so many for whom surgery could do so little – the abdominal cases that died so soon; the brain cases that took so long to die. And of all the dreadful wounds in war the lacerating brain wound is the most harrowing; restless, noisy, delirious, the unhappy victims struggle with the men who would restrain them, babbling of private matters, of domestic things, crying for water and yet spitting it out when brought. Morphia is useless, chloroform alone prevails to still that brain to sleep, for an hour or two, until the morphia acts. But we were never short of morphia or of chloroform; for that we can be grateful.[52]

Captain Robert Dolbey, 2nd King's Own Scottish Borderers, 13th Brigade, 5th Division, II Corps

However, sometimes a doctor could save a man by dint of his direct and skilful action. This helped make it all worthwhile for Dolbey.

Then an officer of the West Kents, Willoughby-Bell by name, was rushed to me in haste by the men of his platoon; he was bleeding furiously from a wound high up in the neck, and his carotid artery was divided. Fortunately I had a bandage and scissors in my hand, and I plugged that severed vessel against the bone of the hard palate. Very seldom is it that a surgeon has the satisfaction of knowing that he has most surely snatched a soul from death; but this satisfaction was mine.[53]

The wounds came upon them in every shape and form. Yet the doctors soon came to discern common elements in the ruined flesh that surrounded them.

> Shrapnel wounds were always bad; the round bullets of lead always ripped and tore the tissues about so terribly. The Mauser bullet did not cause nearly so much damage, but it sometimes produced very lacerating wounds. The Mauser bullet 'turns over' when travelling through a limb, and this turning means tearing of tissues on the path of the bullet, and often a huge jagged wound like that produced by an explosive bullet.[54]
>
> Lieutenant Arthur Martin, 15th Field Ambulance, Royal Army Medical Corps, 5th Division, II Corps

The shells caused indescribable injuries that took almost every imaginable form. Lieutenant Martin discovered no part of the human body was sacrosanct.

> The first case attended to was that of a young soldier of the Norfolks who had been struck by a shell in the abdomen. His intestines were lying outside the body, and loops were inside the upper part of his trousers. Under chloroform we did what we could. He died painlessly four hours afterwards. There were many bad shell wounds of the head; one necessitating a trepanning operation. One poor fellow had his tongue half blown off. The loose bit was stitched on. The compound fractures were numerous and of a very bad type, associated with much shattering of the bone. Four men died during the day, but our arrival and timely help undoubtedly saved many men. We made the poor fellows as comfortable as we could, and we were incessantly busy from the moment we entered this blood-stained place. I personally shall never forget the sight of these poor, maimed, bleeding, dying and dead men crowded together in those outhouses, with not a soul near them to help.[55]

But there were other elements that complicated the treatment of the wounded. New threats, new challenges for the medical profession to overcome. One threat lay in the soil of Flanders itself, as Martin was soon all too aware.

> Gas gangrene was one of the terrors of the doctors at this time. It was a new and totally unexpected complication of the wounds, and at first

we did not know what to do in the face of this pressing danger. The gangrene was caused by a group of bacilli called anaerobes, they are all spore-bearing, and grow in the absence of air. The soil of the trenches is full of these organisms, which, if introduced into an open wound, grow and spread and cause the limb to become gangrenous. When a man got wounded some dirt was bound to get into the wound, for the men's hands and clothes were usually caked with mud. It is a natural movement to clap a hand on the wounded spot. If a man is struck on the face or limbs, he will lay down his rifle or perhaps drop it, and at once put his hand on the injured part to ascertain the extent. It is a movement which is almost involuntary. The hands of the men in the trenches were infected with the bacilli of this gas gangrene and when these infected fingers touched a recent wound, the wound itself became infected with these highly dangerous organisms. Pieces of khaki cloth, caked in mud, were often driven into the wounds with the bullets and shrapnel, and on this cloth there were of course millions of the deadly little beasts. If the case reached us soon after the onset of gangrene a cure could almost certainly be promised. If the case arrived late, when the limbs were dead, amputation was the only 'conservative treatment' that one could adopt. Many of the cases sent to me were beyond any hope of recovery and soon died. All the cases of gas gangrene had a very penetrating putrefactive smell, which is quite characteristic.[56]

As if this was not enough, another old enemy of mankind lay lurking within the mud.

Another complication of our wounds at this time was tetanus – or the so-called lock-jaw. When tetanus manifests itself, when the convulsions and muscular spasms come on, it is a terrible malady to treat, and most of the cases die. At this time the injection of anti-tetanus serum does not ensure a recovery, but if this serum is given to every wounded man, then none will develop tetanus. When it was recognised that the bacillus of tetanus was also found in the soil of France and Flanders, efficient measures were at once adopted to combat its terrible effects. Accordingly anti-tetanus serum was provided at all the base hospitals, clearing hospitals, and ambulances, and every man wounded in France or Flanders gets an injection of this serum within twenty-four hours of the receipt of the wound. No deaths from tetanus have occurred since these measures have been adopted.[57]

The more seriously wounded undoubtedly suffered torments during the whole process of initial treatment and evacuation back to the base hospitals.

> My wounds were dressed with iodine which hurt horribly and I was given some more morphia which had no effect on me, and I was put into an ambulance which I think belonged to an Indian contingent and taken joltingly to Kemmel where I was laid in a chapel and had more iodine applied. I lay there till about 5pm when I was removed in a motor ambulance to Bailleul. It was an appalling journey for me. There were four slightly wounded 'Tommies' in the ambulance which was closed up and all the Tommies smoked Woodbines all the time and our way lay over a much damaged route pavé. Every jolt gave me 'gyp' and I was nearly suffocated and unable to speak. Every time I tried to speak the air blew out from my wounds instead of going through my larynx. By the time I reached the hospital at Bailleul was pretty nearly done. I must have looked hopeless for they did not take the trouble to transfer me from the stretcher to bed and I spent a sleepless night. Next morning I was put on board an ambulance train and sent to Boulogne. I do not remember much about the journey except that I occupied one side of a first-class carriage and a man with a disabled limb occupied the other. I must have been pretty bad because I remember that the RAMC orderly who was looking after us thought it safe enough to go through my pockets and relieve me of £10 or £12 in gold, and a few odds and ends as well. I tried to call the medical officer's attention to this when I got to Boulogne but I could not make myself heard. A strong feeling of furious indignation no doubt helped to increase my exhaustedness – at any rate when I eventually was put to bed in No. 11 General Hospital at the Imperial Hotel at Boulogne I was past knowing much about anything.[58]
>
> Captain Beauchamp Tudor St John, 1st Northumberland Fusiliers, 9th Brigade, 3rd Division, II Corps

Sister Martha Aitken was one of the dedicated staff of female nurses that had to deal with the influx of seriously wounded men back at the base hospitals. She had been posted to a new hospital established at Wimeroux in a former hotel.

> The wounds are fearful in some cases. Huge gashes. All the men without exception say it is not warfare but slaughter. The strongest

machinery against the strongest machinery. There are six bad head cases among them, the men all have huge gashes and one can see the brain pulsating when the dressing is going on. Poor men, and they make such good patients and hardly utter a groan when I am sure they must suffer agonies. One poor man was dreadfully injured. He had a compound fracture of both femurs and the left humerus as well as a hole in his head. Fortunately he soon got quite unconscious and died two days later. These men who are able to be moved are soon sent across the Channel and the others are kept here and nursed till their turn comes. How bravely they bear all their pain and even lie in bed and make jokes about what they have come through. One and all are glad to get into bed and feel that they can sleep and fear no night attack. A clean shirt and bed are all they ask. This morning one of them was sitting up in bed shaving with the aid of a piece of mirror about two inches square. He was quite happy although he had a badly fractured leg.[59]

Aitken found that around this time the concept of a 'Blighty wound' had begun to take hold amongst the men. Part humorous and part deadly serious, it was the idea of a wound sufficiently serious to get a man evacuated back to Britain, but not so bad as to cause life-threatening harm or disability.

After I had got one man into bed and clean, I was surprised to see him lying laughing to himself. On asking the reason, he said it seemed so funny to be in bed and clean after three months in the trenches. His face had been last washed twenty-one days ago and he had washed his hands on the wet grass of the battlefield. He had been wounded at Armentières and says the fighting has been awful. Poor man, he was quite deaf caused by the noise of bursting shells.[60]

Many of the casualties had serious mental traumas that were not easy to understand, being often well beyond the experience of ordinary doctors. Fortunately, many, like Lieutenant Arthur Martin, had the sense to adopt a reasonably sympathetic and patient approach.

I attended one young officer and three men who had been buried in the earth when their trench was blown up. The officer and one man were unconscious, and when the man recovered consciousness he was nervy and excitable. He had a startled, terrified expression, and when in bed he would peer round in a wild, anxious way, and then suddenly pull the blankets well over his head and curl up underneath as if anxious to shut out his surroundings, or what he thought were his surroundings. He seemed really to be living through some terrifying experiences of the past few days antecedent and up to the time when his trench was blown up and he was engulfed in the mud and debris. The officer recovered consciousness more slowly, and spoke in a curious staccato speech; his nerves were completely gone, and he had fine tremors of the lips and tongue and fingers. He told me that his memory had gone, that he had only a hazy recollection of recent things, which seemed far away and dim.[61]

Martin would become familiar with the collation of symptoms of what would be known generically as 'shellshock', which gradually became as familiar to the doctors as the more obvious physical wounds and diseases. Nervous twitches, uncontrollable shouting and screaming, night terrors, and many other afflictions were the result of mental stress and trauma.

A young officer, nineteen-years of age, was standing by a haystack in the north of France when a large 'Black Maria' burst near him, rolled him over, and plastered him with clay, but did not kill him. The concussion had thrown him down. He remained unconscious for half an hour, and when he woke to consciousness he discovered he was blind. His grief was pathetic, and one can easily understand it. A careful examination was made of the interior of the eyes with the ophthalmoscope and nothing was found wrong. He was assured by the medical officers that he would certainly recover after perhaps a week or two of blindness, that it was due to concussion of the nerve of sight, and the delicate structures at the ball of the eye; that nothing was destroyed, and that a complete rest would bring back his vision. Next day he was transferred by hospital train to the Base en route for England. This note, unknown to him, was pinned on his coat: 'Functional blindness. Any medical officer handling this officer please tell him that he will fully recover his sight!' Knowing the kind-hearted nature of the medical profession, one can be sure that he was cheered up all the way to England. I received a letter from this officer's mother some weeks after, saying that her son had completely recovered his vision.[62]

Just as some lost their sight for varying periods, so on occasion individuals lost other senses.

Several cases of deaf mutism have occurred during the hard fighting near Ypres and La Bassée, and these are certainly very curious. The men so afflicted have written down that shells burst near them, that they were thrown down, and remembered nothing more for a time. On coming to again, they were deaf and dumb. These men also show other signs of nerve shock; they are restless, troubled with sleeplessness, and have anxious expressions. Generally all get completely well in a few weeks, but some of the cases remain mute for a much longer time.[63]

Although medical officers like Martin were often sympathetic, they also at times made some underlying assumptions that sound very strange to the modern ear. Traces of special pleading and an arrogant assumption of class-based attributes were evident in some passages of Martin's memoirs.

Many officers and some men have been sent back from the front in France and Flanders suffering from nerves. These men are not 'nervous' as the public generally understand that term. They are brave and courageous men who are anxious to do their duty. I said many officers and some men have been so afflicted, and it is true that the officer is much more prone to get 'nerves' than is the simple soldier. The life of the officer is one of responsibility and worry, but the soldier's mental lot is simpler – he just does what he is told and has not to reason why. The education and upbringing of the officer are different, as a rule, from that of the soldier, and heredity has an influence on a man's nervous organisation. In civil life anyone can call to mind certain boys and girls who are more 'nervous' than others. It may be that our officers who develop neurasthenia at the front are more emotional and imaginative than those who do not, but they are no less courageous.[64]

Such inherent prejudices and preconceptions could lead to less understanding of cases that did not fit the 'pattern', and many ordinary soldiers would suffer from a failure by some doctors to recognise that the working classes could also be sensitive to the stress of modern war.

THE PROBLEM OF MANNING A FRONT line all day, every day, for an indefinite period with a finite body of men was one that made the tired heads of the brigade and divisional staff 'swim' as they tried to work out the intricacies of a policy that would work – without failure – in practice.

Should a brigade stay in one place and move battalions in and out of the line? or should a division circulate the brigades? There were arguments in favour of both points of view.

> We are apparently to stay on this line for some time and 5th Division arrangements for two brigades to be in front line and one brigade in reserve entirely throughout. Very inconvenient for troops. It would be much better to have three sections, each brigade having its own section resting. Tried to get this done but unsuccessfully. Romer, who is a moderate staff officer rather prevented it. One scheme has advantage, that you have your own trenches, communications, huts, washing arrangements, billets etc., presumably, the other is in the main impossible for all and has few, if any advantages.[65]
>
> Brigadier General Stanley Maude, Headquarters, 14th Brigade, 5th Division, II Corps

In the event the wider flexibility of moving whole brigades and divisions around would be the way forward, allowing them to have periods right out of the line for training and real rest periods away from even the longest range shells. The actual mechanics of organising a relief were of a mind-boggling complexity.

> The reliefs made one's head whirl. It was all right to start with, two battalions in the trenches (i.e., fire-trenches, support-trenches, and reserve – trenches), and two battalions in reserve at Dranoutre or thereabouts – four days about, each battalion, in eight-day reliefs, or three days about in twelve-day reliefs. This was simple. But when our line was lengthened to a three-battalion length it became much more difficult, especially when one battalion was much weaker than the other three. It was very difficult to fit everything in so that each battalion had its fair share of duty and of rest. Even with the best intentions matters did not always pan out straight, for considerations of strength, of comparative excellence, of dangerous and of safe localities, of morale, of comfortable or uncomfortable trenches, of spade-work and of a dozen other things, had to be fitted together like a Chinese puzzle. There was a particularly dangerous and uncomfortable length which was given to the best battalion to hold. On its relief, who should hold it? The next best, who was badly wanted somewhere else, or another one weak in numbers and consequently unfit? And when the relief came again, was the best battalion always to be doomed to

the worst and most dangerous trenches, merely because it was the best? Hardly an incitement to good work. And when the battalions did not fit their length, were you to add or subtract a company from somebody else, or would you put some in reserve out of their turn, thereby inflicting unfair hardship on another battalion?[66]

Brigadier General Lord Edward Gleichen, Headquarters, 15th Brigade, 5th Division, II Corps

When the men came out of the line they were not necessarily beyond the reach of tiny enemies. They soon became aware in many of their billets that 'they were not alone'.

We went back to shelters in the sparse wood on the leeside of the Scherpenberg – where we all became thoroughly 'lousy'. These shelters were in the nature of primitive huts rising three or four feet above the level of the ground with a shallow trench running down the centre of each. They would have disgraced the most primitive African kraal. Who the previous inhabitants were I do not know but they left us a heritage which we could gladly have avoided. The whole of the Scherpenberg must have been alive with body lice. They seized upon us as virgin soil and avidly planted their vile eggs in our protesting flesh. The kilt pleased them enormously, for the thickness of the cloth and the numbers of the folds in the neighbourhood of the waist, provided both 'funk holes' and heat. What more could the pioneering spirit of the enterprising louse desire? We scratched and we swore, we swore and we scratched.[67]

Private Harold Stainton, 10th King's Liverpool Regiment, 9th Brigade, 3rd Division, II Corps

Wherever possible the men would be billeted in barns, farm outbuildings, or houses in the villages located a fair distance behind the lines. The accommodation was plain enough, but welcome for all that after the hell of the trenches.

Our billets were small cottages sparsely and crudely furnished and with bare floor boards. But should we ever again experience such a feeling of luxurious indulgence as we did that evening when after a hot meal we sat playing cards in the warmth given out by the projecting stove? This was indeed paradise and for a brief period a feeling of contentment and well-being pervaded the billet.[68]

Private Clifford Lane, 1st Hertfordshire Regiment, 4th Guards Brigade, 2nd Division, I Corps

But most billets were rarely free of lice for long and this would indeed become an endemic problem. As a partial solution the army soon organised bath facilities, using existing communal facilities or impromptu arrangements to allow the men – who had had no chance to wash or bath in the line – to get cleaned up from head to foot.

Had a lovely hot bath and change of clothing this morning. On arrival at the brewery we undressed in a room taking off everything except shirt and boots. Our khaki coat, trousers and cap, less the chinstrap, were tied in a bundle and placed in a fumigator and vest, pants and socks were carted off, lice and all, for boiling. We then had to go out into the open along the towpath for about fifty yards, in full view of the ladies on the bank. We had only a shirt on and it was windy and bitterly cold so we did not loiter for their benefit. The high wind did not help our modesty. The bathtubs were large beer vats and ten men were allotted to each vat. We were soon in like a lot of excited kids. Every now and then we had a peep over the side to see if our boots were OK, as we were told they were likely to be pinched. We were now a very lousy crowd for the lack of washing had bred lice by the thousand and the surface of our bath water was soon a thick scum of these vermin. We scratched each other's backs to ease the itching. Towels and soap were ready and when we were dry we got a clean shirt. Then we had to go back along the canal bank where the girls were still waiting. It must have been very cold for them but I suppose they thought it worthwhile. We got clean underclothes and our uniforms came out all steaming hot. What a sight we looked with our clothes all creases and our caps all shapes.[69]

Private Arthur Cook, 1st Somerset Light Infantry, 11th Brigade, 4th Division, III Corps

It was an efficient process that allowed a whole company of men to be washed and changed in less than ninety minutes.

The men were not free of duties even when out at rest. Many of the simple tenets of military discipline were reintroduced to the irritation of the men.

When we were in reserve this officer decided to have a kit inspection. You had to show your emergency rations: a tin of bully, biscuits, tea and sugar. Most of them had eaten the tin of bully and the biscuits – I had as well! The punishment was this: he ordered two two-gallon jars of rum – it was over-proof rum mind you – to be brought out. There was the Regimental Sergeant Major Thompson, he had to take the cork out and they deliberately poured that four gallons of rum out there in front of our eyes. Something should have been done about that – he should have been shot. This here Thompson had his own little individual trench when we were in reserve. The next morning when he got up, about six feet from him somebody had put a tent peg with a field post card. On it was written:

This place marks the spot
Where many a young soldier lost his tot
It was poured out in damned dirty fashion
Because he'd eaten his emergency rations!

He never found out who did but he went livid! It was very appropriate wasn't it?[70]

Lance Corporal Joe Armstrong, 1st Loyal North Lancashire Regiment, 2nd Brigade, 1st Division

The continued necessity for working parties could cause friction as well, although few officers would take the robust measures adopted by the pugnacious Major Gerald Burgoyne of the 2nd Royal Irish Rifles.

This morning I saw a fatigue party marching off, the men all over the place, no discipline, and the Corporal in charge, useless. I called out to them, but one man took no notice, so I ran out and gave him two under the jaw. They pulled themselves together then and marched off something more like soldiers. On parade this afternoon I saw another man scrim-shanking. Had seen the Company parading but was 'just getting a drop of tea hotted'. I lifted him a couple of the best and kicked him till he ran, and then I spoke a few well-chosen words to the men. Told them that if they did not play the game to me, I'd lead them a dog's life, and if they 'played up well', I'd look after them well. I am sure my little show of firmness had its effect. All men like an officer who compels obedience, and it's no use punishing a man on active service as one does in peace time; the only thing is to hit him at once and hard, and if the men see their officer takes a real personal interest in them, as I think I do, or at least try to do, well these Irishmen of mine will follow me, I am sure.[71]

While they were out of the line and at rest, the men would take the opportunity to post their letters home to their families, although first they had to be read and censored by their officers.

> Every three or four days we have to censor the men's letters to see that they do not mention where we are or anything like that in them. Some of these letters are most amusing and nearly all end up with rows of crosses – for kisses – and remarks like, 'Roll on Xmas!' and 'I hope this will find you well, as I'm thankful to say, it leaves me at present!'[72]
>
> Second Lieutenant Lionel Tennyson, 1st Rifle Brigade, 11th Brigade, 4th Division, III Corps

The men were soon visiting estaminets, small cafés set up by local Belgians and French civilians with an eye of profiting from the situation they found themselves in. Drink was one pleasure that dulled the senses and provoked at least a kind of forgetting. Sex was another time-honoured release of tension – the soldier's base idea of women's war work. Then there was always the final sinful pleasure of cards.

> I began to realise the tremendous importance, amounting almost to an absolute necessity, of packs of playing cards among the troops during the war. Every odd half-hour was put into a rubber of 'Van John' as Vingt-et-un' was called among the men.[73]
>
> Private Douglas Kingsley 1st Honourable Artillery Company, 8th Brigade, 3rd Division, II Corps

Sometimes they would get a chance to play football. Kick-a-bouts were common, but Signaller John Palmer was good enough to be selected for the battery team.

> I had erected goalposts consisting of our telephone poles with tape across the top. Centre and corner flags were also in position. I had a rare job selecting my team as only one apart from myself had ever played in a match prior to the war. Our opposition were in a far better position. It was a great game and at back I had plenty to do as our opponents were pressing strongly all the time. Our goalie played the game of his life and at half time there was no score. At that period we held a confab and Lieutenant Gardner, asked me to go up forward with him. He said that between us we might score a breakaway goal or two. This proved correct as I did get the opportunity to slip the ball between

their backs for him to pounce on like a terrier and crash it between their posts for a great goal. However the 116th Battery ran out winners eventually as our defence could not stand the strain of the constant pressure. To lose by only 3-1 when some of our lads hardly knew the difference between a cricket ball and a football was not too bad.[74]

There was, however, one more fly in the ointment for Palmer and his friends, even out of the line. This was a visit by King George V. The required spit and polish proved onerous for tired soldiers.

It was darned hard on those troops who had come straight from the firing line, tired, torn out and soaked to the skin. That they should have to work from morn until night to get themselves spruced up for the inspection was a scandal. Why should he only be allowed to see us all dressed up, why not as we really were when we came out of action? If it is the wish of general headquarters, or those responsible, that he should become decidedly unpopular, well they look like getting their wish. Well, we saw the King, he was thrown off his horse, had it been one of us we should have heard a sarcastic voice shout, 'Who the hell told you to dismount?' and probably have a few extra riding school lessons thrown in.[75]

Only one thing might have cheered Palmer and his friends up: the thought that the Germans were suffering as much as they were – and in that they were surely right. The Great War inflicted misery on both sides.

Things have got very much worse: Flanders is just one great morass and all military operations have been brought to a standstill by the mud. Day and night we stand up to our knees in mud and water. We have to wrap our legs up to our thighs in sandbags just to survive. The rain pours incessantly from above, while beneath us the water-table has risen to just below ground level. The lookout positions have been raised up on stilts and the water is baled out of the trenches using pots and pans and any container to hand. If only there were such things as pumps in the trenches! In the communication trenches we have built raised walkways because it is simply impossible to drain them. On top of all this the mad gun-battle goes on across this forsaken plain, stretching out in front of us as flat as a table-top, where it is dangerous even to raise your head above ground during the day.[76]

Pioneer Friedrich Nickolaus, 53rd Reserve Pioneer Company

War, it seemed, was a hell on earth for everyone.

14

STAGNATION

The fighting around Ypres once more proved the strength which
the defence had acquired through the development of fire-power
and especially that of machine guns. The offensive had not
gained in any similar proportion. Out of this situation there
arose the long period of stagnation of the two opposing armies,
during which a new sort of warfare came into existence, the
war of position, as opposed to the so-called war of movement.
Some way had to be found which would enable the offensive to
surmount the obstacle and break through the shield which the
ground everywhere afforded the soldier – some way of dealing
at close quarters with that unreachable weapon, the machine
gun, which, even when blindly directed, inexorably swept the
battlefield with a rain of bullets. In other words, munitions had
taken on a character of vital importance in war.[1]

General Ferdinand Foch, Headquarters, Northern Group of Armies

IT MIGHT WELL BE CONSIDERED that the BEF was lucky to achieve a
state of stagnation after the terrible fighting of October and November
1914. Part of the reason they were able to survive, bolstered as they were
by copious French reinforcements, were the preparations made before the
war to augment the Regular Army on the Western Front in its time of
need. One of the most crucial interventions came from the timely arrival
of the Indian Corps (Lahore and Meerut Divisions) and the Indian Cavalry

Corps in October. Haig had laid plans for the deployment of two Indian divisions during his period as Chief of General Staff in India from 1909. The plans had been put aside on the orders of the Viceroy, who feared that such overt intentions might prove overly provocative to the Germans. They had, however, reappeared at the hour of need. The mobilisation was carried out with such efficiency that the Lahore Division was embarked on troopships at Karachi as early as 24 August. After a long voyage in convoy, they disembarked at Port Tewfik, Egypt, to spend a brief period in Cairo. They then re-embarked at Alexandria to finally reach Marseilles on 26 September. Here they were joined a couple of days later by their designated commander Lieutenant General Sir James Willcocks. Born in 1857, he had joined the Leinster Regiment, before seeing extensive active service in various colonial units and a multiplicity of campaigns across the British Empire. This marked him out as an obvious candidate to take command of the Indian Corps. After a period completing their transport provision, the first two brigades of the 3rd Lahore Division finally moved up into the front line area for the first time on 22 October.

Many of the older BEF regulars had served in India, but even for those whose feet had never touched Indian soil, there was an emotional reaction to the arrival of the long marching columns. For them this was the spirit of the Empire made flesh before their eyes.

> I happened to turn from a lane on to the straight road which connects
> Neuve Chapelle and Estaires. To my astonishment I saw a column
> of Indian infantry swinging through the flat prosaic country as
> unconcernedly as if they were marching down the Grand Trunk Road
> in the swirling dust beneath the peepal trees and brazen sun. No
> tribute could have been more fitting than that which India paid to
> the altar of the British Empire when at the hour of destiny her armed
> manhood arrived to hold the sagging line against the assaults of the
> mighty enemy. And no pathos more poignant than the fate of these
> soldiers who crossed the oceans to die in the mists of a strange land.[2]
>
> Captain Cecil Brownlow, 40th Brigade, RFA, 3rd Division, II Corps

It proved to be the Jullundur Brigade of the Lahore Division. The reinforcements were more than welcome given the desperate straits all along the II Corps line in late October. But some of the cooler heads pondered on how well the Indians would cope as winter loomed.

We knew that the Indian Divisions from Lahore and Meerut were shortly coming to strengthen this part of the line. This was distinctly satisfactory from our point of view; but I was not entirely happy, for I was very doubtful how far these untried Indian troops would stand up to what was evidently going to be a very difficult situation if the Germans went on attacking as they had been doing. Fresh troops, it is true. But they had had no experience of this sort of fighting, nor of trenches, nor of cold wet weather: and they were going to have all three.[3]

Brigadier General Lord Edward Gleichen, Headquarters, 15th Brigade, 5th Division, II Corps

The Indian troops may not have had much experience of modern warfare – heavy shell fire, machine gun bursts, aircraft up above and the siege tactics of trench warfare – that was true enough, but then neither had any of the British troops thrust into combat on the Western Front.

On 24 October, the Jullundar Brigade was moved up to relieve French cavalry units nestling between II and III Corps. Further north, one of the first real tests occurred during the First Battle of Ypres. The Ferozepore Brigade had been attached to help the 2nd Cavalry Division hold the line on the Messines Ridge. On 30 October came the splurge of heavy artillery fire that presaged one of the great German attacks. Lieutenant Harold Lewis had been in support when the attack began. His men were soon moved forwards.

On my arrival the trenches in the salient were being very heavily bombarded: many were obliterated. Captain Dill with his machine guns and most of his men were, however, still in action. I brought up two platoons from the support to reinforce but could not find a yard of trench for them to occupy. The ground was levelled. For want of a better place the men lay down in the open near the farm in the salient in which were some men of the machine-gun sections filling belts. The farm was cut in half by a shell and caught fire and the occupants burnt before our eyes. Wounded were numerous, and as, owing to casualties, stretchers had not arrived from the supports, I ran back to fetch some. Coming up again with the stretchers I saw English, Indian and German troops together coming out from the salient. These wounded and the men burnt in the farm account for most of our 'Missing' on this day.

Each man extricated himself as best he could from this melee and fell back on a position 600 yards behind.[4]

Lieutenant Harold Lewis, 129th Duke of Connaught's Own Baluchis, Ferozepore Brigade, Lahore Division, Indian Corps

By the time they fell back towards Hollebeke, the young Lieutenant was commanding his company, as Major George Humphreys[5] had been killed by shrapnel. Just a day later, Lewis would take part in a frenetic 03.00 counter-attack on 1 November, after another farm position held by the 129th Baluchis had been inadvertently delivered up to the Germans rather than the intended French relief force.

> The Colonel decided to attack the farm. I took about 150 men to the left, Potter was on the right and the Colonel in the centre. We came up quite close and rush in. The Germans rushed out and fired into us at about ten yards. I dashed down to the left to cut off any escaping, I passed an open door on the way – I saw Germans inside, so blazed off my revolver. I saw a flash and felt a blow in the stomach, then I fired again and again I saw and felt a flash – and saw I was bleeding. Then I passed the door. Well both those shots fired at five yards were smashed to fragments on the steel frame of my field glasses – and the blood was simply from the bullet grazing my right thumb. I could never imagine greater luck! I lay as close to the ground as I could because my own men's bullets were whistling over my head. I got off about seven more rounds at some of them who escaped – and the man I fired at in the farm had a bullet through his heart. We captured the farm, capturing twelve Germans, killed ten and wounded a lot.[6]

The timely arrival of the Lahore Division was followed by the Meerut Division, which had reached Marseilles on 11 October and was ready for action at the front on 29 October. That very night, they and the Jullundur Brigade were assigned to relieve the exhausted II Corps from Givenchy by the La Bassée canal in the south, past the hotly contested villages of Richebourg L'Avoué and Neuve Chapelle to run along the shallow Layes valley to the hamlet of Rouges Bancs. The influx of Indian troops certainly made an impact on Private Dominik Richert of the 112th Infantry Regiment.

> All of a sudden, we were informed that the English trench was occupied by black people – Indians. And sure enough, here and there

we noticed a turban – their head-cover. As we did not trust them, half of us had to do sentry duty at night. One dark night, suddenly one of the Indians jumped into our trench and held his hands in the air. Nobody had heard him coming. He kept pointing towards the English lines and made a sign of cutting their throats. A soldier who had signed up for a year, who understood English, was fetched, and as the Indian could also speak some English, the two of them could make themselves understood. The Indian said that he and his comrades hated the English and that they all wanted to cross over to us and fight against them. We believed him and let him go to fetch his comrades, as he had said he would do. We listened out into the night to find out whether they were coming. Soon a peal of mocking laughter showed us that the black man had really fooled us.[7]

As is often the case, rumours endowed the Indian troops with near-supernatural powers to cloak their movements in the darkness of night, as illustrated by Richert.

One night I was sent with eight others to cover the pioneers who were working out front. We stood about six metres behind them with our guns at the ready and listened out into the dark night. We could not see or hear anything. Suddenly two dreadful screams, which came from our pioneers, sounded through the night. We shot quickly into the darkness and then jumped to help our pioneers. But both of them lay on the floor of the sap, the one dead, and the other seriously wounded. Both had been stabbed by Indians who had crept up on them.[8]

The Germans were not slow to test the mettle of their new opponents, launching a series of vicious night attacks that often triggered bitter fighting lasting for several days.

In response, on the night of 9 November, the Garhwal Brigade ordered a raid by the 1/39th and 2/39th Garhwal Rifles to be carried out on a new German trench facing Richebourg L'Avoué. The task was given to Major Guy Taylor, an experienced 41-year-old career officer from the 2/39th Garhwal Rifles. He considered that this was going to be a risky endeavour.

The enemy had been making a trench parallel to ours for three or four days and I received orders to seize it and fill it in, no explosives being available. I asked for fifty men, and for a similar number from the 1/39th Garhwal Rifles to co-operate. I arranged for ten men behind each party to carry several shovels each and to follow when we had taken the trench. There being a shallow drain leading up to centre of enemy's trench, I took this as my directing mark on my right, and the l/39th G. were to keep in touch with it, keeping it on their left. The ground we had to move over was open, with no concealment but a few turnips. The ground on the right of the drain (where the l/39th were) had more cover from view, being covered with high cabbages and other vegetables. The night was clear, moonless and the distance to be traversed in the open about fifty yards.[9]

Major Guy Taylor, 2/39th Garhwal Rifles, Garhwal Brigade, 7th (Meerut) Division, Indian Corps

Some of the men were assigned to carry picks and shovels to fill in the German trench once it had been overrun. The raiders first lined up in a convenient irrigation ditch in front of the British trenches. It had been intended to launch the attack at 18.00, but frustrating delays meant that some time had elapsed before they embarked on their mission. All too aware of what would happen if they were sighted, Taylor and his men spared no efforts in crossing No Man's Land unseen.

The advance was slow as we crawled along on our stomachs, the l/39th men keeping more upright, but losing connection several times. There was no wire or other entanglement, and eventually we crawled on to the enemy's parapet itself or just below it and lay waiting for the l/39th party to join up. During our advance several rounds had been fired from their loopholes, but was evidently the usual sniping, and their sentries could not have been very alert, as though we lay on the parapet some time no alarm was raised. I could hear the Germans talking, and on being scolded by an officer or NCO they kept quieter.[10]

The tension must have been excruciating as they lay there, just yards from the Germans, waiting for the 1/39th Garhwal Rifles to get into position to their right. At last the moment came.

I fired my revolver at a German who appeared in the passage of the trench and shouted, 'Charge!' The men charged and moved further on to the parapet. Many of the enemy fired at us at close range, one round or so, and then bolted. We fired a few rounds after them, and

I fired at six men who appeared in the trench below me in turn with my revolver. We then entered the trench and my party captured at once three prisoners. On our charge the 1/39th party also cheered and advanced to the trench. I heard firing and shouting on their part. It was seven or eight feet deep, revetted, roofed, loop-holed and quite shrapnel proof. Also it was at least 150 yards long, and there was a deep, roofed communication trench leading to the rear. All this time the din was terrific: rifle, machine gun fire and now shells devoted their energies to us. Luckily, the ground being low and by keeping down and in the enemy's trenches, few casualties occurred to the 2/39th party. Seeing that to fill in the trench with the few men with me would be a task of days, not of hours, also seeing that even if we filled it in, it would be a task of no difficulty and danger for the enemy to sap again from their communication trench and make the trench as good as before in a very short time; also the fact that the fire was getting heavy, and the Germans attacking, induced me to give the order to both parties to retire. I sent the prisoners off and collected some men to carry Naik Lai Sing Bisht, who was badly wounded. We brought in one German rifle, three pickelhaubes, six prisoners and one pair of shoulder straps.[11]

Although they had only suffered four casualties, nothing much had been achieved of military value. Indeed Taylor took care to incorporate a warning for the future into his subsequent report on the raid.

In conclusion, I would mention that the trench seemed to be full of men; I presume nearly one hundred, if not more, and had they kept efficient watch or had any obstacles or warning apparatus, we must have suffered a severe loss. Now that the Germans have been warned it is not likely that a similar proceeding could be carried out again in the same way.[12]

In view of the explicit nature of his final paragraph, it is somewhat frustrating to recount that four days later a near-identical operation was launched on the night of 13 November by the 2/3rd Gurkha Rifles with the support of fifty men from the 2/39th Garhwal Rifles – led once again by Major Guy Taylor. This time they were supported by a short artillery barrage before they went over the top at 21.15. All this did was forewarn the Germans, who had augmented their defences with both a machine gun and a searchlight. The sepoys struggled across the open turnip fields under a withering fire and in the fighting that followed the Germans took a severe toll. Amongst the numerous dead was Major Guy Taylor.[13]

Both sides were engaging in this kind of harassing raid on their opponents, and on the night of 22/23 November it was the turn of the German 112th Infantry Regiment, who attacked a trench near Richebourg L'Avoué. They had borrowed one of the favourite tactics of siege warfare, digging out a series of saps, pushing them out from the German front line and deep into No Man's Land before connecting the heads of the saps to form a new front line. Having narrowed the gap to about fifty yards, a final series of saps would be pushed out to within a few yards of the Indian front line. Then another old weapon – the grenade – was put into deadly action. Amongst the attackers was Private Dominik Richert.

> From the saps, hand grenades, which I saw in use for the first time, were thrown into the Indian trenches. Then we jumped across and drove back the Indians in the trench. In a dead-end trench leading to the latrine we were able to take more than sixty of the brown fellows. One of our young Lieutenants, who had only been in action for a few days, climbed out of the trench and called to the Indians 'Hands up!' in English. But some shots were fired and the Lieutenant tumbled head-over-heels into the trench. My company, which had been brought back up to a strength of two hundred and forty men, only lost three men and the Lieutenant. In the trench lay several dead Indians; the older ones had long hair, while the younger ones' hair had been cropped short. They were all wearing new clothes and had really only been in the trenches for a short time. Scattered around in the trench were lots of new woollen blankets and lots of their food, which I could not identify. We took the English loopholes and built them in on the opposite side, facing the Indian troops, who had occupied another trench about 200 metres further back.[14]

The Germans knew that a counter-attack was all too likely; after all it was what they would have done themselves. Richert was distinctly nervous.

> I was on duty between four and six o'clock in the morning. As I did not trust the Indians, I peered out into the night. Suddenly I thought I heard a noise ahead of me. The next sentry to me, who was only two metres away, asked me whether I had had heard anything. When I said that I had, we undid our safety catches, got ready to fire and tried to

penetrate the darkness with our eyes. For about half an hour we did not see or hear anything and we were feeling more relaxed again.[15]

The attack finally burst upon them.

Suddenly the loud sound of a whistle pierced the peace of the night. At the same moment, a salvo burst close to us and with a fearful, shrill scream the Indian soldiers stormed towards us. We were completely surprised and many of us lost our wits. I quickly fired off my five bullets and then fitted my bayonet and placed myself at the front wall of the trench. The Indian soldiers were firing down into the trench, but as we pressed ourselves forward against the wall of the trench, their bullets flew over us. They could not see us in the dark trench, while we could see them clearly as they were outlined against the sky. We shot and stabbed above us and none of the Indians dared to force his way into the trench. Soon, however a terrible yelling told us that about thirty metres away from us the Indian soldiers had made their way into the trench.[16]

There was immediately panic in the German trench as they tried to get away. The frenzied mayhem of night fighting in the enclosed environs of the narrow trenches was not yet as familiar as it would become. Men were terrified, desperate to get away from the bullets and bayonets.

The Indian soldiers fired into the trench from ahead, from behind, and from the side. We all rushed towards the communication trench leading back to our previous position. The people who were hit fell and were trampled to death. Everyone was screaming and shouting. There was a terrible crowd at the entrance to the trench; everyone wanted to get through first, but the entrance was so narrow that people could only get in one at a time.[17]

After a frantic scramble both Richert and his friend Zanger managed to make it back to their former trench line, but they seemed to have lost most of their comrades. This was just another incident in the ever-unfolding pattern of trench warfare.

The Indian Corps played a truly vital role. It added two infantry divisions to the meagre strength of the BEF and relieved II Corps in the line when its fighting strength had been drained to almost nothing. Without the contribution of the Indian Corps it is difficult to imagine how the

BEF would have coped, although we must never forget that somehow Joffre may well have conjured up a couple of divisions to cover the gap. The French Army, after all, was a huge continental army, as opposed to the BEF which was being built up through a series of ad hoc measures.

THE OTHER GREAT SOURCE OF SOLACE to Sir John French was the arrival at the front of several specially selected territorial battalions. For this, too, he was indebted, at least in part, to Haig, who had played such a major role in the creation of the Territorial Force during his stint as Director of Military Training back in 1907. During the last months of 1914 no less than twenty-two territorial battalions were despatched out to the Western Front. Upon arrival, these units were placed in the line attached to regular battalions to allow them to gain the practical experience of war. Thus the regulars of the 1st East Lancashires had the territorials of the 5th (Rifle Brigade) London Regiment attached to them. Private Edward Roe was appointed to act as mentor to a young gentleman he referred to as 'Hubert S'.

> We have got to initiate them into the art of trench warfare. They soon resigned themselves to the hardships of trench – or canal – warfare. They are a fine lot of fellows, well educated. Some can speak three or four languages, all can speak French, and they have a superior bearing. Why send these fellows in to die with people who only possess Army thirds,[18] and most none at all? I do not mean that they should not die, or take equal risks, but they could be better employed and would be of more benefit to the State were they trained and employed as officers. I have shown Hubert how to make a 'Bully Beef Stew', or 'Stew-a-la-Plugstreet! I crawled out last night, got some potatoes from a pit in front of our firing line, some leeks from a cultivated patch, and commenced the stew at 11.30 am, using both our mess tins. He pronounced it, 'Top hole!' gave me his address, and when the war is over we are going to have a 'blowout' in Frascatis in Oxford Street![19]

This truly was another world for Roe to contemplate. Whether either would survive to sample the proffered 'blow out' was a moot point. Private Douglas Kingsley of the Honourable Artillery Company (despite its name an infantry battalion), was attached to the 2nd Royal Scots. Here he discovered that many of the regular soldiers had not survived the campaigns mentally unscathed.

Our first few days in the trenches were spent with the Royal Scots, to help break us in, but unfortunately for us they had suffered so heavily, and had had such a terrible time, both during and since the retreat from Mons, that they were very nervy, and far more inclined to frighten us than to steady us. However, they taught us many little 'tricks of the trade', if such a phrase may be applied to soldiering, particularly in regard to cooking our rations and keeping our rifles clean – for these men knew the value of having a ready and handy weapon.[20]

This was not an uncommon problem. Men seemed to have a limited amount of personal courage and could not endure battle indefinitely.

There was also a very real issue with the quality of the replacement drafts sent out from the regimental depots to the regular battalions at the front. Major Gerald Burgoyne was particularly scathing on this matter.

There will be heavy fighting yet before the War is over. I confess that with my company I sincerely hope I shall see little of it. So many of them are far too old and stiff to move quickly; they can't run, much less make a charge. A number of them really haven't the heart to go on, and I suppose if 20% of the Battalion advanced to the attack, it's as many as we could expect. We all loud and strong curse the War Office, the recruiting officers and the commanding officers for sending out drafts of such 'miserable things'. Why, a number of them ain't even fit for the lines of communication; simply too lazy and spiritless to do anything; a proper lot of curs; just old age and intemperance – Belfast and Dublin corner boys. A whole crowd of them, ex-regulars who were chased out of the 1st and 2nd Battalions ten or fifteen years ago, as useless. But the majority of our regular battalions now, are almost as bad, as they are all more than half 'S' reservists.[21]

Many of the men sent were the very reservists who had been too unfit or ill-trained to be sent with the original battalions in August.

An even more pressing difficulty lay in the shortage of officers. The nature of the fighting and frequent necessity for the officers to lead from the front had cut a vast swathe through their ranks. Captain Henry Jackson began to clamour to return from the RFC to his regiment, not just because it was evident that the promotion prospects for a man of his experience would be better, but because he felt that he could do more for the war effort by taking on the responsibility of command.

At the beginning of the war I would have agreed that, 'The front was the first rate club where you meet all your friends!' Every day's casualties make this less and less possible, and I dread the answer which I so often get whenever I enquire after a friend. It grieved you to see so many boys of nineteen and twenty in the list of killed. It is sad, but they can be replaced, but we have lost so terribly in senior officers, and they cannot be replaced. A Divisional General like Hubert Hamilton, a Brigadier General like Charles FitzClarence, a Colonel like McMahon, a staff officer like Jenkinson – and all the good regimental officers – cannot be replaced by boys from Sandhurst. I don't think that I am exaggerating when I say that there is not a single regiment out here commanded by a Colonel. I have just been down to the Adjutant General's office to see the casualty lists for the last fortnight. Both our battalions have lost heavily – and at the moment I should be commanding the one and second in command of the other! Can you wonder that I have again asked to be allowed to go back? Here I command nothing. Don't think me discontented. I know that I should be of more use there than I am here – now that we have so much bad weather. I have a certain power of command over men – the great essential in a regimental officer as opposed to a staff officer. You will also appreciate what the regimental tie is – the nearest approach to a family tie there is.[22]

The shortage of officers caused anxiety throughout the BEF. Given the severe losses and the awful conditions in the trenches, the men needed good leadership more than ever.

We had suffered fearful casualties and the proportion of losses in officers was higher than in any other rank, and it was going on every day. I was really positively at my wits' end, suffering almost agony, to know where I could get officer reinforcements. You all know how any fighting force must deteriorate, and deteriorate badly, unless this supply of officers is kept up properly and regularly.[23]

General Sir John French, General Headquarters, BEF

These serious losses amongst the officer corps were exactly what Haig had – rightly or wrongly – been concerned about in early August 1914, fearing the consequences of expending valuable resources before the full strength of the British Empire could be deployed in battle. Yet French managed to come up with a coherent solution after being impressed by what he had seen and heard of the 28th (Artists Rifles) London Regiment. He believed that this elite Territorial Force unit was full of the 'right sort' of men to provide officers for the denuded regular battalions. Lieutenant Colonel Henry May described French's proposal.

> I would undertake to pick out the very best men we had in the regiment, and, I assured him, every officer and NCO in the regiment would assist me to select the best. I reminded him that our men had had no extensive military training, only what a good territorial regiment can give to its men in times of peace, added to a few weeks of practical experience since mobilization, but I informed him that I would personally guarantee that every man I sent him would be of the proper class, and would, 'play the game', also that I would guarantee his character as a man, his 'grit', his common sense; that he would always behave himself as an officer and a gentleman, and that except for his want of military training, he would never let down the regiment he might be posted to, or give them any occasion to be ashamed of him. It was thereupon arranged that I should at once select fifty young men – roughly, one for each company in the 7th Division – who were to join their respective regiments as officers at once, i.e., the same day. Lord French agreed with me that it would be better not to denude our battalion by sending away any of our officers, or, except in special circumstances, our NCOs. I then enquired if I was to have the power to at once make officers of the young men selected, and to put a star on their shoulders before they left us, as I thought this would make all the difference to their reception by their new units – i.e., that they should join as officers, and not as young men who hoped someday to be made officers.[24]
>
> Lieutenant Colonel Henry May, 28th (Artists Rifles) London Regiment

The officers generated by the Artists Rifles were a considerable success, and subsequently the battalion was utilised as an Officers Training Corps based at Bailleul. Such measures helped, but were only the start of an ongoing process that would eventually see a less class-based orientation to officers' messes later in the war. First the products of good grammar schools, then the educated clerical and commercial classes, finally anyone who showed leadership and dash – all could be promoted to feed the need for officers.

THE ACCEPTANCE OF STALEMATE IN THE long term was not really in accordance with British military doctrine as expressed in Field Service Regulations Part I. It was considered that standing on the defensive was only a temporary expedient, for battles could not be won by standing fast. 'Every commander who offers battle, therefore, must be determined to assume the offensive sooner or later.'[25] It was accepted that when faced with overwhelming numbers, defence was the only sensible option, but if the battle, or war, was to be won, then one must attack eventually. The question – given the existence of German trenches, barbed wire, machine guns and artillery – was how? Despite his relatively lowly level in the scheme of things, even Private Edward Roe of the 1st East Lancashires could see the problem.

> Brigadier Hunter Weston is a constant visitor and is a source of worry to his staff as he always hangs about the most dangerous points. He remarks to us as he strolls along the trench, 'Well lads you're going through it here, but I'll let you get your own back, I'll let you in with the bayonet on the first opportunity!' Dear old Hunter – we've been 'in with the bayonet' – we know what it means! Cavalry and infantry charges are a thing of the past, unless you have an overwhelming preponderance of artillery. Mud, barbed wire, magazine rifles and machine guns have shorn cavalry and bayonet charges of all their glamour and glory. Hunter dear, we may take a couple of hundred yards of waterlogged ditch, but our losses are out of all proportion to our gains.[26]

Even organising a small-scale raid was a real challenge. Brigadier General Stanley Maude had been promoted to command the 14th Brigade, when he found that he was required to take action to identify the German units facing them across no man's land.

> General Morland came at about 10 and is anxious that we should attack one of the German trenches so as to get a prisoner. Somewhat a mad scheme involving certain loss while the prisoner will be a doubtful quantity. Some of the higher commanders have not got down to sufficient bedrock to realise the difficulties arising from darkness, or moonlight, wire entanglements, exposed stretches of ground over which advance has to be made, use of illuminants by enemy etc., to say nothing of the difficulty of preventing our own men from firing into each other. However, am quite ready to take it on and do the best we

can. My only point is that the game scarcely seems worth the candle. But careful reconnaissance and careful plans are essential to ensure success or minimise the risk of failure. So asked that I might put it off till tomorrow night. As a matter of fact the trench is opposite the Norfolks on our left and they belong to the 15th Brigade. But we can do it by arrangements with them. My proposal approved. Had conference of three Commanding Officers at Wulverghem at 5.30pm to formulate our plans and impress on them the necessity for reconnaissance of the various points to be studied.[27]

The raid was carried out by the 2nd Manchesters on the night of 9 December. Lieutenant Williamson and forty-five men crept out at 18.30 to attack a trench some 300 yards away. Despite his reservations, Maude had done his level best to gain success.

Manchesters carried out the operation (to attack a German trench) which Sir Horace and General Morland were anxious for them to do. Quite futile of course and had no results. Planned it very carefully to give it best chance of success possible. Bedfords to support them with fire on their left if necessary and Devons sent two platoons forward and machine guns to occupy position to support them on right if necessary. From report received, platoon got up to trench and got through a wire entanglement, but were stopped by a second and had to retire losing one officer and one man wounded and five men missing.[28]

This chastening experience was probably on Maude's mind when he put forward his own ideas on how a successful attack could be achieved. At every level of command, the more intelligent officers were putting their minds to solving this most intractable of problems.

Wrote to divisional headquarters to say that, in view of shortage of howitzer ammunition, in my opinion best way to attack would be to send men forward under cover of darkness to cut enemy's wire. Then for assault to be delivered in the half-light in morning, or by moonlight just after moon had risen, attacks to be continuous over as long a front as possible consistent with our strength both in men and guns and not piecemeal. Artillery to give the signal to commence attack by a salvo as nearly as possible at a given time and to fire at will over the heads of the infantry.[29]

It is interesting to see that Maude, as an intelligent officer, has already felt his way to an appreciation that narrow-front attacks merely allowed the Germans to concentrate their fire on the attacking troops from both the front and both sides. Yet tucked away in his note were the words 'consistent with our strength both in men and guns'. Wide-frontage attacks demanded large numbers of troops, guns and ammunition. None of these were available. Furthermore any gap torn in the German front line would be fairly easy to plug by the Germans with local reserves until a counter-attack could be organised. A few days later came a request that showed that the risk of localised attacks had not yet been realised by his superiors.

> Towards evening 5th Division asked whether we could take an odd trench opposite us. Replied that we certainly could if desired, but that we should not be able to hold it permanently in all probability and that net result would be nil except for casualties. Suggested that if necessary to attack at all along our front, we should make a general attack along whole line, as being the only sound military proposition.[30]

By the middle of December, the desire to show a more offensive spirit was beginning to take hold. Smith-Dorrien found himself selected to take the plunge.

> Towards the middle of December the Chief decided that we should make an attack with a view to effecting a lodgement on the Wytschaete Ridge. The day selected was the 14th December. I had had conversations with General D'Urbal, the commander of the French Army on my immediate left, and with General Grossetti commanding the XVI French Corps, the corps actually touching me and on the 12th Grossetti had dined with me to discuss details. We concluded dinner by drinking, 'The King'. I was to conduct the operation as far as the British troops were concerned. Besides my own corps I was given extra guns and a reserve of 6,000 dismounted men of Allenby's Division.[31]

It was not French that had initiated these operations. They originated in orders from Joffre for a wide-ranging offensive designed to pin the German Armies to the Western Front in an effort to prevent them reinforcing to any great extent their forces on the Eastern Front. Major attacks were to be launched by the French Tenth and Fourth Armies in the Artois and

Champagne sectors, respectively. To disperse the German efforts across as wide a region as possible, secondary operations were also to be undertaken by the French Second and Eighth Armies – it was as part of this subsidiary effort that the BEF were to make an attack. It is crucial to realise that the BEF was not at the epicentre of affairs, but right on the periphery of events. The intention was to launch an attack by the 8th Brigade, which, given success, would then stretch southwards to take the whole of the Messines Ridge. This was extremely ambitious. Smith-Dorrien was by no means enamoured at the prospect that lay before his men and by no means surprised by the overall failure of the operation on 14 December in the Locre sector, when it was launched at 07.45 by the 1st Gordon Highlanders against the bare knoll of Maedelstede farm, while the 2nd Royal Scots attacked the Petit Bois trenches. Although the artillery of three divisions was directed against the objectives, this merely flattered to deceive as the bombardment only lasted forty-five minutes due to the terrible shortage of ammunition. As Smith-Dorrien recounts the attempt was a debacle.

> It was an exceedingly difficult position to attack. The enemy's trenches were mostly on higher ground than ours, and had a fine field of fire, especially at what was known as Hill 75, whilst our troops had to cross an open valley except opposite the Petit Bois. The state of the ground was awful, knee-deep in mud. My headquarters were on a prominent hill called the Scherpenberg. It was decided that to cross the open ground would be impossible until we had entered the Petit Bois and got forward in it, and until the French on our left had made headway. I had about 180 guns, and at 7am on the 14th all of them bombarded, and at 7.45 the Royal Scots and Gordons rushed forward into Petit Bois and towards Maedelstede farm to the south of it. The Royal Scots and left of the Gordons established themselves in the Petit Bois, but the right of the Gordons could not make much headway against the many hostile machine guns across the open ground in spite of the most devoted efforts; for our bombardment had not been very effective.[32]

Later in his career, Smith-Dorrien looked back on the operation with some dismay.

> Later on in the war we should never have attempted such an operation without a much more serious artillery preparation and many more

troops. Personally I had never been in favour of the attack, and did
not expect it to be successful. The French made no headway at all.
That afternoon another attempt was ordered by the Commander in
Chief, and from 3.30 to 4.15pm another intense bombardment took
place and apparently our infantry made a successful advance, but after
dark I found they had, except in the Petit Bois, to fall back on their
own trenches. I then went to General Grossetti's headquarters, to find
the French had failed too, with 600 casualties. Next day the Chief
decided that another attempt to get forward would be useless unless
the French made headway, and, as they made none, our men remained
in their trenches and the attempt to get forward was given up. As a
matter of fact, the French on our left had come to the conclusion that
any further attempt at a direct attack was useless, and had decided to
devote themselves to working forward by sapping, an operation which
was possible for them, as the ground in their area was better drained
and of a more solid nature than in ours. Getting possession of the Petit
Bois had, however, been an important gain – but our casualties in the
two days had been nineteen officers and 499 men. I consider we got out
of it very lightly in view of the nature of the enterprise.[33]

From afar, Haig took a waspish view of the attack by II Corps, but he, like
Maude, was obviously aware of the futility of such a narrow front attack.
Furthermore, it is clear that Haig too was working towards possible solutions.

Very little energy displayed by the 8th Brigade of the 3rd Division,
II Corps in pressing the attack. Their methods are much the same as
at Spion Kop and Vaal Krantz in South Africa where the whole Army
looked on at a couple of battalions attacking. So at Le Petit Bois the
attack was made by the Royal Scots and Gordon Highlanders, and
when the latter lost some 200 casualties, operations ceased, and the
Gordons fell back to their original trenches! In my opinion there are
only two ways of gaining ground either, (a) a general offensive all along
the front, with careful preparation of artillery at special chosen points
in order to dominate the enemy's artillery at specially chosen points,
[and] use of trench guns, mortars, hand grenades, etc. to occupy the
enemy's attention everywhere, and press home in force at certain
points where not expected. The other method (b) is to sap up, as in
siege warfare. This is a slow business especially in wet ground. It is sad
to see the offensive movement by the British Army 280,000 strong
resolve itself into an attack of two battalions![34]

The tragedy of the Great War was that while the generals wrestled with these complex problems, the men in the trenches paid a grim price in blood when things went wrong. After 14 December, the repercussions of the slaughter of the Gordons lingered on for days. In the early afternoon of 17 December, Major Gerald Burgoyne of the 2nd Royal Irish Rifles (who had taken over the front line) discovered a desperate wounded survivor still trapped in no man's land.

> A moment ago word was given up to me that there was a wounded Gordon in front crying for help. I ran up the line, stripped off my overcoat and had a look, and sure enough saw the poor devil's face about fifty yards in front of us, just beyond our wire entanglements, peering over the top of a shell hole. At my call all the men near volunteered to fetch him in. I took two and went out to him. We found the poor fellow, shot in the groin, lying in the muddy water of a shell hole, and had been there since Monday! My two men picked him up, and wound or no wound, ran him smartly into our trenches, where he stood a moment and stoutly cursed the Gordon Highlanders for leaving him there. He was so grateful to us.[35]

Even that was not the end of it. Next day another Gordon was heard moaning from amidst the corpses that littered No Man's Land. This time Burgoyne followed Major Arthur Festing out into no man's land.

> Festing crawled out. I at once followed and fell over him and nearly yelled with fright; thought I was on top of a huge corpse. After a hideous crawl on hands and knees through a turnip field we found the two men, amid an awful stench; discovered one man was reclining on a very dead German. They were nearly done, and had had no food since Monday, the 14th, except the tea given them yesterday morning. Festing sat down with them and sent me for the stretchers. He remained an hour and then returned to me. No word of the stretchers. We dozed all through the night and at dawn I told him we must get them in in ground sheets. So out he and eight men went again, I staying inside to assist them over the parapet and after nearly 115 hours lying wounded and starving out in the winter damp and cold, these poor fellows reached the dressing room station. One man was hit in the groin, and the other in the knee, and it must have hurt awfully bringing them in over the parapet, poor fellows.[36]

What the wounded suffered lying out for three to four days in the freezing cold of No Man's Land is almost beyond comprehension.

A similar narrow-front attack was launched on 16 December by the Ferozepore Brigade on two German saps in the Givenchy sector to the right of the Indian Corps sector. The 129th Baluchis were to lead the attack, racing across a narrow No Man's Land of just twenty-five to thirty-five yards, going over the top at 06.30 well before dawn. Digging parties would stand ready to connect the front line to the saps once they had been overrun.

> The method of attack was similar against each sap-head, viz. the four platoons of a company to issue from our trenches one after the other, to charge down on either side of the sap, and to seize the points in the enemy's trench where the saps joined it. The attack was timed to take place as soon as the light was enough for the men to distinguish their objective, of which they had otherwise no knowledge, nor had they seen the ground. Both companies were timed to start at the same moment. This time was altered by 10 minutes owing to one company going wrong in the darkness so that it was nearly light when the attack started. Only two platoons could be packed into the front trench; the other two platoons were placed in the support trench, from which each platoon in turn filed into the front trench, extended and went forward. The first two platoons went forward on the minute, and in each case made good the sap-head and the major portion of the sap. The third platoon also made good, and a few men succeeded in reaching the main trench. By the time the fourth platoon was in position to go forward it was daylight, and the enemy brought a heavy cross-fire with machine guns to bear on the spaces between the sap-heads and trench. Both platoons lost heavily; a few men did reach the sap-heads.[37]
>
> Major John Hannyngton, 129th Duke of Connaught's Baluchis, Ferozepore Brigade, Lahore Division, Indian Corps

Although they had taken the two saps, the Baluchis then found they were trapped. This exemplified the problem with narrow-front attacks: shot at from three sides they were totally isolated. Under such heavy fire, the digging of the communication trenches from the Indian lines across No Man's Land out to the saps was excessively costly. Meanwhile the Germans were counter-attacking, feeling their way forward through the trenches amidst vicious bomb and bayonet fighting. Sadly, the Baluchis had very few hand grenades, which made their position even more tenuous.

> For some three hours before darkness fell, we watched them from loopholes, imprisoned in the German sap-head. A German arm appeared above a traverse, a bomb was thrown, a scuffle among our men, and perhaps the bomb was thrown out to explode immediately just outside. Lance-Naik Sahib Jan on several occasions relieved the situation by charging single-handed with fixed bayonet down the sap. And all the time we, in our trench about twenty yards or so away, were digging like maniacs, but otherwise powerless to help, except by raising cheers to keep up their spirits and to make the Germans less cock-a-hoop.[38]
>
> Lieutenant Harold Lewis, 129th Duke of Connaught's Baluchis, Ferozepore Brigade, Lahore Division, Indian Corps

In the end the right sap would be abandoned. Of the eighty men who had occupied the sap, only eighteen would return. After much severe fighting the forty-yard sap on the left was successfully connected to the British lines.

> The sap was packed with the living, the dead and men. As I went along I remember the advice given me by the sepoys I met, 'You can walk on him, Sahib, he is dead! No, not on that one, he is terribly wounded but not dead yet!' They were so packed one could not get along in any other way.[39]
>
> Captain Ronald Davies, 129th Duke of Connaught's Baluchis, Ferozepore Brigade, Lahore Division, Indian Corps

A follow-up attack on the morning of 18 December failed to achieve much improvement in the position, but on 20 December the Germans struck back. After a heavy artillery bombardment they charged forward to deadly effect. The shock of it threw the Baluchis into a state of total confusion.

> The right and centre companies of the firing line suddenly appeared retiring in good order. Some of the men said the order had been given to retire by a British officer, but I could not discover whether such order had been given or not. Anyhow the Germans were on the top of

them; their rifles missed fire owing to having no bolt covers, and the only thing to do was to continue the retirement holding on to every bit of cover until the canal was reached. Artillery support was almost nil owing to lack of ammunition and want of communication, due to the destruction of the telephone wires. Owing to the surprise of this retirement some documents were left behind in the drawer of a table in the regimental headquarters and the loss was not discovered till late in the evening. One of the regimental signallers who was employed in the office volunteered to go up to Givenchy that night, and although the place was in the hands of the Germans he succeeded in rescuing the papers and returned with them in the early morning.[40]

Lieutenant Colonel Southey, 129th Duke of Connaught's Baluchis, Ferozepore Brigade, Lahore Division, Indian Corps

In these small-scale affairs, the Germans had a supreme advantage in their possession of a dominating mass of artillery, coupled with plenty of hand grenades, which it was already apparent would be crucial in close-quarter trench fighting.

UP AND DOWN THE LINE, SENIOR officers of the BEF were coming to terms with the situation that faced them. But their attempts to solve the problem were handicapped by the scale of the resources that would be required to make any serious impression on the German lines. The French, on the other hand, still had some spare military capacity. During December 1914 they had launched a series of full-scale offensives on the German lines. On 17 December the Tenth Army attacked in the Artois region with the intention of wresting the heights of the Vimy Ridge from the Germans. Like the Germans, they too sapped forward across No Man's Land to reduce the distance to be covered in the open by their attacking troops. they also amassed their guns to deliver what it was hoped would be an utterly devastating artillery bombardment before the infantry went over the top. A second offensive began on 20 December 1914 when the Fourth Army of some 258,000 troops backed by over 700 guns attacked on a twenty-five-mile front in the Champagne area. The end result was piecemeal gains, but they could not break through the German trench lines. Already the French had moved to the next stage of development of trench warfare: a starkly attritional method of warfare, seeking to use the power of the guns to blast their way through. But for every minor advance, there was a vicious German counter-attack, small villages, woods, and hills of previously negligible importance became the focus of severe fighting, with casualties measured in thousands upon thousands. All seemingly for nothing. The British did not have the men, guns, or munitions to participate in such fighting. Many of the officers were well aware that much more would be required before the war was done.

> What we want out here are, men, guns and ammunition – not cigarettes and mufflers! The sooner England wakes up to this serious state of things, and to what is really demanded, the better. The country seems to think (from reading the papers) that all is going well and that the war will be over in six weeks or two months. It will last at least another year. I do not mean to say that things are going badly or that we are beaten by any means, but we are only hanging on by the skin of our teeth, and if we want to attain decisive results we must have many more men, and the country must exert itself to provide them.[41]
>
> Major General Hubert Gough, Headquarters, 2nd Cavalry Division

On a visit back to London in early December, Haig tried desperately to get George V to understand the stern nature of the fighting, drawing on the vivid experiences during the First Battle of Ypres to impress on his monarch that not all of the troops could stand up to the terrors of war.

> The King seemed very cheery but inclined to think that all our troops are by nature brave and is ignorant of all the efforts which Commanders must make to keep up the 'morale' of their men in war, and of all the training which is necessary in peace in order to enable a company for instance to go forward as an organised unit in the face of almost certain death. I told him of the crowds of fugitives who came back down the Menin road from time to time during the Ypres battle having thrown everything they could, including their rifles and packs, in order to escape, with a look of absolute terror on their faces, such as I have never before seen on any human being's face.[42]

Haig was not a man to let grass grow underfoot. On 24 December, he held a conference of his divisional commanders and key officers from the specialist arms to thrash out the best method of carrying on operations under the new conditions. Here he sums up the discussion.

We discussed:

1. a) Trenches. Size, depth and state, nature of revetment etc.
   b) Care of men. Not to put into wet trenches up to their knees in water as has been done in parts of this front.
2. Nature of Defence
   It must be active, otherwise enemy will advance and blow in our trenches with minenwerfer as he did to the Indians.
3. Trench Mortars. Personnel to be gunners or specialists.
4. Hand Grenades. Keep enemy at a distance as long as possible. Use outposts entrenched.
5. Local Attack. As in the old days Bomb throwers. Bayonet party. Attacking body, with flank detachments etc.
6. General attack. I asked General Officers Commanding to get to know the ground so as to be ready for a general advance when the time comes.[43]

These are not the reactions of men hidebound by tradition, or unable or unwilling, to understand the new state of warfare that had engulfed the BEF.

The same day, 24 December, also saw Wilson receive a great disappointment in his ongoing campaign to replace the underperforming and exhausted Murray as Chief of Staff. Wilson's response as recalled in his diary is surely indicative of both his character and the dysfunctional nature of the GHQ.

> Sir John sent for me at 10.20am. He said that no man had ever given another more loyal and valuable help than I had given to him. He said so long as he was alive and had power my future and my promotion were assured. He went on in this way for some time and then came to the real point. He said the Government and Kitchener were very hostile to me. They said my appointment would be very repugnant to the Cabinet and would shatter confidence in the Army! That I was the principal cause of all the Ulster troubles and was therefore dangerous. In short neither Kitchener or 'Squiffy'[44] will have me. I feel highly complimented and told Sir John so. I care not a rush for the opinions of either of these two men.[45]

The hapless Murray was thus temporarily confirmed in his position, although he would shortly afterwards be replaced by the far more magisterial figure of Sir William Robertson in January 1915. Robertson began a process of reform to the dysfunctional clutter that was the GHQ, having taken the wise precaution of first removing Wilson as 'Sub-Chief'.

Even as these military and 'political' discussions were going on, the BEF was expanding around them. Indeed, with the arrival of the 27th Division, Sir John French was able to begin forming a new V Corps, which meant that the original two corps of the BEF had swollen to a total of six corps, which was far too great a burden for the GHQ to shoulder. On 26 December, the situation was rationalised with the formation of the First and Second Armies, each reporting directly to French at GHQ. The First Army would be commanded by Haig, the Second Army by Smith-Dorrien. And there was more to come, much more. Yet the vast expansion that was already underway brought other problems in its train. Who would lead the new armies, corps and divisions? There was a serious lack of officers with sufficient operational experience, coupled with the capability, intelligence and steely nerves necessary to step up to these levels of command. Indeed, how were the great masses of partially trained recruits, not really soldiers yet at all, to be turned into warriors capable of facing the most dangerous opponent in the world – the German Army? And then there were disquieting rumours that the politicians were looking for an easier way to victory, one that involved attacking almost anywhere, or anyone, but the Germans on the Western Front. Haig had good reason to be worried.

> Lord Kitchener has recently published in the press that six armies
> will be formed each of about three corps! We all think that these
> new formations with (rather elderly) doubtful Commanders and
> untrained staff a great mistake. It was folly to send out 'the New Army'
> by divisions and armies. Much better to send out battalions, or even
> brigades, for incorporation in our existing divisions and corps. C-in-C
> wished to say he had the Army Commanders in agreement with him
> on this. We all quite concurred, and thought that the new corps and
> new armies [which are insufficiently trained] might readily become
> a danger! French also read a letter from Kitchener in which the latter
> hinted that his New Army might be used better elsewhere than on the
> eastern frontier of France. A suggestion was made of co-operating with
> Italy and Greece. I said that we ought not to divide our military force,

but *concentrate on the decisive front* which was on this frontier. With more guns and ammunition, and more troops we are bound to break through.[46]

Thus many of the key themes of the Great War were already being explored at the end of 1914. It would be a gargantuan conflict, involving millions at the front, the mobilisation of whole populations behind the wheel of conflict. The intractable problems of trench warfare were apparent; what was not yet so obvious was the malleable resistance of the German Army. This was not a static problem with a single solution. This was an interminable struggle, with constantly evolving defence tactics that thwarted every new tactical initiative. But before that fateful year ended, there was an unimportant event that the sentimentalists would assert indicated that somehow the men in the trenches did not really feel a real hatred towards each other, that perhaps the war was all just some kind of terrible mistake.

1. Generals pondering. Left to right: General Sir Douglas Haig, Major General Charles Monro, Brigadier General John Gough and Brigadier General Edward Percival. (© IWM, Q54992)

2. Field Marshal Sir John French on his arrival at Boulogne at 17.00 on 14 August 1914. (© IWM, Q55512)

3. General Sir Horace Smith-Dorrien commanding II Corps in August 1914. (© IWM, Q70054)

4. General Alexander von Kluck, commander of the German First Army, August 1914. (© IWM Q52083)

5. Lieutenant General Sir Douglas Haig commander of I Corps. (George Grantham Bain Collection, Library of Congress, LC-DIG-gg-bain-18014)

6. General Helmuth von Moltke (the Younger) German Chief of the General Staff. (George Grantham Bain Collection, Library of Congress, LC-DIG-ggbain-16768)

7. A German troop train. (© IWM, Q81763)

8. Germans of the 47th Infantry Regiment. (© IWM, Q53422)

9. The 9th Lancers arriving at Mons on 21 August 1914. (© IWM, Q83051)

10. Private Carter of the 4th Middlesex Regiment on sentry duty, 22 August 1914. (© IWM, Q70070)

11. Men of 4th Royal Fusiliers resting in the Grand Place at Mons on 22 August 1914. Next day they would be fighting for their lives in the Battle of Mons. (© IWM, Q70071)

12. Officers of the 1st Cameronians in conference before the Battle of Le Cateau on 26 August 1914. (© IWM, Q51480)

13. Driver Job Drain of 37th Battery, RFA who was awarded the VC for his courage at the Battle of Le Cateau on 26 August 1914. (© IWM, VC349)

14. Atmospheric photo of the 1st Cameronians on the march on 6 September 1914. (© IWM, Q51486)

15. Men and horses at rest of the 11th Hussars, 2 September 1914. In the foreground is Captain Charles Mulholland. (© IWM, Q51224)

16. British 18-pounder guns in action during the Battle of the Marne, 8 September 1914. On the left are men of the 1st Cameronians. (© IWM, Q51488)

17. The pontoon bridge used by the 2nd Division to cross the Aisne River in September 1914. The old demolished bridge is seen in the background. (© IWM, Q54988)

18. A British cavalryman and his horse taking a break. (© IWM, Q53324)

19. Sergeant Clifford Malins and Second Lieutenant James Nicholl of the 1st Cameronians looking for snipers in the wonderfully named 'Cabbage Patch Trench', 5 November 1914. (© IWM, Q51524)

20. Men of the Royal Naval Division in their trenches at Vieux Dieu at Antwerp, 7 October 1914. (© IWM, Q14774)

21. British, Belgian and French soldiers fraternising together. (© IWM, Q53334)

22. Indian soldiers of the 129th Baluchis in trench on the outskirts of Wytschaete in October 1914. (© IWM, Q60744)

23. An Indian cavalryman at Messines, October 1914. (© IWM, Q56301)

24. Wounded men of the 7th Division in October 1914. (© IWM, Q57209)

25. Wounded heroes 'after the battle'. (George Grantham Bain Collection, Library of Congress, LC-DIG-ggbain-17239)

26. Men of the 2nd Scots Guards carrying out a reconnaissance toward the village of Gheluvelt on 20 October 1914. Shortly after this photo was taken Drummer Charles Steer was killed by a shell. (© IWM, Q57222)

27. The corpse of Drummer Charles Steer lying in the field. He was buried in the German cemetery of Kruiseecke and subsequently reburied in the Zantvoorde British Cemetery. His parents were Sidney and Gertrude Eleanor Steer, of 71, Coulsdon Rd., Caterham, Surrey. (© IWM, Q57224)

28. Men of the 2nd Royal Scots Fusiliers in the trenches. (© IWM, Q49104)

29. Men of the 1/5th London Rifle Brigade resting in a dugout at Ploegsteert Wood. (© IWM, Q11727)

30. View across No Man's Land taken from trenches held by the 1st Royal Scots Fusiliers. The German trenches run along the line of trees. (© IWM, Q49102)

31. Men of the 1st Cameronians in the trenches at Houplines in December 1914. (© IWM, Q51550)

32. Officers' mess of the 1st Cameronians at Houplines on 18 November 1914. (© IWM, Q51528)

33. Men of the 1st Cameronians in the trenches at Houplines in December 1914. (© IWM, Q51558)

34. British 18-pounder in action in the Ploegsteert Wood sector, October 1914. (© IWM, Q51223)

35. A British 18-pounder and crew in a gun emplacement in the Armentieres sector, 7 December 1914. (© IWM, Q51542)

36. Machine gunners of the 11th Hussars in the trenches at Zillebeke in the Ypres sector. (© IWM, Q51194)

37. British and German soldiers fraternising in No Man's Land at Ploeg-steert Wood during the Christmas Truce. (© IWM, Q70074)

15

CHRISTMAS TRUCE

Xmas morning in the trenches. Just imagine our feelings when
we thought of home and looked at our bleak surroundings.
A yard or so from where I was standing a German soldier had
been buried, and his foot had actually been sticking out in our
trench until we had covered it up with earth. The stench at times
was almost unbearable, and the trenches were infested with huge
rats who fed off the corpses.[1]

Sergeant Frederick Brown, 1/2nd Monmouthshire Regiment, 12th Brigade,
4th Division

BY LATE DECEMBER THE WAR had been raging for nearly five months.
If anyone had really believed that it would be 'all over by Christmas'
then it was clear that they had been cruelly mistaken. With the strength
of Imperial Germany now evident to all, there appeared to be no chance
of victory in the foreseeable future. By this time men were beginning,
almost despite themselves, to gain a kind of grudging respect for their
opposite numbers lurking across No Man's Land. They were enduring the
same terrible weather, the same dreadful living conditions and, after all,
they had managed to fight each other to an absolute standstill. The earlier
rumours of atrocities, knavish tricks and the callous use of 'dum-dum'
bullets had abated, as more experience was gained of the destructive
power of high-velocity bullets, shrapnel bullets and shell fragments when

they smashed into the frail human body. The war had become the new reality for countless men, as they were wrapped up into the stultifying routines and deadly horrors of trench warfare. There seemed to be no respite in sight, but it was critical to maintain a high level of watchfulness, or else the consequences were often fatal.

> The absence of shellfire made our fellows a bit careless I think, and the German snipers took full advantage of this. In shallow parts of our trench, unless one ducked when passing along it, the head would be brought above the top of the parapet. Only for a second or two perhaps, but in that brief moment the crack of a rifle would be heard and another of our chaps had paid the penalty for being careless. These snipers seldom missed. Their guns were fixed during the day to aim at a certain spot, and then during the hours of darkness they would fire at short irregular intervals, hoping to catch some of us who were moving about. We lost a lot of men sniped, among them my chum Frank. On the night of December 21st a ration party returning along our trench let slip that the snipers had caught three more of our chaps in 'D' Company, and I pricked up my ears when I heard my chum's surname mentioned. There was only one man of that name in the battalion: it was him alright. I got further particulars and found that he had been shot clean through the head and had collapsed and died without a sound. It was a shock to me, and I was not able to see the rough wooden cross that marked his grave till some days later. When I did the ground was under a foot of water, and just the tap of the cross showing, made from old ammunition boxes, trimmed up with a jackknife or bayonet. I read the inscription marked on the rough wood with indelible pencil: 'RIP, Pte. F. Toull, 2nd Batt. Bedf. Regt. Killed in Action. Dec. 21st. 1914.' With mixed feelings I thought of his parents at home and wondered how I was to inform them, for I knew that my letter would be the first intimation of his death, and not till some time later would the official notice from the War Office be despatched. One's thoughts were, always, not so much for the man killed, who was beyond all need for sympathy, but for those left behind to mourn him.[2]
>
> Private William Quinton, 2nd Bedfordshire Regiment, 21st Brigade, 7th Division, IV Corps

The unfortunate Private Frank Toull is now buried in the Rue-David Military Cemetery.[3] It would be a miserable Christmas for his parents living in Tottenham when they got that letter from Quinton.

Amidst the continuing fighting, there was also a growing evidence that in some localised sectors of the line, the two sides were edging to a modus vivendi that helped ameliorate some of the worst aspects of trench life. Many Germans could speak English and there had been a fair number of German soldiers who lived and worked in Britain before the war. Sometimes it seemed almost natural for an attitude of 'live and let live' to creep in. Breakfast time seemed to be quieter, latrine breaks were respected, and men engaged in mundane tasks were left in peace. Soldiers would shout banter to each other across No Man's Land, and there were even rumours of informal shooting contests at impromptu targets displayed in each other's trenches. Such behaviour attracted the attention of Smith-Dorrien, who issued orders to try and eradicate such relaxed practices.

> Experience of this, and every other war proves undoubtedly that troops in trenches in close proximity to the enemy slide very easily, if permitted to do so, into a 'live and let live' theory of life. Understandings – amounting almost to unofficial armistices – grow up between our troops and the enemy, with a view to making life easier, until the sole object of war becomes obscured, and officers and men sink into a military lethargy from which it is difficult to arouse them when the moment for great sacrifices again arises. The attitude of our troops can be readily understood and to a certain extent commands sympathy. So long as they know that no general advance is intended, they fail to see any object in undertaking small enterprises of no permanent utility, certain to result in some loss of life, and likely to provoke reprisals. Such an attitude is, however, most dangerous, for it discourages initiative in commanders, and destroys the offensive spirit in all ranks. The Corps Commander, therefore, directs Divisional Commanders to impress on all subordinate commanders the absolute necessity of encouraging the offensive spirit of the troops, while on the defensive, by every means in their power. Friendly intercourse with the enemy, unofficial armistices (e.g., 'we won't fire if you don't' etc.) and the exchange of tobacco and other comforts, however tempting and occasionally amusing they may be, are absolutely prohibited.[4]

It is interesting to note the understanding tone taken in this order: this was not the knee-jerk reaction of high command of popular imagination.

On 24 December there was a severe frost and in some places it began to snow. As the water froze in the trenches around their feet, the troops seemed to have little, or nothing, to look forward to. From the perspective of the trenches of the Western Front, the onset of Christmas – the season of peace and goodwill to all – seemed almost surrealistic. Peacetime Christmas celebrations seemed a world away. Nevertheless, that day, Leutnant Walther Stennes noticed a distinct change in the tempo of the war. In German households it was traditional to celebrate on Christmas Eve; that was when families would open their presents and have a celebratory dinner.

> On Christmas Eve at noon, fire ceased completely. We had received mail from Germany, there were heaps of parcels coming in. Later on when it became dusk we opened the parcels and tried to be a little like at home – write letters. Of course it was unusual that the opposite side also ceased fire because they always maintained sparse rifle fire. Then my officer controlling the sentries came in and asked, "Do you expect a surprise attack? Because it's very unusual the situation?' I said, 'No I don't think so! But anyhow everybody's awake, no one is sleeping and the sentries are still on duty. So I think it's alright!' The night passed, not a single shot was fired.[5]
>
> Leutnant Walther Stennes, 16th Infantry Regiment, 27th Brigade, 14th Division, VII Corps, Sixth Army

The British too were being inundated with letters and parcels containing presents from home. There was even a special gift commissioned for every soldier originating from Princess Mary – a tin containing tobacco, cigarettes, or sweets, amongst other ephemera that would be issued on Christmas Day to troops in the field. All told, there was a strange atmosphere – an awareness that something was in the air. The question was what? Perhaps a gesture of friendship, but equally possible was a sudden deadly attack to capitalise on the kind of lethargy identified by Smith-Dorrien. As they pondered, there were strange sights and sounds emanating from the German trenches.

> Something in the direction of the German lines caused us to rub our eyes and look again. Here and there showing just above their parapet we could see very faintly what looked like very small coloured lights. What was this? Was it some prearranged signal, and the forerunner

of an attack, or was it to make us curious and thus expose ourselves
to a sudden raking of machine gun fire? We were very suspicious and
were discussing this strange move of the enemy, when something even
stranger happened. The Germans were actually singing! Not very loud,
but there was no mistaking it. We began to get interested. The enemy
at least were going to enjoy themselves as much as the circumstances
would permit. Suddenly, across the snow-clad No Man's Land, a strong
clear voice rang out, singing the opening lines of 'Annie Laurie'. It was
sung in perfect English and we were spellbound. No other sound but
this unknown singer's voice. To us it seemed that the war had suddenly
stopped! Stopped to listen to this song from one of the enemy. Not a
sound from friend or foe and as the last notes died away a spontaneous
out-burst of clapping arose from our trenches. Encore! Good old Fritz![6]

Private William Quinton, 2nd Bedfordshire Regiment, 21st Brigade, 7th
Division, IV Corps

There were several reports of trees being erected in the German front lines
to brighten up the dark miserable night.

Then suddenly lights began to appear along the German parapet,
which were evidently makeshift Christmas trees, adorned with lighted
candles, which burnt steadily in the still, frosty air! Other sentries had,
of course, seen the same thing, and quickly awoke those on duty, asleep
in the shelters, to 'come and see this thing, which had come to pass'.
Then our opponents began to sing 'Stille Nacht, Heilige Nacht. This was
actually the first time I heard this carol, which was not then so popular
in this country as it has since become. They finished their carol and we
thought that we ought to retaliate in some way, so we sang 'The First
Noel', and when we finished that they all began clapping; and then
they struck up another favourite of theirs, 'O Tannenbaum'. And so it
went on. First the Germans would sing one of their carols and then
we would sing one of ours, until when we started up 'O Come All Ye
Faithful' the Germans immediately joined in singing the same hymn to
the Latin words 'Adeste Fideles'.[7]

Rifleman Graham Williams, 5th (London Rifle Brigade) London Regiment,
11th Brigade, 4th Division, III Corps

It was ironic that several much-loved 'British' Yuletide customs, including Christmas trees and coloured fairy lights, had been imported from
Germany during the Victorian era through the influence of Prince

Consort Albert of Saxe-Coburg and Gotha. In some sectors there was no doubting the underlying friendly intent, and soon there were fraternal demonstrations from both sides.

> Here were the 'Deutchers', who are supposed to regard us with bitter hate, first of all shouting across at us. One of our fellows yelled out, 'Come and have a drink!' The answer was, 'Come and have some plum pudding!' Then we called out, 'Waiter!' Answered by, 'How do you like your eggs boiled?'[8]
>
> Lieutenant Wilfred Barham, 1st East Kent Regiment, 16th Brigade, 6th Division, III Corps

Shouting out invitations and merry quips was all very well, but the men that took the initiative in initiating the truce were brave – or foolish – men. To show themselves above the parapet meant breaking the ingrained habits from painful experiences of the accuracy of snipers. Still, the distinct signs of a thaw in relations meant that some men were tempted to test the waters, despite the obvious risks. Curiosity was like a naked flame burning within them. What were their foes really like? Did they suffer equally from the torments of trench warfare? Were they really the monstrous pikelhaubed creations of propaganda? Or just ordinary soldiers like themselves? Yet the risks were still very real, as was illustrated when Sergeant Frederick Brown of the 1/2nd Monmouthshire Regiment watched Sergeant Frank Collins take his first steps out into no man's land.

> A rumour went round that an armistice was to take place from 9am until 12 noon, in order that the Germans could bury their dead, who were lying between the trenches. Really this was necessary, as when the wind was in our direction the stench was pretty bad, in fact some of it was present all the time. About 8am voices could be heard shouting on our right front, where the trenches came together to about thirty-five yards apart, German heads appeared, and soon our fellows showed themselves and seasonal greetings were bawled back and forth, evidently Xmas feeling asserting itself on both sides. Presently, a Sergeant Collins stood waist high above the trench waving a box of Woodbines above his head. German soldiers beckoned him over, and Collins got out and walked halfway towards them, in turn beckoning someone to come and take the gift. However, they called

out, 'Prisoner!' and immediately Collins edged back the way he had
come. Suddenly a shot rang out, and the poor Sergeant staggered back
into the trench, shot through the chest. I can still hear his cries, 'Oh
my God, they have shot me!' and he died immediately.[9] Needless to
remark, every head disappeared in a trice with very bitter feelings on
our part.[10]

This was not a unique occasion. Despite the friendly overtures on the
front of the East Kent Regiment, there was a breakdown in trust, and
Lieutenant Wilfred Barham's mood soured in a savage moment.

One of my Sergeants woke me up with, 'A Merry Christmas, Sir, under
the circumstances, this morning!' I asked him what was the matter
with the circumstances. 'Too beastly cold, sir!' Twelve o'clock. One silly
fool has just tried to go over to their lines; absolute madness, because
sniping has been going on; he got about fifty yards when they shot
him. That did not matter so much, but a Corporal started out to fetch
him in, and he was shot through the head as soon as he put it over the
parapet – he was killed instantly. I have just been up there and could
hear the other man groaning, but he deserved every bullet he got. At
5.30 two men brought the fellow in, but he died soon after; he was hit
in three places.[11]

Here there was now little sympathy for those trying to institute a truce.
Yet, despite the obvious risks with occasional outbursts of firing emanating from up and down the line, men were still tempted into making
approaches to their enemies. Individuals would get out of the trench,
then dive back in, gradually becoming bolder.

We'd been standing up on the firing parapet and nobody was shooting.
So one or two fellows jumped out on top; another two stopped in the
trench with their rifles ready. But they didn't need. As these two fellows
got up others followed and there were scores of us on top at the finish.
It was grand, you could stretch your legs and run about on the hard
surface. We tied an empty sandbag up with its string and kicked it
about on top – just to keep warm of course. And Jerry – he was sliding
on an ice pond just behind the line – we could tell the way he started
off, went so gently across to the other end and then another followed.
We did not intermingle. Part way through we were all playing football,
all on top. Some Germans came to their wire with a newspaper, they

were waving it. A corporal in our company went for it, went right to the wire and the Germans shook hands with him, wished him 'Merry Christmas' and gave him the paper. Of course we couldn't read a word of it so it had to go to an officer. It was so pleasant to get out of that trench from between them two walls of clay and walk and run about – it was heaven.[12]

Private George Ashurst, 2nd Lancashire Fusiliers, 12th Brigade, 4th Division, III Corps

In the sector held by the 2nd Royal Welsh Fusiliers, the officers had issued stern orders that there was to be no fraternisation. But would the orders hold? The mists that wreathed the ground around the low-lying valley of the River Lys meant that no one realised what was happening until after lunch.

The sergeant on duty suddenly ran in and said that the fog had lifted and that half a dozen Saxons were standing on their parapet without arms, and shouting that they did not want to fight. I ran out into the trench and found that all the men were holding their rifles at the ready on the parapet, and that about half a dozen Saxons were standing on their parapet and shouting, "Don't shoot! We don't want to fight to-day!"[13]

Captain Charles Stockwell, 2nd Royal Welsh Fusiliers, 19th Brigade, 6th Division, III Corps

For a moment the situation stood in the balance: then Stockwell reports the Saxons made an offer that broke the ice; unquestionably it was an offer that some of the Welshmen could not resist.

The Saxons began shouting, 'Don't shoot, we will bring you some beer if you will come over!' Whereupon some of our men showed above the parapet and waved their hands. Then the Saxons climbed over the parapet and trundled a barrel of beer to us. Then lots of them appeared without arms and of course our men showed themselves. Then though we had been warned that the Germans would attack us, two of our men broke out of trench and fetched the barrel. Then another broke out and brought back a lot of cigars. All the Saxons then came out of their trenches and called out to us to come across.[14]

In places the festivities took on an a more cultural tone as the finest singers on both sides vied in their performances.

> All our men got out of their trenches and sat on the parapet, the Germans did the same, and they talked to one another in English and broken English. I got on top of the trench and talked German and asked them to sing a German *Volkslied*, which they did, then our men sang quite well and each side clapped and cheered the other. I asked a German who sang a solo to sing one of Schumann's songs, so he sang *The Two Grenadiers* splendidly. Our men were a good audience and really enjoyed his singing. The Germans sang, *Die Wacht Am Rhein*, it sounded well. Then our men sang, *Christians Awake*, it sounded so well. It was a curious scene, a lovely moonlight night, the German trenches with small lights on them, and the men on both sides gathered in groups on the parapets.[15]
>
> Captain Reginald Armes, 1st North Staffordshire Regiment, 17th Brigade, 6th Division, III Corps

Although such friendly overtures and resulting fraternisation in No Man's Land were not universal, there is no doubt that a fair proportion of the British battalions in the front line, particularly in III and IV Corps areas, were involved to some degree. Some officers tried to direct what was going on, but they were soon swept along by the press of events. One such was Lieutenant Sir Edward Hulse of the 2nd Scots Guards.

> By 8am there was no shooting at all, except for a few shots on our left. At 8.30am I was looking out, and saw four Germans leave their trenches and come towards us; I told two of my men to go and meet them, unarmed (as the Germans were unarmed), and to see that they did not pass the halfway line. We were 350–400 yards apart at this point. My fellows were not very keen, not knowing what was up, so I went out alone, and met Barry, one of our ensigns, also coming out from another part of the line. By the time we got to them, they were three-quarters of the way over, and much too near our barbed wire, so I moved them back. They were three private soldiers and a stretcher bearer, and their spokesman started off by saying that he thought it only right to come over and wish us a happy Christmas, and trusted us implicitly to keep the truce. I was dressed in an old stocking-cap and a man's overcoat, and they took me for a corporal, a thing which I did not discourage, as I had an eye to going as near their lines as possible![16]

Hulse returned to the trenches after giving instructions that the Germans should not be allowed past a house that marked the halfway point across No Man's Land. Then he went back to report to his battalion headquarters. On his return, he found that the truce had moved on apace in his absence.

> I was surprised to hear a hell of a din going on, and not a single
> man left in my trenches; they were completely denuded (against my
> orders), and nothing lived! I heard strains of *Tipperary* floating down
> the breeze, swiftly followed by a tremendous burst of *Deutschland über
> Alles* and as I got to my own company headquarters dugout, I saw, to
> my amazement, not only a crowd of about 150 British and Germans
> at the halfway house which I had appointed opposite my lines, but six
> or seven such crowds, all the way down our lines, extending towards
> the 8th Division on our right. I bustled out and asked if there were
> any German officers in my crowd, and the noise died down (as this
> time I was myself in my own cap and badges of rank). I found two,
> but had to talk to them through an interpreter, as they could neither
> talk English nor French. They were podgy, fat bourgeois, looking very
> red and full of sausage and beer and wine, and were not over friendly.
> I explained to them that strict orders must be maintained as to meeting
> halfway, and everyone unarmed; and we both agreed not to fire until
> the other did, thereby creating a complete deadlock and armistice – if
> strictly observed. These two fat swine would vouchsafe no information,
> and, beyond giving me a very nasty cigar, did nothing, and returned
> to their trenches. Meanwhile Scots and Huns were fraternizing in the
> most genuine possible manner.[17]

With, or without, the presence of officers and NCOs, the truce proved to be an organic process, taking on its own impetus and expanding beyond the control of individuals. It was not planned or controlled, it just happened. That it was the same for both sides was vouchsafed by Leutnant Walther Stennes of the German 16th Infantry Regiment.

> The whole thing was an absolutely spontaneous action. Not even the
> officers knew anything about it. When I rushed out of the dugout,
> I found many of my company standing in the open, waving and
> saying, 'Merry Christmas!' On the other side some Indians were
> standing up and waving! The men hesitantly advanced to the middle,
> first hesitating, then later on stepping freely forward and in the middle

of No Man's Land they met, shook hands and then began talking. Then more men came out. Suddenly No Man's Land was covered with Indian and German soldiers. I met some English officers, we shook hands, offered cigars and talked as much as we could. Anyhow we understood each other. Of course everybody was unarmed – not even a knife – that was given out as a rule. But the sentries they were standing on duty, rifle at the ready on both sides.[18]

There is no doubt that precautions were taken in the opposing trenches against the very real possibility of betrayal. Chastened by the death of their comrade, many of the Monmouthshires would remain on their guard against any more of the 'mistakes' of the kind that had cost Frank Collins his life. Certainly Sergeant Frederick Brown was unimpressed by the belated German overtures.

Later, in spite of what had happened, at 9am all shooting stopped and Jerry came out in hundreds into No Man's Land, ostensibly to bury their dead. Actually all they did was to collect up rifles and equipment, and to fraternize with a lot of our chaps, who also went out| mostly to collect souvenirs in the shape of helmets, etc. Cigarettes were exchanged, apologies made for the shooting of Collins and general conversation took place. It was surprising how many of the enemy could speak English. They were mostly Bavarians, and were of good physique, and outnumbered us by at least three-to-one. I did not leave the trench myself, feeling too sick at what had happened to Collins and thinking some of us had better be ready in case of any other treacherous act.[19]

Even senior officers recognised that there was little that could be done in this strange state of affairs. Brigadier General Lord Edward Gleichen accepted the truce as a fait accompli, but was still keen to ensure that the Germans did not get too close to allow them a view of either the ramshackle British trenches or indeed how few men were left to defend them. He saw this as a very practical reason for allowing his men to meet the Germans halfway across no man's land.

They came out of their trenches and walked across unarmed, with boxes of cigars and seasonable remarks. What were our men to do? Shoot? You could not shoot unarmed men. Let them come? You could not let them come into your trenches; so the only thing feasible at the moment was done – and some of our men met them halfway and began talking to them. We got into trouble for doing it. But, after all, it is difficult to see what we could otherwise have done, unless we shot the very first unarmed man – who showed himself – *pour encourager les autres*; but we did not know what he was going to do. Meanwhile our officers got excellent close views of the German trenches, and we profited accordingly; the Bosche did not, for he was not allowed close enough to ours.[20]

As the troops fraternised, the British officers certainly took unfair advantage, covertly trying to determine what they could about the state of the German defences and to judge the state of their morale. Second Lieutenant Bruce Bairnsfather of the 1st Royal Warwicks was almost unrecognisable as an officer in his filthy khaki uniform, sheepskin coat and balaclava helmet.

I joined the throng about halfway across to the German trenches. It all felt most curious: here were these sausage-eating wretches, who had elected to start this infernal European fracas, and in so doing had brought us all into the same muddy pickle as themselves. This was my first real sight of them at close quarters. Here they were – the actual, practical soldiers of the German army. There was not an atom of hate on either side that day; and yet, on our side, not for a moment was the will to war and the will to beat them relaxed. It was just like the interval between the rounds in a friendly boxing match. The difference in type between our men and theirs was very marked. There was no contrasting the spirit of the two parties. Our men, in their scratch costumes of dirty, muddy khaki, with their various assorted headdresses of woollen helmets, mufflers and battered hats, were a light-hearted, open, humorous collection as opposed to the sombre demeanour and stolid appearance of the Huns in their grey-green faded uniforms, top boots, and pork-pie hats. The shortest effect I can give of the impression I had was that our men, superior, broadminded, more frank, and lovable beings, were regarding these faded, unimaginative products of perverted kulture as a set of objectionable but amusing lunatics whose heads had got to be eventually smacked.[21]

Second Lieutenant John Wedderburn-Maxwell gained a rather better impression of the Germans he encountered while acting as a forward observation officer for his artillery battery in the Laventie sector.

I met a small party and they said, 'Oh, come along into our trenches and have a look at us!' I said, 'No! I'm quite near enough as it is!' I gave them some English tobacco they gave me something German. One was an American; another was a waiter at the Ritz! There were several of them talked to me, who talked quite a bit of English. They looked very good: well turned out, clean, good uniforms, healthy – they looked all right. Some very young; one or two very young ones, eighteen if not younger. We just said how bloody it was in that mud; how we hated it all. They said, 'We are Saxons – you are Anglo-Saxons – why are we fighting! The Russians can't fight, the French won't fight, and you're the only people who do fight, why are we doing it?' We laughed and chaffed each other for about half an hour in No Man's Land! We then we shook hands, wished each other luck! One fellow said, 'Will you send this off to my girlfriend in Manchester?', so I took his letter, franked it and sent it off when I got back![22]

Second Lieutenant John Wedderburn-Maxwell, 5th Battery, 45th Brigade, RFA, 8th Division

Lieutenant Sir Edward Hulse was also probing away for low-level intelligence as he chatted to the Germans he encountered as he strolled about in no man's land.

The little fellow I was talking to, was an undersized, pasty-faced student type, talked four languages well, and had a business in England, so I mistrusted him at once. I asked them what orders they had from their officers as to coming over to us, and they said none; that they had just come over out of goodwill. They protested that they had no feeling of enmity at all towards us, but that everything lay with their authorities, and that being soldiers they had to obey. I believe that they were speaking the truth when they said this, and that they never wished to fire a shot again. They said that unless directly ordered, they were not going to shoot again until we did.[23]

Hulse also had a very interesting exchange of views concerned the use of dum-dum bullets, although the two sides could not quite agree.

We talked about the ghastly wounds made by rifle bullets, and we both agreed that neither of us used dum-dum bullets, and that the wounds are solely inflicted by the high-velocity bullet with the sharp nose, at short range. We both agreed that it would be far better if we used the

old South African round-nosed bullet, which makes a clean hole. I told
them of various sweet little cases which I have seen for myself, and
they told me of English prisoners whom they have seen with soft-nosed
bullets, and lead bullets with notches cut in the nose; we had a heated,
and at the same time, good-natured argument, and ended by hinting
to each other that the other was lying![24]

Another practical reason for embracing the truce was the opportunity it
presented for burying the dead that littered No Man's Land. Both sides
had emotional and practical reasons for clearing away the corpses. Private
William Quinton of the 2nd Bedfords was one of those sent out on a
burial fatigue party that Christmas morning.

As daylight crept in, we were surprised to see the Germans waist-high
out of their trenches, gazing across at us with impunity. Imagine
the position: whereas yesterday the mere sight of a bit of field-grey
uniform would have caused a dozen British rifles to crack, here was
the enemy in full view of us, gazing serenely across No Man's Land
at us, and we at him. To us in the front-line the whole world had
changed. We could take stock of our surroundings at our leisure. At
9 o'clock precisely, the German burying party climbed from their
trenches, shovels and picks on their shoulders. They advanced about
ten yards in our direction and waited expectantly. A word from our
company officer and our party were soon out. The officers looked on
apparently conversing, The digging party soon lost interest in their
task and before long were busy fraternising. Cigarettes were being
exchanged and they seemed to be enjoying themselves immensely!
Needless to say, before very long we in the trenches were soon out on
top, sauntering about in the snow, but keeping this side of our wire
entanglements. Likewise the Germans. For the whole of that day and
for many days to come, friend and foe mixed freely out on No Man's
Land. Except for the fact that a few of the enemy could speak a little
English, we found the language difficulty a bar to conversation, but
we made do with signs and gestures. I remember distinctly a German
holding out an opened box of chocolates for me to take one! The
Germans wanted to play us a football match on No Man's Land, but
our officers would not allow it![25]

Private Henry Williamson of the 5th (Rifle Brigade) London Regiment
was also assigned to a burial party in No Man's Land. This miserable task

even triggered a somewhat philosophical debate with a German soldier, a trenchant exchange of views that seems to have given Williamson some pause for thought.

> The Germans started burying their dead which had frozen hard, and we picked up ours and we buried them. Little crosses of ration box wood were nailed together, quite small ones, and marked in indelible pencil. They were putting in the Germans, 'Für Vaterland und Freiheit!' 'For Fatherland and Freedom!' I said to a German, 'Excuse me, but how can you be fighting for freedom? You started the war, and we are fighting for freedom!' He said, 'Excuse me English comrade, but we are fighting for freedom for our country! I have also put, "Here rests an unknown hero known to God!" Oh yes, God is on our side!' But, I said, 'He is on our side!' And that was a tremendous shock – I began to think that these chaps were like ourselves and who felt about the war as we did. They said, 'It will be over soon because we shall win the war in Russia!' And we said, 'No, the Russian steamroller is going to win the war in Russia!' 'Well, English comrade, do not let us quarrel on Christmas Day!'[26]

The idea that football matches were played between the British and Germans in No Man's Land has taken a strong hold, but the evidence can now seem a little intangible. Yet there are several semi-feasible accounts, including one interview recorded in the 1960s by Leutnant Johannes Niemann of the Saxon 133rd Regiment, who told of a game with Scottish Highlanders in No Man's Land between Frelinghien and Houplines.

> A Scottish soldier appeared with a football which seemed to come from nowhere and a few minutes later a real football match got underway. The Scots marked their goal mouth with their strange caps and we did the same with ours. It was far from easy to play on the frozen ground, but we continued, keeping rigorously to the rules, despite the fact that it only lasted an hour and that we had no referee. A great many of the passes went wide, but all the amateur footballers, although they must have been very tired, played with huge enthusiasm. Us Germans really roared when a gust of wind revealed that the Scots wore no drawers under their kilts – and hooted and whistled every time they caught an impudent glimpse of one posterior belonging to one of 'yesterday's enemies'. But after an hour's play, when our commanding officer heard

about it, he sent an order that we must put a stop to it. A little later we drifted back to our trenches and the fraternisation ended. The game finished with a score of three goals to two in favour of 'Fritz' against 'Tommy'.[27]

Another impressionistic oral history account was supplied by Private Ernie Williams of the 1/6th Cheshire Regiment.

The ball appeared from somewhere, I don't know where, but it came from their side – it wasn't from our side where the ball came. It was a proper football. They took their coats off some of them and put them down as goalposts. One fellow went in goal and then it was just a general kick about. I should think there would be at least a couple of hundred taking part. I had a go at it – I was pretty good then at nineteen. Everybody seemed to be enjoying themselves. There was no sort of ill-will. There were some of the Germans could speak English, I don't think many of our side could speak German! No referee, we didn't need a referee for that kind of game. It was like playing as a kid in the streets, kicking the ball about and the referee being the policeman and chasing you off. There was no score, no tally at all – it was simply a melee. As far as I was concerned it didn't last a long time, I'll be quite frank I didn't trust them.[28]

However, the bulk of games reported in eyewitness accounts seem to have been confined to impromptu games on their own side of the wire. Whatever the truth about the fabled football matches, one strange sporting episode in No Man's Land was recorded – indeed triggered – by Lieutenant Edward Hulse.

An old hare started up, and seeing so many of us about in an unwonted spot, did not know which way to go. I gave one loud 'View Holloa!' and one and all, British and Germans, rushed about giving chase, slipping up on the frozen plough, falling about, and after a hot two minutes we killed in the open, a German and one of our fellows falling together heavily upon the completely baffled hare. Shortly afterwards we saw four more hares, and killed one again; both were good heavy weight and had evidently been out between the two rows of trenches for the last two months, well fed on the cabbage patches, etc., many of which are untouched. The enemy kept one and we kept the other.[29]

Apparently neither side had entirely lost their zest for blood sports.

Of course not everyone was involved in the truce and some battalions remained collectively aloof, rising above such dalliances. Private Clifford Lane and his comrades were simply not in the mood for a truce after what, by any standards, was an extremely trying day.

> About an hour before dawn on Christmas day we set out to relieve the Grenadier Guards who were holding the line near the Rue du Bois. Our section was detailed to occupy what was described as a sap head in No Man's Land. This was in fact a natural drainage ditch which ran from our forward trench right into the German front line with a sandbag block midway. The communication trench from the support line to the forward trench was almost knee-deep in water and the water in the forward trench itself came well over the ankles, but in order to reach the sandbag block at the sap head we had literally to wade through water waist-high. Two men were stationed at the sap head and the rest were strung out at intervals along the ditch and told, to take up positions on the bank. We were warned to keep down as low as possible as two men on the bank had been shot through the head the previous day. The bank consisted of slimy mud and our constant struggles to avoid sliding into the water, while at the same time keeping sufficiently low to prevent offering a target to enemy snipers took on the quality of a nightmare. We all survived however, and when relieved by another section after dark returned to the forward trench, soaked to the waist and plastered with mud as we were, the few inches of water in this trench seemed comparatively comfortable and later we were able to dry out by standing round a brazier. We were now ready to enjoy what the English newspapers described as our Christmas dinner! This consisted of the usual bully beef and hard biscuits with the addition of a lump of cold Christmas pudding about the size of a tennis ball. There wasn't even a rum issue! The night was completely silent apart from the occasional rifle shot fired by a nervous sentry, but towards midnight there seemed to be some commotion in the enemy trenches and shortly afterwards a Chinese lantern was raised above the enemy parapet and shouts of, 'Zum wohl!'[30] were heard. We were immediately ordered to open fire, and thus, what was undoubtedly a friendly gesture was brutally repulsed.[31]

> Private Clifford Lane, 1st Hertfordshire Regiment, 4th Guards Brigade, 2nd Division, I Corps

This unfriendly attitude was the case where the British battalions were facing Prussian units, who were generally considered far more dangerous opponents than the Saxons or Westphalians. In fact, Haig's I Corps was unaffected by the truce, as was most of Smith-Dorrien's II Corps.

The truce lasted for a varying amount of time. In some areas it was just Christmas Eve or Christmas Day itself. But elsewhere the truce endured for several days. Thus Josef Wenzel was surprised to find a state of truce existing when his unit moved up into the line at 04.00 on 26 December.

> I expected to come under heavy fire, but to my astonishment there was no firing. The men we relieved explained to us that they had swapped things with the British and I should not have believed it, had I not found proof in the form of some English cigarettes in my dugout, which I much enjoyed. Hardly had day dawned than the British began to wave to us and our men returned the gestures. Gradually they left their trenches. Our men took out a Christmas tree complete with candles, which they placed on a wall and lit up. They then rang bells and everyone moved out of their trenches; nobody thought of opening fire. That which only hours ago I should have thought was nonsense I now saw with my own eyes. A British soldier, who was then joined by a second man, came from our left and crossed more than halfway into No Man's Land, where they met up with our men. British and Bavarians, previously the worst of enemies, stood there shaking hands and exchanging items. More than half of my platoon went out. Because I wanted to take a closer look at these chaps and obtain a souvenir, I moved towards a group of them. Immediately one came up to me, shook my hand and gave me some cigarettes; another gave me a handkerchief, a third signed his name on a field postcard and a fourth wrote his address in my notebook. Everyone mingled and conversed to the best of their ability. One British soldier played the mouth organ of a German comrade, some danced around, whilst others took great pride in trying on the German helmets. One of our man placed a Christmas tree in the middle, pulled out a box of matches from his pocket and in no time the tree was lit up. The British sang a Christmas carol and we followed this with, 'Silent Night, Holy Night'. It was a moving moment; between the trenches stood the most hated and bitter enemies and sang Christmas carols. All my life I shall never forget the sight.[32]

> Josef Wenzel, 16th Bavarian Reserve Regiment, 6th Reserve Division, XIV Reserve Corps

Indeed, once the truce was established, the new status soon achieved a strange 'normality' for those taking part. However, other motivations lurked below the surface as both sides seized the opportunity to bring up supplies of building materials and set to work on improving their sorry trenches. Hulse was typical of this pragmatic approach.

> We improved our dugouts, roofed in new ones, and got a lot of very useful work done towards increasing our comfort. Directly it was dark, I got the whole of my company on to improving and remaking our barbed wire entanglements, all along my front, and had my scouts out in front of the working parties, to prevent any surprise; but not a shot was fired, and we finished off a real good obstacle unmolested. Although I do not trust them a yard, I am convinced that all they want is to see us making ourselves thoroughly comfortable and to assure themselves that we are not going to attack; so much so, that I honestly believe that if we had called on them for fatigue parties that night, to help us put up our barbed wire, they would have come over and done so. They are, I am sure, pretty sick of fighting, and found the truce a very welcome respite, and were therefore quite ready to prolong it; in fact made us prolong it by continually coming to talk. One way and another, they were quite ready to have a respite and to improve their own comforts and trenches like us.[33]

It is crucial to realise that, for the vast majority of the participants, the truce was a matter of convenience and maudlin sentiment. It did not mark some deep flowering of the human spirit rising up against the war or signify political anti-war emotions taking root amongst the ranks. The truce simply enabled them to celebrate Christmas in a freer, more jovial and, above all, safer environment, after all the exhausting torments they had been enduring. It also allowed them to satisfy their natural curiosity about the Germans. Finally, it let them to carry out vital construction works, which would have been nigh impossible under the constant threat of snipers.

In these circumstances the truce could not last. It was a break from reality, not the dawn of some brave new peaceful world. The gradual end of the truce mirrored the start: it too was a dangerous business, where a mistake could cost lives if the firing opened up while men were still milling about between the trenches. For Captain Charles Stockwell of the 2nd Royal Welsh Fusiliers, the truce ended early on Boxing Day, and the transition was handled with a consummate courtesy.

> Not a shot all night: our men had sing-songs – ditto the enemy. He
> played the game and never tried to touch his wire or anything. At
> 8.30am I fired three shots in the air and put up a flag with 'Merry
> Christmas' on it, and I climbed on the parapet. He put up a sheet
> with, 'Thank you' on it, and the German captain appeared on the
> parapet. We both bowed and saluted and got down into our respective
> trenches – he fired two shots in the air and the war was on again![34]

In other sectors, the artillery behind the lines opened up and the bursting
shells soon shattered the truce. At times the changeover of battalions in
the front line brought in a new unit that had not 'shared the moment' and
was hence not inclined to compromise. On some occasions, an embittered
individual could not resist the chance to kill a German. One such incident
was witnessed by Private Edward Roe of the East Lancashire Regiment on
28 December.

> About 9.30 am a shot is fired from the direction of our company
> headquarters and a German falls. That started the war again. Three of
> our men, who were out looking for doors to roof some dugouts, were
> caught in the open coming back, and two were wounded. We found out
> who fired the shot. It was a young fellow, about sixteen or seventeen
> years of age and a lance corporal. He was acting as a kind of ration
> corporal to the company quartermaster sergeant. The only qualifications
> he possessed for either his lance stripe or his employed job were his good
> looks. He got a couple of tots of buckshee rum and he got brave. It was
> a wonderful achievement to shoot down a man standing behind his
> trench unarmed and smoking, a man that placed his trust in us. The
> young lance corporal thought he had performed a wonderful deed. We
> did not like the idea of being the first to break the mutual agreement.
> The honour of the British Army was at stake, and we lost it.[35]

Soon war had regained its grip on the whole of the British sector. When
it came to it, the troops went back to war willingly enough. Many would
indeed have rejoiced at the end of the war, but they still stood fast alongside
their friends – their comrades – in the line, still willing to accept the orders
of their NCOs and officers, still willing to kill Germans. It is this last that
must give most pause for thought for those who believe the truce to have
been some kind of moral epiphany. If that was true, then it was short-lived
and shallow indeed; even after meeting and 'putting a face' on their enemies,

the average British soldier was more than willing to shoot them the moment the truce was over. Belgium and a good part of northern France were still occupied; German aggression had not visibly diminished. The Germans and French were still embroiled in what they perceived to be a war of national survival. As such the truce had changed nothing and meant nothing.

The year ended with another strange interlude on the front held by the 1st Scots Guards. Their response to the New Year was orchestrated by Captain Sir Edward Hulse.

> Punctually at 11pm (German war time is an hour ahead of ours), the whole of the German trenches were illuminated at intervals of fifteen or twenty yards. They all shouted, and then began singing their New Year and patriotic songs. We watched them quietly, and they lit a few bonfires as well. Just as they were settling down for the night again, our own midnight hour approached, and I had warned my company as to how I intended to receive the New Year. At midnight I fired a star shell, which was the signal, and the whole line fired a volley and then another star-shell and three hearty cheers, yet another star-shell, and the whole of us, led by myself and the Platoon Sergeant nearest to me, broke into *Auld Lang Syne*. We sang it three times, and were materially assisted by the enemy, who also joined in. At the end, three more hearty cheers and then dead silence. It was extra-ordinary hearing *Auld Lang Syne* gradually dying away right down the line.[36]

Next day, thousands of men looked to the future and wondered what it held for them, their families and their country. One of them was Captain Sir Morgan Crofton of the 2nd Life Guards

> The first day of the New Year. I wonder what it will bring. Let us hope that 1915 will be as destructive to Prussian militarism, as 1815 was to French.[37]

It was a fond hope, but alas it was not to be. Hopes of a victory in 1915 would soon be extinguished as the realities of the new warfare resumed: a grinding existence of trenches, barbed wire, machine guns, mud, blood, and, above all, the infernal thunder of the guns. Nearly four long years of war lay ahead of them.

16

EPILOGUE

We had not gained a great victory over the enemy, but we had prevented him from gaining one over us.[1]

General Ferdinand Foch, Headquarters, Northern Group of Armies

THE BATTLE OF MONS, THE Great Retreat and the First Battle of Ypres are all enshrined as British legends of the Great War. Tales of inspiring heroism that have become a comfortable metaphor for what some perceive as a very British way of life: a peace-loving country unprepared for war, dependent for survival on the supreme competence of their elite regular soldiers, but tormented in battle by the knavish unreliability of its allies. As we have seen, the British cannot be portrayed as entirely innocent and had prepared for war; the problem was that they had not prepared for the type of war that would face them in 1914. British statesmen had chosen to devote unprecedented amounts of Treasury money to the construction of a Grand Fleet that was second-to-none. They were unwilling in addition to pay for a large army, well equipped and trained; this was a decision taken at the highest level and it reflected the preoccupations of the British nation. Conscription, the only feasible route to a continental-size army in times of peace, was resolutely opposed. As a result the BEF originally placed in the field had totalled just four infantry and one oversize cavalry division, a force dwarfed utterly by the French and German armies. The generals who presided over the bedlam spreading across the Western

Front, the men who decided the fate of nations on the battlefields – these men would be French and German.

Then again the Germans were no cartoon hordes of poor-quality soldiers, but a well-trained army that was capable on occasion of integrating artillery, machine guns and infantry to devastating effect even in the early stages of the war. This was not due to some inherent martial superiority but to a carefully planned programme of national investment in military resources and expensive field exercises. The Imperial German Army was a fearsome beast, as Sir John French somewhat glumly recognised.

> It was commanded and led by a Sovereign who possessed absolute authority – military and civil. Its Emperor and Commander in Chief was served by a great General Staff which had been steadily and vigorously preparing for this tremendous trial of strength for a period of over 40 years. This great collision of nations in arms had been kept steadfastly in view. In the preparation of the German Army for this supreme moment not a chance had been thrown away. In manpower, armament, training, and equipment; in the instruction of leaders and officers; on the choice of commanders and every other element which makes for efficiency in an army, the most laborious thought and care had been expended. Compare with this the conditions in which the French and British Armies had been brought up to this fateful hour – systems, staffs, military policy, even money grants, all undergoing constant and drastic change year after year with every fresh wave of popular opinion and every fresh clamour, whilst the intrigues which run riot in all branches of the public service when 'votes' rule everything, exercised their usual baneful influence.[2]

Yet the German war machine was not quite so perfect as some would have it. The overall strategic vision had been a response to the difficult conundrum of war on two fronts, but the Schlieffen Plan demanded wonders of the men who would have to carry it out. Indeed, the German Army, huge as it was, nevertheless lacked sufficient troops to carry out the 'full plan'. The German soldiers would also have to march much further, endure more and fight far harder than their opponents if they were to triumph. What is more, having pinned his faith in his latest version of the plan, von Moltke failed to follow the in-built precepts for victory, weakening the right flank and allowing his subordinates to throw troops away in

428 ❖ FIRE AND MOVEMENT

unnecessary offensives on the left. German generals made too many mistakes in the field, failing to correctly divine what the Allies were doing, making faulty judgements and committing tactical errors that exposed them to the spectre of defeat. This was inevitable: no practice on the training grounds could mimic the sheer chaos of war conducted in real time, where the consequences of even a small mistake could be catastrophic. At the lower tactical levels, although they did often demonstrate enviable skills, they also made mistakes; they were after all human, not the automatons of legend.

It is also crucial to comprehend that the French Army – far from being unreliable – had been the solid bedrock of the Allies on the Western Front in 1914, bearing the brunt of the fighting and suffering almost inconceivable casualties. The Allied heroes were the likes of Joffre and Foch, not the somewhat hapless Sir John French. Joffre was the man who held the French together after the mortifying disaster of the Battle of the Frontiers, the man who had the vision to implement the strategy that led to the defining moment of the war at the Battle of the Marne. Foch fought hard in numerous capacities, but excelled in overseeing the defence of Ypres: without the introduction of copious French troops to bolster the British line, the Germans would have surely broken through. But that is after all what allies do, as the British too would come to appreciate later in the war when they willingly took up far more of the burden themselves.

An assessment of the British High Command is difficult without relying on copious amounts of hindsight. It is generally considered that French performed badly, that he failed to understand the situation, ignoring evidence that should have helped him in determining what was happening. Furthermore, he did not provide leadership to his corps commanders at key moments in the campaign. His attention seemed focussed at times on demonstrating 'leadership' by meeting his men in the field rather than carrying out command functions at GHQ. It is therefore ironic that he was unable to demonstrate his personal leadership skills by creating a harmonious working environment amongst his senior staff officers, who were allowed to degenerate into a somewhat dysfunctional group of individuals. The failures in communication between GHQ and I and II Corps made the task of Haig and Smith-Dorrien even more difficult, in what was already often a threatening situation. Both corps commanders were 'guilty' of mistakes, making decisions that in the cold light of day can be picked apart and criticised.

But this is to ignore the dreadful reality of command and control in a campaign where they were being pressed by German forces that threatened the envelopment and total destruction of their forces. With little effective guidance from Sir John French, minimal intelligence of German dispositions, poor communications with each other, stressed beyond measure by their onerous responsibilities, Haig and Smith-Dorrien still came to their decisions in a coherent manner. A serious command error could have had utterly disastrous consequences that would doom tens of thousands of their men; yet, a failure to respond to a situation could be equally fatal to all concerned. 'Damned if you do and damned if you don't!' might best sum it up in the vernacular of the time. In particular, I have come to respect the early performance of Smith-Dorrien, who may or may not have been right to stand at Le Cateau on 26 August, but who nonetheless had the guts to take the decision – and the luck to get away with it relatively unscathed. All this within ten days of taking over command of II Corps after the unexpected death of the intended commander Lieutenant General Sir James Grierson. Haig was steady enough early on, but came into his own at Ypres, where he proved himself a true master of the defensive battle.

Attempts to portray the BEF as the arbiters of destiny in the 1914 campaign, whether at Mons, Le Cateau, the Marne, the Aisne or Ypres, are risible. The BEF was a tokenistic contribution in a battle of the giants, but it was still a tangible symbol of what was to come, and the French valued greatly its presence. Indeed, in cheerfully debunking popular legends, one has to beware of missing some essential points. The British myths are misguided, true, but the fact remains that for the most part the men that fought for the BEF in 1914 conducted themselves with exceptional courage and great adaptability. They may have been sent to war by their country in inadequate numbers, ill-equipped, untrained and inexperienced in many of the basic requirements for success in modern war, but that was not their fault, and they secured the grudging respect of their German opponents. We can surely still admire them, cling to their achievements and, perhaps, excuse their occasional frailties.

Most important of all, when the final crunch came at the First Battle of Ypres, the BEF had not faltered. They had not won, but they had not lost – that was what mattered. Even as they fought and died the New Armies were flocking to the colours. Just as Kitchener had promised, there would be a million British soldiers on the Western Front by the summer of 1915. The BEF would swell up out of all recognition by 1916. They were still only trained in simple military skills, short of guns and munitions, but they would be there when it counted. Many hard battles lay ahead of them but the 'Old Contemptibles' had bought the British Army the time to transform itself into a continental force capable of exchanging meaningful blows with the German Army on the main battlefront side by side with the French Army.

What is unacceptable is allowing British pride in the very real achievements of the BEF to slip into the denigration of the efforts of either the French or Belgian Armies. They too had much to learn, but they fought hard to equal effect. At times, each of the allies had plenty of reason to feel overstretched, neglected or let down by their partners, but that is the very essence of alliance warfare. How much more so when faced with the German Army, the best-prepared and best-equipped army in the world. Facing this behemoth, things would go very wrong and sometimes there was the temptation to look for scapegoats. Foch, the ultimate allied commander, understood the pressures only too well.

> Great wars, especially those in which several allied nations are engaged, as well as the important battles they involve, cannot be considered merely from the viewpoint of one particular participant in the fight. They constitute a whole, a combination of joint actions, which, although extending over large spaces and long periods of time, must necessarily be harmonized, if a favourable result is finally to be attained. Even if one of these actions should come to a standstill, or one group of these forces be particularly tried, the commander of the whole must unflinchingly stand by his general plan, at the same time stimulating or sustaining the failing action; but without ever admitting that it can be wholly renounced or that its weakness causes the relinquishment or change of that plan. Losses suffered at any given moment by a group of forces even so great as an army cannot justify any such disturbance in the combined operations of the other armies, or in actions being pursued for the defence of the allied interests as a whole. The moral to be drawn from this idea – and it is applicable to all degrees in the hierarchy of command – is that the more anxious

and disquieting the situation of his own troops may be, and the more critical the moment then facing him appears, the more urgent it is for any commander to push forward with unshaken energy his share in the general operations.[3]

In truth, all three allied armies, French, British and Belgian, although each wavered at times, played their part to the full in 1914. Equally, all suffered terrible torments in those dreadful campaigns. War against the Germans was always going to be a painful experience, but together they stood firm.

The 1914 campaign would prove decisive to the war. It set the whole tone of the battles that followed. The utter failure of the Schlieffen Plan, designed to secure the rapid defeat of France, meant that Germany would indeed be condemned to ruinous hostilities on two fronts at once. As such, the Battle of the Marne proved to be the great turning-point of the whole war – a battle that truly changed the world in that it confirmed that the Germans were unlikely to win the war. The pre-war predictions from the German strategists that they could not prevail against the combined forces of France and Russia proved to be accurate, especially with, first, the British Empire and, then, the United States added to the list of their enemies. The German Army fought with a sustained skill and endurance that cannot but be admired, but they never quite managed to take advantage of the few fleeting chances for victory that still remained. After 1914, the odds really were stacked against the German Empire.

ACKNOWLEDGEMENTS

FIRST OF ALL I WOULD thank all the veterans who left their memories from that dramatic campaign of 1914. They tell of challenges that I could never have faced and experiences I could not have endured - all these men have my heartfelt admiration. It is amazing just how much of the character of a man can emerge in a short account, especially when describing a life and death occurrence. All of human life is here, on occasion red in tooth and claw, sometimes modest men looking to the gods – or themselves – for inspiration, but all more than interesting in their own right. I have thoroughly enjoyed getting to know them, reading their letters/diaries/memoirs and of course listening to tape recordings. Throughout this book the original quotations have, where necessary, been lightly edited for overall readability. Thus punctuation and spellings have been largely standardised, material has occasionally been re-ordered and irrelevant material has been omitted, usually without any indication in the text. Nevertheless, changes in the actual words used in the original sources have been avoided wherever possible.

As ever I am beholden to the Imperial War Museum, which is the finest treasure trove of archive knowledge on the Great War. In particular, I would signal out Margaret Brooks and Tony Richards of the Sound and Documents Collections. But I wish to dedicate this book to my late friend Rod Suddaby whose hard work and commitment enhanced the magnificent collection of the Imperial War Museum Documents Archive, thereby providing much of the raw materials for countless books written over the last forty years. No academic honours came his way: his reward lay in the esteem of the authors he served so well. He was probably prouder of his record as a fine fast bowler for the IWM cricket team. Rod bowled with red-haired aggression off the wrong foot, to the discomfort of many an opening batsman taken in by his less than athletic appearance. Perhaps to counterbalance his many qualities, he was one of the worst fielders I have ever seen! But in this – as in everything else – Rod always tried his best. A wonderful man. We will miss him.

As to printed sources, Jack Sheldon has written many superb books, and his *The German Army at Ypres, 1914* (Pen and Sword, 2010) and (with Nigel Cave) *Le Cateau: Battleground Europe* (Pen and Sword, 2008) proved invaluable in understanding the German perspective. In addition, Jack was also kind enough to identify and translate German quotations to elucidate key passages on Mons, Nimy and the Aisne. I am greatly in his debt and admire his ability to be deeply immersed in all things German, yet still retain a cool detachment. I would also thank Terence Zuber, whose book *The Mons Myth: A Re-assessment of the Battle* (History Press, 2010) I found both stimulating and irritating. I entirely agree with Zuber as to the bulk of his argument relating to the relative performances of the British and German forces at Mons; I just do not share his Germanophile belief that the Germans were practically perfect in every possible way, capable of nothing wrong in thought or deed in 1914. There is little point in replacing British myths with a whole new polemic of exaggerated hubris. But I do understand why he is enraged at the repeated untruths disseminated and endlessly perpetuated by British authors. Jerry Murland is one of a new generation unwilling to accept wholesale the British myth. He reviews the first few months of the campaign in his *Retreat and Rearguard, 1914* (Pen and Sword, 2011) and *Battle on the Aisne, 1914* (Pen and Sword, 2012). He was also kind enough to help me discover some new sources.

Two excellent, recently published, personal accounts that I found of great value were *The Kaiser's Reluctant Conscript* by Dominic Richert (translated and edited by D. C. Sutherland, Pen and Sword, 2012) and *Diary of an Old Contemptible: From Mons to Baghdad, 1914–1919* by Edward Roe (edited by P. Downham, Pen and Sword, 2004). For recent academic works, I would recommend *From Boer War to World War* (University of Oklahoma Press, 2012) by Spencer Jones, who also edited the rather wonderful collection of essays, *Stemming the Tide: Officers and Leadership in the British Expeditionary Force, 1914* (Helion, 2013).

It is fashionable to denigrate the British official history assembled by James Edmonds, *Military Operations of the Great War, 1914* (vols. 1 & 2), but while I would take issue with some of his judgements relating to the damage inflicted by the BEF on the German forces, I have nonetheless found it invaluable in charting a course through British movements and honest enough as to the results of German attacks on the British. This surely provides yet more evidence that it is easier for contemporary witnesses and reports to discern accurately what is going on within their own camp rather than speculate on the strength, intentions and casualties suffered by opponents – at least before the 'dust' dies down and there is free access to the archives of both parties.

In the process of actually writing the book I must first thank my wife Polly Napper and my two lovely daughters Lily and Ruby Hart who have to put up with me on a daily basis. I am also grateful to all those people who have read early drafts of the book and been most helpful in pointing out my many failings. Amongst these I would particularly mention in strict alphabetic order: Roger Chapman, Jim Grundy, Bryn Hammond, Alan Jeffreys, Polly Napper, John Paylor, John Sneddon and George Webster. Would that I could claim to be my own most strident critic, but that honour falls to Mr Paylor! As ever, they alone are responsible for any remaining errors. My grateful thanks to my agent Ian Drury, who brings a welcome touch of style to any occasion. At Oxford University Press I would thank my editor Tim Bent, his able assistant Keely Latcham, long-suffering production manager Augustine Leo, my super copy editor Cheryl Jung and proof reader Paul State for all their practical help and cheery encouragement. All in all, this book has been a pleasure to write, the 1914 campaign so utterly fascinating that it is with considerable sadness I finish the book.

Peter Hart
London, August 2014

NOTES

Preface

1. Kaiser Wilhelm II was meant to have issued the following order on 19 August 1914: 'It is my Royal and Imperial Command that you concentrate your energies, for the immediate present upon one single purpose, and that is that you address all your skill and all the valour of my soldiers, to exterminate first, the treacherous English, walk over General French's contemptible little Army.' This was quoted in the BEF orders of 24 September but no evidence of such an order by the Kaiser has ever been found. It would seem to have been well-judged British propaganda to inspire their own soldiers to even greater efforts.
2. D. Haig, quoted in J. E. Edmonds, *History of the Great War: Military Operations France and Belgium, 1918*, vol. 2 (London: Macmillan, 1937), 512.

Chapter 1

1. Lord Palmerston, speech to House of Commons, 1 March 1848 (*Hansard's Parliamentary Debates, 3rd series*, vol. 97, col. 122).
2. O. Parkes, *British Battleships* (London: Seeley Service, 1957), 435.
3. H. Wilson, quoted by C. E. Callwell, *Field Marshal Sir Henry Wilson*, vol. 1 (London: Cassell, 1927), 78.
4. F. Foch, quoted by C. E. Callwell, *Field Marshal Sir Henry Wilson*, vol. 1 (London: Cassell, 1927), 78–79.
5. H. Wilson, quoted by C. E. Callwell, *Field Marshal Sir Henry Wilson*, vol. 1 (London: Cassell, 1927), p.99.
6. W. L. S. Churchill, *World Crisis* (London: Penguin Classics, 2007), 37.
7. W. L. S. Churchill, *World Crisis* (London: Penguin Classics, 2007), 37–38.
8. H. Wilson, quoted by C. E. Callwell, *Field Marshal Sir Henry Wilson*, vol. 1 (London: Cassell, 1927), 104.
9. H. Wilson, quoted by C. E. Callwell, *Field Marshal Sir Henry Wilson*, vol. 1 (London: Cassell, 1927), 105.

Chapter 2

1. H. Musgrave, quoted by W. Raleigh, *The War in the Air*, vol. 1 (Oxford: Clarendon, 1922), 232.
2. J. French, *1914* (London: Constable, 1919), 11.
3. J. E. Edmonds, quoted by J. Charteris, *Field Marshal Earl Haig* (London: Cassell, 1929), 13. Although Charteris is an unreliable biographer and responsible for many of the more colourful myths and misunderstandings about Haig, this story quoted from Edmonds, the editor of the *Official History of the Great War* – even if apocryphal – certainly has the ring of truth in relation to what we know of Haig's character.
4. The title of the excellent biography by John Terraine, *The Educated Soldier* (London: Hutchinson, 1963).
5. D. Haig, quoted by J. Charteris, *Field Marshal Earl Haig* (London: Cassell, 1929), 55–56.
6. General Staff, War Office, *Field Service Regulations, Part I* (London: HMSO, 1909 as amended 1912), 14. It is interesting how this presages the concept of the 'All Arms Battle' of 1918. The various new elements were simply slotted into the original framework.
7. General Staff, War Office, *Field Service Regulations, Part I* (London: HMSO, 1909 as amended 1912), 20.
8. General Staff, War Office, *Field Service Regulations, Part I* (London: HMSO, 1909 as amended 1912), 20.
9. General Staff, War Office, *Field Service Regulations, Part I* (London: HMSO, 1909 as amended 1912), 126–127.
10. I. Hamilton, *A Staff Officer's Scrap-book during the Russo-Japanese War* (London: Edward Arnold, 1906), 108.
11. I. Hamilton, *A Staff Officer's Scrap-book during the Russo-Japanese War* (London: Edward Arnold, 1906), 109–110.
12. The work of my friend and former IWM colleague Stephen Badsey was invaluable in defining my views on the development and role of cavalry before and during the Great War. See his book, *Doctrine and Reform in the British Cavalry, 1880–1918* (Aldershot, UK: Ashgate, 2008).
13. J. French, quoted by S. Badsey, *Doctrine and Reform in the British Cavalry, 1880–1918* (Aldershot, UK: Ashgate, 2008), 184.
14. Thanks to my friend Andrew Whitmarsh whose work has exploded many popular myths concerning the pre-war reaction of British generals to the inherent possibilities of aviation. See his article, 'British Army manoeuvres and the development of military aviation, 1910–1913', *War in History* 14, no. 3 (July 2007).
15. J. Grierson, quoted by W. Raleigh, *The War in the Air*, vol. 1 (Oxford: Clarendon, 1922), 226–227.

16. J. French, quoted by A. Whitmarsh, 'British Army manoeuvres and the development of military aviation, 1910–1913', *War in History* 14, no. 3 (July 2007).
17. W. S. Brancker, quoted by N. Macmillan, *Sir Sefton Brancker* (London: William Heinemann, 1935), 52–53.
18. T. Snow, *The Confusion of Command: The Memoirs of Lieutenant-General Thomas D'Oyly 'Snowball' Snow, 1914–1918*, ed. D. Snow and M. Pottle (London: Frontline Books, 2011), 7–8.
19. D. Haig, quoted by D. Scott, *The Preparatory Prologue: Douglas Haig, Diaries and Letters, 1861–1914* (Barnsley, UK: Pen and Sword, 2006), 253.
20. D. Haig, quoted by D. Scott, *The Preparatory Prologue: Douglas Haig, Diaries and Letters, 1861–1914* (Barnsley, UK: Pen and Sword, 2006), 260.
21. H. Wilson, quoted by C. E. Callwell, *Field Marshal Sir Henry Wilson*, vol. 1 (London: Cassell, 1927), 62–63.
22. D. Haig, quoted by J. Charteris, *Field Marshal Earl Haig* (London: Cassell, 1929), 52.
23. H. Gough, *Soldiering On* (London: Arthur Barker, 1954), 100.
24. IWM SOUND: R. MacLeod, AC 4169, Reel 1.

Chapter 3

1. IWM DOCS: R. H. Owen typescript letters, 2/8/1914.
2. E. Grey in *War Speeches by British Minister, 1914–1916* (London: T. Fisher Unwin, 1917), 158.
3. IWM DOCS: H. Jackson, manuscript letter, 3/8/1914.
4. E. H. W. Hulse, *Letters Written from the English Fronts in France between September 1914 and March 1915* (Privately Printed, 1916), 1–2.
5. D. Lloyd George, 'Speech delivered by the Rt. Hon. David Lloyd George, M.P. (Chancellor of the Exchequer) at the Queen's Hall, London, 19 September 1914.
6. This refers to Brigadier General J. A. L. Haldane, 10th Brigade.
7. IWM SOUND: A. N. Dunton, AC 43, Reel 1.
8. J. L. Dent, quoted by J. P. Jones, *History of the South Staffordshire Regiment* (Wolverhampton, UK: Whitehead Brothers, 1923), 243.
9. E. Roe, *Diary of an Old Contemptible: From Mons to Baghdad, 1914–1919*, ed. P. Downham (Barnsley, UK: Pen and Sword, 2004), 3–4.
10. E. Roe, *Diary of an Old Contemptible: From Mons to Baghdad, 1914–1919*, ed. P. Downham (Barnsley, UK: Pen and Sword, 2004), 5.
11. F. A. Bolwell, *With a Reservist in France* (London: Routledge, 1918), 4–5.
12. H. L. Lincoln, letter enclosed with will, 12 August 1914, Probate Service.
13. E. J. Needham, *The First Three Months: The Impressions of an Amateur Subaltern* (Aldershot, UK: Gale and Polden, 1933), 15–16.
14. IWM DOCS: K. F. B. Tower, manuscript account, 2.

15. H. L. Lincoln, letter enclosed with will, 12 August 1914, Probate Service. Harry Lincoln was killed on 5 May 1915. He has no known grave and is commemorated on the Menin Gate Memorial at Ypres.
16. IWM DOCS: R. H Kelly, typescript letters, 9/8/1914.
17. H. Kitchener, quoted by G. H. Cassar, *Kitchener's War: British Strategy from 1914 to 1916* (Washington, DC: Potomac Books, 2004), 27.
18. IWM DOCS: H. Jackson, manuscript letter, 8/1914.
19. H. Wilson, quoted by C. E. Callwell, *Field Marshal Sir Henry Wilson*, vol. 1 (London: Cassell, 1927), 62–63.
20. W. S. Brancker, quoted by N. Macmillan, *Sir Sefton Brancker* (London: Heinemann, 1935), 66–67.
21. D. Haig, quoted by D. Cooper, *Haig* (London: Faber and Faber, 1935), 129.
22. J. French, *1914* (London: Constable, 1919), 6–7.
23. J. French, *1914* (London: Constable, 1919), 6–7.
24. J. French, *1914* (London: Constable, 1919), 6–7.
25. D. Haig, quoted by D. Cooper, *Haig* (London: Faber and Faber, 1935), 131.
26. D. Haig, quoted by D. Cooper, *Haig* (London: Faber and Faber, 1935), 132.
27. D. Haig, *Douglas Haig: War Diaries and Letters, 1914–1918*, ed. G. Sheffield and J. Bourne (London: Weidenfeld and Nicholson, 2005), 56.
28. D. Haig, *Douglas Haig: War Diaries and Letters, 1914–1918*, ed. G. Sheffield and J. Bourne (London: Weidenfeld and Nicholson, 2005), 58.

Chapter 4

1. A. A. E. Gyde, *Contemptible* (London: William Heinemann, 1916), 19.
2. 'Extract from General Lehman's Diary, August 1914,' *First WorldWar. com: A Multimedia History of World War One*, ed. Michael Duffy, http://www.firstworldwar.com/source/lemandiary.htm. See also Charles F. Horne, ed., *Source Records of the Great War*, vol. 2 (National Alumni, 1923).
3. J. L. Dent, quoted by J. P. Jones, *History of the South Staffordshire Regiment* (Wolverhampton, UK: Whitehead Brothers, 1923), 243–244.
4. A. A. E. Gyde, *Contemptible* (London: Heinemann, 1916), 5–6.
5. E. J. Needham, *The First Three Months: The Impressions of an Amateur Subaltern* (Aldershot, UK: Gale and Polden, 1933), 21–22.
6. D. Haig quoted by I. F. W. Beckett, *Johnnie Gough VC* (London: Tim Donovan Publishing, 1989, 176.
7. W. Robertson, *From Private to Field Marshal* (London: Constable, 1921), 197–198.
8. E. Gleichen, *The Doings of the Fifteenth Infantry Brigade, August 1914 to March 1915* (Edinburgh and London: William Blackwood and Sons, 1917), 12–14.
9. F. Smith quoted in *Nottingham Evening Post*, 8 October 1914. Quote sourced by Jim Grundy.
10. IWM DOCS: J. W. Palmer, typescript diary, 17 August 1914.
11. IWM DOCS: C. J. Paterson, typescript diary, 17 August 1914.

12. IWM DOCS: H. J. Rowthorn, typescript account.
13. Private William Marney died on 17 August 1914. He is buried in the Esqueheries Communal Cemetery.
14. C. Lanrezac, *Le Plan de Campagne français et le Premier Mois de la Guerre, 2nd Août—3rd Septembre 1914* (Paris: Payor et Cie, 1920), 25 and fn.
15. J. Joffre, *The Memoirs of General Joffre*, vol. 1 (London: Geoffrey Bles, 1932), 1161.
16. C. Lanrezac, *Le Plan de Campagne français et le Premier Mois de la Guerre, 2nd Août—3rd Septembre 1914* (Paris: Payor et Cie, 1920), 91–92.
17. IWM SOUND: E. Spears, AC 4231 Reel 1-2 (edited from several takes).
18. J. French, *1914* (London: Constable, 1919), 36–37.
19. A. Grasset, quoted by P. Young, 'Battle of the Frontiers: The Ardennes' (*Purnell's History of the First World War*, vol. 1), 154–155.
20. D. E. Renault, quoted by J. P. Guéno and Y. Laplume, *Paroles de Poilus* (France: Librio, 2003), 27.
21. C. de Gaulle, quoted in P. M. de la Gorce, *De Gaulle entre Deux Mondes: Une Vie et Une Époque* (Paris: Fayard, 1964), 102. Charles de Gaulle saw active service as a junior officer with the 33rd Régiment d'Infanterie from 1914 to 2 March 1916, when, wounded, he was captured during the Battle of Verdun. Jean Lacouture, *De Gaulle: The Rebel 1890–1944*, trans. Patrick O'Brian (London: Collins Harvill, 1990), 21, 37–41.
22. H. Gough, *The Fifth Army* (London: Hodder and Stoughton, 1931), 5–6.
23. G. de S. Barrow, *The Fire of Life* (London: Hutchinson, 1942), 143.
24. A. L. Ransome, quoted by C. H. Dudley Ward, *History of the Dorsetshire Regiment, 1914–1919* (Dorchester, UK: Henry Ling, 1932), 17.
25. IWM SOUND: C. E. C. Rabagliati, AC 4208, Reel 1.
26. IWM SOUND: C. E. C. Rabagliati, AC 4208, Reel 1.
27. D. Haig, quoted by D. Cooper, *Haig* (London: Faber and Faber, 1935), 131.
28. IWM SOUND: E. Spears, AC 4231 Reel 1-2 (edited from several takes).
29. H. Smith-Dorrien, *Isandlwhana to the Great War* (Driffield, UK: Oakpast, 2009), 424.

Chapter 5

1. IWM DOCS: A. N. Ackland, typescript account, 1–2.
2. A. Kluck, *The March on Paris and the Battle of the Marne, 1914* (London: Edward Arnold, 1920), 45–46.
3. IWM DOCS: K. F. B. Tower, manuscript account, 8.
4. IWM DOCS: K. F. B. Tower, manuscript account, 9.
5. IWM DOCS: K. F. B. Tower, Manuscript account, 10.
6. T. Schröder quotation provided and translated by J. Sheldon from *Erinnerungsblätter der ehemaligen Mansteiner 1. Folge Nr. 8* (Hamburg, 1924), 69–70.
7. IWM DOCS: K. F. B. Tower, manuscript account, 10–11.
8. A. P. G. Vivian, *The Phantom Brigade* (London: Ernest Benn, 1930), 152.

9. T. Schröder quotation provided and translated by J. Sheldon from *Erinnerungsblätter der ehemaligen Mansteiner 1. Folge Nr. 8* (Hamburg, 1924), 69–70.

10. Oberleutnant Liebe quote provided and translated by J. Sheldon from *Erinnerungsblätter der ehemaligen Mansteiner 1. Folge Nr. 8* (Hamburg, 1924), 57–59.

11. IWM DOCS: K. F. B. Tower, manuscript account, 10–11.

12. IWM DOCS: T. S. Wollocombe, typescript diary, 23/8/1914.

13. W. Holbrook, AC 9339 Reel 7.

14. W. Holbrook, AC 9339 Reel 7.

15. Captain Walter Bowden Smith died, aged 33 years old, on 28 August 1914. He is buried at Clement House Cemetery, West-Vlaanderen, Belgium.

16. Lieutenant Maurice Dease, 4th Royal Fusiliers who was awarded the first VC of the Great War for his heroic defence of Nimy Bridge, where he was killed 23 August 1914. Buried in St Symphorien Military Cemetery.

17. IWM DOCS: K. F. B. Tower, manuscript account, 11–12.

18. Oberleutnant Liebe quotation provided and translated by J. Sheldon from *Erinnerungsblätter der ehemaligen Mansteiner 1. Folge Nr. 8* (Hamburg, 1924), 57–59.

19. T. Schröder quotation provided and translated by J. Sheldon from *Erinnerungsblätter der ehemaligen Mansteiner 1. Folge Nr. 8* (Hamburg, 1924), 69–70.

20. Private Sidney Godley was awarded the VC for his courage at Nimy Bridge, and one must presume that he managed to throw the detachable firing-lock of his machine gun into the canal before his capture. Godley survived the war.

21. Captain Walter Bowden Smith died, aged 33 years old, on 28 August 1914. He was probably taken prisoner later in the day and died of his wounds. He is buried at Clement House Cemetery, West-Vlaanderen, Belgium.

22. IWM DOCS: K. F. B. Tower, manuscript account, 12.

23. Oberleutnant Liebe quotation provided and translated by J. Sheldon from *Erinnerungsblätter der ehemaligen Mansteiner 1. Folge Nr. 8* (Hamburg, 1924), 57–59.

24. M. V. Hay, *Wounded and a Prisoner of War* (Edinburgh and London: Blackwood, 1916), 37–38.

25. IWM DOCS: S. C. M. Archibald, microfilm account, 81–82.

26. IWM DOCS: B. T. St John, typescript account Pt I 20–21.

27. IWM SOUND: E. E. Dorman-Smith (later known as E. E. Dorman O'Gowan), AC 4184 Reel 1.

28. He refers here to Captain Theodore Wright.

29. Captain Theodore Wright VC was killed, aged 31 years old, on 14 September 1914. He is buried at Vailly British Cemetery.

30. IWM DOCS: B. T. St John, typescript account pt I, 22–23.

31. J. Perryman, *Diary of Lieut. J. B. W. Pennyman* (Middlesbrough, UK: Jordison, 1915), 7–8.

32. W. Bloem, *The Advance from Mons, 1914*, trans. G. Wynne (London: Peter Davies, 1930), 56.
33. M. Cave and J. Horsfall, *Mons: 1914: Battleground Europe* (Barnsley, UK: Pen and Sword, 1999), 67.
34. IWM DOCS: G. Roupell, typescript account, 3–4.
35. IWM DOCS: W. Morritt, manuscript letter, 3/9/1914-4/9/1914.
36. IWM DOCS: B. T. St John, typescript account pt I, 24.
37. IWM DOCS: E. S. B. Hamilton, typescript memoir, 7.
38. IWM DOCS: E. S. B. Hamilton, typescript memoir, 7.
39. Major Charles Simpson of the 1st Gordon Highlanders.
40. IWM DOCS: E. S. B. Hamilton, typescript memoir, 7. Slightly edited using material from typescript letter, 28/8/1914.
41. G. A. L. Brownlow, *The Breaking of the Storm* (London: Methuen, 1918), 46, 48.
42. T. Zuber, *The Mons Myth: A Reassessment of the Battle* (Stroud, UK: The History Press, 2010), 167.
43. H. Smith-Dorrien, *Isandlwhana to the Great War* (Driffield, UK: Oakpast, 2009), 430–431.
44. IWM DOCS: F. H. Le Breton, typescript diary, 24/8/1914.
45. J. L. Dent, quoted by J. P. Jones, *History of the South Staffordshire Regiment* (Wolverhampton, UK: Whitehead Brothers, 1923), 252.
46. A. Kluck, *The March on Paris and the Battle of the Marne, 1914* (London: Edward Arnold, 1920), 48–49.
47. B. de Lisle, quoted by Marquess of Anglesey, *A History of the British Cavalry, 1916–1919*, vol. 7 (Barnsley, UK: Pen and Sword, 1996), 120.
48. IWM DOCS: B. J. N. Marden, manuscript diary, 24/8/1914.
49. F. Grenfell, quoted by Marquess of Anglesey, *A History of the British Cavalry, 1916–1919*, vol. 7 (Barnsley, UK: Pen and Sword, 1996), 122.
50. T. Zuber, *The Mons Myth: A Reassessment of the Battle* (Stroud, UK: History Press, 2010), 186–187.
51. E Broadwood, quoted by J. Callcut, *A Village at War: Newdigate in World War One* (Brighton, UK: Reveille Press, 2011), 48.
52. F. Grenfell, quoted by Marquess of Anglesey, *A History of the British Cavalry, 1916–1919*, vol. 7 (Barnsley, UK: Pen and Sword, 1996), 123.
53. F. Grenfell, quoted by Marquess of Anglesey, *A History of the British Cavalry, 1916–1919*, vol. 7 (Barnsley, UK: Pen and Sword, 1996), 123.
54. E. Broadwood, quoted by J. Callcut, *A Village at War: Newdigate in World War One* (Brighton, UK: Reveille Press, 2011), 48–49.
55. D. C. Boger, quoted by A. Crookenden, *The History of the Cheshire Regiment in the Great War* (Chester, UK: Evans, 1939), 17–18.
56. H. Smith-Dorrien, *Isandlwhana to the Great War* (Driffield, UK: Oakpast, 2009), 430–431.
57. T. Snow, *The Confusion of Command*, ed. D. Snow and M. Pottle (London: Frontline, 2011), 14.
58. T. Snow, *The Confusion of Command*, ed. D. Snow and M. Pottle (London: Frontline, 2011), 18.

59. A. Johnston, quoted by E. Astill, *The Great War Diaries of Brigadier General Alexander Johnston, 1914–1917* (Barnsley, UK: Pen and Sword, 2007), 8–9.
60. A. Johnston, quoted by E. Astill, *The Great War Diaries of Brigadier General Alexander Johnston, 1914–1917* (Barnsley, UK: Pen and Sword, 2007), 8–9.
61. General Staff, War Office, *Field Service Regulations, Part I* (London: HMSO, 1909 as amended 1912), 96.
62. A. Johnston, quoted by E. Astill, *The Great War Diaries of Brigadier General Alexander Johnston, 1914–1917* (Barnsley, UK: Pen and Sword, 2007), 9.
63. IWM DOCS: F. H. Le Breton, typescript diary, 25/8/1914.
64. E. J. Needham, *The First Three Months: The Impressions of an Amateur Subaltern* (Aldershot, UK: Gale and Polden, 1933), 29.
65. Sergeant Thomas Secrett was Haig's servant.
66. Major Eugene (Micky) Ryan, the medical officer of Headquarters, I Corps.
67. J. Charteris, *At GHQ* (London: Cassell, 1931), 17.

Chapter 6

1. C. Fussell, quoted by B. Gillard, *Good Old Somersets: An 'Old Contemptible' Battalion in 1914* (Leicester, UK: Troubador, 2004), 25.
2. H. Smith-Dorrien, *Isandlwana to the Great War* (Driffield, UK: Oakpast, 2009), 438–439.
3. H. Smith-Dorrien, letter to J. Vaughan, 12 June 1919.
4. H. Smith-Dorrien, *Isandlwana to the Great War* (Driffield, UK: Oakpast, 2009), 445–446.
5. H. Smith-Dorrien, *Isandlwana to the Great War* (Driffield, UK: Oakpast, 2009), 450.
6. H. Smith-Dorrien, *Isandlwana to the Great War* (Driffield, UK: Oakpast, 2009), 448.
7. G. A. L. Brownlow, *The Breaking of the Storm* (London: Methuen, 1918), 79–80.
8. T. Snow, *The Confusion of Command,* ed. D. Snow and M. Pottle (London: Frontline, 2011), 17.
9. IWM DOCS: J. Headlam, typescript address 4/12/1918.
10. T. Snow, *The Confusion of Command*, ed. D. Snow and M. Pottle (London: Frontline, 2011), 22.
11. G. R. Parr, quoted by B. Gillard, *Good Old Somersets: An 'Old Contemptible' Battalion in 1914* (Leicester, UK: Troubador, 2004), 18.
12. A. Johnston, quoted by E. Astill, *The Great War Diaries of Brigadier General Alexander Johnston, 1914–1917* (Barnsley, UK: Pen and Sword, 2007), 10–11.
13. IWM SOUND: R. MacLeod, AC 4169, Reel 1.
14. IWM SOUND: R. MacLeod, AC 4169, Reel 1.
15. T. Snow, *The Confusion of Command,* ed. D. Snow and M. Pottle (London: Frontline, 2011), 23–24.
16. IWM DOCS: W. Read, transcript diary, 26/8/1914.

17. IWM SOUND: R. MacLeod, AC 4169, Reel 1.
18. J. H. C. Drain, *Essex Weekly News*, 1915.
19. T. Snow, *The Confusion of Command,* ed. D. Snow and M. Pottle (London: Frontline, 2011), 33.
20. M. V. Hay, *Wounded and a Prisoner of War* (Edinburgh and London: Blackwood, 1916), 61–62.
21. M. V. Hay, *Wounded and a Prisoner of War* (Edinburgh and London: Blackwood, 1916), 62–63.
22. M. V. Hay, *Wounded and a Prisoner of War* (Edinburgh and London: Blackwood, 1916), 64.
23. M. V. Hay, *Wounded and a Prisoner of War* (Edinburgh and London: Blackwood, 1916), 64.
24. Lieutenant Schacht, quoted by N. Cave and J. Sheldon, *Le Cateau, 26 August 1914: Battleground Europe* (Barnsley, UK: Pen and Sword, 2008), 52.
25. Lance Sergeant John Fair, 2nd Argyll and Sutherland Highlanders, killed 26 August 1914. He has no known grave and is commemorated on the La Ferté sous-Jouarre memorial.
26. C. Ditcham, AC 374 Reel 6.
27. H. Smith-Dorrien, *Isandlwana to the Great War* (Driffield, UK: Oakpast, 2009), 448.
28. IWM DOCS: L. G Lutyens, microfilm, 30.
29. Lieutenant Schacht, quoted by N. Cave and J. Sheldon, *Le Cateau, 26 August 1914: Battleground Europe* (Barnsley, UK: Pen and Sword, 2008), 52–53.
30. IWM DOCS: L. G Lutyens, microfilm, 33–34.
31. H. K. O'Kelly, quoted by C. D. Bruce, *History of the Duke of Wellington's Regiment (1st & 2nd Battalions), 1881–1923* (London: Medici Society, 1927), 90–91.
32. J. H. C. Drain, *Essex Weekly News*, 1915.
33. Driver Benjamin Cobey died aged just 19 years old. He has no known grave and is commemorated on the La Ferté sous-Jouarre memorial. This rectangular block of stone, 62 feet by 30 feet and 24 feet high, commemorates nearly 4,000 officers and men of the BEF who died in August, September, and the early part of October 1914 and who have no known grave.
34. IWM DOCS: H. E. Trevor, typescript letter, 26/9/1914.
35. R. Sinclair, quoted by M. V. Hay, *Wounded and a Prisoner of War* (Edinburgh and London: Blackwood, 1916), 70–71.
36. IWM DOCS: T. S. Wollocombe, typescript diary, 26/8/1914.
37. IWM DOCS: C. Helm, typescript account, 7.
38. H. O'Kelly, quoted by C. D. Bruce, *History of the Duke of Wellington's Regiment (1st & 2nd Battalions), 1881–1923* (London: Medici Society, 1927), 91.
39. Recent research by Nigel Cave and Jack Sheldon has revised this estimate down to approximately 5,000, but they also assert that more research needs to be carried out.

Chapter 7

1. E. Roe, *Diary of an Old Contemptible: From Mons to Baghdad, 1914*–1919, ed. P. Downham (Barnsley, UK: Pen and Sword, 2004), 30.
2. J. French, *1914* (London: Constable, 1919), 84.
3. H. Gough, *The Fifth Army* (London: Hodder and Stoughton, 1931), 32.
4. H. Gough, *The Fifth Army* (London: Hodder and Stoughton, 1931), 34.
5. I. Maxse, quoted by J. Baynes, *Far from a Donkey* (London: Brasseys, 1995), 115.
6. E. Gleichen, *The Doings of the Fifteenth Infantry Brigade, August 1914 to March 1915* (Edinburgh and London: William Blackwood and Sons, 1917), 62–64.
7. A. Mainwaring, quoted by J. Hutton, *August 1914: Surrender at St Quentin* (Barnsley, UK: Pen and Sword, 2010), 134.
8. J. Elkington, quoted by J. Hutton, *August 1914: Surrender at St Quentin* (Barnsley, UK: Pen and Sword, 2010), 134.
9. A. Osburn, *Unwilling Passenger* (London: Faber, 1932), 78.
10. T. Bridges, *Alarms and Excursions* (London: Longmans, 1938), 87.
11. T. Bridges, *Alarms and Excursions* (London: Longmans, 1938), 87.
12. IWM SOUND: W. Holbrook, AC 9339 Reel 7.
13. T. Snow, *The Confusion of Command,* ed. D. Snow and M. Pottle (London: Frontline Books, 2011), 38–39.
14. J. French, *1914* (London: Constable, 1919), 88.
15. J. L. Dent, quoted by J. P. Jones, *History of the South Staffordshire Regiment* (Wolverhampton, UK: Whitehead Brothers, 1923), 256.
16. J. French, *1914* (London: Constable, 1919), 87.
17. C. Lanrezac, *Le Plan de Campagne français et le Premier Mois de la Guerre, 2nd Août–3rd Septembre 1914* (Paris: Payor et Cie, 1920), 211–212.
18. J. Joffre, *The Memoirs of General Joffre,* vol. 1 (London, Geoffrey Bles, 1932), 185.
19. J. Joffre, *The Memoirs of General Joffre,* vol. 1 (London, Geoffrey Bles, 1932), 190.
20. J. Joffre, *The Memoirs of General Joffre,* vol. 1 (London, Geoffrey Bles, 1932), 195.
21. V. Huguet, quoted by J. Joffre, *The Memoirs of General Joffre,* vol. 1 (London, Geoffrey Bles, 1932), 203.
22. C. Lanrezac, *Le Plan de Campagne français et le Premier Mois de la Guerre, 2nd Août–3rd Septembre 1914* (Paris: Payor et Cie, 1920), 215–217.
23. C. Lanrezac, *Le Plan de Campagne français et le Premier Mois de la Guerre, 2nd Août–3rd Septembre 1914* (Paris: Payor et Cie, 1920), 218.
24. D. Haig, quoted by D. Cooper, *Haig* (London: Faber and Faber, 1935), 161.
25. J. French, quoted by D. Cooper, *Haig* (London: Faber and Faber, 1935), 161.
26. J. French, quoted by D. Cooper, *Haig* (London: Faber and Faber, 1935), 162.
27. D. Haig, quoted by D. Cooper, *Haig* (London: Faber and Faber, 1935), 162
28. IWM DOCS: H. Rees, transcript memoir, 'A Personal Record of the First Three Months of the War', 27/8/1914.

29. IWM DOCS: D. M Laurie, typescript diary, 27/8/1914.
30. IWM DOCS: H. J. Rowthorn, typescript account.
31. IWM DOCS: H. J. Rowthorn, typescript account.
32. IWM DOCS: J. McIlwain, typescript diary account, 27/8/1914.
33. W. Robertson, *From Private to Field Marshal* (London: Constable, 1921), 210
34. IWM DOCS: S. C. M. Archibald, microfilm account, 90.
35. IWM SOUND: T. Painting, AC 212 Reel 4.
36. IWM DOCS: H. Rees, transcript memoir, 'A Personal Record of the First Three Months of the War', 7–8.
37. H. Yates, quoted by C. H. Dudley Ward, *Regimental Records of the Royal Welch Fusiliers* (London: Forster Groom, 1928), 51.
38. IWM DOCS: J. W. Palmer, typescript diary, 27/8/1914.
39. J. L. Dent, quoted by J. P. Jones, *History of the South Staffordshire Regiment* (Wolverhampton, UK: Whitehead Brothers, 1923), 260–261.
40. W. Cook, quoted by B. Gillard, *Good Old Somersets: An 'Old Contemptible' Battalion in 1914* (Leicester, UK: Troubador, 2004), 35.
41. IWM DOCS: J. McIlwain, typescript diary account, 2/9/1914.
42. E. J. Needham, *The First Three Months: The Impressions of an Amateur Subaltern* (Aldershot, UK: Gale and Polden, 1933), 36.
43. E. Roe, *Diary of an Old Contemptible: From Mons to Baghdad, 1914–1919*, ed. P. Downham (Barnsley, UK: Pen and Sword, 2004), 29–30.
44. A. A. E. Gyde, *Contemptible* (London: William Heinemann, 1916), 59–60.
45. IWM DOCS: T. S. Wollocombe, typescript diary, 30/8/1914.
46. W. A. T. Synge, quoted by E. Wyrall, *The History of the King's Regiment (Liverpool) 1914–1919* (London: Edward Arnold, 1928), 29.
47. IWM DOCS: H. Smith-Dorrien, manuscript letter, 29/8/1914.
48. IWM DOCS: R. Rolleston West, typescript memoir, 57.
49. IWM DOCS: R. Rolleston West, typescript memoir, 58.
50. IWM DOCS: R. Rolleston West, typescript memoir, 58–59.
51. IWM DOCS: R. Rolleston West, typescript memoir, 59–60.
52. IWM DOCS: R. Rolleston West, typescript memoir, 60.
53. IWM DOCS: W. Clarke, typescript questionnaire.
54. Leutnant von Zitzewitz quote provided and translated by J. Sheldon from *Bund der Königin-Kürassiere Geschichte des Kürassier-Regiments 'Königin' (Pommersches) Nr. 2 Teil III 1904–1909* (Stettin), 83–85.
55. J. Giffard, quoted by S. Giffard, *Guns, Kites and Horses: Three Diaries from the Western Front* (London: Radcliffe, 2003), 50.
56. J. Giffard, quoted by S. Giffard, *Guns, Kites and Horses: Three Diaries from the Western Front* (London: Radcliffe, 2003), 50–51.
57. Captain Edward Bradbury died, aged 33 years old, on 1 September 1914. He and his men are commemorated on a memorial in the Néry Communal Cemetery.
58. IWM DOCS: W. Clarke, typescript questionnaire.
59. Lieutenant Claude Norman de Crespigny was killed, aged 26 years old, on 1 September 1914. He was initially buried at Néry but disinterred by

his grieving family and returned home to be buried at Champion Lodge, Maldon in November 1914. This practice would be forbidden in early 1915.

60. IWM DOCS: W. Clarke, typescript questionnaire.
61. Kürassier Soltzien quote provided and translated by J. Sheldon from *Bund der Königin-Kürassiere Geschichte des Kürassier-Regiments 'Königin' (Pommersches) Nr. 2 Teil III 1904–1909* (Stettin), 83–85.

Chapter 8

1. IWM DOCS: H. Wilson, diary, 5/9/1914.
2. J. French, quoted by J. E. Edmonds, *History of the Great War, Military Operations, France and Belgium, 1914*, vol. 2 (London: Macmillan, 1925), 474–475.
3. H. Kitchener, quoted by J. E. Edmonds, *History of the Great War, Military Operations, France and Belgium, 1914*, vol. 2 (London: Macmillan, 1925), 475.
4. J. French, quoted by J. E. Edmonds, *History of the Great War, Military Operations, France and Belgium, 1914*, vol. 2 (London: Macmillan, 1925), 476.
5. J. French, quoted by J. E. Edmonds, *History of the Great War, Military Operations, France and Belgium, 1914*, vol. 2 (London: Macmillan, 1925), 476.
6. J. French, *1914* (London: Constable, 1919), 99–100.
7. J. French, *1914* (London: Constable, 1919), 100.
8. H. Kitchener, quoted by J. E. Edmonds, *History of the Great War, Military Operations, France and Belgium, 1914*, vol. 2 (London: Macmillan, 1925), 245.
9. J. French, quoted by J. E. Edmonds, *History of the Great War, Military Operations, France and Belgium, 1914*, vol. 2 (London: Macmillan, 1925), 245.
10. A. von Kluck, *The March on Paris and the Battle of the Marne, 1914* (London, Edward Arnold, 1920), 69.
11. A. von Kluck, *The March on Paris and the Battle of the Marne, 1914* (London, Edward Arnold, 1920), 77.
12. A. von Kluck, *The March on Paris and the Battle of the Marne, 1914* (London, Edward Arnold, 1920), 91.
13. Quoted by J. E. Edmonds, *History of the Great War, Military Operations, France and Belgium, 1914*, vol. 2 (London: Macmillan, 1925), 264.
14. A. von Kluck, *The March on Paris and the Battle of the Marne, 1914* (London, Edward Arnold, 1920), 96–97.
15. J. French, *1914* (London: Constable, 1919), 110.
16. IWM SOUND: E. Spears, AC 4231 Reel 1-2 (edited from several takes).
17. J. Joffre, *The Memoirs of General Joffre*, vol. 1 (London: Geoffrey Bles, 1932), 254–255.
18. J. Joffre, *The Memoirs of General Joffre*, vol. 1 (London: Geoffrey Bles, 1932), 255.
19. J. French, quoted by J. E. Edmonds, *History of the Great War, Military Operations, France and Belgium, 1914*, vol. 2 (London: Macmillan, 1925), 498.
20. D. Haig, quoted by D. Cooper, *Haig* (London: Faber and Faber, 1935), 166.

21. H. Gough, *The Fifth Army* (London: Hodder and Stoughton, 1931), 43.
22. A. von Kluck, *The March on Paris and the Battle of the Marne, 1914* (London: Edward Arnold, 1920), 98–99.
23. A. von Kluck, *The March on Paris and the Battle of the Marne, 1914* (London: Edward Arnold, 1920), 98–99.
24. D. Haig, quoted by D. Cooper, *Haig* (London: Faber and Faber, 1935), 168–171.
25. J. L. Dent, quoted by J. P. Jones, *History of the South Staffordshire Regiment* (Wolverhampton, UK: Whitehead Brothers, 1923), 263.
26. K. von Bülow, quoted by J. E. Edmonds, *History of the Great War, Military Operations, France and Belgium, 1914*, vol. 2 (London: Macmillan, 1925), 299.
27. K. von Bülow, quoted by J. E. Edmonds, *History of the Great War, Military Operations, France and Belgium, 1914*, vol. 2 (London: Macmillan, 1925), 303.
28. Minutes of R. Hentsch First Army briefing, 9/9/1914, quoted verbatim by A. von Kluck, *The March on Paris and the Battle of the Marne, 1914* (London: Edward Arnold, 1920), 138.
29. Rittmeister von der Horst quote provided and translated by J. Sheldon from E. v. Trauwitz-Hellwig, *Das Königlich Preußische Husaren-Regiment Königin Wilhelmina der Niederlande (Hannoversches) Nr. 15 im Weltkriege 1914–1918* (Wandsbek, 1929), 136.
30. IWM DOCS: A. N. Ackland, typescript account, 5–6.
31. IWM DOCS: C. Helm, typescript account, 15.
32. J. Perryman, *Diary of Lieut. J. B. W. Pennyman* (Middlesbrough: Jordison, 1915), 29–30.
33. IWM DOCS: J. W. Palmer, typescript diary, 8/9/1914.
34. IWM SOUND: T. Painting, AC 212 Reel 4.
35. W. A. T. Synge, quoted by E. Wyrall, *The History of the King's Regiment (Liverpool) 1914–1919* (London: Edward Arnold, 1928), 53.
36. T. W. Sheppard, quoted by E. Wyrall, *The History of the King's Regiment (Liverpool) 1914–1919* (London: Edward Arnold., 1928), 51.
37. D. Haig, *Douglas Haig: War Diaries and Letters, 1914–1918*, ed. G. Sheffield and J. Bourne (London: Weidenfeld and Nicholson, 2005), 69.
38. F. Foch, *The Memoirs of Marshal Foch* (London: William Heinemann, 1931), 108.

Chapter 9

1. IWM DOCS: C. J. Paterson, typescript diary, 16/9/1914.
2. A. von Kluck, *The March on Paris and the Battle of the Marne, 1914* (London: Edward Arnold, 1920), 151.
3. The appointment of Falkenhayn was kept secret until November 1914.
4. IWM DOCS: L. Tennyson, manuscript diary, 12–13/9/1914.
5. A. Hunter-Weston, quoted by R. Berkeley, *The History of the Rifle-Brigade in the War, 1914–1918*, vol. 2 (London: Rifle Brigade Club, 1927), 25.

6. IWM DOCS: L. Tennyson, manuscript diary, 12–13/9/1914.
7. Private C. Gregory, killed 13 September 1914. Buried in Vauxbuin French National Cemetery.
8. IWM DOCS: L. Tennyson, manuscript diary, 13/9/1914.
9. Captain Douglas Lucas-Tooth recorded by the Commonwealth War Graves Commission as having died on 14 September 1914, aged 33 years old. He is buried in Moulins New Communal Cemetery. Both his brothers were killed in the war.
10. IWM DOCS: B. J. N. Marden, manuscript diary, 13/9/1914.
11. A. Osburn, *Unwilling Passenger* (London: Faber and Faber, 1932), 78.
12. C. J. O'Sullivan, quoted by H. F. N. Jourdain and E. Fraser, *The Conaught Rangers*, vol. 2 (County Cork, IE: Schull Books, 1999), 425.
13. IWM SOUND: W. Holbrook, AC 9339 Reel 8.
14. Major Maywald quote provided and translated by J. Sheldon from *Das 8. Lothringische Infanterie-Regiment Nr. 159 im Frieden und im Weltkrieg* (Berlin: Officers Association I.R. 159, 1935), 66–70.
15. IWM DOCS: W. A. T. Synge, transcript diary, 14/9/1914.
16. E. J. Needham, *The First Three Months: The Impressions of an Amateur Subaltern* (Aldershot, UK: Gale and Polden, 1933), 55.
17. Lieutenant Herbert Loomes died 14 September, aged 25 years old. He has no known grave and is commemorated on the La Ferté-sous-Jouarre Memorial to the Missing.
18. J. G. W. Hyndson, *From Mons to the First Battle of Ypres* (London: Wyman and Sons, 1933), 49–50.
19. An Indian Army term for a gully or valley.
20. J. G. W. Hyndson, *From Mons to the First Battle of Ypres* (London: Wyman and Sons Ltd, 1933), 51–52.
21. F.A, Bolwell, *With a Reservist in France* (London: Routledge, 1918), 52.
22. E. J. Needham, *The First Three Months: The Impressions of an Amateur Subaltern* (Aldershot, UK: Gale and Polden, 1933), 57.
23. I. Maxse, quoted by J. Baynes, *Far from a Donkey* (London: Brasseys, 1995), 118.
24. IWM DOCS: H. Rees, transcript memoir, 'A Personal Record of the First Three Months of the War', 19–20.
25. G. D. Melville, quoted by T. O'Marden, *The History of the Welch Regiment, Part II, 1914–1918* (Uckfield, UK: Naval and Military Press, 2009), 306.
26. IWM DOCS: R. Blewitt, manuscript letter, 14/9/1915.
27. E. G. Hamilton, quoted by H. F. N. Jourdain and E. Fraser, *The Conaught Rangers*, vol. 2 (County Cork, IE: Schull Books, 1999), 428–429.
28. E. G. Hamilton, quoted by H. F. N. Jourdain and E. Fraser, *The Conaught Rangers*, vol. 2 (County Cork, IE: Schull Books, 1999), 430.
29. J. Joffre, quoted by J. E. Edmonds, *History of the Great War, Military Operations, France and Belgium, 1914*, vol. 2 (London: Macmillan, 1925), 368.
30. Second Lieutenant Gilbert Amos died, aged 18 years old, on 14 September 1914. He is buried in the Vauxbuin French National Cemetery.

31. R. V. Dolbey, *A Regimental Surgeon in War and Prison* (London: John Murray, 1917), 55.
32. R. V. Dolbey, *A Regimental Surgeon in War and Prison* (London: John Murray, 1917), 56.
33. J. B. W. Pennyman, *Diary of J. B. W. Pennyman* (Middlesbrough, UK: Jordison, 1915), 36.
34. R. V. Dolbey, *A Regimental Surgeon in War and Prison* (London: John Murray, 1917), 56–57.
35. J. B. W. Pennyman, *Diary of J. B. W. Pennyman* (Middlesbrough, UK: Jordison, 1915), 36.
36. R. V. Dolbey, *A Regimental Surgeon in War and Prison* (London: John Murray, 1917), 59–60.
37. Musketier Kubina quotes provided and translated by J. Sheldon from *Das 8. Lothringische Infanterie-Regiment Nr. 159 im Frieden und im Weltkrieg* (Officers Association I.R. 159: Berlin, 1935), 81–84.
38. Musketier Kubina quotes provided and translated by J. Sheldon from *Das 8. Lothringische Infanterie-Regiment Nr. 159 im Frieden und im Weltkrieg* (Officers Association I.R. 159: Berlin, 1935), 81–84.
39. IWM SOUND: J. Armstrong AC 10920 Reel 2.
40. J. French, quoted by J. E. Edmonds, *History of the Great War, Military Operations, France and Belgium, 1914*, vol. 2 (London: Macmillan, 1925), 523.
41. J. French, *1914* (London: Constable, 1919), 154.
42. F. S. Maude, quoted by A. Syk, *The Military Papers of Lieutenant General Stanley Maude, 1914–1917* (Stroud, UK: History Press/Army Records Society, 2012), 34–35.
43. F.A. Bolwell, *With a Reservist in France* (London: Routledge, 1918), 56–57.
44. IWM DOCS: L. Tennyson, manuscript diary, 6/10/1914.
45. J. French, *1914* (London: Constable, 1919), 144.
46. IWM DOCS: C. Lowther, typescript diary account, 15/9/1914.
47. Captain William Cecil, 2nd Grenadier Guards, killed 16 September 1914. Buried Soupir Communal Cemetery.
48. IWM DOCS: F. A. Firks, manuscript letter in the private collection of E. R. Meade-Waldo, 25/11/1914.
49. IWM DOCS: S. Knight, typescript diary, 18/9/1914.
50. IWM DOCS: J. McIlwain, typescript diary account, 17–21/9/1914.
51. A. Osburn, *Unwilling Passenger* (London: Faber and Faber, 1932), 133–134.
52. A. Osburn, *Unwilling Passenger* (London: Faber and Faber, 1932), 134–135.
53. Second Lieutenant George Taylor-Whitehead died, aged 21years old, on 29 September 1914. He is buried in Longueval Communal Cemetery.
54. IWM DOCS: J. W. Palmer, typescript diary, 15/9/1914.
55. IWM DOCS: F. Pusey, typescript account, 13.
56. IWM DOCS: F. H. Le Breton, typescript diary, 17/9/1914.
57. F. S. Maude, quoted by A. Syk, *The Military Papers of Lieutenant General Stanley Maude, 1914–1917* (Stroud, UK: History Press/Army Records Society, 2012), 34–35.

58. IWM DOCS: W. Read, transcript diary, 16/9/1914.
59. IWM DOCS: W. Read, transcript diary, 120/9/1914.
60. IWM DOCS: W. Read, transcript diary, 25/9/1914.
61. IWM DOCS: H. Jackson, Manuscript letter, 27/9/1914.
62. For the complete lyrics, see *Make 'Em Laugh*, 'The Prime Minister of Mirth, George Robey,' http://monologues.co.uk/George_Robey/Archibald_Certainly_Not.htm
63. IWM DOCS: W. Read, transcript diary, 30/9/1914.
64. W. Raleigh, *The War in the Air*, vol. 1 (London: Hamish Hamilton, 1969), 341.
65. This would be the 'clock code' which came into use in 1915. It was a system based on the numbers of a clock, with the 12 o'clock as true north from the target at the centre of the clock face, while a series of imaginary lines at various distances from the centre of the target allowed further adjustments.
66. IWM DOCS: J. L. Mowbray, typescript diary, 2/10/1914.
67. IWM DOCS: E. A. Luther, typescript account, 2.
68. Captain Gilbert William Mapplebeck, No. 4 Squadron, RFC. Mapplebeck would be killed on 24 August 1915.
69. IWM DOCS: F. H. Le Breton, typescript diary, 21/9/1914.
70. IWM SOUND: C. E. C. Rabagliati, AC 4208, Reel 1.
71. W. Congreve, quoted by T. Norman, *Armageddon Road* (London: Kimber, 1982), 34–35.
72. Captain Robert Parker died, aged 35 years old, on 17 September 1914. He has no known grave and is commemorated on the La Ferté–sous-Jouarre Memorial.
73. E. J. Needham, *The First Three Months: The Impressions of an Amateur Subaltern* (Aldershot, UK: Gale and Polden, 1933), 60.
74. E. J. Needham, *The First Three Months: The Impressions of an Amateur Subaltern* (Aldershot, UK: Gale and Polden Press, 1933), 61.
75. L. H. B. Burlton, quoted by Anon in *The Northamptonshire Regiment, 1914–1918* (Uckfield, UK: Naval and Military Press, 2005), 42–43.
76. L. H. B. Burlton, quoted by Anon in *The Northamptonshire Regiment, 1914–1918* (Uckfield, UK: Naval and Military Press, 2005), 43–44.
77. IWM DOCS: J. G. Stennett, manuscript diary letter, 17/9/1914.
78. Second Lieutenant Cosmo Gordon died, aged 20 years old, on 17 September 1914. Buried at Vailly British Cemetery.
79. E. J. Needham, *The First Three Months: The Impressions of an Amateur Subaltern* (Aldershot, UK: Gale and Polden, 1933), 61.
80. E. J. Needham, *The First Three Months: The Impressions of an Amateur Subaltern* (Aldershot, UK: Gale and Polden, 1933), 61.
81. IWM DOCS: C. J. Paterson, typescript diary, 18/9/1914.
82. IWM DOCS: R. H Owen typescript letters, 24/9/1914.
83. IWM DOCS: J. W. Palmer, typescript diary, 19/9/1914.
84. IWM DOCS: F. H. Le Breton, typescript diary, 20/9/1914.

85. IWM DOCS: W. A. T. Synge, typescript diary account, 12.

86. IWM DOCS: R. H Owen, typescript letters, 24/9/1914.

87. A. A. E. Gyde, *Contemptible* (London: Heinemann, 1916), 197–198.

88. F. S. Maude, quoted by A. Syk, *The Military Papers of Lieutenant General Stanley Maude, 1914–1917* (Stroud, UK: History Press/Army Records Society, 2012), 36.

89. F. S. Maude, quoted by A. Syk, *The Military Papers of Lieutenant General Stanley Maude, 1914–1917* (Stroud, UK: History Press/Army Records Society, 2012), 37.

Chapter 10

1. F. Foch, *The Memoirs of Marshal Foch* (London: William Heinemann, 1931), 131.

2. J. Joffre, *The Memoirs of General Joffre*, vol. 2 (London: Geoffrey Bles, 1932), 282.

3. J. French, *1914* (London: Constable, 1919), 156–157.

4. This was not an unusual expression of frustration with Sir John French. On 17 September his diary reports tersely that, 'Sir John is simply stupid'. IWM DOCS: H. Wilson, diary, 17/9/1914.

5. IWM DOCS: H. Wilson, diary, 25/9/1914.

6. J. Joffre, *The Memoirs of General Joffre*, vol. 2 (London: Geoffrey Bles, 1932), 294.

7. J. Joffre, *The Memoirs of General Joffre*, vol. 1 (London: Geoffrey Bles, 1932), 303.

8. J. Joffre, *The Memoirs of General Joffre*, vol. 1 (London: Geoffrey Bles, 1932), 294.

9. E. M. Lockwood, quoted by D. Jerrold, *The Hawke Battalion* (London: Ernest Benn, 1925), 18.

10. E. M. Lockwood, quoted by D. Jerrold, *The Hawke Battalion* (London: Ernest Benn Ltd, 1925), 19.

11. R. Brooke, letter, 17 October 1914, *The Letters of Rupert Brooke*, ed. G. Keynes (London: Faber and Faber, 1968), 622.

12. R. H. Shelton, quoted by D. Jerrold, *The Hawke Battalion* (London: Ernest Benn, 1925), 20.

13. H. Asquith, quoted by M. Gilbert, *Winston S. Churchill*, vol. 3 (London: William Heinemann, 1971), 113.

14. R. H. Shelton, quoted by D. Jerrold, *The Hawke Battalion* (London: Ernest Benn, 1925), 20–21.

15. IWM DOCS: H. Mellanby, transcript account.

16. R. Brooke letter, 17 October 1914, quoted in *The Letters of Rupert Brooke,* ed. G. Keynes (London: Faber and Faber, 1968), 624.

17. R. Brooke letter, 17 October 1914, quoted in *The Letters of Rupert Brooke,* ed. G. Keynes (London: Faber and Faber, 1968), 624–625.

18. R. Brooke letter, 11 November 1914, quoted in *The Letters of Rupert Brooke,* ed. G. Keynes (London: Faber and Faber, 1968), 632.
19. R. H. Shelton, quoted by D. Jerrold, *The Hawke Battalion* (London: Ernest Benn, 1925), 21.
20. W. Henderson, quoted by L. Sellars, *RND: Antwerp, Gallipoli and the Western Front, 1914–1918* (Leigh on Sea, UK: Len Sellars, 1998), Issue 4, 273–275.
21. R. H. Shelton, quoted by D. Jerrold, *The Hawke Battalion* (London: Ernest Benn, 1925), 22.
22. H. Asquith, quoted by M. Gilbert, *Winston S. Churchill,* vol. 3 (London: William Heinemann, 1971), 130.
23. D. Jerrold, *The Royal Naval Division* (London: Hutchinson, 1923), 39.
24. D. Richert, *The Kaiser's Reluctant Conscript,* trans. by D. C. Sutherland (Barnsley, UK: Pen and Sword, 2012), 31.
25. IWM DOCS: B. T. St John, typescript account, pt. II, 15–18.
26. H. R. Sandilands, *The Fifth in the Great War* (Dover, UK: Grigg and Son, 1938), 47.
27. IWM DOCS: C. Helm, typescript account, 28–29.
28. J. French, *1914* (London: Constable, 1919), 222.
29. IWM DOCS: C. Helm, typescript account, 32.
30. IWM DOCS: W. Read, transcript diary, 22/10/1914.
31. D. Richert, *The Kaiser's Reluctant Conscript,* trans. D. C. Sutherland (Barnsley, UK: Pen and Sword, 2012), 31.
32. R. V. Dolbey, *A Regimental Surgeon in War and Prison* (London: John Murray, 1917), 113–114.
33. R. V. Dolbey, *A Regimental Surgeon in War and Prison* (London: John Murray, 1917), 116.
34. R. V. Dolbey, *A Regimental Surgeon in War and Prison* (London: John Murray, 1917), 117–118.
35. D. Richert, *The Kaiser's Reluctant Conscript,* trans. D. C. Sutherland (Barnsley, UK: Pen and Sword, 2012), 33.
36. D. Richert, *The Kaiser's Reluctant Conscript,* trans. D. C. Sutherland (Barnsley, UK: Pen and Sword, 2012), 34.
37. D. Richert, *The Kaiser's Reluctant Conscript,* trans. D. C. Sutherland (Barnsley, UK: Pen and Sword, 2012), 35.
38. D. Richert, *The Kaiser's Reluctant Conscript,* trans. D. C. Sutherland (Barnsley, UK: Pen and Sword, 2012), 35–36.

Chapter 11

1. IWM DOCS: W. A. Quinton, typescript account, 16.
2. R. G. A. Hamilton, *The War Diary of the Master of Belhaven, 1914–1918* (Barnsley, UK: Warnecliffe, 1990), 3.
3. IWM DOCS: H. Mattison, typescript account, 27.

4. E. Pickard, quoted by H. C. Wylly, *The Green Howards in the Great War, 1914–1919* (Richmond, UK: Regiment, 1926), 36–37.

5. E. von Falkenhayn, quoted by R. Foley, *German Strategy and the Path to Verdun: Erich von Falkenhayn and the Development of Attrition, 1870–1916* (Cambridge, UK: Cambridge University Press, 2005), 102.

6. J. French, *1914* (London: Constable, 1919), 223.

7. J. French, *1914* (London: Constable, 1919), 224–225.

8. R. G. A. Hamilton, *The War Diary of the Master of Belhaven, 1914–1918* (Barnsley, UK: Warnecliffe, 1990), 13.

9. IWM DOCS: H. Mattison, typescript account, 46.

10. R. G. A. Hamilton, *The War Diary of the Master of Belhaven, 1914–1918* (Barnsley, UK: Warnecliffe, 1990), 17.

11. R. G. A. Hamilton, *The War Diary of the Master of Belhaven, 1914–1918* (Barnsley, UK: Warnecliffe, 1990), 18.

12. R. G. A. Hamilton, *The War Diary of the Master of Belhaven, 1914–1918* (Barnsley, UK: Warnecliffe, 1990), 20–21.

13. IWM DOCS: H. Rees, transcript memoir, 'A Personal Record of the First Three Months of the War', 32.

14. IWM DOCS: S. Knight, typescript diary, 21/10/1914.

15. Vizefeldwebel Frischauf, quoted by J. Sheldon, *The German Army at Ypres* (Barnsley, UK: Pen and Sword, 2010), 100.

16. W. Kahl, quoted by J. Sheldon, *The German Army at Ypres* (Barnsley, UK: Pen and Sword, 2010), 105–106.

17. E. J. Needham, *The First Three Months: The Impressions of an Amateur Subaltern* (Aldershot, UK: Gale and Polden, 1933), 88–89.

18. E. J. Needham, *The First Three Months: The Impressions of an Amateur Subaltern* (Aldershot, UK: Gale and Polden, 1933), 92–93.

19. IWM DOCS: C. J. Paterson, typescript diary, 17/8/1914.

20. IWM DOCS: H. Rees, transcript memoir, 'A Personal Record of the First Three Months of the War', 33.

21. IWM DOCS: F. Packe, letter, 26/10/1914.

22. IWM DOCS: C. J. Paterson, typescript diary, 22/9/1914.

23. IWM DOCS: H. Rees, transcript memoir, 'A Personal Record of the First Three Months of the War', 34–35.

24. IWM DOCS: J. W. Palmer, typescript diary, 23/10/1914.

25. H. M. Dillon, quoted in *The Oxfordshire and Buckinghamshire Light Infantry Chronicle, 1914–1915*, vol. 24 (London: Eyre and Spottiswood), 186.

26. H. M. Dillon, quoted in *The Oxfordshire and Buckinghamshire Light Infantry Chronicle, 1914–1915*, vol. 24 (London: Eyre and Spottiswood), 186–187.

27. IWM DOCS: J. McIlwain, typescript diary account, 23/10/1914.

28. H. M. Dillon, quoted in *The Oxfordshire and Buckinghamshire Light Infantry Chronicle, 1914–1915*, vol. 24 (London: Eyre and Spottiswood), 187–188.

29. H. M. Dillon, quoted in *The Oxfordshire and Buckinghamshire Light Infantry Chronicle, 1914–1915*, vol. 24 (London: Eyre and Spottiswood), 188.

30. IWM DOCS: C. J. Paterson, typescript diary, 24/10/1914.
31. Captain Charles Paterson, killed 1 November 1914, aged 26 years old. Buried in Ypres Town Cemetery.
32. V. D'Urbal, quoted by J. E. Edmonds, *History of the Great War, Military Operations, France and Belgium, 1914,* vol. 2 (London: Macmillan, 1925), 192.
33. IWM DOCS: H. Mattison, typescript account, 60.
34. IWM DOCS: J. W. Palmer, typescript diary, 26/10/1914.
35. IWM DOCS: J. L. Mowbray, typescript diary, 2/10/1914.
36. D. Haig, *Douglas Haig: War Diaries and Letters, 1914–1918,* ed. G. Sheffield and J. Bourne (London: Weidenfeld and Nicholson, 2005), 75.
37. IWM DOCS: H. M. Dillon typescript letters, 41.

Chapter 12

1. F. Foch, *The Memoirs of Marshal Foch* (London: William Heinemann, 1931), 168.
2. L. Klein, quoted by J. Sheldon, *The German Army at Ypres* (Barnsley, UK: Pen and Sword, 2010), 165.
3. Captain Charles de la Pasture died, aged 35 years old, on 29 October 1914. No known grave and commemorated on Menin Gate.
4. IWM DOCS: C. E. Green, typescript diary, 29/10/1914.
5. Lieutenant Godfrey Macdonald died, aged 35 years old, on 2 November 1914. No known grave and commemorated on Menin Gate.
6. Private Alfred Stringer died, aged 19 years old, on 29 October 1914. Buried in Perth Cemetery (China Wall), Ypres.
7. IWM DOCS: J. Garvey, typescript account.
8. IWM DOCS: C. E. Green, typescript diary, 29/10/1914.
9. Private H. Bain was killed on 29 October 1914 and is buried in the Zandvoorde British Cemetery.
10. This could have been one of two men named Private William Bruce, or Private Fred Bruce – both men serving with the 2nd Gordon Highlanders and killed on 29 October 1914.
11. Lieutenant James Brooke was posthumously awarded the VC for his actions in leading the counterattack and organising the resistance to the German attacks. He was killed on 29 October 1914 at Gheluvelt and is buried at the Zantvoorde British Cemetery.
12. J. F. Bell, quoted by C. B. Purdom, *Everyman at War* (London: J. M. Dent, 1930), 17–18.
13. J. F. Bell, quoted by C. B. Purdom, *Everyman at War* (London: J. M. Dent, 1930), 18–19.
14. J. F. Bell, quoted by C. B. Purdom, *Everyman at War* (London: J. M. Dent, 1930), 19–20.
15. C. Berkeley, quoted by T. O'Marden, *The History of the Welch Regiment, Part II, 1914–1918* (Uckfield, UK: Naval and Military Press, 2009), 316.

16. Captain Richard Slater was killed, aged 34, on 27 July 1916 on the Somme. By this time he had been awarded the MC and twice mentioned in despatches. He has no known grave and is commemorated on the Thiepval Memorial.
17. Thomas Painting AC 212 Reel 6. Interview recorded for the IWM by Martin Brice.
18. IWM DOCS: C. S. Baines, typescript account, 2–3.
19. IWM DOCS: P. N. Baldwin, Midshipman's Log, 27/10/1914.
20. IWM DOCS: P. N. Baldwin, Midshipman's Log, 28/10/1914.
21. IWM DOCS: P. N. Baldwin, Midshipman's Log, 28/10/1914.
22. T. B. S. Marshall, quoted by T. O'Marden, *The History of the Welch Regiment, Part II, 1914–1918* (Uckfield, UK: Naval and Military Press, 2009), 320.
23. IWM DOCS: H. Rees, transcript memoir, 'A Personal Record of the First Three Months of the War', 38.
24. Captain Rubenbauer, quoted by J. Sheldon, *The German Army at Ypres* (Barnsley, UK: Pen and Sword, 2010), 172.
25. IWM DOCS: H. Rees, transcript memoir, 'A Personal Record of the First Three Months of the War', 33.
26. IWM DOCS: R. Blewitt, typescript account, 3.
27. IWM DOCS: R. Blewitt, typescript account, 3.
28. IWM DOCS: R. Blewitt, typescript account, 4.
29. J. D. Boyd, quoted by H. C. Wylly, *History of The Queen's Royal Regiment* (London: Gale and Polden Ltd, 1925), 24–25.
30. F. A. Bolwell, *With a Reservist in France* (London: Routledge, 1918), 88.
31. F. A. Bolwell, *With a Reservist in France* (London: Routledge, 1918), 88.
32. IWM SOUND ARCHIVE: J. Armstrong, AC 10920, Reel 3.
33. F. A. Bolwell, *With a Reservist in France* (London: Routledge, 1918), 89.
34. IWM DOCS: J. W. Palmer, typescript diary, 31/10/1914.
35. IWM DOCS: J. W. Palmer, typescript diary, 31/10/1914.
36. IWM DOCS: J. W. Palmer, typescript diary, 31/10/1914.
37. IWM DOCS: J. W. Palmer, typescript diary, 31/10/1914.
38. Lieutenant General Samuel Lomax died at 59 years of age back in England on 10 April 1915. He is buried in Aldershot Military Cemetery.
39. J. French, *1914* (London: Constable, 1919), 248–259.
40. F. Foch, *The Memoirs of Marshal Foch* (London: William Heinemann, 1931), 174–175.
41. F. Foch, *The Memoirs of Marshal Foch* (London: William Heinemann, 1931), 168.
42. J. Charteris, *Field Marshal Earl Haig* (London: Cassell, 1929), 118–119.
43. D. Haig, quoted by G. Sheffield, *The Chief: Douglas Haig and the British Army* (London: Aurum, 2011), 95.
44. W. Finch AC 8280: edited from Reel 2–3.
45. W. Finch AC 8280: edited from Reel 2–3.
46. W. Finch AC 8280: edited from Reel 2–3.

47. IWM DOCS: H. M. Dillon, typescript letters, 44–45.
48. IWM DOCS: V. Fleming, typescript letter, 6/12/1914.
49. IWM DOCS: V. Fleming, typescript letter, 6/12/1914.
50. H. Kitchener, quoted by G. H. Cassar, *Kitchener: Architect of Victory* (London: Kimber, 1977), 249.
51. F. Foch, *The Memoirs of Marshal Foch* (London: William Heinemann, 1931), 183–184.
52. IWM DOCS: H. Rees, transcript memoir, 'A Personal Record of the First Three Months of the War', 45–46.
53. IWM DOCS: H. Rees, Transcript memoir, 'A Personal Record of the First Three Months of the War', 50.
54. Colonel Norman McMahon, killed 11 November 1914. He has no known grave and is commemorated on Panel 1 of the Ploegsteert Memorial.
55. IWM SOUND: W. Holbrook, AC 9339 Reel 8.
56. E. G. Hamilton, quoted by H. F. N. Jourdain and E. Fraser, *The Connaught Rangers*, vol. 2 (County Cork, IE: Schull Books, 1999), 438.
57. IWM DOCS: J. McIlwain, typescript diary account, 11/11/1914.
58. H. R. Davies, quoted in *The Oxfordshire and Buckinghamshire Light Infantry Chronicle, 1914–1915,* vol. 24 (London: Eyre and Spottiswood), 202.
59. Second Lieutenant Francis Pepys was killed, aged 23 years old, on 12 November 1914. He has no known grave and is commemorated on the Menin Gate Memorial at Ypres.
60. IWM DOCS: H. M. Dillon, typescript letters, 48–49.
61. IWM DOCS: H. Rees, transcript memoir, 'A Personal Record of the First Three Months of the War', 53–54.
62. F. Foch, *The Memoirs of Marshal Foch* (London: William Heinemann, 1931), 196.
63. H. Horne, 'The Great Commander', *The British Legion Earl Haig Memorial Number* (March 1928): 238.
64. E. G. Hamilton, quoted by H. F. N. Jourdain and E. Fraser, *The Connaught Rangers*, vol. 2 (County Cork, IE: Schull Books, 1999), 434.
65. F. Foch, *The Memoirs of Marshal Foch* (London: William Heinemann, 1931), 206.

Chapter 13

1. G. A. L. Brownlow, *The Breaking of the Storm* (London: Methuen, 1918), 210–211.
2. IWM DOCS: E. D. Kingsley, typescript account, 10–11.
3. IWM DOCS: H. H. Stainton, typed account, 18–19.
4. IWM DOCS: H. H. Stainton, typed account, 27.
5. E. Roe, *Diary of an Old Contemptible, From Mons to Baghdad, 1914–1919,* ed. P. Downham (Barnsley, UK: Pen and Sword, 2004), 67–68.

6. E. Gleichen, *The Doings of the Fifteenth Infantry Brigade, August 1914 to March 1915* (Edinburgh and London: William Blackwood and Sons, 1917), 256–258.
7. E. H. W. Hulse, *Letters Written from the English Fronts in France between September 1914 and March 1915* (Privately Printed, 1916), 33.
8. IWM DOCS: A. N. Ackland, typescript account, 31.
9. F. S. Maude, quoted by A. Syk, *The Military Papers of Lieutenant General Stanley Maude, 1914–1917* (Stroud, UK: History Press/Army Records Society, 2012), 50–51.
10. IWM DOCS: M. Aitken, typescript account, 19.
11. G. A. L. Brownlow, *The Breaking of the Storm* (London: Methuen, 1918), 193–194.
12. E. H. W. Hulse, *Letters Written from the English Fronts in France between September 1914 and March 1915* (Privately Printed, 1916), 33.
13. E. H. W. Hulse, *Letters Written from the English Fronts in France between September 1914 and March 1915* (Privately Printed, 1916), 48–49.
14. E. Roe, *Diary of an Old Contemptible, From Mons to Baghdad, 1914–1919,* ed. P. Downham (Barnsley, UK: Pen and Sword, 2004), 61–62.
15. IWM Docs: R. M. Synge, typescript account, 16–17.
16. E. H. W. Hulse, *Letters Written from the English Fronts in France between September 1914 and March 1915* (Privately Printed, 1916), 45.
17. IWM DOCS: H. H. Stainton, typed account, 28.
18. B. Bairnsfather, *Bullets and Billets* (London: Grant Richard, 1916), 55–56.
19. IWM DOCS: F. A. Brown, typescript memoir, 4–5.
20. IWM DOCS: E. D. Kingsley: typescript account, 17.
21. E. Roe, *Diary of an Old Contemptible, From Mons to Baghdad, 1914–1919,* ed. P. Downham (Barnsley, UK: Pen and Sword, 2004), 66.
22. IWM DOCS: G. Roupell, typescript account, 60–61.
23. IWM DOCS: G. Roupell, typescript account, 60–61.
24. J. H. Marshall-Cornwall, quoted by P. Liddell, *Captured Memories, 1900–1918* (Barnsley, UK: Pen and Sword, 2010), 102.
25. IWM DOCS: B. J. N. Marden, manuscript diary, 18–19/11/1914.
26. W. Smalley, quoted in *Nottingham Daily Express,* 8 December 1914.
27. Second Lieutenant William Smalley killed, aged 23 years old, on 9 December 1914. Buried at Cabaret-Rouge British Cemetery, Souchez.
28. IWM DOCS: E. D. Kingsley: typescript account, 10–11.
29. Trooper Herbert Boyce was killed on 18 November 1914. He has no known grave and is commemorated on the Menin Gate, Ypres.
30. M. Crofton, quoted by G. Roynon, *Massacre of the Innocents: The Crofton Diaries, Ypres, 1914–1915* (Stroud, UK: Sutton, 2004), 25–26.
31. IWM DOCS: F. A. Brown, typescript memoir, 4.
32. E. Gleichen, *The Doings of the Fifteenth Infantry Brigade, August 1914 to March 1915* (Edinburgh and London: William Blackwood and Sons, 1917), 273.
33. IWM DOCS: L. Tennyson, manuscript diary, 12/11/1914.

34. G. Burgoyne, *The Burgoyne Diaries* (London: Thomas Harmsworth, 1985), 20.
35. G. Burgoyne, *The Burgoyne Diaries* (London: Thomas Harmsworth, 1985), 21.
36. IWM DOCS: L. Tennyson, manuscript diary, 7/11/1914.
37. IWM Docs: F. G. Chandler, typescript letter, 17/12/1914.
38. Captain Horace Herd died, aged 31 years old, on 27 December 1914. Buried at Brown's Road Military Cemetery, Festubert.
39. IWM DOCS: H. Rees, transcript memoir, 'A Personal Record of the First Three Months of the War', 65.
40. D. Haig, *Douglas Haig: War Diaries and Letters, 1914–1918,* ed. G. Sheffield and J. Bourne (London: Weidenfeld & Nicholson, 2005), 84.
41. J. G. W. Hyndson, *From Mons to the First Battle of Ypres* (London: Wyman and Sons, 1933), 118–119.
42. IWM DOCS: P. Whitehouse typescript account, 37–38.
43. IWM DOCS: P. Whitehouse typescript account, 38–39.
44. IWM DOCS: J. W. Palmer, typescript diary, 13/11/1914.
45. IWM DOCS: J. W. Palmer, typescript diary, 19/11/1914.
46. IWM DOCS: J. W. Palmer, typescript diary, 19/11/1914.
47. IWM DOCS: J. W. Palmer, typescript diary, 28/10/1914.
48. IWM DOCS: B. T. St John, typescript account pt. II, 45–47.
49. A. Martin-Leake, quoted by A. Clayton, *Martin-Leake: Double VC* (Barnsley, UK: Pen and Sword, 1994), 134–135.
50. IWM DOCS: J. McIlwain, typescript diary account, 11/11/1914.
51. IWM DOCS: J. McIlwain, typescript diary account, 12/11/1914.
52. R. V. Dolbey, *A Regimental Surgeon in War and Prison* (London: John Murray, 1917), 58.
53. R. V. Dolbey, *A Regimental Surgeon in War and Prison* (London: John Murray, 1917), 56–57.
54. A. A. Martin, *A Surgeon in Khaki* (London: Edward Arnold, 1917), 192–193.
55. A. A. Martin, *A Surgeon in Khaki* (London: Edward Arnold, 1917), 97–98.
56. A. A. Martin, *A Surgeon in Khaki* (London: Edward Arnold, 1917), 186–187, 189.
57. A. A. Martin, *A Surgeon in Khaki* (London: Edward Arnold, 1917), 192.
58. IWM DOCS: B. T. St John typescript account, pt. II, 47–48.
59. M. Aitken, typescript account, 14.
60. M. Aitken, typescript account, 19.
61. A. A. Martin, *A Surgeon in Khaki* (London: Edward Arnold, 1917), 205.
62. A. A. Martin, *A Surgeon in Khaki* (London: Edward Arnold, 1917), 202–203.
63. A. A. Martin, *A Surgeon in Khaki* (London: Edward Arnold, 1917), 206.
64. A. A. Martin, *A Surgeon in Khaki* (London: Edward Arnold, 1917), 211–212.
65. F. S. Maude, quoted by A. Syk, *The Military Papers of Lieutenant General Stanley Maude, 1914–1917* (Stroud, UK: History Press/Army Records Society, 2012), 50–51.
66. E. Gleichen, *The Doings of the Fifteenth Infantry Brigade, August 1914 to March 1915* (Edinburgh and London: William Blackwood and Sons, 1917), 262–263.

67. IWM DOCS: H. H. Stainton, typed account, 16–17.

68. IWM DOCS: C. J. Lane, typescript account, 4.

69. A. Cook, quoted by B. Gillard, *Good Old Somersets: An 'Old Contemptible' Battalion in 1914* (Leicester, UK: Troubador, 2004), 125–126.

70. IWM SOUND: J. Armstrong AC 10920 Reel 2.

71. G. Burgoyne, *The Burgoyne Diaries* (London: Thomas Harmsworth, 1985), 24–25.

72. IWM DOCS: L. Tennyson, manuscript diary, 25/10/1914.

73. IWM DOCS: E. D. Kingsley, typescript account, 7.

74. IWM DOCS: J. W. Palmer, typescript diary, 24/11/1914.

75. IWM DOCS: J. W. Palmer, typescript diary, 23/12/1914.

76. F. Nickolaus, quoted by M. Brown and S. Seaton, *Christmas Truce: The Western Front, 1914* (London: Pan Macmillan, 2001), 23.

Chapter 14

1. F. Foch, *The Memoirs of Marshal Foch* (London: William Heinemann, 1931), 201–202.

2. G. A. L. Brownlow, *The Breaking of the Storm* (London: Methuen, 1918), 192.

3. E. Gleichen, *The Doings of the Fifteenth Infantry Brigade, August 1914 to March 1915* (Edinburgh and London: William Blackwood and Sons, 1917), 193–194.

4. H. V. Lewis, quoted by W. S. Thatcher, *The Fourth Battalion Duke of Connaught's Own Tenth Baluch Regiment in the Great War* (Cambridge, UK: Cambridge University Press, 1932), 16.

5. Major George Humphreys died, aged 41 years old, on 30 October 1914. He is buried at Kemmel Churchyard.

6. IWM DOCS: H. V. Lewis, letter, 2/11/1914.

7. D. Richert, *The Kaiser's Reluctant Conscript,* trans. D. C. Sutherland (Barnsley, UK: Pen and Sword, 2012), 36.

8. D. Richert, *The Kaiser's Reluctant Conscript,* trans. D. C. Sutherland (Barnsley, UK: Pen and Sword, 2012), 38.

9. G. H. Taylor, quoted by D. H. Drake-Brockman, *With the Royal Garhwal Rifles in the Great War, 1914–1917* (Uckfield, UK: Naval and Military, 2006), 130.

10. G. H. Taylor, quoted by D. H. Drake-Brockman, *With the Royal Garhwal Rifles in the Great War, 1914–1917* (Uckfield, UK: Naval and Military, 2006), 130–131.

11. G. H. Taylor, quoted by D. H. Drake-Brockman, *With the Royal Garhwal Rifles in the Great War, 1914–1917* (Uckfield, UK: Naval and Military, 2006), 131.

12. G. H. Taylor, quoted by D. H. Drake-Brockman, *With the Royal Garhwal Rifles in the Great War, 1914–1917* (Uckfield, UK: Naval and Military, 2006), 131.

13. Major Guy Taylor died, aged 41 years old, on 14 November 1914. He has no known grave and is commemorated on the Neuve Chapelle Memorial.

14. D. Richert, *The Kaiser's Reluctant Conscript*, trans. D. C. Sutherland (Barnsley, UK: Pen and Sword, 2012), 38–39. This is dated by Richert as 21 November but seems better to fit the events of the capture of the night of 23 November.
15. D. Richert, *The Kaiser's Reluctant Conscript*, trans. D. C. Sutherland (Barnsley, UK: Pen and Sword, 2012), 40–41.
16. D. Richert, *The Kaiser's Reluctant Conscript*, trans. D. C. Sutherland (Barnsley, UK: Pen and Sword, 2012), 40–41.
17. D. Richert, *The Kaiser's Reluctant Conscript*, trans. D. C. Sutherland (Barnsley, UK: Pen and Sword, 2012), 40–41.
18. Army Third Class educational certificates.
19. E. Roe, *Diary of an Old Contemptible, From Mons to Baghdad, 1914–1919,* edited by P. Downham (Barnsley, UK: Pen and Sword, 2004), 65.
20. IWM DOCS: E. D. Kingsley, typescript account, 10.
21. G. Burgoyne, *The Burgoyne Diaries* (London: Thomas Harmsworth, 1985), 41.
22. IWM DOCS: H. Jackson, manuscript letter, 18/11/1914.
23. J. French, quoted by H. A. R. May, *Memories of the Artist Rifles* (London: Howlett and Son, 1929), 147.
24. H. A. R. May, *Memories of the Artist Rifles* (London: Howlett and Son, 1929), 143.
25. General Staff, War Office, *Field Service Regulations, Part I* (London: HMSO, 1909 as amended 1912), 126.
26. E. Roe, *Diary of an Old Contemptible, From Mons to Baghdad, 1914–1919,* ed. P. Downham (Barnsley, UK: Pen and Sword, 2004), 63.
27. F. S. Maude, quoted by A. Syk, *The Military Papers of Lieutenant General Stanley Maude, 1914–1917* (Stroud, UK: History Press/Army Records Society, 2012), 52.
28. F. S. Maude, quoted by A. Syk, *The Military Papers of Lieutenant General Stanley Maude, 1914–1917* (Stroud, UK: History Press/Army Records Society, 2012), 53.
29. F. S. Maude, quoted by A. Syk, *The Military Papers of Lieutenant General Stanley Maude, 1914–1917* (Stroud, UK: History Press/Army Records Society, 2012), 53.
30. F. S. Maude, quoted by A. Syk, *The Military Papers of Lieutenant General Stanley Maude, 1914–1917* (Stroud, UK: History Press/Army Records Society, 2012), 54.
31. H. Smith-Dorrien, *Isandlwhana to the Great War* (Driffield, UK: Oakpast, 2009), 529.
32. H. Smith-Dorrien, *Isandlwhana to the War* (Driffield, UK: Oakpast, 2009), 529.
33. H. Smith-Dorrien, *Isandlwhana to the Great War* (Driffield, UK: Oakpast, 2009), 529–530.
34. D. Haig, *Douglas Haig: War Diaries and Letters, 1914–1918,* ed. G. Sheffield and J. Bourne (London: Weidenfeld and Nicholson, 2005), 84–85.

35. G. Burgoyne, *The Burgoyne Diaries* (London: Thomas Harmsworth, 1985), 17.
36. G. Burgoyne, *The Burgoyne Diaries* (London: Thomas Harmsworth, 1985), 17.
37. J. A. Hannyngton, quoted by W. S. Thatcher, *The Fourth Battalion Duke of Connaught's Own Tenth Baluch Regiment in the Great War* (Cambridge, UK: Cambridge University Press, 1932), 28–29.
38. H. V. Lewis, quoted by W. S. Thatcher, *The Fourth Battalion Duke of Connaught's Own Tenth Baluch Regiment in the Great War* (Cambridge, UK: Cambridge University Press, 1932), 16.
39. R. D. Davies, quoted by W. S. Thatcher, *The Fourth Battalion Duke of Connaught's Own Tenth Baluch Regiment in the Great War* (Cambridge, UK: Cambridge University Press, 1932), 16.
40. W. M. Southey, quoted by W. S. Thatcher, *The Fourth Battalion Duke of Connaught's Own Tenth Baluch Regiment in the Great War* (Cambridge, UK: Cambridge University Press, 1932), 33.
41. H. Gough, *The Fifth Army* (London: Hodder and Stoughton, 1931), 74.
42. D. Haig, *Douglas Haig: War Diaries and Letters, 1914–1918*, ed. G. Sheffield and J. Bourne (London: Weidenfeld and Nicholson, 2005), 83–84.
43. D. Haig, *Douglas Haig: War Diaries and Letters, 1914–1918*, ed. G. Sheffield and J. Bourne (London: Weidenfeld and Nicholson, 2005), 87.
44. 'Squiffy' was the common nickname for Prime Minister Herbert Asquith due to his reputed alcohol intake.
45. IWM DOCS: H. Wilson, diary, 24/12/1914.
46. D. Haig, *Douglas Haig: War Diaries and Letters, 1914–1918*, ed. G. Sheffield and J. Bourne (London: Weidenfeld and Nicholson, 2005), 92–93.

Chapter 15

1. IWM DOCS: F. A. Brown, typescript memoir, 5.
2. IWM DOCS: W. A. Quinton, typescript account, 23–24.
3. The Commonwealth War Graves Commission has the date of death for Frank Toull as 20 December 1914. He was 20 years old.
4. H. Smith-Dorrien, quoted by M. Brown and S. Seaton, *Christmas Truce: The Western Front, 1914* (London: Pan Macmillan, 2001), 35–36.
5. IWM SOUND: W. Stennes, AC 977, Reel 1.
6. IWM DOCS: W. A. Quinton, typescript account, 23–24.
7. G. Williams, quoted by M. Brown and S. Seaton, *Christmas Truce: The Western Front, 1914* (London: Pan Macmillan, 2001), 58–59.
8. W. S. Barham, *The Diary of Wilfred Saxby Barham during the Great War, 1914–1915* (London: Thomas, 1918), 48–49.
9. Sergeant Frank Collins, killed 25 December 1914. Buried at Calvaire (Essex) Military Cemetery.
10. IWM DOCS: F. A. Brown, typescript memoir, 5–6.
11. W. S. Barham, *The Diary of Wilfred Saxby Barham during the Great War, 1914–1915* (London: Thomas, 1918), 49–50.

12. IWM SOUND ARCHIVE: G. Ashurst, AC 9875 Reel 6.
13. C. I. Stockwell, quoted by C. H. Dudley Ward, *Regimental Records of the Royal Welch Fusiliers* (London: Forster Groom, 1928), 112.
14. C. I. Stockwell, *RWF Regimental Journal*, 2 September 1966.
15. IWM Docs: R. J. Armes, manuscript letter, 24–25/12/1914.
16. E. H. W. Hulse, *Letters Written from the English Fronts in France between September 1914 and March 1915* (Privately Printed, 1916), 56–57.
17. E. H. W. Hulse, *Letters Written from the English Fronts in France between September 1914 and March 1915* (Privately Printed, 1916), 58.
18. IWM SOUND: W. Stennes, AC 977, Reel 1.
19. IWM DOCS: F. A. Brown, typescript memoir, 6.
20. E. Gleichen, *The Doings of the Fifteenth Infantry Brigade, August 1914 to March 1915* (Edinburgh and London: William Blackwood and Sons, 1917), 272–273.
21. B. Bairnsfather, *Bullets and Billets* (London: Grant Richard, 1916), 92–95.
22. J. Wedderburn-Maxwell, AC 9146 Reel 3. Interview recorded by Lyn Smith for the IWM.
23. E. H. W. Hulse, *Letters Written from the English Fronts in France between September 1914 and March 1915* (Privately Printed, 1916), 56–57.
24. E. H. W. Hulse, *Letters Written from the English Fronts in France between September 1914 and March 1915* (Privately Printed, 1916), 57.
25. IWM DOCS: W. A. Quinton, typescript account, 24–26.
26. H. Williamson, AC 4297 Reel 1. Interview recorded for the BBC Great War Series broadcast in 1964.
27. J. Niemann quoted in *We Were There: An Eyewitness History of the Twentieth Century*, ed. Robert Fox (London: Profile, 2010), 46–47.
28. IWM SOUND: E. Williams, AC 25228, Reel 1.
29. E. H. W. Hulse, *Letters Written from the English Fronts in France between September 1914 and March 1915* (Privately Printed, 1916), 59–60.
30. A traditional German toast meaning, 'Cheers!' or 'Good health!'
31. IWM DOCS: C. J. Lane, typescript account, 5.
32. J. Wenzel quote provided and translated by J. Sheldon from F. Solleder, *Vier Jahre Westfront: Geschichte des Regiment List Reserve Infantry Regiment 16* (Munich, 1932), 91–92.
33. E. H. W. Hulse, *Letters Written from the English Fronts in France between September 1914 and March 1915* (Privately Printed, 1916), 61, 67.
34. C. I. Stockwell, quoted by C. H. Dudley Ward, *Regimental Records of the Royal Welch Fusiliers* (London: Forster Groom, 1928), 113–114.
35. E. Roe, *Diary of an Old Contemptible, From Mons to Baghdad, 1914–1919,* ed. P. Downham (Barnsley, UK: Pen and Sword, 2004), 76–77.
36. E. H. W. Hulse, *Letters Written from the English Fronts in France between September 1914 and March 1915* (Privately Printed, 1916), 72.
37. M. Crofton, quoted by G. Roynon, *Massacre of the Innocents: The Crofton Diaries, Ypres, 1914–1915* (Stroud, UK: Sutton Publishing, 2004), 104.

Epilogue

1. F. Foch, *The Memoirs of Marshal Foch* (London: William Heinemann, 1931), 200.
2. J. French, *1914* (London: Constable, 1919), 140.
3. F. Foch, *The Memoirs of Marshal Foch* (London: William Heinemann, 1931), 134–135.

INDEX

Page numbers followed by n indicate notes. Page numbers in *italics* indicate maps.